The Anonymous L[

A.E. Hackford

Un' omaggio dalla
Collega di un
[omo]fil[i]o

Siena, 23.10.58

The Anonymous Leader

Appointed CEOs in
Western Local Government

*Edited by Kurt Klaudi Klausen
and Annick Magnier*

Odense University Press 1998

© The Authors and Odense University Press 1998
Set and printed by Narayana Press, Gylling, Denmark
ISBN 87-7838-413-3

Odense University Press
Campusvej 55
DK-5230 Odense M

Phone: 66 15 79 99
Fax: 66 15 81 26
E-mail: press@forlag.ou.dk
Internet-bookstore: www.ou.dk/press

Contents

Preface   7

Introduction   8

1. The Anonymous Leader   11
   by Kurt Klaudi Klausen and Annick Magnier

2. The Challenge of Constant Change: The Australian
   Local Government CEO   31
   by Rolf Gerritsen and Michelle Whyard

3. Local Authority Chief Executives: the British Case   49
   by Michael Goldsmith and Jon Tonge

4. Power with Responsibility: The Role of the Manager in Irish
   Local Government   64
   by Andy Asquith and Eunan O'Halpin

5. United States of America: Similarity Within Diversity   78
   by James Svara

6. The Danish Local Government CEO: From Town Clerk
   to City Manager   97
   by Niels Ejersbo, Morten Balle Hansen and Poul Erik Mouritzen

7. The Strong CEOs of Finland   113
   by Siv Sandberg

8. The Norwegian CEO: Institutional Position, Professional Status,
   and Work Environment   128
   by Harald Baldersheim and Morten Øgård

9. Turbulence as a Way of Life: The Swedish Municipal CEO   140
   by Roger Haglund

10. No More Double Dutch: Understanding the Dutch CEO   159
    by Jaco Berveling, Marcel van Dam, Geert Neelen and Anchrit Wille

11. The Belgian Municipal Secretary: A Manager
    for the Municipalities?   173
    by Yves Plees and Thierry Laurent

12. The Asymmetric Interdependence Between two Powerful Actors:
    The CEO and the Mayor in French Cities   188
    by Jean-Claude Thoenig and Katherine Burlen

13. Italian Local Democracy in Search of a New Administrative
    Leadership   204
    by Maurizio Gamberucci and Annick Magnier

14. Portuguese Chief Administrative Officers: Between Rationalization
    and Political Struggles   220
    by Manuel da Silva e Costa, Joel Felizes and José P. Neves

15. Functions and Duties of Funcionarios Directivos Locales
    (Local Chief Officers)   238
    by Irene Delgado, Lourdes López Nieto and Eliseo López

16. Executive Management at the Political-Professional Interface:
    CEOs in Israeli Local Government   253
    by Nahum Ben-Elia

17. The New Mandarins of Western Local Governments –
    Contours of a New Professional Identity?   265
    by Kurt Klaudi Klausen and Annick Magnier

Technical Appendix   285
    by Lene Anderson and Poul Erik Mouritzen

List of Participants   312

Preface

Local government has a primary role in the implementation of new policies in most welfare states. Although it is probably not unimportant to understand how they are managed, we know comparatively little about this topic.

This book focuses on the top civil servants, those who are linking the administrative and the political system at this, the lowest level of public administration. Even if the study "covers the globe" they are all appointed Chief Executive Officers (the highest ranking appointed official) in "Western" local government. While their worksituations may differ, they are likely to share several features not found in other parts of the world. We have included fifteen countries in this comparative study which is based on a joint survey and other qualitative studies. The countries are Australia, Belgium, Denmark, Finland, France, Great Britain, Ireland, Israel (the only country which did not conduct the survey), Italy, Norway, Portugal, Spain, Sweden, the Netherlands and the United States of America.

While these CEOs hold important positions in the local administrative and political life, we know little about who they are, how they are recruited, the way in which they view their own positions and particularly their relative position vis-à-vis the political system and the mayor. We set out to explore these features country by country, and in two overview chapters, in this first book from the project. Subsequent volumes will take up specific comparative issues in more detail.

We have named the project the *U.DI.T.E. Leadership Study* after the Union des Dirigeants Territoriaux de l´Europe, whom we thank for their moral support. Every book has a life of its own, and this one is no different. Bringing together research groups from many countries making them work jointly on a project is no easy task. We wish to thank all the national teams for their great collaborative efforts and for their swift responses to troublesome queries from the editors. We also wish to thank Steven Sampson for his valuable work on copy-editing the manuscripts and Vibeke Pierson for her patient and competent work with the many revisions and technical details in the manuscripts.

It has been a pleasure working on this project, and we readily admit that we also enjoyed the hospitality of Florence and Odense on more than one occasion.

Odense and Florence, August 1998

Kurt Klaudi Klausen and Annick Magnier

Introduction

In the Fall of 1991 the Local Government Research Unit at Odense University was asked to carry out a study of the five Danish associations heads of municipal administration. By the end of 1992 the immediate results of the research were reported and this promoted an action plan for the future integration of the five associations. The research was based on documents, qualitative interviews and a survey comprising all the members of the five associations.

In 1993, the Odense research team proposed to extend the research to other European countries, a proposal which was endorsed by the board of directors of U.DI.T.E. – the Association of the European Local Government Chief Executives (*Union des Dirigeants Territoriaux de L'Europe*). The board recommended that national associations gave their support to the research project which was now labelled *The U.DI.T.E Leadership Study*.

Originally, the study was intended to cover only eight of the U.DI.T.E. membership countries, Belgium, Denmark, Spain, France, Italy, the Netherlands, Portugal and the United Kingdom. Later on more countries have joined the project which now also includes Sweden, Norway, Finland, Ireland, the USA and Australia. It is possible that Germany and Canada will be covered at a later stage.

The U.DI.T.E. Leadership Study covers many aspects of the daily life of the local government CEO: work values, role perceptions, relations between administrators and political leaders, career and mobility, leadership styles, cultural values, administrative reforms, decentralization, networks, influence patterns and social characteristics. One of the immediate problems that had to be solved by the international research group was to define the "population". Who are the CEOs? First it is important to note that we agreed to use the term CEO for the object of the study. This was the most neutral term which could be found while terms such as "city manager", "kommunaldirektør" or "city clerk" would carry quite different connotations across countries. In this context, it is important to note that our respondents are not necessarily the persons who have full responsibility over all executive functions in their municipality. In fact, one of the main questions which is going to be answered by the U.DI.T.E. Leadership Study is exactly what is the role – formally as well as informally – of the highest ranking appointed administrative official in western local governments? This also indicates how the population is defined: Our respondents are the *highest ranking appointed administrative officials in municipalities*.[1]

---

[1] In some countries it is not even clear who this person is. In the Netherlands, the Mayor is appointed but is considered as belonging to the group of politicians rather than administrative officials.

The U.DI.T.E. Leadership Study is mainly based on three types of data sources: a survey, intensive interviews and a job-posting analysis. The data and the procedures used are explained in the technical appendix which also contains the English version of the joined questionnaire.

Over the period 1995-1998 the participating researchers have spent around 14 days together in six meetings planning the details of the research. Furthermore, a data confrontation seminar was organized in Hanstholm, Denmark, January 20th-26th 1998 where about 20 participants worked day and night on the survey data in order to develop a common understanding of the data and the problems associated with the analysis of the data.

In order to facilitate the application of a common coding procedure, our research assistants spent almost a week together in Odense in early 1996. They brought with them 100- 200 of the completed questionnaires from their own country and started the actual coding. Several joint session were held every day during which common coding problems were solved and a codebook for the various open-ended questions was developed. After the coding session the national files were finished by each participating team and, finally, they were merged at Odense University. Altogether the file now contains the responses from 4353 CEOs in 14 countries.

The intensive interviews have been conducted in several of the participating countries ranging from 2 to more than 20 in one country. Most of them were taped and transcribed and in some cases English resumes were developed and shared among participants. The question guide used in the intensive interviews is also found in the technical appendix.

The job posting analysis has been completed in seven countries, Denmark, Finland, France, England, Norway, Sweden and the Netherlands. Job advertisements, which were selected to represent three periods, the 70's, the 80's and the 90's, have been coded according to a common framework (cf. the technical appendix).

The present volume, organized country – by – country, is the first of four planned books from the U.DI.T.E. Leadership Study. The three remaining books will focus on specific topics and are expected to be published during 1999. These are:

- *Social Bonds to City Hall: How Appointed CEOs Enter, Experience, and Leave Their Jobs in Western Local Governments* (edited by Peter Dahler-Larsen).
- *The Nexus of Leadership: Administrators in the Political Process in Western Local Governments* (Poul Erik Mouritzen, James Svara and Jean-Claude Thoenig with contributions by Marcel van Dam, Geert Neelen and Siv Sandbjerg).
- *New Public Management and the CEO: Managing Change in Western Local Governments* (edited by Michael Goldsmith).

In September 1996, the preliminary results from ten countries were presented at the third U.DI.T.E. Congress in Odense, Denmark. A report from the Congress is available in Danish, French and English.[2] The planning, as well as the content and aftermath of this congress, is an indication of the excellent relationship between the researchers and the practitioners which has persisted throughout the project. The international research group extent their warm thanks to the U.DI.T.E. board of directors, and to the national associations of local government CEOs who have all recommended their members to participate in the study. Finally, we want to thank Jørgen Norup, former president of the Danish Association of Local Government Chief Executives, who acted as an effective liaison between the world of the administrative leaders and the world of the researchers and who fully understood that the conditions under which research takes place are rarely the same as the conditions under which top administrators work.

Odense, July 1998

Poul Erik Mouritzen
Coordinator of the U.DI.T.E. Leadership Study

---

2 Michael Goldsmith and Poul Erik Mouritzen eds. (1997): *The U.DI.T.E. Leadership Study. Report from the 3 rd Congress 6-7 September 1996,* Odense, Denmark (available from the National Association of Chief Executives in Denmark).

CHAPTER 1

The Anonymous Leader

by Kurt Klaudi Klausen and Annick Magnier

Global Approaches to Local Leadership

"Town meetings are to liberty what primary schools are to science; they bring it within the people's reach, they teach men how to use and how to enjoy it. A nation may establish a free government, but without municipal institutions it cannot have the spirit of liberty. Transient passions, the interest of an hour, or the chance of circumstances may create the external forms of independence, but the despotic tendency which has been driven into the interior of the social system will sooner or later reappear on the surface" (Tocqueville 1991, p. 61). Dropping the hypothesis of a generic delocalization of social links, social sciences are rediscovering the Tocquevillian problem of the local bases of democracy (Putnam 1993, 1995; Etzioni 1993; Bellah et al. 1995; Kymlicka 1995, Fukuyama 1995). In the process, however, we have also discovered that, even within the narrow confines of our own developed societies, our knowledge of local democracies is still extremely limited.

Advocates of the formation of supranational institutions call for convergence, cohesion and integration (Leonardi 1994), but there is a marked contrast between the rhetoric of globalization often associated with the global change in administrative cultures, ascribed to the influence of New Public Management models (Aucoin 1990; Barzelay 1992, Osborne and Gabler 1992), and the global change in political cultures, associated with the development of new communitarian movements (Lawson-Merkl 1988) and the dominant domestic orientation of the empirical research on local government. Our "primary schools" of democracy are being subjected to strong pressure for change: in each country, their transformation is still described in terms of national models and specific disciplinary and methodological traditions; in cross-national perspective, we observe difficulties in comparing the efficiency and values they promote. On the one hand, we know that public sector reforms are taking place throughout the Western world, and that new regionalization and levels of government and governance are being established (Bullman ed. 1994, Marks 1993, Massey ed. 1997). On the other hand, it is to be expected that these reforms, often referred to as a modernization of the public sector, assume different forms (Olsen 1991), being culturally plural rather than homogeneous (Hood 1995) resulting in a mixture of international trends

(Naschold 1995) rather than a linear homogeneous trend in public sector development.

Local government was not specifically incorporated into the surveys on political cultures (e.g. Almond and Verba 1963 and on) which stressed local activism as a distinctive feature. After this period, comparative inquiries on local democracy which went beyond the bi-national or tri-national dimension were rare. A few initiatives managed to promote new hypotheses and renew research interest (Tarrow 1977, Page and Goldsmith 1987, Wolman and Goldsmith 1992), but they failed to address central questions generated by new developments. In Europe, the emergence of a supranational and multilevel level of government and governance (Marks, 1993; Marks, Hoghe and Blank 1996) and the search for new principles of sovereignty and territorial division of competence require us to explore the foundations of local democracy in the continent and its metamorphoses. Only a few comparative projects (Mouritzen 1993, Goldsmith and Klausen eds. 1997) and a few now classic handbooks (Mouritzen-Nielsen 1988, Humes 1991, Norton 1994) offer references in this direction.

Classical studies in public administration and management have set the tone of the discourse, but have not made an effort to differentiate between different layers of government. This is as true for the classical studies of bureaucracy e.g. Weber, Gulick and Urwick as it is for neoclassical studies by for example, Simon and March. Textbooks, such as those of Harmon and Mayer (1986) and Heffron (1989), usually stress the special public context (in contrast with the private and the voluntary nonprofit sectors). This difference is implied by Allison (1979), who, following Sayre, poses the question: "Public and private management: are they fundamentally alike in all unimportant respects?" Nevertheless, many of the recommended techniques are generic in their intent; that is, they are thought of as universally applicable and therefore encourage institutional isomorphism (DiMaggio and Powell 1983).

At first glance, administrative studies could seem to have gone further in the description of what seems to be a global uniform change: like the old icons of POSDCORB and Management by Objectives stemming from classical public management, new icons like Total Quality Management and New Public Management models form common reference points for administrative innovations, a basis for a national and international debate and a common language in the professionalization of administrations. Research obviously echoes these debates. However, after the fall of the American comparative administration project, comparative administration has also often been denounced as "a series of excursions into the exotica of world political systems" (Peters 1992, p. 88): descriptive and country-based, rather than widely analytic and comparative. We must observe that although Public Administration reform has recently become a growing focus of comparative scientific interest (Kickert 1997, Lane 1997, Olsen and Peters 1996), the comparative effort is rarely based on empirical inquiries, and local administration remains neglected, despite the fact that local authorities in the Western world represent from 10 to 60% of public manpower (Page-Goldsmith

1987, p. 187) and constitute the interface between citizens and their State. As a result of this neglect, our comparative models of public administration are founded on the analysis of central bureaucracy. This is the case with the seminal studies of the Comparative Elites Project of Putnam et al. (Putnam 1973, 1976; Mellbourn 1979; Aberbach, Putnam, and Rockman 1981; Eldersveld-Kooiman, and van der Tak 1981) and of the major comparative studies and analyses which have been developed from the 1970s onward (Armstrong 1973, Dogan 1975, Suleiman 1984). We find only few recent exceptions to this, such as the studies of the Nordic "free-commune" reforms (Baldersheim and Stålberg eds. 1994), studies of urban innovation and city management (Clark ed. 1994) and anthologies on trends and developments (e.g. Batley and Stoker eds. 1991).

The Uncertain Ecology of Local Political-Administrative Systems

Studies of local government and administration traditionally stressed two main structural distinctions, which variously combine to offer geographical system typologies: the boundaries of "civic" culture and those of "classic" administration are the ideal lines we find in all the available descriptions of local democracies.

The model of "classic" administrative systems, or of the so-called "Wilsonian-Weberian" systems, grew in its popular version quite freely from its supposed original political and sociological formulation. Both its distinct versions, the French and the German (Heady 1979), assume a contrast between a discontinuity in politics, and continuity in administrative areas, emphasizing a confidence of tenure on a life-time basis and lack of partisan and unionist activities by bureaucrats (no strike, no participation in political activities). The difficulties that these bureaucracies have in adjusting to change and their dramatic balancing between extreme routine and crisis seem to remain typical, notwithstanding the ambition of the most prestigious *corps* to profess themselves to be the promoters of the modernization (Crozier 1995). Traditionally, the main differences pointed out between the German and the French cases concern the relations between Centre and Periphery. The German model emphasizes hierarchical authority, but allows for a considerable decentralization in operations; and it leads to a strict departmentalization into "divisions". Dogmatism, rigidity and intolerance are considered the German bureaucrat's features, but the literature also insists on his strong motivation for performance. Twenty years ago, Putnam and his colleagues demonstrated nevertheless that neither in France nor in Germany did top bureaucrats cluster heavily round the "classical bureaucrat" (Aberbach, Putnam and Rockman 1981).

The administrations of the Anglo-Saxon countries are often defined as "civic administrations". They are not obliged to replace ineffectual party or elected bodies, as was the case in France or Germany. This gives a clear advantage over the American bureaucracy in terms of prestige and status, and a rigidly external selection of the top management, mitigated only through the reforms of the 1970s in favour of internal promotion. Hence the British "citizenry regards the bureaucracy as performing in a service capacity and being properly subjected to firm political control, however expert the bureaucrat may be" (Heady 1979, p. 200). In contrast, the spirit of the American tradition is represented, according to this point of view, by more specialized and practical examinations for the selection, by channels for the career advancement much less planned and more haphazard than in the British system (ibid. p. 203). While old patterns of deference persist among British civil servants, more impersonal rules are enforced in order to achieve the same results in the United States; the American choices would have produced a "more internally competitive, a more experimental, a noisier and less coherent, a less powerful bureaucracy within its own governmental system, but a more dynamic one" (ibid. p 203).

In the traditional handbooks on comparative administration, the other Western administrative systems are considered to be mixed combinations of these two fundamental configurations. Current reflections on public administration reforms introduce to the debate other distinguishing features derived mainly from the debate on the new developmentalist approach upon which, for example, the OECD PUMA group reports are grounded. This debate drops the question of the relationship and similarities on differences between political and bureaucratic work – on which the Wilsonian-Weberian dichotomy was grounded – and instead attaches importance to an old basic problem, the problem of the relationship and the differences and similarities between public and private management (Sayre 1951, 1958, Allison 1979, Perry and Kraemer 1983). In this model of administrative change, the industrialized countries are placed along a continuum between the old administrative management on the one hand and the New Public Management, the entrepreneurial bureaucratic culture and practice of a lean state on the other (OECD 1994, 1996); this dichotomous model points to Anglo-Saxon experiences as the end of a modernizing process. The recent OECD report on Performance Management Practices (OECD 1997, p. 28) for example, proposes a semi-traditional clustering of Western countries which is clearly developmentalist according to their "management focus" (from "rule and norm management" to "performance management"). This model outlines 4 groups: Anglo-American, Scandinavian, Continental and Latin. However, these are "Implications without proof. The industrialized countries are quite plainly following different courses of development" according to some observers (König 1997, pp. 213-4). Furthermore, the lack of evaluations of the reforms going in the direction of New Public Management would make the identification of the real changes difficult. Other observers stress the differences between reform initiatives in North-America and a European trend of reform, and the ambiguous position of Great Britain in this general framework (Peters 1997). The diversity of patterns of change would become clearer were we to consider the single areas of institutional reform (for example, the differentiated adoption of the agency model in the European area, underlined by Peters 1997, p. 252) or if we look at the modernization strategies not at a macro-level – nation-state level – but at the local differences, at "the micro-level strategies of one part of a political system which allows us to use the microscope" (Klages and Löffler 1994 quoted in Flynn and Strehl 1996, p. 5). Hence, recent attempts to model comparative administration underline the importance of local practices and links (Peters 1997).

The available typologies of local governments follow a similar trajectory toward growing differentiation and uncertainty. The ideal starting point is not very clear. A trivial but necessary premise would be to say that even if we limit the focus to Western democracies, the spectrum of countries taken into consideration varies from one overview to another. Classical typologies distinguish the geographical areas of influence of each country which had the capacity to influence the political-administrative history of whole regions (e.g. France, England, Spain, the United States), in the case of Humes and Martin (1961) for example, this leads to four groups of countries within the Western World (Anglo-Saxon, Northern Europe, Central and Northwestern Europe, Southern Europe). Furthermore, we find typologies trying to combine historical considerations on administrative cultures and intergovernmental relationship, such as Bennett's subsequent attempts based on the individualization of two historical cleavages in the European region (Bennett 1989, 1993): the Reform led to a rapid secularization of the administration in Protestant (Northern and Western) Europe, in contrast to the persistence of a more hierarchical, separate structure in the more Catholic Southern and Eastern Europe. The latter found its form and was imposed by the French revolution and Napoleon's intervention, in a vast area of invasion and influence (France, Italy, Belgium, the Netherlands, northwestern Yugoslavia and Prussia, but also Spain, Portugal and Turkey, Austria-Hungary). Here the "excessive" decentralization of the Revolution was quickly replaced by the "fused system", with prefects and mayors as decisive central nominees, bureaucracy constituted a force which inhibited representation and self-governance. In contrast to this group of European states, two other distinct groups formed according to Bennett, namely those of the Scandinavian countries (Norway and Sweden) and Great Britain. These two models are labelled as "dual", and they are governed mainly by committees of local councillors. The Scandinavian model differs from the British one in terms of the influential presence of an executive authority (a governing board led by an elected chief executive) and in the strength of "peasant politics" favoured by the popular movements and a long distance from the central administration. Observations based on functional and financial measures of decentralization traditionally stress the North-South contrast within Western Europe, variously placing the United States and Britain in an Anglo-Saxon group. Hesse and Sharpe (1991), for example, propose a tripartite typology: the Anglo-Saxon area, according to their data, contrasts sharply with the Franco-group (France, Italy, Spain, Belgium, Portugal, and in part Greece) and with Central Europe. Focusing on the concrete intergovernmental relations, on decentralization in its multifarious dimensions, Page and Goldsmith provide further evidence of the contrast between Northern and Southern European Unitary States: "In the North European countries, by which we mean Britain, Denmark, Norway and Sweden, local government has traditionally had more extensive functions than in the South, including France, Italy and Spain, where local government had responsibility for a narrow range of functions until the end of the 1970s, since when sub-national government (but not necessarily the traditional municipalities) has received a number of additional functions. There are no clear differences in the degrees of discretion enjoyed by local authorities in the seven countries.... However, the types of limitation on discretion in Scandinavia and Britain differ from those in the South European states because there is greater emphasis in the former on specifying through general norms, statutes and regulations criteria that must be observed (statutory regulation); in the latter, many decisions of local authorities involve the intervention of central officials at an earlier stage in the policy process (administrative regulation).... The strength of direct channels of access, based on the importance of local politics and local legitimacy for national careers, encouraging the development of close links between the centre and specific localities through party or bureaucratic channels, distinguishes the South from the North" (Page and Goldsmith 1987, pp. 161-2). "Legal" or "political" localism is a distinction developed from a very different empirical and theoretical matrix, which reminds us of another "North-South" divide, the distinction between "civic" cultures and the others ("parochial", "subject" cultures (Almond and Verba 1963, Verba 1965), or, according to resuscitated terminologies, cultures labelled as "patrimonial"). The idea of a different quality of democracy in the "Northern world", in areas of the West not contaminated by the "Roman" influence, forms a ritual (more or less explicit) reference in the analysis of local government: the dichotomy offered, even before Almond and Verba, are "elementary categories" of the social and scientific interpretation of local politics.[1]

This almost obligatory reference – which the non-dual typologies also refer to, as we have seen above – is being used with increasing caution. Trends toward uniformity, and toward inversion of the traditional tendencies are being increasingly emphasized. Page and Goldsmith themselves have already suggested such a revisionist attitude in the conclusion of their report, with respect to intergovernmental relations: "In recent years, however, these contrasting patterns seem to have been reversed: in South Europe, despite fiscal stress, central government

---

[1] Thus, the contrast between France and the United States is underlined by Tocqueville "the New Englander is attached to his township not so much because he was born in it, but because it is a free and strong community, of which he is a member, and which deserves the care spent in managing it" (p.66). Just to give one more recent example, Gasser (1949) describes the world of triumphing "communalism" already as a "civic culture" ahead of its time: "the healthy democracies of our time (the Scandinavian States, the Anglo-Saxon world (Great-Britain, Canada, Australia, New Zealand, South Africa, the United States of America), plus the Netherlands and Switzerland), in which the inferior subdivisions are vivid organs, whose administrative autonomy is fully assured", which never knew the "imperative bureaucracy, imposed from the top, the allochtone management which peremptorily cuts the questions of regional and local administration" (p. 14) are also those countries in which "one is used to trust in the good faith of everybody towards the whole and of the whole towards everybody" (p.77).

has been devolving functions to subnational level, and is beginning to distance itself from the details of the locality, if not the region. In Northern Europe, despite some earlier decentralization, patterns of enhanced central control over local government have emerged, which have begun to involve the centre far more in the details of the locality" (Page and Goldsmith 1987, p.168).

It is interesting to observe, for example, that Humes has recently tried to integrate his previous typology with further reflections upon the internal municipal power-structure (though still referring mainly to its formal definition) and proposing a typology based on configurations of forms of control (Humes 1991). He examines 1) a British model of "inter-organizational (regulation)" in which the local executive is fully responsible to a council (not directly to a higher authority), 2) a "hybrid" German model of "subsidiarization" in which the local executive is responsible to the council for most functions, but is also responsible to a higher authority for the implementation of specific central policies, and 3) another "hybrid" French model of "supervision" in which the local executive is partially responsible to the council and, as a designated agent of a central authority or as a member of a central hierarchy, is directly responsible to it – and supervised by it.[2]

This not altogether convincing attempt to integrate or bridge classical cleavages echoes an emerging interest in further ecological reflections on local democracies. Norton faces the problem explicitly (Norton 1994). Having identified five main traditions of Local Government (South European, North European, British, North American and Japanese), specifying that the Federal Republic of Germany shows characteristics of both Southern and Northern European groups, Norton observes that "the classification resembles to most others that are known in identifying a Southern European group (Hesse and Sharpe 1991, Humes 1991, Page and Goldsmith 1987)". Norton goes on to say that the emphasis on the prefectural role in these analyses is now out of date, but not the close organic relationship between national, regional and local levels. "A reformulation is needed which fully takes into consideration the evolution of relationships between central, regional and local governments arising from the decentralization policies of the last twenty years and distinguishes France from other Latin nations in which *cumul des mandats* has had much less significance and in which regionalization has been more fundamental in its effects. In many respects, the latter countries are closer to Germany in their constitutions and their regional, electoral, political systems (p.13)". Furthermore, the Anglo group should be split in two: the North European group is closer to central Europe and should therefore be defined as a German/Scandinavian group, and, finally, Finland has developed a "special approach" to local democracy.

---

2 All three models obviously contrast with the Soviet "intra-organizational (subordination)" model whereby the local executive is part of the central hierarchy and wholly subordinated to a central authority.

To sum up, it emerges that in the overlapping of numerous stages of change and in their apparent recent acceleration many configurations have lost their clear-cut properties. Moreover we also observe a general obsolescence of the instruments of analysis. Many traditional indicators on which the functional typologies of local governments were based have now become – principally as a consequence of privatization and contracting out – difficult to interpret and difficult to use; an examination of the most recent and complete picture proposed by Norton (1994, pp. 63-66) sufficiently illustrates this difficulty. Indicators related to the actors' influence, to their behaviour and to their values seem in the end to be relatively more significant. This suggests a return to a more strictly "politological" analysis of local democracies and to more classic instruments of analysis in the field. The literature on the processes of decentralization/recentralization, of privatization and contracting out, on new forms of governance, on trends toward professionalization, has grown substantially over the last years; but a large and synthetic check of the transformations which they brought to local government (and which should not only go beyond the boundaries of the traditional "regional" aggregates of developed nations, taking into account a large variety of cases, but also beyond the traditional disciplinary boundaries between administrative studies and political analysis) may be helpful in reconstructing the new ecological picture of local governments.

The Comparative Strategy

The aim of the U.DI.T.E. project is to identify and describe the roles and functions of local government Chief Executive Officers and to understand how local authorities view their situation. By *Chief Executive Officers* are meant those actors who formally head the administrative apparatus in the municipalities. This category includes the American city manager, and the Belgian, French, Spanish and (for the moment) Italian *Secrétaire Général*, whose functions of coordination are not clearly defined and whose role is predominantly considered that of control: they are *Chief Administrative Officers* rather than *Chief Executive Officers*. Nevertheless, these actors hold the highest bureaucratic position with general functions in their municipalities (Mouritzen 1995). This stratum of bureaucrats has often been neglected in the national analyses of local government, and generally overlooked in the comparative studies. They are the "anonymous leaders". In the classic overviews previously mentioned, they appear only as dummy figures in a wide comparison between fused and dual systems and as a more or less influential element of the mechanism of internal coordination using a rough distinction between the national cases in which they are *primus inter pares* and in which they are "the hierarchical superior of all, or most, of the department heads" (Humes and Martin 1961, pp. 158-161). The scientific interest for this "category" in Humes' and Martin's study was to view the chief executive as an element in the professionalization of local government, to be studied in relation to the contemporary (and different) process of professionalization to which the political area was subjected. The "growing importance" it acquired in Western local governments was interpreted as "a result of the need for the type of top administrative leadership which can usually be best supplied by full-time officials who have trained for and have experience in the field. The development of council-appointed chief executives (elected officials, expected to be primarily a leader in the representative aspect of the local government process, editor's note) and the growing importance of the central administrative officer are inter-related trends with the same underlying causes" (ibid. p. 159).

Conducted with the moral support of the Union des Dirigeants Territoriaux de l'Europe and of its National Associations, and for this reason enigmatically called the U.DI.T.E. Leadership Study, this project was initially developed in the eight countries in which U.DI.T.E. was active. Subsequently, it has been extended throughout Europe including a few more Western countries which provide valuable reference points for the analysis of local political-administrative systems: the study now includes fifteen countries, studied by fifteen national research teams. Altogether more than four thousand *Chief Executive Officers (CEOs)* have been included in the survey.

The description of the category planned in the U.DI.T.E. Leadership Study project (Mouritzen 1995, Goldsmith and Mouritzen eds. 1997) includes many facets of the role and of those individuals holding it (cf. the survey questions in the appendix). The research design allows for both exploratory and explanatory efforts. It is an exploratory endeavour insofar as we are trying to identify who the CEOs are and how they view their world. It is explanatory because the many data and comparisons make it possible to test hypotheses and theories. It is only exceptional that we find studies based on an empirically founded comparison and identification of, e.g., new public managers, as does Farnham et al. (1996). Farnham and his colleagues identify managers in eight European countries who conform to NPM features, but they are not conducting comparative research along a joint research design. Most traditional studies of management and leadership, however, refer to leaders in private firms, and at best (as in Kickson ed. 1993) they are country to country studies; i.e., they are neither comparative nor built around a shared project design with a common methodological and theoretical framework. This is true for all the dominant schools on leadership (see e.g., Yukl 1989, Bryman 1996), such as: 1) the "traits approach" which dominated until the late 1940s (and where scholars sought to find specific traits of successful leaders); 2) the succeeding "style approach" which lasted until the late 1960s (where the choice of the right leadership style was seen as promoting well-functioning organizations); 3) the "contingency approach" which has been influential until today (where management is supposed to adapt to changing circumstances); and lastly 4) in the various modes of "New Leadership Approaches" which came to prominence in the 1980s and 1990s (emphasizing among other things charismatic leadership and value-oriented leadership). All these approaches are generic. What we set out to do is to explore who the CEOs of local government are, and to what extent they differ from one another and from leaders in other settings. Furthermore, we seek to explain the findings by testing various hypotheses grounded in theories as diverse as those of nation-building (Tilly ed. 1975), networks (Rhodes 1997) and national cultures (Hofstede 1980).

In this way, the intention is for this special but significant category of bureaucrats to contribute to improving our comparative knowledge in classical areas of the sociology of bureaucracy: the collected data relate to recruitment, attitudes, behaviour, structure of administrative systems, and bureaucratic outcomes. Referring to the main models offered by the current literature, it deals with the perceived roles, management styles and organizational cultures; special attention is paid to behaviour, a relatively neglected area in comparative administrative studies (Peters 1992). The data provide a vivid image of institutions and of everyday life in the municipalities, of the concrete structure of the political-administrative system, the processes of influence, relations to citizenship and administrative work.

The European surveys of the 1970s represent a permanent implicit reference which the project has modestly tried to renew in a field which has been marginal to comparative political sociology and comparative administrative studies. Permanent care was taken, in order to avoid the methodological amnesia which according to many observers is typical of the comparative tradition, and especially of the comparative survey tradition (Scheuch 1989, Kuechler 1987) so as to utilize the critiques of the previous generations of surveys (Przeworski-Teune 1970, Berting 1979, Niessen-Pieschar 1982, Ragin 1987, Sztompka 1988). The diversity of the disciplinary approaches and of the national traditions represented by the national teams (cf. appendix) contributed immensely to enriching the apparatus of questions and the common point of view, in contrast to the minimalist strategy often considered as an unavoidable feature for large surveys (Merritt-Rokkan 1966, Berting 1979, Niessen-Pieschar 1982). The consciousness of diversity dominated the definition of the research design and was confirmed and enriched during the process, while aiming at being a truly "cooperative" research effort (Rokkan 1968, Rokkan-Verba-Viet-Almasy 1969, Smelser 1976, Rose 1991). The result is that the research has been open, not only to questions which arose – more or less explicitly – in the international debates over the last years, but also to the specific national scientific problems, while less known, these are nevertheless stimulating at an international level (every questionnaire was composed of shared core questions and specific national questions). Similarly, the national reports included in this book were based on a common schedule of items corresponding to the comments of the collected data in the "core" part of the questionnaire and on the free choice of some key issues by the national teams. It is the responsibility of the national teams to summarize the results, to evaluate features they evoke, to reflect on the possible fallacies, and to evaluate the quality of the sample. Two distinct weighing procedures were defined in the elaboration programme, relevant to the dimensional-institutional characteristics of the municipalities (cf. appendix); nevertheless we decided for the first publication to allow the national teams to reflect freely on the data collected, on the possible bias of the sample and on the explanatory significance of the variables. This book, the first of the series based on the U.DI.T.E. Leadership Study, is the product of this attempt at a careful contextualization, being a first step in the cautious interpretation of the numerous data collected from the more than four thousand Chief Executive Officers who participated in the inquiry.

Local Government CEOs and Local Democracy

We have commented upon some of the data we collected through secondary analysis, interviews, job posting and the surveys, in order to answer several basic questions such as: 1. What does the system of local government look like? 2. What is the position of the CEOs in this system? 3. Who are they and where do they come from? 4. What do they do? 5. What do they think about politics? 6. What do they think about their own influence? 7. Who do they relate to and depend on? 8. How do they perceive the development of their roles?

This book faces these questions – which will be treated in comparative detail in the subsequent volumes from the project – from a specific point of view: it focuses on the diachronic and contextual dimensions of the collected data. We are mainly interested in change and its representations in one area of local government, the top leadership of local bureaucracies. To describe this area comparatively while observing our dual concerns for contextualization and diachrony, we carry out the secondary analysis offering normative and diachronic information, the network analysis and the interpretation of the role on the basis of the distinction between what we, using Putnam's (1975) dichotomy, call the political and the classical bureaucrat – derived from the classical divide between a more or less neutral and politicizing bureaucrat (See, eg., the discussion in Aberbach, Putnam and Rockman 1981 – also similar to elaborations about the spheres of elected officials and administrators, Svara 1990).

Studies of local government which systematically use network analysis are still not numerous. After the pioneer studies of the 1970s (Kotter and Lawrence 1974, Becquart-Leclerq 1976, Grémion 1976), the technique of network analysis became fashionable in the sense of the policy networks perspective (Rhodes 1997), i.e., it became an instrument to refine decisional analysis. Our questionnaire, thanks to two questions about "influence" in budgeting and in economic local policies, is informed by this kind of perspective; but the technique is used mainly to describe more institutionally, through his regular contacts, the CEO's position, inferring his (personal or institutional) resources of influence in local government from his daily activity (Laumann and Pappi 1976, Eulau 1986). The technique has never been systematically used in comparative analyses on local government. Tarrow's bi-national comparison was based on limited observations of the relations between local and national officials and party representatives (Tarrow 1977).

The comparison of the "average" networks of local CEOs in fifteen Western countries offers not only a good picture of the organization forms of administrative leadership (and coordination), but also an original insight into the structures of influence in local governments. To obtain such a picture, we were forced to reduce the complexity of the normative structures to standardized categories of actors. We chose to define a limited number of key figures uniformly present (mayors[3], department heads, opposition politicians and other politicians, employees, citizens, representatives of central government, representatives of other levels of government, business representatives, the press, trade unions, associations). But the national teams each specified relevant categories, subdividing them into several positions (the prefect and the other representatives of central bodies for example: a distinction used in the "franco-group"), or consolidating positions (such as the members of the municipal executive). This offered the possibility of comparison without too much reduction in the national significance of the results. In the network analyses we consider three dimensions of the contacts (frequency, importance and cooperation); the collected data are therefore rich and complex. The information gathered through the networks of local CEOs offers an opportunity to reconsider the ecology of local political-administrative systems on a more concrete basis. As we shall see, one of the important dimensions confirmed by the network analyses is related to the degree of influence of the "first citizen". The traditional American distinction between "strong mayor" and "weak mayor" systems is significant in every context.

For this book two different concepts of roles have been elaborated.[4] The first is the distinction made by Putnam (1975) seeing the CEO as a *classical bureaucrat versus a political bureaucrat* (constructed from key question number 23 cf. table 1.1). The second set of roles is connected to the role of the politicians as seen from the perspective of the CEO. Here we distinguish between roles emphasizing administration, representation, governance or stability (constructed from key question number 36 cf. table 1.2).

The emphasis the CEOs put on the different roles is indicated as an index-number. For more information on how these numbers are constructed, see the technical appendix at the end of this book.

---

3 The President of the Finnish Municipal Council was included among the "mayors" for the occasion: the data collected, as we shall see, underline nevertheless the arbitrariness of the definition.
4 In the chapter about the Swedish CEOs, the use of the role concept is different (cf. chapter 9). Australia, Ireland and Spain did not include the ideal role concepts of the politicians in their chapters. The Israeli contribution is an exception as well, insofar as no survey was carried out here – but the survey questions were used in qualitative interviews.

Table 1.1 The classical and the political bureaucrat. Key question 23:

"Chief executives must necessarily decide the priority of various tasks. Please indicate how much emphasis you in your daily work put on each of the tasks listed below?" (Cf. questionnaire).

The classical bureaucrat	The political bureaucrat
4. Guide subordinate staff in day-to-day handling of activities 8. Manage economic affairs, accounts and budgetary control 9. Ensure that rules and regulations are followed 10. Provide the mayor with legal, economic and other kinds of technical advice	3. Formulate ideas and visions 5. Promote and encourage new projects in the community 11. Provide the mayor with political advice 12. Be informed about citizens' viewpoints 13. Develop and implement norms concerning the proper roles of politicians vis-à-vis bureaucrats 14. Influence decision-making processes in order to secure sensible and efficient solutions

Table 1.2 The roles of the ideal politician. Key question 36:

"Politicians must give priority to different tasks in their daily work. As a local government official, to which tasks do you think the leading politicians ought to attach particular importance?" (Cf. questionnaire).

Administration	Representation
7. Be a spokesperson for local groups or individuals who have issues pending decisions by the authority 11. Lay down rules and routines for the administration 12. Taking decisions concerning specific cases	1. Be informed about citizens' views 2. Represent the municipality to the outside world 5. Defend the authorities' decisions and policies externally 9. Be a spokesperson for their political party 13. Be a spokesperson vis-à-vis the press

Governance	Stability
6. Implement the program on which he/she has been elected 8. Decide on major principles 10. Have a vision of the way in which the municipality will develop in the long run	3. Create stability for the administration 4. Formulate exact and unambiguous goals for the administration

The ideal roles of the politicians were created on the basis of factor analyses in order to distinguish between ideal roles in which politicians were seen by the CEOs to be more or less oriented towards administration (direct involvement in concrete administrative affairs), governance (policy-orientation, particular interest in long term development), representation (emphasizing the role of being someone's representative) and stability (playing the role of creating stability). The two polar role-types of the CEO distinguish between the roles associated with the classical bureaucrat (who is procedure and rule oriented – the loyal and neutral civil servant) and the political bureaucrat (who is problem and program oriented – the policy-oriented civil servant). While the former is mentally above politics the latter recognizes the inherent inseparability of administration and politics.

We are aware that there may be a problem regarding the pertinence of defining the areas of politics and bureaucracy which is nowadays generally solved in favour of a definition of policy action and governance in which a large configuration of actors intervenes at various levels (Pressman and Wildavsky 1973, Lipsky 1979, Barrett and Fudge 1981, Rhodes 1997). We have already observed that the ideal boundary between the world of "classic" bureaucracy and the world of "civic" bureaucracy has lost its clear geographical significance in the comparative overviews of local political-administrative systems. For several reasons, however, this does not mean that the distinction between policy and its implementation is no more useful in the analysis of public action or in the analysis of bureaucratic attitudes. First, if it is trivial to observe that bureaucrats intervene in the definition of policies everywhere, the question of "how much" and "how" they are influential in this definition remains a central problem in the analysis of democratic processes. The "classical-political bureaucrat" dichotomy and the description of the tasks on which it is based, remains a valuable reference for a rapid evaluation of this influence and of its forms. Second, the separation between politics and administration reappears periodically as a political theme which inspires different programmes of modernization of bureaucracy, asked either by bureaucrats or by politicians, according to the circumstances and the contents. Recently, in many countries, and especially at local levels, a recurrent theme has been the attempt to fight against the invasion of party politics in daily administration and to moralize local systems. The growing influence of bureaucracy in the definition of policies seems to be the result of a growing incapacity to generate decisions in an increasingly complex political arena. At the local level, this may also be seen as a consequence of a declining interest for politics and of growing difficulties in recruiting professionalized or competent elected officials. The limits ascribed to their own role and to the politicians' role by the bureaucrats are important components of their role perception, while the values to which these perceptions refer are important indicators of their conception of democracy. As we shall see, the national research teams' reactions to the results obtained in this part of the questionnaire offer interesting information about the dominant interpretations and about the variables that could affect them.

To conclude, our national reports offer mainly three kinds of comparative material: 1) a description of the institutional transformation (each chapter opens with a description of the CEOs' political-administrative environment and of the main changes which have affected it recently), 2) the justification proposed for it (information about the motives for action of the institutional entrepreneurs), and 3) the CEOs' own description of values related to their roles (especially those values concerning the definition of the specific fields of the administrators', and of the politicians' activity). This self-description is portrayed through network analysis of their behaviour and an implicit comparison between their ideal and their real roles. We shall see that at these three levels, the patterns of homogeneity and differences are slightly different, crudely suggesting the necessity of a serious refining of our national models and research instruments. A renewed attention to cooperative cross-national research strategies may meet this need.

We have chosen to arrange the chapters in an order which in part reflects the groupings of countries which emerges from the project. We have chosen to call our CEOs anonymous leaders because even though they are the formally appointed heads of the local government administration and therefore quite "visible" within the political and administrative system itself, they are little known, virtually unscrutinized by research and invisible to the public at large. It is the mayor who is visible, not the CEO. So the title "anonymous leader" also denotes an expectation regarding the overall role of the CEO: maybe he runs the city, but nobody knows!

Bibliography

Aberbach, Joel D., Robert D. Putnam, and Bert A. Rockman (1981): *Bureaucrats and Politicians*, Cambridge, M.A.: Harvard University Press.

Allison, Graham T. Jr. (1979): Public and Private Management: are they fundamentally alike in all unimportant respects?, in Jay M. Shafritz and Albert C. Hyde (eds.) (1987), *Classics of Public Administration*, Chicago: The Dorsey Press, pp. 510-528.

Almond, Gabriel A., and Sidney Verba (1963): *The Civic Culture; Political Attitudes and Democracy in Five Nations*, Princeton: Princeton University Press.

Armstrong, John Alexander (1973): *The European Administrative Elite*, Princeton: Princeton University Press.

Aucoin, Peter (1990): Administrative Reform in Public Management: Paradigms, Principles, Paradoxes and Pendulums, in *Governance: An International Journal of Policy and Administration*, Vol. 3, No. 2, pp. 115-37.

Baldersheim, Harald and Krister Ståhlberg (eds.) (1994): *Towards the Self-Regulating Municipality. Free Communes and Administrative Modernization in Scandinavia*, Aldershot: Dartmouth.

Barrett, Susan, and Colin Fudge (eds.) (1981): *Policy and Action*, London: Methuen.

Barzelay, Michael (1992): *Breaking through Bureaucracy: A New Vision for Managing in Government*, Berkeley: University of California Press.

Batley, Richard, and Gerry Stoker (eds.) (1991): *Local Government in Europe. Trends and Developments*, New York: St. Martin's Press.

Becquart-Leclercq, Jeanne (1976): *Paradoxes du pouvoir local*, Presses de la Fondation Nationale des Sciences Politiques.

Bellah, Robert et al. (1995): *Habits of the Heart: Individualism and Commitment in American Life*, Berkeley: University of California Press.

Bennett, Robert J. (ed.) (1989): *Territory and Administration in Europe*, London: Pinter.

Bennett, Robert J. (ed.) (1993): *Local Government in the New Europe*, London: Belhaven.

Berting, Jan et al. (eds.) (1979): *Problems in International Comparative Research in the Social Sciences*, Oxford: Pergamon Press.

Bryman, Alan (1996): Leadership in Organizations, in Stewart R. Clegg, Cynthia Hardy and Walter R. Nord (eds.) (1996): *Handbook of Organization Studies*, London: Sage, pp 276-292.

Bullman, Udo (Hrsg.) (1994): *Die Politik der dritten Ebene. Regionen im Europa der Union*, Baden-Baden: Nomos Verlagsanstalt.

Clark, Terry Nichols (ed.) (1994): *Urban Innovation. Creative Strategies for Turbulent Times*, Thousand Oaks: Sage.

Crozier, Michel (1995): *La crise de l'intelligence: Essai sur l'impuissance des élites à se réformer*, Paris: Interéditions.

DiMaggio, Paul J., and Walter W. Powell (1983): The Iron Cage Revisited: Institutional Isomorphism and Collective Rationality in Organizational Fields, in *American Sociological Review*, vol. 48, pp. 147-60.

Dogan, Mattei (ed.) (1975): *The Mandarins of Western Europe: The Political Roles of Top Civil Servants*, Beverly Hills: Sage.

Eldersveld, Samuel J., Jan Kooiman, and Teo van der Tak (1981): *Elite Images in Dutch Politics*, Ann Arbor: University of Michigan Press.

Etzioni, Amitai (1993): *The Spirit of Community: Rights, Responsibilities and the Communitarian Agenda*, New York: Crown.

Eulau, Heinz (1986): From Labyrinths to Network. Political Representation in Urban Settings, in R. Waste (ed.), *Community Power Structure*, Beverly Hills: Sage.

Farnham, David (1996): *New Public Managers in Europe. Public Servants in Transition*, Basingstoke: McMillan.

Flynn, Norman, and Frenz Strehl (1996): *Public Sector Management in Europe*, Harvester Wheatsheaf, Prentice-Hall.

Fukuyama, Francis (1995): *Trust: The Social Virtues and the Creation of Prosperity*, New York: The Free Press.

Gasser, Adolphe (1946): *L'autonomie communale et la reconstruction de l'Europe, Principes d'une interprétation éthique de l'histoire*, 2nde éd., Neuchatel: Baconnière.

Goldsmith, Michael, and Kurt Klaudi Klausen (eds.) (1997): *European Integration and Local Government*, Cheltenham: Edward Elgar.

Goldsmith, Michael, and Poul Erik Mouritzen (eds.) (1997), *The Udite Leadership Study*, Copenhagen: Kommunaldirektørforeningen i Danmark.

Grémion, Pierre (1976): *Le pouvoir périphérique; Bureaucrates et notables dans le système politique français*, Paris: Seuil.

Harmon, Michael M., and Richard T. Mayer (1986): *Organization Theory for Public Administration*, Glenwiew: Scott, Foresmann and Co.

Heady, Ferrel (1979): *Public Administration, A Comparative Perspective*, 2nd ed., Albuquerque: University of New Mexico.

Heffron, Florence (1989): *Organization Theory and Public Administration*, Englewood Cliffs: Prentice-Hall.

Hesse, Joachim Jens, and Lawrence James Sharpe (1991): Local Government in International Perspective: Some Comparative Observations, in J. J. Hesse (ed.), *Local Government and Urban Affairs in International Perspective*, Baden Baden: Nomos Verlag.

Hickson, David J. (ed.) (1993): *Management in Western Europe. Society, Culture and Organization in Twelve Nations*, Berlin: Walter de Gruyter.

Hill, Larry B. (ed.) (1992): *The State of Public Bureaucracy*, Armonk: E.M. Sharpe.

Hofstede, Geert (1980): *Culture's Consequences*, London: Sage.

Hood, Christopher (1995): Contemporary public management: a global paradigm? pp 104-17 in *Public Policy and Administration*, Vol.10, No. 2, Summer 1995.

Humes, Samuel, and Ellen M. Martin (1961): *The structure of Local Government Throughout the World*, Den Haag: Nijhoff.

Humes, Samuel (1991): *Local Governance and National Power, a Worldwide Comparison of Tradition and Change in Local Government*, New York: Harvester Wheatsheaf.

Kickert, Walter J.M. (ed.) (1997): *Public Management and Administration Reform in Western Europe*, Cheltenham: Edward Elgar.

Klages, Helmut, and E. Löffler (1994), *Public Sector Modernisation in Germany, Recent Trends and Emerging Strategies,* IIAS Working Group on Public Sector Productivity, Helsinki (July 1994).

König, Klaus (1997), Entrepreneurial Management or Executive Administration: The Perspective of Classical Public Administration, in Kickert (ed.) 1997, pp. 213-232.

Kotter, John P., and Paul R. Lawrence (1974): *Mayors in Action: Five Approaches to Urban Governance*, New York: Wiley.

Kuechler, M. (1987): The Utility of Surveys for Cross-National Research, *Social Science Research*, XVI, 3, September pp. 229-244.

Kymlicka, Will (1995): *Multicultural Citizenship*, Oxford: Oxford University Press.

Lane, Jan Erik (ed.) (1997): *Public Sector Reform: Rationale, Trends and Problems*, London: Sage.

Laumann, Edward O., and Franz Urban Pappi (1976): *Networks of Collective Action*, New York: Academic Press.

Lawson, Kay, and Peter H. Merkl (eds.) (1988): *When Parties Fail, Emerging Alternative Organizations*, Princeton: Princeton University Press.

Leonardi, Robert (1994): *Convergence, Cohesion and Integration in the European Union*, London: St. Martin's Press.

Lipsky, Michael (1979): *Street Level Bureaucracy*, New York: Russell Sage Foundation.

Mellbourn, Anders (1979), *Byråkratins ansikten*, Stockholm: Liber.

Marks, Gerry (1993): Structural Policy and Multilevel Governance in the EC, in Alan W. Cafruny and Glenda G. Rosenthal (eds.) (1993): *The State of the European Community*, vol 2, Boulder: L. Rienner.

Marks, Gerry, L. Hoghe, and K. Blank (1996): Between Nation-State, Regionalism and World Society: The European Integration Process, *Journal of Common Market Studies*, vol. 34, no. 3, pp 341-378.

Merritt, Richard L., and Stein Rokkan (eds.) (1966): *Comparing Nations: the Use of Quantitative Data in Cross-National Research*, New Haven: Yale University Press.

Mouritzen, Poul Erik (1995): *A Comparative Research Project on Chief Executives in Local Government: the Udite Leadership Study*, Odense: Odense University.

Mouritzen, Poul Erik (ed.) (1993): *Defending City Welfare*, Beverly Hills: Sage.

Mouritzen, Poul Erik, and Kurt Houlberg Nielsen (1988): *Handbook of Comparative Urban Fiscal Data*, Odense: DDA.

Niessen, Manfred, and Jules Peschar (eds.) (1982): *International Comparative Research; Problems of Theory, Methodology and Organisation in Eastern and Western Europe*, Oxford: Pergamon Press.

Norton, Alan (1994): *International Handbook of Local and Regional Government; A Comparative Analysis of Advanced Democracies*, Aldershot: Edward Elgar.

OECD (1994): *Performance Management in Government: Performance Management and Results-Oriented Management*, Paris: OECD.

OECD (1996): *Performance Management in Government: Contemporary Illustrations*, Paris: OECD.

OECD (1997): *In Search of Results, Performance Management Practices*, Paris: OECD.

Olsen, Johan P. (1991): Modernization Programs in Perspective: Institutional Analysis of Organizational Change, in *Governance: An International Journal of Policy and Administration*, Vol. 4, No. 2, pp. 125-149.

Olsen, Johan P., and B. Guy Peters (1996): *Lessons from Experience – Experiential Learning in Administrative Reforms in Eight Democracies*, Oslo: Scandinavian University Press.

Osborne, David, and Ted Gaebler (1992): *Reinventing Government. How the Entrepreneurial Spirit is Transforming the Public Sector*, Reading: Addison-Wesley.

Page, Edward C., and Michael Goldsmith (eds.) (1987): *Central and Local Government Relations: A Comparative Analysis of West European Unitary States*, London: Sage.

Perry, James L., and K.L. Kraemer (1983): *Public Management: Public and Private Perspectives*, Palo Alto: Mayfield PC.

Peters, B. Guy, (1992): Comparative Perspectives on Bureaucracy in the Policy Process, in Hill (ed.), pp. 87-110.

Pressman, Jeffrey, and Aaron Wildavsky, (1973): *Implementation*, Berkeley: University of California Press.

Przeworski, Adam, and Henry Teune. (1970): *Logic of Comparative Inquiry, Comparative Studies in Behavorial Science*, New York: Wiley.

Putnam, Robert D. (1973): *The Beliefs of Politicians. Ideology, Conflict and Democracy in Britain and Italy*, New Haven: Yale University Press.

Putnam, Robert D. (1975): The political attitude of senior civil servants in Britain, Germany and Italy, in Mattei Dogan (ed.) 1975 pp. 87-128.

Putnam, Robert D. (1993): *Making Democracy Work: Civic Traditions in Modern Italy*, Princeton: Princeton University Press.

Putnam, Robert D. (1995): Tuning In, Tuning Out: the Strange Disappearance of Civic America, *Political Science Review*, 28, 4.

Putnam, Robert D. (1976): *The Comparative Study of Political Elites*, Englewood Cliffs: Prentice-Hall.

Ragin, Charles C. (1987): *The Comparative Method, Moving beyond Qualitative and Quantitative Strategies*, Berkeley: University of California Press.

Rhodes, Roderick A.W. (1997): *Understanding Governance. Policy Networks, Governance, Reflexivity and Accountability*, Buckingham: Open University Press.

Rokkan, Stein (ed.) (1968): *Comparative Research across Cultures and Nations*, Paris: Mouton.

Rokkan, Stein, Sidney Verba, JeanViet and Elina Almasy (1969): *Comparative Survey Analaysis*, Den Haag: Mouton.

Rose, Richard (1991): *Comparing Forms of Comparative Analysis*, Glasgow: University of Strathclyde.

Sayre, Wallace S. (1951): Trends of a decade in administrative values, *Public Administration Review*, 11, 4, pp. 1-9.

Sayre, Wallace S. (1958): Premises of Public Administration: Past and Emerging, *Public Administration Review*, 18, 2, pp. 102-5.

Scheuch, Erwin K. (1989): Theoretical Implications of Comparative Survey Research: Why the Wheel of Cross-Cultural Methodology Keeps on Being Reinvented, *International Sociology*, IV, 2, pp. 147-167.

Smelser, Neil J. (1976): *Comparative Methods in the Social Sciences*, Englewood Cliffs: Prentice-Hall.

Suleiman, Ezra N. (ed.) (1984): *Bureaucrats and Policy-Making: A Comparative Overview*, New York: Holmes and Meier.

Svara, James (1990): *Official Leadership in the City. Patterns of Conflict and Cooperation*, New York: Oxford University Press.

Sztompka, Piotr (1988): Conceptual Frameworks in Comparative Inquiry: Divergent or Convergent?, *International Sociology*, III, 3, pp. 207-218.

Tarrow, Sidney (1977): *Between Center and Periphery; Grassroots Politicians in Italy and France*, New Haven: Yale University Press.

Tilly, Charles (ed.) (1976): *The Formation of National States in Western Europe*, Princeton: Princeton University Press.

Tocqueville, Alexis de (1991): *Democracy in America*, (18th print., trans. H. Reeve, rev. F. Bowen, ed. P. Bradley), New York: Knopf.

Verba, Sidney (1965): *Political Culture and Political Development*, Princeton: Princeton University Press.

Wolman, Harald, and Michael Goldsmith (1992): *Urban Politics and Policy: A Comparative Approach*, Oxford: Blackwell.

Yukl, Gary A. (1989): *Leadership in Organizations*, London: Prentice-Hall.

CHAPTER 2

The Challenge of Constant Change: The Australian Local Government CEO

by Rolf Gerritsen and Michelle Whyard

Introduction

Over the past 15 years, there have been two interacting phenomena that have reshaped the role of the Australian local government CEO: the "managerialist" and the "privatisation" revolutions – both of which have implications for the workplace practices and careers and the roles and accountability of CEOs. Overlaying these factors are the new demands created by the legislative enhancement of public participation, the expansion of the functional roles of local government, in part a result of some concurrent functional devolution of central government functions to local government (traditionally a sphere of Australia's States), and the new demands of local government regionalism. Local government continues to suffer resource scarcity, mostly imposed by the other tiers of Australian government.

Within this general framework, there is great diversity in the roles and power of Australian CEOs. This diversity is partly to do with the differing scales of local government relative to their State governments and partly to an urban-rural divide (which in some States is reflected in widely differing sizes of and populations within local governments).

Australia's Diverse Local Government Systems
Australia, like Germany and the USA, is a federation. This affects local government because State governments have legislative control over their local government system. This means that Australia has, in effect, seven (eight if we include the partly separate Indigenous local governance structures) distinct local government systems.

Australia began its modern history in 1788 as an English penal colony, with only gradual decentralisation of political power from the imperial metropole to Colonial governments. For administrative purposes these governments established administrative or police districts (Power, Wettenhall & Halligan 1981: 7), which later often became the foundation of the areas for incorporated local authorities. The first conventional local government was established in Melbourne in 1842 (Bowman 1983: 166). This municipal government was modelled on England's Boroughs Act of 1835[1] and provided what now would be called urban services. Municipal forms of local government then spread throughout the large towns of New South Wales and Victoria again following English models, which continued to dominate Australian local government structures (if not functions) until the post-World War II period and which were not completely exorcised until the 1980s (when the States granted local government constitutional recognition). In some rural areas local farmers cooperated to establish Roads Boards or Roads Trusts. These authorities had the power to build roads and for a time to levy road user tolls as well as property rates to pay for the road construction. The Colonial governments encouraged local communities to form local governing authorities to provide basic urban and roads services (Halligan & Wettenhall 1989).

Nevertheless, local governments remained weak, usually being too small, parochial and under-resourced to be effective service providers. Yet more were created. It was not until a decade after World War 1 that the trend to reduce the number of local authorities commenced[2]. The centralised institutional control over local government was continued by the State governments of the Twentieth Century, and these often established State Trading Enterprises to carry out the services normally associated with English local authorities. The temptation for State governments to redefine local government boundaries to increase their geographic and population scales (and hence resources) remained a constant refrain, this being most spectacularly exhibited in the drastic, compulsory Council amalgamations in Victoria in 1994[3]. Since 1906 the average population of Australia's local governments has increased from 3,000 to 23,500. However this masks considerable divergence between States, with Western Australian median about 12,500 and Victoria's about 35,000 (with ranges from a low 500 in WA to a high of 150,000 people in Victoria).

After World War II many local governments moved to expand their functions. They began to move beyond their traditional "roads, rates and rubbish" focus, initially to include town planning functions such as zoning, building and health standards creation (Lang 1991) and later personal services (especially recreation

---

1 This established the English model of Crown-conferred local government (ie., that local governance was within the grant of the national state) rather than constitutionally derived local government, which was based on rights under natural law (Norton 1994: 9).
2 This is a highly simplified account that understates the substantial differences within Australian colonies/-States. For some elucidation of these see the individual State chapters in the Power, Wettenhall & Halligan 1981 ACIR volume.
3 The 210 Councils were amalgamated into 78 by legislative fiat of the State government, which appointed Commissioners to run the new Councils for two years before the process of electing new Councils was carried out over 1996 and 1997.

and sports facilities), welfare services (ALGA 1993; Ohlin 1992; Roberts 1989) and economic development. This trend has been uneven, being more marked in the most populous States (especially Victoria) and in the nation's metropolitan and large provincial city local authorities (Cutts & Osborn 1989: Table 2.1.1, pp 13-16). In the rural areas local government has been much more focused upon roads provision and other services have received far less priority (and are usually only undertaken when Federal or State payments provide the fiscal resources under specific purpose programs).

If we look at the inter-State comparisons we see that there is still considerable variation within Australian local government (Cutts & Osborn 1989). Taking comparative per capita expenditure data (for example) reveal the fact that – notwithstanding a decade of nationally similar reform – the States still have their own policy priorities and preferences, mostly following an inertial legacy of past practices (Australian Bureau of Statistics, 1993-94 Government Finance Statistics Australia – Catalogue 5512)

It is apparent that even after a decade of intensive (and on-going) reform, Australia's seven systems (including the Northern Territory) of local government have retained much of their traditional focuses of concern. Though the reforms had common national elements, they did not produce uniform results. For example, Western Australians appear to cling tenaciously to their tradition of small local governments (Park Report 1996).

It is not just in its services organisation, size and population that Australian local government is very diverse.

Until 1986 (when WA abolished the property qualification and introduced the universal franchise) the representative basis of local government in Australia was not uniform across all the States. Even now only in NSW, Queensland and Victoria does the State Government declare all Council seats vacant at each local government election (Cutts 1995). The degree of formal political party involvement ranges from overt in Brisbane, Sydney and Melbourne to almost nonexistent in most rural Shires. Historically the degree of land use planning carried out by local government differed widely between States and even within them. The size of local authorities varies from one square kilometre (Peppermint Grove in WA) to several hundreds of thousands of square kilometres (East Pilbara in WA). Similarly the population range can be from a few hundred (eg., the Ngaanyatjarraku Shire in WA) to the almost one million people in the Brisbane City Council. The uneven resource endowments of local authorities has always been a problem. During the 1970s the Federal government recognised this by providing horizontally equalising general purpose Financial Assistance Grants (FAGs) to the States for on-passing to local government (Bowman 1983: 174-75).

Finally, though not included here, from the late 1970s a system of Indigenous local governance has emerged. This system has evolved considerably to the present, though it is largely confined to the northern areas of Australia (Gerritsen forthcoming).

The Indigenous local government sector has the effect of making the determination of the number of local authorities difficult. Also, this is a constantly moving field. Local governments are being amalgamated and – in the case of the Towns of Cambridge, Victoria Park and Vincent excised in 1994 from the City of Perth – "de-amalgamated" continuously. This makes any global figures subject to continuous revision. However, at present in Australia there are about 700 mainstream local governments (including the 30 Community Governments in the NT) and some 70 other Indigenous local governing authorities that have statuses separate from those defined under the relevant State Local Government Acts. So, depending upon the definition of local government, Australia has between 675 and 775 local governments.

For present purposes Indigenous local government CEOs were excluded from this survey. So our Australian sample is based on 246 responses from the 675 mainstream Councils and is broadly representative of Australian local government.

The CEO's Politico-Administrative Context
Over the past two decades the broad functions and operations of Australian local government have changed radically (Jones 1993). This means that the job of the local government CEO is unrecognisable from that of a generation ago.

The roles of local government have generally expanded beyond direct provision of physical infrastructure and garbage services especially into community welfare and environmental services (Osborn & Cutis 1995). In the community services area, local governments can choose to involve themselves in the provision, management or operation of "service" functions such as: community services, public health, cultural, educational and library services; public transport; sport, entertainment and recreation; and housing. In practice there is a wide range of local government services in Australia. Queensland local governments, and the larger local governments of Victoria and NSW tend to provide the widest range of services. The less-populous States, with their smaller property rates base and State governments unwilling to provide local government with program funding, tend to have a narrower range of services.

At present the Federal government provides local government with roads funding and some Specific Purpose Payments for the operation of childcare and multicultural community services (Bowman 1985; AUDR 1994). To achieve some horizontal equalisation, the Federal government also provides general purpose Financial Assistance Grants (Maskell 1989). Federal contributions average 15 per cent of local government revenues, though this ranges from about six per cent for the larger, better-resourced Councils to over 80 per cent for some large, under-populated rural Shires in the remote areas of Australia.

This provides the CEO with an elaborate and sometimes confusing web of accountability. For example, in delivering aged care services under the Home and Community Care program, the CEO can be accountable simultaneously to his/her Council as well as to State and Federal government program officers.

The Normative Framework
The normative framework of the local government CEO has changed over the past two decades. In part this has been because of the re-formulation of the CEO role under the new State government's Local Government Acts and in part because of the influence of "managerialism" and the "privatisation" of many local government functions.

The major statutory change has been the codification of the "Westminster" distinction between policy and implementation. Now the elected Councillors are expected to make policy, with the CEO responsible to the Council for implementation of that policy. In addition local government now faces a variety of statutory demands for community consultation and participation, which complicates the CEO's life (McKenna 1995).

The effects of "managerialism" has been to reshape the workplace and organisational structures of local government. There is an increasing emphasis upon formal qualifications in the training and recruitment of local government CEOs. A slight majority (and a great majority of younger CEOs) have a university degree, usually in management (especially those under 45 years old) or engineering. The local government CEO is now expected to be an educated "generalist" manager and not necessarily equipped with skills or particular knowledge of any of the Council's service activities. Recruitment of CEOs from outside the local government sector is now common.

The "privatisation" of local government services (ERC 1990) has also redefined the role of the CEO. In particular, the use of the distinction has made CEOs (now the purchaser rather than the provider) contract managers and blurred – even contradicted – the formal accountability requirements of local government CEOs.

The CEO's Career and Status

Although Local Government has traditionally been a sector where a great deal of mobility is expected in order to be able to progress within the structure, eighty per cent of the respondents spent at least part of their childhood in the state where they presently work. From the information collected on previous employment, seventy per cent moved into their present position from another municipality, where a majority of them (56%) were either the CEO or Deputy CEO. It appears therefore that the mobility is intra-State, which is not surprising considering the Australian local government legislative structure where each State has a separate and unique Local Government Act.

Relations between the CEO and the Mayor in Australian local government vary widely between States and within them. However, generally Australian local government is characterised by an absence of overt partisan political affiliation, by either the CEO or the Mayor. Only in the three major coastal cities of the east coast – Sydney, Melbourne and Brisbane – are the relations affected by the party political affiliations of the Mayor. Even in the LGAs in these cities the CEO usually affects party neutrality. Consequently, relations between the CEO and the Mayor are primarily determined by their respective personalities, personal reputations and local influence.

The status of the local government CEO varies. It is highest in the four less populous States (and the Northern Territory) and lowest in the two large States, NSW and Victoria, where there are larger State government and private sector bureaucracies. The status of the CEO is also partly inverse to the degree of organised political party involvement in local government elections. This is mostly confined to Victoria and NSW and to the larger local governments of Queensland. Within States the CEOs of the large (mostly metropolitan and provincial city) Councils is high, as is the status of the CEO of small rural shires, where the Shire General Manager is a significant local figure in a small, parochial political arena (Gray 1991). The lowest status element is for the mid-range of metropolitan and provincial municipal Council CEOs.

Australian local government has been historically a male preserve. Recently women have secured a greater proportion of elected Council positions. This feminisation of Councils has not yet extended to Council CEOs. Even now only four per cent of CEOs are female, most of these coming from a human services background. In this gender imbalance Australia differs significantly from European local government.

Local government managers work hard, the range reported to us being from 38 to 80 and the average 50 hours per week. On average CEOs spend six years in their job (as they did in their previous position) and most feel that they will move on before completing their career. Historically, mainly because of the statutory, industry-specific qualifications required of local government CEOs, they have come entirely from within the local government sector. This has changed dramatically because of the managerial reforms of the past 20 years, with only 40 per cent of local government CEOs now coming from within the sector.

The Employment Structure of Australian Local Government
Though it is by far the smallest of the three tiers of government, historically Australian local government has been a significant local employer (Osborn 1995). The employment structure of local government was dominated by the distinction between "inside" (ie., clerical and management) and "outside" (labourers, plant operators etc.) staff.

Because of its organisation and minimal resources as much as its functions, local government workforces were different from those of the Federal and State spheres of government. The major differences were:

- Local government had the lowest proportion of professionals, para-professionals and managers/administrators;
- Local government had a higher proportion of its workforce occupied by plant/-

machine operators, drivers and related workers (reflecting the property service/infrastructure provision roles of Councils); and
- Local government had the lowest proportion of female workers in the public sector.

In rural and remote region Councils the proportions of "outside" staff (principally workers and plant operators on roadmaking gangs) was higher and the educational qualifications of clerical, professional/managerial staff lower than the average for the local government sector as a whole. Professionals and para-professionals outside the traditional Council Engineers and Council Clerks were concentrated in the expanding community services areas, which were mainly the province of larger urban Councils, particularly in Victoria.

During the 1980s the workforce structure began to change. In part this change followed the gradual expansion of the role of local government. As it moved into human services and community development, local government began to employ more professionals and para-professionals. More than previously, these new employees were women, particularly in the human services areas. A few of these women have since become CEOs. The gathering reforms of the 1980s also changed the structure of the workforce. Contracting out rubbish collection, for example, replaced "outside" labourers and plant operators with clerical and managerial staff (Gerritsen & Albin 1993). These changes added to the pressures for reform, some of which – such as the introduction of contracts and performance-based management – were common to all Australian public sector employees (Crawford 1996: 43-49).

The managerial reform of the local government sector over the last decade has been profound. Changes in work practices, organisational restructuring, staff evaluation and staff training have all been part of this package, albeit unevenly applied (AUDR 1994: Table 12, p.57). This evolution is often expressed in professional circles as one from administration to management. In this matter local governments and their CEOs have responded to the same microeconomic reform agenda as the other spheres of Australian government (Crawford 1996), though more wholeheartedly and completely. Like most other public and private enterprises, local government has been affected by the broad evolution of human resource management over the past decade or so. Examples of such influences have been Federal initiatives such as Equal Employment Opportunity, Occupational Health and Safety measures and the 1992 Disability Discrimination Act. These have introduced new demands upon local government CEOs.

However the essence of the management reforms that have particularly affected local government have been (Martin 1997: 209, passim):

- a focus on service delivery outcomes rather than administrative process;
- a change in the nature and organisation of local government employment;
- a more comprehensive evaluation of private versus public costs; and
- a transfer of significant service delivery functions to the private sector, with

the CEO overseeing this delivery and accountable for it to the elected Councillors.

Most of the new State Acts have imposed business-like frameworks on local governments, both in their staffing reorganisation and the requirement to prepare corporate plans and to base their budgets upon those plans (AUDR 1994: chapter 10). Most States have encouraged a redefinition of local government service delivery. Some States (ie., Victoria) have imposed Compulsory Competitive Tendering on local government, seeking to accelerate the contracting-out of local government services. Other States, such as South Australia, have achieved similar outcomes to the Victorian ones (AUDR 1994: Table 12, p.57) but without the compulsory element.

The "Privatisation" of the Local Government State
Usually described as "contracting out", this phenomenon in particular has reshaped the local government workforce in recent years.

One consequence of contracting out waste disposal and some other services is that managers/administrators, other professionals and para-professionals now constitute about 27 per cent of the local government sector workforce, not too far away from the same measure for the Federal government (38%), but still some distance away from State governments (56%). The local government CEO, rather than directly controlling the workforce and its service delivery, now oversees a group of professionals, many supervising contracts with private sector enterprises that deliver these services. This means that the CEO now supervises persons and activities in which he/she has no direct competence, adding both to the complexities of the job and leading to a change in its definition – from direct supervisor to generalist manager.

Local Government Workplace Reform
This is often defined broadly to encompass matters such as: the changing roles of the elected Members, human resource development, intergovernmental initiatives, the entrepreneurial activities of local government, and the role of unions (Martin 1997: 214). Where this is more narrowly defined it usually includes:

- more flexible patterns of workplace organisation, specifically the introduction of purpose-specific, program-based, organisational units and the recognition of part-time work;
- the enhanced utilisation of output-oriented performance measurement and evaluation and the linking of executive remuneration to the results of this evaluation; and
- the reduction of "professional" workplace barriers and restrictions and an emphasis upon corporate culture and objectives, the latter including internal processes of consultation and participation in designing work.

Because many local governments do not have the resources either to engage in direct workplace bargaining to secure enterprise agreements or to be represented at industrial tribunals, the sector has largely relied upon the State/Territory Local Government Associations for the carriage of industrial agreements. The nature of workplace contracts is still largely outside the powers of the local government CEO, though he/she remains responsible for their performance.

The Roles and Values of the CEO

The roles of the CEO are now more analogous to the private sector manager than was historically the case. Our sample of CEOs define their priorities with an outcomes orientation rather than the process orientation more prevalent a decade ago.

In terms of establishing priorities in their daily work, accomplishing tasks efficiently and quickly easily topped the list as our CEOs first priority, followed by ensuring wide involvement in the decision-making process (the new statutorily required public participation factor). Observing established rules and procedures came a distant third in prioritising these three considerations.

Overall, making assisting in formulating policy for the Mayor and Council and ensuring that resources are used efficiently are overwhelmingly given the most emphasis in the CEOs daily work. Table 2.1 indicates the ranking that CEOs place on a variety of tasks and places them within the framework of the classical and political bureaucrat.

It appears that Australian CEOs are different to their European counterparts. The political bureaucrat scores high and they place far less emphasis upon the *administrator* and *integrator* aspects of their role than do the South European CEOs. For the Australian CEO the leadership or *entrepreneur* role is important. The *fundraiser* and *adviser* roles are in the mid- range of importance.

Some of the reform impetus of the recent past has clearly changed CEO behaviour. Thus the CEOs ranking of their task priorities clearly reflects "managerialist" changes as well as the new demands of accountability and public participation, which have introduced the necessity for the CEO to be a community leader.

Table 2.1 The roles of the CEOs, Australia

The classical bureaucrat		62
Guide subordinate staff in day-to-day handling of activities	52	
Manage economic affairs, accounts and budgetary control	65	
Ensure that rules and regulations are followed	54	
Provide the mayor with legal, economic and other kinds of technical advice	77	
The political bureaucrat		70
Formulate ideas and visions	86	
Promote and encourage new projects in the community	73	
Provide the mayor with political advice	49	
Be informed about citizens' viewpoints	77	
Develop and implement norms concerning the proper roles of politicians vis-á-vis the bureaucrats	56	
Influence decision-making processes in order to secure sensible and efficient solutions	76	

Relationship with the Elected Members
The majority of the "political" tasks of the CEO can be broken up into three activities: council relations, community leadership, and administrative activities. There is an overwhelming feeling that managing relations with the Councillors is the most important in terms of ensuring job success.

With this in mind, it is interesting to look at how CEOs feel about their relations with the Councillors. There is strong agreement (71%) that it is the politician's duty to decide on principal issues and to leave routine matters to the bureaucratic arm. This opinion is certainly an offshoot of the new Local Government Acts which legislate the responsibilities of the elected Councillors as analogous to those of Boards of Directors – to be planners, not implementers. The implementation role is for the CEO.

Likewise, there is strong agreement that the CEO should assume leadership in shaping municipal policies and be a prime mover in adapting the local authority to changes in society. Thus, CEOs see themselves as advisers to the policy arm. It is their opinion that recommendations presented to the elected members be based on non-partisan expert opinion and promote policies that are of benefit to the community, not simply those that are in line with the politicians' interests.

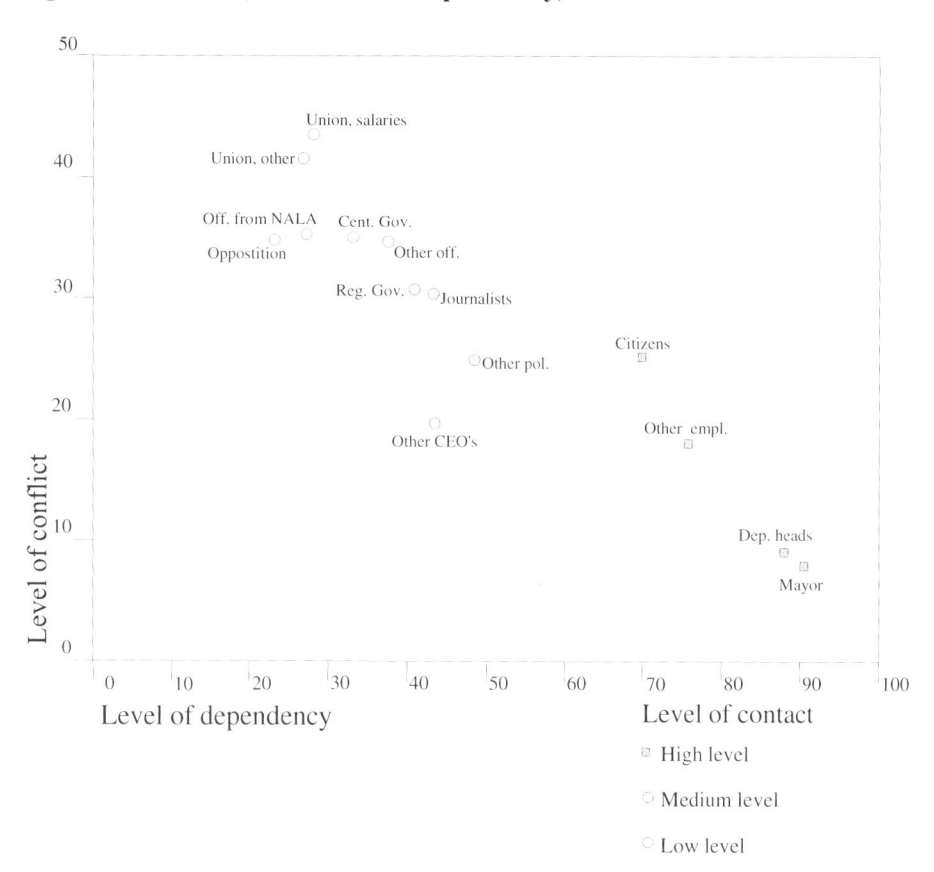

Figure 2.1 Contact, conflict and dependency, Australia

Scatter plot with axes "Level of conflict" (y-axis, 0–50) and "Level of dependency" / "Level of contact" (x-axis, 0–100). Legend: High level, Medium level, Low level.

Points plotted:
- Union, salaries (~25, 43) – Medium
- Union, other (~18, 40) – Medium
- Off. from NALA (~18, 35) – Medium
- Cent. Gov. (~28, 35) – Medium
- Opposition (~20, 33) – Medium
- Other off. (~33, 33) – Medium
- Reg. Gov. (~28, 30) – Medium
- Journalists (~33, 29) – Medium
- Citizens (~72, 25) – High
- Other pol. (~45, 24) – Medium
- Other CEO's (~38, 19) – Medium
- Other empl. (~75, 18) – High
- Dep. heads (~85, 8) – High
- Mayor (~87, 6) – High

These opinions are consistent with the amount of influence the CEO feels is brought to bear in both the budget making process and in local economic development. In both cases, they rate themselves as being the most influential in terms of policy making. In regard to the budget, the departmental heads and rank and file employees are given greater influence in the budget making process, followed only then by the Mayor and members of Council. The situation is similar in terms of economic development with the inclusion of a high degree of influence being wielded by local private business interests.

The amount of influence attached to each of the above interests is mirrored in the relationship between contact, conflict and dependency (figure 2.1) and by the extent to which good relationships are important in order to fulfil the functions of the CEO. Ninety-five per cent of the respondents indicated that their relationship with the Mayor (or Shire Chairman/President in rural local governments) was either very important or important. Similarly, ninety-four per cent felt the same regarding their relationships with the heads of departments within their organisation. Rates of contact by meetings, phone calls, discussions, etc, support the importance of these relationships. Forty-eight per cent communicate with the

Mayor daily, with a further forty-six per cent speaking with him between two and four times per week. Department heads are spoken to by eighty per cent of the CEOs daily. In both cases the CEOs reported a high degree of cooperation with each of the groups. In fact the only group which seemed to create any sense of conflict were the trade unions. Although several individuals did indicate some conflict with some actors and interest groups in the municipal arena, sixteen per cent reported a conflictual relationship with the union over salaries and twelve per cent over other issues.

Values
In socio-economic terms, Australian Local Government CEOs are an unusual group of professionals. They are less educated (in the sense of having a tertiary education qualifications) than are State and Federal officers with similar levels of responsibility. Of course this may merely reflect the old Town/Shire Clerk professional training system (Solomon 1993) and could be expected to change in the near future as the older generation of CEOs retires. More striking, however, is the proportion of CEOs who come from a small business parental background. Thirty-two per cent of CEOs (54% in non-metropolitan Councils) come from a household where the head ran their own business. In a society where the self-employed are about 6 per cent (or 12 per cent if you count farmers) of the workforce, this is an intriguing result and may explain the general support of CEOs for the "privatisation" of local government functions and the more private sector-like restructuring of local government workplace organisation.

In Australia a small business background usually denotes a conservative political allegiance. Yet 87 per cent of our CEOs have never been a member of a political party, higher than for any European country in the U.Di.T.E. study. This reflects the apolitical traditions of Australian local government administration, even in those States where there is overt political party electoral involvement in local government. Only about six per cent of our CEOs think that a major task of their elected Councillors is to be a spokesperson for a particular party, a much smaller proportion of the sample than work in Councils where active political allegiances apply to Council elections. Indeed Australian CEOs appear to be technocratically managerialist and anti-political to the point of cynicism in their orientation. Only about 35 per cent believed that elected Councillors should implement the platform upon which they had been elected!

Most of the negative comments made by CEOs about their job in our survey concentrated upon the heavy workload and the changes in the norms and cultures of local government administration. The most positive aspect of the CEOs' evaluation of their jobs was in the increased autonomy and legitimacy for their role as a result of recent reforms of the States' Local Government Acts.

As a leader within the administrative structure, the CEO has a variety of management techniques at his fingertips which he can use in his daily work. When asked to prioritise aspects of leadership, it becomes very apparent that there is a strong reliance on motivation through commendation and individual reward.

Formal power is given very little priority, with most of the CEOs depending on strong personal relationships rather than official authority. This partly reflects broader Australian politico-administrative cultural traditions, which discourage the overt, public application of power.

CEO Networks and Influence

As nearly 40 per cent of Australian CEOs identified their first job as being one in local government, they generally have some experience in recognising and organising local networks and community groups. This aspect of the Australian CEO's duties has been given increased emphasis since the 1980s.

Mainly because of the generally minimal role played by political parties in Australian local government[4], the CEO is at the centre of interest intermediation in local politics. This tendency has been strengthened by the legislative requirements for community consultation and participation introduced over the past decade. Here the legislative requirement is in advance of political practice (McKenna 1995). Australians generally have little interest in local government. Voter turnout at local government elections ranges from 12 to 65 per cent, with averages usually in the low 30s percentage range (Gerritsen & Osborn 1997: 66-67). For most rural local governments only a minority (average about 30%) of Council seats are contested at each election. Even for urban local governments up to 40% of seats will probably be uncontested (Cutts 1996). So Council memberships are relatively stable, with high rates of long-term incumbency. This leads to stable and predictable patterns of political demands. Consequently, community participation in local government and the introduction of new issues is dominated by the activities of pressure groups, usually pursuing a single interest (eg., a residents association formed to oppose a proposed development project). This means that the formal requirements for community-wide consultation are belied by the realities of local politics.

This vacuum creates a need for the CEO to be proactive in seeking community opinion and involvement (Jaboor 1996: 24). The CEO has to be a community leader and to mediate between different community interests. This creates an incentive for the CEO actively to encourage community organisations and exhibit a community leadership role. In effect, the Australian CEO has to create his/her own community networks. If the CEO is successful at this, and expert at mediating between interests and mobilising support groups, then he becomes a person with considerable influence in local affairs.

In the broader State and Federal milieu, the CEO has limited influence. The tendency of Australian politics is for State and Federal politicians to dictate to

---

4 For example, the seminal survey of Australian Local Government (ALGA 1989) provides only passing references to political parties, concentrating instead on finances.

local government (Balmer 1989; Gerritsen & Osborn 1997: *passim*). This was again illustrated recently when the Federal government sanctioned the overhead roll-out of pay television cable despite vehement protests from local governments, whose formal control over building approvals was thereby overridden. The CEO's interaction with State and Federal programs is one of accountability to these superior jurisdictions for the proper discharge of the program funds provided. So, while there has been some devolution of functions from higher to lower tiers of government over the past two decades, the historical reality of the administrative subordination of local government (Chapman & Wood 1984) continues to be the central feature of central-local relationships.

The major external ally the CEO has is the Institute of Municipal Management, which is an association of senior local government personnel and represents them industrially and politically. The Institute also has stewardship of the professional development of local government administrators (Carroll 1989: ch. 21). The other significant professional association is the Australian Local Government Engineers Association. There are also minor associations (eg of librarians, social workers and childcare professionals) comprising various occupations that are not exclusively represented in local government services administrations (Osborn 1989).

Challenges to the Local Government CEO

The majority of Australian CEOs have at least 15 years experience in local government administration. Given this experience, they are in a good position to have some historical perspectives on the changes in the sector over the past two decades. The survey results indicate some polarisation but with no significant inter-State or urban-rural differences.[5] While 55 per cent feel that the job of the local government CEO is more attractive than ten years ago, 41 per cent feel that it is less attractive. The most positive are the young CEOs aged 35-45 years (29% of our sample), the least CEOs over 55 years old (17% of the sample). There is also a positive correlation between the level of formal education (a university degree and/or a postgraduate qualification) and approval of the reforms of the past decade. It appears that the older generation of CEOs, brought up in the traditional, now-supplanted Town Clerk/Shire Clerk role, with its industry-specific systems of professional recognition and qualifications, are the most negative about the challenges faced by the modern Australian local government CEO.

When asked to rate factors which have negatively impacted on their ability to perform their jobs, CEOs emphasized: "New regulations from upper-level gov-

---

5 A higher proportion of Melbourne metropolitan CEOs were unhappy than in the sample at large, but they were too small a proportion of our sample to draw firm conclusions.

ernments" (57%), "Cuts in grants from upper-level governemnts" (40%) and "Federal and / or State government control of local government finances" (39%). Factors such as: "Financial problems" (23%) "Lack of clear political goals" (19%), "Unemployment and social problems" (12%), and "Conflict between political parties (6%)" caused less problems. The percentages indicate a composite score pulling together the respondents from the very high extent and high extent categories.

From this data it is obvious that the controls and impositions of upper levels of government are the major factor in producing problems for Australian local government CEOs.

Notwithstanding this there are problems – in the development of human resources, in possible role conflicts between CEOs and Councillors, and in the resource scarcity afflicting local government – that will increasingly challenge Australian CEOs in the near future.

Given the differing emphases on service delivery in the three spheres of government, particularly in the provision of infrastructure and health and educational services, then the recent growth in the proportion of professionals within the local government workforce is seen as providing future tests for human resource development, especially as resource difficulties constrain education and training opportunities. This means that professional recruitment will be from outside local government, which may create management problems for the CEO with existing staffs and their unions.

If Councillors are removed from interfering with service deliver by policy-administration dichotomy, and the local administrators removed from direct responsibility by the purchaser-provider distinction, then some concerns about accountability and democratic participation will inevitably arise to bedevil the future role of Australian local government CEOs.

The continuing problem (eg., see Self Inquiry 1985; Howard 1985) of the mismatch between financial resources and the citizenry's service demands will shape the future role of the CEO. This is exacerbated in some States by populist State government restrictions on property rate increases, the main source of local government revenue. The local government response to this problem has been the increased use of user charges and the privatisation of many services over the past decade. In part this is a nationally-imposed policy agenda, currently labelled National Competition Policy (Aulich 1997). The privatisation reaction has an element of "bureau-shaping", in which professional administrators have enhanced their job prospects at the expense of lower level staff (Albin 1991). Some of the recent regulatory reforms, such as privatising building inspection functions (Sproats & Crichton 1997) also exhibit this tendency.

Resource shortages have provided an incentive for the strong movement by Australian local governments to form Voluntary Regional Organisations of Councils. Originally formed for the purposes of resource sharing, the more successful of these have expanded into regional strategic economic and environmental management planning (Cutts 1996). However, most of these regional organisations have few dedicated staff and add considerably to the workload of the participating local governments' CEOs.

Conclusions

Australian local government has undergone a veritable revolution in the last ten to twenty years. Aspects of this revolution – the introduction of new local government functions and the contracting out of the more traditional physical services – have reshaped local government workforces and management structures. Some of this has been driven by policy agendas not created by local government. The "political" environment of the local government CEO has been altered by the new requirements for community consultation and participation and the (to us artificial and contrived) codification of the relationship between the CEO and the elected Councillors, both factors complicating the accountability of CEOs. The new conservative Coalition Federal government elected in 1996 is seeking to reverse the trend of Federal funding of specific purpose programs, initially replacing the money amounts thus lost with general purpose funding. Inevitably local government will see Federal funding cuts in the near future. Yet the services and facilities provided by 25 years of Federal SPPs have created public demands and expectations that will not similarly recede. This tension between declining resources and expanding demands is going to create management pressures for Australian local government CEOs.

Many of the problems that the revolution of the past two decades will pose for the Australian local government CEO are only now becoming evident. It is probable that local government CEOs will face difficult, and as yet unrealised, challenges in the immediate future as the full implications of this revolution become more apparent.

Bibliography

Albin, Stephen (1991): *Bureau-Shaping and Contracting Out: The Case of Australian Local Government*, Canberra: Australian National University, Public Policy Program, Discussion Paper No. 29 (January).

ALGA (1989): *The Australian Local Government Handbook*, Canberra: Australian Government Publishing Service.

Aulich, Chris (1997): Competition in Local Government, in Brian Dollery and Neil Marshall (eds.), *Australian Local Government*, Melbourne: Macmillan.

AUDR (1994): *Financing Local Government: A Review of the Local Government (Financial Assistance) Act 1986*, Melbourne: Australian Urban & Regional Development Review, Discussion Paper No. 1.

Balmer, Colin (1989): Local Government in the Federal System, in *The Australian Local Government Handbook*, Canberra: Australian Government Publishing Service.

Bowman, Margaret (1983): Local Government in Australia, in Margaret Bowman and William Hamptin (eds.) *Local Democracies: A Study in Comparative Local Government*, Melbourne: Longman Cheshire.

Bowman, Margaret (1985): Local Government and Specific Purpose Grants: Structure, Finance, Coordination and Development, in *National Inquiry into Local Government Finance: Research and Consultancy Reports, Vol. 2*, Canberra: Australian Government Publishing Service.

Carroll, Brian (1989): "A Very Important and Influential Body": A History of the Institute of Municipal Management, Melbourne: Institute of Municipal Management.

Chapman, Ralph J.K., and Wood, Michael (1984): *Australian Local Government: The Federal Dimension*, Sydney: George Allen & Unwin.

Crawford, Peter J. (1996): *The Serious Business of Governing. Reform in Government & Transformation in the Public Sector*, Erskineville, NSW: Hale & Iremonger.

Cutts, Llois, and Osborn, Dick (1989): Diversity in Local Government Systems, in *The Australian Local Government Handbook*, Canberra: Australian Government Publishing Service.

Cutts, Llois (1995) Having a Go: Standing for Local Government Election, in Dick Osborn and Llois Cutts *Enhancing Local Government's Effectiveness in Natural Resources Management (Vol. 2)*, Canberra: University of Canberra, Australian Centre for Regional and Local Government Studies.

Cutts, Llois (1996): *Evaluation of the Voluntary Regional Cooperation Program*, Canberra: National Committee on Regional Cooperation/Australian Centre for Regional and Local Government Studies.

ERC (1990): Evatt Research Centre, *Breach of Contract: Privatisation and the Management of Australian Local Government*, Sydney: Pluto Press.

Gerritsen, Rolf (forthcoming): *Aboriginal Governance in Australia: Cause for Hope?*, Canberra: University of Canberra, Australian Centre for Regional and Local Government Studies, Monograph.

Gerritsen, Rolf, and Osborn, Dick (1997): The Reform of Local Government in Australia, in *Comparative Study of Local Government in Japan, Australia and New Zealand*, Sydney: Council of Local Authorities for International Relations/Japan Local Government Centre.

Gerritsen, Rolf, and Albin, Stephen (1993): Privatisation: Economic Cure-all or Ideological Dogma?, in Peter Vintilla, John Phillimore and Peter Newman (eds.), *Markets, Morals and Manifestos: Fightback & the Politics of Economic Rationalism in the 1990s*, Murdoch, WA: Murdoch University, Institute for Science & Technology Policy.

Gray, Ian (1991): *Politics in Place: Social Power Relations in an Australian Country Town*, Sydney: Cambridge University Press.

Halligan, John, and Wettenhall, Roger (1989): The Evolution of Local Governments, in *The Australian Local Government Handbook*, Canberra: Australian Government Publishing Service.

Howard, John (1985): Local Government Revenue Raising, in *National Inquiry Into Local Government Finance, Research and Consultancy Reports (Vol. 2)*, Canberra: Australian Government Publishing Service.

Jaboor, Bill (1996): Changing Role for the Local Government, *Local Government Management*, May, pp. 24-26.

Jones, Michael (1993): *Transforming Australian Local Government: Making it Work*, Sydney: Allen & Unwin.

Lang, Jill (1991): *Local Government's Role in Urban Infrastructure*, Canberra: Australian Government Publishing Service.

Martin, John (1997): Workplace Reform: HRM and Enterprise Bargaining, in Brian Dollery and Neil Marshall (eds.), *Australian Local Government*, Melbourne: Macmillan.

Maskell, Charles (1989): The Inter-State Distribution of General Purpose Funds for Local Government, in *The Australian Local Government Handbook*, Canberra: Australian Government Publishing Service.

McKenna, Brent (1995): *Community Participation in Local Government: A Research Report and Critique*, Canberra: Australian Centre for Local Government Studies.

Norton, Alan (1994): *International Handbook of Local and Regional Government. A Comparative Analysis of Advanced Democracies*, London: Edward Elgar.

Ohlin, Jackie (1992): *A Change of Culture: Local Governments Planning for Life*, Hobart: Municipal Association of Tasmania.

Osborn, Richard (1989): Local Government and Support Networks, in *The Australian Local Government Handbook*, Canberra: Australian Government Publishing Service.

Osborn, Richard (1995): What do Local Governments do?: They Employ People, in Dick Osborn and Llois Cutts, *Enhancing Local Government's Effectiveness in Natural Resources Management (Vol. 2)*, Canberra: University of Canberra, Australian Centre for Regional and Local Government Studies.

Park Report (1996): *Advancing Local Government in Western Australia. Report of the Structural Reform Advisory Committee*, Perth: Western Australian Department of Local Government.

Power, John; Wettenhall, John, and Halligan, John (1981): Overview of Local Government in Australia, in J. Power, R. Wettenhall and J. Halligan (eds.), *Local Government Systems of Australia (ACIR Information Paper No. 7)*, Canberra: Australian Government Publishing Service.

Roberts, Joan (1989): Local Government and Community Development, in *The Australian Local Government Handbook*, Canberra: Australian Government Publishing Service.

Self Inquiry (1985): *National Inquiry Into Local Government Finance*, Canberra: Australian Government Publishing Service.

Solomon, Keith J. (1993): *Higher Education Needs and Provision for Australian Local Government Councils and Officers*, Canberra: Australian Local Government Training Board.

Sproats, Kevin, and Crichton, Roslyn (1997): Regulatory Reforms: Balancing Interests, in Brian Dollery and Neil Marshall (eds.), *Australian Local Government*, Melbourne: Macmillan.

CHAPTER 3

Local Authority Chief Executives: the British Case

by Michael Goldsmith and Jon Tonge

Introduction

One of the more constant features of British local government over recent years has been their chief executives. Whilst the system over which they exercise considerable influence has been constantly changing over the last twenty years or so, British local government chief executives remain one of the corner stones of the system.

The emergence of a chief official, something more than primus inter pares, effectively dates from the start of the period of constant change, namely the reform of local government in early seventies by the then Conservative government. It is somewhat ironic that it is another Conservative government, within a decade, which was to accelerate the process of change through which British local government has passed and continues to do so.

It was the 70s reforms which created the large local governments for which Britain stands out from local government in most other countries. Within the U.Di.T.E. comparative study, the smallest British local authorities, at around 25000 population, would be larger than the majority of local governments in all the other countries included. The 1972 reforms, as well as giving Britain large local governments, epitomised the management thinking of the time, and saw the internal running of local governments as something to be undertaken by a small policy committee made up of the leading elected members on the one hand, and supported by powerful chief officers under the overall leadership of a chief executive who would oversee the administration of policy (Bains: 1972).

The mix of just over five hundred local governments created in Britain at this time represented the high point of the form of local government whose primary concern was the delivery of those services associated with the welfare state – education, public housing, transport, social welfare as well as more basic services such as refuse collection and disposal, consumer protection and environmental health, were all the responsibility of local government, even if income transfers such as unemployment benefit or disability allowance were still provided by central government agencies. It should be remembered that Britain has effectively four different systems of local government – one for England, another very similar but smaller in scale for Wales, a completely different system for Scotland, and a fourth and different system in Northern Ireland. In the case of the latter, there are only twenty six local governments with minimum responsibilities such as refuse collection and disposal and leisure and recreation services, with the big services being provided through a series of appointed boards. This method of service delivery was introduced in 1972, as a consequence of the religious discrimination which existed in service provision and which gave rise to the protest and conflicts of the late sixties, conflicts which have bedeviled the province ever since.

Scottish local government was reformed at the same time as that in England and Wales but given a different regional form. The 9 regions and 3 island councils were powerful bodies with nearly all the important services located at this level. They were large in population and land, with Strathclyde Region covering virtually half of Scotland in these terms. Below the regions were 53 district authorities. From studies made of the system in operation, the Scottish regional system appears to have been relatively successful. But much of it was controlled by either the Labour or Scottish National parties, and the present conservative government felt encouraged to reform the system still further in the early nineties, abolishing the two tier regional system and replacing it with a series of 32 large unitary authorities in 1996.

Outside London and the major English cities, local government in England and Wales has largely involved a two tier system of counties and districts. The scale of these has been smaller in Wales, with its eight counties and 37 districts. However, the Welsh system was also abolished in 1995 and replaced with a unitary system of 22 larger district councils in April 1996, a reform not enthusiastically welcomed by either many Welsh elected officials nor by all the population at large.

Paralleling the Scottish and Welsh reforms, the government established a Local Government (Banham) Commission to review the 35 English counties and 274 districts and to suggest reforms. Earlier in 1986 the Thatcher government had abolished the Greater London Council (established as one of the first metropolitan wide governments in the world in 1966) and the 6 metropolitan counties, leaving London's government in the hands of 32 London boroughs and that of the other metropolitan areas in those of the 36 metropolitan districts. So since the middle eighties the structure of British local government has been undergoing change. But so have both the financial and the functional systems. In its attempts to control and reduce public expenditure, the Thatcher government of the early eighties introduced both caps on expenditure and local taxation by local governments and went on to restrict capital expenditure further. In part Mrs Thatcher's downfall was brought about by the experience of the ill-fated community charge or poll tax as it was more popularly called.

In functional terms, one of the first pieces of legislation passed under the 1979

Conservative government introduced the compulsory sale of public housing, thus effectively forcing local governments to sell their stock of housing to sitting tenants at heavily discounted prices as against the market value of the property. Boosted by subsequent legislation, it also had the effect of taking local governments out of housing provision, putting the provision of social housing into the hands of voluntary sector housing associations. Similarly the privatisation of public transport, which obliged local governments to run their municipal bus services along market lines rather than permitting any fare subsidy out of local taxation, opened up the way for the private sector takeover of many municipal bus services.

The introduction of compulsory tendering and the requirement to contract out services saw many services previously provided by blue collar municipal workers, such as refuse collection, school meals and cleaning services, pass to the private sector. Even though many municipalities saw contracts being won by their own workforces, this was often achieved by a lowering of wages and by the loss of at least some jobs. More recently, central government has required local authorities to put core white collar services, such as planning and legal services, out to compulsory competitive tendering. Finally the 1988 Education Act effectively moved responsibility for primary and secondary education out of the direct control of local governments and placing it in the hands of school governors and head teachers, whilst the 1991 Act placed further education under the control of local governors appointed by the Secretary of State for Education and moved the former higher education polytechnics firmly into the university world, also with appointed boards of governors. The one important function which local government was given during this period was responsibility for care in the community of the elderly and the physically and mentally handicapped. The view underlying this development was that essentially people could be better looked after within their own homes or in the community than they could be inside institutions.

In other areas the government has introduced new single purpose agencies, either to run new functions or to work alongside existing local government provision. Examples include the Training and Enterprise Councils, responsible for much workplace and training activity for the unemployed, as well as local economic development and aid to small enterprises; the Urban Development Corporations and many other similar bodies. In the nineties municipalities have been invited to bid for limited capital funds under such banners as city or regional challenge, often with the result that the winners end up with slightly enhanced funds, perhaps for projects which they might have given the same priority if left to their own devices, whilst the losers find they have less capital funds than would have otherwise been the case.

The effect of all these changes has been to transform the essential nature of British local government from the large service producing organisations which they had become by the sixties and continued to be through most of the seventies into what came to be called enabling authorities who essentially decide what level of services they want and can afford and set about finding the best means of providing them. But there have been local political changes as well, the most important of which has been the growing number of hung authorities in which no one political party holds a majority. Of the respondents to the U.Di.T.E. survey, no less than 40% of responding chief executives were working in authorities where no single party was in control. Allied to this has been the widespread decline in recent years in the number of local governments controlled by the Conservative party. In a country where there is a long-standing tradition of party rule in local government, albeit within locally well defined frameworks and rules, the emergence of multi-party government has posed a number of problems. The British have no tradition of such coalition government. As a result there have been occasions when the party with the largest number of seats has refused to both to take office and do a deal with one of the other minority parties, and on other occasions no single party has been willing to take office at all. Decision making in these circumstances becomes tortuous and unpredictable, and the chief executive is often the one person who can negotiate a route through the partisan muddles. As the Widdicombe Report (1986) showed, British local government has not only become more partisan, it has also become more politicised. Today more chief executives are used to dealing with hung councils.

The Local Government Chief Executive in Perspective

In all this process of change the one person who has remained a constant figure has been the local government chief executive. As the chief administrative official – often referred to as head of the paid service – it has been this official above all others who has been responsible for seeing that local governments adapt to the changes either thrust upon them by central government or to the other changes which follow from changes in the local economic and social environment. Yet the notion of a chief officer who is something more than first amongst equals dates only from the early seventies. And even over the last twenty years it is clear, as we shall show, that both the job and the kind of person who undertakes it have also changed.

In the nineteenth century, as local government grew in importance, the task of the town clerk, as the most important local official, was largely concerned with legal matters. For much of the century, and certainly in the growing urban towns and cities, the legal skill of the town clerk was paramount in ensuring that the locality increased its powers and functions through the promotion of local Acts of Parliament. Providing street lighting; gas and electricity, running municipal libraries, museums and art galleries all followed from such acts. Legal qualification has remained the main requirement for town clerks through much of the twentieth century, as a recent study has shown (Travers et al.: 1997), and even today a significant proportion of chief executives have a legal background.

It was local government reorganisation in the early nineteen seventies which saw the change from town clerk to chief executive, seeing the holder of the office move from being at best first amongst equals to the senior paid official. At that time (1972), the work of local government was essentially undertaken by committees, who oversaw the work of departments, produced policy proposals for approval by the full council. The key working relationship was between the chief officer in charge of the service department and his committee chair. The town clerk was no more than one officer amongst many, and there were major problems of policy coordination, the over-involvement of council members in matters of service detail and insufficient attention being given to major policy matters and strategy. All of these weaknesses were identified in the report of the Bains committee on the internal working arrangements of the new, reformed local authorities due to come into operation in 1974.

The emphasis in the new structure was on a separation of policy from detailed administration, with the encouragement of delegation to (chief) officers over matters of detail. Councillors – or at least the leading group of committee chairs and the leader of the council – were expected to concern themselves with policy matters in a new style policy committee, setting the overall strategy and objectives for the local government. In turn the chief officers, headed by the new chief executive, would work as a management team to implement the policy decisions of the council.

The theory may have been fine, but the practice was somewhat different. Not all councillors accepted the idea that they should be excluded from policy matters and be left to play a kind of backbench role in the council chamber. Many authorities claimed to accept the Bains proposals, but in practice retained over-elaborate committee structures. And over time some authorities began to question the need for a powerful management team and powerful chief executive officer – whilst some service chief officers resented the introduction of the new chief executive. But by the late seventies and early eighties it would be true to say that most local governments had moved along the lines suggested by Bains. The problem was that a new government was in power, determined to challenge what it saw as the entrenched and powerful interests of local government, interests dominated by the professional officers who it was believed largely determined actual service standards and modes of provision in ways which were not in the interest of the people using the services. But the Thatcher government was not alone in such a criticism, which was also voiced by many on the left.

In essence, however, the left and right have differed in their approach to the problem and the management structure and practices which follow. For the Right, both under Thatcher and Major, it has been a question of fragmenting the structure of local government, by introducing a number of single purpose bodies responsible for services previously provided by elected local governments, and by encouraging local governments to become more market orientated and more consumer aware...local governments supposedly became enablers rather than providers. And individuals were to become consumers, able to exercise choice, rather than clients who had to take what was offered.

This view has been the dominant one in determining how British local governments work in practice. It has involved a cultural change on a scale which could not have been imagined even ten years ago, setting the context for understanding much of the material which follows. But the left has not been uninfluential in the debate, with a number of local governments experimenting with an alternative perspective, arguing for more participatory processes, which in effect encourage a view of the individual as citizen rather than as consumer. Such an emphasis is likely to encourage chief executives to believe that increased citizen involvement in their local government's affairs is to be encouraged, and again this is reflected in some of what follows.

The Present Day Chief Executive

Surveys of British local authority chief officers have become commonplace over recent years. At the time of the U.DI.T.E. survey, the Rowntree Foundation funded a study of some aspects of the work of the chief executive, which also involved a national survey. The Society of Local Authority Chief Executives (SOLACE) conducted its own survey in the early 1990s. An earlier survey was undertaken by Norton and Mills in 1988 and reported in 1990. At that time John Stewart could write articles entitled "In Search of a Role" (Stewart: 1990), and there was much discussion amongst chief executives and their association on what the role of the premier official should be. Respondents to the Norton and Mills survey suggested the core of the job was essentially threefold: leading the management team and being involved in its appointment and appraisal; promoting constructive relationships between members, officers and members; and strategic policy formulation and planning, as well as providing general policy advice and translating political requirements into management action. Other tasks thought to be essential but of a lower priority included the promotion of professional values and practices; promoting innovation and organisational change, and representation of the authority externally (Norton and Mills: 1990, 12 -13).

Today, the typical British local government chief officer is likely to be male (92.%)[1]; aged around 50 (over two thirds are between 45 and 55); have been educated to degree or degree equivalent level, with over a quarter (27%) having a legal background – twice as many as any other qualification. Over a quarter (27%) are likely to have been in post for under two years, though 16% of respondents had also been in post for more than ten years. Before coming to their present post, overwhelmingly most had been employed in local government pre-

---

1 Data refer to the findings of the British version of the U.DI.T.E. survey. Questionnaires were sent to all local authority chief executives in England, Wales and Scotland in December 1995 and January 1996, with a reminder being sent out approximately one month later. Responses were received from over 300 chief executives, with completed questionnaires being returned by 284, a return in excess of 60%.1 School districts,

viously (84%), with just under a third (30%) having worked in the same municipality before reaching their present position, and over half (54%) having worked in another local authority.

Of these almost forty per cent had worked as an assistant, deputy or chief executive before coming to their present job, with finance (13%) and a technical background (planning; environmental health for example)(12%) being other previous job background. Many had come into their job because the previous incumbents had left the job either because of their age or from taking early retirement (54%), though a few had come into the post because the previous incumbents had left to advance their own careers (15%). But almost a quarter (23%) claimed that their predecessor had left because he or she could not work well with the local politicians. Workloads are significant, with most chief executives working either between 45 and 50 hours a week (26%) or between 55 and 60 hours (24%). Almost two thirds live within their municipal boundaries (63%), with 27% having lived in the area as a child. Most are politically neutral, both in partisan terms (fewer than one in five had been a member of a political party) whilst over half (54%) claimed to belong to no local organisations whatsoever. But by contrast over half had been active in some way within SOLACE, the British association of local authority chief executives (of which 51% of respondents were also members), and many were also members of other professional bodies. Fewer than one in five (18%) were actively seeking another job elsewhere, whilst 30% were definitely not going to seek another position.

In what kind of political environment were our respondents working? Reference has already been made to the growing number of British local governments where no one party is directly in control. In over two authorities out of five (41%), chief executives were working where no one party was in control. Of the remainder, one party, frequently the Labour party (66% – 109 authorities – of party controlled councils), was in control. These two extremes – working where no clear partisan leadership was provided or the party in control was in opposition to the governing party at Westminster – could generate an environment in which either the chief executive was working without any clear direction from political masters or else was working where the direction might be clear but was likely to be opposed to official government policy. Nevertheless, our results suggest that such a picture would be misleading, and that despite the highly centralised nature of British local government, at the local level both partisanship and politicisation is now less important as a divisive factor that was suggested by the Widdicombe Report in the middle eighties. For example, over a third (36%) of our respondents suggested that there were few party conflicts at the local level, whilst only 13% suggested that there were many or frequent party conflicts within their municipality. Almost half (47%) suggested that there were some partisan conflicts, however.

Relationships with Council Leaders

A partial explanation for this situation might lie in the way in which many leaders of council are seen by their chief executives as being currently unchallenged in their position: 46% of respondents suggested that their political leaders were in this position. Given that over a quarter (27%) of such local leaders had been in office for a year or less, and that a further 48% had held office for between 2 and five years might offer some explanation for the apparently secure position many local political leaders occupy. Put another way, only 13% of such leaders were seen as being in a weak position by their chief executives, and only 10% had been in office for more than ten years.

The relationship with the political leader of the municipality is often a key to the successful chief executive. Over three quarters of respondents (76%) suggested that this relationship was very important to their job – a far higher response than for any other item. Only heads of departments (58%) came anywhere as close, whilst the relationship with other politicians – including opposition party leaders – were seen as important in only 31% of cases. The ability to work with political leaders was brought out in a number of our more detailed interviews with a small number of chief executives in the North West of Britain – in one case, for example, one chief did not expect to remain in his job for much longer following a change of political leadership and control, where the new leader believed that the post was a redundant one! Another said "You do need extraordinary political sensitivity" in dealing with leaders in a hung authority, whilst a third, longstanding CEO described his working relations with politicians as the most difficult thing he had had to learn and develop. Nevertheless, most chief executives (57%) described their relationship with their political leaders as very cooperative: only one described it as being extremely conflictual. Again only departmental heads (54.6%) came into the same category, despite a tendency amongst respondents to regard a large number of people as either cooperative or very cooperative. Only union representatives discussing pay (8%) or other matters (7%); central government officials (8%) and opposition party leaders (5%) were at all regarded by respondents as producing conflicts in their dealings with chief executives.

Chief executives strongly agreed that politicians, and particularly the council leader, are expected to undertake what might best be described as a governance and representational role, as table 3.1 indicates. Additionally they are expected to provide a stable internal environment within which the CEO and the professional staff can undertake their work: council leaders and local politicians are not expected to be involved in the routine administration of the municipality. As one CEO put it "... there has to be a degree of trust, that's what it boils down to. The leader's job and mine are so wide ranging. He has to trust the management team and I have to trust the leader ... we try not to supervise each other ..." Or as another said "I have good relationships with council members. It's robust and fairly contested and one has to avoid getting caught in the political crossfire. The politicians and the leader have to provide guidance ..." Or another ... "with 48 Labour and no Conservatives, the decision making mechanisms are pretty clear, as is the framework within which members wish to operate. I see the leader pretty well every day to sort out strategy..." And in this context another CEO said that "a CEO is a bit like Moses ... a bridge requiring confidence on both sides."

Table 3.1 The ideal politician, Great Britain

Administration		36
Be a spokesperson for local groups or individuals who have issues pending decision by the authority	42	
Lay down rules and routines for the administration	26	
Taking decisions concerning specific cases	40	
Representation		71
Be informed about citizens' views	84	
Represent the municipality to the outside world	74	
Defend the authorities' decisions and policies externally	72	
Be a spokesperson for their political party	64	
Be a spokesperson vis-á-vis the press	63	
Governance		78
Implement the program on which he/she has been elected	63	
Decide on major policy principles	87	
Have a vision of the way in which the municipality will develop in the long run	84	
Stability		67
Create stability for the administration	63	
Formulate exact and unambiguous goals for the administration	70	

The CEOs' View of the Job

How do British municipal chief executives view their job? A third (33%) thought the job had become more attractive over the last ten years. By contrast, however, 50% thought it had become less attractive. Given the changes through which British local government has passed in recent years, this latter result is not altogether surprising. The trend towards centralisation (stressed by 88% of respondents); the loss of status brought about by the growth of other special purpose and non-elected local bodies, and the financial restraints under which local government has operated all offer partial explanations. Of the things which respondents thought had impacted negatively on their ability to do the job, 75% suggested that central government control was a very important factor; 60% mentioned new central government controls or regulations, and 59% mentioned cuts in government grants as being similarly important – all far ahead of other possible causes. This is despite the fact that over three-quarters of respondents said their authority had undergone privatisation and contracting out; 54% though such moves had been important in reducing staffing levels, and 70% drawing attention to increased delegation from politicians to officials.

Job Priorities

In terms of their daily priorities, British chief executives placed greatest importance on the ability to influence decision making processes, followed by the need to formulate ideas and promote vision, with the need to promote interdepartmental cooperation coming third. Perhaps reflecting some of these priorities, chief executives saw such things as good personal relationships (62%) in the job as an important source of job satisfaction, as was accomplishing tasks efficiently (57%). These results are, probably not all that dissimilar from many other people in similar positions in other situations. Over a third (34.5%) believed providing motivation was important, whilst 31.7% thought ensuring satisfaction with decision making important.

The Chief Executive's Role

In terms of the different roles which chief executives might play, one key distinction is between what Putnam (1975) has called political and bureaucratic roles. In the first case, the role involves the provision of leadership, vision, initiative; the promotion of new projects, as well as exercising some influence over decision making in the municipality. To these would be added a desire to have an influence over resource allocation; to see that they are used efficiently, whilst also expecting to be aware of the views of the public.

Table 3.2 The roles of the CEOs, Great Britain

The classical bureaucrat		53
Guide subordinate staff in day-to-day handling of activities	46	
Manage economic affairs, accounts and budgetary control	51	
Ensure that rules and regulations are followed	45	
Provide the mayor with legal, economic and other kinds of technical advice	68	
The political bureaucrat		69
Formulate ideas and visions	84	
Promote and encourage new projects in the community	69	
Provide the mayor with political advice	56	
Be informed about citizens' viewpoints	73	
Develop and implement norms concerning the proper roles of politicians vis-á-vis the bureaucrats	48	
Influence decision-making processes in order to secure sensible and efficient solutions	85	

As far as the bureaucratic role is concerned, one would expect such chief executives to place a greater stress on establishing administrative norms and routines; improving departmental cooperation; introducing new routines; providing technical advice and overseeing financial matters.

Whilst clearly the two roles are not incompatible, nor mutually exclusive, British chief executives now clearly expect to perform a role closer to the first specification than the second. Table 3.2 below lists the mean scores according to the importance given to a number of tasks by our respondents.

As table 3.2 reveals, the present day chief executive is heavily concerned with what might be called the pro-active aspects of the job, rather than with routine matters. As such, they fit Putnam's (1975) description of the political bureaucrat. It is doubtful whether it was ever different in many respects. The comparison with the Norton and Mills' 1990 survey is interesting. The core task of strategic policy formulation remains important – and is possibly strengthened, in that present day chief executives put influencing decision making and formulating new ideas at the top of their list of tasks. But efficiency arguments also come through clearly – especially in terms of the use of resources – something also highlighted by Norton and Mills' data. The latter survey placed less stress on the promotion of personal relationships and the attraction of external resources – again both things the modern chief executive is expected to do.

The classical bureaucrat tasks receive lower scores and reflect the increased delegation within local governments which many of our respondents mentioned. With more things delegated to middle and junior officials, the chief executive spends less time ensuring rules are followed, or managing financial details, or issuing directions to staff and is able to concentrate on what he sees as the important strategic issues. Again this feature was brought out in a number of the personal interviews we conducted. Nearly all our interviewees stressed not only the distance they had moved when they came into the job, but also the extent to which one of their main tasks was to ensure that problems were handled at the appropriate level by the appropriate staff. As one newish CEO said "I've made a few changes and management board members now feel a bit more involved. I would like to introduce more empowerment, persuading chief officers and others to take *their* decisions ... I still have some difficulty with this."

The Influence of Local Actors

How do chief executives view their own influence and that of others over different policy areas? We investigated this issue through two policy areas – influence over the budget and on local economic development. The findings reveal, as one might expect, that the council leader and majority party group are believed to exert the greatest influence on both areas, though their influence over local economic development is considerably less than it is over the municipal budget. The only other actor considered to exert considerable influence over both areas is the CEO, also considered as the person with the largest influence over local economic development. Committee chairs and departmental chief officers are two other groups of actors seen to exercise influence, though more so on the budget than on local economic development. The influence of external groups, such as parties, users/clients and private business interests is generally not seen as high, though the latter are considered more influential over matters relating to local economic development – again as one might expect.

One reflection of the importance of various actors is the frequency of their interaction with the CEO as well as the dependence of the CEO on these actors, details of which are given in Figure 3.1. Clearly it is the council leader and those departmental heads with whom the CEO meets most frequently who are the most important and on whom the CEO depends most heavily in his daily work. All others pale into insignificance by contrast.

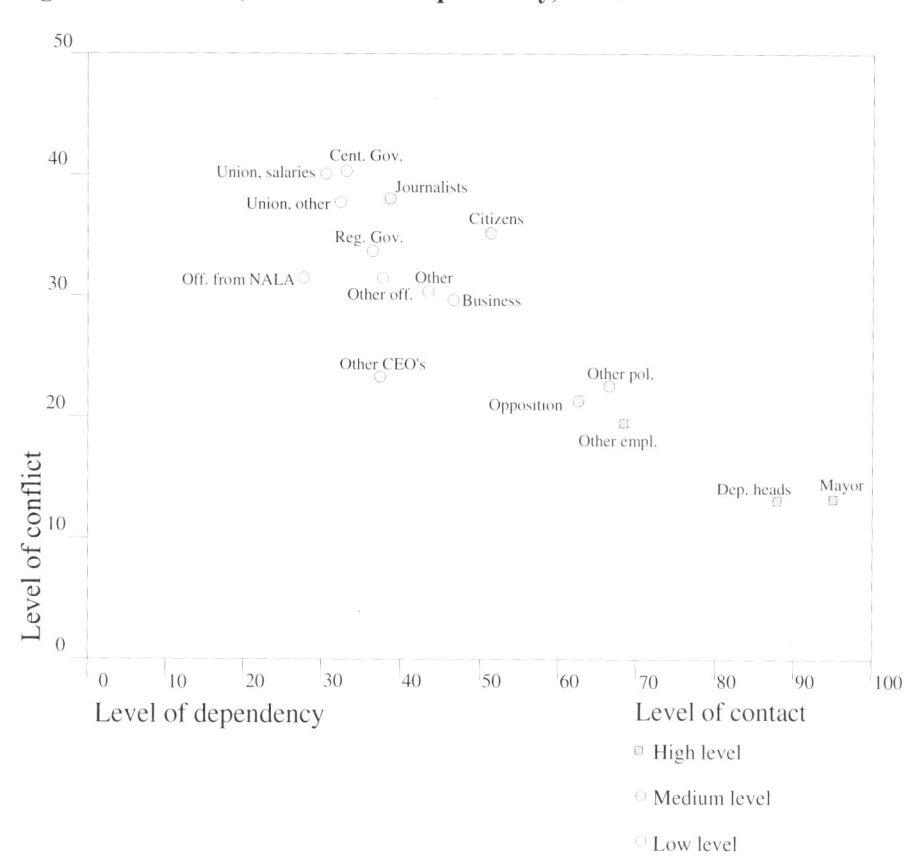

Figure 3.1 Contact, conflict and dependency, Great Britain

[Scatter plot with x-axis "Level of dependency" / "Level of contact" (0 to 100) and y-axis "Level of conflict" (0 to 50). Points plotted:
- Cent. Gov. (~30, 40)
- Union, salaries (~22, 40)
- Union, other (~22, 37)
- Journalists (~40, 38)
- Citizens (~55, 35)
- Reg. Gov. (~35, 33)
- Off. from NALA (~18, 30)
- Other (~42, 30)
- Other off. (~37, 28)
- Business (~50, 28)
- Other CEO's (~35, 23)
- Opposition (~52, 20)
- Other pol. (~72, 21)
- Other empl. (~68, 18)
- Dep. heads (~80, 13)
- Mayor (~90, 13)

Legend: ▫ High level, ○ Medium level, ○ Low level]

Given the recent growth of non-elected local institutions, we might expect chief executives to engage in extensive networking, building relationships with bodies outside the local government, especially as local government generally has lost or had to share powers and functions over recent years. This topic is extensively reviewed in the Rowntree study (Travers, Jones and Burnham: 1997), but the U.DI.T.E. survey also reveals how this activity has increased in importance. We noted that business interests were seen as influential actors in relation to the economic development of the community and the survey reveals that chief executives regard cooperation and a good relationship with such interests as important in terms of their ability to do their job – coming ahead of officials from other public bodies or from regional and central government offices. Something of the flavour of this important relationship comes from our interviews with chief executives. As one chief executive put it: "... these are some of the most important people we do business with, and the good of the town depends on different organisations pulling together. A lot of what is done is quiet...behind the scenes, not really visible." Another described his role in such networks as "setting the tone, facilitating, maintaining and changing relationships, all directed towards locally desired outcomes...brokering, compromising, building goodwill."

A preliminary analysis of job advertisements also stresses this change: many of the more recent ones stress how chief executives are expected to "work with business, central government agencies" or to "forge public and private partnerships." Chief executives are having to perform more of a broker kind of role on behalf of their local government in relation to other agencies and the private and voluntary sectors than has been true in the past, with them spending considerable time networking extensively between these different groups. In a sense, however, the CEO has always had an important public relations or ambassadorial role to play: as Boynton (1986: 105, 106)) put it, the CEO "should be the PRO for his authority" and should "never let it slip from the priority list". What has changed is the complexity of the networks and the degree to which the CEO is a key brokerage actor in them.

Conclusion

The modern British local government chief executive is a middle aged, well educated male who has served in local government for most of his life. There is a one in four chance that he will have a legal background; a two in five chance that he will be working for a council where no one party is in control, or else he will most likely be working for a Labour-controlled authority. He will probably have been in his present post for around five years, having served either as a deputy CEO or else a CEO elsewhere. He is not likely to be politically active, either in the partisan or associational sense, except within his professional association. His also unlikely to be actively seeking employment elsewhere, but if the right opportunity occurs he is likely to take it up. He will be working with a council leader who will probably have been in office for a shorter period than himself, in an environment which is perceived as heavily dominated by the actions and outlook of central government. Certainly one in two chief executives are likely to think the job less attractive than it was ten years ago.

Yet these same chief executives have a clear sense of their priorities and what they see as the key tasks, relationships and difficulties with which they must deal. They are essentially political bureaucrats rather than classical ones: managers and leaders rather than simply following their master's instructions. They seek to influence decision making processes and to formulate new ideas. They seek to promote cooperation internally and externally. They want to see that resources are employed efficiently. Satisfaction comes from promoting good personal relationships, be they with politicians or professional colleagues.

British CEOs regard the council leader, the majority party, central government and chairs of committees, as well as themselves as particularly important actors influencing the municipal budget, adding private business interests to this list when the question of local economic development is considered. This sense of importance is echoed by the frequency of contact which the CEO has with these different actors – and some of these reflect the increasing networking role which chief executives have to play in the increasingly fragmented system of local governance which has developed in Britain over the last fifteen years.

Bibliography

Audit Commission (1989): *More Equal than Others: The Chief Executive in Local Government*, London: HMSO.

Bains Report (1972): *The New Local Authorities: Management and Structure*, London: HMSO.

Boynton, J. (1986): *Job at the Top*, Harlow: Longman.

Cochrane, A. (1993): *Whatever Happened to Local Government?*, Buckingham: Open University Press.

Gyford, J. (1991): *Citizens, Consumers and Councils: Local Government and the Public*, London: Macmillan.

Gyford, J., Leach, S., and Game, C. (1989): *The Changing Politics of Local Government*, London: Unwin Hyman.

Headrick, T.E. (1962): *The Town Clerk in English Local Government*, London: Allen and Unwin.

Hill, D. (1994): *Citizens and Cities: Urban Policy in the 1990s*, Hemel Hempstead: Harvester Wheatsheaf.

Morphet, J. (1993): *The Role of Chief Executives in Local Government*, Harlow: Longman.

Norton, A., and Mills, L. (1990): The British local authority Chief Executive: some new survey evidence, *Local Government Policy Making*, 17, 1, 9-18.

Pratchett, L., and Wilson, D. (eds.) (1996): *Local Democracy and Local Government*, London: Macmillan.

Putnam, R. (1975): The Political Attitudes of Senior Civil Servants in Britain, Germany, and Italy, in Mattei Dogan *The Mandarins of Western Europe: The Political Role of Top Civil Servants*, New York: John Wiley & Sons.

Rhodes, R.A.W. (1988): *Beyond Westminster and Whitehall*, London: Unwin Hyman.

Stewart, J. (1990): In Search of a Role, *Local Government Policy Making*, 17, 1, 3-9.

Stewart, J., and Stoker, G. (1995): *Local Government in the Nineties*, London: Macmillan.

Stoker, G: (1991): *The Politics of Local Government*, (2nd Edition), London: Macmillan.

Svara, J. (1990): *Official Leadership in the City: Patterns of Conflict and Cooperation*, New York: Oxford University Press.

Travers, T., Jones, G., and Burnbaum, R.: (1997): *The Local Authority Chief Executive*, Rowntree Foundation.

Walsh, K. (1995): *Public Services and Market Mechanisms*, London: Macmillan.

Widdicombe Report (1986): *The Conduct of Local Authority Business*, London: HMSO.

Wilson, D., and Game, C. (1994): *Local Government in the United Kingdom*, London: Macmillan.

CHAPTER 4

Power with Responsibility: The Role of the Manager in Irish Local Government

by Andy Asquith and Eunan O'Halpin

In Ireland local affairs and national politics are inextricably interlinked. To win election as a TD (MP) in the Dail (the lower house of parliament), and to stay there, politicians nurse the local vote with extraordinary gusto: "observers have often remarked on what they see as the overconcentration by Dail deputies on constituency business" (Gallagher, 1993, p. 151). Almost all politicians first establish themselves through running in elections to local authorities (councils), and the great majority retain council membership when they win seats in the Dail: until 1991 even serving ministers were allowed to hold their council seats. It is, therefore, striking that these same politicians have acquiesced in the development of a highly centralised administrative system, in which local government for the most part acts simply as a provider of services the nature and standard of which are decided and financed at national level in the departments of the Environment and of Finance (Barrington, 1980, p. 3; Desmond Roche, 1982, pp. 27-92; Dick Roche, 1992, pp. 21-6). Opinions differ about the consequences for Irish democracy and for the efficient administration of public business. Localists claim that local government endures perpetual bullying from the centre, is hopelessly underfunded, and is unable to respond quickly and imaginatively to local needs and to local wishes; central government maintains that as the main financier of local authorities it has a duty to ensure that public money is properly spent, and that as the guarantor of national equity and wellbeing it is obliged to insist on uniform standards of service throughout the state.

These arguments will be familiar to students of central/local relations in any European country. What differentiates Ireland from most of her European neighbours, however, is the sheer and growing extent of central government's control. Since the state came into being in 1922 local representative government has lost almost all its functions in respect of the administration of justice (1924), in health services (1971), and most recently in environmental protection (1992), while its autonomy in other areas such as physical planning and roads development has been steadily eroded. With the exception of justice matters, such functions have been entrusted to national or regional statutory authorities which are not accountable to electorates (Boland & O'Halpin, 1991). Local government's capacity to levy local taxes has been severely reduced, most notably through the effective abolition of local property taxes in 1978, contributing to chronic financial difficulties, to the progressive attenuation of the democratic link between local taxation and local representation, and to the burgeoning of anti-tax sentiment amongst the electorate. The only domestic property tax which now exists is one imposed by central government, and even it is shortly to be abolished due to its perceived inequity between urban and rural dwellers and to widespread public hostility to this form of taxation. When European Community funding for economic and social development at sub-national level became available to Ireland first through the regional and then through the structural funds, the government channelled most of this away from the formal political and administrative structures of local government and into the hands of ad hoc, unelected groups, frequently of doubtful representativity and administrative competence. This trend is set to continue, if a recent report on rural development by the authoritative National Economic and Social Council is any guide. It speaks of "the anxiety that an increased local authority role could damage the innovative or collaborative nature of many recent initiatives", observes that "while the conduct of rural and local development policy by local authorities may ensure propriety, it is unlikely to meet the criteria of effectiveness or accountability", and argues that "an increased role for local authorities in rural and local development should only occur" following "reform of local government" (National Economic and Social Council, 1994, pp. 21 and 155).

In recent years central government has acknowledged that local government is in crisis, but it has yet to come forward with a solution. In 1991 a powerful committee, composed mainly of advocates of local government reform, made recommendations for wide ranging change. Apart from the division of the unitary Dublin county council into three councils, something which has already been agreed in principle, only limited action followed: while local authorities did gain some new statutory powers in economic regeneration and development, one member of the committee wryly observed that its most tangible achievement had been to win local authorities the power to erect their own road signs without having to seek the permission of the Department of the Environment (private information, September 1996). In 1995 the government established a "devolution commission" to identify powers which could be transferred from the centre to local government, and in 1996 the Minister for the Environment sought all-party consensus for the rational reform of local government finances (and implicitly for the reintroduction of some form of local property tax). No informed commentators expect much to emerge from these initiatives, which have already been attacked by the state's largest political party (Ahern, 1996). The evidence of recent years suggests that, while Irish people want more and better local services, they also expect central government to pay for them. It seems most unlikely that any government will risk grasping the local taxation nettle without all-party support, while the rhetorical willingness to devolve significant powers from Dublin is very likely to be constrained by other administrative and political considerations.

In addition to coping with Dublin's innate centralism, local government has also had to meet the demands of its communities for an increasing range of sophisticated services. It has simultaneously had to cope with financial pressures through reducing its labour costs (and thereby weakening its hallowed role as a local employer of last resort in hard economic times), although it still provides work for almost 10 per cent of the labour force. Many local authorities have also had to contract out services such as refuse collection, and a number have introduced deeply unpopular fixed charges for refuse and water collection. Some authorities have also reacted positively to their public funding crisis by forging new partnerships with private capital to develop and operate new facilities such as toll roads and bridges, and small ferries, and most have become far more active in their handling of public assets such as land and buildings. It is now quite common for authorities to complete property sales or make land exchanges with private interests, and authorities frequently acquire assets in order to sell them on in order to promote infrastructural or economic development in their localities.

The thirty five managers (CEOs) of Irish local authorities operate within considerable systemic constraints, fiscal, legal and political. However, they also have some advantages: their powers and responsibilities are defined in law, they are almost entirely free from local political control, and they have a good deal of administrative discretion. The apparent complexity of the local government system, with its limited powers, its financial problems and its hierarchy of authorities, masks the reality that managers are in a commanding position. These points merit separate consideration.

The discussion below is based largely on the authors' interviews with a selection of managers during 1996. Those interviewed work in both rural and urban authorities in various parts of the country, and provide a good cross-section of the present cadre of managers.

The Political-Administrative System Surrounding the Manager

The Irish system of local government remains clearly a product of British rule. In the nineteenth century, a combination of political, administrative, geographic and economic considerations saw the growth in Ireland of relatively interventionist central government. Matters such as primary and secondary education, policing, the fostering of local industry, and welfare, which in Britain itself were largely the business of local government, in Ireland were handled from the centre.

The 1898 Local Government (Ireland) Act for the first time defined a coherent set of tiers of local administration in urban and rural Ireland. While it transformed Irish popular politics, by providing new local authorities elected on a relatively broad franchise, its administrative impact was limited because so many aspects of local affairs were already subject to central intervention and control. At the pinnacle of the structure established by the 1898 act was the administrative county, that is the county council or in large urban areas the county borough [i.e. the city]. Because of local political sensitivities governments have been very reluctant to alter this structure, which still pertains despite seven decades of national independence, a remorseless increase in services, and fitful experimentation with alternative and supplementary forms of sub-national government.

Irish local government now operates at a number of levels of representation defined by numbers, by geography and by accidents of legal history. These are the town (what we term here the "electoral town"), the urban district council (UDC) or borough corporation, and at the highest level the county council or county borough. The smallest electoral unit of Irish local government is the town, with a population of at least fifteen hundred and not more than eight thousand people who have the right to elect town commissioners. Most such electoral towns, however, came into being in the latter half of the nineteenth century. After independence in 1922 the government dissolved a number on grounds of their inefficiency, corruption or incapacity to provide local services, and for decades avoided creating new ones on the grounds that the unit of governance involved was too small for administrative effectiveness and that the powers of town commissioners were so limited. (The government was, also, undoubtedly wary of creating additional local political platforms). Consequently many towns which meet the legal requirements for elected self-government do not have any such representative structure, while even those that are notionally run by town commissioners, including a number established in the last two decades as a result of local pressure and litigation, are in practice administrative clients of the larger authorities within whose boundaries they lie, and which possess the necessary resources and expertise to provide services effectively.

Ascending the scale, the next unit of local government is the urban district council (UDC). The UDC is, generally speaking, the first effective level of local administration, in that the model /is designed for towns of at least eight thousand people with a sufficient revenue base to allow for the provision of some local services. There are currently forty nine such UDCs. Comparable in power, though more exalted in status, are borough corporations, of which there are presently five. These owe their existence to charters granted individually over the last five hundred years, the most recent being in 1930. In the last ten years two such borough corporations have, as a result of spectacular population growth, been further elevated, now being administered respectively as a county borough [i.e. a city] and a county.

Unlike the subordinate tiers of local authorities the "county" is largely an accident of medieval judicial history. It is not defined by size of population, by geographic area, or even by natural boundaries. While all counties are equal in status and powers, they vary dramatically in size, circumstance and population. Thus a poor and depopulated county such as Leitrim, with just 26,000 people, has precisely the same legal and administrative structures as a county such as Kildare with five times as many people and vastly greater resources. For many years after 1940 some small counties were paired for administrative and representative purposes and were served by a single administrative structure headed by a county manager, but by 1982 all such counties had been de-coupled. While no council areas now cross the historic county boundaries, two of the twenty six historic counties are divided internally for representative and administrative purposes. As recently as 1993, the old county area of Dublin was split into three administrative counties as a belated response to suburban sprawl outside the boundaries of Dublin city. Twenty six county Ireland thus has twenty nine county councils, in addition to the five county boroughs of Dublin, Cork, Limerick, Waterford and Galway. The administrative leadership in each of these councils is provided by a manager.

At each formal level of local government, business is transacted in the name of an elected body; in reality, however, operational control of local administration lies not with local politicians but with local authority officials working under the ultimate direction of the manager. A legal divide exists between policy and executive functions, and between the corresponding rights and duties of elected politicians and of officials. It is this division which lies at the heart of the "management system", an approach to public business which some regard as a remarkable achievement, and others as the negation of democratic politics. Administrative rationalists applaud the combination of impartiality and initiative which it confers on local officials; local politicians, preoccupied with brokerage activities, argue that it deprives them of power over the detailed decisions which actually matter most to their constituents.

The concept of "management" was first applied successively in the state's four largest urban authorities between 1929 and 1939. It followed other measures introduced in the 1920s to force local authorities to use competitive tendering procedures, and to ensure that senior officials were selected and appointed on the basis of professional merit rather than of political persuasion. This was largely a response to widespread disquiet about the quality and integrity of local administration under the old system where much executive power lay with committees of councillors. In 1942, the depoliticisation process was completed with the introduction of county management throughout the state. Under the management acts, all policy matters or "reserved functions" are determined by elected councillors; the manager and his officials simply administer affairs in the light of policy decisions. In practice this gave managers enormous powers, because it kept councillors away from control of day to day administration. The first generation of managers antagonized many local councillors, who felt themselves entirely excluded from local decision making. An effort was made to redress the balance in 1955 through strengthening the power of councillors to vote to direct a manager to act in a particular manner where lawful. However, this procedure

– which quickly became known as "Section 4" – became associated with suspicions of political abuse and even of corruption in physical planning matters, because some authorities repeatedly used it to sanction individual construction projects which contravened their own statutory development plans and the advice of engineers, town planners and other council professionals. Such conflicts had a corrosive effect on manager/councillor relations, and managers interviewed deplored the loss of "trust" which resulted. The law was changed in 1991 to make the "Section 4" process less open to abuse. The fact that this was deemed necessary, in an era when the rhetoric of central government is thick with devolutionist phrases, demonstrates the continuing fears of local corruption which partly explain the continuing strength of the managers in local administration: in the last resort they are trusted to be impartial where local councillors are not. One manager applauded the virtual demise of "Section 4s" not only because it lessened impropriety but because it cleared the agenda for council meetings and encouraged a more strategic focus in council debates.

The managers' legal position is buttressed by other factors. Firstly, the elected councillors naturally devote a good deal of their time to interparty conflict, and even within parties councillors may compete for the loyalty of their electorates (for examples in the 1991 elections see Rafter and Whelan, 1992, pp. 52 and 202). Secondly, in the larger towns and cities the chairmanship/mayoralty is rotated amongst councillors each year; similarly, the chairmanship of county councils passes from one person to the next each year. Furthermore, these offices have considerable representational and ceremonial functions, which may distract the holder from seeking involvement in policy issues. Some of the managers interviewed described their chairmen's evident powerlessness as something of an embarrassment in meetings with visitors from other countries with very different systems of local government, though no manager was disposed to argue that the powers of chairmen in council affairs should be increased.

The managers interviewed all spoke of marked changes in relations with councillors. Where the first generation of managers acquired a reputation for a somewhat legalistic and autocratic approach to their dealings with councillors, the emphasis is now on constructive collaboration and on "give and take". One long serving manager said he always made a point of informal consultations with councillors before taking a decision concerning their localities, even where they had no legal right to consultation. This enabled him to draw on their "intimate local knowledge" in taking decisions, so improving both the quality of administration and its legitimacy on the ground. It also promoted good relations with councillors, and so facilitated the conduct of business. Other managers made similar points, one using a fishing analogy: "You must show them enough of the bait but not too much". Managers stated that factors such as the development of local radio and the growth of local pressure and self-help groups had had an important educative effect both on the people generally and on local politicians, who were now subject to more public scrutiny and who were more willing to consider decisions from a strategic perspective.

The Career and Status of Managers

The current cadre of managers have come to the top positions by much the same routes as have their predecessors since 1942. The great majority entered local authority service at clerical level, and worked their way up through the system while studying for third level qualifications in commerce, accountancy or public administration at night. A minority worked initially in the civil service or in the private sector before securing a middle level local authority post. All managers are, like other public servants, debarred from party political activity of any kind and are bound to discharge their duties in an impartial manner. All managers have had a peripatetic career, with successive promotions involving moves around the country from one authority to another. (Dublin city has always been a partial exception to the rule that promotion requires mobility, as the city's size and complex administrative structure provides officials with the broad range of experience thought necessary for those aspiring to the highest posts). Those managers interviewed laid stress on the importance of mobility for the career development of officials, despite the upheaval which it can cause for families. As well as exposing officials to a wide range of tasks in a variety of authorities, it facilitates networking and promotes the diffusion of ideas throughout the system. There has even been a pattern of mobility at the manager level, with some moving on from smaller to larger counties or cities: all those interviewed had already been managers when appointed to their current posts.

One incentive is money – the managers of the largest authorities receive considerably higher salaries than their peers; in interviews factors more frequently stressed were the enhanced status and greater challenge which someone might see in running a big city or county. It should be noted that, however desirable in terms of the breadth of experience which it imparts, career mobility is yet another factor which limits the opportunities for women to rise through the local government hierarchy. It may also serve as an effective barrier for private sector applicants for the top positions. One striking characteristic of Irish local authority service are the methods of recruitment of officials. Entry to even the most junior grades in the administrative and technical hierarchies is by competitive examination and interview, an approach imposed by central government in the 1920s despite bitter resistance from local authorities in order to combat local nepotism and corruption. The more senior the post, the greater the degree of central control over an appointment. The same approach applies to professional positions such as architects and engineers where recruitment is at graduate level. Vacancies in senior administrative and professional positions are open to applicants from any local authority, and are filled through the medium of the Local Appointments Commission (LAC), a national body with powers analogous to the Civil Service Commission responsible for recruitment to central administration. A local authority cannot refuse the candidate selected by the LAC. Thus a county council does not select its own manager, secretary, county engineer or librarian, though in the last decade the job specifications for such positions have become somewhat less generic and now reflect the particular circumstances of the authority in which a vacancy has arisen.

1992 saw one very significant change in the employment conditions of managers, when the government ordained that all new appointments should be on fixed term contracts in some cases not exceeding five and in others seven years, after which incumbents would be eligible to compete for that or for another post provided they were still under retirement age. Interviews suggest that managers viewed this development with mixed feelings: one said it had been announced in a "brutal" fashion, while another described it as "bordering on draconian", and complained that able managers might be "thrown out on the street". While those interviewed all saw the case for some time limit on service, most thought five years too short a period in which to make a strategic impact in the complex world of local administration. Historically, managers have reached that rank in their mid to late forties, and so have had an assured period of 10 to 15 years for which to plan: the doyen of the current managers has held that rank for over twenty years, and has several years to go before retirement). Those interviewed also complained that the early retirement package which underpins the new fixed term contracts was imposed without serious negotiation with the managers' association. These contracts will have the effect over time of increasing the turnover of managers and consequently the opportunities for promotion or recruitment to the top posts.

Managers have always been public figures to some extent. This is due both to their statutory functions, and to the fact that they attend council meetings and speak on the record, sometimes in the face of very vigorous comments from councillors, and so are in the public eye in a way that civil servants are not. They also have the advantage of long incumbency, whereas the chairmanship of councils changes each year. Most of those interviewed, while they stressed the importance of being accessible to the media, felt that at public functions and the like, managers should take care always to be one pace behind the politicians and should never seek the limelight.

Roles and Values of Managers

The interviews and survey data reflect considerable changes in the role of managers over the last decade or more. In many respects the pattern conforms to developments seen in other countries as the approaches of New Public Management (NPM) succeed the more traditional ways of public administration (Hughes, 1994). Managers attribute these developments to a combination of factors. These include the size and complexity of authorities; the impact of fiscal drought on operations; the rise of local community and pressure groups outside the formal political system; the European Commission's overly sentimental "people power" approach to the promotion of local economic and social development, which frequently bypasses local authorities altogether; the need to build a constructive partnership with councillors to promote development and to strengthen the manager's hand in dealing with central government; increased public consciousness of citizens' rights; increased scrutiny of administrative actions by the courts, and since 1986 by the ombudsman; and a general recognition within local government of the need to view matters more from the "customer's" or "client's" perspective. As can be seen in table 4.1 the Irish CEO puts even emphasis on the two roles of the classical and the political bureaucrat – he can identify with both.

The daily routine of a manager is a function of a number of factors including individual management style, the complexity and geographic extent of different local authorities, and the date of the next council meeting. A manager in a rural authority will generally spend rather more time travelling than will one in a city (although urban managers interviewed stressed the importance of getting out and about). The importance for councillors of public ceremonial activities means that a manager is frequently dragged away from his desk in order to form part of the photographic backdrop. In the days preceding a council meeting, most managers will devote considerable time to preparatory discussions with the chairman of the authority. The biggest change in the pattern of their work perceived by both urban and rural managers is a shift towards concentrating more on strategic issues, particularly the improvement of services and the development of collaborative links with other bodies, public and private, in order to foster economic and social development.

The managers interviewed expressed mixed feelings about the local government system's chronic financial problems. While all argued that an equitable local tax was the only means by which local government could operate effectively, they also commented on the need to achieve greater value for money in council operations. The sheer shortage of money contributed to a climate in which strict financial management had become politically acceptable: one manager spoke of having had to "force" councillors to make a budget (local authorities must make a balanced budget each year, and risk suspension or dissolution if they fail to do so). This in turn has had beneficial effects on the overall efficiency of his local authority's operations. So too, according to another manager, have the activities of the revamped local authority audit group, which since 1993 has been using VFM techniques and comparative studies to examine the performance of authorities and to formulate constructive suggestions for improvements. Managers were quite happy about other trends including the increased use of private contractors for operational purposes, especially in the areas of construction and of roads development and maintenance. These provided an element of "benchmarking" for a council's own direct labour organisations and introduced a useful element of competition.

Table 4.1 The roles of the CEOs, Ireland

The classical bureaucrat		71
Guide subordinate staff in day-to-day handling of activities	64	
Manage economic affairs, accounts and budgetary control	85	
Ensure that rules and regulations are followed	65	
Provide the mayor with legal, economic and other kinds of technical advice	68	
The political bureaucrat		71
Formulate ideas and visions	92	
Promote and encourage new projects in the community	87	
Provide the mayor with political advice	35	
Be informed about citizens' viewpoints	71	
Develop and implement norms concerning the proper roles of politicians vis-á-vis the bureaucrats	60	
Influence decision-making processes in order to secure sensible and efficient solutions	81	

All the managers spoke of the crucial importance of local authorities' unacknowledged role as promoters of local economic development. Anecdotal evidence suggests that some managers adopted a pro-active approach years ago, whereas others have been persuaded more recently. The great asset which local authorities bring to economic development tasks is their powers in respect of physical development, including the provision of facilities and the acquisition or disposal of property. Progress in this area is, they maintained, being hampered by the preference of national government and of the European Commission for funding ad hoc bodies outside the formal local structures. This has, managers claimed, resulted in a proliferation of small, inexperienced and unaccountable bodies engaged in largely unco-ordinated activities, attempting to address problems of economic underdevelopment and social exclusion which local authorities would be far better placed to tackle given the same resources. It appears that neither Dublin nor Brussels shares the managers' views on this.

The managers interviewed all spoke of a growing problem of "remoteness" which needed to be addressed. They argue the need to reach out to the ordinary citizen, and they linked this with the need to make authorities more efficient by reorganisation, by promoting cross-functional teams to tackle projects, and by getting officials out of headquarters and into localities. This would be done by the creation of appropriately located and computer networked "one stop shops" throughout each local authority area; by the "flattening" of hierarchies within local authorities to release administrative energy and to push decisions downwards; by the encouragement of officials to be pro-active and decisive in their work; by placing more emphasis on outcomes than on processes; and by appropriate training for all employees in how to deal with the public. Managers were optimistic that the public, as well as local politicians, will support such developments.

The managers were clear that they have to act as agents for change within their organisations, providing leadership to their subordinates and, as we have already noted, also to councillors. One commented that his first task was to get everyone in the council – politicians as well as officials – thinking "strategically".

Patterns of Influence

When looking at the networks of the Irish CEO´s (figure 4.1) it becomes clear that there is a direct relationship between the dependency and the level of conflict. Managers identified four crucial personal links: with each other; with elected councillors, with central government, and with their own staffs. Of these the first is the easiest to characterise: the County and City Managers Association is a powerful cohesive force amongst the managers, all of whom are members and the majority of whom meet every month. The CCMA also fosters links with managers associations abroad (Asquith and O'Halpin, 1996). It is less easy to generalise about managers' relations with councillors, but the general trend is clearly towards a more consensual style than before, relying more on mutual trust and less on the legal division of powers. The managers interviewed spoke surprisingly positively about their relations with central government, which again is something of a novelty: they described officials of the Department of the Environment as generally sympathetic, and said that they have easy access to ministers who are inclined to take them more seriously than they do importunate councillors. But this, while it indicates the high regard in which managers are held, also illustrates the problem that central government still has no time for local politicians. The final set of links is with their own staff: here managers emphasised the importance of getting the message across about becoming customer conscious, about being pro-active and about learning to explain matters clearly to the public and the media.

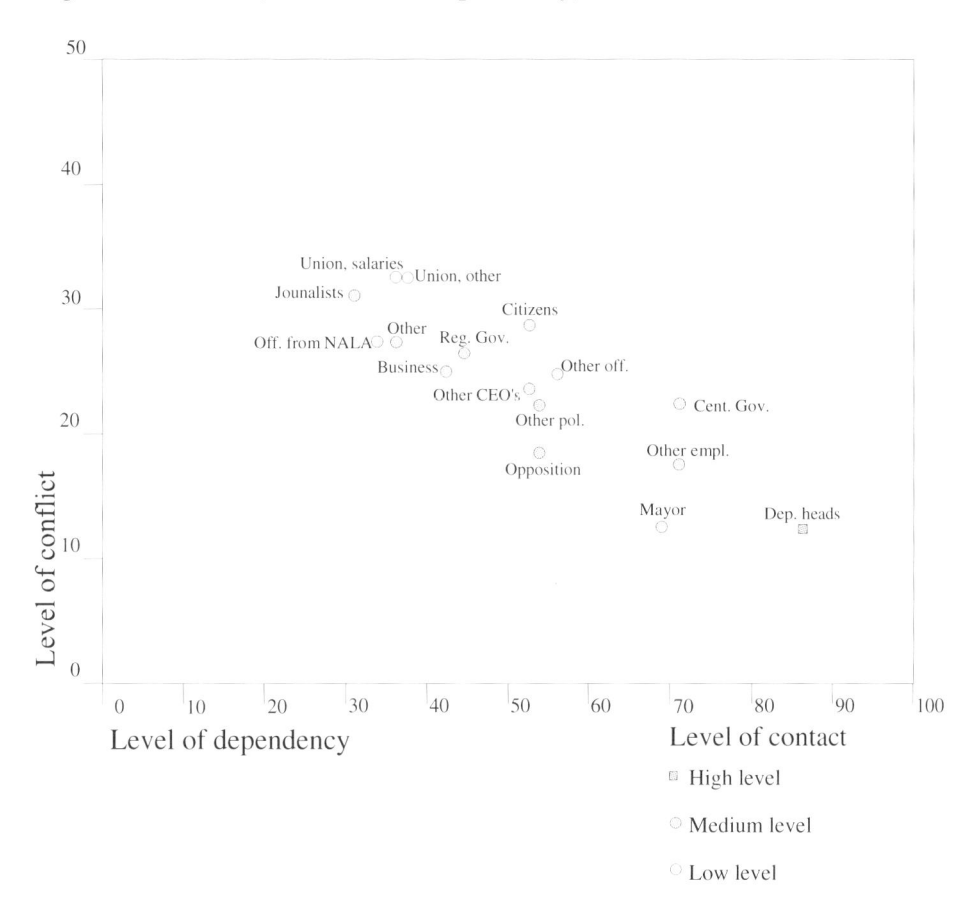

Figure 4.1 Contact, conflict and dependency, Ireland

[Scatter plot with x-axis "Level of dependency" / "Level of contact" (0–100) and y-axis "Level of conflict" (0–50). Data points: Union, salaries; Union, other; Jounalists; Citizens; Off. from NALA; Other; Reg. Gov.; Business; Other off.; Other CEO's; Cent. Gov.; Other pol.; Opposition; Other empl.; Mayor; Dep. heads. Legend: High level, Medium level, Low level.]

Challenges

Irish managers evidently assume that local authorities will have to do more with less in the future. They are conscious of a gap which must be bridged between local administration and the ordinary citizen, and are very aware in a general sense of the opportunities which information technology may offer for improved administration and for increasing public access to local bureaucracy (though no local authority has yet put a customer oriented IT strategy into operation). Managers remain fatalistic about the prospects for the proper reform of local government funding, and they anticipate further difficulties with sometimes contradictory public expectations: for example, it will be difficult to maintain the traditional role of local authorities as major employers of direct labour, given the pressures now generated by commerical competition.

The managers interviewed indicated a number of key challenges which they face both within and outside their organisations. Within the organisations, the challenges are to get people to accept more responsibility, become pro-active, and work across hierarchies in order to achieve results; to flatten the administrative hierarchy; and to bring local authorities physically and culturally closer to their customers. Externally, the challenges identified are to persuade government to grasp the nettle of local government financial reform; to increase local authority participation in economic and social development, particularly through greater involvement in nationally funded and EU-funded projects; and generally to increase the range of competence of local government.

Conclusion

The role of Irish managers has changed substantially in recent years for a number of reasons. The 1970s and 1980s brought a combination of fiscal crisis and expanding demand for local services which required a reorientation of local authority priorities. While this led to cutbacks in employment and in some services, and to the introduction of elements both of contracting out and of straightforward private sector provision, there is little doubt that it has resulted in an overall increase in efficiency and in a reorientation in thinking within local authorities. Where once the proper discharge of duties in compliance with the law was the order of the day, concepts such as strategic thinking, team-work, partnership with councillors, and customer-orientation are now part and parcel of a manager's discourse. Yet for all these developments, Irish managers remain recognisably the same powerful administrative figures which they were a generation ago. While they may be more willing to delegate, they have no intention of abandoning their leadership role. It is precisely the enduring strength of local authority management which gives confidence that, despite all the problems, Irish local government will survive and will improve its services to its customers.

Bibliography

Ahern, B. (1996): Interview with Bertie Ahern TD, leader of Fianna Fail, Radio One, 17 Sept. 1996.

Barrington, T. (1980): *The Irish administrative system*, Dublin: Institute of Public Administration.

Boland, J., and O'Halpin, E. (1991): A chronology of local government, 1918-1990, in *City and county management, 1929-1990: a retrospective*, Dublin: Institute of Public Administration.

Gallagher, M. (1993): Dail deputies and their constituency work, in J. Coakley and M. Gallagher (eds.), *Politics in the Republic of Ireland*, Dublin: PSAI Press/Folens.

Hughes, Owen P. (1994): *Public management and administration: an introduction*, Basingstoke: Macmillan.

National Economic and Social Council (1994): *New approaches to rural development*, Stationery Office, Dublin.

Roche, Desmond (1982): *Local government in Ireland*, Dublin: Institute of Public Administration.

Roche, Dick. (1992): Irish local government: controlled to a virtual standstill, in K. Rafter and N. Whelan (eds.), *From Malin Head to Mizen Head: the definitive guide to local government in Ireland*, Dublin: Blackwater Press.

CHAPTER 5

United States of America: Similarity Within Diversity

by James Svara

The study of the CEO in the United States is complicated by the fact that cities use different forms of government. In the council-manager cities, there is a true appointed CEO – the city manager – along with a non-executive mayor. The mayor-council cities included in this study, on the other hand, have chief administrative officers (CAO); they serve along with the mayor who is the elected CEO. The respondents to the U.DI.T.E. survey include 485 city managers and 172 CAOs from cities with a population of 2500 or more, along with 39 in cities with some other form of government. Although there is diversity in form of government, the analysis demonstrates that there is substantial similarity in roles and attitudes of the top appointed official in council-manager and mayor-council governments.

The Historical and Institutional Context

The position of municipalities in the United States is shaped by a complex set of intergovernmental relations. There are over 19,000 municipalities, although almost half are under 1,000 population. The status of municipalities is characterized by contradictions. On the one hand, municipal governments are the most important provider of the distinct services needed by their residents. On the other hand, they are legally dependent on state governments. They employ only 14% of the public sector workforce which constitutes just one fifth of the total workforce.[1] Many basic human services are the responsibility of another local government – the counties that are usually but not always larger in area than municipalities – as well as the state and national government.

The United States Constitution delegates certain powers to the states and

---

[1] School districts, which are usually not part of municipal government, employ an additional 27 percent of the public sector workforce. Counties employ another 12 percent.

retains others as the legal prerogatives of the federal government. There is no constitutional protection for local government. Rather, cities and other local governments are the creatures of state government. How much power the states delegate to localities and how closely they control local governments varies from state to state. There has been a general trend toward expanded "home rule" which allows city governments to change their charters – the legal documents under which they operate. Local choice, however, is much more likely to pertain to the structure of the government rather than to their fiscal affairs or to the functions cities provide.

To understand the position of cities, it is important to identify the division of functions among levels and types of governments in the United States. The *national government* provides programs to support the economic security and health of the poor, the disabled, and the elderly and transfers funds to states and local governments, although the amount of federal financial assistance has been shrinking over the past twenty years. The *states* tend to directly provide economic and natural resource development, higher education, highways, courts and corrections, and certain aspects of land use management, particularly to protect environmentally sensitive areas. Through counties, the states are responsible for human services, education, and enforcement of environmental regulations. In addition, they provide assistance to local governments and manage federal government programs. The *counties* deliver human services for the state, maintain records, and provide rural law enforcement and roads. In urban areas, counties have developed a wide range of functions and often provide city-type services, for example water, sewer, and recreation, to residents of the county who live in areas that are not within the boundaries of a municipality. Public education is provided by 14,556 *school districts*. Most are "independent," i.e., separate units of government found in almost three fourths of the states; in the remaining states, the district is "dependent" and under the control of a city or county government. In addition, over 33,000 other *special districts* provide usually a single governmental function, e.g., water and sewer, for a geographical area that does not necessarily correspond to any other governmental jurisdiction. They are used extensively in three quarters of the states.

City governments – municipalities – serve a dual purpose and provide two types of functions: governmental, as an agent of the state, and proprietary, as an agent of the local inhabitants providing services for their convenience. Cities continue to be the most important "local" government in the sense of responding to the needs of residents of the locality by means of programs and services that are locally determined. Cities offer public works and physical services, police and fire protection, recreation and cultural programs, planning and housing, neighborhood improvement, and city-wide economic development. They oversee or provide basic utilities. American cities like those in Australia and Canada are urban support systems – emphasizing those services needed to support the distinctive needs of their residents and which promote the development of the city itself. These systems are different from the "welfare state" systems of

Scandinavia and Britain or the "clientelistic" systems of southern Europe.[2] Only the small number of cities that also have the powers of county government (e.g., New York, Philadelphia, St. Louis, Indianapolis, Richmond) offer a full range of human services. In only 12 states are any cities directly involved in providing public education.

There is usually a fairly high degree of fragmentation among governments in urban regions. For all residents classified as living in metropolitan areas in the United States, only 40% reside within the central cities of these areas.[3] The remainder live in suburban jurisdictions or unincorporated areas outside the central city. Counties and special districts are providers of at least some local services in these residents. In addition, there are typically many municipalities which geographically divide the provision of city functions in a given urban region. Nowhere in the United States does one major city government have jurisdiction over its entire urban region.

The fiscal position of city governments also illustrates their mixture of independence and dependence. At the turn of the century, local governments raised over half of all government revenues and the states just ten percent. In 1970, on the other hand, the national government raised 62% of all government revenue, the states 20%, and local governments 18%. In 1992, the local share was approximately the same but the federal portion had decreased to 56% and the state share had increased to 25% of total revenues.

With this shift of resources upward, there were also expanded transfers downward but that trend has ended. In 1980 – just after the peak of federal contributions – state and federal funds accounted for 37% of municipal budgets. In 1992, intergovernmental revenues had dropped to 28% with all the drop coming in federal funds which declined from 16 to seven percent. City governments are increasingly relying on their own resources to replace lost intergovernmental revenues. The transition has been difficult for many city governments. Service cutbacks and staff reductions have been common. Despite these trends, local government administrators view centralized control as a greater problem than reduced funding from the national government. In this survey, new regulations from upper level governments and their control of local government finances were ranked second and fourth, respectively, among factors which have negatively affected the ability of top administrators to perform their jobs. In contrast, cuts in grants ranked ninth among fourteen factors.

Even in the absence of actual fiscal constraints, there is also strong popular

---

2 Goldsmith (1991, p. 8) provides these labels although he uses the term "regime and growth coalition systems" to refer to the ideal type that includes the United States. The services provided by municipalities may be harnessed to a growth agenda when the constellation of interests supports this approach – as they often do – but some governments promote stability and others amenities over growth. Some even seek to limit growth.
3 U.S. Bureau of Census, *State and Metropolitan Area Data Book, 1991*. (Washington, D.C.: U.S. Government Printing Office, 1991). Calculated from data provided on pp. 180-200.

sentiment for tax cuts and reduction in the size of government in many states and localities. Anti-tax and anti-government sentiment ranked third.

Contracting out to private companies and nonprofit agencies is commonly practiced in response to new fiscal and political pressures as well as changes in management thinking. Privatizing or contracting out has been used by 80% of the council-manager cities and 62% of the mayor council cities, and by approximately 90% of cities over 50,000 in population regardless of form of government. Two-thirds of all administrators feel that these practices have been at least moderately important in reducing the number of municipal employees.

The CEOs in the Political-Administrative System

The structure of city government in the United States was transformed by a movement to improve and reform government that started in the late nineteenth century as part of the broader "progressive era." The target of the reform movement at the local level was corrupt and ineffective governments often dominated by political party machines (see Stillman, 1974, and Svara, 1994, for a more complete discussion). Through so-called Model City Charters in 1897 and 1916, the reformers sought to centralize authority through first the strong mayor-council form and then the council-manager form of government, reduce the importance of political parties through nonpartisan elections, and expand the size of constituencies through at-large elections. Reformers also advocated city planning and selection of staff based on merit.

The council-manager form of government – the centerpiece of the second model charter – distinguished "legislation" from "administration," naturally assigning the former to the council and the latter to the manager. The council would exercise regular and comprehensive supervision, so there was no presumption that the manager would handle the administrative affairs of the city in isolation from the council. Conversely, the manager was called upon to offer policy advice and recommendations to the council in its enactment of legislation. The commentary on the second model charter contains numerous references to the manager's policy role. Overall, the manager must "show himself to be a leader, formulating policies and urging their adoption by the council" (Woodruff, 1919: 130). The reformers did not intend to simply add an administrative technician who would take charge of implementation of policies.

The council-manager form was rapidly adopted in a growing number of cities. The mayor-council form of government is more commonly used than the council-manager form in small cities and in very large cities. In cities with population between 10,000 and 500,000, on the other hand, the council-manager form is used more often.

The reform movement also had an impact on the mayor-council form. Increasingly, cities that used this form concentrated power in the mayor's office and many added a chief administrative officer to the government to assist the mayor. Approximately 35% of the mayor-council cities with a population between 10,000 and 50,000 have a chief administrative officer (CAO) as do 39% of the mayor-council cites over 50,000 in population.[4] Other elements of the reform plan, particularly the merit system, financial accounting, and city planning were widely introduced in "traditional" mayor-council as well as council-manager cities. Nonpartisan and at-large elections are still more common in council-manager cities, although the number that use districts has been increasing since the sixties.

The two forms of government offer a clear contrast between the unitary model in the council-manager form and the separation of powers model in the mayor-council form as the basis for organizing government. The mayor-council form of government is based on separation of powers with authority divided between the executive and the legislature. The strong mayor-council version of this form has separation of powers between, on the one hand, a mayor with extensive powers and integrated administrative control over staff and, on the other, the elected legislative body. The council in mayor-council cities is confined to a more limited role and is more or less dependent on the mayor.[5] Since the purpose of offsetting powers is to permit one set of officials to hold the other in check, it is common for conflict to arise in the relationship between the mayor and the council in mayor-council cities (Svara, 1990).

The scope of the position and the duties depend on what responsibilities that are assigned by the officials who appoint the CAO. These usually include authority over implementation of programs, day-to-day administrative concerns, and budget formulation, as well as playing an advisory role in developing other policy recommendations. It has been common to assume that the CAO is appointed by the mayor, derives his or her influence from the mayor, and the CAO operates within the orbit of the mayor (Hogan, 1976). In the present study which includes smaller cities than Hogan included, 51% of the CAOs are appointed by the mayor with the approval of the city council, and another 38% are nominated by the city council. Only 11% are appointed by the mayor alone, although direct mayoral appointment is found in half of the cities over 30,000 in population.

The council-manager form is based on the unitary model of organizing government. The council possesses all governmental authority, except as it delegates authority to the manager, and, thus, there is no separation of powers or checks and balances in the system. The council and mayor occupy the overtly political roles in government, set policy, oversee administration, and select the city manager. Only 4% of the city managers are nominated by the mayor. The mayor is typically the presiding officer of the council and has no formal powers different from those of other council members, except for the veto power in 13% of council-manager cities.[6] Mayors, directly elected in 62% of these cities, can

---

4 Estimate based on data provided by the National League of Cities, 1996.
5 There are also "weak" mayor-council governments commonly found in very small cities. Authority in these cities is widely shared among elected officials.

exercise facilitative leadership and be an important source of policy guidance and coordination of participants, although they rarely exercise any administrative authority (Svara and Associates, 1994). The city manager provides policy advice and recommendations to the council and directs the administrative apparatus. The structure of council-manager government and prevailing values within the form promote cooperative relationships among officials.

The Recruitment of CEOs

In the initial decades of council-manager government, city managers usually had technical training in engineering and often moved into city management laterally from a managerial position in business or some other governmental agency. They were more likely to be "administrative generalists" who moved from one administrative position to another inside or outside government in the same city rather than "careerists" who were committed to municipal administration and moved from one city to another. In addition, there was a group of "local appointees" often without training or experience but selected because of strong local ties and support (Stillman, 1974: pp. 81-82). Presumably, the proportion of careerists is increasing at the expense of both generalists and local appointees.

In comparison to chief administrative officers (CAO) found in mayor-council cities, the city manager has greater professional qualifications although both groups have been become better educated. In the late seventies, over half the managers had masters or other advanced degrees in comparison to 29% of the CAOs (Svara, 1990: 179). In the present study, 70% of the city managers have a graduate degree compared to 53% of the CAOs. The difference between forms, however, is strongly related to the age of the administrator. Among those under 40 years of age, a higher percent of CAOs have a graduate degree (75%) than city managers (64%). Over seventy percent of the city managers over 40, on the other hand, have a graduate degree compared to 47% of CAOs. The most common field of graduate study is public administration; 64% of those with a graduate degree received the MPA. Administrators with the MPA degree represent approximately half of all top administrators.

The average tenure of city managers has fluctuated from 7.8 years in 1974, to 4.2 years in 1980, and by 1984 back to 5.4 years. In the present study, the average number of years in the current positions is 6.9 years for city managers and 6.5 years for CAOs. In cities over 50,000, the tenure drops to 6.4 for council-manager cities and 4.3 years for mayor-council cities. In comparison to managers, CAOs are not as upwardly or geographically mobile. When they do move to other municipal governments, they tend to move to cities with the council-

---

6 Veto and election and veto statistics from Charles R. Adrian, "Forms of City Government in American History," *Municipal Yearbook, 1982* (Washington: International City Management Association, 1982), 10.

manager form of government. According to analysis of career patterns among ICMA members in 1995 (DeSantis and Newell, 1996), CAOs are more likely to move to council-manager cities than city managers are to move to a mayor-council city. Of course, there are more city manager than CAO positions available in American cities. Two fifths of those who had previously been CAOs in mayor-council cities were city managers in 1995. Only 22% of those who had previously been city managers, on the other hand, had become CAOs in mayor-council cities. The same pattern is present for former assistant or deputy managers or administrators: all of those from council-manager cities took city manager positions whereas the assistant or deputy CAOs were evenly split between city manager and CAO positions. These findings together with information about education level suggest that young administrators with graduate degrees may find positions in relatively small cities as CAOs early in their careers but over time seek to move into positions in council-manager cities.

Top administrators are primarily recruited from other public sector positions with only 10% moving from the private sector into their current position. Over half came from other cities (55%) rather than moving into the top spot from a subordinate position in the same city (20%). One in ten come from a public agency other than a city – most from counties. Overall, 37% served as the top administrator in their previous position, 17% served as an assistant manager or CAO, and 8% served as part of the staff of the top administrator. City managers are more likely to have served as the chief administrator in their previous post than CAOs (40% vs. 31%) or as the assistant manager (11% vs. 5%). On the other hand, 17% of CAOs come from the private sector compared to 8% of the city managers. When cities over 20,000 in population are examined, these differences are much more pronounced: 59% of city managers compared to 15% of CAOs were executives or assistants in another city. Over one quarter of CAOs as opposed to only 5% of city managers came from the private sector; 38% of the CAOs occupied other positions in the same city government compared to 25% of the city managers in cities with population over 20,000. Thus, in larger cities, CAOs are more likely to be drawn from the locality where they work and/or the private sector whereas city managers in these cities have served top or assistant administrators in other cities. Thus, the "careerist pattern" is still somewhat more common among city managers than CAOs.

Job Postings
Council expectations for the city manager are reflected in the way openings are announced in job postings. Although a systematic analysis of job postings has not been conducted in the United States, an informal assessment has been made by James Brimeyer (1993), a former city manager who now heads a private consulting firm which assists cities in recruiting managers. In 1978, councils looked for experience in economic development, in dealing with labor unions, and in obtaining grants; they preferred a style of leadership and management which stressed maturity, a low profile, diplomatic skills, an aura of authority, a steady

career path, and skill in promoting unity within the city council. In 1988, elected officials wanted experience in protecting neighborhoods, negotiating labor contracts, dealing with environmental issues – especially recycling of solid waste – , assisting the governing body with goal setting, and establishing strong customer service orientation. The preferred leadership and management style was ability to persuade, a high level of energy, sensitivity to political realities, and skill in conflict resolution. In 1993, elected officials were looking for managers who are visionary, oriented toward staff development, possess skills in collaboration, and are experienced in financial management, development and redevelopment. They want a manager who can share leadership roles and empower staff, view the governing board and staff as a team, encourage citizen participation, develop partnerships, resolve conflicts, be sensitive to issues of racial and sexual diversity, and possesses a strong commitment to ethics. Brimeyer interprets these changes to indicate that the council wants more active leadership from the city manager with less of a distinction in roles between the council and the manager. In a sense, the manager is expected to be more of an equal with the council. At the same time, however, the manager is also more vulnerable to removal by elected officials if they feel that the manager is not "in tune" with the council. The formal and hierarchical distance between the city council and the city manager still evident in 1978 is shrinking.

Salary

The average salary of American city managers in 1995 was $69,330; for CAOs, it was $58,201. By contrast, the mayor in council-manager cities averages $5,520, and in mayor-council cities (including those without CAOs) averages $15,926.[7] The average salary had increased 20% for city managers and 26% for CAOs, respectively, between 1990 and 1995. The following are the average salaries for managers and CAOs in various population categories:

Population size	*City Managers*	*Chief Administrative Officers*
Over 100,000	$117,297	$83,372
25,000-99,999	$90,251	$68,208
10,000-24,999	$70,489	$60,815
2,500- 9,999	$52,869	$44,914
Source: "Salaries of Municipal Officials, 1995," *Municipal Year Book 1996* (Washington, D.C.: International City Management Association, 1996), pp. 74-75. Average of mean salaries for population categories.		

---

[7] For comparison, the average salary for an elementary school teacher (grades kindergarten-8) was $34,611 in 1993-94.

Turnover

The city manager in the United States has always been subject to close scrutiny by the city council.[8] City managers "serve at the pleasure" of the council, and elected officials exercise their authority to remove the manager for whatever reason. City managers may be attracted to positions that offer more attractive opportunities, i.e., they are "pulled" to a new position, or they may be fired or otherwise "pushed out" of the office. The impression one gets from interactions with city managers and some scattered evidence is that forced manager turnover is increasing at the present time. There are, however, few systematically collected data. On the one hand, a study from 1992 found 60% turnover in the formerly secure village manager positions in Illinois (reported in Golembiewski and Gabris, 1994: p. 529.) In a 1993 national survey of city managers, on the other hand, Wheeland (1995: pp. 14-15) found that only 9.6% of cities over 20,000 in population had three or more managers between 1988 and 1993. Among the managers who responded, two-thirds had been managers before their current position. Of these, only 10% reported being fired or pressured to resign and only five percent left a city to escape conflict within the council. In general, the greater the political instability in the city, the greater the likelihood of managerial turnover (Whitaker and DeHoog, 1991).

In the present study, 23% of the immediate predecessors of the current administrators left for career advancement to a higher or better paid position. In council-manager cities, 47% of the predecessors had experienced problems in the relationship with the city council – higher than in any of the other fourteen countries in the U.DI.T.E. study. In the mayor-council cities, 27% of the CAOs left because of conflict with the council and 24% because of conflict with mayor. Only 15% of the city managers departed because of conflict with the mayor. Problems with department heads were a factor in turnover in only 9% of the cities with no variation by city government form. Only 8% of the previous managers retired – lowest (along with Australia) among the study countries.

Attractiveness of Job

The prevailing opinion among city managers is that the job of the highest appointed official in local government has gotten worse over the past ten years. Over half – 53% hold this view -and 23% feel that it has remained the same. Only 24% feel it has gotten better. CAOs have a more positive assessment: 38% feel the job has gotten better, 26% feel it has not changed, and only 36% feel it has gotten worse. The factor most commonly mentioned to explain the negative change is increasing demands for services from cities, although only one in eight offered this explanation. Less frequently mentioned were declining financial resources, poorer relations with elected officials, and tensions in relationships with citizens.

---

8 In the 1920s and 1930s, over forty percent of the separations of city managers resulted from firing or forced resignation as opposed to voluntarily moving to a new position.

Roles and Values of CEOs

The role definition of the city manager and the relationship of this official to the governing board has been a critical issue throughout the history of the council-manager form of government. As we have noted, a policy role for the city manager was explicitly supported at the time of initial endorsement of the council-manager form of government by the National Municipal League in 1916. The advocates of the form, however, promoted its acceptance in the twenties and thirties by stressing that the city manager was a neutral official not involved in policy formation. These years corresponded with the period of orthodoxy in American public administration, and a retreat into a role restricted to "administration" occurred. When this view was strongest in the thirties, a publication of ICMA asserted that the manager should not "let himself be driven or led into taking the leadership or responsibility in matters of policy." The 1938 Code of Ethics of ICMA stated unequivocally "the city manager is in no sense a political leader." A dichotomy between politics and administration – not present in the thinking of the founders of the form – had appeared (Svara, 1998).

The problem with this view is that most city managers have always been policy leaders whose contributions go beyond offering technical advice. There is extensive empirical evidence of such leadership in research throughout the history of council-manager plan – even during the time when the dichotomy concept was accepted doctrine. The experience of city managers since the late twenties, therefore, has been schizophrenic: officially they are neutral administrators who stay out of policy; in practice they have been influential in policy formulation as well.

Given this background, it is not surprising that city managers have virtually identical scores on indices of the "classical" and the "political bureaucrat." To state the generalization differently, city managers are equally active as organizational leaders and providers of technical information, on the one hand, and as policy leaders, on the other. These results are indicated in table 5.1, column A. Among the indicators of the classical bureaucrat, they are most active in fiscal management and giving the mayor and council technical advice. They give moderate importance to more detailed aspects of management. These tasks are presumably delegated to assistant managers (in larger cities) and department heads. The score for the "political bureaucrat" role would be even higher if one activity were removed. City managers assign little importance to giving the mayor political advice, a finding consistent with the tradition of partisan neutrality and noninvolvement in electoral matters. Without that activity, the score would be 72 rather than 64, i.e., an indication that these activities taken together have great importance to the city manager. The most prominent of these activities is formulating ideas and visions. In other research as well, I have shown that city managers are highly involved in helping to shape the mission of city government, i.e., its purposes, goals, and strategies (Svara, 1989.)

Table 5.1 The roles of City Managers (Council-ManagerCities) and CAOs (Mayor-Council Cities), USA

	A: City-Manager	B: CAO
The classical bureaucrat	65	67
Guide subordinate staff in day-to-day handling of activities	54	58
Manage economic affairs, accounts and budgetary control	77	75
Ensure that rules and regulations are followed	59	62
Provide the mayor with legal, economic and other kinds of technical advice	69	74
Provide the council with legal, economic and other kinds of technical advice*	75	73
The political bureaucrat	64	63
Formulate ideas and visions	81	77
Promote and encourage new projects in the community	69	65
Provide the mayor with political advice	23	32
Be informed about citizens' viewpoints	77	73
Develop and implement norms concerning the proper roles of politicians vis-á-vis the bureaucrats	59	54
Influence decision-making processes in order to secure sensible and efficient solutions	72	74

* Not included in the summary index score for the classical bureaucrat

As the size of the city increases, city managers place greater importance on the political dimensions of the position and less importance on the management dimensions. To illustrate, 23% of the managers in cities over 50,000 in population assign little importance to guiding subordinate staff, whereas only 10% of the managers in smaller cities consider it to be unimportant. On the other hand, 48% of the managers in the over 50,000 category consider formulating vision to be of utmost importance compared to 35% of the managers in smaller cities.

City managers are slightly more active in most of the "political" aspects of the position than are CAOs, with one important exception – offering political advice to the mayor. (See column B in table 5.1.) The CAOs, on the other hand, give slightly greater emphasis to most of the "classical" roles. On the surface, this is a surprising result given the common association of the CAO with the mayor; the CAO would be expected to act as the political agent of the mayor. As we noted earlier, however, most CAOs are appointed or confirmed by the city council. Although CAOs overall assign more importance to giving political advice to the mayor, there is substantial variation among the CAOs themselves depending on the mayor's level of authority over their appointment. If appointed by the council, the importance index for offering political advice to the mayor is 24; if appointed by the mayor with approval of the council, the index for this role is 29; and if appointed by the mayor, the value is 47. Thus, the CAOs appointed by the council are virtually identical to the city managers in avoiding political advice to the mayor; if approved by the council, the CAO is similar to the city manager. Only those appointed directly by the mayor assign more importance to this role. In general, the presence of a mayor with executive authority in the mayor-council cities constrains the CAO. The executive mayor is the source of policy initiation, and CAOs confine themselves somewhat more to the internal management activities associated with the classical bureaucrat.

The structure of council-manager government and prevailing values within the form promote cooperative relationships among officials. When the city manager's interaction with other officials in city government is examined, the cooperative pattern is apparent. (See figure 5.1.) The city manager has very high dependency on the council (other politicians), the mayor, and department heads. The contact with them is high, and the level of cooperation with all three is very high. In contrast, leaders of the political opposition are not an important factor in the contacts of city managers. There is little contact, no dependency and a neutral relationship with them. (Other relationships will be considered in the next section.)

CAOs, who are not included in figure 5.1, have equivalent dependency but slightly less cooperation with the mayor and department heads, and only a medium level of contact with other members of the city council. Still, their interactions with these key actors inside government are also essentially positive. When CAOs are appointed by the mayor, they have more contact, greater dependency on the mayor, and closer cooperation. The only other internal contact that is affected by the method of appointing the CAO is cooperation with department heads. When the CAO is directly appointed by the mayor, there is lower cooperation than there is between department heads and CAOs appointed or approved by the city council.

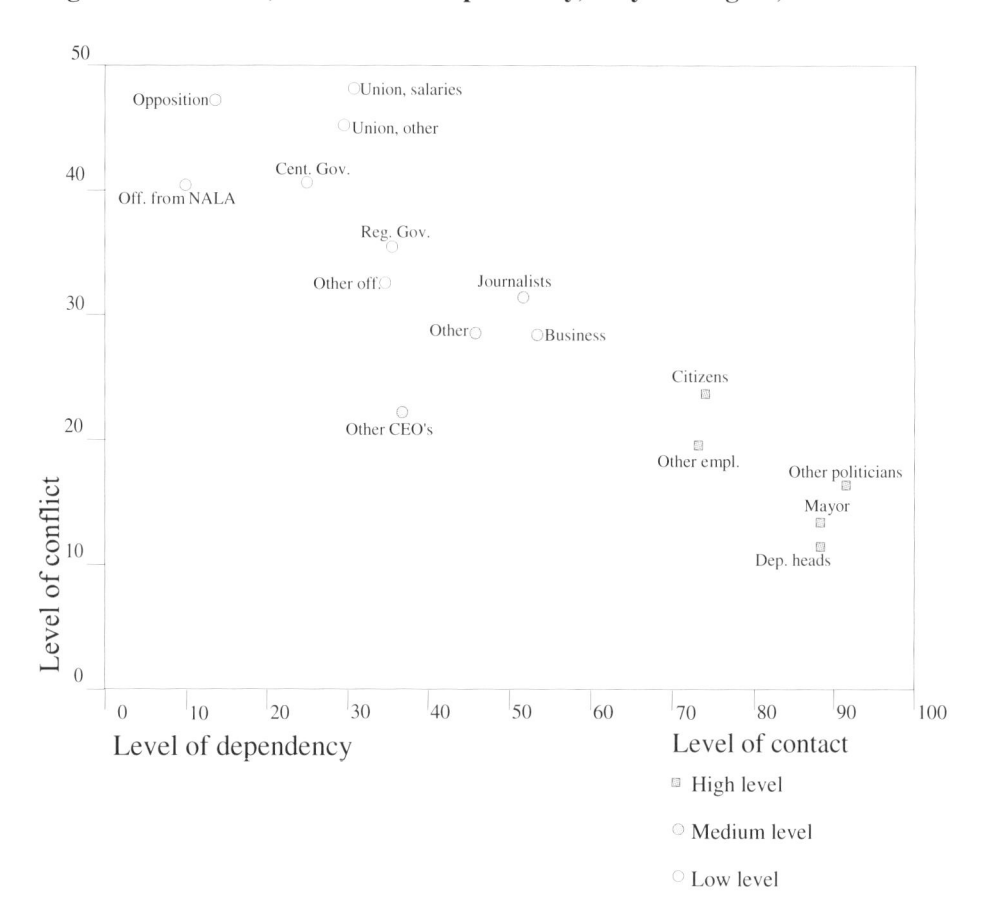

Figure 5.1 Contact, conflict and dependency, City Managers, USA

[Scatter plot with axes "Level of conflict" (y-axis, 0–50) and "Level of dependency" / "Level of contact" (x-axis, 0–100). Data points:
- Opposition (low level): ~(10, 45)
- Union, salaries (low level): ~(35, 46)
- Union, other (low level): ~(37, 42)
- Cent. Gov. (low level): ~(27, 40)
- Off. from NALA (low level): ~(15, 39)
- Reg. Gov. (low level): ~(37, 36)
- Other off. (low level): ~(32, 31)
- Journalists (low level): ~(50, 31)
- Other (medium level): ~(40, 28)
- Business (low level): ~(55, 28)
- Citizens (high level): ~(72, 23)
- Other CEO's (medium level): ~(32, 21)
- Other empl. (high level): ~(72, 18)
- Other politicians (high level): ~(88, 16)
- Mayor (high level): ~(83, 14)
- Dep. heads (high level): ~(82, 11)

Legend: ■ High level, ○ Medium level, ○ Low level]

In addition to their role preferences for themselves, city managers and CAOs also have expectations regarding the roles to be filled by elected officials. (See table 5.2.) There are no substantial differences between the preferences of city managers and CAOs. All administrators feel that council members should attach the most importance to governance roles, especially deciding on major policy principles and having a vision of the way that the municipality should develop in the long run. Creating stability for administration and formulating exact goals are also assigned great importance. They would prefer that council members assign only moderate importance to implementing the program on which they were elected. Among other representational activities that council members could pursue, being informed about citizens' views is very important, representing the municipality to the outside world and defending the authority's decisions and policies externally are quite important, and being a spokesperson vis-à-vis the press is moderately important.

James Svara

Table 5.2 The ideal politician in Council-Manager and Mayor-Council Cities, USA

	A: Council-Manager	B: Mayor-Council
Administration	39	43
Be a spokesperson for local groups or individuals who have issues pending decision by the authority	37	41
Lay down rules and routines for the administration	29	32
Taking decisions concerning specific cases	52	55
Representation	55	54
Be informed about citizens' views	83	83
Represent the municipality to the outside world	68	67
Defend the authorities' decisions and policies externally	67	68
Be a spokesperson for their political party	12	17
Be a spokesperson vis-á-vis the press	43	36
Governance	70	71
Implement the program on which he/she has been elected	51	56
Decide on major policy principles	77	77
Have a vision of the way in which the municipality will develop in the long run	81	81
Stability	69	65
Create stability for the administration	72	69
Formulate exact and unambiguous goals for the administration	65	61

Given very little weight by the appointed administrators is being a spokesperson for the political party. CAOs assign slightly more importance to this role (a rating of 17 versus 12 for city managers), but there is a pervasive agreement among appointed administrators in the United States that council members should "rise above" party, just as the administrators themselves are nonpartisan.[9] Of least importance overall is filling administrative roles. Speaking for groups or individuals who have decisions pending before the city government and laying down rules and routines for the administration should not have much importance in the view of administrators, although taking decisions concerning specific cases is assigned moderate importance. This is one of the activities that the formulators of the council-manager form assigned to the city council. Administrators consider the resolution of specific problems by the council to be fairly important.

When the preferences of municipal administrators for themselves and elected officials are compared, their shared and complementary roles are apparent. Both will be highly involved in setting the broad direction of their government, and the council will make major policy decisions in response to the administrator's proposals. It is much more important that council members be informed about citizens' views rather than acting on their campaign promises; it is unimportant for council members to promote their party's position. Indeed, generally parties are viewed as irrelevant to city government concerns. Creating stability for the municipal government is fairly important and resolving specific cases is moderately important. Administrators expect that elected officials will be actively engaged in setting the direction and determining policy for the city in active partnership with the administrators themselves. Both will also be highly attentive to citizens. The dichotomy model that held sway from the thirties through the fifties – and continues to receive some support – has largely been supplanted by a restored model of complementarity.

Networks and Influence: External and Internal

Beyond the roles filled by city managers in their relationships to elected officials, city managers are also important community leaders and organizational directors.

Community Leadership
The importance of community leadership is reflected in the attitudes of practising local government managers and in the organizational norms of ICMA. The ICMA Future Visions Consortium (Newell, 1993: p. 8) recommended that city managers fill the following roles in order to meet the challenges of their cities: consensus builder, educator on community issues, translator/interpreter of community values, problem solver, process leader, convener of interested parties and diverse community groups, team builder/mentor, source of empowerment, change agent, champion of new technologies, facilitator of conflict resolution,

---

9 71% of the administrators feel that most or all of their council members do not consider party affiliation to be important.

bearer of ethical standards, and champion of leadership development within the community. All of the roles deal directly or partially with the community leadership sphere.

The positive involvement of city managers in the community is reflected in interactions with citizens. (See figure 5.1.) Despite widespread reports of popular discontent with government, city managers report high contact with and dependency on citizens as well as cooperative relations with them. Although city managers have medium levels of contact with journalists, private business interests, and other community leaders, the extent of their communication with them is in the top three ranks compared with the CEOs in other countries. The relations with all are cooperative. City managers also have extensive dealings and very positive relations with other chief administrators in their urban area. City managers do not depend much on other external actors – staff in the national association of cities or officials with regional government, regional councils, or other government officials. Relations with them are cooperative to neutral. CAOs (not included in Figure 5.1) have slightly less contact with other CEOs than city managers. Otherwise, their external relations are similar to those of city managers.

Organizational Leadership

The final sphere of managerial leadership is the organization. Here, the city manager has had the traditional advantage of strong formal authority. Generally, city managers develop the budget, appoint department heads, and determine the administrative organization. In this survey, a comparison of the authority of the city manager and CAO shows the stronger formal position of the city manager. More city managers than CAOs propose the executive budget (95% vs. 83%), direct all or most departments (98% vs. 83%), and have authority to reorganize departments (88% vs. 58%). City managers appoint 76% of the departments heads in their governments compared to 22% appointed by CAOs in their cities.

It would be a mistake, however, to overstate the degree of managerial autonomy of city managers in the administration and management. Even when the formal authority over budget, appointments, and reorganization is present, city managers are probably engaging in more informal interaction with the council over the exercise of this authority, and in some areas community groups are involved as well. It is common in larger cities, for example, for candidates for police chief to be interviewed by a wide range of citizen organizations. Furthermore, other pressures on the manager leave less time for internal management. As we have seen, the larger the city, the more the manager sets the tone and establishes general direction and devotes less attention to internal management.

The internal relationships of the city manager and CAO are similar. Both report high interaction, dependency, and cooperation with department heads and other employees. For both, unions of city staff are not salient actors. Despite the importance of unions in some cities, they are not a major actor in most cities.

Conclusion

City managers in the United States have always been caught between the being narrow and broad leaders. The original intention of the reformers who invented the council-manager form of government was for city managers to be comprehensive professional leaders. Richard Childs, one of the important early proponents of the form, had high aspirations for the new city management profession. At a meeting of the fledgling organization of city managers in 1918, he stated his position eloquently.

Some day we shall have managers here who have achieved national reputation, not by saving taxes or by running their cities for a freakishly low expense per capita, but managers who have successfully led their commissions into great new enterprises of service. . . . (quoted in White, 1927: p. 143)

The reformers sought to strengthen leadership and were immediately successful. Adrian (1987: p. 452) concludes that "by the 1920s, the city manager had become a firmly established community leader." The emerging dichotomy concept, however, suggested a withdrawn, reactive stance. This became the public face of the management profession during the thirties, and, though regularly renounced, persists to this day. A leading scholar and practitioner felt it was necessary in 1993 to proclaim in ICMA's monthly magazine that "The Policy-Administration Dichotomy is Bunkum" (Murray and Banovetz, 1993). City managers are broadly engaged and proactive but they have had trouble altering their public image to match their actual role and behavior.

CAOs have had a different image problem. They have commonly been seen as closely linked to mayors and their political agenda. Although this is true to some extent among the CAOs in large cites who are appointed by the mayor, most of the top appointed administrators in mayor-council cities are confirmed or appointed by the entire council. Their behavior is similar to city managers. Overall, CAOs are somewhat more oriented to internal management, somewhat less involved in guiding policy, and, if appointed by the mayor, more engaged in offering political advice to the mayor. They have slightly less formal education and somewhat shorter tenure. They are more likely to be drawn from other positions in the same city or from the private sector. Still, in most respects they are a variation on the city manager as professional administrator rather than being a nonprofessional and primarily political administrator.

Within the divergent structures of municipal government in the United States, there is substantial similarity among the top local government administrators. The presence of an elected executive mayor in mayor-council cities limits the scope of the CAO's actions and produces greater emphasis on the internal management dimensions of the position. City managers are chief executive officers with extensive organizational authority. They help to frame the agenda of issues for their cities and formulate policy alternatives. Compared with other countries, they are among the most active in contacts with citizens, the media, business, and nonprofit and voluntary organizations. CAOs have similar levels of community contact. City managers have very positive relations with their councils but are also very dependent on them. If the working relationship sours, city councils commonly exercise their prerogative to remove the city manager. CAOs take into account support from the mayor and well as the city council. In the final analysis, both city managers and CAOs are comprehensive leaders who must balance relations with elected officials, the community, and the organization.

Bibliography

Adrian, C. (1987): *A History of American City Government*, New York: University Press of America, p. 452.

Brimeyer, J. (1993): Council-Manager Relations: Time for Adjustment, Before It Is Too Late, *Public Management*, 75: 10-12.

DeSantis, V., and Newell, C. (1996): Local Government Managers' Career Paths, *Municipal Yearbook 1996*, Washington: International City Management Association: 3-10.

Goldsmith, Michael, (1991): *Options for the Future? – Local Democracy Abroad*, The Belgrave Papers, No. 5. The Local Government Management Board.

Golembiewski, R.T., and Gabris, G. (1994): Today's City Managers: A legacy of Success-Becoming-Failure, *Public Administration Review*, 54: 525.

Hogan, James B. (1976): *The Chief Administrative Officer*, Tucson: University of Arizona Press.

Murray, S., and Banovetz, J. (1993): The Policy-Administration Dichotomy is Bunkum. *Public Management*, 75: 14.

Nalbandian, J. (1991): *Professionalism in Local Government*, Jossey-Bass, San Francisco.

Renner, T (1991): Appointed Local Government Managers: Stability and Change, *Municipal Yearbook 1991*, Washington: International City Management Association.: 41-52.

Schellinger, M. (1985): Local Government Managers: Profile of the Professionals in a Maturing Profession, *Municipal Yearbook 1985*, Washington: International City Management Association.

Stillman II, R. J. (1974): *The Rise of the City Manager*, Albuquerque: University of New Mexico Press, p. 51, pp. 43-53.

Stillman II, R. J. (1977): The city manager: Professional helping hand, or political hired hand? *Public Administration Review*, 37 (November/December): 659-670.

Stone, H. A., Price, K. A., and Stone, K. H. (1940): *City Manager Government in the United States*, Chicago: Public Administration Service, p. 247.

Svara, James H. (1989): Policy and Administration: Managers as Comprehensive Professional Leaders, in H. George Frederickson (ed.)., *Ideal and Practice in City Management*, Washington: International City Management Association, pp. 70-93.

Svara, James H (1990): *Official Leadership in the City: Patterns of Conflict and Cooperation*, New York: Oxford University Press.

Svara, James H (1994): The Structural Reform Impulse in Local Government, *National Civic Review*, 83 (Summer-Fall): 323-347.

Svara, James H (1998): The Politics-Administration Dichotomy Model as Aberration, *Public Administration Review*. 58 (forthcoming).

Svara, J. H. and Associates (1994): *Facilitative Leadership in Local Government: Lessons from Successful Mayors and Chairpersons in the Council-Manager Form*, San Francisco: Jossey-Bass Publishers.

Wheeland, C. M. (1995): Council Evaluation of the City Manager's Performance, *Municipal Year Book 1995*, Washington: International City Management Association: 13.

Whitaker, G., and DeHoog, R. H. (1991): City Managers Under Fire: How Conflict Leads to Turnover, *Public Administration Review*, 51: 156-165.

White, Leonard. (1927): *The City Manager*, Chicago: University of Chicago Press.

Woodruff, C. R. Ed. (1919): *A New Municipal Program*, New York: D. Appleton and Company.

CHAPTER 6

The Danish Local Government CEO: From Town Clerk to City Manager

by Niels Ejersbo, Morten Balle Hansen and Poul Erik Mouritzen

The Historical Context

The municipalities in Denmark constitute the largest organizational field in the country. They employ more than 16% of the total workforce (482,679 full time equivalents) and spend more than 33% of the gross national product. Municipalities are responsible for primary schools, day-care institutions, all programs for the elderly (such as home-help, residential homes, old age pensions and other forms of economic support), social assistance, libraries, cultural activities, water supply, public parks, roads, refuse collection, and environmental protection, to mention the more important tasks. All these programs are provided by an organization formally directed by the city council and supported by a professional administration.

The individual municipality can decide the level of service (spending, quality, coverage, etc.) on a large number of the services which are central to the welfare state. Municipalities have a great deal of autonomy with regard to services produced by municipal institutions, and relatively little when it comes to income transfers. Furthermore, autonomy vis-à-vis central state authorities is granted by the rights of local governments to fix their own tax rate. The typical Dane thus pays around 20% of taxable income to municipalities and an additional 10% to the counties. The municipal tax rate varies from around 17% to 22%. Revenue from taxation covers about half of the municipal spending, the rest being covered by grants from the central government and fees and user charges (Jørgensen & Mouritzen 1993).

Not all the tasks presently carried out by the municipalities have always been handled by them. A major reform in 1970 radically altered the Danish local governmental system. In this context, the most interesting features were the reduction in the number of municipalities from around 1300 to 275, the decentralization of tasks from the central government to the municipalities, and the creation of a shared political and administrative structure for the municipalities. These reforms produced large, professional organizations at local levels and in many ways also created the CEO position as we know it today. The consequences for CEOs and the effects on CEO recruitment will be discussed in the following sections. Below we will focus on the structure of the political and administrative organization.

Following the 1970 reform, the majority of municipalities at the political level had a finance committee and four standing committees covering the traditional areas of social welfare and health, primary schools and culture, technical services and, finally, municipal property. Each standing committee was matched by a department at the administrative level. Until the late 1980s this was the structure of the political and administrative organization in the majority of the Danish municipalities. Since the late 1980s, many municipalities have begun to reduce the number of committees and departments, resulting in a far less homogenous structure in the municipalities. From 1970 to the late 1980s the political and administrative structure of the municipalities reflected the reform in 1970. Today it is much more difficult to point to one structural arrangement which describes the Danish municipalities.

The CEO's Position in the Political-Administrative System

In strictly legal terms, the Danish local government CEO (*kommunaldirektøren*) does not exist. The CEO is not mentioned in the Local Government Statute, *Den kommunale Styrelseslov*, which exclusively regulates the political structure of the municipality and the authorities of the various political bodies. Nevertheless, in most municipalities the CEO holds an important and often powerful position. This apparent paradox is due to the fact that the CEO's influence is derived from the mayor. To understand the position and the roles of the CEO thus requires an understanding of the structure of governance in general, and of the mayor's role within that structure in particular.

According to the Local Government Statute "municipal affairs are governed by the city council". The city council, typically composed of 11-17 members, is elected every four years. At its first meeting after the election, the council elects the mayor and members of the various standing committees by and among themselves. Each standing committee (typically 5-7 members) is responsible for the "immediate administration" of affairs defined by the council via the municipal ordinance. This means, that cases brought to the political system by the administrative organization will typically be decided by a committee. It also entails, that cases to be decided by the council will be prepared by the relevant committee. The finance committee, chaired by the mayor, has a special status, for it supervises all financial and administrative matters. The finance committee prepares the annual budget proposal and handles all cases which have financial or administrative consequences. Appointment of personnel rests with the finance committee, except when it comes to the appointment (and dismissal) of the CEO and the department heads. In these cases the city council makes the decision (le Maire and Preisler 1996:135).

The position of mayor is considered a full time job and is paid accordingly. The mayor is the chairman of both the city council and the finance committee. The mayor convenes the council, prepares the agenda and is responsible for the minutes. The mayor may also decide on matters which cannot be delayed. Finally, the mayor is the "head of and daily leader of the municipal administration". The mayor has limited veto powers in the sense that he or she can block the implementation process only if decisions are obviously problematic in terms of their preparation. Despite the authority given to the finance committee and to the mayor, it would be incorrect to describe their relation to the standing committees as hierarchical. The finance committee cannot interfere in cases which are the responsibility of a standing committee. The mayor cannot instruct the standing committees nor can he or she tell the department heads to make specific recommendations to the committees, nor reverse or veto decisions made by the committees.

There is no doubt that the decision-making authority in Danish local government rests with the city council. The location of the executive function, however, is more ambiguous as it is partly shared among the city council, the standing committees, the finance committee and the mayor.

Within the framework defined by the Local Government Statute, the individual local government can define the responsibilities and duties of the CEO rather freely – actually it can decide to abolish the position altogether. However, there are certain commonalities which are found in most municipalities. First, the CEO is almost always present at council and finance committee meetings. Second, the CEO usually directs the meetings of the department heads (the management team). Third, the CEO chairs the so-called works and safety committees composed of elected employee representatives (typically covering various unions) as well as representatives from management. Finally, the CEO is usually formally responsible for policies regarding human resource management within the (often wide) boundaries stipulated by the finance committee. The division of labor between the mayor and the CEO often reflects the particular style of the mayor (and in some instances the style and influence of the CEO). At one extreme, the CEO will act as a de facto executive; at the other extreme, the CEO's position can best be described as a staff assistant to the mayor. We shall return to this issue at the end of the chapter.

An example of the dual position of the CEO is that on the one hand he is appointed by the council and expected to provide advice and administrative services to the whole council, while on the other hand he is extremely dependent on and subordinate to the only full time politician, the mayor. The dilemmas stemming from this dual relationship between CEO and mayor should be kept in mind for further discussion.

The Recruitment of CEOs

The position of today's chief executive officer has evolved from the old position as *town treasurer/town clerk* (kæmner). The town clerk was the leading appointed official in most municipalities; the position was not, however, as strong and powerful as the current CEO position. The town clerk was head of the financial department and the secretariat of the town council. The typical town clerk began as a trainee in the municipal organization around the age of 17, followed by periods as assistant and municipal bookkeeper before reaching the top position as town clerk, typically within the same locality. In the large cities the leading, appointed official would in some cases have a university degree, typically in law.

In 1980 less than 20% of the Danish CEOs held academic degrees. Today this figure is close to 50%, and if we take CEOs appointed after 1989 (that is with less than six years of experience in their present position) the CEOs with an academic background account for 56%. The most common academic degree is still in law (about 1/3); however, CEOs with degrees in economics and political science are gaining ground, accounting for 1/4 and 1/5 respectively of those CEOs with academic degrees. In contrast, the proportion of CEOs who have followed the classical pattern, beginning as a municipal traineee, has dropped drastically, from 3/4 in 1980 to less than half in1992. Among the CEOs appointed after 1989, only about 1/4 began as trainees.

In 1980 close to half the CEOs were recruited from within the municipality. Fifteen years later that figure was 38%. The trend is clear. Over the last five years a mere one out of four CEOs has been internally recruited, while six out of ten have come from other municipalities. However, there is no trend indicating that the barriers to other parts of the public sector have broken down, on the contrary, we observe an influx of CEOs from the private sector.

The turbulence of the job is indicated by the fact that a disproportionately large proportion of the CEOs, namely 71%, have acquired their position within the last ten years. This in striking contrast to the situation in the beginning of the 1980s where the position could be characterized as a life-long secure employment in the public sector. During the ten years from 1971 to 1981, only around 40% of the municipalities had CEO job openings (Riiskær, 1982: 113). Resignations during the 1970s seem to have been caused mostly by "natural" causes such as age. During this period only 15% of the resignations made reference to problems of cooperation as a cause of resignation (Riiskjær, 1982: 116). In 1995 cooperation problems were mentioned by 25% of the respondents concerning relations to politicians, and by 15% concerning relations to fellow bureaucrats. Looking at the resignations which have taken place during the last five years, however, more than 1/3 seem to have been caused by problems of cooperation with politicians and about 1/4 by conflicts with fellow bureaucrats.

Part of the change in recruitment and job security can also be explained by new demands on the CEOs. In the 1970s job announcements for local government CEO's were rather short, and no specific function was emphasized (Dahler-Larsen, 1997). In the 1980s functions as "be in charge of the administration", "secretary for the political body", "coordinate branches of administration" were significant. In the 1990s especially significant were tasks such as "adviser to the mayor" and "develop services in the municipality". We can also see a marked change in the personal qualifications required of the CEOs. Today the CEO should be visionary, have communication skills, be able to motivate and have a sense of humour.

Part of the background of the increasing job insecurity for CEOs are new conditions of appointment. More specifically, it has become easier to fire them. Until a few years ago CEOs (and department heads) were appointed as civil servants with more or less life-long job security due to the fiscal burden imposed upon the municipality by pre-retirement termination of employment. Today, an increasing number of CEOs are appointed on a contract for a fixed period of time, typically for six years, where the increased insecurity in the job is compensated by a higher yearly salary.

Despite the increasing job insecurity, Danish CEOs generally find that the job has become more attractive over the years. More than 60% indicate that they find the job "much more" or "somewhat more" attractive over the last ten years. Less than 20% indicate that the job has become "somewhat less" or "much less" attractive. The most common causes given for the negative assessments refer to relations to politicians or conflicts between the political parties. Only a few respondents refer to the lack of job security (mentioned by 3 out of 36 respondents).

As the major reasons given for the positive assessments, most CEOs refer to changes in the content of the job, such as increased competence, more autonomy on the job, more influence, variations in the job and the introduction of modern management practices in local government. Very few (six out of 115 respondents) refer to better salary conditions. It is a fact, however, that salaries have improved considerably over the last ten years, both in absolute terms as well as relative to other categories of employees. Generally, the salary of a CEO depends on the number of inhabitants and the conditions of employment, but in recent years more and more variation can be found due to individual supplements. In a municipality with less than 10,000 inhabitants the yearly salary including supplements is around 450,000 DKK a year for the CEO and around 400,000 for the mayor. In municipalities with 75,000 inhabitants the CEO's annual salary amounts to 690,000 DKK compared to the mayor's approximately 530,000 DKK. A primary school teacher at the top of the scale earns approximately 256,000 DKK a year.

The Roles and Values of the CEO

The Danish local government CEO is the main link between the political superiors and the administration. In that respect it is relevant to evaluate how the CEO views his own role as bureaucrat as well as the proper role of local government politicians.

Looking at the CEO's perception of his own role as bureaucrat, a distinction can be made between the "classical bureaucrat" and the "political bureaucrat". This typology will structure the first part of the discussion. The analysis of the CEO's perception of the proper role of local government politicians will concentrate on the following four sets of roles: administration, representation, governance and stability. Finally, we will examine the tasks CEOs emphasize in relation to the administration.

Table 6.1 The roles of the CEOs, Denmark

The classical bureaucrat		48
Guide subordinate staff in day-to-day handling of activities	33	
Manage economic affairs, accounts and budgetary control	41	
Ensure that rules and regulations are followed	33	
Provide the mayor with legal, economic and other kinds of technical advice	84	
The political bureaucrat		73
Formulate ideas and visions	83	
Promote and encourage new projects in the community	76	
Provide the mayor with political advice	68	
Be informed about citizens' viewpoints	69	
Develop and implement norms concerning the proper roles of politicians vis-á-vis the bureaucrats	61	
Influence decision-making processes in order to secure sensible and efficient solutions	83	

Table 6.1 shows how Danish CEOs emphasize individual tasks and the two resulting roles. The figures shown are calculated as index values.[1]

The classical bureaucrat scores 48, indicating the component tasks are perceived as having moderate importance only. The four tasks, however, are not emphasized equally. In particular we note the strong emphasis attached to the technical advice given to the mayor. The political bureaucrat, on the other hand, scores 73 on the index, indicating that the CEOs perceive the tasks to be very important. Apparently the Danish CEO accords high priority to tasks where he or she can act as a policy leader and get closely involved in the political process. This may give the impression that the Danish CEO acts as a "Politicus". However, the picture is much more varied. There is considerable variation among the variables used to construct the two types of bureaucrats. For example, CEOs indicate that giving the mayor legal, economic and other kinds of technical advice – part of the classical bureaucrat role – is the most important task. This indicates that on average, the CEO leans towards the political bureaucrat, but the classical bureaucrat is present in many municipalities. When examining those variables in the questionnaire that relate to the CEO's political involvement this variation is also evident.

Even with the reservations just mentioned, there is a clear tendency towards the political bureaucrat. We suspect that this differs from the situation 10-15 years ago. We have no prior studies that enable us to make an exact comparison over time. However, a study of local government department heads in 1982 (Riskjær 1992) clearly supports the supposition that Danish CEOs have evolved a political character.

At the moment, the proper role of local government politicians is one of the most intensely discussed issues in Danish municipalities. One of the main positions in this discussion is that elected officials should fulfil a new role where they are expected to concentrate on major principles and to help formulate visions for the municipality instead of dealing with administrative matters and constituency cases. The pressure on elected officials to act according to this new role has been intensified with the decentralization of economic competence to municipal service institutions, and with the amalgamation of political committees and legislation requiring municipalities to inform citizens about objectives for different services performed by the municipalities.

As shown in table 6.2, Danish CEOs take a clear stand in the debate on the proper role of elected officials. From the viewpoint of the CEO, elected officials should first and foremost concentrate on the representation and governance role. Their role in relation to the administration should be to create stability and to formulate exact and unambiguous goals. Clearly, the Danish CEOs do not want the elected officials to interfere in administrative matters.

---

1 The value 100 indicates that all respondents attach utmost importance to tasks, while the value 0 indicates that all respondents attach very little or no importance to the task. More specifically, the response categories have been coded as: 0-"Very little or no importance", 25-"Little importance", 50-"Moderate importance", 75-"Very important", and 100-"Utmost importance".

Table 6.2 The ideal politician, Denmark

Administration		21
Be a spokesperson for local groups or individuals who have issues pending decision by the authority	26	
Lay down rules and routines for the administration	20	
Taking decisions concerning specific cases	17	
Representation		72
Be informed about citizens' views	84	
Represent the municipality to the outside world	73	
Defend the authorities' decisions and policies externally	74	
Be a spokesperson for their political party	60	
Be a spokesperson vis-á-vis the press	70	
Governance		75
Implement the program on which he/she has been elected	56	
Decide on major policy principles	84	
Have a vision of the way in which the municipality will develop in the long run	84	
Stability		62
Create stability for the administration	59	
Formulate exact and unambiguous goals for the administration	65	

The CEOs' views on the proper role of elected officials indicate a traditional separation of politics and administration. Other studies, however, (Ejersbo 1996) suggest that elected officials are highly dependent upon the input from CEOs in fulfilling their representation, governance and stability roles. At the same time, survey data indicate that in their daily work, elected officials place only moderate emphasis on the three roles just mentioned. On the contrary, Danish elected officials seem to concentrate on the administration role. Combining these conclusions with the above findings on the CEO as a political bureaucrat, we find a relationship between politics and administration which is intertwined instead of the clear separation of the two as originally intended. The unfulfilled expectation that elected officials can and will formulate general principles and visions for the municipality makes the elected officials even more dependent on the CEO and his views.

Finally, a few comments on the different tasks that the CEO emphasizes in relation to the administration. These functions concern CEOs as de facto leaders of the administration and their relations downwards in the organization. Traditionally, an important task for CEOs has been to manage economic affairs, cf. the traditional recruitment pattern. This task clearly plays a less important role for CEOs today. Tasks such as stimulating cooperation between departments, being informed about viewpoints of employees and solving problems and conflicts of human relationships, are emphasized to a much greater extent. This development can be explained in several ways. Municipal administrations have grown and more municipalities have separate economic/financial departments taking over the responsibility for economic affairs. Second, the many changes of the organizational structure and amalgamation of departments have put greater emphasis on aspects related to human resource management. Finally, the development away from budgeting and control corresponds with new trends within public management. Yet even with the clear pattern of emphasizing "human resource management" tasks, CEOs are still very concerned with efficient use of resources in the traditional, economic sense of the word. They serve both concerns.

Networks and Influence

In this section our analysis of the formal rules and roles of the CEO is related to a broader and more informal network perspective. The networks of the CEO are constituted by the importance and frequency of relations to others actors.

These networks are important because: (a) the CEO exerts influence through them, (b) the role of the CEO varies between networks, (c) cross-pressure often arises from having different roles in different networks, (d) CEOs' attitudes are shaped by the people with whom they interact, and (e) new ideas and practices diffuse through these networks of interaction.

Figure 6.1 provides an overview of the CEO's perception of the average level of contact, conflict and dependency to selected actors.

The figure indicates that the higher the level of contact, the higher the level of dependency and the lower the level of conflict. This intuitively appealing covariance will be scrutinized below on the basis of interviews and observations.

We will structure the discussion of the networks of the Danish CEOs according to three types og arenas: (a) the municipal political system, (b) the municipal organization, and (c) the environment.

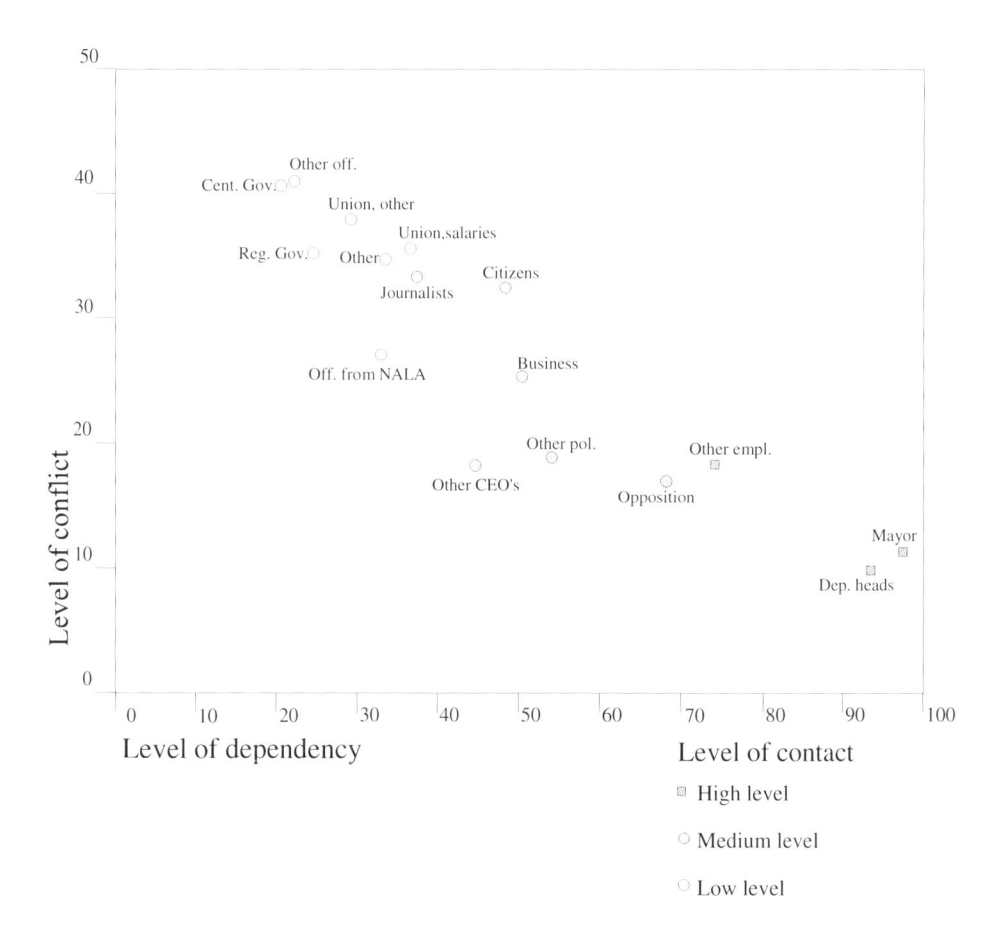

Figure 6.1 Contact, conflict and dependency, Denmark

[Scatter plot with x-axis "Level of dependency" / "Level of contact" (0-100) and y-axis "Level of conflict" (0-50). Data points:
- Cent. Gov. (~20, 40)
- Other off. (~30, 41)
- Union, other (~30, 36)
- Reg. Gov. (~22, 34)
- Other (~30, 34)
- Union, salaries (~42, 36)
- Journalists (~38, 31)
- Citizens (~50, 32)
- Off. from NALA (~32, 25)
- Business (~55, 25)
- Other pol. (~52, 19)
- Other CEO's (~43, 17)
- Other empl. (~75, 19)
- Opposition (~68, 17)
- Mayor (~95, 11)
- Dep. heads (~92, 9)

Legend: ■ High level, ○ Medium level, ○ Low level]

These three network arenas are distinguished from each other because the interaction within each network is structured by very different rules.

The analysis of the networks and actors is ordered according to the importance attached to them by the CEOs. Those networks perceived to be the most important are treated first. A brief presentation of each network is given, followed by an analysis of actors perceived to be most important.

The Municipal Political System
The political network is the most formalized network. The formal relations within this network are described above. The CEO cannot change the rules of the game, which provide the basic structure of the interaction within this network. The rules are backed by democratic norms and traditions. The CEO is the subordinate in this network, since he is hired and fired by the city council. A large part of the CEO's influence, however, derives from this network. The CEO is the bureaucrat with the most comprehensive knowledge of political intentions and

possibilities. The formal and informal mandate from the political decision-making bodies provides him with authority in the two other types of networks. When the CEO deliberately tries to exert his influence in this network it is through the preparation of agendas and information for the political meetings and through rational argumentation in informal settings. But in such efforts the CEO must be careful not to lose the basic trust of the politicians and especially that of the mayor.

The mayor is without question the most important individual in the CEO's network. As many as 97% of the CEOs regard the relation to the mayor to be either extremely or very important for their work.

There are at least four potential areas of conflict between the mayor and the CEO. First, the mayor may fail to understand the conditions under which the administration works, or the CEO may lack political flair and the two may not be capable of supplementing each other. A second and more serious problem for the CEO arises if the mayor has little political influence or is not trusted by the other politicians. Under these circumstances it is often difficult for the administration to obtain clear guidelines from the politicians. Seen from an administrator's point of view, a good mayor is a person who can and will stick to his agreements with the administration in a political conflict. Third, the mayor can have made unfortunate mistakes which the CEO has to rectify. Fourth, disagreements or uncertainty about the division of work between the CEO and the mayor may lead to conflicts.

Although the observations and interviews indicate the potential for these conflicts between the mayor and the CEO, the survey does not suggest that conflicts are common. Only 5% of the CEOs regard their relationship with the mayor to be conflictual, while 89% describe the relationship as either cooperative or very cooperative. These figures, of course, may be interpreted in at least two ways: either the CEO has to have a reasonably good relationship with the mayor in order to keep his position, or, they may have underestimated the level of conflict, given the precarious character of the question, the mayor is after all their superior.

The second most important group of actors in the political system are the political leaders from other political parties. About three out of four CEOs meet leaders from other political parties at least once a week. In more than two-thirds of Danish municipalities, the mayor, and hence, the CEO, is dependent on leaders from the opposition, as the mayor's party does not have the majority. These opposition politicians often hold positions as chairmen of one of the standing committees, positions which provide them with an important platform for exercising influence in the policy-making process.

The meetings in the municipal political system structure the work of the CEO in important ways. The meetings are the formal decision arenas and therefore provide important deadlines around which the CEO necessarily has to structure his work.

The CEO is almost always present at council and finance committee meetings, and he is responsible for the preparation of the agenda and for taking the minutes of these meetings. In this respect the CEO is clearly acting as the right-hand man of the mayor, cf. the competences of the mayor in the Local Government Statute; however, many mayors do not seem to become heavily involved in these functions. Only about 30% of the mayors are involved in the preparation of minutes for council meetings to a "very high" or "high" extent. As regards the preparation of minutes, less than 10% of the mayors are controlling the minutes to a "very high" or "high" extent.

At the meetings the CEO usually just listens and takes the minutes. Sometimes the CEO presents information regarding economic or legal issues, but it is unusual for the CEO to present any personal opinions regarding a subject. At these meetings the CEO acts as the loyal civil servant who respects the rules of democracy.

Outside the political meetings, relations between the CEO and the politicians are somewhat ambiguous. The politicians do not have any formal authority outside the meetings. Some of them work for the municipality as teachers, nurses, etc., and are in a way subordinates to the CEO, while very few of them work in jobs with a higher status than the municipal CEO. Perhaps the best way to describe the CEO's relationship to the politicians outside the meetings is as a delicate balance between trust-building and decoupling. On the one hand, the CEO pays attention to the politicians and tries to build a relationship of trust with them, on the other hand, the CEO tries to ensure that the politicians do not interfere too much in the work of the administration.

The CEO depends upon a relationship of trust with both the mayor and the city council. The fact that the CEO is appointed by the council and is expected to serve both the council in general, including the political opposition, and the mayor in particular, provides a potential dilemma in the work of the CEO. This statement by one of the Danish CEOs clearly reflects the dilemma:

> "I am of the opinion that a CEO, of course, is CEO for the city council as such; however, I am also of the opinion that the loyalty of the CEO should be directed primarily towards the mayor."

The dilemma of loyalty manifests itself particularly in municipalities where the council is marked by intense political conflicts. In such situations, the working conditions of the CEO may be affected in several ways. First of all, the CEO, as well as the department heads, has to make sure that proposals are prepared thoroughly and that facts and arguments are presented in an exhaustive and objective way. If there are any weaknesses, the CEO and the administration immediately become involved in a political game. Second, due to his commitment to the mayor, the CEO will often find it necessary, or find himself forced, to protect the mayor against political attacks. Third, the administration will be affected in its daily routines by unclear and shifting political signals, as the opposition leaders will often have their own power bases as committee chairmen, and by a flood of single issues/cases. Finally, the CEO must find a delicate balance in his capacity as advisor to the mayor. A few CEOs establish this balance by a very simple rule: never engage in political advice. Others, in fact the majority of CEOs, stress their advisory role vis-á-vis the mayor. About 25% consider political advice to the mayor as "extremely important" and another 36% characterize this task as "very important".

The Municipal Organization

The municipal organization consists of an administration and a number of implementing units which deliver municipal services. In principle, the municipal organization is the instrument through which decisions in the political system are implemented. In reality, a number of decisions are in fact made within the administration. This is due to the overload of the political system in which the only professional full-time actor is the mayor. In contrast, the organizational municipal network consists of full-time employees. Interaction within this network is also very formalized, but in contrast to the political network, the CEO is in a position to change many of the rules. After the mayor, the CEO is largely the superior in these network relations, although his formal authority over the department heads is somewhat ambiguous.

Besides the mayor, the department heads are the most important counterparts in the network of the CEO. Ninety-eight per cent regard the relations to the department heads to be either "extremely important" or "very important" for their work as CEOs. The unclear hierarchical relationship between the CEO and the department heads is due to the ambiguous hierarchical relations between the standing committees and the financial committee. The most influential actors in the municipal organization are the mayor, the CEO, the department heads, and the committee chairs, but the actual sharing of managerial functions within this group is very much determined by the individuals who occupy each position, and especially by the preferences of the mayor. In general, and especially in the budgetting process, the distinction between "champions" and "guardians" (Wildawsky 1974) seems appropriate. The natural role for the mayor and the CEO is as guardians who try to coordinate and ensure that the municipal budget is respected. The natural role for the department heads and committee chairs is to be champions who try to make sure that their sector is delivering services of high quality. In the late 1980s the role as guardian has been strengthened because of efforts to restrict and reduce public spending.

The heads of departments, together with the CEO, form the management team (*ledergruppen*), an important though informal institution in the municipality, which gained increasing importance in the late 1980s as a means of coordinating efforts to reduce spending. Meetings of the management team often constitute the forum in which the CEO and the department heads decide principles for interacting with the political system. The management team handles conflicts between the various sectors, administers and elaborates strategies and policies for personnel development, discusses organizational change etc. In some municipalities, the mayor will participate in these meetings as an observer or active participant, while in others the mayor does not participate in the meetings of the management team.

The CEOs consider themselves, the department heads and the chairmen of the standing committees to have approximately equal influence on the municipal budget, and to have considerably less influence than the mayor. The survey supports the conventional view that the persons who hold the formal leading political and administrative positions are the most influential actors in the budgetary process.

The Environment
Publicly, the CEOs are relatively anonymous. Behind the scenes, however, the CEOs represent the municipality in a number of external relations. The CEOs do not consider these external relations to be as important to their work as the internal relations, a strong internal position may provide the necessesary basis for the external work of the CEO.

The environmental network consists of a number of actors in the local/regional environment and in the national/international environment. The nature of the interaction within this network varies considerably. The personal priorities of the CEO are more important in this external network, since it is not as formalized as in the two other networks, and relations are often ad hoc and more uncertain. In contrast to the two former networks the CEO have no hierarchical authority in most of these relations, the CEO merely represents his or her municipality.

The counterpart considered to be most important in the environment is private business interests. As many as 74% of CEOs surveyed consider this interaction to be important to at least some extent. The relationship concerns subjects such as specific business projects, more permanent business relations, recurring meetings in the trade or tourist association, or informal exchange of ideas and information. Some CEOs have an important function as a catalyst for job-creating business projects in the municipality.

The CEOs' most frequent counterpart in the environment, and the second most important according to the survey, are the citizens. This interaction is considered important to some extent or more by 70% of the CEOs. Much of this interaction has a ceremonial character: the officiating at a wedding ceremony, the opening of a new institution, public meetings, etc.

Third, 60% of the CEOs consider their interaction with CEOs from other municipalities to be important at least to some extent. This interaction concerns the association of Danish CEOs, various forms of cooperation between municipalities, informal exchange of information, or various conferences and seminars.

Fourth, 49% of the CEOs surveyed consider interaction with journalists to be important to some extent or more. The content of this interaction, of course, is to present a public image of the municipality. CEOs, in municipalities characterized by a higher level of conflict, due to party competition or internal conflicts in the municipal administration, attach greater importance to this relationship than do CEOs in municipalities with few conflicts.

Lastly, around 5-10% of the CEOs are very active at the national level and can be considered to be part of the national decision-making system. Municipal CEOs participate in committees for education programmes for municipal employees, in government commissions dealing with various issues, etc.

Conclusion

The municipalities have gradually become the largest administrative sector in Denmark, and in this context the Danish municipal CEO holds a leading position. In the typical Danish municipality the CEO mediates the interactions among elected officials, approximately 1,000 municipal employees and key external actors.

Formally speaking, the CEO has a weak position. In reality he derives his influence from the mayor, and his hierarchical competence gravitates between a role as de facto executive position and as a staff assistant to the mayor. In most cases the CEO is highly dependent on the mayor as well as on the leaders of the political opposition. Historically, the system of governance in Danish municipalities has always been marked by a high degree of consensus. This consensus also characterizes the relations between the CEO and the mayor (as well as CEO relations with leaders of the opposition). In recent years this consensual relationship has come under attack. The role and working conditions of the CEO have changed. A group of modern managers, who play a more important political role, are entering the scene at the expense of the traditional administrator. As a consequence, the position of CEO has become more attractive but as indicated by the high degree of turnover in later years, also more vulnerable.

Bibliography

Albæk, Erik, Rose, Lawrence, Strömberg, Lars, and Ståhlberg, Krister (1996): *Nordic Local Government*, Helsinki: The Association of Finish Local Authorities.

Dahler- Larsen, P. (1997): Udviklingen i kravene til danske kommunaldirektører de seneste tyve år belyst ved stillingsannoncer: en social konstruktion, *Nordisk Administrativt Tidsskrift* No. 2/97 78.

Ejersbo, Niels (1996): *Den Kommunale Forvaltning under Omstilling*, Odense: School of Business and Economics, Odense University.

Ejersbo, Niels (ed.) (1997): *Politikere, Ledere og Professionelle i Kommunerne – effekter af strukturændringer*, Odense: Odense Universitetsforlag.

Elklit, Jørgen and Pedersen, Mogens N. (eds.)(1995): *Kampen om Kommunen – ni fortællinger om kommunalvalget i 1993*, Odense: Odense Universitetsforlag.

Gundelach, Peter, Jørgensen, Henning, Klausen, Kurt Klaudi (eds.)(1997): *Det Lokale*, Ålborg: Ålborg Universitetsforlag.

Hansen, Morten Balle (1995): Kommunaldirektørens Roller i den Kommunale Organisation. *Kommunalpolitiske Studier* No. 7, Odense: School of Business and Economics, Odense University.

Jørgensen, T. B, and Mouritzen, P.E. (1993): *Udgiftspolitik og budgetlægning*, Herning: Systime.

Knudsen, Tim (ed.)(1991): *Welfare Administration in Denmark*, Copenhagen: Department of Political Science, University of Copenhagen.

le Maire, Emil, and Preisler, Niels (1996): *Lov om kommuners styrelse med kommentarer*, Forlaget: DJØF.

Mouritzen, Poul Erik (1991): *Den Politiske Cyklus*, Århus: Politica.

Mouritzen, Poul Erik (1991): Economics and Politics in Local Fiscal Policy-making. Some Findings after 15 years in the Treadmill, in *Festskrift til Krister Ståhlberg*, Åbo: Åbo Akademiske Forlag.

Nielsen, Jørn Flohr (1985): *Kommunal Organisering*, Århus: Politica.

Riiskær, Erik (1982): *Kommunale forvaltningschefer*, Århus: Politica.

Wildawsky, A. (1974): *The Politics of the Budgetary Process*, Boston: Little, Brown and Co.

CHAPTER 7

The Strong CEOs of Finland

by Siv Sandberg

Introduction

The notion of strong municipalities attributed to the Scandinavian welfare state model is particularly well-founded in the Finnish case. Finnish municipalities perform a wide range of functions, from public schools to waste removal, fire protection and specialized health care, yet the Finnish municipal system has only a single tier. Primary municipalities are responsible for most of the tasks that in the other Nordic countries are handled by the county level. This may sound paradoxical, considering the fact that Finland has such a large number of municipalities: 452 including the 16 municipalities of the Åland islands, and they are rather small. The number of inhabitants in a typical Finnish municipality is about 5,000 (median), the mean value being approximately 11,000. The practical problem of many tasks and small size is solved through various cooperative arrangements. For some services, joint municipal authorities are established, in other cases one municipality sells services to its neighbour municipalities. Over the years there have been several attempts to reduce the number of municipalities, but since the principle of voluntarism has been widely accepted, no major amalgamation reform has been implemented.

The municipal mandate is twofold. The general mandate allows the municipalities to assume functions within the framework of local self-government on a voluntary basis. The special mandate means that municipalities are obliged to perform functions stipulated for them in legislation, for example health care and fire protection. The budget of the municipalities derives from two main sources, municipal taxes and state grants. The local tax rate varies between 15 and 20 percent. The state grant system underwent a major change in 1993, with the move from earmarked grants to block grants. Fiscal austerity at the state level has caused a noticeable reduction of grants-in-aid to the municipalities throughout the 1990s. The general economic recession in the beginning of the 1990s, with high rates of unemployment and thereby lower tax revenues, has affected the economies of the municipalities. Thus cut-backs in management has become a central theme in the management of municipal affairs. When asked about factors negatively affecting their job as CEO during the last years, 64% of the CEOs consider the reduction of state grants as a severe problem, followed by unemployment and social problems. The general impression, however, is that the municipalities have managed the fiscal crisis quite well. In 1996, 45 municipalities decided on a lower tax rate for the year 1997, while only 10 municipalities decided to impose a 1997 tax rate higher than in 1996 (*Suomen Kuntaliitto* 1996).

According to the CEOs surveyed, the last decade has been a time of increased decentralization. Decentralization has been significant both in the relation between the municipalities and the central level and within the municipalities. While detailed regulations and extreme sectorization characterized the municipalities during the 1970s and early 1980s – the main expansion phase of the Finnish welfare municipalities – the trend over the past ten years has been towards deregulation and flexible modes of organizing policies and services. The socalled Free Commune Legislation, launched in 1989, gave all muncipalities, not only the 56 Free Communes, the right to individualize their administrative structures (Sandberg 1992). The most visible effect has been the dramatic reduction in the number of standing committees, and thereby in the number of political appointees holding office (Ståhlberg 1994, 1999). Recent legislation concerning the municipalities leaves them with a great deal of authority in deciding how to run the business. From a researcher point of view, obtaining an overview of municipal administration has become more difficult, since there are, if not 452 different models, at least many more solutions than at the end of the 1980s. This observation is an illustration of the general conclusion that the autonomy of the Finnish municipalities has grown considerably during the last decade.

The CEO's Position in the Political-Administrative System

The duality between the political and the administrative leadership, if not absent, is much less visible in the Finnish municipalities than in municipalities in many other countries. This is due to formal reasons. The political leadership is in the hands of collective bodies, especially the executive board, while one person – the CEO – holds a powerful position as the administrative leader of the municipality. Thus, the politics-administration axis is represented not by two persons, the Mayor and the CEO, but by a collective body of politicians and the CEO.

The two most important political bodies in the Finnish municipalities are the municipal council and the executive board. The municipal council is elected every fourth year in general, proportional elections and comprises from 13 to 85 members, depending on the number of inhabitants in the municipality. The inhabitants are supposed to vote for a single candidate who usually, but not necessarily, is a representative of a political party. The political parties at the local level are the same as those at the national level. Decision-making authority of the municipal council concerns among other things plans and budgets, general goal-setting and the organization of the municipal administration. The executive board, one of the few compulsory representative bodies, is appointed by the municipal council. The executive board prepares and implements the council's decisions, and is in general expected to function as a representative of the municipality. Coalition government is the rule at both local and national levels in Finland. The seats in the executive board (and other appointed bodies) are shared among the parties represented in the municipal council in proportion to the number of seats each party has obtained. In a typical Finnish municipality, an average of five parties or groups are represented in the municipal council.

The municipal council and the executive board are chaired by different persons. The chairmen, as well as the other politicians in the municipality, are lay politicians, i.e. there are no paid full-time politicians whatsoever in Finnish municipalities. The chairman of the municipal council is appointed from among the elected members of the council. The members of the executive board, including the chairman, may be appointed among non-council members as well. In 85% of the municipalities, the chairman of the executive board usually is a member of the municipal council. The chairman of the municipal council holds the most important formal political position, while the chairman of the executive board usually is in a position to influence the day-to-day handling of municipal matters. Forty-nine per cent of the CEOs surveyed considered that the chairman of the executive board is the leading politician in their municipality, 38% answered "the chairman of the municipal council" and 11% held the opinion that someone else is the leading politician. This might illustrate our hesitancy in naming the politician equivalent to "the Mayor" when constructing the Finnish questionnaire. However, we hypothesize that the chairman of the executive board has most in common with the Mayor because of his closer connection to the daily operation of municipal administration.

The history of the Chief Executive Officer in Finland is nearly as old as the existence of Finland as an independent nation. A committee appointed by the first Finnish government in 1918 reformed the administration of the cities, by introducing the office of a city manager, *kaupunginjohtaja – stadsdirektör*, into all cities. The system was considered well-functioning, and the rural municipalities were also given the possibility to employ a Chief Executive Officer in 1948. From 1977 on, all municipalities where obliged to have a CEO (*kunnanjohtaja – kommundirektör*) (Pikkala 1993, 74-75).There have been slight variations in the formal position of the CEO during the years. The first city managers and CEOs were expected to be members of the executive board, that is, they held a political position as well as an administrative one. By the Local Government Act of 1976, a strict separation was made between politics and administration. The Local Government CEO was first of all expected to be an administrative officer, which meant that he was no longer allowed to be a member of the executive board. Later reforms have blurred this strict distinction between politics and administration. The present Local Government Act, from 1995, gives the concept of CEO a broader meaning. Still, as a subordinate of the executive board, the CEO is the daily leader of the administrative, economic and other activities of the municipality. The municipal council, however, can decide to give this leadership different frameworks. According to the Local Government Act three models are possible:

1) the traditional model, where the CEO is appointed for an indefinite period of time;
2) the managerial model, where the CEO is appointed for a defined period, usually 5 or 7 years;
3) the "mayoral" model, with a CEO appointed for the four-year period by the municipal council, also functioning as chairman of the executive board.

In practice, the second model has gained wide-spread acceptance, while no municipality, according to our knowledge, has yet introduced the third model. A recent survey among politicians and administrators in 47 Finnish municipalities showed low acceptance of the mayoral model (VILU -95). The fact that the alternative models were written into the Local Government Act reflects the focus on leadership in the Finnish debate over the last five years. One concern has been the introduction of more private sector-like leadership, another about strengthening the political leadership. Two regulations written into the Local Government Act, the first concerning the hiring of CEOs, the second related to the suspension of CEOs, signify this attempt to strengthen the political leadership. The municipal council has been given both the possibility of employing a CEO for quite a short period, and the instruments for dismissing the CEO, if he no longer has the confidence of two-thirds of the municipal council. The CEOs do not seem to appreciate the higher degree of instability. Nearly 80% of the CEOs find their jobs less or somewhat less attractive than ten years ago, the most common reasons mentioned being the reforms of the legislation concerning their job.

The formal role of the CEO is that of leading administrative officer. The Local Government Act states that the CEO is the daily leader of the administration, the economy and of other activities of the municipality operating as a subordinate to the executive board. Every municipality decides the exact implementation of the statements, and sets the CEOs' salary and other benefits. The CEO is present at the meetings of the municipal council and the executive board and takes the minutes. According to the legislation, the executive board is in charge of representing the municipality and of speaking on behalf of the municipality. In practice, much of this is done by the CEO, to whom a share of the decision-making power of the executive board has usually been delegated. Thus, the position as CEO is highly visible. Although the CEOs themselves claim that their job has lost some of its former respect among people, the status of the job is still considered high in small municipalities as well as in larger ones.

The Background and Career of the Finnish CEO

Earlier studies have described the Finnish CEOs as a very homogenous group regarding their educational background and career pattern (Pikkala 1993, 78-84). Our study verifies rather than falsifies this finding. The typical CEO is male, 49 years old, holds a university degree in social sciences from the University of Tampere and has made a career within municipal administration. The Local Government Act contains no statement at all regarding the formal competences of the CEO, thus, the municipalities are allowed to establish the principles guiding the appointment of the CEO. In a comparison of job-postings from the years 1983 and 1993, Pikkala found that municipalities now tend to place more emphasis on educational competence and personal qualities than they did ten years ago (Pikkala 1994). The proportion of Finnish CEOs holding university degrees, either at a higher (Master) or lower (Bachelor) level is very high. Social sciences (usually political or administrative science) is the most common field, 75% of the CEOs have a university degree in social sciences. A law degree forms the second largest group, with about 7% of the CEOs. The dominance of social scientists seems to be stable. There is no significant difference in exam field between older and younger CEOs, but the share of persons with a university degree is higher among the newly employed CEOs (Pikkala 1994). The degree of homogeneity is accentuated by the fact that one university, the University of Tampere, has been the dominant "supplier" of CEOs. Of the population of Finnish CEOs, 63% have got their education from the University of Tampere. The educational product, a specialized municipal exam at bachelor level offered by the university, seems to have been a formidable success!

The social background of the Finnish CEOs reflects the rapid urbanization of Finnish society. Nearly 40% of the CEOs come from farm households. The post-war baby-boom generation pioneered in opening access to a university education for people from all social classes and all parts of the country. The burgeoning welfare state was in desperate need of educated people. The baby-boomers still dominate the public sector. Of the CEOs in office in 1996, 13% were born in the 30's, the majority, 56%, in the 40's, 27% in the 50's, and only 5% in the 60's. Within the next ten to fifteen years many muncipalities will therefore be looking for a new CEO. The share of women among the CEOs is about 6% today, and 10% among the CEOs recruited during the last three years. In 1990 the share of women was 2% (Pikkala 1993).

The introduction of New Public Management ideas in the municipalities gave rise to a wide-spread assumption that municipalities, especially successful ones, recruit their leaders from the business sector. The assumption is partly myth. A career within the municipal world is still the best guarantee for getting a job as a CEO. Of the CEOs, 78% held their previous position in a municipality, 61% in a different municipality than the present one. In addition, 14% were formerly employed by a joint municipal authority. The most common previous position, 29% of the respondents, was in fact CEO in another municipality. Career advancement after age/retirement is the most common reason for their predecessor's resignation. More than half the CEOs surveyed consider seeking another position if the right opportunities arises. The high degree of mobility may indicate that there are different strata of municipalities. Moving from being CEO in a small municipality to CEO of a big city means climbing upwards in the hierarchy. The share of private sector previously held jobs is 5% of the whole sample of CEOs. The myth described above is true in the sense that the share of CEOs recruited from the private sector is increasing: of the CEOs who have been in office up to 3 years, 8% come from the private sector, compared with 2% among the CEOs holding office more than 15 years.

The willingness to attract more public personalities to the CEO jobs seems to be growing. As management of local government affairs nowadays increasingly involves fundraising and entrepreneurship and fewer traditional bureaucratic tasks, and the competion between municipalities in attracting different resources is becoming more intense, municipalities put their trust in the CEO. A dynamic and well-known CEO, if not a guarantee of success, is at least an advantage for the municipality in relation to the outside world. There are some extreme examples of this trend. Recently, a former Miss Finland (beauty queen) was appointed CEO of a small municipality in eastern Finland. More usually, municipalities try to attract influential politicians or businessmen to the post as leader of municipal administration. Among the CEOs today are a handful of former members of parliament and ministers. Of the 200 members of the Finnish parliament (*Eduskunta*) about ten have a civil career as a Local Government CEO.

Although the CEO is not allowed to participate as an elected or appointed member of the political bodies of the municipality, most of the CEOs have a partisan commitment. Sixty-six per cent are presently members of a political party, 12% have previously been party members. In comparison with the Finnish electorate as a whole – 13% are party members (Katz & Mair 1992) – the CEOs are definitely "overpoliticized". The most popular party among the CEOs is the Centre Party which is also the largest party at the municipal level. Of the CEOs who are members of a political party, 59% are members of the Centre Party. Having the right party commitment usually strengthens a candidate's possibilities of becoming a CEO. There is a strikingly close match between the largest party in the municipal council and the party commitment of the CEO. In municipalities where the Social Democratic Party holds the largest number of seats in the municipal council, 53% of the CEOs are Social Democrats. In municipalities dominated by the Centre Party, the share of Centre Party CEOs is 58%. Roughly speaking, in municipalities with a right-wing majority, 58% of the CEOs are members of right-wing parties, 5% of left-wing parties, and 36% do not have a party commitment. In municipalities with left-wing parties in majority, 76% of the CEOs have a left-wing party commitment, 17% are members of right-wing parties and the share of non-party members is 7%.

The Roles and Values of the CEOs

Several characteristics, among them the homogeneous educational background and the high rate of involvement in the association of CEOs (86% are members of the association), suggest that Finnish CEOs are very close to forming a profession, comparable, for example, to teachers or nurses (Pikkala 1993). Representatives of the national association of CEOs strongly emphasize that the CEO is a professional manager, not any kind of leader; hence, the association has been opposed to changes of legislation aimed at giving the political bodies more power to influence the office of the CEO. The "hands-off" attitude towards other groups is characteristic of professions, and is clearly visible when analyzing the Finnish CEOs' views about their own jobs and about the relation between politics and administration. In the following section the highlights will be on the CEOs' perceptions of their tasks and on their expectations towards the leading politicians. To keep in mind the framework for understanding the roles and values of the Finnish CEOs, I want to repeat and emphasize some of the circumstances shaping the CEOs' working environment:

- the important position of the municipalities in the Finnish system of governance;
- the traditionally strong, legally mandated, position of the CEO;
- the absence of a strong political leader, a "mayor";
- the fact that most CEOs have academic backgrounds;
- the CEOs' high level of party-political involvement.

Putnam's distinction between classical and political bureaucrats (Putnam 1975) may serve as a tool in positioning the Finnish CEOs in the universe of bureaucrats. I do not think the tool is exact enough, at least not operationalized by the questions in the U.DI.T.E questionnaire. I will elaborate on these critical points later. Initially, however, the distinction is a fruitful one. It is not at all surprising – considering the above description of the position of the Finnish CEO – to observe that Finnish CEOs score higher on items describing the political bureaucrat than on questions describing the classical bureaucrat.

Finnish CEOs find it more important to be policy leaders in their municipality – to formulate ideas and visions, to promote new projects, to influence decision-making – than to engage in the daily paper-work at the local government office. They are not particularly interested in guiding subordinate staff or in ensuring that rules and regulations are followed. The political bureaucrats dominate among the Finnish CEO: well over 90% of the respondents are political bureaucrats rather than classical bureaucrats. This means that there are only minor differences in role orientations between CEOs in different parts of the country and between CEOs with varying length of duty. Older CEOs in small municipalities might have a tendency to orientate themselves more like classical bureaucrats towards their role, but in general variations are marginal and seldom significant.

Table 7.1 The roles of the CEOs, Finland

The classical bureaucrat		45
Guide subordinate staff in day-to-day handling of activities	33	
Manage economic affairs, accounts and budgetary control	72	
Ensure that rules and regulations are followed	38	
Provide the mayor with legal, economic and other kinds of technical advice	38	
The political bureaucrat		66
Formulate ideas and visions	84	
Promote and encourage new projects in the community	78	
Provide the mayor with political advice	17	
Be informed about citizens' viewpoints	71	
Develop and implement norms concerning the proper roles of politicians vis-á-vis the bureaucrats	66	
Influence decision-making processes in order to secure sensible and efficient solutions	81	

The table shows one outlier item in each of the roles, although Finnish CEOs are classical bureaucrats only to a small extent, management of economic affairs is a highly preferred task, and although a political orientation is common, giving political advice to the mayor is not considered important. This indicates that the operationalization of the distinction between the classical and the political bureucrat does not completely fit the Finnish context. The second comment has an obvious explanation. Since the chairman of the executive board in the Finnish municipalities is not mayor in the traditional sense, questions about political and technical advice to the mayor (in the Finnish questionnaire the chairman of the executive board) seem irrelevant. More relevant would have been a question about advice to politicians in general, even if my guess is that CEOs would hardly prefer this task more than giving advice to the mayor. In view of the highly political background of the Finnish CEOs, one could expect the CEO to readily engage in political advice, but this does not seem to be the case, or in any case the CEOs do not want to admit it. The other exception from the classical-political scheme calls upon a more thorough examination of the role orientation of the Finnish CEO. A factor analysis of the 18 items concerning job preferences results in five distinct roles, showing that management of economic affairs is something beyond the mere day-to-day dealing with checks and balances. Economic administrations is strongly associated with the item "securing the economy of the municipality" which makes up a distinctive, economic profile. Since the focus on economic matters has been strong in the municipalities during the last years, my judgement is that the CEOs' concern about economic matters does not necessarily represent a classical bureaucratic orientation. The distinct economic orientation, however, is not the one emphasized the most among the CEOs. The most accentuated factor is made up of items concerning entrepreneurship: formulating ideas and visions, promoting new projects, attracting resources from external sources, activities together with the other municipalities in the area etc. Altogether, the analysis draws a picture of a CEO less concerned with what is going on inside the town hall than with matters of the outside world, more interested in visions than details, rather a political "Mr. Municipality" than a neutral civil servant.

The Finnish CEO's desire to play an active and visible role in the governance of the municipality is obvious. It is also obvious, according to the responses of the CEOs, that they themselves recognize that their position as CEO is extremely influential. For example, where influence over the budget and the municipal economy is concerned, the Chief Executive Officer is that actor ranked most influential, above political parties, central government and leading politicians (see also Tuittu 1995). Formally, however, the municipal council and the executive board – thus the leading politicians – are superior to to the CEO. This makes the relation between the administration and the politicians interesting. In the following section the CEO's views about the proper division of tasks between politics and administration will be examined.

Generally, the Finnish CEOs' opinions as to what politicians should do can be summarized in one of the items in our questionnaire "It is the politicians' duty to decide only on major principal issues and not on routine matters". According to the CEOs, politicians should *not* concentrate too much on administration, that is, it is not important that politicians lay down rules and routines for administration or that they act as spokespersons for people who have issues pending decisions by the authority. Nor should they, rather surprisingly, be too political. Issues such as "being a spokesperson for their political party" are not considered important. In this respect, the CEOs' expectations on the priorities of the leading politicians resemble their own job priorities. In fact, several studies have shown that the members of the executive board and the CEO share many of the same priorities and opinions (Pikkala 1995, VILU-95). This reflects the similar positions of the highest administrative officer and the leading politicians. Concern for the municipality as a whole does not allow for involvement in details, nor does it call upon extreme engagement in the interests of one's own party.

Table 7.2 The ideal politician, Finland

Administration		37
Be a spokesperson for local groups or individuals who have issues pending decision by the authority	33	
Lay down rules and routines for the administration	21	
Taking decisions concerning specific cases	57	
Representation		56
Be informed about citizens' views	75	
Represent the municipality to the outside world	60	
Defend the authorities' decisions and policies externally	67	
Be a spokesperson for their political party	33	
Be a spokesperson vis-á-vis the press	45	
Governance		59
Implement the program on which he/she has been elected	25	
Decide on major policy principles	68	
Have a vision of the way in which the municipality will develop in the long run	84	
Stability		60
Create stability for the administration	67	
Formulate exact and unambiguous goals for the administration	52	

What should the leading politicians, then, do? Table 7.2 shows that representation, governance and stability are considered almost equally important by the CEOs, and the index averages show that the priorities are not very conclusive. The picture, however, is blurred by the fact that the items concerning party political orientation, as shown above, obtain considerably lower scores than the rest of the items. When these items are left out of the analysis, governance is the dimension that the CEOs think is most important for the leading politicians. That is, the leading politicians are expected to have a vision about how the municipality should develop in the long run and to decide on major policy principles. This argument is in line with the management-by-objectives ideology that has dominated the re-organization of the Finnish municipalities during the last ten years (Naschold 1994). Again, there are only minor differences between different types of municipalities and CEOs regarding the view of the ideal politician. The CEOs in the largest municipalities put somewhat more emphasis on the governance aspect than do the rest, and older CEOs value stability somewhat more than do younger CEOs.

A brief look at the priorities of the members of the executive board in 47 Finnish municipalities concerning their job as leading politicians shows that they fit rather well into the CEOs' vision of the ideal politician. The most important tasks, according to the politicians, are related to the major lines in governing the municipality. The members of the executive board are more concerned with formulating visions and listening to the views of the citizens than with administrative details, and definitely more interested in the municipal totality than in defending specific interests. Yet, contrary to the CEO's picture of the ideal politician, the politicians themselves find it relatively important to engage in party politics (VILU-95). I shall return to the discussion of the relation between politics and administration in the conclusion.

Networks and Influence

The CEO's position as both the highest ranking administrative officer in the municipal organization and the bridge-builder between politics and administration makes him a key player in the municipal team. Many people within and outside the municipal organization are dependent on contacts with the CEO, and in order to perform his duties, the CEO must be in touch with different people and agencies. The CEOs, as we have seen, are well aware of their central position.

The municipality is the centre of the universe for the Finnish CEO, if by municipality we mean both the administrative and political municipal organization and several groups within the geographical borders of the municipality. Roughly speaking, actors within the municipality are more frequently in touch with the CEO than actors outside the municipality, and are often deemed more important by the CEO. The exceptions from this rule are union representatives and representatives of voluntary organizations, who presumably operate within the municipality. The frequency of communication between the CEO and these actors is low. The CEO does not find the relation important and the relationship is more conflictual than other relationships. A ranking of the actors according to a) frequency of interaction and b) importance attached to the relation results in two slightly different lists. The CEOs note the highest interaction frequencies with top executives in the municipality, the economic executive (municipal treasurer) and the heads of various departments. These actors are usually identical with the members of the municipal management group. The CEO communicates several times a week with citizens in the municipality and with the chairman of the executive board. The CEO has at least weekly contacts with other employees of the municipality, private business interests in the municipality, CEOs in other municipalities and journalists.

The CEOs find the relation with the chairman of the executive board most important for their ability to perform their duties. The top executives of the municipality are important as well. This assessment indicates the position of the CEO: between politics and administration. With the job priorities of the CEOs in mind, it is not surprising that their relations with private business interests in the municipality are considered to be among the most important. The special interests of the CEO, economic matters and new projects usually depend on the participation of various private business actors. This observation might also apply to the citizens of the municipality, which is another group considered important by the CEO.

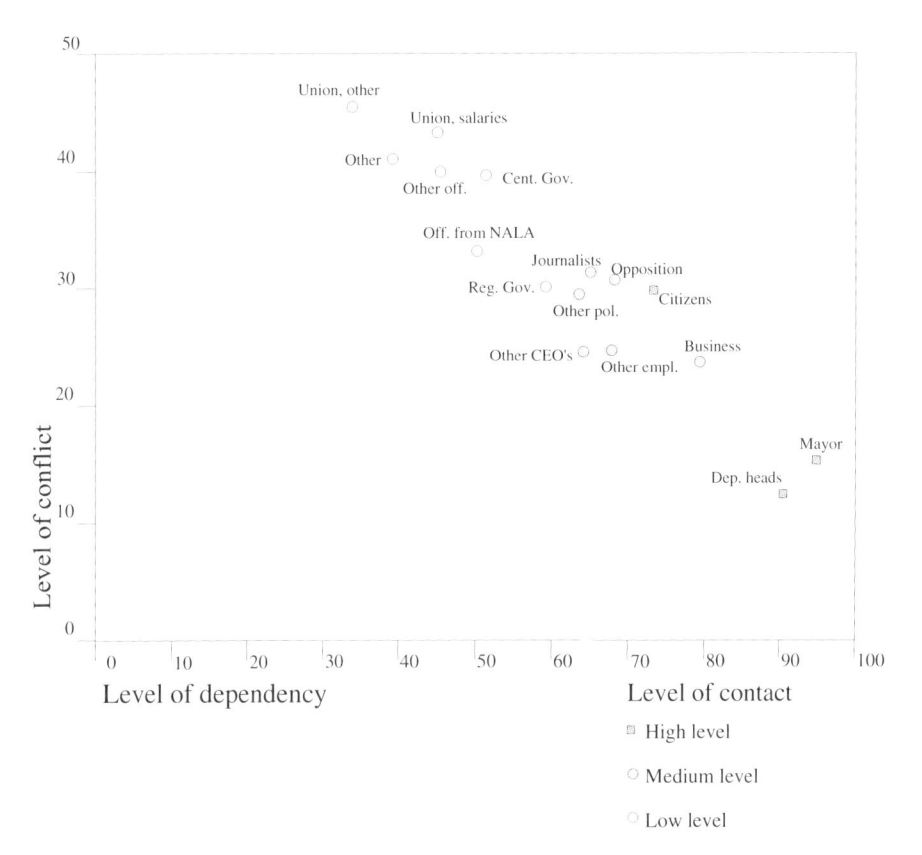

Figure 7.1 Contact, conflict and dependency, Finland

The political network of the CEO is dominated by the chairman of the executive board. Contacts with other politicians are more disperse, a couple of times a month on the average. We did not include the chairman of the municipal council in the list of actors; hence, we are not able to compare the importance of the two major political actors in the municipality from the CEO's point of view. The political actors, leaders of the political opposition (although there usually is no clear majority-opposition constellation in Finnish municipalities) and other politicians are nevertheless considered quite important, more important than actors outside the municipality.

One of the tasks gaining considerable priority among the CEOs consists of planning together with the other CEOs in the neighbouring region. Those other CEOs seem to be the most important actors from the world outside the municipality. Given the situation that many of the municipalities are small and dependent on cooperation with their neighbouring municipalities, the result is quite natural. In municipalities dependent on cooperative arrangements, the CEOs were found to interact slightly more with other municipalities and joint municipal authorities than did the CEOs from municipalities with most of the services inside their own organization. A detail worth noting is that the CEOs seem to accord higher priority to contacts with the regional council, a relatively new municipality-based authority taking care of regional planning and regional policy than to contacts with the county, that is, the state regional authority.

On average, there are few conflicts between the CEOs and the actors in and around the municipality. If the value 0 means "very conflictual" and 100 "very cooperative", the most conflictual relationship – with union representatives – obtains the index value 54, which means neutral. Generally, the conflict-cooperation pattern follows the patterns of interaction and importance described above. Relationships with important and frequently contacted actors are usually considered more cooperative than relationships with less important actors. As most of the actors consist of many individuals, there might be conflicts between, for example, a single politician and the CEO, but not with politicians in general. The comment, written by one of the CEOs when asked about the frequency in his communication with the citizens of the municipality "Not everybody, of course", is applicable also to conflicts.

Concluding Remarks

The relationship between the CEO and the political level has been the main focus of this chapter. It is a somewhat complicated, and hence, very interesting relationship. On the one hand, the CEO is dependent on the political level and stresses the importance of a good relationship with leading politicians in order to function as a CEO. On the other hand, the CEOs show a strong desire to act independently of the political level. They do not want the politicians to involve themselves too much in the running of municipal affairs. Furthermore, they want to play an independent role vis-a-vis the community and the citizens. Not many of the CEOs fully agree with the statement that CEOs should be responsible primarily to the politicians and only secondarily to the local population.

Finnish CEOs have probably never been classical bureaucrats. The earlier system, with the CEOs acting as members of the executive board and the tradition of political recruitment to the position, has consolidated the quasi-political role of the CEO. Traditionally, the CEOs room for maneuvering has been quite large in the Finnish municipalities. Continuity – the CEOs were, until the recent changes of the legislation, appointed for an indefinite period, while politicians are elected or appointed for one four-year term at a time – and knowledge – the politicians are laymen, the CEOs professionals – are two factors determining a comparative advantage for the CEO in relation to the political level. The organizational reforms in the Finnish municipalities – reduction of the number of boards, introduction of management-by-objectives techniques, reform of the budgetary system, etc. – have to some extent made the distribution of power between the political and administrative level more uneven. Especially the municipal council, i.e. the elected politicians, according to many observers, have lost some of their power to the executive board and the CEO. The legislation on the CEO was reformed in order to reestablish the balance between the elected politicians and the Executive. A CEO in fear of losing his position, goes the main line of argument, might be more ready to listen to the signals from the political level. As already noted, the CEOs do not appreciate the new legislation, finding that it weakens their possibilities to act as a professional manager. The combination of – at least in principle – the weakened position of the CEO and the recent economic crisis at the municipal level has caused most CEOs (80%) to view their job as less attractive than ten years ago. A challenge for future research is to investigate whether the changes mentioned have reshaped the power balance in the Finnish municipalities. At present, however, the CEO remains the most influential actor at the local level.

Bibliography

Kommunallagen 365/1995.

Naschold, Frieder, 1995: *The Modernization of the Public Sector in Europe*, Helsinki: Työministeriö.

Pikkala, Sari (1993): *Omgivning, ledarskap och förändring i kommunerna*, Åbo: Åbo Akademi.

Pikkala, Sari (1994): Johtajakuvan muutos kunnallishallinnossa, *Kommunalvetenskaplig tidskrift* 3/1994, 74-83.

Pikkala, Sari (1995): *The Roles of Political and Administrative Leaders in Local Government*, paper presented at the First Annual European Summer School in Local Government Studies, Odense.

Putnam, Robert, D. (1975): The Political Attitudes of Senior Civil Servants in Britain, Germany, and Italy, in M. Dogan (ed.) *The Mandarins of Western Europe*, New York: John Wiley & Sons.

Sandberg, Siv (1992): *Frikommuner och produktivitet – en kontingensteoretisk studie*, Åbo: Åbo Akademi.

Ståhlberg, Krister (1994): The Finnish Case – a reform rather than an experiment, in Baldersheim & Ståhlberg (eds.): *Towards the Self-Regulating Municipality. Free Communes and Administrative Modernization in Scandinavia*, Dartmouth: Aldershot.

Suomen Kuntaliitto (1996): *45 laskee ja 10 nostaa. Kuntien tuloveroprosentti keskimäärin 17,43 ensi vuonna*. Press release 19.11.1996.

Tuittu, Hannu (1994): *Eliitti, valta ja budjetti. Tutkimus budjettieliitin käyttäytymisestä ja valtakäsityksistä suurissa kaupungeissa*, Tampere: Tampereen yliopisto.

VILU-95. *Preliminary results from a survey of ca. 3,000 politicians and administrators in 47 Finnish municipalities*, Åbo: Åbo Akademi.

CHAPTER 8

The Norwegian CEO: Institutional Position, Professional Status, and Work Environment

by Harald Baldersheim and Morten Øgård

Local Government Legislation

The legal foundation for local government in Norway goes back to 1837, when the Local Government Act (*formannskapsloven*) was passed. This act placed responsibility for public administration within a three-tiered system of government consisting of central national government, counties, and municipalities. Directly or indirectly elected political bodies, along with administrative agencies charged with the implementation of political decisions, were to be found at all levels. The original act of 1837 involved a duality of responsibilities. On the one hand, local government received certain specifically designated tasks (such as primary schools). In this respect, local government was treated as a subordinate part of an integrated system of government. On the other hand, local government was also granted the right to undertake any activities not specifically assigned to other bodies or otherwise explicitly prohibited by statutory regulations, a provision known as a negative or residual delimitation of local power (Rose 1996).

Size and Number of Municipalities and Counties

Norway is presently divided into19 counties and 435 municipalities. Counties range in size from roughly 75,000 to 480,000 inhabitants, whereas municipalities may contain populations as little as 300 to over 480,00 inhabitants (Kommunenøkkelen 96/97). If we take a closer look at size measured in land area, we also find considerable variation. The smallest municipality (Kvitsøy) only covers 5.7 square kilometers, while the largest one (Kautokeino) covers over 9,700 square kilometers. The largest of the counties is Finnmark (up in the north) which covers close to 49,000 square kilometers, but contains only 76,688 inhabitants (1.58 inhabitants pr. square kilometer). Oslo, on the other hand is the smallest county in area with only 454 square kilometers but contains over 480,000 inhabitants (1058 pr. square kilometer). If we bear in mind that the whole of Belgium covers 30,519 square kilometers and Denmark 43,069 square kilometers, size, as shown here, might be an interesting variable.

Growth and Responsibility

The post-war period has seen significant growth in the proportion of local government consumption relative to total public consumption, from roughly 45% to approximately 60%. The major part of this growth took place from the end of the 1970s (Rose 1996). Following Rose (1996:163-164) we can identify several factors which underlie this development. In a general sense, however, there is no doubt that this growth is due primarily to the development of the Norwegian welfare state, a state built on an ideology that all citizens, regardless of where they live in the country, are to be ensured equal rights and access to certain social services. National policy-makers have used local governments extensively as a vehicle for implementing this welfare state ideology by providing both municipal and county government bodies with extensive responsibilities for the provision of services across a broad spectrum of activities. As examples can be mentioned: The Act on Social Care (*Lov om sosial omsorg*) from 1964, the Act on Primary Education (*Grunnskoleloven*) of 1969 and the Act on Municipal Health Services (*Lov om kommunale helsetjenester*) from 1985. These acts seem to confirm Rose's observation that "the Norwegian welfare state, in essence, is primarily a municipal welfare state" (1996:164). To handle the new responsibility there has been a huge growth in the number of people employed by the municipalities, from 93,100 full-time positions in1962 to 380,000 full-time positions in 1995 (Hagen og Sørensen 1997).

At present, municipal governments fulfil several tasks: providing pre-school day-care, cultural activities, land-use planning, building control, sanitation, food and veterinary control services, water and sewage treatment, fire protection and general municipal administration. To sum up, we may say that municipal government operates in three major areas of responsibility: 1) basic education, i.e., comprehensive primary education for children from 6 to 16 years of age; 2) primary health care services for all residents, including out-patient medical treatment and nursing home facilities for the elderly; and 3) social service delivery, including care for the elderly (both home care as well as special homes for the elderly) and a variety of services not covered by the regular social security system. Activities within all three areas are generally regulated by national policy decisions and together account for over two-thirds of all municipal expenditures (Rose 1996).

Like the other Nordic countries, Norway also went through an administrative amalgamation period during the late 1950s and 1960s. Over a ten-year period, the number of municipalities was reduced from 744 to 443, though this reduction was not nearly as drastic as similar processes undertaken in Denmark and Sweden at roughly the same time.

Financing

Traditionally, local government expenditures in Norway have been financed by means of three principal sources of revenue: 1) taxes on income and capital, 2) grants or transfer payments from central government, and 3) local fees and charges. During the post-war period we have witnessed a change in the sources of local government financing, the most prominent change being the increase in central government grants. The period most marked by growth in central government transfer payments was the mid-1960s to the late 1970s (Baldersheim 1987, Rose 1996). This shift in local government finances reflects the national assistance given for funding nationally mandated programs, moreover, local governments throughout the country were assured a relatively comparable revenue base in pursuing the goal of equal service availability for all citizens. Tax rates on income are regulated by the state, but local governments have the right to fix their own tax rates within a minimum and maximum level. In 1997 the maximum rate was 11.5% for municipalities and 6.75% for counties. All municipalities and counties operate with the maximum rate (Hagen and Sørensen 1997), which in municipal parlance is often referred to as the "tax ceiling".

Steering Structure

The supreme governing body in the municipalities is a popularly elected municipal council. Election to the council is held every four years according to principles of proportional representation. Local elections are contested on a partisan basis. Most parties represented in Parliament also field candidates in most municipalities. However, purely local lists are also quite common. The council then decides upon other organizational structures of the local authority. According to law, an executive committee (*formannskap*) is elected by and among the members of the council, again applying the principle of proportional representation. Most parties are therefore represented on the executive committee, except the smallest ones. By law, the local council also elects a chairperson or mayor (*ordfører*) from among its own members. The mayors convenes and presides over meetings of the council and executive committee, and is responsible for the preparation of matters to be considered by these bodies. However, the mayor is in most instances "first among equals" and exercises his/her powers in cooperation with other party leaders. This has led several observers to conclude that the position of the mayor is more of a symbolic character rather than that of strong and active leadership (Baldersheim 1990, Larsen 1990).

In addition to the executive committee and mayor, local authorities also establish a variety of standing committees. Presently, most municipalities have several permanent standing committees for educational, health and social welfare, cultural, and technical affairs. At their own initiative, these standing committees may set up various subcommittees in order to facilitate their work. This form of local government is referred to as the "aldermanic model" (*formannskapsmodellen*). It is an arrangement which tends to stress a collective sense of responsibility and is thought to contribute to the consensual character of local politics (Baldersheim 1992, Rose 1996).

Over the past 10 years there has occurred an extensive experimental activity through several programs with the aim of trying out new local government forms/organizational models. The "free commune" program is only one example (Bukve and Hagen 1991). Other examples include a Pilot Commune Project initiated by the Norwegian Association of Local Authorities (Baldersheim et al. 1996), and the Program for Local Government Renewal undertaken by the Ministry of Local Government (Kleven and Hovik 1994). As in the other Nordic countries, the free commune program represented a growing concern with local government capacity to respond to local electorates and consumers, and was an instrument for national and local authorities to co-operate in removing obstacles to better responsiveness at the local level (Baldersheim and Ståhlberg 1994).

By the late 1980s, practically all Norwegian municipalities were organized according to the Principal Standing Committee Model. In the 1990s, however, this model was criticized as it was claimed that it encouraged narrow sectoral views among councillors and too little attention to the municipality as a whole (Baldersheim and Stava 1993). Ideas of a New Public Management lineage are now attracting increased attention in municipal circles.

The experimental programs mentioned above were aimed at offering local authorities greater leeway to experiment with solutions better suited to local conditions, improving on the standardized solutions so often prescribed by national regulations. This experimental activity signalled a growing demand for more municipal autonomy in organizational choice. Increased administrative autonomy was institutionalized through the new local government act that took effect on January 1st, 1993. According to a survey from 1996, however, the dominant organizational form in Norwegian municipalities remains the Principal Standing Committee Model (Gravdahl and Hagen 1997).

The CEO's Position in the Institutional Arrangements of Local Government

Until the passage of the most recent revision of the act on local government, the CEO was formally accorded a strong and independent status. Once appointed by the local council, the CEO was specially protected against dismissal. The new local government act entailed several changes in the position of the CEO (Baldersheim 1992:60):

1) changes in the responsibility for preparing and submitting recommendations to the municipal council;
2) changes in authority over subordinate administrative agencies;
3) changes in the conditions of appointment.

Under the terms of the new act on local government, the CEO no longer has an independent and pre-eminent role in preparing and submitting recommendations to the municipal council. It is now up to each municipality to decide how to allocate responsibility for preparing and submitting recommendations to the municipal council. Revision of the law has strengthened the position of the elected officers in relation to the CEO. It is also possible to argue that the revision has strengthened the CEO's position in relation to other administrative leaders in the municipality. Traditionally, the municipal administration is based on specialized departments with administrative officers serving as directors of each department. The most typical departments are those for education, health and social services, cultural affairs, and technical matters, a division more recently mirrored by the structure of the specialized permanent standing committees of the municipal council referred to above.

The new Act of 1993 stipulates the CEO as the formal leader of the municipal administration. This was not a matter of course earlier, when several department heads could plead for a more autonomous administrative position because of national legislation on special policy issues. These issues often imposed responsibilities on local governments over which neither the CEO nor the local council had any influence. Another change in the law that has strengthened the CEO in relation to other departmental heads is that the law allows the municipal council to delegate decisions to the CEO in matters not of "fundamental interest". The CEO can delegate this power to other administrative departments. This is seen as an expansion of administrative discretion compared to the formulation in the previous act. The changes that we have pointed out are meant to improve the CEO's opportunities to co-ordinate and direct municipal administration (Baldersheim 1993).

Previously, the CEO had a civil service protection (*embetsmannsstatus*) akin to that of higher civil servants in the national government, based on a legal stipulation that gave the CEO the opportunity to appeal a dismissal to the Ministry of Local Government. This was meant to protect the CEO against removal by an occasional majority in the municipal council that happened to disagree with the CEO's recommendation. This possibility to appeal is now abolished. At the same time, the municipal council has been given the opportunity to appoint the CEO on a contractual basis (*åremål*), though not for a period shorter than six years. The new act leaves the politicians more room to shape the role of CEO according to local preferences and circumstances. This flexibility includes how much they want to delegate to the incumbent, and how far they will allow the CEO to operate on the political arena of the municipality.

Who are the CEOs, and How do They Experience Their Jobs?

Traditionally, the position of CEO has been occupied by men. Kjølholdt (1992), for instance, reported a 4% share of female CEOs, while our survey shows the share to have risen to 7%. In other words, the position of CEO is still strongly dominated by men. Moving from sex composition to age, it is interesting to note that age varies from 27 years up to 69. The average age being 49 years. This is close to that reported by Kjølholdt (1992) (47 years) and Askvik et al. (1988) (48 years). The average age of the CEOs has thus been quite stable for the last ten years. When it comes to education, the Norwegian CEOs have an average length of education of 17 years. Our results (in line with previous studies) confirm that it is the candidates with a degree in law (21%) together with candidates from the Municipal Academy (22%) who dominate the educational profile of CEOs. For the first time, the proportion of candidates from the Municipal Academy is higher than the share of lawyers. Still, it is worth mentioning that the share of lawyers holding the position as CEO in Norway is much higher than in the other Nordic countries (Pikkala 1996). Another interesting point is that the share of CEOs with another academic background is high (29%). Furthermore, in this category there is a considerable share of CEOs with a military background. The average CEO in Norway is thus a man in his late 40s with an academic education in law or from the Municipal Academy.

When the CEOs are asked whether the job is *more attractive today than 10 years ago*, the answers can be roughly divided in two categories. Forty-seven per cent answer that the job has become more attractive, while 39% say that it has become less so. Since previous studies (Kjølholdt 1992, Askvik et al. 1988) did not ask this question, we have no previous data with which to compare. However, the fact that 39% say that the job is less attractive today than formerly makes it imperative to make further investigations in order to see if the development has something to do with changes in the CEO's position as a result of the revision of the local government act. Another indicator that might provide a clue is the amount of hours the CEOs work. The answers to this question vary from 38 hours to 70 hours a week. The average CEO works 47 hours a week. Compared to research on managers in the private sector and in central government (Næss and Strand 1992) the average number of working hours for CEOs is lower than that of their colleagues in the above-mentioned sectors.

Why, then, do the CEOs *leave their jobs?* Is it because of the workload and other pressures stemming from the job? Workload is ranked as only the fourth most common reason for resigning. The most common reason is *advancement to higher or better paid office*. The second most important reason given is problems of co-operation with politicians, and the third is age. In other words, problems of co-operation are not unusual reasons for leaving the job. In an earlier discussion of the CEO's career patterns Askvik et al. (1988) do not mention problems of co-operation with politicians at all. They found the most common reason for job changes to be age and career advancement.

The pattern found in our data suggests two hypotheses for further exploration: 1) a generational change among the CEOs occurred in 1980s, and 2) the revision of the local government act may have increased tensions between politicians and the CEOs.

The CEOs' Own Views of Their Role

The discussion of the CEOs' opinions regarding their role may be related to a distinction between two role models: the classical bureaucrat and the political bureaucrat, as suggested by Aberbach et al. (1982). The Norwegian CEOs are divided almost equally between the two models (58% vs. 62%).

The table shows a marked variation in the importance attached to the variables comparing the respective indices. For example, the profile of the CEO as a classical bureaucrat reflects a concern with the management of economic affairs, accounts and budgetary control, while guiding subordinate staff in day-to-day management is given somewhat less attention. The profile of the political bureaucrats is marked by a keen interest in influencing decision-making processes and formulating ideas and visions for the community, whereas they seem less involved in supplying their mayors with political advice.

Table 8.1 The roles of the CEOs, Norway

The classical bureaucrat		58
Guide subordinate staff in day-to-day handling of activities	48	
Manage economic affairs, accounts and budgetary control	66	
Ensure that rules and regulations are followed	53	
Provide the mayor with legal, economic and other kinds of technical advice	64	
The political bureaucrat		62
Formulate ideas and visions	72	
Promote and encourage new projects in the community	67	
Provide the mayor with political advice	25	
Be informed about citizens' viewpoints	61	
Develop and implement norms concerning the proper roles of politicians vis-á-vis the bureaucrats	72	
Influence decision-making processes in order to secure sensible and efficient solutions	74	

Table 8.2 The ideal politician, Norway

Administration		30
Be a spokesperson for local groups or individuals who have issues pending decision by the authority	27	
Lay down rules and routines for the administration	33	
Taking decisions concerning specific cases	30	
Representation		67
Be informed about citizens' views	78	
Represent the municipality to the outside world	71	
Defend the authorities' decisions and policies externally	76	
Be a spokesperson for their political party	50	
Be a spokesperson vis-á-vis the press	62	
Governance		71
Implement the program on which he/she has been elected	53	
Decide on major policy principles	74	
Have a vision of the way in which the municipality will develop in the long run	87	
Stability		76
Create stability for the administration	73	
Formulate exact and unambiguous goals for the administration	79	

What Kind of Politicians do the CEOs See as the Ideal Partner?

Interacting with the politicians is a major part of the job as a CEO. What role expectations do CEOs hold with regard to their political masters? What kind of politicians would they prefer to work with? To analyze this issue, the U.DI.T.E. project has defined four different roles that can be of help. The first role focuses upon the politicians as active players in the administrative arena, the second concentrates on the representative functions of a politician, the third role is that of governance, and the fourth concerned with maintaining the stability of the administrative operations.

The above table indicates that Norwegian CEOs would most of all like to co-operate with politicians concerned with the stability of administrative processes, then governance, representation, and last of all politicians operating in an active administrative role. Seen in light of the main focus in municipal reorganization in Norway over the last 10 – 15 years, i.e., the "free commune" and "pilot commune" projects, this is not surprising. These programs have aimed at separating the political and administrative arenas by developing and implementing structural changes. Naschold (1995) has described them as "moderate and incremental internal modernization". One also finds this internal stability/governance focus in the revised local government act with its emphasis on the separation of politics and administration.

Contact, Conflict, and Dependency

In order to do their job properly, CEOs depend on the co-operation of a number of other actors. Who are these actors and on whom do they depend? To what extent are they able to engage in co-operation? And to what extent are relations conflictual? Figure 8.1 provides an overview of what can be labelled as the networks of the CEOs.

Figure 8.1 indicates two groups of particular interest in regard to the CEOs' contacts and dependencies. Not surprisingly, the CEOs have a very high level of contact with the municipal department heads and with the mayor. Contacts also seem to be quite frequent with other staff members. It is interesting to note that these internal relations are mostly of a co-operative nature, whereas the external or more distant relations can be more conflictual. Such relations include those with regional government bodies, private companies and journalists. Furthermore, levels of contact and dependency are closely related: the CEOs have more contacts with those on whom they depend for doing their job well.

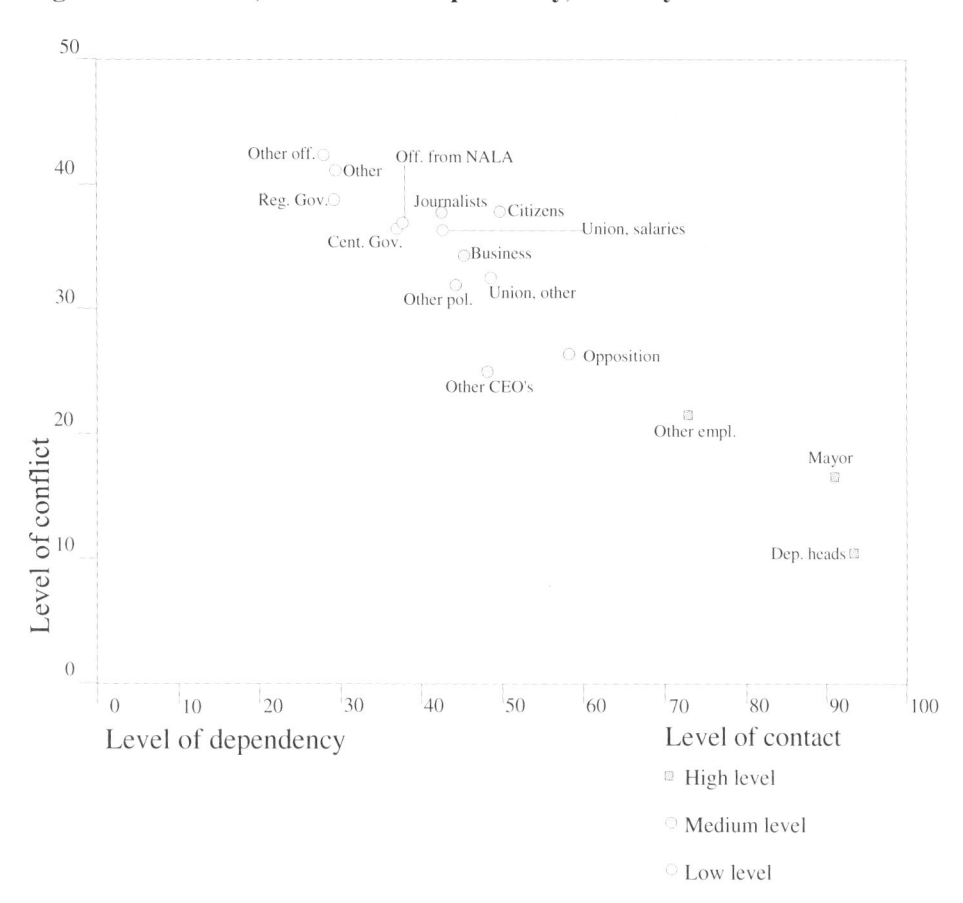

Figure 8.1 Contact, conflict and dependency, Norway

[Scatter plot with "Level of conflict" on y-axis (0-50) and "Level of dependency" / "Level of contact" on x-axis (0-100). Data points include:

- Other off. (≈25, 41)
- Other (≈30, 39)
- Off. from NALA (≈40, 40)
- Reg. Gov. (≈30, 37)
- Journalists (≈37, 36)
- Citizens (≈43, 36)
- Cent. Gov. (≈35, 34)
- Union, salaries (≈70, 35)
- Business (≈43, 33)
- Other pol. (≈38, 30)
- Union, other (≈47, 30)
- Other CEO's (≈42, 24)
- Opposition (≈63, 26)
- Other empl. (≈70, 20) — High level
- Mayor (≈87, 18) — High level
- Dep. heads (≈90, 9) — High level

Legend: ■ High level, ○ Medium level, ○ Low level*

Conclusions

With regard to the status and functions of municipalities, Norway belongs to the Nordic family of local government systems. Local government is closely integrated with welfare state functions. This influences not only citizen expectations, with perhaps lower tolerance of municipal inequalities than in other parts of Europe, but also administrative and political behaviour at the local level. Norwegian local politics and administration have traditionally been imbued with a deep respect for the proper "rules of the game". Recent reforms have aimed at reducing the pressure towards standardization of local operations which the national importance of local government has entailed. The well-known "free commune experiments" are an example of this. Initiatives toward administrative reorganization often look for inspiration to New Public Management. This means that new ideals of administrative as well as political leadership are coming into conflict with old-style local governance. Consequently, though the relationship is still overwhelmingly peaceful and co-operative, tensions between politics and administration may be increasing. CEOs are classical and political in their orientations in almost equal measure. As advisors to the mayor, however, they concentrate on technical issues rather than on political ones. *The picture of the Norwegian CEO that emerges is of an apolitical bureaucrat struggling to become a more modern manager.*

Bibliography

Aberbach, J.D., Putnam, R.D., and Rockman, B.A. (1981): *Bureaucrats and Politicians in Western Democracies*, Cambridge, Mass.: Harvard University Press.

Askvik, S., Espedal, B., Strand, T., and Ulvenes, Å. (1988): *Rådmanns-roller i utvikling*, Bergen: AFF-rapport nr. 2/88-E.

Baldersheim, H. (1990): Den nye kommunen – den politiske bedrift?, in H. Baldersheim (ed.), *Ledelse og innovasjon i kommunene*, Oslo: Tano.

Balderheim, H. (1992): 'Aldermen Into Ministers': Oslo's Experiment With a City Cabinet, *Local Government Studies,* Vol. 18, No. 1.

Baldersheim, H. (1993): Rådmannen – frå politisk embetsmann til lojal manager?, in H. Baldersheim (ed.), *Ledelse og innovasjon i kommunene* (2nd ed.). Oslo: Tano.

Baldersheim, H., and Stava, P. (1993): Reforming Local Government Policymaking and Management through Organizational Learning and Experimentation: the Case of Norway, *Policy Studies Journal,* Vol. 21, No. 1, pp. 104 – 114.

Baldersheim, H., and Ståhlberg, K. (eds.) (1994): *Towards the Self-Regulating Municipality: Free Commune Experiments and Administrative Modernization in Scandinavia*, Aldershot: Dartmouth.

Baldersheim, H., Hovik, S., Tufte, G.C., and Øgård, M. (1995): *Kommunal reorganisering*, Oslo: Kommuneforlaget.

Bukve, O., and Hagen, T.P. (1991): *Nye styringsmodeller i kommunene*, Oslo: Kommuneforlaget.

Gravdahl, H.P., and Hagen, T.P. (1997): *Ny kommunelov, ny organisering?* Oslo: NIBR Notat 1997:105.

Hagen, T.P., and Sørensen, R.J. (1997): *Kommunal organisering* (4th ed.), Oslo: Tano Aschehoug.

Kjølholdt, A. Næss (1992): *Mot en ny administrativ ledelse i kommunene? En analyse av rådmennenes orienteringer*, M.A. Thesis, Department of Political Science, University of Oslo.
Kleven, T., and Hovik, S. (1994): *Til invortes bruk...* Oslo: NIBR Rapport 1994:11

Kommunenøkkelen 96/97, Oslo: Kommuneforlaget.

Larsen, H. (1990): Ordføreren – handlekraft eller samlende symbol?, in H. Baldersheim (ed.), *Ledelse og innovasjon i kommunene*, Oslo: Tano.

Naschold, F. (1995): *The Modernisation of the Public Sector in Europe*, Helsinki: Ministry of Labour.

Næss, S., and Strand, T. (1992): *Kommunale ledere. Forskjeller og likheter mellom ledere i ulike sektorer og innenfor kommunal sektor*, Bergen: LOS-senter Rapport 9209.

Pikkala, S. (1996): Kommundirektörernas ställning och bakgrund, in L. Rose (ed.), *Kommuner och kommunala ledare i Norden*, Åbo: Institutet för jämförande nordisk politik och förvaltning vid Åbo Akademi.

Rose, L. (1996): Norway, in E. Albæk, L. Rose, L. Strømberg and K. Ståhlberg (eds), *Nordic Local Government*, Helsinki: ACTA.

CHAPTER 9

Turbulence as a Way of Life: The Swedish Municipal CEO

by Roger Haglund

The Municipal Context – a Historical Background

Swedish municipalities date back to 1862, when a reform of the local government system took place. With the reform came a greater degree of freedom in relation to the state. The reform gave the municipalities legal authority, taxation rights, communal membership for all inhabitants and a well-defined decision-making body. At this time Sweden had approximately 2,500 municipalities. Of these about 2,400 were very small (Strömberg & Westerståhl, 1983; Strömberg & Westerståhl, 1984).

The need for various kinds of services provided by the municipalities for its members grew during the post-war period. Similar to theories of large-scale production came the idea of creating larger municipalities for more efficient service-production. The main argument here was that larger municipalities would provide a better tax base and that increased economic resources would enhance the possibilities of administrative planning. Moreover, larger municipalities would provide a wider base for the recruitment of representatives for the elected body. As a result of these ideas, two amalgamation reforms were carried out during the 20th century. The first of these reforms was conducted in 1952 and the second completed in 1974. The first reform resulted in a reduction of the number of municipalities by half (from 2,498 to 1,037), while the second reform reduced them to 277 (ibid.; Norell, 1994). Only small adjustments have been made since 1974, and today Sweden contains 288 municipalities.

If one examines the political and administrative structure during this period of almost a century and a half, one sees a change from a system with elected laymen (trustees) towards a system of professional full-time-employed political leaders. In the beginning of the century, administrative staff were seldom found. Large municipalities (i.e., cities and certain boroughs) often had few officials, while the smaller municipalities had none. During the 1920s and 1930s, small municipalities also began to hire administrators, and it was not until the late 1950s when the last municipality left the system with only elected laymen and started to employ professional administrative personnel alongside elected professional politicians. Hereby the structural division between politics and administration was established (Strömberg & Westerståhl, 1983).

Sweden now has quite large municipalities, especially in an international context. In 1995 the number of inhabitants per municipality was 15,731 (median value).[1] Prior to the two amalgamation reforms, the average population was around 1,500, and following the 1952 reform this rose to 4,100. In the discussion concerning the second reform, the central arguments for larger municipalities was the number of inhabitants needed for municipalities to be efficient, and it was set to approximately 8,000 inhabitants. The main argument for large municipalities was based on calculations concerning economy in the school system (ibid.).

Sweden has thus moved from a system with many small municipalities to one of relatively few but large municipalities. At the same time, Sweden has changed from a system with only elected laymen to a system with elected professional party-politicians (some in full-time employment) assisted by numerous professional administrators.

Hand in hand with the amalgamation reforms, more and more tasks have been placed at municipal level. Today public welfare is produced mainly by municipalities. This is also reflected in the taxation system; the typical Swede pays about 30% in local income tax, divided between the municipal and the county level (the municipality takes two-thirds and the county the remaining one-third).[2] Overall, the municipal part of the GDP today amounts to 30%. Of the public spending and investments, the municipalities stand for approximately 50% (SCB, 1993). During the post-war period, the level rose steadily, only to slow down in the late 1980s and early 1990s. Municipalities employ about 46% of all publicly employed personnel and are thereby the largest public employer in Sweden (Svenska Kommunförbundet, 1995).

In a comparative international perspective, Sweden's degree of municipal autonomy could be described as high.[3] In recent years, however, municipal autonomy has been questioned – is it genuine autonomy or is it a false picture? The principle of local autonomy is specified by the Local Government Act (*Kommunallagen*). In recent years a huge amount of responsibilities and tasks have been transferred from central government to the municipalities, though without financial compensation from the state, however. There is also a central decision which stipulates that the level of municipal taxation (which is an important factor for local autonomy) may not rise. We also find other limiting regulations (e.g., the level of social welfare for poor people). The question of Swedish local autonomy could therefore be seen as twofold: formal legislation which ensures autonomy, and regulations and transfers that limit the autonomy in central parts.

---

[1] The mean population was 30,675.
[2] The main task for Swedish counties is to take care of medical needs in society; i.e., administering hospitals.

The CEO and the Municipal Structure

The internal municipal organisation is in fact regulated by the state. Over time these regulations have changed, from a rather heterogeneous system towards a more homogeneous one. Since 1992, however, the system has been loosened up, so that municipalities can now be organised in the way they find most appropriate, except for a few mandatory organisational units, e.g., election board, executive board, and, of course, the council. Examples of reorganisation are municipalities dividing their organisation in two other boards – one for implementing political decisions and one for producing certain services (a sort of internal market system). Another example is the creation of geographical sub-units handling a predefined range of municipal tasks. The main organisation, however, is still divided into different sectors. For example, the School Board takes care of education, and the Social Welfare Board manages social welfare (Haglund & Jaktling, 1993).

Swedish municipalities have many tasks. At the individual citizen's level, when ordinary people contact public authorities, they mainly encounter municipal authorities. Local authorities are thus responsible for childcare, schools (from primary to secondary school), social benefits, services for the elderly, cultural activities and health care. They also handle emergency services, refuse disposal, land and city planning, streets, water supply, housing and local economic development.

The municipal political system is representative. Every four years members of the Municipal Council – *Kommunfullmäktige* – are elected by the people. The Swedish councils vary in size, from 31 to 101 members (depending on municipal size). The Council is the highest decision-making body in our municipalities. The central administrative and executive body is the Executive Board – *Kommunstyrelse* – which is elected by the Council and is often composed proportionally, as is the Council. In this way the Executive Board forms a coalition, where most parties in the Council are represented. The chairman of the Executive Board occupies the leading political position and could thereby be seen as a kind of Mayor, even though Swedish local administration does not in fact have the formal position as Mayor any more. The chairman is usually full-time employed in this function. Virtually every municipality contains an additional full-time employed politician representing the main opposition party and, in large municipalities, additional full-time employed politicians from both the majority party and the opposition (parties).

There is no pure hierarchical relationship between the Executive Board and other boards. The Executive Board cannot formally supervise any other board. I would rather say that they handle different matters. The Executive Board handles budget preparation and matters which concern the entire municipal organisation. Other boards handle tasks concerning their special fields, such as schools, culture and leisure.

If one tries to place the top administrator (the focus of this chapter) into this complex system of politicians and administrators, this person would be situated in between.[4] However, there is at least one problem when it comes to positioning the top administrator. The position of the Chief Executive Officer – *Kommundirektör* – in Swedish municipalities has traditionally been weak. The system of today is a system with no formal standards for this position. A municipality can have a CEO, or it can choose not to have one; the specific role is decided upon by the respective municipalities. The only restriction found is that the person on top of the administration cannot be elected to political positions in the municipality (i.e., the person is the *only* municipal official who cannot be elected). Variations among different municipalities appear just by looking at the title of this administrative position. Most municipalities have adopted the modern title Chief Executive Officer (*Kommundirektör*) clearly associated with private sector management terminology. Thirty-seven per cent of the municipalities use this title. Almost as many (30%) use the term Chief Executive Officer (*Kommunchef*), and the same goes for Administrative Chief (*Kanslichef* 25%). Kanslichef is quite an old term which was frequently used earlier. However, it is ambiguous because it is also used in some municipalities to identify who is in charge of the Central Municipal Office. The title Kanslichef does not for certain indicate whether the person is a CEO or not. Many municipalities have chosen to go their own way and give the position a unique name. Hence, in Sweden the top administrator is not found simply by looking for a title. To this must be added that not all municipalities have a top administrator in the formal sense we are seeking. A handful of municipalities have chosen to skip the function and use a sort of corporate management model instead.

It is the municipality's Executive Board that hires the Swedish CEO, and he has no formal power, unless the board gives it to him. In recent years the trend has been to add more importance to this administrative position, and the ideas behind this stem mainly from the private sector (see for example Brunsson, 1994; Forsell, 1994; Haglund & Jaktling, 1993). Nowadays the focus is on leadership and visions, where focus used to be on the CEO as the filter between the political and the administrative sphere, giving the former well-prepared proposals and the latter instructions (see the section below on job postings).

CEO Recruitment?

As previously mentioned, the Swedish CEO has had a rather weak and unclear position since the amalgamation reforms, though this profession has won respect over the last decade. This increased authority is due mainly to ideas "imported" from the private sector.

---

3 See for example Goldsmith, 1995.

The first striking feature is that almost all CEOs (96%) have a university degree. The remaining 4%, or 10 persons in the survey of late 1995, have either worked their way to the top simply by long municipal affiliation, or have a middle-range education. Thus, Sweden has a quite homogenous group, and this has been the case for quite a long time. In fact, neither age nor the time in present position makes any difference with regard to the level of education.

The CEOs' most common university degree is in political science and public administration. Almost half (47%) of those with academic degrees state this kind of background. Another 12% comprise people with a university degree as a 'socionom', meaning that they are educated at higher schools for social work. An explanation might be appropriate here. Earlier, schools for social work offered two types of education, one for students aiming at social work and one for students aiming at a career in public administration (Ighe & Fridén, 1994). Many public administrators in Sweden have this kind of background. These results correspond quite well to findings by P.O. Norell in the early 1980s (Norell, 1989). Recent years, however, have witnessed an educational diversification among public administrators recruited at all levels.

Even though the majority are well educated, not all CEOs have a university background in public administration, social work or political science. Twenty-eight per cent have economic degrees and another 26% have a degree in law.[5] In addition, a few (2-3%) have non-social science educations such as technical, natural science and humanities/history. Table 9.1 groups the CEOs based on the time they have been in office.

In recent years a change in educational background of CEOs is evident. These figures are in one sense a reflection of what kind of profiles the municipalities are looking for when they recruit new CEOs. If this is a true picture of the demand, one striking finding is a move away from law as educational background. When it comes to the recent growth in the figures on CEOs with a background in economics, one explanation may be the strained economic situation in which the municipalities find themselves.

Another way of looking at the demands on and expectations towards CEOs is to examine the qualifications stated in job advertisements. Yet another way would be to see what a CEO is expected to do, according to written jobdescriptions. The last alternative, however, is not so easy in the Swedish case because they rarely exist. For many municipalities, the only document covering job descriptions is actually the advertisement.

---

4 When nothing else is stated, the data on Swedish CEOs are based on a survey conducted between November 1995 and January 1996. The survey, a questionnaire mailed to all top administrators in each of Sweden's 288 municipalities, yielded a 80.3% response rate.

5 In the survey it was possible to mark the type of university degree which was the focus of the education – nevertheless, many CEOs were unable to select just one due to the fact that university degrees in Sweden often comprise several disciplines. For this reason, the percentage of degrees earned exceeds 100%.

Table 9.1 The division of CEOs classified by university background on lenght of time in present position (percentage)

Degree earned	Total	0-5 years	6-10 years	> 10 years
Law	26	19	34	42
Economy	28	30	20	30
Political science/public administration	47	46	48	49
Technical	4	4	4	0
Natural science	2	3	2	0
Humanities/history	4	4	2	2
Social work and other university degree	23	22	25	26

Comment to the table: The column labelled "Total" should be read as the total dispersion among the respondents on their educational background (e.g., 26% state a degree in law, etc.). Observe that it does not vertically add up to 100% due to the fact that respondents could state more than one field of education. The following columns show the educational background classified according to length of service (e.g., 19% of the CEOs holding their position 0-5 years state a degree in law).

I have analysed three 1-year intervals over a period of 17 years: 1978, 1985 and 1995.[6] In total, there are 64 advertisements: 16 in 1978, 16 in 1985 and 32 in 1995. To describe the findings, the data can be divided into three categories: functions, qualifications and attributes.

When looking at *the functions* that CEOs are expected to perform, one finds that most municipalities advertising for a CEO in 1978 wanted the individual to be "secretary for the political body or the chairman of the Executive Board", "head of administration", "leader", and wanted the CEO "to plan" and "to administer". In 1985, three more functions were significant (the content of more than half of the advertisements): they should "refer/convey matters to the political body or the chairman of the Executive Board", "co-ordinate different branches" and "engage in the local community". In 1995 emphasis was on conducting change, reforming the organisation, and developing services (reorganisation movements) was added. Functions such as political secretary or advisor to politicians have less weight today. Leadership, planning, co-ordinating different branches, together with being a change agent and the ability to develop the organisation are nowadays the main functions for new CEOs.

Among *the formal qualifications* mentioned, the most enthralling finding is the turn from a pure municipal experience to a more broad-based experience. In

---

[6] The same paper for advertisements has been chosen for the period: The weekly KommunAktuellt (the only one of its kind) is published by The Swedish Association of Local Authorities (Svenska Kommunförbundet). The selection of 1978 instead of 1975 has to do with the simple fact that the first paper for advertisements on similar jobs started that year; before there was none.

the mid-1990s, the necessary qualifications are less formalised and more focused on personal qualities; the "right" person can have any type of educational background and any kind of special knowledge. The most important is that he or she is open for change and has the right leadership instinct. Often it is stated without specification that he should have "the right background". It is worth paying special attention to some of the qualifications mentioned. In 1978, municipal experience was often requested. In 1985 this changed to a wider public sector experience, and in 1995 it became a split between private, public or municipal experience. Through the years there has been a focus on leadership experience. And theoretical knowledge is virtually assumed as a necessary base. In almost all the cases from 1978 and 1985, an academic degree is required (88% of all advertisements for these two years have this as a key prerequisite). In 1995 the formalised education requirement is not as prominent as before (though still significant). This has probably to do with the search for "the right person", and with the fact that a university degree is supposed to be obligatory, the latter meaning that everybody applying for such a job has definitely a university degree.

Finally, the *personal qualities* requested are not so often expressed in formal terms in any of the three years. There is a split, however, in the picture on qualities, insofar as some are more present than others. In 1978 the focus was on initiative and co-operative ability. This was also the case in 1985 and in 1995. In 1995, however, there was also a strong desire for leadership.

When summarising the period, one could say that the job has proceeded from an ideal of planning to an ideal of change, and from the bureaucrat towards the entrepreneur.

Another point worth mentioning in connection with job advertisements is the use of consultancy firms in recruiting, so-called "headhunting" firms. Over the period, it is only in 1995 that consultants are mentioned. In that year 15 out of 32 advertisements were drafted and searches conducted by such firms. This corresponds quite well with earlier findings (Haglund & Jaktling, 1993; Solli & Källström, 1995).

Where do the CEOs come from when they are appointed? If one takes a look at their previous post, one can see that they come mainly from administrative jobs (44%). The second is accounting (16%). One interesting finding is that 7% of the CEO candidates come directly from a CEO position in another municipality. This could be be seen in connection with the current turbulence of the position as CEO, or as a normal CEO career move (Norell, 1989). Seven per cent come from juridical work, and the same goes for planning. Six per cent come from a job with personnel. Most come from a leading position (72%) such as a previous position as a manager. Twenty-six per cent come from a middle level and 1% from a low level, such as assistant work. Finally, 34% come from within the same municipality.

Most of the CEOs have a municipal background; 82% come directly from a municipal position, 4% from the counties and 6% from central government (located either in the capital Stockholm or, more commonly, from local branches of central government). Six per cent are recruited from the private sector.

Only 8% of the CEOs are female, all appointed within the last five years. The average age for the entire group is 50 years, and the average age when CEOs were hired is 43 years. When it comes to geographic mobility, very few have spent part of their childhood in the area. Only 22% have grown up close to their present workplace. Even the local connection of today is vague inasmuch as one out of four has chosen not to live in the municipality where he/she works.

The present job and position as local government CEO in Sweden is undergoing great change. This should probably be seen in relation to the fact that since the 1980s CEOs' lifetime tenure has been replaced by contracts for a limited period of time usually six years (Solli & Källström, 1995).[7] The transition to limited tenure should probably be seen on the background of the economic crisis affecting most Swedish municipalities. These crises make the work harder and more conflictual, and the politicians more tense. One indicator of the degree of turbulence is to see how long the CEOs have held their position. The median value is 5 years, which means that half the present CEOs have been in position for less than 5 years. Seventy-five per cent have held their positions for up to 10 years, and a few have held their positions for up to 28 years.

In the questionnaire we asked the CEOs what had happened to their predecessors, i.e., for what reason had their predecessors leaft their positions as CEO? In this way one could manage the turbulence and obtain a clearer picture of the causes. Table 9.2 displays subgroups for a specified illustration.

Age is cited as the major cause for the predecessor's resignation, followed by problems with politicians. The turbulence becomes quite clear in this table. The "age-cause" has diminished, probably because CEOs do not stay in office very long. At the same time, problems with politicians have more clearly become central causes for resignation. More than every fourth CEO in position for less than 5 years mention this as a cause for the predecessor's exit. Another not so significant cause are problems with fellow bureaucrats, mentioned by 8% of our sample. Seen in relation to time in office, it looks as if this is an emerging problem. CEOs with more than 10 years in office (25% of the total sample) have not found this as a cause, and among CEOs with 5 to 10 years only 1% mention this as a cause. By comparison, the "youngest" group mention this cause at a higher rate (10%). Even the "workload and pressure cause" has quite recently become more evident. To sum up the turbulence discussion, the work of a CEO seems to be under pressure. Politicians, fellow bureaucrats and workload have in recent years been causes for resignation. I will return to this issue later on.

---

7 The option of employing CEOs on a limited contract, an option popular a few years ago, has lately proven less attractive, since some municipal councils used it to opt out on financial terms stated in the contract which were very costly for the municipality.

Table 9.2 Reasons given by CEOs for their predecessors exit from their posts, according to length of service (in percent)

Reason given	Percent having served Total	Years served as CEO		
		0-5 years	6-10 years	> 10 years
Career	12	10	18	12
Problems with politicians	22	27	18	12
Problems with bureaucrats	8	10	1	0
Workload/pressure	7	9	4	5
Age	35	31	36	46
Illness/death	5	4	4	9
Don t know	5	5	9	2
Other	13	13	16	9
New position/no predecessor*	14	15	9	14

Comment to the table: The column labelled "Total" should be read as the total dispersion among the respondents regarding their view of predecessors (e.g., 12% state career, etc.). The vertical sum is not 100%, as the respondents could state more than one field of causes. The following columns show the cause of resignation according to length of service (e.g., 10% of the CEOs in position 0-5 years state the cause career).

* New municipalities have emerged where there has been no predecessor. Also, reorganizations have created new offices where the new CEO has been more in focus than before.

Yet another picture of the job as a Swedish CEO is found in their evaluation of the attractiveness of the job over time. We have asked them how attractive, more or less, they think the job as CEO has become over the last 10 years. The picture of their cumulative view is not too bright – 48% say that the job has become less attractive.[8] Another 26% find it more attractive, and the rest, 26%, do not see any change in attractiveness.

Major reasons for the negative assessment could be summarised in relation to these problems:

- The relation to politicians
- The financial crisis and its problems
- Pressure on the individual

---

8 Here I have merged "somewhat less attractive" and "much less attractive" into a single category: "less attractive". The same has been done with "somewhat more attractive" and 'much more attractive'. In this way I obtain three categories instead of the original five in order to obtain an easier and clearer interpretation.

In the words of some of the respondents, the CEO job has become less attractive because the position has been exposed to more pressure: pressure from the politicians, from media, from citizens and from the administration. The general turbulence surrounding the CEO also seems to have had a negative effect and to be part of the pressure. A lot of the pressure seems to have its background in fiscal austerity, which leads to "more liquidation than development", as one respondent puts it. The role-perception is another central problem mentioned in the open-ended questionnaire, inasmuch as the distribution of authority between politicians and the CEO is too unclear. This implies that the CEO does not know what kind of authority he or she really has.

Major reasons for the positive view could be summarised by invoking the virtual other side of the same coin:

- The positive effects of the financial crisis:
    - (i) challenge
    - (ii) adventure
    - (iii) possibilities of exerting influence
    - (iv) responsibility
- Stronger focus on leadership

The positive statements could be described as the other side of the same coin: the problems are looked upon with an optimistic and constructive attitude. Fiscal austerity works as a catalyst for new and brave solutions. With limited resources, one has to come up with really good ideas, and this challenges some of the CEOs. The leadership role has been emphasised and become more focused, and this is seen as a positive change. The possibility to influence has risen, and there is now "more room for influence due to the need for leadership".

Roles and Values Among Swedish CEOs

The CEO is a link between two the political and the administrative arenas. A link is always important because information is filtered there. The information and orders from the politicians to the administration is transformed by the CEO, and the same goes for information and matters in the opposite direction. He also acts as a link to the outside world.

Differing perceptions among CEOs produce different attitudes towards the environment. Separating roles and values among the CEOs can help us to construct a picture of the group as a whole.

One set of roles to analyse concerns the relationship between the CEO and the political sphere. In this area, two roles of interest revolve around the ideas of the classical versus the political bureaucrat. The former view is based on Max Weber's ideal type, which could be summarised as the objective expert with a clear demarcation line between politics and administration. The second role, as the name may imply, is a more political one, a mixture of the bureaucrat and the politician. In this second view, political advice and political influence are correct behaviour (see for example Putnam, 1975).

These two bureaucratic styles can be identified by linking together a couple of survey-items in the 1995 survey, as shown in table 9.3.

Table 9.3 The roles of the CEOs, Sweden

The classical bureaucrat		46
Guide subordinate staff in day-to-day handling of activities	34	
Manage economic affairs, accounts and budgetary control	37	
Ensure that rules and regulations are followed	40	
Provide the mayor with legal, economic and other kinds of technical advice	74	
The political bureaucrat		64
Formulate ideas and visions	78	
Promote and encourage new projects in the community	76	
Provide the mayor with political advice	32	
Be informed about citizens' viewpoints	63	
Develop and implement norms concerning the proper roles of politicians vis-á-vis the bureaucrats	60	
Influence decision-making processes in order to secure sensible and efficient solutions	76	

Comments to the table: The index score can vary from 0 to 100, where 0 means no importance and 100 extreme importance. The summary scores for the classical bureaucrat and the political bureaucrat are averages of included items.

The table indicates a clear predominance of the political bureaucrat among our CEOs. The strength of this predominance, however, is not clear. For the classical bureaucrat one item is of outstanding importance to CEOs – offering the chairman of the Executive Board legal, economic and technical advice. However, to give the chairman political advice is not popular. Hence, one interpretation would be that while we have a predominance of the political bureaucrat type, the terminology "political advice" is beyond what is accepted – it is not "politically correct" to say that you give political advice when you are a Swedish public servant. It could also be a question of terminology: how can we be sure that "legal, economic and technical advice" does not involve political aspects of a problem or an up-coming discussion? The law can always be interpreted in different ways, and the economy of a municipality, at least when it comes to Swedish municipalities, is highly political. A study by P.O. Norell projects the same type of results (Norell, 1989).

Another aspect of the relationship between the CEO and the political arena concerns how he or she views the role of leading politicians – what should these actors be like and how should they behave with regard to certain certain aspects. Two main types can be separated theoretically. One is the politician elected to represent the municipality, i.e., the board member or municipal representative. The other is the politician who represents mainly the party, i.e., the party politician.

In the same fashion as with the role perceptions above, one can use items from our 1995 survey to calculate index tables as shown in table 9.4.

Table 9.4 shows a higher demand among CEOs for municipal representatives than for party politicians. There is some ambiguity, however, in this rather simple interpretation. CEOs do not want the leading politicians to be involved in individual cases or to represent individuals. Considerable emphasis has been placed on the party connection. In this way the CEOs reveal an ambiguous attitude. On the one hand, they want politicians to act for the common good of the municipality, but they want their actions to be channelled through the political parties. The CEOs want the politicians to act as members of a political party in the best interest of the municipality, while running the administration themselves without interference from the political arena. In Sweden, considerable emphasis has been

Table 9.4 Role of the leading politicians · CEOs' perspective

The municipal representative		
		85
Represents the municipality to the outside world	83	
Decides on major policy principles	81	
Has a vision of the way in which the municipality will develop in the long run	93	
The party politician		50
Makes decisions concerning specific cases	35	
Is the spokesman for their political party	71	
Is a spokesman for local groups or individuals	23	
Implements the program on which he/she has been elected	70	

Comments to the table: The index score can vary from 0 to 100, where 0 means no importance and 100 extreme importance. The summary scores for the municipal representative and the party politician are averages of included items.

placed upon moving individual cases from the political to the administrative arena, so that politicians can concentrate on goals and visions, and maybe this is what CEOs are trying to point out. In the follow-up answers to the question on how they see their jobs 10 years from now, many stated that they do not want too many interruptions in their job, but, rather, a more peaceful time of work.

Another question of interest is how the role perceptions towards the administration are focused. One way to address this question is to distinguish between economy and control, on the one hand, and the management of human resources, on the other.[9] Maybe this could be seen in their personal view upon people or staff. Are they lazy or can they be trusted? Do they need to be supervised and controlled, or do they just need the right conditions and to be accepted and believed in? This separation corresponds quite well with *theory X* and *theory Y* presented by Douglas McGregor (McGregor, 1960). His theory X represents the supervising and controlling leadership-style, with theory Y the more humane and believing leadership-style.

Polarity of economy and control could be estimated by items in the questionnaire, as shown in table 9.5.

Table 9.5 Role of the administration – CEOs' perspective

Role expectation

Economy and control		47
To manage economic affairs, accounts and budgetary control	37	
To ensure that rules and regulations are followed	40	
To guide subordinate staff in day to day handling of cases	34	
To ensure that resources are used efficiently	78	
Management of human resources		70
To stimulate co-operation between departments	81	
To be informed about the viewpoints of the employees	67	
To solve problems and conflicts/human relationships	61	

Comments to the table: The index score can vary from 0 to 100, where 0 means no importance and 100 extreme importance. The summary scores for economy and control and management of human resources are averages of included items.

---

9 Whether this is a useful way of separating the roles in Sweden can be questioned. One way of conducting economy and control is to stimulate co-operation and to control simply by giving certain units a bag of money instead of specific orders and regulations.

The management of the human resources point of view seems dominant among Swedish CEOs. The focus on human resources is quite clear. The economy and control view does not appear to be as important, though they say that there is a need for supervising the use of resources. This is probably the case because of the extreme economic conditions for most municipalities in Sweden. Being at the top of the administration, the politicians makes economy a key problem for which the CEOs have a personal responsibility.

Networking and Influence

Our questionnaire asked the CEOs about their relationship with a number of actors. Explicitly, we asked about their level of conflict with these actors, their frequency of contact with them and the level of dependency on each of these actors with regard to the success of CEOs in their work. From these responses, we can assess the network patterns of Swedish CEOs.

In what kind of networks do Swedish CEOs participate and how frequently? And to what extent do they see networks as important? As most people would agree, networks are a good way to receive and spread information. They also operate to shape attitudes, promote influence and are a potential instrument of power. In various networks actors adopt different roles. With this in mind, it would be interesting to see what the network patterns of CEOs look like. Three directions will be in focus: networks aimed at the political system in the municipality, at the administrative system in the municipality, and networks with the outside world.

To begin with the political network, one could say in this network the CEO has a subordinate role and is extremely dependent. This is because it is the politicians (the Executive Board) who hire and fire him. The CEO's subordination is also due to the fact that it is through a link going from the politicians through the CEO (mainly from the chairman of the Executive Board) that the municipality is run administratively. In this sense, the politicians need the CEO to work for them and their intentions, and the CEO can at the same time exert an influence on the decisions. When looking at the turbulence around Swedish CEOs mentioned earlier in this chapter, this network makes the picture a bit clearer. Many of the CEOs' predecessors left their position due to problems centered mainly on this network.

To begin from the top, the chairman of the Executive Board is definitely the most important person in the political network (and in all of the three networks). Eighty-six per cent of the CEOs meet daily with the chairman, and all of them meet him at least 2–4 times a week. The chairman is also the person whom the CEOs regard as the most important one when it comes to the ability to perform their functions as CEOs. All of the CEOs state that their relation to the chairman is of great or very high importance. In contrast to the discussion about career instability, conflicts with the chairman are quite rare; 94% of the CEOs feel that there is a co-operative or very co-operative relationship between them. Only 5% state a neutral relationship, and 1% (two persons) state a conflictual relationship.[10]

The second most important relationship in the political network is with leaders of the political opposition. Seventy-four per cent of the CEOs consider relations with these politicians to be of great or very high importance. However, they do not meet with these actors as often as with the chairman. A little more than half the CEOs (58%) meet some of the leading politicians from the opposition at least 2–4 times a week, while conflicts hardly exist: only 1% of the CEOs see a conflict in this relationship.

Finally, the third part of the political network consists of the remaining politicians in the municipality. This group may occupy third place in importance, but nevertheless 54% of the CEOs find this relationship of great or very high importance, and 10% meet some of them on a daily basis. We do not find a conflictual picture here either. Most of the CEOs see the relationship as co-operative, even though one in four have a more neutral relation to this group of politicians. They probably meet certain politicians in this rather large group more than others. Compared to the party leaders these "other politicians" are a larger group consisting of different types of politicians. A few are active in the Executive Board, but most are active in other boards.

Turning our attention to the second kind of network – the administrative network – the picture focuses primarily on the department heads. These fellow administrators are regarded as highly important by the CEO. Ninety-four per cent of the CEOs see this group of administrators as important to a great or very high extent, and this relationship is definitely of a co-operative kind (98% state co-operative or very co-operative). In communicating with someone from this group, one-third of the CEOs do so daily, and three out of four at least 2–4 times a week.

In terms of communication and daily meetings, the chairman may be the most frequent partner, but close to that comes the chief of economic administration. Ninety-eight per cent of the CEOs communicate with their chief economic administrator at least 2–4 times a week, and 70% daily. The relationship is seen as greatly or very highly important by 88% of the CEOs. And conflicts rarely exist.

Other employees, of course, are also part of the administrative network. In terms of communication, this is done on a regular basis (45% communicate daily), and conflicts are rare. In terms of importance for the CEO and his/her work, 56% see the relationship as important to a high or very high degree.

When trying to point out the last of the three network types – the network including the outside world – three central findings are of interest. First, the

---

10 This could mean that there is only little conflict in this relationship in Sweden. It could also mean that if there are conflicts between the two, one has to leave the system, and it is usually not the chairman.

CEOs are in frequent contact with the municipal citizens. More than half the CEOs talk to citizens several times a week, and one-fourth also find this relation to be important to a great or very high degree. In terms of conflict, citizen contact is for most CEOs a neutral area.

The second finding concerns extent to which CEOs engage with local business interests. Eight per cent of the CEOs communicate daily with representatives of local business, and 35% meet with them several times a week. This has a bearing on the way CEOs look upon the importance of this relationship. Sixty-one per cent find it important to a great or very high extent. As regards conflict, however, it is mainly seen as a neutral relationship.

The third finding of interest concerns journalists or the media. Three out of four CEOs meet with the media at least weekly. The relationship is mostly neutral, but a small number of CEOs note conflictual experiences (4%).

If one turns the perspective upside-down and observes with whom the CEOs rarely communicate, with whom they have conflictual experience, and whom they do not regard as important for their job as CEO, the following is worth pointing out:

In particular, there are two groups of actors with whom CEOs do not normally communicate: civil servants from the counties and civil servants from central government. More than half the CEOs are seldom or never in contact with these officials. This pattern goes hand in hand with the patterns of importance; three out of four CEOs see these two relationships as unimportant or of very little importance. These findings are not surprising. Swedish municipalities have a great deal of independence from the state; therefore, these civil servants rarely come into contact with each other. When it comes to the civil servants from the counties, the explanation is the same; municipalities and counties deal with different parts of the welfare society without an internal hierarchy.

Conflict occurs mainly with representatives of the media and with officials from the national association of local authorities, but it is important to make clear that conflicts are generally rare for the CEOs (if their statements in the survey are trustworthy).

Conflict, dependency and frequency in contact are graphically presented, as shown in figure 9.1. Here we can quite clearly see the linearity between dependency and level of conflict. The third dimension, frequency in contact, also follows the assumed line. There is no natural direction in this causal relationship. Four or five clusters can be of interest.

The most important contacts for CEOs are with the chairman of the executive board. Little conflict, much dependency and frequent contacts are typical. The same picture, but a little less pronounced, is found with the heads of department. The next cluster is a formation of other politicians, employees, local businessmen and politicians from the opposition; some conflict, some dependency and a medium frequency in contact. In the third (or maybe fourth) cluster are citizens and media placed together with a variety of more or less loose contacts. The last cluster contains regional and central government officials.

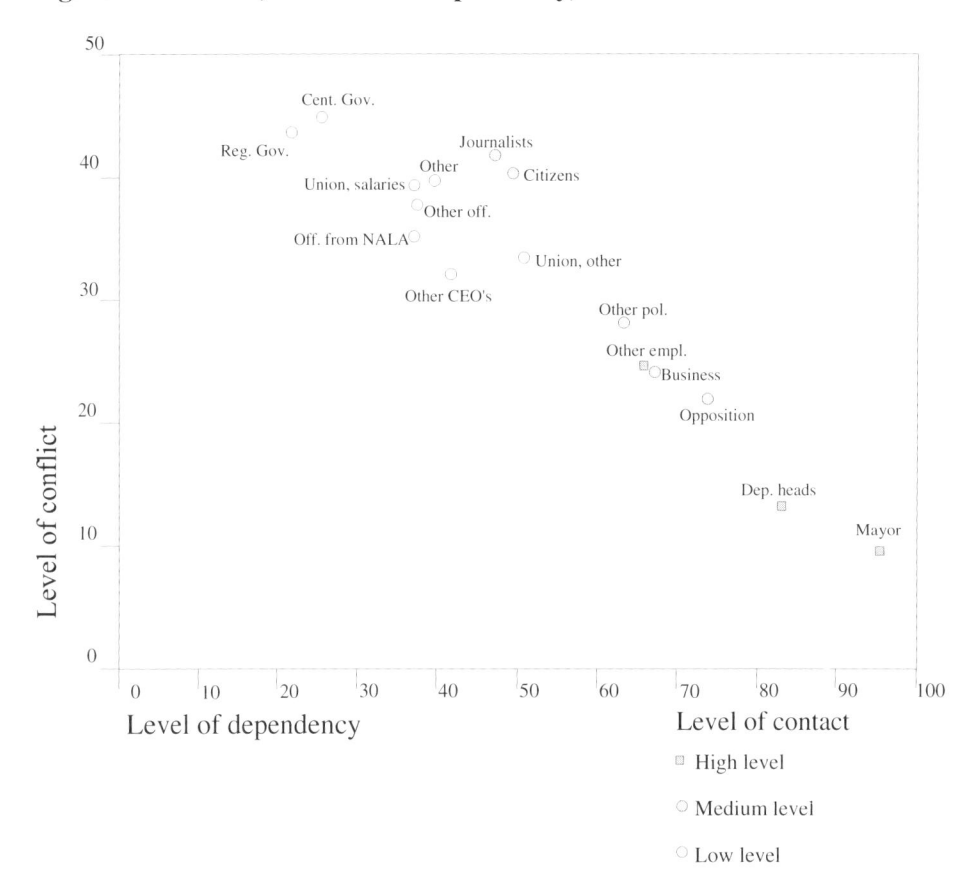

Figure 9.1 Contact, conflict and dependency, Sweden

[Scatter plot with x-axis "Level of dependency / Level of contact" (0–100) and y-axis "Level of conflict" (0–50). Points plotted:
- Cent. Gov. (~25, 43)
- Reg. Gov. (~18, 41)
- Journalists (~42, 41)
- Other (~38, 40)
- Union, salaries (~22, 39)
- Citizens (~52, 39)
- Other off. (~40, 37)
- Off. from NALA (~32, 34)
- Union, other (~55, 33)
- Other CEO's (~38, 30)
- Other pol. (~63, 28)
- Other empl. (~65, 24)
- Business (~68, 23)
- Opposition (~72, 21)
- Dep. heads (~82, 12)
- Mayor (~93, 9)

Legend: □ High level, ○ Medium level, ○ Low level]

The picture, while not surprising, is nevertheless a quite good illustration. The linearity reveals a pattern of centre–periphery in the everyday life of Swedish CEOs. The most important contacts are found in the lower right corner and the least important in the upper left corner. With importance comes frequency in contact.

Some Concluding Remarks

The function of the CEO in Swedish municipalities has changed from a somewhat anonymous administrative position to a more marked and powerful position. Tasks have become more explicit, and there is a greater emphasis on leadership, external representation and on visions and co-operation. The ideas are derived from leadership in the private sector, and the "offspring" of the New Public Management concept has left a profound mark on Swedish municipalities. This change can be seen in many examples of reorganisations, e.g., organising the municipality almost like a group of companies with a focus on central management, where sub-fields have been contracted out (Haglund & Jaktling, 1993). In this perspective, the focus on the CEO can thereby be seen as following the common change among our municipalities. Though the effects on democratic legitimacy have not yet been objectively questioned by observing a CEO acting in the political field, the idea of democratic representation is challenged.

Bibliography

Brunsson, Nils (1994): Politization and 'company-ization' – on institutional affiliation and confusion in the organizational world, *Management Accounting Research* 5/1994, pp. 323–335.

Eldersveld, Samuel J., Strömberg, Lars, and Derksen, Wim (1995): *Local Elites in Western Democracies. A Comparative Analysis of Urban Political Leaders in the U.S., Sweden, and the Netherlands*, Oxford: Westview Press.

Forsell, Anders (1994): Företagisering av kommuner, in Bengt Jacobsson (ed.), *Organisationsexperiment i kommuner och landsting*, Stockholm: Nerenius & Santérus.

Goldsmith, Mike (1995): Autonomy and City Limits, in David Judge, Gerry Stoker and Harold Wolman (ed.), *Theories of Urban Politics*, London: Sage Publications, Ltd.

Haglund, Roger (1997): Turbulens i den kommunala ledningen – självklarhet eller orosmoln?, *Kommunal Ekonomi* 2/1997, pp. 31–32.

Haglund, Roger, and Jaktling, Tomas (1993): *Inventering av 28 kommuners organisationsförändringar. Pilotstudie våren 1993*. CEFOS Arbetsrapport 2/1993, Göteborg: Centrum för forskning om offentlig sektor.

Ighe, Ann, and Fridén, Bertil (1994): *När menighetsbesvär skulle bli tjänstetid*, Göteborg: Institutionen för socialt arbete.

Lundquist, Lennart (1993): *Ämbetsman eller direktör? Förvaltningschefens roll i demokratin*, Stockholm: C.E. Fritzes AB.

McGregor, Douglas (1960): *The Human Side of Enterprise*, New York: McGraw-Hill.

Montin, Stig (1993): *Swedish Local Government in Transition: A Matter of Rationality and Legitimacy*, Örebro: Högskolan i Örebro.

Norell, Per Owe (1989): *De kommunala administratörerna. En studie av politiska aktörer och byråkratiproblematiken*, Lund: Studentlitteratur.

Norell, Per Owe (1994): Communal Administrators – The Swedish Case, *Research in Urban Policy* 5/1994, pp. 137–167.

Putnam, Robert D. (1975): The Political Attitudes of Senior Civil Servants in Britain, Germany, and Italy, in Mattei Dogan (ed.), *The Mandarins of Western Europe: The Political Roles of Top Civil Servants*, New York: Halsted Press.

SCB (1993): *Statistisk Årsbok för Sverige 1994*, Stockholm: Norstedts.

Solli, Rolf, and Källström, Anders (1995): *Kommundirektören. En studie av kommunens högste tjänsteman*. CEFOS Arbetsrapport 8/1995, Göteborg: Centrum för forskning om offentlig sektor.

Solli, Rolf, and Källström, Anders (1997): *Med takt och taktik. Om den ekonomiska krisen, våra kommuner och det kommunala ledarskapet*, Göteborg: BAS.

Strömberg, Lars, and Szücs, Stefan (1993): The Swedish National Report, in Jacob, Ostrowski and Teune (eds.), *Democracy and Local Governance: Ten Empirical Studies*, Honolulu: Matsunaga Institute for Peace.

Strömberg, Lars, and Westerståhl, Jörgen (ed.) (1983): *De nya kommunerna. En sammanfattning av den kommunaldemokratiska forskningsgruppens undersökningar*, Stockholm: Liber Förlag.

Strömberg, Lars, and Westerståhl, Jörgen (1984): *The New Swedish Communes: A Summary of Local Government Research*, Stockholm: Liber Förlag.

Svenska Kommunförbundet (1995): *Perspektiv 99. Kommunerna och Svenska Kommunförbundet 1995-1999*, Klippan.

CHAPTER 10

No More Double Dutch: Understanding the Dutch CEO

*by Jaco Berveling, Marcel van Dam,
Geert Neelen, and Anchrit Wille*

Introduction

There is something mysterious about the position of the civil service in Dutch society.[1] On the one hand, we know relatively little about the daily activities of civil servants. On the other hand, however, civil servants are thought to be highly influential. The image of the civil service as a "fourth power" persists, and the notion that the municipal secretary is an influential actor at the local level is generally accepted (Leemans 1967: 211-222; Weststeijn 1988: 19; Darson 1992: 7; Renou and Lutters 1993: 9). However, some authors (Eijsbouts 1980; Derksen 1992: 15-16; Elzinga 1993; Van der Meer 1995) have argued that his position has been eroded to some extent due to various developments within Dutch municipalities. Since these perceptions of the role of the municipal secretary are contradictory, we will attempt to find out how influential the municipal secretary (thinks he) is. We will do this by addressing the following questions. What is his present position within the political administrative system? How does the municipal secretary perceive his own role and that of local politicians? And finally, with whom does he communicate and how does he value the interactions with the actors in his social network? By reference to these questions we can see how far the municipal secretary may be regarded as a key figure at the local level.

This chapter is based on a survey that was sent to all ordinary members of the Dutch Association of Municipal Secretaries (the VGS).[2] Although there are several studies which deal with the position and functioning of the municipal secre-

---

[1] We would like to thank Ms. Saskia de Haas and Ms. Janny Lens-Mobach who helped us considerably with the survey on which this chapter is based.
[2] We focus purely on the position of municipal secretaries. The position of sub-local secretaries and regional secretaries is not discussed.

tary, until now there had been no comprehensive survey relating to the total population of municipal secretaries.[3]

The Broader Institutional Context: Dutch Municipalities

Before we examine the position of the municipal secretary in the political-administrative system, we will briefly discuss the position of the municipality within the Dutch system of intergovernmental relations, commonly described as "a decentralized unitary state".[4] This system of intergovernmental relationships was established by the Constitution of 1848, the Provincial Government Act of 1850 and the Municipal Government Act of 1851 and is associated with the Dutch statesman J.R. Thorbecke (1798-1872). Nowadays the essential characteristics of the decentralized unitary state still apply, although both the Constitution and organic legislation (legislation with respect to municipalities, provinces and water control boards as forms of functional decentralization) have been replaced and many attempts have been made to change the system of intergovernmental relations.

The present role of the municipality in the Dutch system of local administration can be sketched by reference to the following three concepts: autonomy, co-administration and supervision.

The notion of "autonomy" pertains to the autonomous domain of municipalities, referred to as "open household". Municipalities are free to take policy initiatives in fields they consider to be necessary without having to ask permission in advance from provinces or national government. As a result of this rather open definition of the local domain, it is impossible to enumerate all municipal tasks. They vary from the more classical ones concerning safety, housing, education and infrastructure to tasks typical of modern welfare states, like programs for the elderly and day-care institutions.

"Co-administration" refers to the duty of local governments to make regulations on certain issues and to implement general regulations whenever these are issued by a higher level of government. Although co-administration forces municipalities to direct their attention and activities to certain specific purposes, it should be noted that they are often given rather free rein in the elaboration of the specifically required provisions. Examples of functions performed by municipalities within the context of co-administration pertain to housing, health care and the execution of the Social Security Act.

"Supervision," the third concept essential to the Dutch decentralized unitary state, can take two forms, preventive and repressive supervision. Preventive supervision implies that certain statutory, municipal decisions only take legal

---

3 For a discussion of the survey see the technical appendix.
4 On January 1, 1996, there were 625 municipalities (CBS 1996: 68).

force when they are approved by provincial or central government. Repressive supervision relates in principle to all municipal decisions and implies a stay or nullification of those decisions taken by municipalities that are considered to be in conflict with the law or with the interests of central government.

Since the second world war, the functions in the realm of co-administration have increased significantly. Indisputably, one can observe a centralization trend in The Netherlands brought about by several factors: the expansion of the welfare state, societal enlargement processes, a tendency to equalizing the level of municipal services, and more endogenous factors pertaining to the political and administrative system of central government (Decentralisatienota 1980). This centralization trend is reflected in the intergovernmental financial relationships, especially the relative importance of the two most important sources of income: general and categorical grants, both of which come from central government. The relative size of the categorical grants, referring to specific purposes related to co-administration, have increased from 30% in the 1950s to about 70% in the late 1980s, to the detriment of the general grants which can be freely spent in the context of autonomy. The third income source of municipalities is local taxes (especially the local property tax), fees (for instance on issuing passports and birth certificates) and revenues from local government enterprises. Compared with most Western European countries like Denmark, Germany and especially Spain (Koopmans et al. 1991: 231), this income source is very modest in The Netherlands: only about 15% of the total municipal income (Miljoenennota 1996: 180). Many municipal government decisions, such as those concerning the approval of the annual budget, were until recently subject to preventive supervision.

At the beginning of the 1980s the central government launched the so called major policy operations, which included a decentralization policy. Due to the huge budgetary problems of the central government, changing ideological principles concerning the role of the state in society and due to a widespread uneasiness with the rather monocentric-hierarchical conception of intergovernmental relationships, a wide range of decentralization operations have been issued. These operations pertain to fields such as housing, care for the disabled, education and public transport. Although municipalities have more formal powers of decision in several fields due to the decentralization policy, it should be noted that the actual scope for policy-making is often limited, especially since their financial position has not improved at the same rate as their work load.

The Position of the Municipal Secretary in the Political-Administrative System

According to article 125 of the Dutch Constitution of 1983 the city council has the highest authority in municipalities. Members of the city council are elected at four-year intervals on the basis of a system of proportional representation. Out of the members of the city council, an executive board of aldermen is recruited;

the executive board is completed by the mayor, who is appointed (and often reappointed) by national government for a period of six years. Besides being the chairman of the executive board, the position of the mayor is also a separate function with specific tasks and authorities, of which the maintenance of the public order is most important. In practice, the executive board of mayor and aldermen is considered to be more influential than the city council. This may be explained by the fact that members of the city council are only part-timers and by the assistance given the board by the municipal secretary and the specialized municipal bureaucracy.

The specific position of the municipal secretary is longstanding since it was established in the Municipal Government Act of 1851 and is still described in the latest Municipal Government Act of 1994. His function, appointment and tasks are laid down in articles 100 through 107 and in article 212. The municipal secretary is appointed by the city council (art. 101) and assists the city council, the executive board, the mayor as well as committees established by these actors (art. 103). Furthermore, he is present at the meetings of the city council and the daily board (art. 104) and co-signs the outgoing documents of the city council and the daily board (art. 105). The other articles of the Municipal Government Act of 1994 concern his replacement (art. 106-107), discharge (art. 101), suspension (art. 101), a reference to forbidden operations (art. 102) and incompatible functions (art. 212).

This formal description relates only to the legal position of the municipal secretary. Notice that no references have been made with respect to his position within the administrative organization. Let us now deal with his position in practice. Traditionally, the municipal secretary is seen as the central link between the political and the administrative systems in Dutch municipalities. On the one hand, he is the permanent secretary to both the executive board and the city council while on the other hand he operates as the chief executive of the administrative organization. Whether the municipal secretary should be seen as the central link between the political and the administrative systems is not clear. Dealing with this question, two related developments have affected and probably eroded the position of the municipal secretary to some extent.

The first development refers to the functioning of the executive board. Formally, the juridical fiction of "colleague-like government" or joint decision making still applies to the board. The board and its individual members are accountable to the city council for their policy (art. 169 of the Municipal Government Act of 1994). In practice however, a division of tasks between aldermen is very common, so that many board decisions become a formality. As a result, aldermen have developed intense relationships with those parts of the municipal bureaucracy occupied with functions for which they have been given responsibility. These close relationships were already common with respect to specific municipal agencies such as municipal housing companies, public utilities, etc. but have gradually extended to other fields. With respect to this study, it is important to note that the municipal secretary is now bypassed more and more by aldermen and department heads (Eijsbouts 1980; Derksen 1992; Van der Meer 1995).

Furthermore, and this is the second development since the 1970s, most municipal bureaucracies have been reorganized. Until then the typical municipal bureaucracy consisted of the office of the municipal secretary, occupied with policy making, and a varying number of departments concerned with the implementation or execution of tasks (Van Raay and Wolters 1987: 5-7). Following the reorganizations, most municipal bureaucracies have chosen an organizational structure which is often denoted as a "sector model". In this model, policymaking and implementation have been integrated into larger departments or policy sectors. Often the tasks of the office of municipal secretary are reduced to advising and assisting the board and the city council and to coordinating the policies of the different sectors. Sometimes the municipal secretary is also the head of a policy sector. A new development is the emergence of so-called management teams which comprise the municipal secretary and the heads of the different sectors. The position of the municipal secretary in these management teams varies from a technical chairmanship to a more formal and dominating position depending on personal and specific organizational conditions (Renou and Lutters 1993; Van der Meer 1995).

Although both developments may vary considerably among municipalities, they nevertheless imply that we should be cautious in identifying the municipal secretary as the sole chief executive within the municipal bureaucracy.[5] The remainder discusses the municipal secretary in more detail, using the findings from the survey held among Dutch municipal secretaries. Let us begin with their social and political background.

Social and Political Background of the Municipal Secretary

In order to obtain an impression of who the municipal secretary is, we first need to describe his or her social background. We focus on three demographic characteristics: education, gender and age. The basic tendency is clear. Municipal secretaries are fairly well educated, male and middle-aged. Over 40% of the municipal secretaries have completed their education at university level and two-thirds (68%) have university degrees Law. Although the emancipation of women has been a major issue in Dutch society in the last three decades, the position of municipal secretary is still a male preserve: less than 5% of the secretaries are women. This low percentage should be seen in the light of the large number of

---

5 It has been suggested that a distinction must be made between small municipalities (less than 10,000 inhabitants, for example) and larger ones. In small municipalities, the position of the municipal secretary is probably very strong since the bureaucracy is relatively small and organized as the office of the municipal secretary (called "secretarie") (Van der Meer 1995). Furthermore, the aldermen in small municipalities are often part-timers.

women working within the municipal service generally: in 1990 32% of municipal employees were women (Van der Meer and Roborgh 1993: 286). Not only women, but also young people are poorly represented in this position. The mean age of the municipal secretary is 49 years. About 82% of the municipal secretaries are between 40 and 55, and only 4% are younger than 40 years (see also Darson, 1992).

The survey data also indicates that a high proportion of municipal secretaries are affiliated to a political party. Almost 55% of the municipal secretaries are members of a political party, and another 13% have previously been a member. In view of the fact that only 3% of the Dutch population are members of a political party, it is clear that this proportion is extremely high. Of those who are members of political parties, nearly 44% are affiliated to the Christian-Democratic Party (CDA), 28% to the Social-Democrats (PvdA) and over 16% to the Liberals (VVD). Although the outcome of the last national election in 1994 showed a general decline in support for the party CDA, the proportions in the Dutch survey showed no loss of support for the CDA among municipal secretaries. While at the national level the CDA-party is for the first time in more than 70 years no longer part of the governmental coalition, it is still by far the dominant party among municipal secretaries.[6] The majority of municipal secretaries, while they may have an affiliation to a political party, do not consider this relevant for the recruitment of their job. Two-thirds of all municipal secretaries indicated that political party membership plays little or no role in the appointment of high level officials in their own municipality. Over a quarter (28%) reported to be neutral on this aspect.

To obtain more insight into the career patterns of municipal secretaries, we wanted to know more about their career history. Three-quarters of the municipal secretaries surveyed were formerly employed by a municipal government: 50% of the respondents came from another municipality while 24% had spent their career in their present municipality. There are few or no transfers from the central government or the private sector to the position of municipal secretaries: only 1% formerly held a job at the central level, while 1% held a job in the private sector before they achieved their present position. Over 27% of the municipal secretaries have held a similar position in other municipalities. Asked whether they consider their present position as the last one in their career, more than 40% indicated that they might seek another post and almost 30% definitely planned to seek another job some time. Yet this ambition is clearly linked to age: the older the municipal secretary is, the less plans he has to seek another job. Asked why their predecessors left their position, the response in almost 46% of the cases was "due to retirement".

---

6 Note that this is a comparison of party membership with election outcomes.

Municipal secretaries have more ties to the community than just serving it. One indicator of their orientation towards their local society is their membership in local associations. About 75% of the municipal secretaries reported being members of at least two local associations, and 53% were members of three or more local associations. Almost 90% of the municipal secretaries live within the boundaries of the employing municipalities. This is not surprising since municipal secretaries have been allowed to live outside their own municipality only since 1994, when the residence stipulation was deleted from the Municipal Government Act. Before that, municipal secretaries (just as the mayor) had to reside within the boundaries of the employing municipality.

Role Perceptions of the Municipal Secretary

The many and varied functions carried out by the municipal secretary involve both political and administrative decision-making (Weststeijn 1988: 17). In order to obtain a better understanding of his position, we will analyze the way the municipal secretary perceives his own role and that of local politicians. Both role perceptions are discussed using the indices set out in the introductory chapter.

Starting with the perceptions of his own role, table 10.1 shows that the image of the political bureaucrat – with an average index score of 65 – finds more resonance among our sample than the image of the classical bureaucrat which has an average score of 46. The Dutch municipal secretary attaches priority to the formulation of ideas and visions and to influencing the decision-making process in order to ensure sensible and efficient solutions. He also attaches considerable importance to the other "political" aspects of the job, with the exception of giving "political" advice to the mayor. The latter may be explained by the fact that the adjective "political" is often associated with "party political". The low emphasis put on giving political advice is sensible, since the appointment of the municipal secretary in The Netherlands is not a political one and since the mayor has no strong party political role. Furthermore, table 10.1 shows that most of the tasks associated with the role of the classical bureaucrat are seen as moderately important. The dominant image of the political bureaucrat may be related to the political environment in which the municipal secretary works (Weststeijn 1988: 19). Frequent and substantial contacts between mayor and alderman, which leads to the amassing of political information, give the municipal secretary the opportunity to influence political decision-making. The perceptions of municipal secretaries of their own role did not vary according to such factors as age, sex and size of the municipality.

Table 10.1 The roles of the CEOs, Netherlands

The classical bureaucrat		46
Guide subordinate staff in day-to-day handling of activities	52	
Manage economic affairs, accounts and budgetary control	40	
Ensure that rules and regulations are followed	46	
Provide the mayor with legal, economic and other kinds of technical advice	46	
The political bureaucrat		65
Formulate ideas and visions	74	
Promote and encourage new projects in the community	63	
Provide the mayor with political advice	49	
Be informed about citizens' viewpoints	65	
Develop and implement norms concerning the proper roles of politicians vis-à-vis the bureaucrats	65	
Influence decision-making processes in order to secure sensible and efficient solutions	71	

Given that municipal secretaries consider themselves to be political bureaucrats, what do they expect from their political counterparts at the local level? Both type of role perceptions probably affect their actual work considerably. Table 10.2 shows the relative importance that Dutch municipal secretaries have attached to various aspects of the role of politicians. It may be inferred from table 10.2 that, according to municipal secretaries, politicians should have a future vision of the (development of the) municipality that is strongly based on citizens' views, but must refrain from detailed interference in the work of the administration. In line with new public management ideas, leading politicians should decide on major policy principles and defend these decisions externally, but should leave the implementation and management to the bureaucratic organization. The interpretation of these findings is difficult, however, since the designation "leading politicians" in the questionnaire includes both mayor and aldermen as well as members of the municipal council; two groups whose roles may be perceived quite differently. The respondents most likely had both groups in mind; the low scores on some items seem to imply that they associated politicians with council members (the administration items and the item "implement the program on which he/she has been elected") whereas the low score on another item suggests that they equated politicians with the mayor and aldermen ("be a spokesperson for their political party"). As a result of these ambiguities, the findings of table 10.2 should be interpreted with caution.

Table 10.2 The ideal politician, Netherlands

Administration		31
Be a spokesperson for local groups or individuals who have issues pending decision by the authority	28	
Lay down rules and routines for the administration	18	
Taking decisions concerning specific cases	48	
Representation		68
Be informed about citizens' views	84	
Represent the municipality to the outside world	67	
Defend the authorities' decisions and policies externally	79	
Be a spokesperson for their political party	58	
Be a spokesperson vis-à-vis the press	50	
Governance		75
Implement the program on which he/she has been elected	65	
Decide on major policy principles	73	
Have a vision of the way in which the municipality will develop in the long run	87	
Stability		66
Create stability for the administration	60	
Formulate exact and unambiguous goals for the administration	72	

Communication Networks of the Municipal Secretary

Communication is another important task of a municipal secretary. Yet with whom does he communicate? Communication patterns presumably tell us much about how municipal secretaries function, and with whom they feel their job requires them to maintain contact. To obtain an impression of his communication network, we investigated the contacts which the municipal secretary had with several actors from the political system, the administrative organization, and the political and administrative environment of the municipality. The municipal secretaries are asked about several actors in terms of how often they communicated with them; whether these relationships were conflicting or cooperative; and whether they consider these relations important for their work as municipal secretaries. This last question is used as an indicator of "dependency on a relation". The "dependency" is thus measured by the extent to which a municipal secretary considers a contact important for his ability to perform his function. The results of the analysis are presented in figure 10.1. The figure shows in graphic fashion the degree of contact, conflict and dependency in the communication network of the municipal secretary.

A first category of contacts consists of relations with actors from the municipal political system. Figure 10.1 shows that contacts with the mayor are frequent. Nearly all municipal secretaries meet the mayor daily or 2 to 4 times a week. Renou and Lutters (1993: 19,29) noted that the mayor and the municipal secretary are often a closely knit team. Whereas aldermen come and go, the mayor, who is appointed and not chosen, together with the municipal secretary represents a stable factor in the municipal-political system. Although he may advise the city council, in practice the municipal secretary primarily advises the mayor and aldermen. Not surprisingly, municipal secretaries consider their working conditions highly dependent upon the relation with the mayor. A similar picture emerges with respect to the aldermen: municipal secretaries meet the aldermen quite frequently and are highly dependent on this relationship.[7] In other words, these contacts are considered to be extremely or very important to their work as municipal secretaries. The data in figure 10.1 show that conflicts are not common with these political actors. Most of the municipal secretaries describe the relationship with the mayor as cooperative or very cooperative. In contrast, the municipal secretary communicates less frequently with the members of the political opposition or with other politicians in the municipality. Moreover, they are less dependent on these latter contacts that are still evaluated as fairly cooperative.

---

7 This item was added to the Dutch questionnaire and is not depicted in figure 10.1.

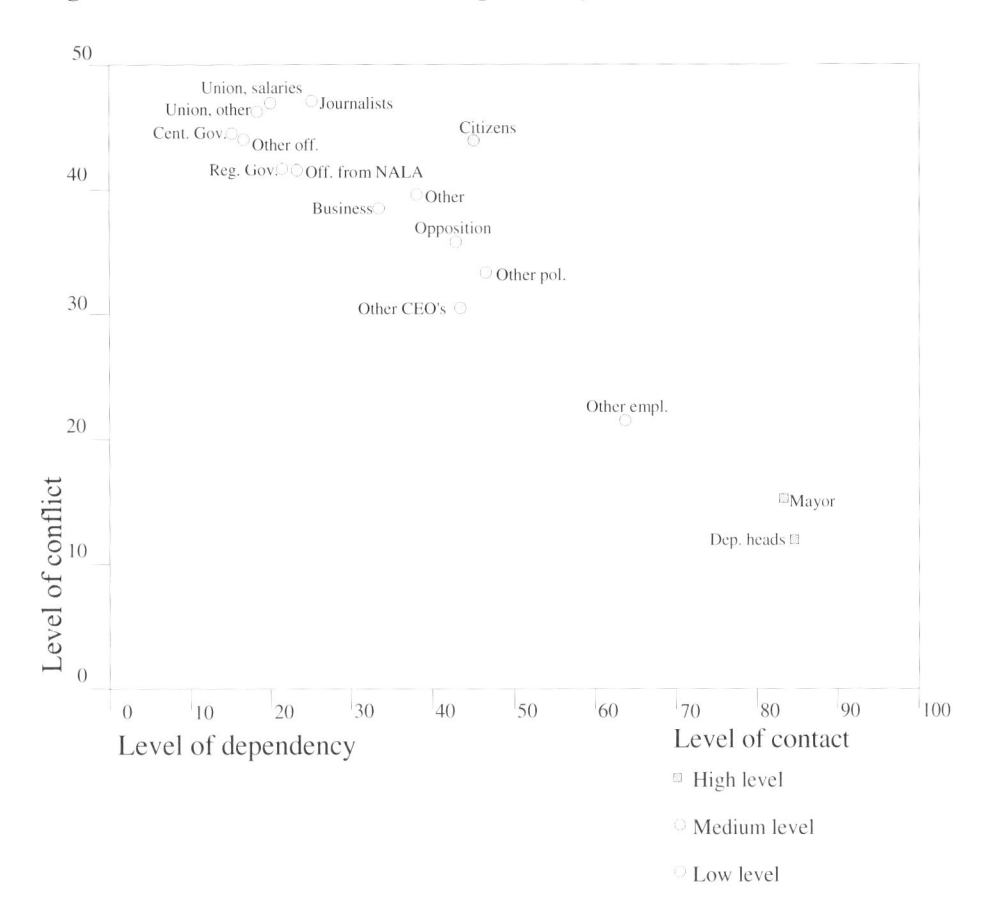

Figure 10.1 Contact, conflict and dependency, Netherlands

[Scatter plot with x-axis "Level of dependency" / "Level of contact" (0-100) and y-axis "Level of conflict" (0-50). Legend: High level, Medium level, Low level.

Data points:
- Union, salaries (~20, 47)
- Union, other (~18, 45)
- Journalists (~28, 45)
- Cent. Gov. (~15, 42)
- Other off. (~22, 41)
- Citizens (~50, 42)
- Reg. Gov. (~22, 38)
- Off. from NALA (~28, 38)
- Other (~43, 37)
- Business (~35, 35)
- Opposition (~47, 33)
- Other pol. (~53, 28)
- Other CEO's (~33, 30)
- Other empl. (~65, 20)
- Mayor (~82, 13) — High level
- Dep. heads (~78, 10) — High level]

A second category of contacts are those with actors within the municipal administrative organization: the heads of departments (or policy sectors) and other employees in the municipal organization. As figure 10.1 shows, municipal secretaries meet departmental heads quite frequently. These contacts are considered important, and municipal secretaries thus depend extensively on these relationships. Contacts with municipal employees are at a medium level. Yet the level of dependency is evaluated as high, though not as high as with the department heads or the mayor. All relations with actors in the municipal organization have a low level of conflict.

A third category in the communication network consists of contacts with administrative actors from outside the municipal organization; for instance, municipal secretaries in other municipalities, officials from the regional and national government and officials from other public sectors. Figure 10.1 shows that municipal secretaries have a low level of contact with all these actors in this category. The municipal secretaries from other municipalities, for example, do not meet frequently, but the dependency on this interaction with others in the same position is considered to be high. Municipal secretaries may advise each other and learn how "peers" deal with similar problems. The relationship is therefore characterized as a cooperative one. The low level of contact with officials from other municipalities, and with officials from the regional and central level is perhaps the result of the delegation of these links to the heads of departments within the municipal organization (see Renou and Lutters 1993: 87). The data in figure 10.1 show that municipal secretaries ascribe low dependency to the relationship with officials from other administrative levels, and that these contacts are considered conflictual.

A final category of contacts consists of actors in the political administrative environment; that is citizens in the municipality, journalists, private business interests and non-profit organizations. Municipal secretaries have low levels of contact with journalists and the level of dependency is low. The level of conflict of these contacts, however, is considered to be high. The same applies to union representatives. Relatively speaking, the most frequently met actors from the political administrative environment are the citizens. However, municipal secretaries indicate that they do not depend on contacts in performing their functions even though such contacts are often quite conflictual.

In short, municipal secretaries attach little importance to external relations. The attention of the municipal secretary is focused mainly on the mayor, the aldermen and the heads of the departments. These are the prime actors within the CEO's network. In contrast, little notice is paid to the officials from other administrative levels and to actors from the political and administrative environment.

The Dutch Municipal Secretary: a Key Figure Within the Municipality?

Let us return to our central question as to whether the municipal secretary is a key figure within the municipality. In section three it was noted that some actors claim that the central position of the municipal secretary has been eroded due to changes within the political-administrative system. However, this suggestion has not been analyzed systematically. We will attempt to shed some light on it using the survey findings.

We asked municipal secretaries about their perception of their own influence over some policies in the community. To make a meaningful comparison, we also wanted to know which persons or groups they consider influential in their communities. Therefore, municipal secretaries were asked to assess the degree of influence of several actors in the community on two domains: the budget, and the economic development of the community.

Municipal secretaries believe that the mayor has extensive influence on both the budget and the economic development of the community. The political parties within the city council are thought to have the highest influence with respect to the budget. According to municipal secretaries, bureaucrats also have a lot of influence. For instance, department heads are considered to be as influential as the mayor in this domain. By contrast, actors from the political administrative environment, such as clients, voluntary associations, trade unions and private business interests, have no influence. When we look at the economic development domain, however, we see an entirely different picture. Here private business interests are considered the most influential actors. The mayor ends up in a second position and upper level governments are a good third. The local political parties, the department heads and the clients of the administration are believed to have only moderate influence.

The municipal secretary does not think of himself as a very influential actor. The municipal secretaries believe that on both domains they are less influential than the executive board of the mayor and the aldermen, the local political parties, the largest political grouping within the council, the department heads, and the upper level governments. Although we are focusing on only two of the many domains at the local level, the survey data suggest that the municipal secretary considers himself to have only limited influence in these areas.

These findings, as well as earlier ones on his limited and inwardly directed social network, are consistent with the claim of some authors that the municipal secretary no longer has a central position within the municipality. In addition, no references have been made in the Municipal Government Act of 1994 with respect to his position within the administrative organization, and we discussed the emergence of management teams that bypass the municipal secretary more and more. However, municipal secretaries have suggested that their influence does not appear directly in such political fields as the ones mentioned in the questionnaire.[8] Rather, his position may be best understood as that of a process manager, since he manages the process through which policies are made and implemented. All reports, letters and advice to the mayor and aldermen are first seen by the municipal secretary, and all the political decisions are passed to the administration by him. Although he is often not involved in preparing most of the reports and advice, he may block or delay them and therefore has considerable influence on the local political agenda. This is much in line with the finding in the section on role perception that municipal secretaries regard themselves primarily as political bureaucrats. However, the designations "process manager" and "political bureaucrats" do not fully correspond to each other since process managers will probably not attach as much importance to the formulation of ideas and visions as do the municipal secretaries (see table 10.1).

Although our data relate to only one point in time, there are some indications that the position of municipal secretary has changed in the last decade. On the one hand, the suggestion made by some observers that his central position has been eroded has found some confirmation in the empirical findings. On the oth-

---

8 These suggestions were made in interviews and in discussions with municipal secretaries in workshops that were organized in relation to the findings of the survey.

er hand, we have argued that nowadays the municipal secretary acts more like a political bureaucrat and to some extent as a process manager. While his influence within the municipal organization has changed in recent years, the foregoing does not imply that his position is powerless. Perhaps he will have to establish his influential position vis-à-vis the other political and administrative actors in a different way than in the past, when his central position was more institutionalized. Testing of this thesis must await future research.

Bibliography

Centraal Bureau voor de Statistiek (1996): *Bevolking der gemeenten van Nederland op 1 januari 1996*, Den Haag.

Darson, L. (1992): *Profielschets van de gemeentesecretaris*, Leiden: 2i Publications.

Decentralisatienota, Tweede Kamer, vergaderjaar 1980-1981, 16492, no. 2.

Derksen, W. (1992): *De gemeente als gemeenschap? Naar een nieuw lokaal bestuur*, 's-Gravenhage: VUGA.

Eijsbouts, T. (1980): Haalt de gemeentesecretaris 1984?, *Binnenlands Bestuur*, vol. 1, no. 6, pp. 8-9.

Elzinga, D.J. (1993): Spil van het bestuur of GA-er met verkeerde schoenen? Positie gemeentesecretaris wankelt, *Binnenlands Bestuur*, vol. 14, no.7, p. 29.

Koopmans, L. a.o. (1991): *Overheidsfinanciën* (7th ed.), Leiden: Stenfert Kroese.

Leemans, A.F. (1967): *De eenheid in het bestuur der grote stad*, 's-Gravenhage: VUGA.

Lutters, A., and Renou, M.(1993): *De verander(en)de gemeentesecretaris*, Oostellingerwerf/Maastricht: VGS.

Meer, F. van der (1995): *The municipal chief executive in the Netherlands*, Leiden University (unpublished paper).

Meer, F. van der, and Roborgh, L.J (1993): *Ambtenaren in Nederland*, Alphen aan den Rijn: Samsom.

Miljoenennota 1996, Tweede Kamer, vergaderjaar 1995-1996, 24400, no. 1.

Raay, W.J.M. van, and Wolters, M.(1987): *Ambtelijke reorganisatie, Een onderzoek naar nieuwe organisatievormen in grote gemeenten*, Alphen aan den Rijn: Samsom.

Weststeijn, G.C. (1988): *De Gemeentesecretaris: zijn benoeming en positie in politiek perspectief*, 's-Gravenhage: Uitgeverij van de Vereniging van Nederlandse Gemeenten.

CHAPTER 11

The Belgian Municipal Secretary: A Manager for the Municipalities?

by Yves Plees and Thierry Laurent[1]

Introduction

While relatively much attention has been devoted to central level civil servants in Belgium, the municipal secretary has never been the subject of a thorough study. Only recently has some attention been paid to this function, which has been grossly underestimated both in scope and importance. In trying to fill this gap, this text highlights the function and profile of the municipalities' chief executive officer, the municipal secretary.

The Chief Executive Officer in the Municipal Organisation

The Municipalities in the Belgian State Organization

Municipalities were already formally organized during the French rule in Belgium. After independence in 1830, the National Congress introduced into the first Belgian Constitution certain key principles concerning the organization and functioning of municipalities: the direct election of municipal authorities; the assignment of everything that comes under "municipal interest" to the municipal councils, and, consequently, the right of the municipalities to manage their own interests; public municipal affairs (meetings of the council, budgets and municipal accounts); the right of municipalities to levy taxes, and, finally, the administrative tutelage of superior authorities in order to avoid municipal councils acting beyond their legal attributions or against general interest.

Belgian municipalities were legally organized six years later by the municipal law of March 30th, 1836. This law was regularly modified, and a newly codified

---

1 We would like to express our gratitude to Elke Van Hamme, Research Assistant at the K.U. Leuven and Kristof De Leemans, Assistant at the Universitaire Instelling Antwerpen for their contribution to this chapter.

municipal law came into effect on January 1st, 1989. However, this new text has already been amended several times since then.

Other laws had a very important influence on the municipal structures. Because of the will to rationalize the operation of local entities, a 1961 law introduced the possibility of mergers. In order to accelerate a too slow process, however, the 30th of December 1975 law dictated a merger plan, and in 1977, on January 1st, the number of municipalities decreased from 2359 to 596, this number being further reduced in 1983 to 589. Finally, we should add that the status of Belgian municipalities is also governed by other stipulations of the Constitution (new articles 39, 160, 162, 168 and 171), the law of July 8th, 1976 organizing the "Centres Publics d'aide sociale – Openbaar Centrum voor Maatschappelijk Welzijn" and the municipal electoral law.

The institutional structure surrounding the municipalities also changed with the times: notably the process of European integration, and, even more importantly, the process of state reform. This process, which began in 1970, gradually transformed the unitary Belgium of the 19th century into a federal system, based on the existence of regions (Vlaanderen, Wallonie and Brussels-capital) and unilingual communities (Vlaamse Gemeenschap, Communauté française and Deutschsprachige Gemeinschaft). In Flanders, the institutions of region and community were subsequently merged. These subnational governments gradually expanded their authorities: the regions in the sphere of territory-related issues (e.g. infrastructure and economics), and the common language communities in the sphere of person-related issues (e.g. culture, education and health-care). In their sphere of authorities, they also have responsibilities in relation to the municipalities. The fact that the regions are responsible for the tutelage and general grants of the municipalities and that the communities subsidize municipal schools are just a few examples of the amplitude of their authorities.

As already indicated, Belgian municipalities have authority with regard to everything that falls under "municipal interest". Consequently, their potential range of power is rather wide. However, this power must be exercised respecting the rules of the superior authorities (provinces, communities and regions, federal state and sometimes the European bodies) which have (within some limits) the right to keep the municipal decisions under their supervision.

Moreover, we should point out the existence of regulated authority, where municipalities have the right to decide if they are performing a certain function, but once this is decided on, centrally fixed rules must be followed. At co-government level, municipalities are strictly obliged to perform certain duties in a certain way on behalf of the central government. An example would be the issuing of passports.

An important difference between the situation of the Belgian CEO and those of other European countries surely lies in his obligation to work within and with those ever changing, hypertrophied and sometimes disjointed, multiple administrative, legal and political structures.

The Municipal Framework Around the CEO

The politico-administrative structures of Belgian municipalities consist of two types of personnel: the local political representatives and the civil servants.

- Politically, municipalities are ruled by decision-making bodies which are changed democratically every six years. Municipal councillors are elected and appoint aldermen (*échevins/schepenen/Beigeordneter*) amongst themselves. These aldermen are selected among members of the political majority: there is no legal requirement (nor practice) to choose aldermen among the political opposition. The size of the Council (councillors and mayor) and the "College" (mayor and aldermen) depends on the number of inhabitants in the municipality. The mayor is not elected but appointed by the King, who theoretically can choose any inhabitant of the municipality. In practice, however, the mayor is a member of the Council and appointed by a majority of the councillors. The "College" exercises in a collegial way the executive power of the municipal authorities.

- Most municipal staff are under the authority of the municipal secretary. There are two exceptions to this. The first is the police superintendent, who is responsible for the local police department. The police superintendent, his deputies and all the policemen receive their orders directly from the mayor with regard to problems of administrative, but not judiciary, police work. The second exception is the municipal "treasurer" who is independent and personally and financially responsible for the validity of municipal revenues and expenses.

There is and always has been considerable variation in the actual organisation of local services. As municipal resources differ, services such as local schools, hospitals, fire brigades and sports facilities or tourist infrastructure are obviously not equally developed everywhere. The Constitution and the law of March 1st, 1922 granted the general rules which made it possible for the municipalities to cooperate in matters of common interest.[2] Practically, such "intercommunales" were created in the medical, social, environmental, energy fields and in regard to regional development.

In each municipality a special body, the "Centre Public d'Aide Sociale – Openbaar Centrum voor Maatschappelijk Welzijn," is responsible for assistance to persons who need economic, social, psychological or medical assistance. This body, created by law in July 1976, is not part of the municipal framework, but closely linked to the municipality, as the latter is financially responsible for it.

---

2 Replaced by the law of December 22nd, 1986. Since the constitutional reform of May 5th, 1993, the regulations on intermunicipal co-operation can be made by regional decree. The regions have authority over the organisation and supervision of intermunicipal co-operation.

On January 1st, 1995, Belgian municipalities had 221,203 employees, 119,406 employed directly by the municipality, 79,406 by the social assistance councils and 22,391 by the various intercommunales (Ministerie van Ambtenarenzaken, *overzicht van de personeelssterkte in de overheidssector,* p.10).

The Belgian CEO: Formal Role
The municipal secretary is the director of the municipal services. He is the obligatory and sole intermediary between local political authorities and the administration which has to implement the decisions of the former. Originally, he was merely described as a kind of official clerk of the local administration. As his functions were only very briefly described in the 1836 law, the major part of them depended on his own initiative and the relationship with the political authorities of the municipality. Consequently, during more than a century, in some municipalities the municipal secretary decided nearly everything because the mayor was only a figurehead without any real knowledge about the legislation.

The October 17th, 1990 law is somewhat more explicit concerning his responsibilities.[3] First, the secretary is responsible for the preparation of matters submitted to the council and the College. He must be present at their meetings, keep the minutes and countersign all municipal acts, rules and mail. Second, under the authority of the College, he manages and co-ordinates municipal services. Nevertheless, the secretary is not allowed to define the fundamental goals of the municipal organisation. The secretary only has to make decisions intended to ensure the efficacy and efficiency of the administrative services. Being a civil servant, the municipal secretary has never had any formal decision powers, nor does he have the right to vote during meetings of the Council or the College. His formal advisory powers are also limited.[4] Hence, even if the decisions of the political authorities are ill-timed, illogical, illegal or contrary to the interest of the inhabitants of the municipality, he must implement them. In practice, however, the municipal secretary often acts as a neutral "legal and technical advisor" and can therefore influence the decisions.

The obligations of the municipal secretary are the following: fidelity with regard to the transcription of decisions, duties of loyalty, reservation, obedience, zeal, professional secrecy, discretion, honesty, neutrality and denunciation of any penal offence.

He is responsible for the assessment of the discipline of the municipal staff. In Flanders, where all staff is evaluated from a Human Resources Management

---

3 The articles organizing the activities of the municipal secretary are the following: Art. 25, 26, 26bis, 28 to 35, 42 to 51, 78, 79, 92,108, 109, 111, 281 to 287.
4 The municipal secretary is a member of a committee in the municipality which gives advice on the legality and effects of the budget plans. Moreover, the municipal council can decide on a regulation which obliges the secretary to give council members, who ask for it, technical information about elements of dossiers in preparation.

viewpoint, he also plays an important role in this evaluation. In this case, the secretary himself is evaluated by the College, just as the treasurer.

Being a civil servant, the secretary has no political responsibility. He has to act according to the instructions of the Municipal Council, the College or the mayor. Moreover, the fact that he may stay in office while political coalitions within the Council (and thus also within the College) change, obliges him to be politically neutral in order to remain efficient. As the CEO has important administrative, civil and penal responsibilities and has to protect the public interest, he cannot conduct commercial activity besides his job, even by means of someone else. His remuneration depends on the size of the population of his municipality. The municipal secretary can be subject to disciplinary sanctions by the Municipal Council, which can suspend him for up to three months, or, in case of a very serious malpractice, decide to fire him.

From a practical point of view, the responsibilities of the secretary have been radically modified by the 1977 merger of the municipalities which has instrumentalised and rationalised the municipal activities. The profile of the CEO also changed because the increasing complexity of local administrative work has forced municipalities to recruit more people with an academic bacground and a knowledge of legal aspects, administrative actors, structures and processes.

The Professional Career of the Municipal Secretary

As indicated in the first paragraph, the municipal secretary has a variety of duties, which requiring a wide range of skills. Here, we will focus on the educational, social and economic background of this professional category.

Recruitment: Formal Requirements
There are two different ways in which a person can become municipal secretary: direct recruitment and promotion. In both cases, the municipal council decides on the conditions which have to be fulfilled by the candidate, but in making these decisions a number of legal stipulations have to be followed (Royal Decree of 20/07/1976, Belgisch Staatsblad 10/08/1976). The secretary must be at least 21 years old at the time of recruitment, of Belgian nationality, been in military service, and in good health and of good moral conduct. In addition, there are several training requirements which differ according to the size of the municipality and whether or not it is a case of promotion or direct recruitment.

- direct recruitment

In municipalities with fewer than 10,000 inhabitants, candidates for the "recruitment exam" must have at least a higher secondary school education and a certificate of a completed study cycle in administrative sciences. In municipalities having above 10,000 inhabitants, a university or equivalent degree and a completed training in administrative sciences are needed. The requirement of the administrative science course is waived for candidates with a university degree, which includes at least 60 hours of lessons in public, administrative or civil law.

• promotion

In case of internal promotion, the candidate must have at least the rank of office manager (bureauchef/chef de bureau), if there are two or more candidates in the municipality with this rank. On top of this, the council can decide on extra requirements, such as a minimum number of years in service.

In some municipalities, however, the council can freely decide which rank the candidates must have. Here candidates must pass an exam, (except if they have already passed an exam for a rank equal to or higher than office manager), and they must have training in administrative science, except if they have a university degree with this component.

When these regulations came into existence, all the secretaries in function were exempt from these rules. This explains why it still is possible to find secretaries who do not fulfil all the requirements.

Recruitment: the Data
Recruitment as CEO without previous professional experience is relatively rare: only 5.0% of all secretaries have been directly recruited as municipal secretary. Most of the CEOs surveyed have a public sector background, roughly 47% as civil servant in a municipality and another 25% in other public employment. Recruitment from the private sector is also rather limited: only 16% of the secretaries previously worked in the private sector. These figures indicate that municipal administration remains a fairly closed system, with limited external recruitment.

Most secretaries begin their career quite young: the average recruitment age is 34 years. The average age is 46 years, which means that the "average" secretary already has 12 years in service. This should not distract us from the fact that nearly one-third of all secretaries have been in office for five years or less.

The job mostly attracts men: only 13% of all municipal secretaries are women. Presently, however, there is an increasing feminization. Indeed, while all CEOs who have been more than 30 years in service are men, this is reduced to 76% for those with less than 5 years in service.

Education and Further Training
On average, a Belgian municipal secretary has had 16 years of full-time training, secondary school included. Currently, more then half the secretaries have a University degree, typically in political science, law or economics. This training is often supplemented by complementary administrative education, e.g. courses organized by provinces or by the federation of municipal secretaries (KFGB, Koninklijke federatie der gemeentesecretarissen van België/Union Royale des

secrétaires communaux de Belgique). Yet there are impressive differences in training among the regions: in Wallonia only 36% of all secretaries have a university degree, compared to 60% for Brussels and 62% for Flanders (in 1985 the average figure was 38% (Hondeghem A. & Robbroeckx M.: 1986: 38). This can be explained by the fact that the average Flemish and Brussels municipality has more inhabitants than the average Walloon municipality. In Wallonia there is a stronger correlation between the size of the municipality, and the fact that the secretary has a university degree. If we examine only those Walloon municipalities having more than 15,000 inhabitants, we find that 64.6% of the Walloon municipal secretaries studied at university, which is far closer to the 72% in Flanders and the 60% in Brussels. A university degree is clearly becoming more typical in this function and gradually replacing the complementary administrative education: indeed, while for all the secretaries this administrative education accounts for 46.5%, this is reduced to 22% for those secretaries below age 35. In this category, the number of people with a university degree is significantly above average (88% versus 52%).

Social Characteristics
The social background of the municipal secretaries varies widely, though middle-class seems to be predominant: more than 40% of the secretaries have a middle-class background, e.g. with the family head occupying functions as employee or self-employed.

With the exception of the mid-70s, when the amalgamation of municipalities was implemented, the job of a municipal secretary is and has been a very stable one. Not only do 71% of the municipal secretaries not search for another post, their predecessors too, only very rarely left their post for another function: 91% of all secretaries in the survey indicated that their predecessor left because of natural reasons (retirement, illness, death). There is a very low turnover, which of course increases stability at the top of the municipal administration.

These figures, however, may be influenced by the fact that in the late 1970s some people "fell ill" or decided to quit (age limit is 65, though one may retire at 60) on learning that they would lose their position as chief executive upon the amalgamation of their municipality with a neighbouring community. This amalgamation had an important influence on the municipalities, and can be considered to be a major step on the way to professionalization of the sector.

As indicated above, the CEOs have a varying and demanding job. In this sense, we can understand the long working hours of the municipal secretaries. On average, a local level CEO works 49 hours a week. Generally, however, the larger the municipality, the more hours the CEO works, and the more seniority he has, the less he works.

The CEOs do not perceive the attractiveness of being secretary to have changed over time. The CEO job is considered only slightly more attractive than 10 years before. As major advantages of the function respondents cite variation in the daily work, the authority of the CEO, and the transition to modern management. Yet the role as CEO also has disadvantages. Most quoted are the long working hours, the legal changes and to a lesser degree the co-operation with politicians. This, of course, can result in stress. Being a secretary in the municipality is indeed a stressful function. In our survey, nearly 40% of all secretaries reported that they were often or always stressed in their job.

Values and Roles

Towards a Typology of Secretaries

As indicated in the first paragraph, Belgian municipal secretaries operate in a structure with a high degree of formalism and hierarchy. In this sense, it should not surprise us if a high number of "classical bureaucrats" could be found. We consider as a classical bureaucrat someone who emphasizes the importance of guiding subordinates in their day-to-day work, managing economic affairs, ensuring that rules are followed and giving the mayor technical advice, in other words, a person oriented towards the internal affairs of his organization and who takes his working environment completely for granted.

Being a classical bureaucrat seems to be inversely linked with the degree of education. In general, the longer the secretary received full-time education, the less he/she scores on the elements which make up the "classical bureaucracy indicator".

For the "political bureaucrat", however, the position does not seem to be associated with any specific pattern of education. We consider characteristic features of this type of secretary to be someone who attaches importance to formulating ideas and visions, promoting and encouraging new projects, giving political advice to the mayor, being informed about the viewpoints of citizens, developing norms concerning proper roles of politicians vis-à-vis the bureaucrats, and influencing the decision-making processes in order to ensure effective and efficient solutions. In other words, the political bureaucrat is more externally oriented.

The classical bureaucrat scores 62 and the political bureaucrat 58 (the range being from 0 – none of the indicators are important to 100 – all indicators are of utmost importance). Hence, the classical bureaucrat is still predominant. However, one has to take into account that within these groups, considerable variation exists between the different variables. Indeed, if we consider the role of classical bureaucrat, we see that the highest score is on the variable "give the mayor legal, economic and technical advice". This might actually create a distortion in the sense that according to legal stipulation this is one of the tasks of the secretary: the secretary prepares the meetings (Art. 26 New Municipal Law of 30/04/1989, *Belgisch staatsblad* 30/05/1989).

Table 11.1 The roles of the CEOs, Belgium

The classical bureaucrat		62
Guide subordinate staff in day-to-day handling of activities	55	
Manage economic affairs, accounts and budgetary control	56	
Ensure that rules and regulations are followed	63	
Provide the mayor with legal, economic and other kinds of technical advice	73	
The political bureaucrat		58
Formulate ideas and visions	68	
Promote and encourage new projects in the community	61	
Provide the mayor with political advice	27	
Be informed about citizens' viewpoints	58	
Develop and implement norms concerning the proper roles of politicians vis-á-vis the bureaucrats	62	
Influence decision-making processes in order to secure sensible and efficient solutions	70	

Using the survey data, we ranked the tasks according to what the secretaries considered most important. As most important tasks, the following were cited: 1) stimulating co-operation among departments, 2) giving the mayor technical, economic and legal advice 3) ensuring the efficient use of available assets 4) influencing the decision-making process in order to ensure rational and efficient decision-making processes, and 5) formulating ideas and visions.

Of course, not every aspect of their tasks is perceived as important: generally, secretaries consider as most important the duty of working efficiently and observing the established rules and procedures. Ensuring that everyone involved is satisfied is not considered very important.

In sum, we could say that the secretary considers his/her main mission to be that of manager of the municipal machinery.

The Secretary and Change
Generally, the secretaries perceive the private sector to be more efficient than the public sector. While the regions do not differ on this, the need for change is perceived differently. Flemish and Brussels secretaries are far more change-minded then their Walloon counterparts. This can be explained by the fact that especially those CEOs with a university degree – more present in Flanders and Brussels

– to a larger extent report that their organization has become less centralized and that a lot still has to change.

Both Flemish and Walloon secretaries strongly disagree with their Brussels counterparts that the small municipalities are too inefficient and should be amalgamated into larger units. This can be explained by the fact that there is a strong correlation between the size of a municipality and the perception of inefficiency of smaller municipalities: secretaries of small municipalities strongly deny that their municipalities are inefficient.

On managing the reform in their organisation, it is striking how much attention is devoted to the opinions of the civil servants involved. Indeed, on a scale of 0-100, the employee involvement is rated 76. Management of change is perceived as a delicate process. They therefore consider it necessary to prepare the change together with a limited number of civil servants, and to proceed rather slowly and stepwise. This slow process might be explained by the way in which the secretaries hope to obtain their goals: they prefer to operate through motivation and personal relations instead of using formal power.

Outsiders are mistrusted. Both the involvement of the trade unions (score 25) and the necessity of a consensus among politicians (score 53) are on the low side. Here it should be noted that the so-called classical bureaucrat and the political bureaucrat hardly differ. The inspiration for the daily activities is found mainly within the their own professional group. Ranked after "own training", most inspiration is obtained from executives of other municipalities (score 71), from the local government association (64) and the federation of municipal secretaries (61). While the private sector is often considered to be more efficient, their managers and consultants are considered to be less inspiring, scoring 33 and 40. Yet the private sector manager is mentioned more as a source of inspiration in the large municipalities. Differences among regions are hardly noticeable in these variables. However, the local government association as a source of inspiration is valued higher in Wallonia. This may again be due to the background variable "size of the municipality".

Within the municipality, a number of changes have occurred: there has been a delegation to the lower hierarchical levels, and a delegation from the political to the bureaucratic level. This delegation to the lower levels makes the position of the heads of departments more important.

The Municipal Secretaries: Their Networks and Influence

As stipulated in their function profile, the CEOs have to work closely with the politicians, especially the College of mayor and aldermen, and direct their staff in their activities. A number of his contacts, therefore, can be considered as "institutional", while other contacts essentially depend on the way the secretary fulfils his duty. The next figure summarises the frequency, the quality, and the dependency of the municipal secretary in his relations with other actors.

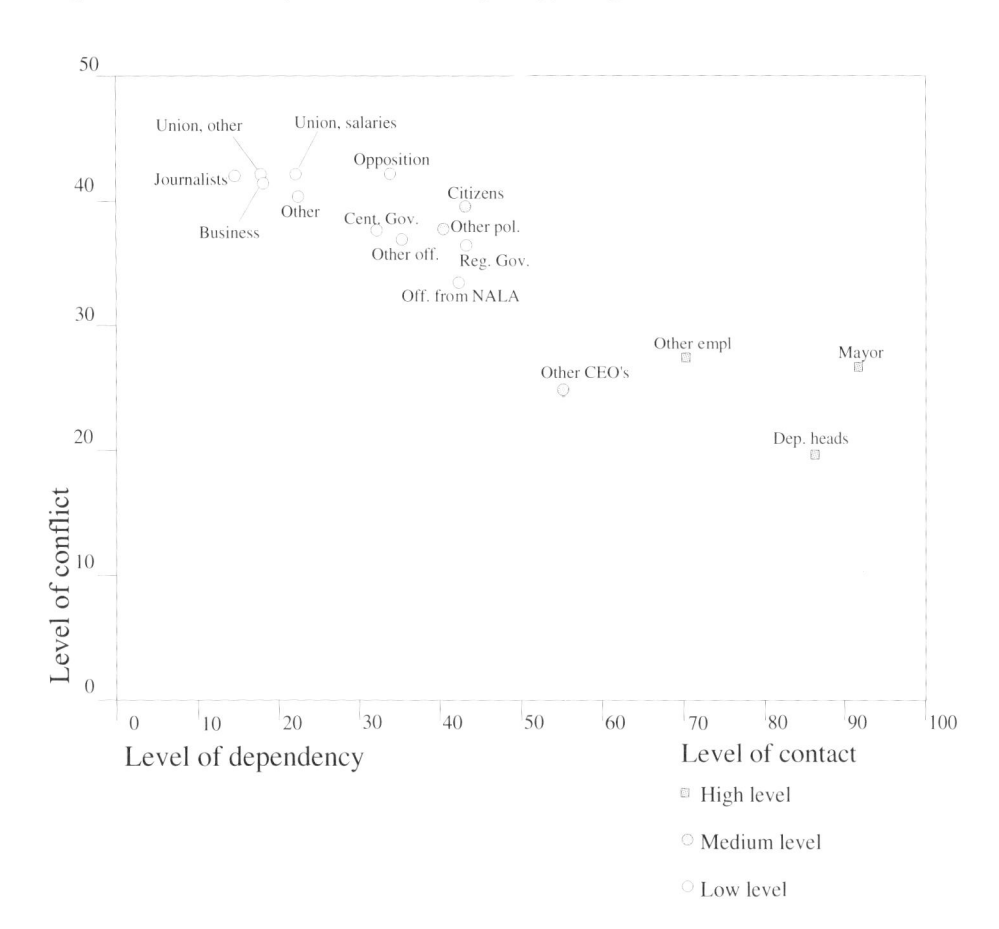

Figure 11.1 Contact, conflict and depency, Belgium

Chart: Level of conflict (y-axis) vs Level of dependency / Level of contact (x-axis). Points include: Union other, Union salaries, Opposition, Journalists, Other, Cent. Gov., Citizens, Business, Other off., Other pol., Reg. Gov., Off. from NALA, Other CEO's, Other empl, Mayor, Dep. heads. Legend: ▫ High level, ○ Medium level, ○ Low level.

The secretaries mainly contact those people, whom they must formally contact according to their job profile, with one exception: the citizens. Indeed, especially in the small municipalities the secretary quite often meets citizens, mainly while dealing with the more complex administrative procedures personally.

Also striking is the lack of contact between the secretary and union leaders. Indeed, this contact tends to occur only in the large municipalities. In this sense, we note that the typical secretary relates inwardly to the organization, with contacts inside the municipal organization.

Yet this perspective is only partial: the frequency of contact does not tell us anything about the importance of these contacts. If we examine the importance of the network of the CEO, we find (not surprisingly) that the mayor is the main contact, followed closely by the department heads and then "other employees". The "other politicians" are mainly aldermen, who have a functional field of competence, and who formally have no direct access to the administration unless via the secretary. To a certain extent, however, aldermen surpass the municipal secretary, and directly interfere in the administration. This happens in 35% of the municipalities to such an extent that we can talk about an "aldermen model" of municipal organisation instead of the "legal" model as described in the law on the municipalities.

The increased role of aldermen is linked to the size of the municipalities. Aldermen in larger municipalities intervene more often then those in the small municipalities, hence, this phenomenon is more noticeable in Flanders than in Wallonia. Also the importance of contacts with the press, unions and business interests is higher in the large municipalities.

It is clear that the importance of contacts is also different in a large town than in a small village, e.g. the role of the heads of service will be completely different.

The local power of the CEO, of course, is also dependent on the degree of conflicts between the municipal secretary and the other actors. Generally speaking, the relation between the secretary and the other actors is considered to be good. Most secretaries co-operate very well with the mayor and the head of departments. Yet the relation to the political opposition and some other politicians – again mainly aldermen – seems to be more conflictual. The relation to the opposition is complicated because political nominations remain a frequent phenomenon, and the secretary may be *perceived* as "belonging to the majority". The fact that the secretary is rarely removed from his position makes it even more complicated.

The Secretary and Politics
As indicated in the first part of the chapter, the formal position of the municipal secretary is that of a neutral, technically well-informed civil servant, who must obey the rules and guidelines (if legal) given by the political level. In this sense, the way in which politicians behave is important for the functioning of the municipal secretary.

The next table describes the role of politicians as perceived by secretaries. The secretaries respect the role of the political level, but want the political level to respect their role as "manager" of the administration as well. This helps us to understand the other elements of table 11.2 The CEO hardly accepts any influence by the politicians in the internal operation of the administration, such as routines or decisions on pending issues. In general, secretaries would prefer the politician to be a strategist, who provides a stable environment in which the administration, headed by the secretary, can work towards clear and unambiguous goals.

Secretaries do not approve of "political games" which may endanger the operation/efficiency of the administration. This is also seen by the low importance they attach to the roles of the politicians as "being spokesperson for their political party", or even "implementing the (political) program on which the politician has been elected".

Table 11.2 The ideal politician, Belgium

Administration		45
Be a spokesperson for local groups or individuals who have issues pending decision by the authority	46	
Lay down rules and routines for the administration	32	
Taking decisions concerning specific cases	58	
Representation		58
Be informed about citizens' views	73	
Represent the municipality to the outside world	59	
Defend the authorities' decisions and policies externally	74	
Be a spokesperson for their political party	35	
Be a spokesperson vis-á-vis the press	47	
Governance		70
Implement the program on which he/she has been elected	54	
Decide on major policy principles	76	
Have a vision of the way in which the municipality will develop in the long run	80	
Stability		74
Create stability for the administration	72	
Formulate exact and unambiguous goals for the administration	76	

Challenges to the Secretary at the End of the 20th Century

As described above, present day municipal secretaries clearly have evolved from being clerks to a more managerial role. Yet at times their formal position makes it hard for them "to manage". The actual situation then depends on the personality of the CEO. There are a number of other challenges. The environment in which they work has changed considerably and will probably undergo further changes in the near future. Here we are thinking especially of the reform of the state structure with its increasing devolution of authority to the regions and municipalities. This will involve a change in importance of contacts, and perhaps in different procedures and rules being applied in the different regions. At this stage, secretaries cite this flood of legislation as one of the most important, though rather negative, aspect of their situation.

The duties of the secretary also increase in scope. In Flanders, for instance, they are responsible for the evaluation of staff. Yet this might create tensions, as hiring and firing of staff remains the responsibility of the political level.

In the near future, we will probably come to a further professionalisation of the municipalities, with a generalist secretary and more specialist department heads. In the long run, this might shift the line of conflict from secretary versus politicians to secretary versus departmental heads.

Conclusion

The role of the municipal secretary has clearly been transformed. There is a professionalisation of the function, with an increasing share of university-educated secretaries. This process is particularly noticeable in the large municipalities. This "new" secretary is more change-minded compared to his colleagues and can hardly be called a classical-bureaucrat. CEOs consider themselves the sole "experts" of municipal administration, whose main focus is to ensure the efficient and legal operation of the municipal administration. If necessary, their ideas can be in opposition to those of the political level, from which they prefer to receive a set of general guidelines about goals, with the implementation left to themselves. In the end, however, they remain loyal to the political level, which has the final word.

Bibliography

Ackaert, J.(1994): *De gemeenten, Wegwijs Politiek*, Leuven: Davidfonds.

Coenen, A.(1994): *Quelques considérations sur le rôle et la responsabilité du secrétaire communal (première partie)*, Brussels: Mouvement Communal, Union des Villes et Communes Belges.

Coenen, A. (1994): *Quelques considérations sur le rôle et la responsabilité du secrétaire communal (deuxième partie)*, Brussels: Mouvement Communal, Union des Villes et Communes Belges.

Collinge, M. (1994): *La commune*, Brussels: Dossiers du CRISP, No. 042, CRISP.

Delperée, F. (1994): *Le nouveau secrétaire communal*, Brussels: Crédit Communal de Belgique.

Depré, R., and Frederickx, R. (1990): De gemeentesecretaris en het management, *Tijdschrift van het Gemeentekrediet*, 4,1990.

Dujardin, J., Somers, W. et al.: (1995): *Praktisch Handboek gemeenterecht*, Brugge: Die Keure.

Dujardin, J., and Vande Lanotte, J. (1994): *De nieuwe gemeentelijke comptabiliteit, wetgeving*. 3de uitgave, Brugge: Die Keure.

Hondeghem, A., and Robbroeckx, M. (1986): *Tewerkstelling van universitairen in de openbare sector*, VLIR-project, synthese van het eerste rapport.

Leboutte J.-M. (1987): Les attributions du secrétaire communal selon la proposition de loi modifiant le titre II, chapitre III, de la loi communale. Bruxelles: Mouvement Communal, Union des Villes et Communes Belges.

Leboutte, J.-M.(1990): *Vers une nouvelle définition légale des missions du secrétaire communal et de celles du receveur communal*. Brussels: Mouvement Communal, Union des Villes et Communes Belges.

Lefebvre, J.-P. (1995): Les secrétaires communaux: véritables boss? – Manager c'est ménager, *Régions et Communes*, Alleur.

Ministerie van Ambtenarenzaken (1995): *Overzicht van de personeelssterkte in de overheidssector*, Brussels: Ministerie van Ambtenarenzaken,

Union des Villes et Communes Belges (1996): Evaluation des fonctionnaires dans le cadre de la RGB (Révision générale des barèmes), *Trait d'Union – La Lettre d'information de l'UVCB*, Brussels.

Ysebaert, Cl. (1995): *Mémento communal 1995-1996*, Brussels: Kluwer Editorial.

CHAPTER 12

The Asymmetric Interdependence between two Powerful Actors: The CEO and the Mayor in French Cities

by Jean-Claude Thoenig and Katherine Burlen

In 1995, France had 36,763 municipalities, by far the largest number within the European Union. France has two more territorial levels above the municipality: the region (21) and the "département" (96).

Such a high density of democratic local authorities may come as a surprise in a nation-state such as France, which conventional wisdom qualifies as being an archetype of political and administrative centralization. Municipalities date their origin back to the century. Public opinion polls suggest repeatedly how closely the population identifies itself with them. On municipal elections day, more than 60% of the registered citizens vote. Municipalities are democracy in everyday life. Their number has not changed significantly. In the last two centuries, their total number has never been reduced by an authoritarian decision of the national authorities, moreover, in France a majority of members of the national parliament simultaneously hold elected local offices as mayors or presidents of regional councils.

All municipalities follow the same pattern, politically and administratively, whether they are a metropolis or a village. Their institutional isomorphism is therefore linked to a high degree of demographic, economic and geographic heterogeneity. Twenty-nine per cent of them have less than 200 inhabitants. Another 29% have from 200 to 499 inhabitants. Only 4.7% have 5,000 inhabitants and more. These cities also include 55% of the total population (Ministère de l'Intérieur 1996).

Since the beginning of the mid 1970s, France has experienced a spectacular revival of local government. The "département", once considered as a rural and sleeping institution, found new blood, resources and policy niches. New institutions such as the region gradually emerged. The municipalities themselves developed new energy and invested in housing, zoning, culture, sports, economic development or social welfare (Lorrain, 1989). This was particularly the case in cities facing massive urbanization. Smaller size municipalities were also active, except in a few very depressed areas. The decentralization policy which took effect between 1981 and 1985 accelerated and legitimized such processes. The government transferred several tasks, as well as introducing block grants and allowing local authorities to make decisions without the need for *a priori* authorization from the prefects and the national ministries (Thoenig 1992).

Today the management of subnational public affairs may be compared to a kind of free market. Municipalities, regions, "départements" as well as the ministries of the central State take initiatives and find policy niches allowing them to intervene. In many cases, joint investment ventures are launched. A sophisticated web of *ad hoc* institutions has been set up, such as "syndicats intercommunaux" or "districts" which allow horizontal cooperation in order to manage tasks, such as refuse collection or economic development. Such cooperation enables the municipalities to utilize economies of scale while avoiding political, administrative and territorial mergers. Even today, and despite tougher financial conditions, the municipalities find room for expansion: while the government faces much tougher budgetary contraints, their fiscal revenues continue to grow.

The study of French municipal CEOs focuses upon municipalities of 5,000 inhabitants or more. It excludes the small municipalities such as villages, where a full-time CEO is rarely employed.

The CEO and the Municipal Political-Administrative System

Formally speaking, a municipality is run by a collegial body: the "Conseil municipal". Every six years, the citizens elect its members. During a two-round ballot, they have to choose between several lists of candidates. One list usually wins an overall majority of the seats. Therefore, partisan coalition building is favored.

The municipal council draws up the budget, makes all the decisions about the portfolio of city affairs and appoints its executive branch. In theory, decisions are the outcome of the aggregation of a majority of individual preferences expressed by council members. A mayor is selected among the members of the majority list as well as several "maires adjoints". The mayor chairs the council and, with the help of the "maires adjoints", supervises the implementation of the council decisions. In cities, this is a full-time paid position.

Figure 12.1 The Institutional Logic of Municipal Affairs

MUNICIPAL COUNCIL --> MUNICIPAL POLICIES

De facto, such a parliamentarian design does not exist. Evidence shows again and again that municipal governance is extremely centralized, effectively in the hands of one person: the mayor. It is around this role that the political-administrative system is structured. On election day, local citizens may select from a list of candidates according to their political orientation, but they also vote for a potential mayor. To a very large extent, it is the candidate for mayorship, whether incumbent or new, who composes a list, forming a coalition with members of various parties and of individuals belonging to various local socio-economic groups. Therefore the "party of the mayor" is as strong as the local national party units. Municipal council members obtain their legitimacy from the visibility of the mayor (Thoenig 1995).

The mayor acts as the main, if not the unique integrator, between various spheres involved in the handling of municipal affairs. In a major way, he governs the majority of the elected council: he sets up the policy agenda, acts as the common denominator between the various interests, allocates more or less – rather less – autonomy to the "maires adjoints". The mayor is the main interface between the council and the municipal bureaucracy: he selects the CEO and the main officers of the administration who will implement the decisions, he controls the feasibility and the opportunity to launch programmes, supervises everyday life and work of the employees, and he knows how to render the various political discussions. He also exerts a rather hegemonious control over the relationship with users and local population. Not only does he appear as the charismatic figure in public, he is also very open to requests coming from citizens or local associations, whom he treats in an individual service manner, acting as problem solver in the municipality. Finally, the mayor maintains a monopoly over external affairs: whenever business requires some help from extramunicipal operators or institutions – such as getting a grant from the government or cooperating with other public authorities – he does it by himself, thus avoiding interference from other members of his coalition and building a network of access to external resources.

Figure 12.2 The Centralization of the Municipal System

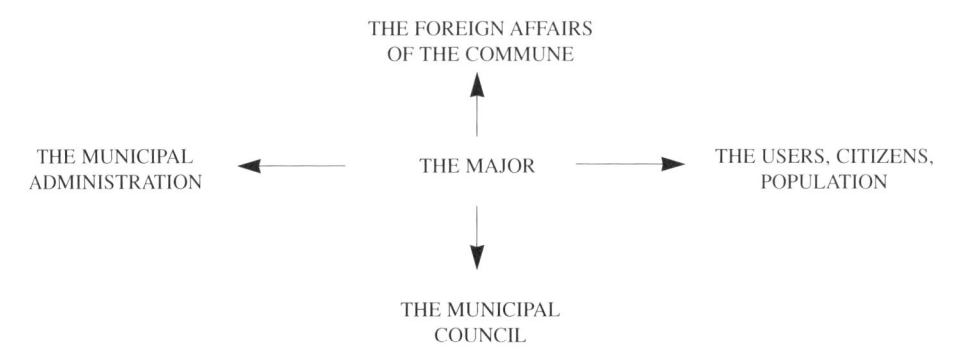

```
                    THE FOREIGN AFFAIRS
                      OF THE COMMUNE
                            ▲
                            │
  THE MUNICIPAL      ◄───  THE MAJOR  ───►   THE USERS, CITIZENS,
  ADMINISTRATION                                  POPULATION
                            │
                            ▼
                      THE MUNICIPAL
                         COUNCIL
```

The role of the mayor is crucial. Such a centralization strategy provides massive power and visibility. It also correlates with long political tenures. Our survey shows that 33% of the mayors are in at least their third consecutive mandate of six years. On top of that, mayors can also fill other elected positions such as members of the national parliament or the regional and "département" councils. In order to perform effectively, a mayor has to rely heavily on somebody who does not belong to the sphere of political competition and whom he can control: this is why the role of CEO is so important in French cities. The CEO is not only an administrative professional; he allows the mayor to be absent from his city or to be preoccupied with various matters while controlling the interface between the political sphere and the administrative sphere of the system.

The CEO is called "secrétaire générale". He can be recruited and fired at the mayor's will. Such a status is rather unique. National laws provide the employes of municipalities with a bureaucratic status which secures them life tenure, protected conditions of remuneration, impersonal selection and promotion procedures based upon merit and seniority, etc. This is not the case with "secrétaires généraux" unless they belong to a "corps" of national or territorial public servants to which they might return in case of disgrace.

Municipalities employ around 900,000 public employees. The size of their personnel has increased at an average annual rate of 1.5% over the last 14 years. Another sign of the active job market they provide is the spectacular increase in the education level and professional diversity of the middle and upper levels of their administrative hierarchies. New experts have been added, from librarians to physicians, from economists to managers of cultural activities. Such an upgrading means that fewer "secrétaires généraux", as well as the second or even third level of managers, started their career at the bottom and climbed the ladder up through seniority and loyalty. Today a university diploma is the average background.

Figure 12.3 The Administrative Hierarchy

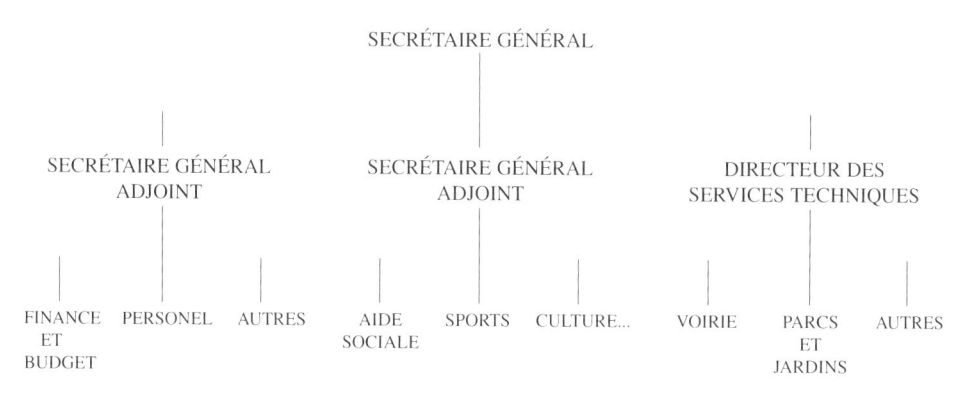

```
                           SECRÉTAIRE GÉNÉRAL
                                   |
        _____|_____
        |                          |                          |
  SECRÉTAIRE GÉNÉRAL        SECRÉTAIRE GÉNÉRAL         DIRECTEUR DES
       ADJOINT                   ADJOINT            SERVICES TECHNIQUES
        |                          |                          |
   _____|_____             _____|_____            _____|_____
   |    |    |             |       |       |            |    |    |
FINANCE PERSONEL AUTRES   AIDE   SPORTS  CULTURE...   VOIRIE PARCS AUTRES
  ET                     SOCIALE                              ET
BUDGET                                                      JARDINS
```

The CEO runs the municipal services. In most cases he or she occupies the top of a rather complex and diversified pyramid which includes dozens of different departments and functions. Control over the finance and budgetary matters, as well as personnel policy are key resources enabling him to integrate an administrative apparatus which can vary from a few dozen to a few thousand employees. The total number of employees varies with the size of the population of the municipality. But the CEO has power and prestige because he is the main channel of communication between the municipal administration and the mayor. He knows how to translate the political wishes of his boss into bureaucratic achievements. He also knows how to decode the political implications of administrative requirements. The larger the municipality, the higher the prestige and the more generous the benefits linked to the position of CEO.

Profiles of CEOs

The "secrétaires généraux" are overwelmingly male. The larger the size of a city, the smaller the presence of women. In our sample of municipalities between 5,000 and 20,000 inhabitants, 18% are women. In cities of 20,000 inhabitants or more only 5% of the CEOs are female. The recruitment of women is also a recent trend, originating in the late 1980s.

The CEOs' family socio-economic backgrounds are diversified. For instance, 10% of the CEOs' fathers were farmers, 14% shopkeepers or independent craftsmen, 10% were born in a family headed by a mid- or higher-level civil servant, 10% had fathers who were rank and file employees in the public sector, 13% had fathers who were skilled workers, etc.

The CEOs' educational background is high. Around 85% had their "baccalauréat", leaving secondary school at the age of 17 to 18 years. Most of them (81%) went to university or an equivalent institution and received a degree. Law degrees are the most common (48% of all CEOs), followed by economics (15%) and political science (9%).

In starting their professional life, most current "secrétaires généraux" began in the public sector. Over 70% had their first job experience in administrative sectors. More than half of the CEOs (56%) started in municipalities, while 14% began in a government agency. By comparison, 17% took their first job in a private firm. One out of five CEOs (19%) started his or her career in the same municipality where they now work as "secrétaire général". Such data suggest a trend toward a progressive widening of the work experience. Socialization into the municipal sector remains strong, but the younger the age of the CEO, the more mobile he has been.

An average "secrétaire général" is 45 years old. Only 7% are 56 years and above. A few are rather young: 5% are below 37 years of age. No relevant age differences exist between men and women.

In our survey, which took place a few months after municipal elections, 16%

of the "secrétaires généraux" had been in office less than 2 years. At the same time, 20% had served 14 years or more. This reflects the importance of electoral cycles. The appointment of a new CEO occurs for basically two reasons: (1) a CEO may have left the position because of retirement or appointment to another job outside the municipality, (2) a new mayor takes office after municipal elections and wants to appoint his own man. Our sample, for instance, shows that 45% of the CEOs have a length of seniority between 2 and 7 years and that 19% have held their positions between 8 to 13 years. Basically, it means that a CEO has filled a position during one, two, three or more political mandates of a municipal council. Under ordinary circumstances, this reveals how much the fate of the CEO is linked to the fate of the mayor, unless a newly elected mayor agrees to work with the already sitting CEO.

The survey sheds light on why CEOs leave their position. Asked why their predecessor left, the current CEOs cite age as the most frequent cause (41%), followed by problems of cooperation with politicians (29%) and advancement to higher or better position as the third (28%).

CEOs face a problem whenever they consider moving to another city: partisan labelling. While they may not be registered as members of a political party, they may still be identified by a prospective employer via the political affiliation of their former employer. It is exceptional for a CEO who has worked for a socialist mayor to obtain a position in a city where the mayor belongs to the center right, or vice versa. The fact is that CEOs are aware of the fragility of their present job. Mobility is constrained and path dependent. While 25% of the CEOs do not intend to seek another position, 53% state that they "may" seek another one, and 22% are actively planning to look for a new position. Such contemplation of job change is impressive, especially in so-called bureaucratic structures. Electoral uncertainties and the relatively young age of some CEOs make mobility an integral part of a CEO's career.

The job situation of the CEOs shows a mixture of universalism and localism. Mobility is part of the career track, which makes it possible to leave the municipality. However, various factors also suggest that local roots, loyalty to a specific municipality or mayor and socialization within the municipal sector, still play important roles. While 59% of the CEOs did not spend a part of their childhood in their present region, 41% did.

The size of the city and of the municipal bureaucracy introduces some nuances into the picture. In municipalities with less than 20,000 inhabitants, 47% of the CEOs are 40 years old or less, as compared with 22% in municipalities with more than 20,000 inhabitants. In municipalities with less than 20,000 inhabitants, 48% of the CEOs have a seniority of 6 years or less, compared with 67% in bigger cities. This suggests once more that there is a dual career track. Young CEOs start in small- and medium-sized cities before moving to larger municipalities. On the other hand, a relevant proportion of older CEOs do not seek mobility pro-actively once they have reasons to hope that the longevity of the mayor is confirmed.

Such mobility perspectives are linked to the size of the municipality. The proportion of CEOs who do not intend to seek another position falls from 30% in cities with less than 20,000 inhabitants to 16% in cities having populations above 20,000. The larger the city, the more volatile the picture. On the other hand, localism is more important in small municipalities. In localities with less than 10,000 inhabitants, 53% of the CEOs spent part of their childhood in the region. In localities above 10,000 people, the proportion is only 34%. It is also true that a large proportion of CEOs who are 50 years old and above (52%) were locals, while only 37% of the younger ones spent part of their childhood in the region.

The job of CEO is considered attractive, even more today than it used to be. While 15% of the CEOs think the job is more or less the same as ten years ago, 62% say it is more attractive and only 19% think it is less.

CEOs are amongst the highest paid public servants in France, though they make 10 – 15% less than they could obtain in the private sector. They also may receive some fringe benefits such as the use of a car or even free housing. They take part in the most important social events in their municipality and are closely associated with the major initiatives taken by the mayor. In most cases, their office is closest to the mayor's office within the "hôtel de ville".

In summary, this picture suggests that:

- the job of CEO is highly valued;

- as a group, CEOs are experiencing a rapid transformation: cosmopolitan, better educated and more mobile persons are making their way onto a market once dominated by local, not very mobile individuals who had come up through the ranks (Lorrain 1991);

- all cities are not equal: small cities do not offer exactly the same work environment as large cities.

CEOs work hard, at least much more than the compulsory 39-hour week: the CEOs themselves estimate their workweek to be about 51 hours. A cross-tabulation by the size of the city nevertheless suggests that in cities with fewer than 20,000 inhabitants, 66% of the CEOs work fewer than 51 hours, whereas in municipalities having more than 20,000 this proportion falls to 39%.

Roles and Values of the CEO

French "secrétaires généraux" of cities are embedded in a peculiar institutional environment: they are simultaneously the formal heads of an important bureaucratic machine and the right hand of a political leader. In order to cope with this dual role, they develop strong professional norms, referring to their peers in other municipalities.

Where politics and partisan interests are part of their daily task environment, they maintain some distance from personal involvement in political matters. Seventy-three per cent of the CEOs say that they have never been a member of a political party, 15% had previously been a member of some party while 12% remain members. This suggests the ambiguity of their legitimacy. On one hand, some mayors are careful not to hire CEOs whose personal opinions are antagonistic to their own political views, at least openly. However, being close to a political movement may help them to obtain or keep the job. On the other hand, too much open partisan activity becomes a disadvantage for the "secrétaire général" as well as for his boss: some degree of neutrality is helpful in establishing bureaucratic legitimacy. Only a small minority of CEOs can thus be called political or partisan militants.

To be a professional executive is a dominant characteristic of their behavior as well as their attitudes. Their view of what an ideal job would be highlights the following items: variety and adventure in the job; good working relationship with the superiors, followed by consultation by direct superiors and good cooperation with the work group colleagues. Working closely with politicians is considered to be of moderate to little importance. Such an ideal shows no relevant differences related to age, size of the municipality or seniority in the job. It is widely shared across the cohort of CEOs.

The same picture emerges from the norms they express about the role of the CEO himself and the way he sets priorities. Technical advice comes out as a major priority (81% of the CEOs consider such a task to be of utmost importance or as very important) while political advice to the mayor is clearly not accepted as a priority (only 6% consider political advice by the CEO as very important).

Other priorities include tasks such as efficiency in the use of resources, influencing decision-making processes in order to secure sensible and efficient solutions, ensuring cooperation between units of municipal administrations, formulating ideas and visions, and attracting resources from external sources. Strict bureaucratic control and command by rule-setting are not the CEOs' cup of tea. They care about local development, coordination of politics, management of human resources, motivation of people and communication with the units. The budget and personnel are his major tools (Maurino, Gaveriaux, Le Perff, 1987).

Putnam's distinction between the classical bureaucrat and the political bureaucrat helps us understand the specificity of the role of the "secrétaire général" as internalized by the current role holders. It suggests that a synthesis or compromise is achieved between technical orientation and environmental sensitivity, between administration of impersonal procedures and management of public policies. The French CEO has to find a subtle balance: he is involved in handling bureaus and routines, but he also participates in the policy-making arena of the city. He is a political actor, but he is not, at least in a vast majority of cases, a partisan activist or silent client of the mayor. In fact, he tries to escape the dilemma between bureaucracy and politics, between neutrality and advocacy. The CEO's dream is to be recognized as a competent, professional public manager.

Table 12.1 The roles of the CEOs, France

The classical bureaucrat		52
Guide subordinate staff in day-to-day handling of activities	65	
Manage economic affairs, accounts and budgetary control	67	
Ensure that rules and regulations are followed	69	
Provide the mayor with legal, economic and other kinds of technical advice	77	
The political bureaucrat		59
Formulate ideas and visions	72	
Promote and encourage new projects in the community	71	
Provide the mayor with political advice	23	
Be informed about citizens' viewpoints	59	
Develop and implement norms concerning the proper roles of politicians vis-á-vis the bureaucrats	55	
Influence decision-making processes in order to secure sensible and efficient solutions	75	

The CEO positions himself as facilitating efficiency, effectiveness and the medium term. He acts as a broker between the bureaucracy and the political sphere with a vision of the general interest and standing on neutral ground.

As perceived by the "secrétaires généraux", the municipal scene outside elections is a stable political arena. This is illustrated by the figure of the mayor. None one of the CEOs consider the mayor of their city to be in a weak position. Ten per cent say that he may sometimes be under attack, but he is in control. Ninety per cent say that he is the clear leader: "No discussion about that".

In reality the mayor is perceived as the key political figure. The vast majority of the "secrétaires généraux" feel that in their municipality, their mayor performs a role which does not interfere with their own. The mayor acts primarily as a politician engaged in political decision-making and emphasizes the promotion of his political platform. Bureaucratic matters are not his favorite occupation.

How far is daily life in line with norms and values? When asked what roles the politicians should play, the "secrétaires généraux" emphasize as main characteristics governance, representation and stability, but not administration. This applies mainly to the figure of the mayor who, in France, emerges as the legitimate, main political actor in the municipality (Dion 1984).

Table 12.2 The ideal politician, France

Administration		44
Be a spokesperson for local groups or individuals who have issues pending decision by the authority	47	
Lay down rules and routines for the administration	35	
Taking decisions concerning specific cases	51	
Representation		65
Be informed about citizens' views	83	
Represent the municipality to the outside world	73	
Defend the authorities' decisions and policies externally	76	
Be a spokesperson for their political party	24	
Be a spokesperson vis-á-vis the press	67	
Governance		81
Implement the program on which he/she has been elected	77	
Decide on major policy principles	78	
Have a vision of the way in which the municipality will develop in the long run	88	
Stability		66
Create stability for the administration	55	
Formulate exact and unambiguous goals for the administration	76	

When asked what priorities the leading politicians of the municipality should emphasize in their portfolio of tasks, French CEOs draw up a clear-cut profile. Priorities are above all to have a long-term vision of the municipalities' development, followed by having information about citizens' views, making decisions on major policy principles, formulating precise and unambiguous goals, implementing the program on which they were elected, and procuring resources from higher level government organs. No priority is given to such tasks as being spokesman for their political party or for local interests, laying down rules and routines for administration and making decisions concerning specific cases.

Such data are evidence that the CEOs want to keep the mayor away from the daily functioning of the bureaucratic machine: this is considered their own turf. However, they also want the politicians, *i.e.* the mayor, not just to be an advocate of sectorial interests and a political operator. They want a boss and partner who shares their own concerns, someone who can deal with policy guidelines, be predictable and keep a steady line of conduct while managing the local political arena. To some extent, they expect the mayor to be the municipal statesman.

CEOs show a high degree of respect for the primacy of politicians. Eighty-three per cent strongly or partly agree with the idea that "the CEO should be primarily responsible to the elected politician, secondarily only to the population". Seventy-eight per cent strongly or partly agree with the idea that public agents, such as CEOs, should not express personal judgments about the actions and decisions made by the politicians. They are legitimists. However, this does not mean that they do not have a duty to express their own judgments, values or opinions if they disagree with the wishes and beliefs of politicians. Eighty per cent of the CEOs strongly or partly agree with the fact that their advice to the mayor should be non-partisan and grounded upon expertise, and 73% disagree or strongly disagree with the idea that CEOs should only make proposals which are in line with the will and intentions of the politicians, while 81% of our CEO respondents strongly agree or partly agree with the idea that CEOs and public servants should be the prime movers in adapting the municipality to societal changes, they also acknowledge that it is an advantage if the CEO shares the same political opinions as the mayor.

The CEOs do not reveal a technocratic syndrome. Their ideal is a balanced dialogue between a public servant who behaves like an executive – themselves – and a strong politician who behaves like a statesman – the mayor – the latter protecting the former from political games and the former helping the latter to beat the bureaucracy.

Length of seniority helps increase the autonomy of the CEO: mayors who benefit from a third or fourth electoral mandate allow more freedom of movement to their right arm. The degree of delegation allocated by the politicians to the administration seems not to be jeopardized. Forty-nine per cent of the CEOs perceive an increase in delegation of authority over the last ten years while 14% think that today there is less delegation (37% see no change). This takes place in an organizational context which followed the same trend within the administrative machine itself. Sixty per cent of the CEOs say that the lower levels of the bureaucratic structure have gained from decentralization, while 23% saw more centralization and 13% noticed no change. Some nuances vary according to the size of the city: the larger the municipality, the more politicians have tended to delegate to administrators and the more decentralization has occurred in the bureaucratic machine.

All in all, values and reality overlap considerably. The pivotal role of the mayor explains most of the variance of the role of the CEO. Reality is not too far from ethos. Eighty-four per cent of the "secrétaires généraux" say that their mayor considers them as a full partner, only 16% that this is not the case.

Openness, Networks and Influence

Municipalities deal with multiple environments. The openness and sensitivity of their political and administrative systems are important issues. The question is also who controls the interfaces with the outside world and how.

The networks are illustrated in figure 12.4. Overwhelmingly, the CEOs consider their relationship with their mayor as crucial: 93% rank it as "important to a very high extent" (and 5% as "important to a high extent"). Heads of administrative departments come second (49% and 43% respectively). Farther back are other politicians in the municipality (9% and 39%), other employees (6% and 34%) and citizens (3% and 16%), not to mention other outside groups and other responsible persons.

The more a specific group or individual is perceived as crucial, the more the relationship with that individual is perceived as cooperative. This is the case for the mayor (80% of the CEOs describe their relationship as "very cooperative" and 16% as "cooperative") and for heads of departments (68% and 30%). As far as other groups or individuals are concerned, if no cooperation exists, relationships tend to remain on a neutral basis. If some moderate degree of conflict is experienced, especially with personnel trade unions, relationships with leaders of the municipal political opposition are mainly experienced as neutral (53%, with but 3% perceiving them as "conflictual").

Sixty-four per cent of our CEOs meet daily with the mayor and 60% with the heads of departments. The second line of partners with whom the CEO interacts are the "maires adjoints" and other employees of the administration (mostly between two to four times a week). Then come the citizens. All these data reflect a rather structured web of relationships. It also reflects his perception of who matters for what.

The budget, for instance, is influenced (in declining order of importance) first by the mayor, then by the CEO himself, moderately by the majority group of the municipal council, on an equal basis by the committee chair of the council and the department heads and marginally by the users. Such results confirm a high degree of polarization of power and influence. The figure of the mayor is central and the role of the CEO highly relevant. To some extent, their activity structures the fate of outside events in the municipality. This is also suggested by the way CEOs perceive the relative influence of local actors on the economic development of the municipality. Here again, the mayor comes overwhelmingly first, but the CEO and the majority group are also perceived as having some role. Second to the mayor as a source of influence, however, are private business interests, a group which formally lies outside the municipal political-administrative system.

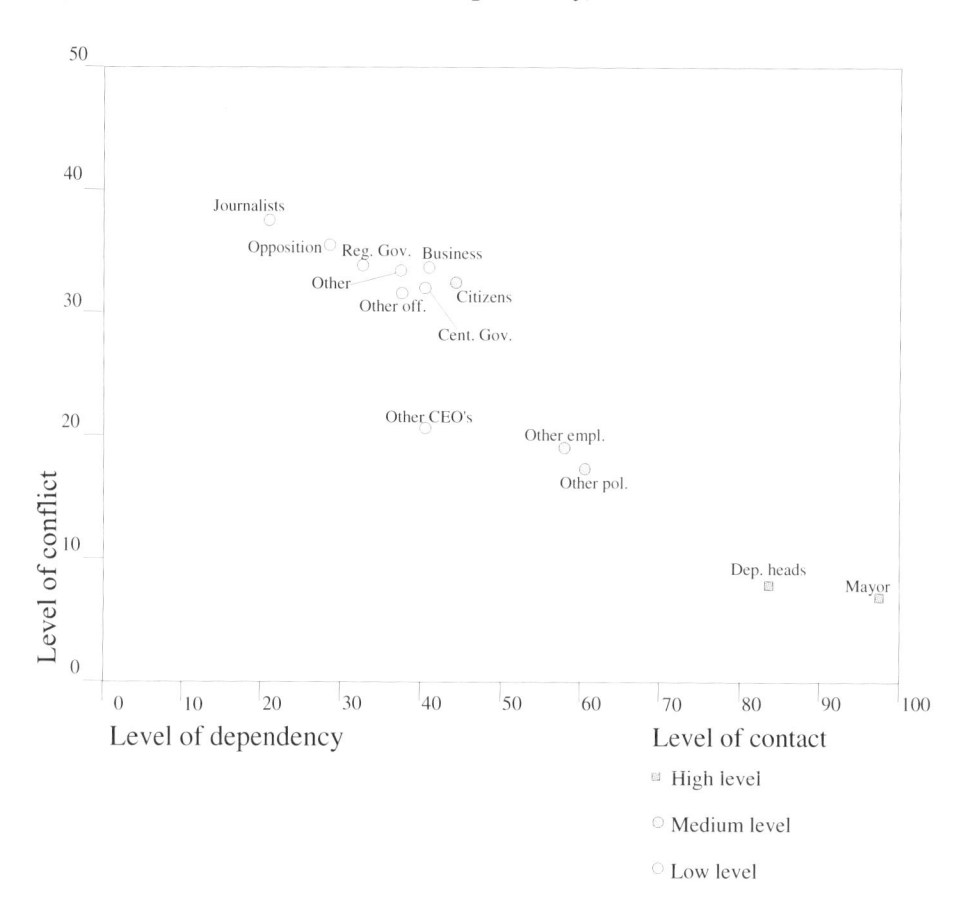

Figure 12.4 Contact, conflict and dependency, France

[Scatter plot with "Level of conflict" on the y-axis (0 to 50) and "Level of dependency" / "Level of contact" on the x-axis (0 to 100). Data points:]

- Journalists (~25, 37)
- Opposition (~28, 33)
- Reg. Gov. (~37, 33)
- Business (~45, 33)
- Other (~28, 30)
- Other off. (~37, 29)
- Citizens (~47, 30)
- Cent. Gov. (~45, 27)
- Other CEO's (~38, 19)
- Other empl. (~60, 18)
- Other pol. (~62, 15)
- Dep. heads (~80, 7) — High level
- Mayor (~92, 6) — High level

Legend:
■ High level
○ Medium level
○ Low level

In many ways, external relations are the central nerve centers of municipalities. The CEOs are part of their management. To some extent, however, they do not value the municipalities as part of their own turf. External relations are managed by the CEOs as a task subcontracted by the mayor. CEOs adapt norms and behaviors which make them spokesmen for their respective mayors. External relations lie at the heart of politics. If a problem becomes too touchy, if something threatening arises and is perceived as a major political issue, the CEO will withdraw and leave room for either the mayor himself or for his "directeur de cabinet", a member of the latter's personal staff. In return, the CEO expects this "directeur de cabinet" not to interfere in running his administration or bypassing him by giving specific instructions directly to the administration. CEOs do not consider the public scene (and direct exposure to the population) part of their professional role and ethos. The mass media are the mayor's domain.

To a great extent, CEOs act in a world which they hope to control. It also means that they are moderately inclined to reduce the size and functions of the administrative machine. User participation or citizen participation may be necessary. Privatization of service delivery may help, but they must not be used as an automatic solution or for ideological purposes. French CEOs do not perceive private management as a relevant source of inspiration. The "municipal way" is still viewed as the ideal solution to master the fate of public affairs. Modernization of administration, efficiency of politics and moderation are better alternatives. Sixty-two per cent of the CEOs disagree with the idea that the public sector has grown too large. Similarly, the same proportion do not believe that the private sector is generally more efficient. Sixty-five per cent doubt that benefits could be gained from contracting out or privatizing municipal tasks. The fact that about a third of the CEOs do not share these views does not mean that neoliberalism is on its way.

One relevant outside network is the network of relationships with other CEOs. The peer group helps to mobilize universal professional norms which legitimize the role of the CEO within the local environment of the municipality. Two channels of relations exist: one is informal, built on specific individuals who know each other, exchange advice, etc. The other one is formal, such as being a member of a professional association.

The survey shows that 64% of the CEOs are members of the national association of city CEOs, 17% are not but may consider joining, 15% are not and do not want to become a member, while 4% have been, but are not any longer. In the CEOs' view the association should accord priority to activities such as influencing the way national laws dealing with the status of CEO are implemented and expressing the voice of the CEOs in Paris whenever new laws are discussed by the parliament and the government. The profession wants to have a strong national lobby.

Conclusion

The French local government scene is characterized by two main factors. Strong political figures such as the mayor govern the municipal arena in a centralized way. And the CEOs occupy a solitary but rather strong and unique position between the mayor and the bureaucratic arena. Their position is strong when they obtain power and legitimacy by acting as the monopolistic channel of interface between the two arenas.

In recent years, the "secrétaires généraux" have developed a strong degree of professionalization. They share common values and skills which lend their role onsiderable specificity. They have engaged in collective action through professional associations. A labor market exists across the various cities.

The most sensitive aspect of the CEOs' position affecting their image and legitimacy is their dependence upon the mayor. However, a mayor also needs a strong CEO insofar as a strong administrator enables the mayor to be successful in his own political entrepreneurship inside the council as well as outside.

Access to the status of general manager and the professionalization of CEOs have been helpful. A kind of technostructure has emerged, appointed by the political owner of the city, which has set up rather solid and subtle standards of conduct, especially in the relationship to politics.

On the other hand, dependence upon the mayor remains strong in terms of hiring and firing. This can be seen when a newly elected mayor with a different political coalition takes office. In an unexpected way, the fact that autonomy and legitimacy have been set up by the "secrétaires généraux" has brought forward a new threat: the personal accountability of the CEO in judiciary cases. The courts fight mismanagement and corruption. In some cases, CEOs have been found guilty of corruption and sent to jail. This reflects the ambiguity of their status but also the fact that today they are major actors in the handling of subnational public affairs.

Appendix

The French Sample

Number of inhabitants per municipality	Number of municipalities in France (1990 census)	Number of questionnaires of CEOs	% of total
5,000 to 9,999	898	86	(10%)
10,000 to 19,999	445	67	(15%)
20,000 to 49,999	293	62	(21%)
50,000 and more	103	51	(50%)
TOTAL	1.739	266	(15%)

The data were collected in December 1995 and January 1996.

Bibliography

Dion, Stéphane (1984): Politique et gestion municipale, *Politiques et Management Public*, vol. 2 (Spring), 3-24.

Lorrain, Dominique (1989): *Les mairies urbaines et leurs personnels*, Paris: Fondation des Villes.

Lorrain, Dominique (1991): De l'administration républicaine au gouvernement urbain, *Sociologie du Travail*, vol. 4, 461-484.

Maurino, Jean D., Gaveriaux, M., and Le Perff, L.(1987): Du secrétariat général à la direction générale: la mutation du management commercial, *Politiques et Management Public*, vol. 4 (Winter), 3-34.

Ministère de l'Intèrieur (1996): *Les Agents des collectivités territoriales*, Paris: La Documentation Française.

Thoenig, Jean-Claude (1992): La décentralisation, dix ans après, *Pouvoirs*, vol. 60, 5-16.

Thoenig, Jean-Claude (1995): De l'incertitude en gestion territoriale, *Politiques et Management Public*, vol. 13 (September),1-27.

CHAPTER 13

Italian Local Democracy in Search of a New Administrative Leadership

by Maurizio Gamberucci and Annick Magnier

Three Classical Issues

There are three reasons why the role of *Segretario Comunale* is currently one of the main issues in the sociological analysis of Italian local government.

First, according to some observers (Bettini 1996, Amorosino 1996, Cerase 1996), "primacy of politics" is one of the main issues in the debate on the reform of the Italian political and administrative system. In their view, politicians have developed projects over the last ten years aiming at consolidating the primacy of politics, thus reinforcing the leadership of visible executive actors against a bureaucracy accused of being the main obstacle in the progress towards greater efficiency in public services. Does the reorganisation of top bureaucracy which began in 1993 strengthen the political scene, or does it strengthen a more autonomous bureaucracy? (See 1 Main act, the Dlgs 29/1993 for comments on the importance of these innovations, see Cassese 1994, Cerase 1994, and D'Orta-Meoli 1994). At the local level, the modification of the rules establishing the role of *Segretario Comunale* (achieved by the recent Bassanini Act) evolved differently through various interpretations. This role is one of the *loci* of change which may allow us to understand the new configuration(s) of the relationship between elected and bureaucratic spheres.

Second, from the fascist period onward, the role of *Segretario* changed to that of a representative of the Ministero dell'Interno and a preventive controller on the acts of the municipality.[1] The improvement of decentralisation is nowadays one of the undiscussed political objectives: decentralisation has been pursued over the last years by the introduction of the statutory autonomy, used hesitant-

---

[1] The Segretario position belongs, with the positions of Segretari Provinciali, to one career of "Segretari Comunali e Provinciali" in which, at the municipal level, we may distinguish between the classes of Segretari Comunali and Segretari Capo (Segretari Comunali with a minimum seniority) and Segretari Generali in municipalities with more than 10,000 inhabitants (Segretari Comunali selected among the Segretari Capo through a special examination).

ly by municipalities but symbolically important, and by the increased opportunities for the municipalities to raise taxes. These changes were not followed by corresponding reforms of the control exercised by higher levels of government over the municipalities, nor were they followed by the autonomy to form municipal policies, or by a break with the Napoleonic principle of uniformity of the municipal system, all of which could have helped the *Comuni* to conform to the substantial differences in size and political circumstance. The relationship between the *Segretario* and the locally elected officials is an indicator of the relationship between central and local government.

Third, the position of *Segretari*, while often criticised for its privileges, is also recognised as one of the few qualified positions in local government.[2] Moreover, it is one of the few positions in Italian administration which is selected through rigid and formal examinations and submitted to further examination throughout the career process. To what extent does this meritocratic selection (closer to foreign models – such as the French one, which is a ritual reference when selecting and training bureaucrats – than to the more usual party-patronage model) conform to the new model of administrative action? This model is stated in the vast and repetitive recent legislation which specifies the constitutional prerequisites for proper state administration: *responsibility* of the bureaucrats vs. the objectives defined by politicians, service orientation, capacity of evaluation of the results in terms of efficiency, *responsibility* in terms of transparency, etc.

Every step in the unsuccessful reform of Local Authorities from the 1990s and onward introduced changes in the role of the *Segretario Comunale*, changes which were often ambiguous, or in contradiction with previous legislative "improvements". This is clearly the case with one of the two recent "Bassanini Acts", aimed at the improvement of decentralisation.

Until the 1980s, the *Segretari Comunali* were recruited every year through a national examination open to graduates with a degree in law or similar field. They were mainly officials of the *Ministero dell'Interno* and worked in a municipality. They were appointed by the town-hall prefect, although their work was evaluated annually by the mayor, and the appointment was generally decided on the basis of informal contacts between the Ministry, the elected officials (also often representatives of the parties) and the *Segretari Comunali* themselves.[3] The power structure in the municipality was fragmented. In theory, the executive body (*Giunta*), composed of *assessori* elected by the council from among its members, was in power, as it defined the political lines of the municipality. In

---

2 The privileges of the Segretari are mainly financial, related to their persistence of obsolete functions, or to the increasing opportunities of participating in numerous commissions and local management organs.
3 On the origins and consequences of the ambiguous position of the Segretario Comunale, reintroduced by the fascist government, see Petracchi 1962, De Cesare 1977, Romanelli 1989, and Cassese 1983. For an auto-description of the role see R. Drago, Ricordi di un Segretario Comunale, 1857-1907, which is presented and extensively commented upon in Mazzanti Pepe 1985, Ferruzza et al. 1966 (especially the abstracts from Giusto Poverotè Ricordi di un Segretario Comunale) and Barbieri 1994.

practice, however, the individualist tradition of the *assessorati* – conceived as small, feudal structures and instruments for the creation of *clientele* and for career advancements – was counterbalanced only by the influence of party organisations. The mayor was only a *primus inter pares* in the *Giunta*, and the municipal council was an *arena* for political exercises (mainly on non- municipal matters) of the youngest and the oldest local activists. Local governments changed according to the rhythms and necessities of the local alliances of the political parties and in accordance with the instability of the executives. The chronic difficulties in decision-making of the main municipal matters and documents, such as municipal budgets and plans, were all correlated expressions of the "pathologies" of the party system. The *responsibility* of municipal bureaucrats was very limited, and the judges were not yet particularly interested in administrative correctness. Bureaucrats referred formally to the mayor ("head of the municipal administration"), but in fact they referred to the *Assessore* who had the authority in their field of activity. In this framework, the role of the *Segretari Comunali* was considered mainly as that of a (often not very useful) supervisor regarding the formal legitimacy of documents. They were seen as controllers "imposed" by the central government, if they did not behave "friendly", or as someone who could help to "respect the procedures" if politically "conform". Experience gained from various previous career positions was used only when cooperative relations could be established with the elected officials.

The Act no. 142, 8 June1990, which introduces the statutory autonomy of the municipalities, stipulates the functions of the *Segretario Comunale*. The *Segretario* is expected to 1) supervise the work of the department heads (*dirigenti*), 2) coordinate their activity in conformity with the directives of the mayor, and 3) to implement the decisions of political bodies. These new functions, if interpreted extensively, may transform a "supervisor" into an organisational leader (art. 52). At the same time, the principle of the responsibility of municipal department heads is introduced: a *responsibility* largely defined with reference to administrative correctness, in terms of the objectives of the municipality and to the efficiency of the management (art. 51, and Dlgs. 29/1993). It is also encouraged to engage external specialists as temporary bureaucratic leaders.

Increased legal control of administrative activities, at the same time as politicians felt their integrity to be under pressure, led to a wish for more qualified legal advice.While not so long ago the perfect *Segretario Comunale* was often a "quiet" *Segretario Comunale*, other characteristics are now required: a *Segretario Comunale* must be well prepared and active. At the same time, many *Segretari Comunali*, availing themselves of the coordinating role as laid down in *Art.* 52 of Act no. 142/1990, act as city-managers and draw heavily on this role.

The incongruity between the current emergence of the role and the ministerial recruitment of the *Segretari Comunali* in a framework of local autonomy has been the central issue of the debate on their status since 1990. This incongruity was further underlined in 1993, when Act no. 81 placed mayors at the centre of the municipal organisation (they are directly elected in the main municipalities, they appoint the *assessori* without submitting the matter to the Council), and, although not very clearly, confirms the changes of the role of *Segretario Comunale*. Some mayors appoint a city-manager, but more often they choose external consultants for administrative reorganisation. The means by which a mayor can ensure that a good *Segretario Comunale* is recruited are limited. From an economic point of view, some municipalities are more appealing to CEOs, and the mayors use this situation extensively. They can offer extra resources by leaving the *Segretario* the taxes collected by the city-hall for *affidavit* or bill protest charges (resources that come from traditional privileges which may be cancelled by the creation of new substituting services) and by multiplying the number of *dirigenti* in order to reduce their legal *responsibility*. There are no legal ways of removing an unwanted or incompetent *Segretario Comunale*. The possibility of implicit removal is revealed in the survey: 12% of the *Segretari* know that their predecessors left because of "bad relations with the politicians"; the threat of a bad "mark" in the annual report is surely less effective than the daily stress of everlasting conflicts. On the other hand, a *Segretario Comunale* who is not on good terms with the now highly visible mayor may become a useful scapegoat, who can be blamed for the negligence of the administration.

Joint decisions between *Segretari*, politicians and representatives of the Ministry, were recently introduced to smooth over the worst consequences of former practices used in connection with the evaluation and nomination of the *Segretario Comunale*.

The Bassanini Act (no. 127/1997) introduces revolutionary requirements to the municipal activities and in the organisation of the administrative leadership of the municipalities, (art. 6(10), 17(67-85) modifying the functions and position of the *Segretari*. The Act redefines the matters and procedures of the control of legitimacy (art.17 (32- 45, 85) to which the political minorities and a revitalized regional ombudsman are called to contribute. In municipalities with more than 15,000 inhabitants, the mayor may engage a "General Director" of the municipalities, a new position which will coexist with the role of *Segretario*, to be maintained in all municipalities (contrary to the fears of the latter) according to a distribution of functions not yet totally defined by the Act. The *Segretari Comunali* are chosen by the mayors and lose their charge with them, but, once appointed, they cannot be removed, except for violations of their official duties.[4] Mayors may choose from a Regional Register of *Segretari*, according to the demographic and structural characteristics of their municipality and the corresponding job qualifications of the *Segretari*. The registers are national and maintained by an Agency, composed of two mayors representing the Association of Elected Officials of Local Government, by one president of a province representing the Association of Elected Officials of the Provinces, by three *Segretari*

---

4 Contradicting article 17(71), clause 72 refers to the case in which the Segretari can be discharged by the agency as a consequence of "failing to obtain the results depending on the Segretari themselves."

Comunali e *Provinciali,* and by two experts nominated for the permanent round table on Local Authorities. The Ministry is no longer in charge of the *Segretario's* career. If the *Segretari Comunali* remain national officials, their careers are regulated by a body in which local representatives have the main influence and the regional dimension of their career path is stressed. All active *Segretari Comunali* and *Segretari Generali* will be included in the register, and, as a significant innovation, so are all the vice- *Segretari* (who are local officials) with sufficient seniority; the *Segretari* who have been passed over by the mayors will be employed by the Agency for other tasks in other administrations.

The *Segretario* used to be defined as "functionally dependent on the mayor". Today, the funcions are defined as follows: "tasks of cooperation and functions of legal and administrative assistance towards the bodies of the municipality with regard to the conformity of the administrative action with the laws, including statute laws and regulations", "supervise the development of the functions of the department heads, and coordinate their activity" – except when a *Direttore Generale* has been nominated. The functions are thus a bit unclear, particularly regarding the "cohabitation" between *Segretario Generale* and *Direttore Generale*, which is a matter delegated to the municipal legislative system and to the decisions of the mayor. The *Segretari* participate on a consultative basis in meetings of the council and the *giunta*, they can sign all contracts in which the municipalities are a part. Additional functions may be assigned to them by the statute, the municipal *regolamenti* and the mayor. One important function (advice on the legitimacy of the documents) is changed: the *Segretario* is no longer an external all-powerful judge, but a legal consultant, whose duties of "assistance" are stipulated, but whose autonomy to act in the name of the municipality depends on the content of the municipal regulations and on the decisions of the political actors. Legal advice becomes one of the many functions of the *Segretari*, the coordinating functions of the department heads now being fully recognised. Nevertheless, these functions are perhaps too ambiguously organised, for a transitory actor as the *Segretario* is now (and will be) in the very stable world of local top bureaucracy. Considering that they are suppressed in favour of the *Direttore Generale* whenever the latter is appointed, they do not yet totally appear as the indubitable "core" of the role. Only practice, depending also on the career paths and the training procedures to be defined by the Agency and the preferences and situation at the political scene, will decide the real characteristics of the managerial dimension of the role.

There are few studies of the top bureaucratic positions in the municipalities, of the large number of municipal *dirigenti* (heads of department) and the "smaller" group of the *Segretari Comunali*.[5] The introductory picture outlined by the U.DI.T.E. Leadership Study on this last figure becomes almost the only reference for an analysis of the current problems of the municipal administrative

---

5 There are also few studies of Italian bureaucracy in general. Despite this general lack of information it is particularly interesting to note the recent sample research promoted by CNR, whose results are published in Cerase 1994, and the historical account by Scamuzzi, 1978.

A Self-Sufficient Profession

Since the 1960s, the *Segretari* have been recruited regularly through a single (ostensibly annual) examination open to graduates in law, political science, economics and sociology: their average age (49), their age distribution and their age distribution on assuming their positions confirm this picture. The average length of the CEOs' studies, 17 years, only lower than the Spanish score among the countries studied in the survey, is a clear indicator of quality (on the basis of this quantitative criterion). The current composition of the *Segretari* population partially reflects the requirements imposed before the last reform of the recruitment procedure (dated 1962): a degree in law or *patentino*, obtained after a long period in local bureaucracy and an examination. Less than 4% of the *Segretari* now in charge have no university degree. In the 1950s the undergraduates represented 29%, dropping to 10% in the 1960s.

There is a striking uniformity in the recruitment following the period of relative *embourgeoisement* and diversification of university training which followed the 1962 reform; this uniformity was broken only by a revolutionary increase in the proportion of females. Today, however, the diversification in the university background is quite noticeable: less than two-thirds of the *Segretari* have a degree in law (one out of five in political science, one out of ten in economics). The predominance of the degree in law, however, does not seem to be threatened anymore.

The social background of the *Segretari* reflects the requirements and characteristics of this job, a proper job for the children of relatively well-off families but not attractive enough to correspond with the ambitions of the "noble idler". The bourgeoisie, the lower middle class and the working class are more or less equally represented, but some sections of the population are especially prominent: 24% are children of shopkeepers and artisans, 12% are children of farmers. On the basis of the Eurostat typology, the term "working class" must be taken in a broader sense, in that it includes many white collar positions which in the ISTAT typology is included in the middle class, but on the whole the working class seems well represented. The national formal examination is a guarantee for social promotion for those who come from families of limited means. On the other hand, the proportion of *Segretari* who are children of professionals is 10%, and the heredity of the position is limited: only 4% of the *Segretari* in our sample are children of *Segretari*. Measured on the basis of the three "classes", social recruitment has not undergone radical changes in the last thirty years: we notice only a modest polarisation of the social recruitment.

More than half (58%) the *Segretari* interviewed spent their childhood in the region where they are presently employed. Italy and Spain, where recruitment and career are dealt with on a national basis, are the only countries where we find a majority of "regional workers" among the people interviewed. These data are in conflict with the low degree of localism shown by other indicators: low membership in local associations and low proportion of *Segretari* who live in the municipality where they work (at 21%, the lowest percentage in Europe).

Measured by the current and past membership in political parties, the degree of politicisation (25%) of Italian CEOs appears to be low. If we consider this category of administrators, Italy is undoubtedly among the few countries with low politicisation. In the Italian case, nevertheless, the quarter of "partisan" bureaucrats (if measured on the basis of party affiliation) is often very close to the political world: 15% of the *Segretari* interviewed have been elected to a local government assembly or have joined a local executive body. This means that in a population largely unfamiliar with political practice, we find a significant group of "semi-professional politicians": one *Segretario* out of eight knows both the political and the bureaucratic scene of his/her local government. Contrary to the dominant scheme of politicisation of bureaucracy, according to which a job as a bureaucrat is the reward for a long and relatively successful political career, or the waiting room where to await new elective opportunities, these *Segretari* enter politics when they are already in an administrative position.

One out of five of our respondents is a woman. This significant proportion – a finding typical of the few European countries where CEOs are recruited through a formal and written examination at national level – is slightly smaller than the actual proportion (28% according to the data of the Ministero dell'Interno), because big cities are overrepresented in our sample. Although the career was opened to women only in 1963, the female presence is now growing rapidly: in the first grade of the career (*Segretario Comunale*) women are more numerous than men; they are slightly less often linked to political parties and slightly more frequently born in the south than their male colleagues. For a long time, the public sector has offered good opportunities for professional autonomy to young women from the south. The examination for *Segretario Comunale* apparently maintains this function, and women are slowly creating a new "southernisation" of the category. As regards the other aspects (social background, university degree) women do not differ from their male colleagues.

A powerful factor promoting homogeneity is the career process. The career remains an exclusive one: an important characteristic in municipalities where politicians after decades of strong professionalisation have often become outsiders (especially mayors, the immediate superiors of the *Segretario*) (Bettin-Magnier 1995). Thirty-seven per cent of our CEOs began their professional activity as *Segretari Comunali*. Among the CEOs who reported having had their first job in the private sector, there is a dominance of those who, after their degree in law, began their training in a lawyer's or legal advisor's office (a necessary step in order to pass the examination to become a professional lawyer). As for those who began work teaching in schools (8%) or in universities (5%), they seem to have experienced only waiting positions before entering a CEO career. The proportion of CEOs who began working in municipalities (7%) – as well as in other public authorities, provinces, regions or in central administration (10%) – is fairly low and lower than one would expect. Previously, local government employees who began their career did not necessarily aim at becoming *segretario*. As the Bassanini reform includes vice-*segretari* with seniority in the register from which *segretari* are recruited, it stresses the possibility of getting on in the local government world.

Half the Italian CEOs consider their jobs less attractive than ten years ago. Perhaps high mobility enables them to reduce the tension in their daily work. On average the CEOs stay in one job six years before moving on in their career. However, half those interviewed have been holding office in the municipality in which they currently work for less than four years (and this is also the case with regard to their previous post). Only a small group of administrators with a satisfied "static ambition" escapes from the law of rapid turnover: one CEO out of ten has been filling the same position over the last fifteen years.

Career patterns are curiously linked with satisfaction: old CEOs are generally less satisfied with their job than younger CEOs. This is not just the case among those who did not advance in their careers, but also among those who reached top positions (*Segretari Generali di prima classe* in big cities). Does satisfied ambition at this level turn to bitterness? Or does the present situation become difficult to deal with for people who were trained for the job in other more stable, if not easier conditions?

Change in Corporate Culture

The so-called "corporate culture" (Gherardi-Mortara 1987, Cerase 1994) of Italian bureaucracy has three features: a) extreme formalism (and low interest in the results of the administrative action) as a consequence of the predominance of juridical education; b) extreme fragmentation of the offices and the duties and weakness of the vertical structure; c) high interaction with the political world – especially at the local level – in a unique *ceto politico-amministrativo* (Segatori 1992). Italian scientific literature describes the Italian bureaucrat as a hybrid animal who gathers the functional inefficiencies of the "political" bureaucrat and of the "classical" bureaucrat (Ammassari et al. 1968, Ferraresi 1980).

The priorities of CEOs when they make decisions in a critical situation are emblematic of a historical shift in values as well as in leadership patterns: the best score (average index values) is obtained by the item "accomplishing tasks efficiently and quickly" (68%), even better than "observing the established rules and procedures" (63%), and is followed by "ensuring consensus" (24%). The leadership pattern is characterised by the use of personalised relations (64%), and mobilisation through recommendation and reward of individuals (57%) rather than by the use of formal power and authority (34%). The factor analysis of these six items reveals two different significant factors: the first is that efficiency is supported by a negative attitude towards consensus orientation and a still more negative one regarding formal authority; the other one is that the observation of the rules and procedures is supported by the formal power and by a very negative attitude towards consensus. The first one could be called an "efficiency-oriented attitude" and the second a "classical authoritarian attitude". The two tendencies are equally represented in the sample with relative concentration on average index values. This indicates the co-existence of the values of the "traditional" *corporate culture*, based above all on the control of legitimacy, with the new trend which stresses efficiency and effectiveness.

The traditional distinction between "classical" and "political" bureaucrat undoubtedly helps us to underline the rejection by the Italian CEOs of the "partisan" dimension of local government. The Italian CEOs remain closer to the "classical bureaucrat" than to the "political". Until 1990 they were not asked to undertake true leadership tasks: "to give political advice" would still be considered as a connivance or an intrusion: the primacy of politics is not at issue. The average scores obtained on the basis of the items chosen to define the two "roles", and the synthetic index deriving from them nevertheless offer an immediate impression of uneasy discrimination. And if we do not consider the heretic item about "political advice" to the mayor, we can see that the difference between the synthetic average scores virtually disappears.

Table 13.1 The role of the CEOs, Italy

The classical bureaucrat		75
Guide subordinate staff in day-to-day handling of activities	71	
Manage economic affairs, accounts and budgetary control	69	
Ensure that rules and regulations are followed	83	
Provide the mayor with legal, economic and other kinds of technical advice	77	
The political bureaucrat		61
Formulate ideas and visions	76	
Promote and encourage new projects in the community	72	
Provide the mayor with political advice	19	
Be informed about citizens' viewpoints	60	
Develop and implement norms concerning the proper roles of politicians vis-á-vis the bureaucrats	75	
Influence decision-making processes in order to secure sensible and efficient solutions	65	

Table 13.2 The ideal politician, Italy

Administration		52
Be a spokesperson for local groups or individuals who have issues pending decision by the authority	62	
Lay down rules and routines for the administration	40	
Taking decisions concerning specific cases	55	
Representation		57
Be informed about citizens' views	73	
Represent the municipality to the outside world	65	
Defend the authorities' decisions and policies externally	74	
Be a spokesperson for their political party	23	
Be a spokesperson vis-á-vis the press	51	
Governance		83
Implement the program on which he/she has been elected	83	
Decide on major policy principles	81	
Have a vision of the way in which the municipality will develop in the long run	85	
Stability		77
Create stability for the administration	71	
Formulate exact and unambiguous goals for the administration	83	

The ambiguous result of the two interpretations of the role ("classical" and "political" bureaucrats) does not indicate a dramatic split in the population of the CEOs. Each item proposed for an ideal definition of the role obtained a good average score, except "give political advice to the mayor". Overall the traditional interpretation of the role (the classical one) coexists with a more active presentation of the job, according to which it is the responsibility of the bureaucrat to stimulate and coordinate projects and to accept the feedback given by the citizens (the political one). This attitude may be interpreted as proof of the inadequacy of the Aberbach's dichotomous model ("classical" versus "political bureaucrat") or as indicating the current indeterminacy of the role (perhaps not only this specific role) in the administrative culture and the poverty of the scientific and political debate on these themes.

Similarly the tasks attributed to politicians provide a clear indication of the various possible interpretations of the roles allowed by the legislative indeterminacy. In principle, the tasks attributed to mayors and councillors are related to the area of the political "mission" and to the definition of "policies" and – to a lesser degree – "to create stability for the administration". Less importance is attributed to the "representative" dimension of the role, an area in which Italian CEOs believe they themselves have a role to play: politicians must principally "be informed about citizens' views" and "externally defend the decisions of the municipality". There is less interest in the classical role of being ambassadors of the community and a negative assesment of the partisan dimension of the role. Nevertheless, the administrative dimension of political roles, if not exactly appreciated, is at least not neglected; these tasks are all strictly related to the administrative leadership, willingly delegated to politicians by Italian CEOs, or tasks for which CEOs desire to be actively supported by the politicians.

Considerable Influence, Low Conflict

Everyday life and behavioural patterns do not totally conform to this image of the role, and, although the standard deviation is low for all the questions related to values and attitudes towards the job, it becomes more significant if we look at the behaviour of CEOs. It is shown that the cultural cohesion correlated to the homogeneity of education, recruitment and career does not exclude a significant variety in the actual interpretations of the role, many of which related to the characteristics of the post, others related to the qualities of the CEOs.

On average, Italian CEOs say they work 45 hours per week, a heavy schedule, but like the Spanish one, slightly less than the European average. Furthermore, Italy and Spain are the two countries where we find that CEOs more often that in the rest of Europe do not live in the municipality in which they work. The main image of the Italian CEO offered through network analysis confirms the obsolescence (or rather the inadequacy) of the traditional stereotype of the *Segretario* as a controller exclusively dedicated to guaranteeing legitimacy. The *Segretario* is a "contact person" at the centre of a large, differentiated and intense network. The narrow convergence on the three dimensions considered (frequency, dependency and conflict) is a characteristic feature of the average configuration of these networks. Three groups of clearly distinct actors appear in these networks: a) actors with a high level of contact, high dependency and low conflict, b) actors with medium level of contact, medium dependency and medium conflict, c) actors considered unimportant, seldomly consulted and considered highly conflicting. Such convergence indicates a surprising lack of "structural" conflict: the Italian local government as a whole maintains a low level of conflict with regard to its significant relations. This is undoubtedly due to the adaptability of the actors, rather than to an extreme selectivity in the choice of the relations (which is at the CEOs discretion for some external groupings but not for the main ones). High mobility, the illusion of the choice of the post and a low personal affective investment in the working sphere are perhaps the main explanations for this general "harmony". Nevertheless, variance in the degree of cooperation is generally high, especially, as could be predicted, as far as relations with the mayor are concerned.

The mayor (consulted nearly every day) is the main person in the working activity of the *Segretari*. This picture is found throughout Europe, but in contrast to other countries the average frequency of contacts found with the department heads is close to the average found for the relationship with the mayor. Many CEOs in charge do not arrange coordinative meetings with the department heads (only 28.4% do so on a weekly basis, 42% monthly). These contacts are mainly informal, person-to-person contacts. Direct contacts with the employees, however, are also very significant, ranking third in importance in the daily life of the CEOs. They illustrate the low degree of verticalisation of the top structure. In short, the activities of the *Segretari* are dominated by contacts with the internal sphere of the municipality, and especially the bureaucratic sphere, with the mayor as the sole but dominating exception.

The second group of relations is quite restricted and significant in its heterogeneity. Here we find, for example, the other politicians who are in majority (among them members of the *giunta*). This means that the relation with the majority is organized mainly by the mayor. But we also find the other CEOs, as proof of the intense interaction among CEOs, and also as proof of the competition between them. This is shown by the level of conflict being surprisingly higher than the conflict they declare to have with the mayor. In this group we also find the citizens, the only sign of the developing ambition of community leadership provided by the data on the networks.

The third group, including the more exceptional relations, illustrates the functions the Italian CEOs do not have. There is hardly any direct contact with politicians from the opposition, but even fewer relations with corporate interests (this indicates the distance between the ideal of community leadership and the actual role). Similarly, there are few relations with the unions, especially with regard to non-organisational problem issues and few relations with other levels of government. The limited relations with the local business world indicate that the Italian CEO is not a fund-raiser. Furthermore, there are no relations with the press, so the *Segretario* is not a representative of the municipality, the "national" roots of the figure are here clearly evident.

Despite recent controversies, we find that the world of the *Segretari* is dominated by a low level of conflict. Few actors are judged extremely cooperative, on average two only. No particular emphasis is placed on conflicts with politicians when the *Segretari* describe their networks.

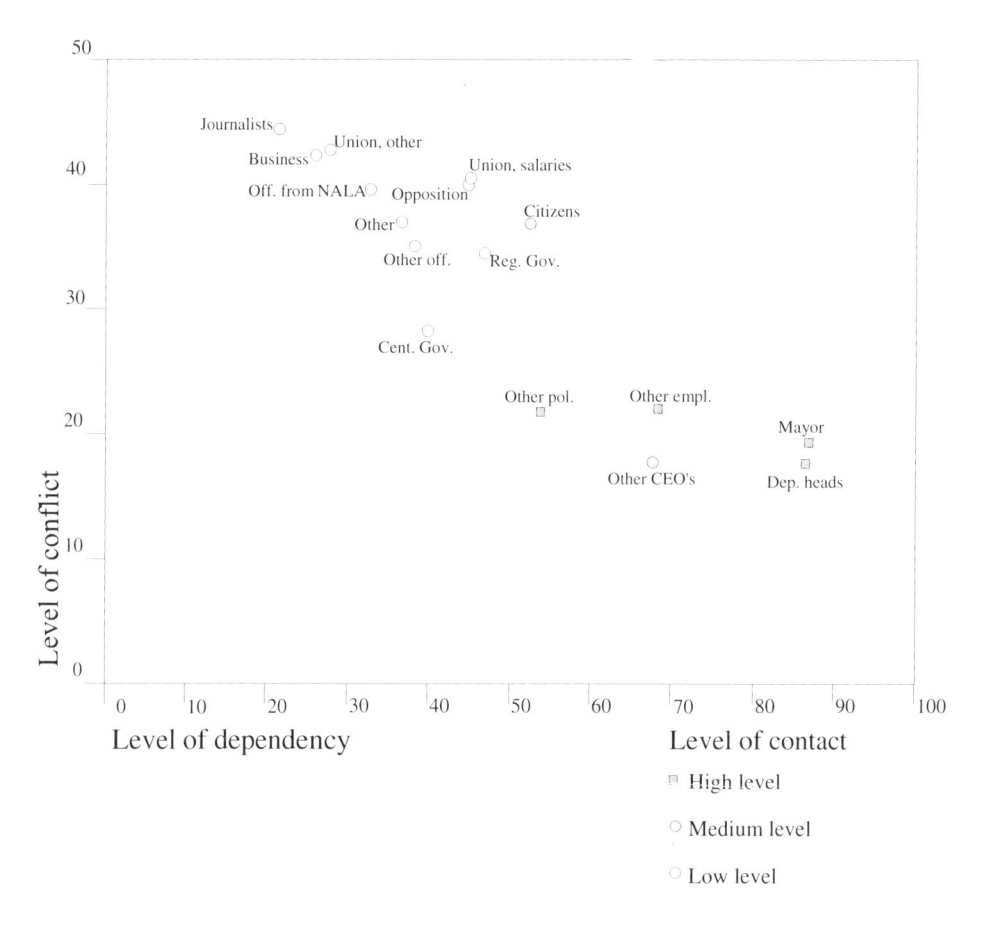

Figure 13.1 Contact, conflict and dependency, Italy

(Scatter plot with X-axis "Level of dependency" / "Level of contact" ranging 0–100, and Y-axis "Level of conflict" ranging 0–50. Legend: ■ High level, ○ Medium level, ○ Low level.)

Data points approximately:
- Journalists (~18, 41) – Medium
- Union, other (~25, 41) – Medium
- Business (~22, 39) – Medium
- Off. from NALA (~22, 36) – Medium
- Opposition (~32, 37) – Medium
- Union, salaries (~55, 39) – Medium
- Other (~30, 35) – Medium
- Citizens (~60, 36) – Medium
- Other off. (~35, 33) – Medium
- Reg. Gov. (~45, 34) – Medium
- Cent. Gov. (~35, 27) – Medium
- Other pol. (~55, 20) – High
- Other empl. (~70, 20) – High
- Mayor (~85, 19) – High
- Other CEO's (~65, 16) – Medium
- Dep. heads (~80, 16) – High

Comparatively, the relations with the political sphere (except the mayor, the pivot of the networks of all our CEOs) grow with age. Newcomers, such as newcomers in local politics, tend to prefer a more "technical" interpretation of the role, that is, they have more contacts with the bureaucrats and less with politicians, especially members of the *giunta*. Gender sems to matter: women are more open (in terms of frequency of contacts, dependency) and have more collaborative relations with the departments and especially with the employees of the municipality, and less interest in the political actors, excepting the mayor. Surprisingly, the networks of CEOs with political experience do not differ from those of their colleagues, indicating further proof of the constraints of the CEO role.

The uniformity of the internal networks is impressive. Variations are found only in extreme cases e.g., in relations with heads of department, which are often not found in the micro-municipalities and in the relations with the workforce where we find a separation in the large cities. A general pattern of equal frequency in relations with the mayor, heads of department, other employees, and the *assessori* is found in small, medium, and large cities. However, the classical, territorial subdivision into four major geopolitical areas remains significant. The networks of the CEOs are much more open to the citizens in Southern and Central Italy. Is this caused by clientelism, or by a civic assumption of responsibility by the CEOs towards the unorganised members of the communities? Or can it be explained by a tendency among the politicians to delegate problematic contacts to bureaucrats? Without excluding the first proposition, we must emphasize that the second and third ones fit with the high level of conflict declared in the very same regions regarding contacts with the "citizens". Though not exactly "pathologic", conflict with the mayor is nevertheless slightly stronger in Southern and Central Italy. Furthermore, in these two areas we can observe a higher degree of "indirect removal", meaning that the mayor ensures their transfer without the formal power to do so.

Towards a New Administrative Leadership?

As might be expected, the main question in Italian local government appears to be the degree of "autonomy" of bureaucracy, established repeatedly through the legislative redefinition of the roles, and considered to be greatly increased by most of the people interviewed (index 70, while an index of 4 is obtained if we consider the increase of autonomy of local governments, and an index of 35 is obtained by the internal decentralisation of the local bureaucratic area). This redefinition nevertheless remains insufficient, as declared by our CEOs, and as confirmed by a description of their networks. While CEOs have the impression from his or her own experience that bureaucracy is more autonomous than it was ten years ago, the level of conflict with the mayor and aldermen ranges from lower (the quantitative relation is high with differences in the index of conflict from 8 to 43) to average. Thus, more autonomy signifies slightly more frequent but minor conflicts in general and better relations with the politicians. The same configuration is found in CEOs' relations with the employees.

On the whole, the personal characteristics of the CEOs have less influence on their behaviour than the characteristics of their environment. Relative homogeneity background and homogeneity of the organisational culture contrast with the high diversity of the municipal situations, not only dimensional, but also geographical and organisational (the forms and the extension of the externalisation).

Going back to the three questions posed by the position of the *Segretario*, we may conclude that: 1) on average, Italian CEOs do not interfere in local politics when considered strictly partisan politics, but have developed an extensive interpretation of their role, even in the transitory period concluded by the Bassanini Act, stressing their ambition to community leadership more than to organisational leadership (contrary to the spirit of that same law); 2) even though they are officials of the central administration, they definitively demonstrate to be a part of the world of local authorities. They have developed horizontal networks, relative accommodation or solidarity towards local politicians and responsiveness to local communities though less to local lobbies. Policy networks in local government do not rely predominantly on bureaucrats, at least not these, transitory, bureaucrats; 3) our data demonstrate the CEOs' openness to the new model of administrative action promoted by recent governments. They also underline problems in the career organisation: in a pluralistic Italy, the problem is the uniformity of the training and the strict separation between the career of the municipal staff, who are locally recruited and promoted, and the career of the nationally recruited and promoted *segretari*.

Even before the Bassinini Act, the Italian *Segretario Comunale* aspired to an effective role of administrative leadership, but he/she is mainly oriented towards giving expert advice, proactivity in organisational management and local development and less to the management of internal (financial and human) resources. The CEO has confidence in the efficiency of the private sector but has doubts about the usefulness of contracting-out municipal services and little interest in the models deriving from the world of private management. Italian CEOs aspire to administrative leadership, yet they interpret it in a somewhat peculiar way, not to be confused with a narrow, "private" interpretation of *management*. The functions related to a routine management (the administrative "management" in the terms of Svara's 1990 definition do not seem to be a main concern, neither for the new Act, nor for the *Segretari Comunali*. The schemes of career and the training procedures do not highlight these capacities particularly. It seems that building the preliminary conditions for the development of a more encompassing administrative leadership in Italian Local Authorities may become one of the main issues of the political agenda in the coming years. Our survey indicates that circumstance undoubtedly demands that we reflect on the specificity of the administrative structure of local power and on the necessary definition of authority in order to avoid generic and ritual references to the international models of new public management. These also include, as demonstrated by our data on conflicts and structural changes, further reforms on the organisation of the political scene adapted to the new configurations of local governance.

Bibliography

Aberbach, J.D., Putnam, R., and Rockman, B.A. (1981): *Bureaucrats and Politicians in Western Democracies*, Cambridge Mass.: Harvard University Press.

Ammassari, P., Grazonio Dell'Orto, F., and Ferraresi, F. (1968): *La burocrazia periferica e locale in Italia: analisi sociologica, Parte II: Il burocrate di fronte alla burocrazia, Archivio ISAP, 4*, Milano: Giuffrè.

Amorosino, S. (1996): In tema di rapporti tra direzione politica e dirigenza amministrativa, *Rivista Trimestrale di Scienza dell'Amministrazione*, 1, pp. 5-17.

Barbieri, A. (1994): *Memorie di un Segretario Comunale*, Firenze: Noccioli.

Bettin, G., and Magnier, A. (1995): I nuovi sindaci: come cambia una carriera politica, *Rivista Italiana di Scienza della Politica*, 1, pp. 91-118.

Bettini, R. (1996): La politica amministrativa italiana tra alibi legislativo e indifferenza/interferenza. Il dirigente politico come free rider?, *Rivista Trimestrale di Scienza dell'Amministrazione*, 1, pp. 137-157.

Camarda, L. (1994): *Il Segretario Comunale e Provinciale a Servizio dell'Ente Locale. Dall'Unità d'Italia ai giorni Nostri*, Bergamo: Cel Editrice.

Cassese, S. (1983): *Il sistema amministrativo italiano*, Bologna: Il Mulino.

Cassese, S. (1994): *Le basi del diritto amministrativo*, Milano: Garzanti.

Cerase, P. (1994): *I dipendenti pubblici*, Bologna: Il Mulino.

Cerase, P. (1996): Deficit istituzionale ed agenda pubblica, *Amministrare*, 3, pp. 425-434.

D'Orta, C., and Meoli, C. (1994): *La riforma della dirigenza pubblica*, Padova: Cedam.

De Cesare, G. (1977): *L'ordinamento comunale provinciale in Italia, Dal 1862 al 1942*, Milano: Giuffrè.

De Marchi, F. (1969): *La burocrazia periferica e locale in Italia: analisi sociologica, Parte I: L'ideologia del funzionario*, Archivio ISAP 5, Milano: Giuffrè.

De Masi, D., and Bonzanini, A. (a cura di) (1988): *Trattato di sociologia del lavoro e dell'organizzazione*, Milano: Angeli.

Ferraresi, F. (1980): *Burocrazia e politica in Italia*, Bologna: Il Mulino.

Ferruzza A., Tani, G., and Coppa, G. (1966): *Gli eroi sconosciuti che fanno in silenzio l'Italia*, Firenze: Noccioli.

Gherardi S., and Mortara, V. (1987): Può il Concetto di Cultura Organizzativa Contribuire allo Studio della Pubblica Amministrazione ed al Suo Mutamento?, *Rivista Italiana di Scienza dell'Amministrazione*, no. 1.

Magnier, A. (1997): *La leadership amministrativa nel Comune Italiano*, Bologna: Compositori.

Massei, A. (1989): La Funzione Dirigente nel Comune; un Modello di Riferimento ed i Risultati di un'Indagine Empirica, *Il nuovo governo Locale*, no.1.

Mazzanti, Pepe F. (1985): *Il personale burocratico e il funzionamento della pubblica amministrazione. Raffaele Drago, Segretario del Comune di Genova (1879-1907)*, Archivio ISAP, 3, *L'amministrazione nella storia moderna, II*, Milano: Giuffrè, pp. 1931-2046.

Ouchi, W.G., and Wilkins, A. (1985): Organizational Culture, *Annual Review of Sociology*.

Petracchi, G. (1962): *Le origini dell'ordinamento comunale e provinciale italiano*, Venezia: Guaraldi.

Romanelli, R. (1989): *Sulle carte interminate, Un ceto di impiegati tra privato e pubblico, I Segretari comunali in Italia, 1860-1915*, Bologna: Il Mulino.

Scamuzzi, S. (1978): Stato italiano, impiegati pubblici e mobilitazione politica, Riflessioni su alcune serie storiche dal 1881 al 1975, *Quaderni di Sociologia*, vol. 27, pp. 154-184.

Svara, J. (1990): *Official Leadership in the City: Patterns of Conflict and Cooperation*, Oxford: Oxford University Press.

CHAPTER 14

Portuguese Chief Administrative Officers: Between Rationalization and Political Struggles

by Manuel da Silva e Costa, Joel Felizes and José P. Neves

Introduction: Theories and Methods

The chief administrative officers (CAO) in Portuguese local government are positioned in multiple frameworks. We deliberately use the term chief administrative officers instead of chief executive officer because the latter role, as we explain below, is fulfilled by the mayor. Our aim is to bring together the global, societal frameworks and the specific contexts influencing CAO's profile and strategies. We then interpret the frameworks characterized by a combination of specific factors (organizational characteristics, national constraints, etc.) linked with a more general structuration.

Drawing on Anthony Giddens' analysis (1987, 1992), we identify three types of frameworks: the pre-modern model (what Giddens calls the "society-like organisation"), the modern model (modern organisations based on rationalisation, drawing on Weber's ideal-type bureaucracy) and a third emergent model, called "reflexive" or "late modernity" (complex and de-territorialised organizations where new forms of life and work are emerging and where a kind of creative disorder occurs). Closing in on our empirical object, we find a diversity of situations that tend to merge different frameworks. In a paradoxical way, the chief administrative officers are influenced by a general trend of modernization, in a context where they are fighting against traditional, pre-modern practices, yet are at the same time guardians of the bureaucratic order, avoiding innovation.

For example, when the issue of local government modernization is under debate, we find a situation of "distortion and confusion between what Chief Executive Officers have to do, what they think they have to do, what they would like to do, and what they do in practice, a situation parallel to what the mayors do in practice.... This scenario quite often produces "schizophrenic" situations for the CEOs where conflicts appear and explains the tensions between CEOs and politicians" (Nieto, 1997: 51). In the Portuguese context, these contradictions are clearly visible among younger chief administrative officers (often having university-level training), who tend to be caught between their idealistic view of the municipality and the more prosaic "pre-modern" or "clientelistic" organisations.

In fact, Portuguese municipal administration reveals a mixture of different time-cultures, a situation different from the one found in other developed countries. As Boaventura Santos wrote (Santos, 1985), drawing on I. Wallerstein's analysis (Wallerstein, 1984), Portugal can be seen as a semiperipheral country, with a structural disarticulation between production and social reproduction, the latter being more developed (reflecting what can be seen as a social "Westernised" normality). The role of the State is to inhibit the gap between the formal ("the law in books") and the informal practices ("the law in action").

Local administration shares some of the features of this context, but there are differences across the country. In the coastal region (including the two metropolitan areas of Lisbon and Oporto) where almost 80% of the population live, the complexity of problems related with this high density and the demands upon relatively large and more professional municipal organisations produce a more modern organisational design, where the gap between the formal and informal practices tends to be reduced. In other municipalities, the organizational processes are centred mainly around the mayor and his influence. According to his profile, the mayor can act as a voluntary agent of modernization, assisted in some cases by the CAO. On the other hand, he can be a kind of clientelistic agent, reproducing a context in which some traces of pre-modernity may be found (although for the past 10 years a new generation of mayors, mostly from the Left-centre wing, are changing this traditional profile).[1]

This can also be seen as a result of a new political trend, common in many other European countries: the "de-ideologisation" of political leadership. The main distinction is no longer between political programs, but between a pragmatic and modernist strategy versus a clientelistic model centred on political control and domination.

Some Notes About the Research Design

In this section, we would like to raise some questions about our main empirical source (the U.DI.T.E. survey), especially about the relevance and reliability of the information gathered in the Portuguese context. In order to avoid simplistic cross-country comparisons based on survey findings, we should be cautious and discuss some *difficulties* observed in the Portuguese case. Knowing that survey results depend largely on the perspective of the person who actually performs the

---

[1] The clientilistic situation is more common in northern Portugal. As Manuel Carlos Silva has written, "the traditional and generally conservative sociopolitical alignment of the inhabitants of contemporary northern Portugal cannot be understood without taking into account the system of bonding to and dependency on influential persons, whether patrons or brokers" (Silva, 1994: 29).

CEO or CAO job, it is important to stress that, *a priori*, we expect different kinds of responses, at least if we compare Portugal with more developed countries. Thus, part of the explanation for the relatively large gap between some quantitative and qualitative findings in Portugal has to do with the different perspectives used by the survey's respondents.

In addition, the vast majority of Portuguese CAOs were informed about the importance of this survey for the promotion strategy of their national association, hence, it is possible that some of the answers were influenced by the respondents' desire to present themselves as active, modern managers.

We should also bear in mind the links between the Portuguese chief administrative officers and their mayors: it was with some surprise that we did not receive only personal and anonymous answers to the survey. Others (almost half of them) were sent through the municipality's official channels (and probably under the control of the mayor).[2]

Thus, it seems that in organizational studies the use of quantitative methods has to be strongly complemented with a qualitative strategy supported mainly by discourse analysis and observation.[3]

When analyzing these findings we will use a frame of values that is implicitly assumed. Usually, the Mediterranean political and administrative agents are seen as having a traditional, clientelistic, non-participatory attitude placed at an early stage of management modernisation. If we see the opposite attitude (common in Northern or Central Europe) not as superior (or inferior), but merely as different, we are giving ourselves an opportunity to see the other side: we *accept* not only the *discourse* of modernisation (present in academic or political discourses), but also the discourse of irrationality, the resistance by those who have no access to the *official* discourse, even if that resistance seems archaic.[4] By doing so, we are reminded that many new social phenomena and movements reveal to us the crisis of the modern *narrative* of progress (about this subject, see, e.g. the work of Lyotard 1984). And this narrative includes some recent managerial discourses (new public management, privatization of local services, and so on).

---

[2] In a study of local elites, Oliveira e Rocha notes that in Portugal it is common to find situations where the local administration is under some kind of "law of silence"; there is a kind of personal and clientelistic domination centred on the charismatic personality of the mayor (Rocha 1988:3).
[3] See also Terry Nichols Clark, who stresses the difference between the rhetoric (discourse) of local officials and what is found when observing their practice (1996:23).
[4] It is interesting to compare this kind of analysis with the discourse of Portuguese central administration regarding local administration. The organisational change in Portuguese local administration was analysed by someone from central administration (regional co-ordination commission) in the following way: "it is common to find situations where the change from an informal organisation into a rational bureaucracy is not achieved through the modernisation of management technologies, where there is no co-ordination to avoid the sectorial segregation; the functions are not defined nor are the procedures modernised; the routines that were proven obsolete carry on" (Couto and Gaio,1990:36).

The Historical Perspective of Portuguese Local Government

History shows us that since the fifteenth century centralisation has become a basic feature of the Portuguese political system. Administrative rationalisation marks the formation of modern Portugal in the seventeenth and eighteenth centuries, developed by the king and aimed at the limitation of the powers held by the nobility and the Catholic Church, leaving unchanged the limited autonomy of local powers.

Recent historical research indicates that local power in Portugal cannot be interpreted as representing the will of the people. On the contrary, the reality of local governments was based on an arbitrary and even tyrannical relationship.

The autonomy of local government (which some historians praise as a long Portuguese tradition) was not a consequence of any deliberate decentralisation, but rather the effect of the central power's inability to intervene in some regions. Some traces of this autonomy are still present, mainly through the influence of the Catholic Church and are not limited to rural areas. Moreover, this inability of central power also favoured the informal production of laws based on communitarian norms, giving way to a dual administration (see, among others, Monteiro 1993 and Capela 1995).

Only after the Liberal Revolution in 1820 and its subsequent Constitution was the country divided into "Distritos" (where central government was represented by general administrators) and "Concelhos" (an earlier form of municipality) with local governments directly elected by the people. The influence of the French model of local administration was now present, trying to define a multiple level administrative structure, with elected members at the local level, however, subordinated to the tutelage of central power or its appointees. This new situation also generated a tension between the increasing influence of central power on the overall territory (directed mainly against the nobility powers) and the increasing individualism (Tocqueville predicted this conflict between the state and the individual as a consequence of this democratic revolution: meanwhile, the intermediate "bodies" were liquidated).

Thus, the Portuguese Liberal period and the early Republic (1910-1926) were characterised by a political struggle between central and local governments. This period ended in 1926 with a coup d'état which brought to power Salazar's dictatorship. Until 1974, Portuguese administration remained highly centralised: local elections were abolished and local authorities nominated by central government. This system also generated practices of nepotism and patronage – central government financial policies were highly discretionary. Local government's share of national expenditure, however, was more or less the same as today (about 10%).

The democratic revolution (1974) saw local self-government as one of its most important achievements. According to the new Constitution, local governments are territorially based collective entities, pursuing specific goals for their respective populations, whom they represent through elections. Local governments also have property and finances of their own and legislative autonomy. According to Law 25/85 (which rectified some aspects of Law 100/84, both laws resulting from the first one, Law 79/77), local governments have the following duties: the administration of property, development, public supply (e.g. marketplaces), public health and sewage, education and schooling, care of children and the elderly, culture, leisure and sports, environment and protection of the quality of life, and civic protection. These somewhat vague obligations are transferred to a complex set of regulations that define local governments' frame of action (and are limited mainly by the law on local finance, Law 1/87). Some of their activities and decisions are subject to approval by various ministries (Finance, Planning and Territorial Administration) and by the Court of Auditors (e.g. municipal annual accounts are given *a posteriori* approval). Nevertheless, some traces of the *Salazarist* regime, such as centralised and bureaucratic structure, were *inherited* by the democratic system.

In sum, we see that the Portuguese case presents a specific dualism between the highly bureaucratic organisational models and the informality linked to the oligarchic models of local domination. Local brokers (influential persons) are thus essential to understanding administrative action, since they work as mediators in the central-local relation.

The changes in this context tend to combine the pre-modern background and late modern complexity introduced by organisational rationalisation, new technologies, European integration and other factors (see, e.g., Martins 1993, and, on the effects of European integration, Costa, Felizes and Neves 1997). In this way, the organisation can be seen as a time-space discursive rationalisation where past and present are linked in a complex manner.

The Local Political-Administrative System

Portuguese local administration can be divided into four levels. First, there are *Freguesias* (parish-based units), the lowest tier of public administration, with limited autonomy. Having very limited financial resources, *Freguesias* can be more or less favoured by municipal administration according to the decentralisation policy pursued by the mayor. Second, there are the *Municípios* or *Concelhos* (municipalities): Portugal has 305 municipalities, 30 of them in the archipelagos. They are the most important level of local government. The municipality has two elected governing bodies: the *Assembleia Municipal* (municipal assembly) and the *Câmara Municipal* (chamber). The latter is led by a *Presidente* (chairman, the mayor) who, together with the powers vested in him, holds an important *symbolic* office. There are also two other more ambiguous units: the *Distritos* or districts, created by the 1822 Constitution. Today they represent a *relic* of the legal system, since they are to be replaced by *administrative regions*. Finally, there are the *Regiões* or regions. In Portugal there are two *autonomous regions* (the archipelagos of Azores and Madeira), with elected governments and a limited revenue raising power mainly from customs and fuel duties. There are also the controversial *administrative regions*, only legally defined in the Constitution of 1976.

Financial Situation

Nowadays, Portuguese local government consumes a relatively small part of public expenditure (8%), corresponding to around 4% of the gross domestic product.

Local government financial resources are divided mainly into three types of resources. First, there are the self-generated resources: property taxes (since 1987 the property transaction tax became the most important – about 35% of total); vehicle tax; tourism tax (in 1987 it was replaced by a 37,5% share in the V.A.T. generated by local tourism); a share in enterprises' income (which is the only – however limited – tax that municipalities can introduce autonomously), and other minor taxes. Second, there are the European Union funds. And third, a complex *equalisation financial fund*, granted from the national budget and distributed mainly according to the size of the municipalities' population, which is crucial for the less developed municipalities.

In the first years after the democratic revolution, Portuguese municipalities were involved in actions relating to the solution of the main structural problems (e.g. road construction and repair, water and electricity supply, etc.). Lately they have been asserting their role in local economic development, upholding new industrial or other activities. However, if we compare the percentage of municipalities' capital investment (around 40% of total investments), we see the persistence of that *infrastructural* stage: excluding education and recreation investment (increasing from 7% to 13%, from 1983 to 1991), the other domains maintain their traditional *profile*.

A brief examination of the statistics shows that Portuguese local governments have been improving their financial standing, following the national economy's general improvement. The composition of their income (which is steadily growing) is less dependent on the equalisation fund, since other sources have become increasingly more important. This partially explains why municipalities became an important agent of the *modernization* mentioned above. However, this is a controversial issue, since local governments' revenues have been decreasing over the last years, while public expenditures have risen, causing a financial strain that remains to be solved, as municipalities are responsible for a major portion of general investment and employment.

Municipalities' Internal Organisation

Before analysing the position of the chief administrative officers, we present an overview of the internal organisation of the municipalities. As mentioned, the municipality is divided into two major political structures: the municipal assembly and the chamber. The chamber has a limited number of councillors (aldermen): from 4 to 16 *Vereadores*, according to the municipality's number of voters.

The chamber is the executive body of Portuguese municipalities. It is led by the mayor (formally, the first name on the list presented by the winning party of the local election for the chamber), but includes other councillors according to a proportional system (which in some cases prevents the formation a single party majority). According to Law 18/91 (replacing Law 100/84, improving the mayor's powers) the chamber is the body responsible for executing and faithfully pursuing the assembly's decisions and planning annual activities, with its respective budget.

Most of the chamber's powers can be delegated to the mayor, with one important exception: the elaboration and execution of the annual plan of activities. The mayor has specific duties: besides representing the municipality and co-ordinating the chamber's activity, he has to submit the accounts to the assembly (for approval) and then to the Court of Auditors. Analysing recent changes on local government's legislation, we note that the mayor's powers have been increased. He has become the real chief executive officer of the municipality, since he is also responsible for the management and direction of human resources, and he has the power to "change or revoke acts carried out by municipal personnel" (see Article 53 of the reviewed Law 100/84). Finally, only the mayor can delegate part of his powers to other elected members, such as councillors obliged to present detailed reports on their activity.

We can distinguish a range of strategies used by mayors: 1) those who do not delegate powers to the opposition councillors, although they have the majority in the chamber; 2) those who, despite having the majority, try to create more consensus and delegate some powers (not the very important powers) to the opposition; 3) mayors who are forced to negotiate with the councillors of the "opposition", as they hold only a relative majority.

The administrative structure can be divided into four different sections. First, there are the municipal services (general administration, treasury and other special services). Second, there are municipalised services (not autonomous since they are directed by the mayor or by an alderman (economic activities such as water supply, sanitation, public transportation, etc.). Third, some municipal services can be replaced by public municipal enterprises (having administrative and financial autonomy). Finally, there are in some cases private enterprises with a concession (usually awarded by municipalities' associations) to provide services such as waste disposal or water supply.

How can we understand the relations between these agents inside the municipality? Here we should define different levels drawing on Mintzberg (1979), where the head of administration may have different roles (see Alfaiate, 1988).

First there is the political level of direction (the "strategic apex"), where the mayor may share his powers with other persons, including the chief administrative officer who in some cases becomes a real chief executive officer, or in other cases a mere bureaucrat, holding limited powers.

Second, we find the intermediate level ("the middle line"), where the technical expertise is often linked more with the conception than with the execution of specific projects. Here, the head of administration is concerned mostly with technical details. However, this kind of work tends to become a more or less deliberate barrier to the political direction's objectives (mostly if these objectives prove difficult to achieve).

Third is the "operating core", where, on one hand, we find manual workers, usually complaining about their work conditions, but also seeing their role as an active one in the execution of the projects; on the other hand, lower level officers who tend to react more passively. This usually occurs if they perceive that possible changes in the municipality may affect them negatively. In these cases, it is possible that they may try to oppose changes, namely through the intervention of their union.

Fourth, we find the "technostructure" and logistical services. Placed in a peripheral position, this level plays a supporting role. When, however, there is a staff closer to the political direction (giving advice about the organisational design), the head of administration may see his role reduced to that of executing orders which he has not even had the opportunity to discuss.

The Situation of Chief Administrative Officers in the Local Political-Administrative System

Until 1984, the administrative functions of Portuguese municipalities were under the responsibility of a chief secretary, a job similar to that of a CEO in other countries. In reality, however, their work was somewhat limited by the demands of a highly bureaucratic organization. This chief secretary belonged to a national board placed under central government control: his status and functions were defined by national administrative law, which was applicable countrywide. This situation began to change with the democratic Constitution of 1976, since it proclaimed the principle of decentralisation and local autonomy, and stipulated that municipalities should have their own personnel, whom they should manage and pay.

After 1984 this principle was applied to local administration. Each municipality was to set up and elaborate its own organisation and personnel.

The chief administrative officers' activities may vary from municipality to municipality. Generally, they participate in the drawing up and carrying out of the municipality's policies and budgets, they also participate in human resource management and supervision, managing also organisations that belong to the general direction of the department, division or area under the authority of the mayor (or other councillors). Furthermore, the head of administration usually has the following powers: 1) notary public in contracts involving the municipality; 2) adjudicating fiscal disputes (debts); 3) state delegate to exhibitions; 4) secretary of council meetings (usually responsible for the minutes); 5) supervisor of specific tasks relating to the management of human, financial and patrimonial resources; 6) proposing of possible improvements of structures, work methods and equipment; 7) certification of the facts and acts belonging to municipal records.

Nevertheless, an important change concerning administrative leadership was introduced, and the new chief administrative officers lost the ability to control the municipal organisation. According to the chairman of the Portuguese association of municipal officers: "in Portugal, after 1984, the head of administration no longer holds the overall control of the co-ordination between municipal services" (Dias, 1995: 6). Besides, in many cases, when the CAO belongs to a political party different from that of the recently elected mayor's party, the new mayor may change the internal administrative set-up, i.e., via a request made to the Ministry of Administration for a special temporary appointment of chief administrative officers from other places, who can replace the existing CAOs.

A closer look at the legal framework allow us to conclude that in important aspects the CAO's status was preserved.[5] Moreover, financial and, mainly, legislative knowledge make him a strategic agent, even when his position is held in low esteem by the mayor's personal staff. In conclusion, it is not evident, as some CAOs maintain, that their importance is decreasing. In small municipalities (and when they have the confidence of the mayor in political matters) they can be real chief executive officers through their personal influence, through what we can term their "symbolic capital", a concept discussed by the French sociologist Pierre Bourdieu and the American political scientist Clarence Stone.

The Background and Values of Heads of Administration: Survey Findings

The Background

Our findings show that the typical Portuguese chief administrative officer is a middle-aged man (50 years old), trained in law or economics, having recently been appointed to his present position (5 years ago on average). Almost one-third are women, and about 60% do not have university degrees.

It should be noted, however, that according to our survey there has been a recent "rejuvenation" change in age composition, as many of the municipalities' former chief administrative officers recently faced retirement.

---

5 We tried to understand what happened during this transition and found two different laws in a one-and-half-year period: Law 116/84 on the "Organisation and Functioning of the Technical-Administrative Services in Local Government" (6 April 1984); then, another law (amending some articles of Law 44/85 of 13 September 1985). Six years later, another decree, 198/91 (29 May 1991) amended two previous laws. Finally, the government passed Law 198/95 (29 May 1995). One of the main reasons for these changes was the temporary situation of the former Chefes de Secretaria (appointed by a national board since 1936), who could serve as CEOs. At the same time the ATAM (Portuguese Association of Municipal Chief Administrative Officers) changed its statutes in order to integrate all administrative officers. In fact, a major change from Law 116/84 to Law 44/85 relates to their financial situation: instead of earning up to the limit of 50% of their basic wage from their function as notary in municipal contracts, the limit was increased up to 70%. Many of the changes were indeed centered on the improvement of the chief administrative officer's position. Even if the changes are not very important, they can be interpreted as being influenced by CAO lobbying. The current chairman of the Portuguese CAO association told us that this relationship with the central power (mainly with lower political levels) is very important to the association.

Based on their background we find two important types of chief administrative officers. On one hand, we find those who worked their way up through the ranks; on the other hand, we find the chief administrative officers holding a university degree who are usually younger than the former. We should note that according to Law 198/91, municipalities can recruit chief administrative officers from persons holding a university degree (or equivalent), or from personnel already making an administrative career.[6] In this way, the young graduates can be seen as promoters of changes in the *establishment*.

The survey also tells us that a vast majority of chief administrative officers were recruited from the public sector's administrative career (only 23% came from the private sector), local administration being the most important source: one-third had their first job here and 49% had their previous job in the present municipality or in another).

Thus, it seems that the identity of the Portuguese chief administrative officer is largely influenced by the tradition built around a local government career system and preserved by its older members. Furthermore, the Portuguese Association of Municipal Officers (ATAM) is mainly led by this kind of self-made professionals.

We find a significant difference between 1) the more traditional background, originating from within municipal or central administration, and concerned mainly with legal procedures and 2) the professionals who are mainly concerned with the results of municipal activities as a whole. Returning to our findings, the causes cited for resignation provide interesting information about this process. In fact, 11% acknowledged co-operation problems with politicians as the cause of the former chief administrative officer's resignation, which indicates a conflict with politicians caused probably, as suggested above, by the administrative apparatus' resistance to its colonisation by a clientelistic system centered on political control and domination.

Role Perceptions: the Chief Administrative Officer and the Politicians

Analysing the CAO's daily activities, we noted above that as a strategic agent influencing local government's policies, he holds limited autonomy. If we com-

---

6 Concerning the chief administrative officers' training, there are two major institutions in Portugal: CEFA (Centre for Municipal Studies and Training), which organizes courses on municipal affairs, and the above mentioned ATAM (Association of Municipal Administrative Officers), organizes regional meetings for professional improvement and courses for local officers, supported by European Union funding. CEFA's courses (a school directed both by central government and by the National Association of Municipalities) are officially recognised for the purpose of recruiting municipal personnel. This centre is an important agent for the local government's modernisation in Portugal. However, when we interviewed some of the graduates, they told us that there is a gap between what they were taught and the reality of local administration. Recently, CEFA's policy is to favour technical instead of organisational theory courses.

Concerning their salaries, the head of department and the head of division earn 80% and 70% respectively of the central administration's general director's wage; some of the CAOs may also earn up to the limit of 70% of their basic wage from their function as notary public in municipal contracts. We may thus conclude, and the majority of the respondents confirm, that the job is attractive.

pare the municipality with a private enterprise, the CAO would be subordinated to the general manager (the mayor). In this way, his roles are limited to day-to-day management. Apparently, the considerable volume of legislation with which he must deal forces him to work mainly as a legal advisor to the chairman.

Table 14.1 shows some results about the way Portuguese CAOs perceive their own roles. Based on the two ideal-types suggested by Putnam's classical work, it seems that the classical bureaucrat type is preferred to the political bureaucrat. In other words, according to the scale presented in the survey, the neutral-role model, centred on the technical and administrative functions, receives an average preference of 78 (on the 0-100 index), although the value found for the other model (the political bureaucrat) is also significant (66).[7] If we disregard the "political advisor" role, the result would be closer to the one found for the "classical bureaucrat" model (73). A possible explanation to this ambiguity is the CAO's desire to gain political support: as mentioned earlier, their present condition is perceived as one of a certain degree of disempowerment caused by the abolition (in 1984) of the municipal secretary and the reinforcement of the powers of local politicians.

Looking at the specific variables in table 14.1, we find a *dissonant* statistic: giving political advice to the mayor is seen as having little importance (28). Our interpretation of this score is that the word "political" has a meaning often related (at least in Portugal) to political parties and to local elections. The administrative leader thus chooses to operate on a neutral basis, outside political struggles. Nevertheless, preferring the classical bureaucratic role (in the Weberian sense), the CAO displays a growing concern with some of the strategic tasks performed on the basis of the profile of the political bureaucrat.

Therefore, if we note the emphasis placed on the correct implementation of rules and regulations (the second highest score: 81), it is somewhat contradictory with the high emphasis also placed on the formulation of ideas and projects: moreover, data from our qualitative research reveal that Portuguese chief administrative officers tend to present themselves as partisans of modernization and the improvement human relations. This reinforces our initial argument about the structural ambiguity found in these professionals.

The distinction between a classical or a political bureaucrat could lead to a dubious conclusion in this situation. We must bear in mind the legal limits preventing the chief administrative officer from becoming a real political bureaucrat. Instead, he may hold a symbolic leading office as the administrative ally of the mayor besides his role as an agent of rationalisation.

---

[7] The average scores have been estimated on a range variation from "0" (very little or no importance) to "100" (utmost importance). The other results from the U.Di.T.E. Leadership Study follow the same presentation scheme.

Table 14.1 The roles of the CEOs, Portugal

The classical bureaucrat		78
Guide subordinate staff in day-to-day handling of activities	75	
Manage economic affairs, accounts and budgetary control	74	
Ensure that rules and regulations are followed	81	
Provide the mayor with legal, economic and other kinds of technical advice	82	
The political bureaucrat		66
Formulate ideas and visions	78	
Promote and encourage new projects in the community	69	
Provide the mayor with political advice	28	
Be informed about citizens' viewpoints	68	
Develop and implement norms concerning the proper roles of politicians vis-á-vis the bureaucrats	78	
Influence decision-making processes in order to secure sensible and efficient solutions	72	

Complementary to these ideas, we present in table 14.2 some findings about the way CAOs perceive the ideal role of leading politicians.

First, we note the CAOs' negative attitude toward assuming a role as elected representatives of their political party (37). Thus, the mayor and the councillors should be above all members of the whole managing board, dealing with every aspect of municipal policy and having a comprehensive view of the development strategy (87). This perception induces a high valuation of the role of creating stability: we interpret this as based on the respondents' assumption that politicians should not interfere with the administrative machine. This position can be understood as a way of enlarging the CAO's influence in the more concrete aspects of municipal affairs. However, this tendency is not clear since the decision on specific cases is still seen as an important prerogative for politicians (70).

In conclusion, the ideal role for the politicians does not seem to reveal a specific profile. Instead, we arrive at a more negative definition: beyond fulfilling their legal obligations, politicians should avoid interference from both political parties and local groups.

Nevertheless, we still maintain that these explanations imply a deeper exploration of our survey and other qualitative data.

Table 14.2 The ideal politician, Portugal

Administration		63
Be a spokesperson for local groups or individuals who have issues pending decision by the authority	49	
Lay down rules and routines for the administration	69	
Taking decisions concerning specific cases	70	
Representation		67
Be informed about citizens' views	83	
Represent the municipality to the outside world	78	
Defend the authorities' decisions and policies externally	75	
Be a spokesperson for their political party	37	
Be a spokesperson vis-á-vis the press	62	
Governance		79
Implement the program on which he/she has been elected	77	
Decide on major policy principles	73	
Have a vision of the way in which the municipality will develop in the long run	87	
Stability		86
Create stability for the administration	84	
Formulate exact and unambiguous goals for the administration	87	

Networks

In this section, we would like to discuss our initial idea of a dualistic political structure.[8] We know that beyond the empirical findings we are dealing with traditionally informal networking practices which in Portugal tend to reproduce clientelistic traditions. We are also aware that great changes are taking place with regard to strategies directed towards the promotion and shaping of bureaucratic procedures.

However it is wishful thinking to assume transparency and equality in the discussion when we analyze political processes, and particularly their implementation. Perhaps a more probing perspective would be to assume a *diversity* of ways in which policies are implemented regardless of the context. Thus, it may be argued that we never have a stable framework for the political dimension. To talk about politics means talking about a series of dynamic processes.

We have here a combination based on two democratic ideal-types: the archetypal ancient Greek city-state (in the writings of Rousseau, Montesquieu or Tocqueville considered an example of participatory democracy) and the liberal-democratic representative system, considered by R. Dahl (1989) as an adaptation of the previous model to complex contemporary societies.[9] Both these ideal-types are now resuscitated by the necessity to manage public economic resources in accordance with budgetary requirements. Today we see this as the ideal model of democracy, commonly, and more or less explicitly, accepted by contemporary social and political scientists.

Next, we choose as an important dimension of the chief administrative officer's network the pressures from specific problems on his job. In the questionnaire we asked whether the following items influenced the daily work of the chief administrative officer in a negative way: demands for better services, unemployment and social problems, pressures from local organized interests. We found that none of the three issues seemed to disturb the bureaucratic machine (an average score of 23).

An additional finding may help us confirm this impression. Looking at figure 14.1, we are not surprised to observe the decreasing level of conflict perceived in the relation between the CAOs and the actors investigated in the survey. As shown in the figure, almost none of the respondents claimed to have conflicting relations with different actors. Most of the responses concerning journalists, trade unions or other public officers were in the category of moderate conflict. Moreover, the level of conflict varies inversely with the level of dependency (how important are the relations with the several agents) and with the level of contact.

---

8 This part of the chapter is partially based on Maurizio Gamberucci's contribution to a paper presented together with Joel Felizes at the Oslo Summer School on Local Government Studies (Gamberucci and Felizes, 1997).

9 For a critical approach to the classical theories of democracy, and for the relation between social complexity and democracy, see Zolo (1992).

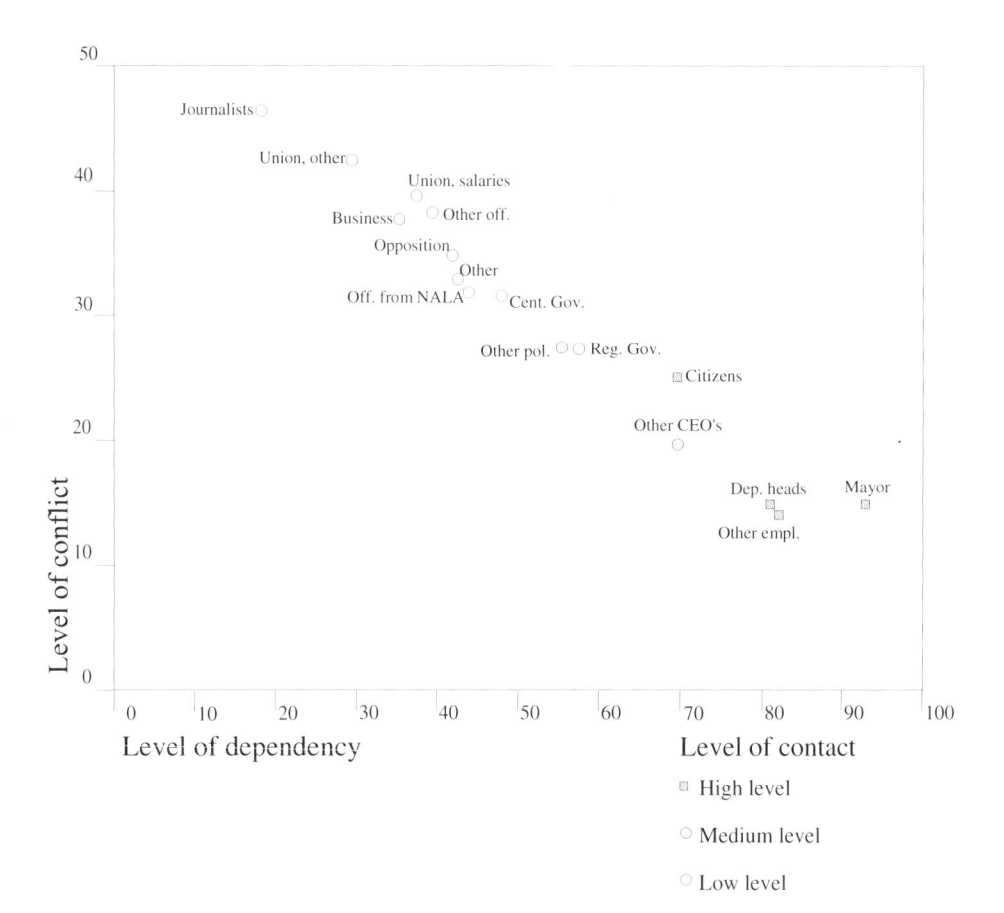

Figure 14.1 Contact, conflict and dependency, Portugal

[Scatter plot with x-axis "Level of dependency" / "Level of contact" (0 to 100) and y-axis "Level of conflict" (0 to 50). Data points plotted:
- Journalists (~20, 45)
- Union, other (~25, 40)
- Union, salaries (~35, 38)
- Business (~30, 36)
- Other off. (~40, 36)
- Opposition (~35, 33)
- Other (~40, 31)
- Off. from NALA (~30, 30)
- Cent. Gov. (~45, 30)
- Other pol. (~40, 25)
- Reg. Gov. (~45, 25)
- Citizens (~65, 24)
- Other CEO's (~60, 20)
- Dep. heads (~70, 14)
- Mayor (~85, 14)
- Other empl. (~70, 12)

Legend:
■ High level
○ Medium level
○ Low level

How can we explain this apparently ambiguous phenomenon? How can we define local authorities' attitudes according to which segments of the community the doors of the Town Hall seem to be open, but at the same time being closed to conflicts? Again, as previously indicated, this ambiguity can be seen as a result of a pragmatic turn to politics. Yet we nevertheless maintain our skepticism: we should not assume the possibility of the dyad *politics-consensus*.

Instead, we interpret this conflict avoidance as reflecting a "paternalistic" strategy. The paternalism stems from the authorities' belief that they "know best" how to manage municipal affairs. Research conducted under a developmental perspective on English local government found this attitude present among local officials dealing with the public in the 1970s. At that time this was related to a recent administrative reorganization of the offices, resulting in bureaucratic professionalisation. All this promoted an attitude toward the public as if it were composed of "clients" without any real authority as to who should "accept the superior judgement of the professional" (Gower Davies, 1974, quoted in Burns *et al.,* 1994: 40). The authors stressed a transformation of the relations with the public, passing through different styles of government in the 1980s and 1990s: the "new right" extended market models, treating people as "consumers", the new managerialism considered the public as "customers", and, finally, what they call extended democracy, dealing with "citizens" who have the real right to express their voice.

Our purpose here is not to define narrow evolutionist patterns of development: instead, we intend to discuss some possible interpretations of the present situation, based on the evidence we found. We expect to find *hic et nunc* a paternalistic attitude, although we are aware of the shifting context with which we are dealing.

Conclusion

We have tried to analyze and characterize the surveyed Portuguese local administration, focusing on the chief administrative officer's position and perspective. We have shown that the context surrounding the chief administrative officer is largely influenced by the legal framework and by the relation that he maintains with the mayor. We also noted that in different ways this context combines practices relating to what we termed a pre-modern background and to a late modern complexity.

One of the most sensitive issues deals with the chief administrative officers' powers, leading us to dismiss their specification as chief executive officers, since this function is usually under the mayor's control. In some (usually smaller) municipalities, however, the chief administrative officer can operate as a real chief executive officer, using his *symbolic capital*.

One possible conclusion for our study is inspired by our theoretical framework in its close relation with our empirical sensitivity. In other words, we developed our argument around the *constructed* intuition that the Portuguese chief administrative officer is mostly worried about the *reproduction* of the system, stressing its normative structure, but at the same time producing a modernizing discourse, which justifies the gap between *saying* and *doing*. This gap is more or less reduced according not only to the chief administrative officer's background but also to the organisational model in which he is placed. This explains our hesitation to construct a clear typology combining more or less modern organizations with the different kinds of chief administrative officers.

Bibliography

Alfaiate, José (1988): O funcionalismo administrativo autárquico, *Revista Crítica de Ciências Sociais*, no. 25-26.

Burns, D., Hambleton, R., and Hoggett, P. (1994): *The Politics of Decentralisation. Revitalising Local Democracy*, London: Macmillan.

Capela, José V. (1995): *O Minho e os Seus Municípios*, Braga: Universidade do Minho.

Clark, Terry Nichols (1996): Small is innovative: local government innovation strategies in the United States and other countries, in Nahum Ben-Elia, *Strategic Changes and Organizational Reorientations in Local Governments. A Cross-National Perspective*, London: Macmillan Press, pp. 21-39.

Costa, Manuel S., Felizes, Joel, and Neves, José P. (1997): European integration and local government: the (ambiguous) Portuguese case, in Michael Goldsmith and Kurt Klausen (eds.), *European Integration and Local Government*, Cheltenham: Edward Elgar pp. 172-188.

Couto, Margarida, and Gaio, Carlos (1990): Informática nas autarquias municipais, *Informação Regional*, Porto, no. 1.

Dahl, Robert A. (1989): *Democracy and Its Critics*, New Haven and London: Yale University Press.

Dias, Artur Vieira (1995): Nota de abertura, *XV Colóquio Nacional da ATAM – Setúbal/95. Comunicações*, Santarém: ATAM.

Gamberucci, Maurizio, and Felizes, Joel (1997): *Political and administrative leaders in Italy and Portugal: local participated democracy as a challenge*. Unpublished paper presented at the Third Annual European Summer School in Local Government Studies, Oslo.

Giddens, Anthony (1987): *Social Theory and Modern Society*, Oxford: Polity Press.

Giddens, Anthony (1992): *As Consequências da Modernidade*, Lisbon: Celta.

Lyotard, Jean-François (1984): *The Postmodern Condition: A Report on Knowledge*, Manchester: Manchester University Press.

Martins, Moisés L. (1993): A identidade regional e local e intervenção autárquica. Da ideia polarizada de desenvolvimento (paradigma centro/periferia) à definição da comunidade como experiência translocal, in Manuel S. Costa and José P. Neves (eds.), *Autarquias Locais e Desenvolvimento*, Porto: Afrontamento.

Mintzberg, Henry (1979): *The Structuring of Organizations*, Englewood Cliffs, N.J.: Prentice-Hall.

Monteiro, Nuno Gonçalo (1993): Os concelhos e as comunidades, in José Mattoso (ed.), *História de Portugal*, Lisbon, Círculo de Leitores, vol. 4, pp. 303-332.

Nieto, Lourdes López (1997): The Spanish Workshop, in Michael Goldsmith and Poul Erik Mouritzen (eds.), *The U.DI.T.E. Leadership Study. Report from the 3rd Congress, 6-7 September 1996, Odense, Denmark*, Odense: Kommunaldirektørforeningen i Danmark.

Rocha, J. Oliveira (1988): *Contributo para o estudo das elites locais: o caso da elite Administrativa de Braga*, Mimeo.

Santos, Boaventura de Sousa (1985): Estado e sociedade na semiperiferia do sistema mundial, *Análise Social*, no. 87-88-89, vol. 21, pp. 869-901.

Silva, M. Carlos (1994): Peasants, patrons and the state in northern Portugal, in L. Roniger and A. Günes-Ayata (eds.), *Democracy, Clientelism and Civil Society*, Boulder: Lynne Rienner, pp. 29-47.

Wallerstein, Immanuel (1984): *The Politics of the World-Economy*, Cambridge: Cambridge University Press.

Zolo, Danilo (1992): *Democracy and Complexity*, Cambridge: Polity Press.

CHAPTER 15

Functions and Duties of Funcionarios Directivos Locales (Local Chief Officers)

by Irene Delgado, Lourdes López Nieto and Eliseo López

The Municipalities and the Decentralisation Process

Two decades after the enforcement of the new institutional rules by which the 1978 Constitution established a new territorial structure, the result is more of a fragmentation than an orderly distribution of spheres of power. Simply from reading newspapers, it becomes clear that we are confronted with a difficult distribution of powers and spheres of action between actors and levels of government. If we add to this that Spain joined the European Community and that, consequently, Spain is involved in transnational politics, the idea of a complex administrative situation becomes evident. The predominant features are an overlapping of authorities and regulations, competition for power and resources, and governmental officials acting with increased freedom and capability of exploiting the various representative and governmental institutions at each level (ERA, 1997). With regard to public expenditures, approximately 88% of the resources in 1980 were managed by the central administration and the remaining 12% by local governments. Of over one-and-a-half million public employees, 1.3 million were in the central administration and approximately 350,000 in the municipalities. In 1996, the 17 *Comunidades Autónomas* (Autonomous Municipalities or AACC), controlled more than 26% of the country's public expenditures and employed more than 600,000 persons. For their part, local authorities had around 167,000 employees, a figure which has now risen to 425,000. Actually, the officers currently working for the AACC and local authorities equal the number working for the State central administration. This is why the progressive consolidation of AACC affects the functioning of local authorities.

Spanish local authorities are numerous, a feature they share with other countries in the Napoleonic tradition. The more than 8,000 municipalities are distributed unequally if compared to the populations living in them.[1] This complex local structure is formed by 50 other authorities as well, the provincial councils, whose functions consist in cooperating with municipalities by providing support for the supply of certain services. The mobility of the Spanish population in the 1960s was not accompanied by new territorial organizations as occurred in many Western democracies. Such reforms have not been carried out, so the territory is still highly fragmented, and this affects the execution of the functions attributed to the municipalities. While the consequences of the processes of decentralizing have been criticized, this does not diminish its general legitimacy. Critics point out that there has been an increase in administrative levels without a simultaneous local restructuring and administrative reform. The decentralizations have been rather costly, because neither the efficiency nor the productivity of local management has increased. This is due mainly to the fact that decentralization has been implemented with little firmness and plenty of hesitation when it was time to introduce a new kind of authority. The old ways of making politics, mainly those of "party power", have also survived without generating new patterns of participation. Finally, the contemporaneous occurrence of these processes with the crisis of the Welfare State has caused a reduction in the provision of social services, as functions were transferred without the necessary resources to accomplish them. The number of political leaders increased as the administrative corporate system and patron-client relations became more solid. Moreover, private actors have now acquired a legal status, leaving only support or coordination functions for public administrations to perform (Borja, 1985).

Although experts are in favor of reforming the municipal structure in order to promote the formation of stronger organizations, which will be the basis of a new local system, political forces have given up proposing drastic and complex solutions in this field (Font i Llovet, 1992:31). Apart from the topics mentioned above, this "impasse" is a consequence of the leading role that municipalities and provincial councils have always had in Spanish political history and also of the patron-client relations in financial and political fields.[2]

Since 1982, socialist majority governments paid more attention to matters related to the autonomous decentralisation than to municipal matters, although this was not a priority process on their political agenda. This is proven by the fact that although the Spanish Constitution recognizes municipal autonomy, no basic local rules were approved until 1985. Therefore, municipalities essentially main-

---

[1] Municipalities with over 100,000 inhabitants (1.2% of the total) elect 2.1% of the councillors, representing 41.3% of the population. Municipalities of 20,000 to 100,000 inhabitants (2.8%), elect 8.1% of the councillors, representing 22.9% of the population. Finally, 96.5% of the municipalities with less than 20,000 inhabitants (4% of the population) elect 89.1% of the councillors (Capo, 1991; Vallés y Sánchez, 1994; Delgado, 1997).

[2] The processing of the last population census by the superior institutions (National Institute of Statistics, INE, and the AACC) revealed an increase of one million "non-existent" inhabitants, owing to the fact that many municipalities chose not to delete from their records many deceased or non-resident inhabitants. The number of inhabitants is one of the main criteria used in allocating public funds.

tained their limited authority. Legislation on local finances was not reformed until 1988, when the AACC asked for financial matters to be transferred to them. When during the 1992-93 economic crisis the central government was obliged to restrict municipal borrowing, municipalities had to increase the rates of the (few) taxes they collected directly. This situation caused a protest from local governments for a more equitable distribution between revenues and expenditures derived from service provision.

Since 1993, national governments have been minority governments, and until today the autonomous decentralization is not yet complete and local autonomy is still "under way". This ambiguity on the part of the State also extends to the power of mayors, who have exercised it unequally; they have at times performed their functions extensively, while the State was passive; this caused tensions with the autonomous governments because in practice, local governments despite their scarce legal, human and material resources had to solve many problems in order to provide services. The "local agreement" was then entered on the political agenda in order to solve these problems. After the 1991 elections, within the Spanish Association of Municipalities and Provinces (FEMP), mayors agreed to ask the central government to be granted the same status as the AACC in public spending: in practice, they demanded 25% of total public expenditures. During the previous years, the two biggest parties the Socialist Party, and the conservative Popular Party agreed on the following distribution of public funds: 50% to the State, 25% to the AACC, 25% to the local governments. In practice, however, these proposals are not applied. The failure to apply this agreement is advantageous to regional governments, which try to obtain the powers demanded by the municipalities. Possibly, in a not too distant future, the AACC might be granted the power to "administer the tranfer" of authority, which would increase regional inequality even further. Although the law grants local authorities the right to look after the municipality's own interests, the control of these interests varies significantly between them.

Mayors and Funcionarios Directivos (FD) in the Spanish Local System

The Spanish municipal system, established in the 19th century on the basis of the Napoleonic model, recognizes the principle of equality of all municipalities (Botella, 1994: 105). However, experience shows that the disparities existing between municipalities make it difficult to analyse complex political relationships. The local political elite is formed by 8,088 *alcaldes* (mayors) and over 57,000 *concejales* (councillors). The councillors are directly elected by citizens, through a proportional representation system of closed and blocked lists, in which 5% of all the votes cast are needed to have access to the distribution of seats.

Spanish mayors have traditionally played a very important role, equivalent to a semi-presidential model. The mayor is the candidate of the party with the most votes and is elected by a majority of votes after the council has been established. Once elected, the council can exercise control over the mayor only through the approbation of budgets and motions of censure.[3]

The mayor can also count on the support of a staff of public administrators who have specific non-political functions. Among them are approximately 6.800 local CEOs (FD) with national qualifications, representing only 1.4% of the total amount of local government officers. Most of them work as FD in municipalities with less than 5,000 inhabitants.[4] From a formal point of view, their functions enable us to recognize them as local chief officers. The Local Government Act stipulates that the basic functions of these officers working for local authorities are "exercise of authority, certification of documents, compulsory legal advice and control; internal supervision of the economic-financial management; budget, accounts and treasury control as well as those generally reserved to officials for a better guarantee of objectivity, impartiality and independence while performing their functions" (Art. 92.2). In small municipalities employees are in charge of all these tasks, while in larger towns treasurers and auditors are in charge of fiscal matters.

The most influential FDs are those working in small municipalities. They usually perform more functions than those legally assigned to them because mayors have a lower level of education (Delgado y López Nieto, 1994).[5] On the other hand, the other *Funcionarios Directivos* play a more neutral role while carrying out their work, owing to the fact that mayors can use their semi-presidential powers more extensively.

The recruitment system is implemented through a complex process which requires the possession of certain prerequisites: FDs should have at least a first university degree and pass an examination to enter the Institute of Local Government Studies. In this national institution they are trained and examined in different "subclasses", and both the ranking obtained in the test and the curriculum vitae are taken into account. They can eventually choose to apply for different posts where specific qualifications are required (in recent years the State has delegated its participation in the recruitment process to the AACC). This type of access is spreading and allows the FDs a higher level of mobility in their professional careers. Today, most FD positions are occupied by lawyers or economists, although access to third grade positions requires only a three-year university course degree or a few years' working experience in a similar position.

---

[3] The regulation of motions of censure was first introduced by the 1985 Electoral Law; one-third of the votes in favour was required to replace a mayor. Political practice in the years that followed has shown the ineffectiveness of these rules. Therefore, the 1991 electoral reform was introduced to strengthen these regulations and make them equal to the votes of constructive motions regulated by the Constitution.

[4] Most FDs who are "third grade" secretaries, work in municipalities with less than 5,000 inhabitants; "second grade" secretaries work in towns with 5,000 to 20,000 inhabitants, and "first grade" secretaries in towns of more than 20,000.

[5] In 1991, 44% of mayors of towns with less than 20,000 inhabitants still had only a basic education; this percentage was lower in previous elections.

Over the last decades, these formal recruitment systems, meant to guarantee the political neutrality of FDs and ensure State control over the management of municipalities and mayors, have coexisted with other forms of recruitment because of the uncertainty and ambiguity of central governments with regard to municipalities. This has not been favourable for the recruitment of FDs. Examinations to enter the AACC or the State, for example, have not been organized as had been planned. Consequently, there have been an increasing number of interim officers who, in many cases, do not possess the qualifications of an FD. Since 1992, some mayors have chosen personal appointment, which has as its main consequence that the appointed "managers" are politically identified with the mayors (this system is awaiting legal ruling by the Constitutional Court). The current reform of the Statute of Public Administration will undoubtedly have to resolve this problem.

Professional Career and Social Setting

According to socio-demographic data, the average age of Spanish FDs is 54 years; 75% are under 44 and started performing their functions after age 25, due to the training requirements of this profession.[6] Within a group mostly formed by men, 27% of the FDs are women. They are comparatively younger and more numerous than the European average. The FDs come from middle-class families: in 24% the household head was a clerk or a skilled worker, in 16.5% a small entrepreneur or shopkeeper, in 18.5% a farmer or independent fisherman, and in 7% a liberal professional. The current earnings of FDs are higher than those of their fathers; consequently, it can be stated that these professionals have risen up the social scale.

Most FDs are university graduates (78%) and among these 61.5% have a law degree. The data show that these officials have undergone a substantial turnover compared to preceding periods. Those who have the specific skills for these positions have achieved them by studying and training for an average period of 19 years. Once the first position is obtained, only one-third attend any additional course on administration.

Spanish FDs are characterized by a certain isolation from other actors. This is also manifest in the limited possibilities to attend refresher courses. The demand for in-service training is precisely one of the priority demands to the *Asociación Nacional de Funcionarios Directivos*. At this point it should be noted that

---

6 The analysis made in the following pages is based on the data from a questionnaire sent to 5,000 FDs in December 1995, within the U.Di.T.E. project, with the collaboration of the Colegio Nacional de Funcionarios de Administración con Habilitación de Carácter Nacional. Of the responses of the sample 68.5% come from municipalities with less than 5,000 inhabitants, 17.4% from municipalities with 5,000 to 20,000 inhabitants, and 14.1% from municipalities with more than 20,000 inhabitants.

because of their geographical dispersion, they meet with great difficulties in attending those refresher courses which are not intensive or distance-learning courses. FDs do not always have easy access to the towns where the courses are held. Attendance at the courses increases when FDs have the prospect of a promotion. This is why 74% of the FDs do not follow any course on local government administration and attach greater importance to learning at their own place of work (27.8%) and to self-training (31.6%). In short, they are basically self-taught.

Most of the municipalities where FDs work are very small, a feature which influences their isolation. It should not be forgotten, however, that the main feature of these municipalities is their heterogeneity, which prevents any generalization. Working in these municipalities has its advantages and disadvantages. Among the former is the presumably higher social consideration in which the FD is held in small towns compared to big towns. Even if they are junior officers, (*secretarios-interventores* i.e., clerks-auditors), they enjoy higher social status, though some say this aspect is not as pronounced as in the past. Other aspects imply advantages and disadvantages at the same time; for example, it is easier to know the citizens' demands, but also easier to experience friction between the local administrators and the citizens when the decisions of the former have "negative" effects on the latter (e.g., the legality of an urban renewal plan). To avoid this, 60% of the FDs reside outside the municipality where they work. Labour mobility is scarce outside the region of origin, which explains why 67% of FDs work in the Autonomous Municipality where they have lived for part or all of their childhood. One of the consequences is that only one-third of them are members a local association (neighbourhood, consumer or parental association). It must be remembered, however, that associational life does not play a relevant role in the Spanish political and social culture. The isolation of these professional actors might, in theory, be an impediment to the performance of their tasks.

Another disadvantage is that daily practice leads the FDs to do all types of clerical work, even if this is not their main responsibilty as leaders and managers. Moreover, as may be expected, 61% of *secretarios-interventores* work with a very small staff – no more than 5 employees with clerical functions. Sometimes this situation causes conflicts between *alcaldes* and FDs when the FDs perform more functions than the law prescribes.

In general, Spanish FDs believe that today's working conditions are worse than they were 10 years ago; nevertheless, they welcome the acquisition of technology and the material changes which have taken place and appreciate the better training of their staff. The complex relationships with politicians, which has an apparent negative effect on the evaluation of their jobs, might be due to changes in the mayor's performance of his functions as head of local government in the aftermath of the 1985 legislation.

Additional evidence of the complex relationship with politicians is the high degree of FDs' geographical mobility: 49.5% have spent less than 6 years in the municipality where they now work and 10% even less than a year. This situation will probably continue, because 20% definitely wish to leave their present job, and 51.5% would not mind doing so were they given other opportunities. Partly, it may be attributed to their dissatisfaction with their present position, but it may also be due to their aspiring to a promotion, as happened to 23% of those who had occupied the same positions before them. Geographical mobility is not caused by job insecurity because employment as officials is secure per se.

The FDs' professional career has a low degree of interprofessional mobility because this is their objective when they finish their studies, perhaps because their expectations regarding promotion are high. In many cases it is their only working experience, as 57% had their first job as FD, 14% had another type of position in the (same) local authority, and another 9% started in other local authorities. Only 9.5% had previously worked in the business sector.

Factors, such as geographical mobility, lack of relationship with local citizens, strained relations with politicians, and absence of contact with other local levels of government, all strengthen the impression of isolation. On the other hand, FDs have had experience in other positions in the local authority where they carry out their professional activity, which is neutral, technical and does not risk being compromised within a politicised, tense and complex environment for decision-making. Perhaps this is why Spanish FDs' ideal job would be one which is secure, which would allow them the collaboration of their few colleagues and free time to spend with their families. They also value good physical conditions, relations with their superiors and opportunities for promotion.

Functions and Values of Funcionarios Directivos

Comparative studies on the functions of FDs in Europe have established a typology which distinguishes five types of functions (administrator, advisor, auditor, manager and tax collector). The combination of political practices and rules regulating the tasks of these local chief officers makes it difficult to fit them into defined models for any national analysis. However, it has been decided to establish a dual typology with comparative effects: the typical bureaucrat and the political bureaucrat.

The function of "bureaucrat" applies when the following functions are considered the most relevant: to provide daily guidance to employees, to organize and monitor economic and budget matters, to ensure rules are obeyed and provide the mayor with legal, technical and economic advice. Instead, a "policratic" FD would choose to develop mainly the following tasks: formulating ideas and programmes, promoting new projects in the community, providing the mayor with political advice, keeping informed of citizens' needs and demands; developing and implementing regulations on the relationships between politicians and bureaucrats, and influencing the decision-making process with the aim of ensuring effective solutions.

In Spain the distribution of authority between actors and levels of government is very complex and remains a subject of debate.[7] On the other hand, it should not be forgotten that the heterogeneity of the Spanish municipalities as a whole, their geographical position, size of population and economic aspects, are elements which make it difficult to make any generalizations.

Table 15.1 The roles of the CEOs, Spain

The classical bureaucrat		77
Guide subordinate staff in day-to-day handling of activities	64	
Manage economic affairs, accounts and budgetary control	77	
Ensure that rules and regulations are followed	78	
Provide the mayor with legal, economic and other kinds of technical advice	87	
The political bureaucrat		56
Formulate ideas and visions	70	
Promote and encourage new projects in the community	60	
Provide the mayor with political advice	16	
Be informed about citizens' viewpoints	55	
Develop and implement norms concerning the proper roles of politicians vis-á-vis the bureaucrats	64	
Influence decision-making processes in order to secure sensible and efficient solutions	69	

---

[7] A new statute of public administration is currently being debated which might in practice affect public management in various government activities. The implementation of local agreements and other political-administrative initiatives such as "the single window" are elements which influence the complex situation we are now analyzing.

Taking all these factors into account, the three functions considered most important by the FD in their daily work are: 1) to give legal, economic and technical advice to the mayor; 2) to guarantee efficient use of financial resources; and 3) to ensure observance of rules and regulations. Hence a profile of typical and perfectly identified functions have been allocated to the FDs by the laws which regulate this profession. FDs are essentially advisors – though completely excluding political advice to the mayor – and administrators, as they ensure that rules are obeyed and manage economic matters and budget control. To a lesser degree, FDs perform "integrative" functions, as they do not promote human relations among the municipal employees.

It might therefore be possible to attribute to Spanish FDs a "bureaucratic" profile, in its most typical sense, even though this conclusion should be compared with facts, that is to say, we should look into whether they perform these functions in their daily activity or whether they actually carry out more tasks.

The FDs laid down a clear outline of politicians' priorities concerning matters and functions that both politicians and they themselves normally carry out. They seem to have a clearer idea of the role that politicians should play than of their own functions. Therefore they believe that mayors should obtain external financial resources, preferably from other levels of governments, and also be informed of citizens' opinions. On the other hand, FDs would keep routine work for themselves, give priority to the development of the local authority's working methods and would also continue to have an important role in the granting of external financial resources. The lack of clarity about responsibility sharing between politicians and officers is undoubtedly the main problem the FDs face when they perform their duties. Moreover, this prevents the municipality's objectives from being achieved in coordination with the local authority's human resources. Nearly half the FDs believe that the existence of conflicts between the political parties of the municipality affects the development of their work.

Networks of Influence

The networks of the FD are directed mainly towards the municipal political system where the FDs perform their tasks and are in close touch with the mayor, but also towards the purely administrative context in which they carry out their activities and, to a lesser degree, towards other social actors. However, the isolation in which FDs work in the municipalities, is strikingly different from the situation of some decades ago when FDs were in charge of maintaining the town-hall and therefore resided there and looked after municipal properties.

When we talk about their relations to the political aspects of the municipal system, it is necessary to distinguish between the close contacts established with the mayor and those established with the opposition. The centrality of the mayor and the close relationship between conflict and dependency is illustrated in figure 15.1. In 70% of our sample, the governing party has the absolute majority, making the opposition of minor importance. On the political scene of the municipality, with the intention of taking part in local government, coalitions between political forces have entered upon agreements that have later been "exported" to higher levels of government. In all types of local governments, however, the mayor is of great importance. The stability of majorities in plenary assemblies, together with the excessive political importance of the figure of the mayor to the other political actors of the municipality, lead FDs to communicate mainly with the mayor. Relationships with the opposition are less important, if they were intense they would disappoint the mayors and endanger relations between FDs and mayors. Moreover, in most municipalities, politicians, who do not hold important political posts, have a professional position which leaves them little time for politics and for being in contact with FDs.

Figure 15.1 Contact, conflict and dependency, Spain

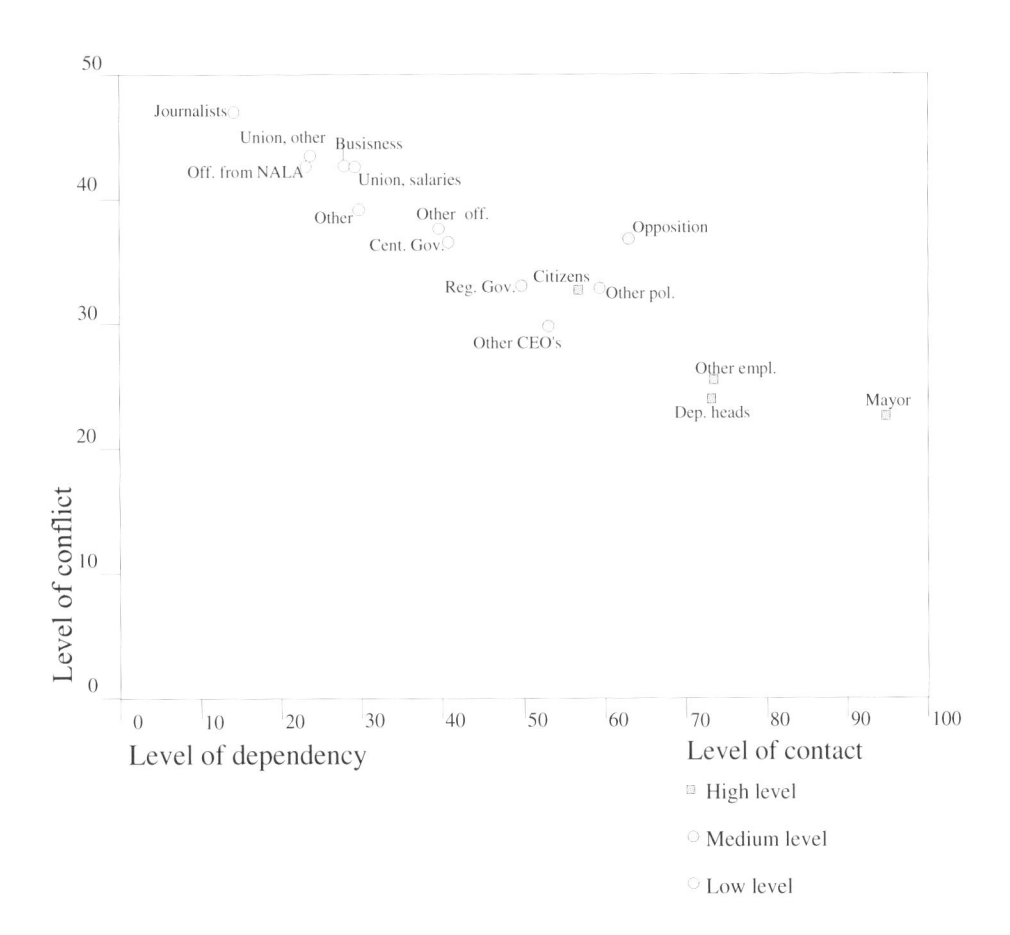

Three-fourths of the FDs (77%) communicate daily with the mayor, although the bigger the municipality, the less important the relation between them. Contacts with opposition groups and other municipal politicians are less frequent: only 34% meet every day; 23% never have contacts with the opposition and 35% have only occasional contacts. It can be deduced from the above that the FDs' relations are made up exclusively of very frequent contacts with the head of the local government and that they consider this relation important and positive for the implementation of their functions. However, although 82% define these relations as "cooperative", this response is conditioned by several factors: the neutral character they pretend to have while performing their duties; the mayor's political behaviour; the possibilities of moving within the country and within the same administration; the wage linking to the mayor, etc. In any case, these matters demand more complex and careful study and will not be dealt with in the preliminary part of this study.

It should be pointed out that, generally speaking, FDs expect politicians to delimit their own administrative authority: in this sense they think that the priority tasks that politicians should have are the following: first, "an overall view of the municipality's development in the long-term" (89.5%), and second, "formulate concrete and clear objectives for their administration" (88.7%). In short, the great majority agree with the idea that a local administration should not initiate important political changes without political guidelines. In the administrative environment, relationships between the FDs, the senior officials of the departments and the municipal employees are quite different. Here a closer "collaboration" takes place, more bureaucratic and less political, as their functions are closely connected. FDs, however, have hardly any relation with officers from other administrations.

Compared to the rest of the actors with some kind of influence on municipal life – pressure groups, citizens, journalists – FDs are not frequently in contact with them. This also adds to their isolation. Nonetheless, some social and political actors have a considerable influence over the budget and over the degree of economic development of the municipality. The logic of the economic component reappears as a decisive element in government activity and municipal administration. The budget is undoubtedly a subject of special importance, in which both politicians and FDs have interest. The mayor is the most influential person for making decisions to prepare the budget, then comes the majority political party and finally the FD. A total of 46.9% of the FDs believe that the mayor influences municipal budget matters considerably, even more so than higher government levels and local political parties. This influence is lower as far as the economic development of the municipality is concerned. The FDs believe that the widest range of influence rests with the mayor (71%). Private entrepreneurs are ranked above higher government levels (68%): they are those who start up the businesses which will influence the municipality; this influence is not due to their interactions with the local administration, but because they are considered essential actors for the strengthening of the environment; FDs rank behind the municipal majority party before the local political parties.

The Municipal Management and Its Challenges

There is no single standard for comparing priorities and control of management in the past and today as far as political decentralisation and distribution of functions are concerned. There is a split regarding the development of decentralization in so far as 42% were of the opinion that there has been a decentralisation to municipalities from other levels of government over the last decade, whereas 37% believe that a decentralization has not taken place. Moreover, 48% believe that there has been no change whatsoever in their municipalities with regard to delegation of functions in the lower levels of hierarchy, although 31% reported some changes. Neither was political delegation to the FDs identified by the majority of FDs (46%). In the Spanish local environment, the organization of the internal bureaucracy of a municipality depends on the municipality itself. The discretionary power to develop more decentralized forms of management does not seem to have been used. The weight of decision-making falls upon mayors, and the political environment prevails on the administrative one. The disparity of the standards found is important because new structures have been established. The AACC have adopted varying attitudes towards the municipalities. Furthermore, the indisputable formal decentralisation implemented by the State has not always been accompanied by the necessary resources, all of which limits the scope of decentralisation.

Economically, the municipalities are no longer solely dependent upon central government, but also on the AACC, and this dependence is even higher in smaller municipalities, even if they are now supposed to have more political and administrative autonomy. Nevertheless, municipalities may contact the *diputaciones provinciales* (provincial council), which are local institutions integrated by the municipalities. Their role is to obtain and distribute economic resources coming from higher-level administrations for service delivery to the municipalities or to the citizens when the municipalities cannot. In the *diputaciones,* however, large municipalities are more influential than the small, and regional and central organizations of political parties are more influential than local organizations.

The FDs' views on the debates on and processes of local administrative reform are fragmented. This is largely because these processes depend, as already pointed out, on the behavior and decisions of each mayor. In this sense, 56% feel that politicians have encouraged the participation of users, while 34% have not noticed any change. Fifty-seven per cent believe that a concern for efficiency in service delivery has increased, while 31% see no changes in the attitude of politicians. Quick decision-making is considered useful to improve management practice by 46%, but 39% believe there has been no change. According to the FDs,

49% of local authorities have attached more importance to goals such as providing equal access to public services, while 40% have not found any such changes.

The ideas FDs have about public administration reform are also contradictory. Two-thirds believe that the public sector has grown too much and that the private sector is more efficient, but at the same time two-thirds also believe that the need to change and reorganise local government has been overstated. Moreover, there is a split opinion between those who think that contracting-out is not very profitable and the 40% who do not agree with this statement. These apparent contradictions leave many interesting questions open for investigating local realities and current processes of administrative reform.

Spanish FDs are also divided when asked if the union of municipalities should encourage the improvement of efficiency of public services: 46% are for and just as many opposed. It is true that this problem is not among the priority issues on the Spanish political agenda; therefore one might be led to believe there are no definite opinions on the matter. The "formulas" of *mancomunidades* (union of municipalities or provinces) for service delivery turn out to be options to solve the inadequacies caused by the size of the municipalities. These options are being promoted by some autonomous governments, albeit with different mechanisms and objectives.

The fundamental problem as to how to improve the management of public municipal matters is a complex issue which at the same time should try to clear up the administrative and political functions, the distribution of financial resources and decrease municipal dependence on other levels of government.

Concluding Remarks

Heterogeneity, the predominant feature of Spanish municipalities, conditions any research on local realities.

The difference between what FDs do, the functions they would like to perform, and those they actually perform, is linked to the behaviour and political experience of the mayors. This situation often produces a "schizophrenia", which is the result of the conflicts and tensions between FDs and politicians; in practice, there is no delimitation of the authority granted to them by the law, partly because of the lack of flexibility in the relationships between the parts involved.

In this context, the professional future of Spanish FDs is uncertain. Meanwhile, there is no political will on the part of national political parties to implement agreements that would guarantee the principle of constitutional autonomy. At the same time, however, their problems are raised in the debate on the functions of public administration in Spain and in the persistence of the criterion which says that the bureaucratic machine acts in a "blind" or indifferent manner (Subirats, 1992: 47). Moreover, it is known that in practice, formal powers and informal/real powers do not always coincide in the Spanish administration, all of which makes it more difficult to exercise control procedures.

Bibliography

Baena, M. (1977) (ed.): La burocracia en España, Número monográfico de *Información Comercial Española*, no. 522.

Baena, M. (1984): *Estructura de la Función Pública y Burocracia en España*, Oñate: Instituto Vasco de Administración Pública.

Bañón, R. (1988): *Poder de la burocracia y Cortes franquista 1943-1971*, Madrid: Instituto Nacional de Administración Pública.

Bañón, R., and Carrillo, E. (1997): *La nueva administración pública*, Madrid: Alianza.

Batley, R., and Stoker, J. (ed.) (1991): *Local Government in Europe. Trends and Developments*, Houndmills: MacMillan.

Beltrán, M. (1977): *La élite burocrática española*, Barcelona: Ariel.

Beltrán, M. (1985): *Los funcionarios ante la reforma de la Administración*, Madrid: CIS-Siglo XXI.

Borja, J. (1985): Descentralización. Cuestión de método, *Autonomíes*, no. 2-3, pp. 21-46.

Botella, J. (1994): Local government in Catalonia: the making of a political élite, 1979-1991, in L. López Nieto (ed.) *Local Elections in Europe*, Barcelona: ICPS.

Capo, J. (1991): Elecciones municipales pero no localesn, *Revista Española de Investigaciones Sociológicas*, no. 56, pp. 143-164.

Chandler, J.A. (1993): *Local Government in Liberal Democracies*, London and New York: Routledge.

Delgado, I. (1997): *El comportamiento electoral municipal español, 1979-1995*, Madrid: Centro de Investigaciones Sociológicas.

Delgado, I., and López Nieto, L. (1994): Innovación urbana española: ¿una nueva clase política?", *Revista de Estudios Políticos*, no. 86, pp. 313-343.

ERA (1997): 15 años de experiencia autonómica. Un balance, *Informe España 1996. Una interpretación de su realidad social*, Madrid: Fundación Encuentro, pp. 373-385.

Fossas, E.-Colomé, G. (1993): *Political Parties and Institutions in Catalonia*, Barcelona: ICPS.

Groppi, T. (a cura di) (1993): *Il sistema di distribuzione delle competenze tra lo Stato e le Comunità Autonome*, Torino: C.EL.DA.B.

Iacometti, M. (1993): *L'ordinamento locale spagnolo*, Milano: Giuffré.

Linz, J.J., and De Miguel, A. (1968): La élite funcionarial española ante la reforma administrativa, *VV.AA. Sociología de la Administración pública española*, Madrid: Centro de Estudios Sociales.

Sheldrake, J. (1992): *Modern Local Government*, Aldershot: Dartmouth Publishing Company, Ltd.

Subirts, J. (1989): *Análisis de políticas públicas y eficacia de la Administración*, Madrid: INAP.

Subirts, J. (1991): La Administración pública como problema. El análisis de las políticas públicas como propuesta, *Documentación Administrativa*, no. 224-225, pp. 15-58.

Subirts, J. (1992): *Un problema de estilo. La formación de políticas públicas en España*, Madrid: Centro de Estudios Constitucionales.

Vallés, J.M., and Sánchez, J. (1994): Las elecciones municipales en España entre 1979 y 1991: balance provisional, in P. del Castillo (ed.) *Comportamiento Político y Electoral*, Madrid: Centro de Investigaciones Sociológicas, pp. 365-381.

CHAPTER 16

Executive Management at the Political-Professional Interface: CEOs in Israeli Local Government

by Nahum Ben-Elia

The multi-purpose nature of local government, the departmental structure and the problematic interface between elected officials and professional staff in Israel as elsewhere indicate the need for an effective corporate center. In the Israeli case, the need for a coordinating, integrating and control function – in the form of a Chief Executive Officer (CEO) – has been underlined by the fundamental changes affecting local government. Since the 1970s, Israel has witnessed the emergence of local government as the most active and entrepreneurial force in the public scene. This still unfolding change expresses a fundamental reversal of its historical subordinate role, vis-à-vis the central government. A variety of independent and disjointed forces – political, institutional and economic – have been moulding a new type of local government characterized by greater autonomy, public assertiveness and functional responsibilities. Local government has grown both in quantitative and qualitative ways. The increasing complexity of local affairs, the continuing demands for improved services to a growing population and the ongoing financial constraints require a greater capacity for guidance and control. As these requirements bring to their limit the capability of the mayor, as the leading executive figure, to handle efficiently the conduct of affairs, there has been a clear trend to introduce a CEO function. The number of municipal CEOs is still small. Only 42 out of 263 local authorities have appointed CEOs, mainly at the municipal level. Yet their relative importance in the local government scene is growing not only because of their personal standing but because of their impact on the shaping of local management. In this chapter I will analyze the CEO function in Israeli local government, in its contextual, behavioral and personal dimensions. The analysis is based on the results of a field survey conducted in 1996 using the methodological framework

---

1 The survey covered sixty-nine per cent of the total population. It followed the U.Di.T.E. joint questionnaire, with the exception of its last questions – questions 50 and onwards – related to the National Association of Local Government CEOs. The survey was conducted during the months of June to November 1996. A previous analysis of similar issues conducted in 1992 by the author added further information to the issues discussed.

of the joint U.DI.T.E. questionnaire and in-depth interviews within a smaller sub-sample.[1] The discussion is preceded by a background introduction to the main characteristics of the Israeli municipal system.

Institutional Background

The Municipal System

Israel's 263 local authorities include 61 municipalities, 147 urban local councils, 53 rural regional councils and 2 industrial local councils. Eighty-two local authorities are Arab and Druze (within the pre-1967 borders). Formal local government was introduced in Palestine in the second half of the last century by the Ottoman rulers. However, it was the British Mandate (1917-1947) that encouraged the development of local authorities and provided the legal and institutional blueprints (Gutman, 1958; Elazar and Kalchheim, 1988). The establishment of the State in 1948 and the creation of a central government hampered for many years the development of the local authority as a responsive local government and as an effective local administration. Public functions that in the past were the responsibility of local communities became the realm of national bodies. The rapid growth of the population, a result of massive immigration, increased the size and roles of national ministries, and their relative powers. The concentration of power at the national level weakened local government and left it with a subordinate role (Elazar and Kalchheim, 1988). Since the late 1970s, Israel experienced a fundamental reversal of historical central-local government relations. The ongoing tensions between the structural constraints of the public economy and the commitments of the welfare state, the managerial limitations of the central ministries to cope with a more complex reality, and the greater political assertiveness and functional capabilities at local level have resulted in an unfolding decentralization process. This process is not an output of positive policy-formulation, but, rather, an unplanned outcome of governance constraints – that is, *decentralization by default* (Ben-Elia, 1993, 1996)

From a functional perspective, local authorities in Israel are partly co-producers of key national services – mainly education and social welfare – and direct delivery agencies for a variety of services including local land-use planning, infrastructure maintenance, sanitation and environmental control, all under formal and informal regulation by central ministries. During the last decade they have been actively involved in economic development. By and large, Israeli local authorities are dependent on central government financing and highly exposed to national stabilization policies. Local budgets are a result of centrally determined frameworks, based partly on historical arrangements, and active negotiations between the local authority and the national ministries. Despite serious efforts in the last years to achieve an equitable allocation, inequalities still exist among local authorities, mainly because of differential local-taxation capabilities (CBS,

1996). Central funding has two main roles: to finance (up to seventy-five per cent) through earmarked grants the provision of national services and to balance, through a general grant, the gap between total income and expenditures. The balancing task has rarely been achieved, and most local authorities have shown annual deficits. The financial cutbacks and restrictions on public spending forced local authorities to increase the share of locally generated income. During the 1980s, local revenues grew in absolute and relative terms, and in the largest and wealthiest cities reached more than two-thirds of the ordinary budget's total resources. However, anti-inflationary considerations and protests from interest groups brought the government to tax-capping. Because of the political, negotiated nature of central-local relations, financial crises have been periodically avoided, and no major breakdowns in the provision of local services have taken place. Lacking the political will (or actual power) to induce the necessary changes, the Ministry of Interior and the Treasury – with the tacit consent of the local authorities – have succeeded in avoiding the financial crisis.

The Structure of Local Government
From a political perspective, the local authority is based on a directly elected executive mayor and an elected (list-based) council as corporate body. The mayor acts as the chairman of the council. Although the mayor is responsible for the execution of council decisions, it is the mayor who shapes the decision-making process and has the executive powers to lead and manage the local authority. This influential status follows the introduction of personal direct elections for the post of mayor (1975), a legal change that granted the incumbent a unique degree of public legitimacy and power. The law allows for the appointment of salaried and non-salaried deputy mayors among the council members, an effective political device in the context of coalition-based local authorities. The deputy mayors usually have a portfolio responsibility, granted by the mayor. The functional duties and powers of the council are organized according to a variety of statutory and voluntary committees.

The professional-administrative structure of Israeli local authorities varies greatly depending on their size and the scope of responsibilities. They are usually organized by functional divisions such as general administration, financial affairs, education, social services, city-planning, municipal infrastructures, sanitation, and various maintenance and supportive services. Despite considerable investments in organizational development and significant advances, most local authorities still suffer from a problematic interface between the political and professional domains, a lack of distinction between staff and line functions, and organizational dysfunctionalities concerning the placement and functional responsibilities of specific units. At the policy level, these deficiencies result in underdeveloped strategic planning capabilities and a strong tendency to short-term solutions. At the management level, they are manifested in serious coordination and integration problems.

The CEO Position

The Emergence of the CEO Position

The CEO position was developed as an experimental project in Jerusalem in 1971. The CEO initiative was a local attempt to cope with fundamental problems of coordination and integration, at a critical time for the city and the municipality. The initiative was supported by the Ministry of the Interior (in charge of local government) and was closely watched. An evaluation commission headed by the Ministry's Director General presented a summary report two years later (Ministry of Interior, 1973). While framed in the Jerusalem context, the report endorses the concept of the CEO position as an integral component of Israeli local government and advanced a very clear policy statement on the subject. The commission's recommendations were presented as suggestive rather than compulsory. That is, they were not translated into a general policy to be enforced nationwide, but, rather, left at the discretion of the individual local authorities to consider whether the suggested changes suited them, and whether the right conditions existed for their successful adoption.

The Consolidation of the CEO Position

The Jerusalem experiment did not result in an immediate or widespread adoption of the new concept. Although there is no reliable mapping of the diffusion process, all indications suggest that it was in the 1980s that the idea finally captured the attention of local incumbents. The first survey on the subject (1992) identified 24 local authorities with CEOs (Agmon and Ben-Elia, 1992). Some of these positions were filled by town-clerks who considered the new job a natural upgrading of their municipal status, but most of them were manned by outsiders brought in by newly elected mayors (see below). As already mentioned, the number of present (1997) CEOs has reached 42, a significant increase in a period of less than 5 years.

The Role of City Size

As the following table illustrates, the size of the local authority (as measured by population size) to a great extent determines whether or not a local authority will appoint a CEO. There are no CEOs in local authorities with less than 15,000 inhabitants. Over this threshold and up to 20,000 inhabitants only 12% of the relevant local authorities have instituted the CEO function. The relative proportion steadily increases, reaching a total coverage in cities with over 100,000 inhabitants.

Table 16.1 CEOs by size of local authority

Population size	No. of local authorities	No. of local authorities having CEO	Relative percentage
Less than 10,000	181	0	0
10,000 – 14,999	29	0	0
15,000 – 19,999	17	2	12
20,000 – 29,999	17	8	47
30,000 – 49,999	15	11	73
50,000 – 99,999	9	8	88
100,000 - 199,999	9	9	100
200,000 - 499,999	2	2	100
500,000 and over	1	1	100
Total	362	42	

It is not that there is any need or even demand for a CEO position in small municipalities. As will be pointed out later, the problem is that the executive role of the mayor is such that to a large extent he acts as the authority's CEO (the use of a male reference in this paper is for purposes of convenience. The content refers to incumbents or professionals of both sexes). In a large municipality, the public and organizational demands are such that the mayor is "forced" to appoint a CEO. Even if such an appointment implies that the mayor has relinquished power, his status and overall responsibility are not impaired. In a smaller local authority, the appointment of a CEO implies a more limited role for the mayor, a situation that few mayors are willing to accept. Moreover, the financial costs of such an appointment might raise eyebrows both at home and in the Ministry of the Interior, which balances the financing of the local authority.

The Nature and Conditions of the Function

As mentioned, the CEO position in Israeli local government is not formally required and therefore lacks the formal legitimacy and structured definition of other key functions (e.g., the chief financial officer, the town-clerk, the city planner or the legal counselor). In close similarity to Stewart's characterization of the role of the CEO in British local government (Stewart, 1988), this function is better understood by its organizational position than by the activities performed, shaped by relationships rather than functional tasks, made rather than predetermined and inherently ambiguous (see Norton 1991 for a similar interpretation).

Legitimacy and Content: the Political Interface

The CEO position is "political" by nature. The CEO is appointed by the mayor and his tenure is determined by his willingness to endorse the service of the senior manager. The mayor can also end the CEO's appointment and even eliminate the position entirely. Fundamentally, it is the mayor who will set the basic conditions and the content of the role. The relative importance of the mayor-CEO relation is fully evident in the CEO's own assessment: nearly all (96%) the CEOs interviewed see the relationship with the mayor as extremely important. A host of factors will affect the mayor's conception of the job and its functional content, among them the mayor's personality, his managerial style (centralism/decentralism), the length of his office, the political climate, etc.

The dual nature of the CEO role, being both a mayor-dependent function and a personal appointee, poses problems of legitimacy. The CEO's main source of power is a function of his personal link with the mayor, but this dependency means that strained relationships between them will affect the legitimacy of the CEO. His organizational legitimacy will be dependent on the continuity of the political tenure of the mayor who appointed him. A change of political incumbents (i.e., a new mayor) will probably affect the status of the CEO.

Even if the CEO's authority and power can be seen as a derivative of the mayor's standing, it would be wrong to assume that the CEOs are simple agents of their political principal. Whatever their dependency on the mayor, the CEOs see themselves as professionals with distinct values and responsibilities. This self-perception is reinforced by a more general view of politics and administration as discrete realms.

The vast majority of the CEOs interviewed believe that the administration should be non-partisan and only base its recommendations on expert opinion. Politicians, according to a greater majority, should maintain a clear separation of roles by centering their main efforts on policy-making (i.e., decisions on major issues) and not on the routine conduct of municipal affairs. Notwithstanding their political dependency, most of them draw a clear line between their personal-functional allegiance to the political incumbents and to the public interest: in our survey two-thirds of them reject the idea that CEOs should be primarily responsible to the political leadership and only secondarily to the local population. When asked about the relative importance of providing the mayor with political advice, the CEOs ranked the issue as one of very little importance. At the same time, providing the mayor with professional advice was considered 'very important'.

CEOs' expectations regarding the political level stress the importance of leadership, steering, consistency, stability and procurement of resources. According to the CEOs, politicians ought to:

- provide the local authority with a vision of long run development;
- decide on major policy principles, taking into account citizen's views; formulate unambiguous goals;

- defend decision and policies;
- create stability for the administration;
- represent the municipality to the outside world; and
- procure resources from the national government.

Despite the attempt to establish distance line between the CEO as professional manager and the politicians, the actual tensions between politics and administration emerge in many undecided issues, such as the extent to which the CEO should submit proposals in line with political intentions or the relative advantage of political affiliation (same as dominant party). The overall relation between present CEOs and elected members is surprisingly non-conflictual. Eighty-three per cent of the CEOs characterized their relations with the mayor as being "very cooperative" and an additional seven per cent as "cooperative". Only a single respondent described his relations with the mayor as very conflictual. The same non-conflictual relations seem to characterize the CEOs' contacts with other elected members. The range of responses concerning this issue range from "correct" to "extremely cooperative", with a more positive bias in the case of non-opposition members.

Legitimacy and Content: the Professional Interface
Paralleling the impact of the political interface between the CEO and the elected members on the CEO's role development, the professional interface (between the CEO and the municipal personnel) makes its unique contribution to the shaping of the role and the conditions of performance. As the leading figure of the professional structure and as the key person responsible for managing internal relationships, the importance of the professional interface is critical. With no more than the formal legitimacy of the mayor, the casting and consolidation of the position is affected by the quality of relations between the CEO and the municipal staff, mainly the middle managers.

The scope of authority of the CEO in Israeli local government is partially determined by functional boundaries set by the position of others. As already mentioned, there are numerous formally defined and legally binding functions based on professional expertise. The CEO might be concerned, for example, with financial issues, but he is not expected to be actually involved in such affairs as they are the formal and public responsibility of the chief financial officer (the city treasurer). In the same way, the CEO might be interested in, say, the quality of the physical environment, but the wise CEO will be extremely careful not to enter the professional domain of the city planner. A new CEO will gradually test the relative boundaries of the various professional turfs and discover (or create) activity areas of his own.

The personal and professional background of the CEO plays an important role in the shaping of the position. Those who enter the job from within the organization will enjoy the benefits of a history of personal contacts with other fellow officials (or suffer from it, if their relation has been problematic). Professionalism also plays an important role. A previous experience with municipal-related areas of expertise strengthens the position of the CEO as one who understands the "business".

The positive moulding of the role is a gradual process based on previous experience, the expectations of the mayor, the pressing needs of the organization and the professional socialization through experts and the peer group. The role of previous experience as a model is evident among those with a military background, in the context of a mayor with a similar past. In this case, the first attempt will be to shape the role according to the model of "chief of staff", as in the military organization. The problem is that the "staff", as mentioned, is rather autonomous and in the multi-purpose nature of the local authority each executive officer has an agenda of his own.

The moulding process improves when the CEO gradually realizes both his limitations and opportunities. Here the CEO develops his role by maximizing inherent potential of the general managing function (Kotter, 1982). The "non"-professional basis of the CEO (i.e., his lack of direct responsibility for functional activities) allows him to exercise his unique position as a:

- dual communication channel between elected officials and professional staff;
- political buffer between political incumbents and the professional staff;
- coordinator and integrator of complex organizational efforts;
- supportive force in organizational maintenance and development;
- leader of innovative projects.

In contrast with other professional roles in local government, which depend on increased resources and activity expansion as personal and functional strengthening devices, the role of the CEO is built and enhanced by his value-added contribution to the general steering and performance of the local authority as well as the smooth administration of functional services.

Personal Profile

Demographic Characteristics
CEOs in Israeli local government constitute a relatively young cadre, with ages ranging from 30 to 52 years and an average of 40 years. This is mostly a male group, with a single female indicative of the gender imbalance. To a large extent this sexual division parallels the minimal representation of women at the top levels of the municipal job hierarchy.

Education
By and large this is an educated group whose formal education ranges from 13 to 20 years in school and an average of 16 years. Close to a third of them hold an academic degree in economics or finance, 24 per cent have a degree in polit-

ical sciences, public administration or public policy, while another 20 per cent hold degrees in the field of the humanities. Only 7 per cent hold technical degrees (engineering or architecture).

Professional Background

Close to 60 per cent of the CEOs surveyed are professionals who previously held a senior job in their local authority; only 10 per cent of them previously occupied the position of town-clerk. Some of them (21 per cent) have spent their entire occupational life in the present local authority. Over 20 per cent of the present CEOs have previously been in the private sector.

The analysis of their professional background based on the sector in which they worked most years points out that half of them have worked for the central government, most as professional (paid) officers in the Israeli armed forces. Israel's armed forces tend to release their paid officers at an early age. At the age of 40 or earlier, the vast majority of them join the civilian labour-force. Only 7 per cent have spent most of their professional life in the private sector.

It is worthwhile noting the presence of a minority who previously served as CEOs in another local authority, a suggestive indication of the CEO's function as an emerging profession (more on this later).

Residency

Slightly over half the CEOs live in the locality they serve. Less than a third were born or raised in the locality.

Political Involvement

Local government CEOs are hardly apolitical civil servants. Fifty-five per cent of them declare that they have a political membership presently and an additional seven per cent have been members of political parties in the past. This political involvement is far greater than the one to be expected from trends at large (the general public) or at the municipal level (municipal employees). My hypothesis is that local political activity works in favor of those who were closely related to the election (or reelection) of the incumbent mayor.

Tenure Length

The CEO position has been held for an average of 4.8 years. Twenty per cent of the present CEOs have been on the job for a year or less. This limited tenure points to the close relation between the mayor and the CEO. The 1992 general municipal elections created the position of the CEO in 14 per cent of the relevant local authorities and new appointments in two-thirds of those local authorities in which the position already existed. This relative turnover is a compound result of political outcomes and the problematic nature of the position.

The Reality of the Job

An Elastic Agenda

The reality of the job is characterized by a mixed daily agenda of organizational and personal priorities. The open-ended nature of the CEO's role is reflected in the multiple activities which require his attention. The CEO's unique relation with the mayor heavily affects his actual tasks. The issues that fill the mayor's daily agenda, the complaints and the special requests forwarded to him as well as his personal priorities constitute an important part of the CEO's own schedule. The mayor's influence is illustrated by the frequency of contacts between the CEO and the mayor. Sixty-five per cent of the CEOs report daily meetings, the rest between two and four times a week. A similar phenomenon takes place at the CEO-staff interface as the CEO's agenda is partially set by organizational needs. According to their own report, close to 60 per cent of the CEOs have daily contacts with the senior staff and an additional 24 per cent meet with them from 2-4 times a week. Although many of these contacts are initiated by the CEO, there is a clear tendency among senior officers and other staff members to bring to the CEO's attention problems considered to have organizational implications – either because of their true nature or as a "problem-exporting" device for difficult issues at the departmental level. Unexpected events and issues that nobody else feels authorized to deal with add an additional component to the inherent flexibility of the CEO's agenda. The factotum nature of the CEO results in long working days: Israeli CEOs report an average 62-hour work week.

Personal Priorities

Irrespective of the degree of autonomy that the CEO enjoys in setting his formal agenda, the CEO has priorities of his own. These priorities, resulting either from his own definition of the role or from personal style, show a clear preference for issues that have a strategic dimension rather than involvement in routine operational matters. This is not to say that the organization does not force the CEOs to deal with operational issues, particularly operational failures, but given the opportunity, they will prefer to expend their energy on subjects of strategic importance. The analysis of the relative priority that CEOs grant to different tasks illustrates this general preference. CEOs put a distinct emphasis on:

- policy support (i.e., influencing decision-making processes);
- organizational steering and coordination (e.g., formulation of ideas and vision; improved cooperation among departments, development and implementation of new working processes);
- resource management (i.e., efficient use of existing resources);
- advancement of new projects at the local level.

Professional Support
Despite their high-ranking position, the CEOs have practically no supporting staff beyond secretarial assistance. To the extent that their work requires professional inputs, the CEO mostly relies on the expertise of other staff members. This relative weakness is partially solved by incorporating, when possible, or coopting non-committed staff functions (such as strategic planning units) or by enlisting the services of professional consultants.

Conclusion

The CEO function is a relatively recent phenomenon in Israeli local government and its gradual consolidation is another expression of the growing managerial demands facing local authorities. These demands are a direct outcome of the institutional strengthening of local government as well as the relative expansion of municipal responsibilities due to decentralization.

The position is structurally constrained by the power of an executive, political mayorality on the one hand, and functional chief officers of independent status on the other hand. Nonetheless, the potential capability of CEOs to develop and sustain their unique position is substantial. This potential emerges from the fundamental tensions and requirements of the local authority as a political and multi-purpose functional organization. The gradual expansion of the role, in terms of the growing number of local authorities adopting it, illustrates its need. The consolidation of the CEO position is achieved through the personal contributions of those holding it. The lack of a formal, compelling definition of the role impels CEOs to make personal interpretations of their role: These are a compound result of local organizational conditions (power balances, personalities and dominant organizational values) as well as the personal stature of the CEO as a leader and as a professional.

Externally, the CEOs are turning their role into a profession. Since the beginning of the decade, Israeli CEOs have organized themselves and created a professional forum of their own. The forum is an active arena for the institutionalization of the role as a distinct municipal profession. Active discussions have taken place concerning fundamental aspects of the role, proper conduct of affairs, qualifications and ethical considerations. Furthermore, they have propagated a national legislation that will grant the CEOs the same statutory basis granted to other key municipal positions. It is to be hoped that these overall efforts will go beyond "syndicalist" interest and contribute to the further development of the CEO position as a transformational force in Israeli local government.

Bibliography

Agmon, O., and Ben-Elia, N. (1992): *CEOs in Local Government*, Jerusalem: Center for the Advancement of Management in Local Government (Hebrew).

Ben-Elia, N. (1993): Policymaking and Management in Israeli Local Government: Evolving Trends and Strategic Challenges, *Policy Studies Journal*, 21,1,115:125.

Ben-Elia, N. (1996): *Strategic Changes and Organizational Reorientations in Local Government – A Cross National Perspective*, London: Macmillan.

Central Bureau of Statistics (1996): *Local Authorities in Israel – Financial Data*, Jerusalem.

Elazar, D., and Kalchheim, Ch. (eds.) (1988): *Local Government in Israel*, Boston: University Press of America.

Gutmann, E. (1958): *The Development of Local Government in Palestine*, (Ph.D. thesis, Columbia University) Ann Arbor: University of Michigan. (microfilm).

Kotter, J.P. (1986): *The General Managers*, New York: The Free Press.

Ministry of Interior (1973): *Report on the CEO Function at Municipality of Jerusalem*, Jerusalem (Hebrew).

Norton, A. (1991): *The Role of Chief Executive in British Local Government*, Birmingham: Institute of Local Government Studies.

Stewart, J. (1988): *Understanding the Management of Local Government*, Harlow: Longman.

CHAPTER 17

The New Mandarins of Western Local Government – Contours of a New Professional Identity?

by Kurt Klaudi Klausen and Annick Magnier

Patterns Within Diversity

Structural Diversity
Reviewing the national reports in this volume there seems to be a huge variety and diversity in the settings of the CEOs. We find variety between countries – insofar as some of our localities have a large number of inhabitants as in Great Britain and Ireland (where most municipalities have more than 50.000 inhabitants) compared to 5.000-30.000 inhabitants of most our sample, with only the Spanish sample covering very small municipalities (49% of the Spanish sample have less than 1000 inhabitants). Furthermore, some of our local governments cover a fairly small geographical territory, as in Belgium and Denmark, whereas municipalities in Australia and Sweden cover vast regions of land. In some countries, local authorities spend a considerable amount of the GNP: the Nordic countries spend close to one-third. Economic resources are less excessive in Portugal and Spain which spend less than five percent of their GNPs. Similarly, some local authorities like Great Britain and the rest of Northern Europe have more public employees, while the municipalities in Southern Europe and Australia have fewer public employees.

The contextual variety between countries thus reflects the entire historical, structural and organizational setup of state and local government relations mentioned in the introductory chapter and in the beginning of each national report. Furthermore, we find similar variations, if not cleavages, within countries, resembling the differences between the very small and the very large cities and municipalities in the United States and France (here the small ones have been omitted in this study) between small municipalities and huge counties in Australia or between north and south in Italy. Australia, the U.S. and Sweden reveal differences along the urban-rural and centre-periphery divides. In the federal systems of Australia and the U.S., each state has its distinct features, and in the U.S. case Svara has to distinguish between council-manager cities and the mayor-council cities in which the mayor is the elected CEO and the appointed top official is the chief administrative officer (CAO). Moreover, in some countries such structural features manifest themselves as distinct institutional disparities. This is clearly depicted in the Portuguese case, where Costa, Felizes and Neves emphasize the duality and the meeting of the great narratives of a pre-modern/clientelistic tradition and the proposed modernization of local government, between the bureaucratic models of organization and the oligarchic models of local domination. Thus we find that at one level of abstraction every unit is unique, while at another level of abstraction we find patterns and clusters of similarity within diversity. Such patterns are often historically grown just as in the huge processes of state- and nation-building.

It is important to understand and keep track of the internal as well as external contexts – the municipality as a microcosm and society at large, being it local community or country – and of the development in this context. As an example, a crucial development has been Britain's transformation from a unitary service delivery system (similar to the Scandinavian ideal type welfare model) to a much more fragmented system in which the role of local authorities has changed from that of producer role to a management role. Similarly and consequently, the role of the local head of administration has changed over the past 20 years from that of being the first among equals (the town clerk) to Chief Executive Officer. Other developmental trends are found when we observe that whereas the trend and the agenda in some parts of Europe is about amalgamating smaller municipalities with others through mergers, the trend in the United States, for example, is to split local governments into smaller units as occurs in big cities and their surrounding areas.

These structural features may be of some importance, since the work environment is likely to influence the range of managerial action creating both limitations and opportunities for the individual CEO. This again can be expected to create different roles and functions of action, specific patterns of recruitment, and a variation in the perceptions of selected issues. Hence, we might expect such features to produce specific national and regional patterns, but also to bridge some of the regional as well as national cleavages. The latter, however, will not be dealt with here (such features will be taken up in more detail in subsequent volumes of the U.DI.T.E. project). Instead, we will concentrate on national disparities and clusters of similarity within diversity at this level of analysis.

Initially, however, it is necessary to emphasize that despite disparities we are indeed looking at CEOs who can be compared. They are comparable because they are in fact the highest ranking officers at the lowest tier of government, linking the administrative apparatus which they head with the political system they must obey.

That we are in fact studying people who can be compared becomes evident when looking at their environment. They share common features both with regard to their distant and close environment insofar as they are all facing the megatrends of our time, trends we shall return to at the end of this chapter, and insofar as they are all part of local networks of a certain similarity. One of the shared megatrends is decentralization. It is a common view of the CEOs that there has been more decentralization within local government in recent years. At the same time, however, we find (with the exception of Finland, Norway and to a lesser extent Ireland and the U.S.) that there has been a simultaneous centralization in relations between states and local government. Hence, the CEOs generally share features of both centralization (vis-à-vis the state) and decentralization (within the municipality). The analyses of networks/ relationships and conflicts in the previous national analyses (cf. the charts) are strikingly similar, implying that the CEOs must manuever within much the same political-administrative environment, having to cooperate with individuals, internal and external groups and (interest) organizations. Here again we find that the relation to the political system and notably the mayor is critical in all instances (except maybe the Finnish case). These features distinguish local government CEOs from leaders and managers in private firms and voluntary nonprofit organizations.

This makes it possible through this study to determine similarities and dissimilarities and to discuss the extent to which they are related to the variations in the structural national background and their situation, the local context.

Similarity within Diversity
Who are the CEOs of Western democracies? If we examine their age, gender, social and educational background they constitute a fairly homogeneous group – on first sight. They are overwhelmingly male, with an average age in the late 40s, and have a varied social/family (middle class) background and educational backgrounds often within the "municipal system" itself or in academia (mostly law and economics). This fairly homogeneous picture, however, can easily be subdivided into patterns of differences, exceptions and trends.

The average age is much the same throughout the surveyed countries, the only exceptions being Ireland and Spain where the CEOs are about 6 years older and younger, respectively. But when it comes to gender there is a distinct and somewhat curious pattern. Women are clearly underrepresented in all the countries surveyed. However, there is a pattern which is somewhat different from what one might expect. It is well known that the Nordic countries for many years have taken pride in a very deliberate policy to promote women. For instance, there are 7 female ministers out of 20 in the Danish government and roughly 40% female representation in the parliaments of Sweden and Finland. In contrast females represent less than 10% in countries like Britain, France, Belgium, Italy and Portugal. Therefore, it is to be expected that we will find more female CEOs in the liberal Scandinavian countries than elsewhere, and certainly more than in traditionally patrimonial southern Europe. Astonishingly enough, we discover that the picture is reversed. In all the countries except the "South European group" women constitute less than 10% of the sample (with one women out of 42 CEOs in Israel and Australia scoring only 4%). These figures change dramatically the further south we go in Europe: Belgium 13% female CEOs, France 12%, Italy 23%, Spain 27% and Portugal 31% female CEOs. Preliminary analyses suggest that this is not simply due to the fact that some of these countries have a large number of very small municipalities, though the percentage of female CEOs in France rises to 18% when looking at municipalities having between 5.000 and 20.000 inhabitants, in Italy the real percentage is 28% instead of the 23% in the sample, which has an over-representation of cities.

Equally important and interesting, however, is that the national studies reveal a clear tendency in some countries for women to have entered the position as local government CEOs in an increasing number over the past few years. This is also the case in countries where their representation is diminutive. As an example, the 8% female CEOs in Sweden have all come into office within the last 5 years. The figures for Finland were 2% in 1990 and 6% in 1996 – a small revolution!?

On first sight, the CEOs also have a similar social and educational background insofar as they are very heterogeneous. There is only one clear, yet at the same time somewhat astonishing, feature of the social and family background. The vast majority of CEOs stem from "petite bourgeoisie" insofar as in most countries (except Great Britain) between one-third and one-half of the CEOs grew up in families where the father was self-employed (it should be mentioned, however, that we do not have these data for all the countries involved in this study). As one might have expected, it is not an upper-middle class family background in which the father was a public employee. About one-fourth have a municipal apprenticeship, and fewer than one might expect have a managerial/academic education. However, this is changing rapidly. In France, for example, a university diploma is now the standard background of the "secrétaire général". Among those with university degrees, the study of law is the most common. This is clearly the case in Italy, Portugal and Spain. There are some characteristic features whereby some countries stand out. For instance more than 90% of the Swedish CEOs have university degrees (50% of these in political science). In the U.S. 91% have 4-year degrees and 65% graduate degrees (often an MPA). About 50% of Belgian CEOs have a private administrative education, and in Spain more than 50% have a background in law – this has recently become a prerequisite in Spain.

Of special importance is the trend reported in (almost) all the national studies saying that newly employed CEOs increasingly have an academic background and/or a professional managerial training, and that a (more targeted/specialized) training/reeducation is going on among CEOs already in office. Some schools, the University of Tampere in Finland, for example, have specialized in the education and training of municipal leaders, and in most countries there are specialized training academies for leaders in local government. We may thus conclude that CEOs are increasingly becoming a profession of hardworking executives with an average work week of about 50 hours.

Even if the overall picture is one of similarity within diversity, meaning that the CEOs share a number of traits, on the issue of gender we find the first sign of a north-south pattern.

There are some overall trends emerging from this analysis, trends which are slowly but steadily penetrating the world of local government CEOs. First, even if women are still seriously underrepresented, more and more women are entering the world of local government CEOs. Second, even if educational backgrounds vary, more academics are recruited to new positions. And third, this can also be seen in terms of an overall professionalization of the CEOs.

Status and Power

Most of the CEOs are recruited from within the municipal system. In most countries, more than one-third have their first job in a municipality after finishing full-time education, and only in Belgium, France, Great Britain and Italy did about one-third have their first job in the private sector. Furthermore, most of the CEOs surveyed entered their present position after having served in a leading position either in their own or in another municipality. This results in the CEO's long work experience in and knowledge about local government affairs. They can provide continuity vis-à-vis the political system, which may at times be more fluctuating with shifting political coalitions. This knowledge, and the personal networks stemming from this preoccupation, constitutes a strong powerbase for the CEOs.

The picture is confirmed when we examine their tenure in office. On average the CEOs stayed in their previous job for about 6 to 7 years and have been in their present position a bit longer. However, the patterns of turnover and job mobility may be changing. Apart from the Irish, Belgian, Italian and Portuguese cases, more than half the CEOs are inclined to seek another job in the future. Their predecessors did not leave their jobs only because of age; in many instances, about one-third left because of problems in the cooperation with either the political or the administrative system.

Ranking the CEOs may be a difficult and somewhat dubious enterprise, since there are always exceptions and since such typologies can never be fully sensitive to real life. Nevertheless, it is of some value in creating an overview of the similarities and differences among our CEOs. Table 17.1 illustrates this in various ways vis-à-vis the political and administrative system – i.e., the mayor and heads of departments – following the formal descriptions as well as their own estimates.

Table 17.1 Ranking of the CEOs vis-à-vis the mayor and the heads of department

Potential authority in relation to subordinates (heads of departments)	Potential authority based on municipality /city government structure	CEO self-reported influence compared to mayor[1]	CEO's average level of influence (budget and economic development)
CEO weaker on budget · Sweden · the Netherlands · Italy · Portugal	Low: weak CEO/ Strong mayor · France · Spain · Portugal · Italy · Israel · Belgium	CEO lower on both: · Spain · France · the Netherlands · Denmark · Sweden · Portugal · Italy · Belgium	Low: 56 or lower · Spain (51) · the Netherlands (49) · Portugal (52) · Italy (56)
	Moderate: Weak CEO/weak mayor · Sweden · the Netherlands · Norway	CEO higher on budget · Norway	Moderate: 57-65 · France (63) · Sweden (65) · Denmark (58) · Belgium (65)
	Moderately high: Strong CEO/ strong mayor: · Denmark · Great Britain	CEO higher on econ. development: · Great Britain	Moderately high: 66-75 · Norway (68) · Great Britain (74)
Stronger on budget · Finland · Norway · Great Britain · Denmark · Ireland · Belgium · France · Australia · USA · Spain	High: Strong CEO/weak mayor · USA [c-m] · Finland · Ireland · Australia	CEO higher on both · USA [c-m] · Finland · Ireland · Australia	High: 75 or over · Australia (81) · USA (86) · Finland (90) · Ireland (91)

1 Relative influence of mayor and CEO on budget formation and economic development.

The first column depicts the relationship with the department heads with regard to the budget. Most CEOs evaluate themselves as being more influential on budget matters than their department heads – not surprising since they are after all the heads of administration. More important in regard to their relative range of maneuvering, however, is their relationship with the mayor, as described in detail in the national reports. Here we provide a broad overview based on the formal structure (second column), on the self-reported influence vis-à-vis the mayor on the budget and on economic development (third column) and, finally, the total self-estimated score on the CEOs' isolated influence on both budget and economic development (fourth column). The last three columns give us a somewhat clearer picture of different clusters.

By abstracting from these findings we arrive at a generalized picture in which those CEOs with the strongest position are from Australia, Finland, Ireland, the United States and perhaps including Great Britain, while the weaker positioned CEOs are found in Belgium, France, Israel, Italy, Portugal and Spain. In between we find Denmark, Great Britain, Norway, Sweden and perhaps the Netherlands. These data seem to confirm the hypothesis regarding clusters of countries based on the history, culture and formal political and administrative systems: configurating a South European group of countries, a North European and Nordic group, and finally an Anglo-American group including Australia (for a more elaborate discussion of such models see the introductory chapter).

However, there are exceptions to the above picture. The exception of Finland from the north-south pattern may be explained by its belonging to a group of city-manager-type CEOs. Furthermore, there are overlaps and fluid borderlines between the groups as indicated by the positions of Great Britain and the Netherlands where the former might be placed in the Anglo-American group while the latter on some dimensions might fit in with the South European group (Berveling, van Dam, Neelen and Wille conclude that the Dutch CEOs do not perceive themselves as being very influential). The Belgian CEO, as described by Plees and Laurent, is in a weak position formally, while in reality he exerts great influence and in many respects may be stronger than the mayor due to longer tenure in office and based on his knowledge about the internal life of the municipality. Furthermore, while the two groups of relatively strong and relatively weak CEOs, respectively, stand out fairly clear, the in-between group by no means constitutes the same position and potential managerial situation for the CEO inasmuch as there are great differences between a CEO who is in a position of medium potential influence because both the mayor and the CEO are weak versus a position in which they are both strong. The latter allows ample room for managerial action if there is a good atmosphere and well functioning cooperation between the CEO and the mayor and may therefore resemble the situation where the CEO has a strong position.

If we examine the roles that the CEOs would prefer the politicians to perform, we see both uniformity and a picture which confirms the north-south pattern. As shown in figure 17.1 there is only little variety in the importance which they believe the politicians should attribute to the roles of representation, governance and stability, whereas they strongly differ when it comes to the importance and/or acceptance of the politicians performing administrative roles such as laying down rules and routines for administration. On this dimension, the Northern and Southern European ends of the spectrum stand out clearly.

In analyzing status and power, we can confirm north-south clusters and observe trends pointing towards more uncertainty and higher turnover (except perhaps in Belgium). On the other hand, it may be argued that because of the increased professionalization and because of rapid administrative changes and developments, the CEOs may in the long run gain more power, discretion and autonomy vis-à-vis the mayor and the political system. The present situation offers them an opportunity to become administrative entrepreneurs and for some, as we shall see shortly, to become (anonymous / behind-the-scene) political entrepreneurs.

Figure 17.1 The ideal politician

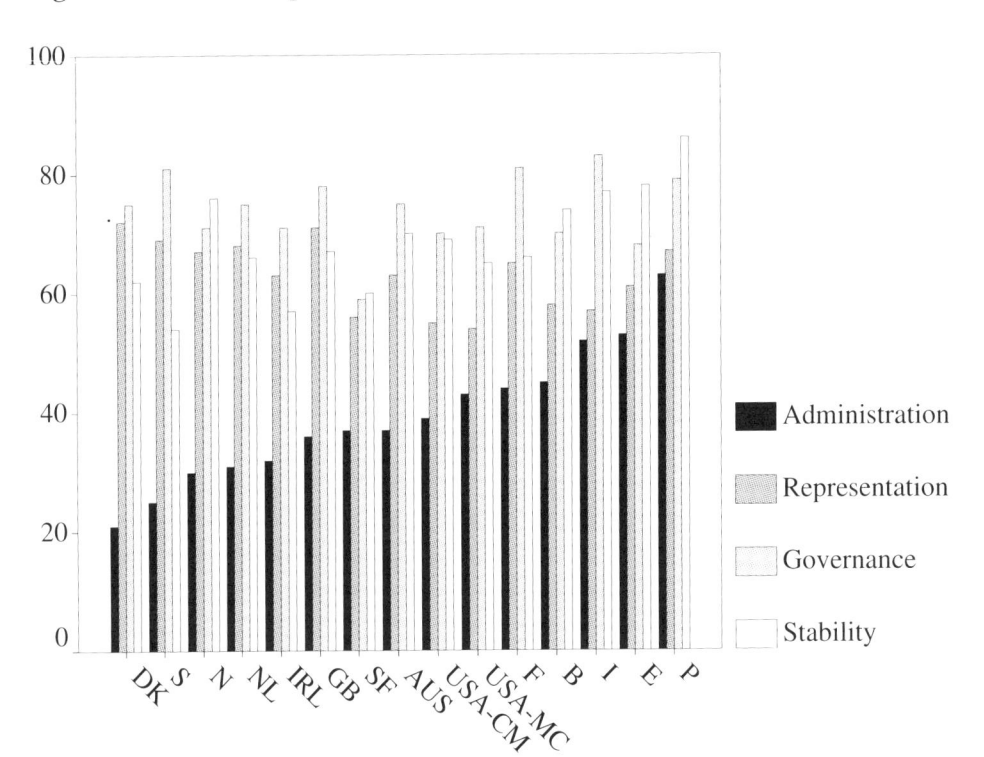

Classical versus Political Bureaucrat?

Each national report sought to analyze the CEOs' various role perceptions based on the emphasis they themselves place on various issues in their daily work. Based on the relative priority which the CEOs gave to tasks such as solving human relationships, formulating ideas and visions, guiding subordinate staff, giving the mayor political advice, the relative importance of two general role-models, the classical and the political bureaucrat, was depicted. This distinction is classical in public organization theory. Figure 17.1 summarizes these data and arranges the countries in the order in which they emphasize the role of the classical and political bureaucrat, respectively. It should be noted that the CEOs can identify with the features constituting both roles, since they all grant them some value. It is the variation, however, which makes for interesting differences. There are some methodological considerations regarding the way in which some of the questions may have been interpreted and answered in the various national reports. Here we choose to compare and interpret the findings disregarding these matters because we find some fairly distinct patterns, patterns we have seen before.

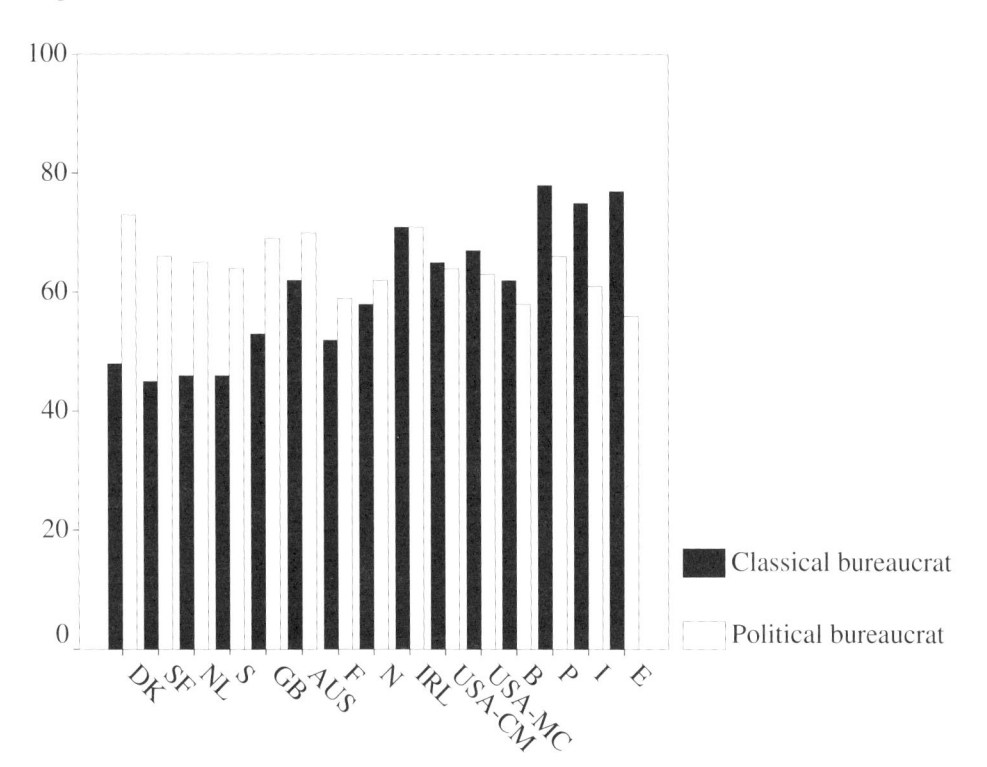

Figur 17.2 The roles of the CEO

Again, the findings suggest similarities at first because the scores are to a large extent almost even on both categories – they are not necessarily antithetic roles but, rather, supplement each other. On closer examination, however, we find dissimilarities. The Southern European CEO identifies more with the role of the classical bureaucrat and the Scandinavian CEOs, notably the Danes, can identify with the role of being a political bureaucrat. Once again we thus find a clear division between the North European group, encompassing Denmark, Finland Sweden, Great Britain, the Netherlands and Norway, and a South European group including France, Italy, Spain and Portugal. Within this perspective, Finland clearly fits the Nordic pattern.

This divide between north and south may be interpreted, as does Goldsmith in the British case, as having been caused by the relatively higher degree of internal decentralization in the north. Such decentralization would allow for more strategic thinking and political advice, and less inclination towards observing rules and regulations.

Figure 17.3 The two-dimensional roles of the CEOs

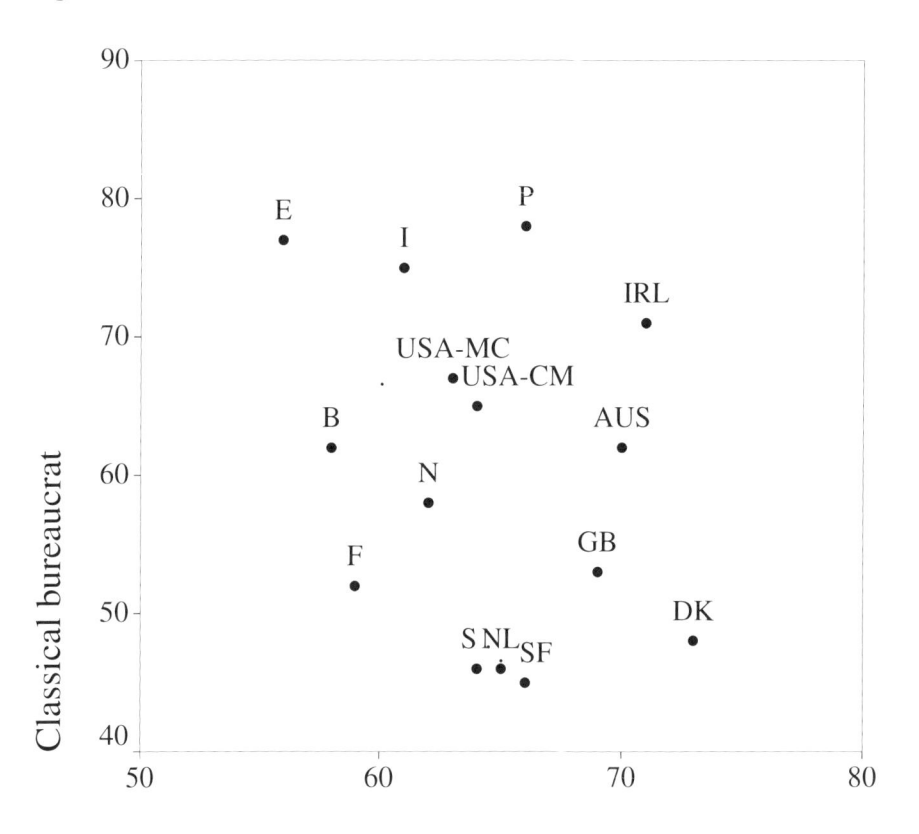

Even so, this overall picture becomes somewhat blurred as we discover that Belgium is caught between the two roles, while Australia may fit in with the Nordic group since they put slightly more emphasis on the political bureaucrat than on the classical bureaucrat whereas the United States may not. These features and (new) clusters become visible when arranging the countries in a chart like figure 17.3. As Svara notes, however, the score would have been in favor of the political bureaucrat had just one topic been omitted, namely that of giving the mayor political advice (overall the American CEO is much involved in formulating ideas and visions, a tendency which increases with the size of the city). Ireland also constitutes a puzzle insofar as the roles are given even weight. It seems as if Ireland belongs to the South European group, in which the classical bureaucratic virtues are held high, yet at the same time belonging to a northern group in which new, more political roles come to the fore. It may be the case, however, that this merely illustrates that these roles are supplementary and not complementary. The CEOs are not torn between these roles. Rather they utilize and master them to varying degrees.

Do these findings correspond to the previous findings regarding the relative power of the CEO vis-à-vis the mayor? Do relatively weak CEOs feel more inclined to play the role of the loyal, technical administrator – the classical bureaucrat? On the other hand, it would be only natural to practice the role of the political bureaucrat for those CEOs working in a context where both he and the mayor were either weak or strong at the same time. Here their mutual dependence and cooperation would seem more important than in the other instances. Furthermore, this would all be of less importance for the strong CEO, which might explain why they fall outside the standard picture.

The distinction between a classical and a political bureaucrat works in the sense that some CEOs give more emphasis to one than the other. Our research on local CEOs, as opposed to administrators at higher levels, reveals a number of deviations from standard expectations about the distinction. First, in half the countries, the political bureaucrat score is higher than that of the classical bureaucrat. Cross-cutting this divergence are five countries in which the two scores are very similar; i.e., they differ by less than ten points. Second, there is greater variation in the classical than the political measure. It is more common for the CEOs to be involved in a close relationship with the mayor and council over matters of policy and political choice than it is for them to be heavily involved in managing the organization. Even in those countries with the lowest scores, we find CEOs who attach more than moderate importance to the activities of the political bureaucrat. This involvement hardly corresponds to the traditional dichotomy. Third, when the specific activity of providing political advice to the mayor is removed, the other indicators of political bureaucracy are even higher and more uniform across the countries.

The categories of classical and political bureaucrat thus make sense in the context of local government CEOs. After all, they are head of the administration while at the same time the political context in which they work makes their relation with political leaders, and the mayor in particular, a sine qua non for their managerial conduct. The variation in the classical bureaucratic emphasis follows a north-south pattern, with the CEOs of other countries in the middle.

Our research shows that we need a more elaborate classification of the roles of the CEOs in order to better understand their activities and how they operate in different dimensions of the position. This will indeed be one goal of subsequent volumes in the project. As a first approximation, however, the two roles continue to have relevance even if they do not generally correspond to the traditional dichotomy.

It might be expected, due to a growing and intertwined complexity of administration and policymaking, that bureaucrats would become more politicizing and politicians become more oriented towards administration i.e., that the roles of the politicians and leading bureaucrats would become more similar (see Aberbach, Putnam and Rockman 1981). This expectation can not be confirmed by our study. What we can say, however, is that in the northern group of countries there seems to be a willingness on behalf of the CEOs to engage in policymaking activities (given that certain ethical precautions are taken) while they do not accept that the politicians engage themselves in their domain. On the other hand, we find a southern group of countries in which the picture is reversed (here, there seems to be a greater acceptance regarding intervention by the politicians), and, finally, we find a third group where the borderlines between the roles are clearer and the domains remain more separate.

Job Satisfaction and Impediments to Success

A number of measures do not conform with the "classical clusters", but seem to constitute similarity rather than divergence in the context and environment of the CEOs. This is seen in the level of satisfaction with their job as CEO. About half the CEOs find their job less attractive today than 10 years ago, whereas the other half find it more interesting. In the national descriptions, however, it becomes clear that the CEOs in both instances find that the (often diverging) pressures and expectations upon them have increased. When asked about the importance of performance goals, such as user and citizen participation, efficiency of service production, protection of minority interests, they all had the impression that their importance had increased. Hence, the expectations and importance regarding the achievement of new goals are increasing. Certain factors have been a common impediment to the successful performance of the CEO, and certain factors that could have caused difficulty have only rarely caused widespread problems on a national basis, although they could have been serious problems in specific communities. Among the latter, the average rating from CEOs indicates only a minor negative effect (i.e., an average score of under 40) in the following cases: demographic changes (23), conflicts between the political parties (27), conflicts between departments (27), pressures from local organized interests, business and the like (28), demands for better service (33).

Unemployment had an aggregate average rating of 33 although in one country, Finland, it was viewed as a fairly serious problem by over half the CEOs. On the other hand, the top two problems were considered to be at least moderately negative by over half the CEOs in nine and seven countries, respectively. Both of these, as well as the fifth-ranking problem, involved actions of higher level governments: new regulations, cuts in grants, and upper-level government's control of local finances. Financial problems and difficulties with elected officials, unclear goals and unclear division of labor were fairly common problems. Comparing countries, Italy had five items that were considered to be a moderate or greater problem to half or more of the CEOs, Norway and Great Britain had four, and Finland had three of such problems. There is variation in the extent and the distribution of the factors that could impede performance.

Re-centralization and Regionalization
As indicated in the factors that impede performance, CEOs often view the relations with higher level governments as a source of difficulty. Our study confirms the findings referred to in the introductory chapter regarding the development of multilevel governance, regionalization and a combined decentralization and re-centralization in the relationship between centre and periphery.

The national reports illustrate the paradoxical features of the centralization-decentralization processes which the Western political systems have undergone in recent decades. At the local level, we find decentralization to lower levels of authority in all cases except for Belgium and Spain. Our descriptions stress only in a few cases re-centralization vis-à-vis the state, confirming the so-called "British exceptionalism", an exceptionalism to which the Dutch case belongs. The Belgian and the Spanish would be linked to this as a consequence of the transfer of authority to regional bodies. The interviewed CEOs propose a picture which is more oriented towards re-centralization than the survey figures indicate. As referred to in the introductory chapter, the tendency towards regionalization can be found throughout Europe and is strongly stimulated by the structural policy of the EU.

Towards a New Shared Professional Identity?

Megatrends
Recent developments and the identification of changes in the similarity and dissimilarity among Western local government CEOs should be seen not only against the backdrop of traditional national differences (which we have stressed both here and in the introductory chapter), but also in light of the widely shared

megatrends of decentralization, internationalization (including regionalization and integration) and modernization (including liberalization/privatization/commodification on the one hand and communitarian measures on the other; that is, empowerment of/responsiveness towards citizens and new ideas about governance). These megatrends are all facilitating the diffusion and adoption of a shared set of new ideas on (proper) management (particularly managerialism/NPM on the one hand and human resource management policies on the other).

As emphasized in what follows these environmental/institutional megatrends have been observed in all the country studies in this book. They seem to penetrate Western democracies as widely shared ideas about modernizing the public sector. In many ways they represent what Costa, Felizes and Neves in the Portuguese case call a de-ideologization of politics. To what extent the new measures are actually implemented is an other issue. As a general methodological observation it should be noted that leaders often know less about their own organization than they think they do, and furthermore, they often know less about their own leadership role and style than they think they do. This should be born in mind when drawing conclusions about reality from the perceptions of the CEOs as comprised in this study. Nevertheless, we have chosen to believe in the general patterns which emerge from the study. What we do find in this study is that there is a widely shared identification of these new ideas among the CEOs, and that they are to a certain extent influencing the world of the CEOs.

Convergence or Parallel Tracks?
This leaves room for the discussion of the position of the CEOs as being more or less similar and more or less convergent. Their perception of their own role, the ideal role of politicians, the importance of performance goals, and the analyses of the networks indicate that the worlds of the CEOs seem very similar, that they are in fact living in a world with some of the same constraints and important political environments with key internal and external interest groups/stake-/shareholders. And even if we know that their managerial situations vary considerably with situational factors such as structure, size, local democratic and administrative culture and resources, we find numerous traits of convergence.

It can of course be argued that what we are witnessing is in fact not a case of convergence but parallel trajectories. This may be argued first as an example of a parallel but autonomous/independent development reflecting similarities in environmental changes in each individual case and in each individual country; and secondly, as an argument saying that it makes no real change and particularly no change towards isomorphy, i.e., that the differences are not being diminished. Nevertheless, we dare talk about convergence in perceptions of the CEOs in Western local democracies regarding present challenges and future developments. We dare do so because of the above-mentioned megatrends, insofar as we both find challenges which are shared and because we se traces of developments pointing in the same direction.

We shall point at two such shared traits: the clear evidence of ongoing professionalization and the introduction of concepts associated with New Public Management. Whereas the first tendency is universal – the CEOs are being increasingly professionalized with regard to both educational background when recruited, because of in-service training, shared learning processes in their professional networks and certain shared norms, the second trend is less uniform and open for discussion.

New Public Management
There are some common traits/signs of convergence in the findings and analyses of the situation in each country and with regard to changes in the position and attitude of local chief executives. We find that shared ideas on the role and challenges penetrate local government CEOs in the Western world. This becomes apparent in the perceptions of reform and change, and in the scope of these ideas which conform with the standards long advocated by institutions such as the OECD and the World Bank, ideas which have gained governmental support and generated administrative modernization measures throughout the Western world over the past two decades. These ideas, which have also been labelled with the concept of New Public Management, now penetrate local government and seem to be a common feature of some importance both in the perception of the proper role of the CEO and in the reform of local government.

Gerritsen and Whyard emphasize two interacting phenomena that have reshaped the role of the Australian local government CEO over the past 15 years, the "managerialist" and the "privatization" revolutions. Both conform to the contents of New Public Management. The managerialist revolution has helped reshape the workplace and organizational structures of local government and at the same time caused a change in the patterns of recruitment and reeducation. CEOs are expected to be educated generalist managers, and in the Australian case it is now common to recruit CEOs from outside local government (though this is not shown by the figures). Gerritsen and Whyard go so far as to say that the Australian CEOs have now become analogues of private managers and that they are now more outcome- than process-oriented. At the same time, however, they provide political advice. They have become entrepreneurs.

The privatization revolution, including features such as contracting out and establishing competitive systems has changed the role of the CEO in some countries e.g., Great Britain and Australia, from one of being the producer and provider of services to that of being the purchaser. Goldsmith and Tonge argue that the growing market orientation and consumer awareness in the British case has created a "cultural change on a scale which could not have been imagined even ten years ago."

In Sweden, contract employment of CEOs has been introduced. The turnover is high, and resignation is more often caused by conflicts with the politicians – a picture we also find in Denmark. As Haglund puts it, "the offspring of the New Public Management concept has left a profound mark on Swedish municipalities."

We also find that local authorities have actually privatized or contracted out some of their services. This is the case in more than half the municipalities in each country (except for Portugal). However, such measures and the above shared features of New Public Management should not overshadow the specific context and belief in the assets of the public sector. There is no overwhelming support for a statement that the public sector has grown too large (only in Denmark, Finland, Sweden and Spain is this statement approved of by a little more than 50 percent). Furthermore, it is only in the countries of our South European group (including Belgium, Italy, Portugal and Spain, though not France) that we find massive support for a statement saying that the private sector is generally more efficient than the public sector. Hence, there is neither support for the classical critique of the public sector nor for the myth about the private sector being much more efficient. Thoenig states this very bluntly when saying that the "municipal way" is still viewed as the ideal solution to master the fate of public affairs, and that modernization of administration and efficiency of politics are better alternatives than privatization.

Moreover, it is questionable whether the liberal ideas of New Public Management are the only important legitimate traits/tendencies presently haunting Western public managers. Certainly there are other legitimate ways of conduct, as is clearly shown in the Portuguese and Italian cases. Furthermore, it is debatable whether the self reported attitudes and perceptions in line with the ideals of New Public Management are "real", in the sense that they are actually altering the behaviour of the CEOs. They could just be fatamorganic, symbolic, adaptations of a new dominant rhetoric. Nevertheless, the penetration of the ideas seems to be indisputable throughout the Western world, where new leaders are recruited, new leadership teams formed, new organizational reforms implemented, new managerial instruments such as MBO and TQM are used, and terms such as management, strategy and vision are no longer alien words on the local public scene. Far from being only neutral, administrative servants, the local government CEOs of today may be called professional managers and even entrepreneurs.

Professionalization
There seems to be ample ground for saying that the CEOs are both a reflection of their historical past, of the tradition and culture in each country, paving the way for national and regional disparities, and that they also reflect present day developments which to a larger extent are the expression of shared features such as New Public Management. The professionalization of the CEOs is one such feature leading in the direction of convergence.

As Sandberg emphasizes in the Finnish case, there are several characteristics, among them the homogeneous educational background and high rate of involvement in the association of CEOs, that suggest that Finnish CEOs are very close to forming a profession, comparable, for example with teachers or nurses. Furthermore, representatives of the national association of CEOs strongly emphasize that the CEO is a professional manager.

Moreover, even if Belgium belongs to the South European group and the Belgian municipal secretary scores high on the classical bureaucrat scale, a new and more change-oriented CEO is emerging in Belgium. As stated by Plees and Laurent, there has been a clear change over time, "there is a professionalization of the function, with an increasing share of university-educated secretaries". This is particularly the case in large municipalities.

Thoenig emphasizes the professionalization of the French CEOs which has taken place within a shared job market and in which the "secrétaire généraux" have developed "shared common values and skills which lend their role considerable specificity". Furthermore, they have engaged in collective action through their professional associations.

The tendency towards professionalization is shown in the new patterns of recruitment, in the entry demands on CEOs, and is also brought about by reeducation and exchange of experiences, both nationally and internationally. In this respect, an important role is to be played by the national as well as the international associations of local government CEOs.

In addition to higher qualifications as a sign of professionalism, there are also certain shared values and attitudes that mark the emergence of a professional identity. A majority of CEOs in all countries agree with a number of norms. To suggest a traditional division of labor with elected officials: the council should decide only major policy issues and not routine matters, and the administration should be nonpartisan and base its recommendations on expert opinion. On the other hand, a majority in each country also tend to agree that the administration should be the prime mover in adapting the local government to changes in society. CEOs almost universally attach great importance to formulating ideas and visions for their municipality and encouraging new projects in their community. They generally feel it is very important not only to stress efficiency, but also to stress cooperation between departments. CEOs have progressed from many different starting points. In many countries, the training was mixed and the position was that of a clerk to the council or legal adviser and first among equals in relationship to other department heads. Today the CEOs generally have substantial education and training, and they commonly see themselves as advisors to elected officials who are also leaders in their communities and integrative managers of their organizations.

Bridges and Cleavages – Defining Structures
Depending on the perspective a study can direct more or less attention to differences and similarities. It is worth noting that we have included in this study only "Western" local governments (i.e., not other parts of the world such as Asian, African, Arab or Latin American countries) – thus, the patterns we find are of course "unique" for these countries, and both the similarities and dissimilarities

might have been different had we included more countries outside the "Western" part of the world.

At one level of abstraction, the micro level, we find that each and every CEO is unique, at other levels, the regional and national levels, we find patterns of similarity. We even find similarities among groups of states. And, as noted, we might have discovered differences between different parts of the world had we included more countries – i.e., in that perspective our countries would have appeared more alike. There will always be differences, so the crucial question is whether it is possible to point out tendencies which are qualitatively new and capable of identifying new patterns, patterns which are bridging the differences both at micro and macro level.

In this study we have (re)identified some of the old clusters of groups of countries – the classical clashes of civilizations (Huntington 1996) – within the Western hemisphere. We find the traces hereof in the political and administrative systems of local government, in the relative position of the CEOs and in their views on their own roles and upon those of the politicians. These clusters of countries can be explained by the interwoven "old, huge" structures of religion (catholic versus protestant), of culture (more or less paternalistic, clientelistic etc.), of empires (Roman, Viking, Napoleonic, British) and their subsequent legal and administrative structures, all of which is analyzed in the studies of state- and nation-building (Tilly ed. 1975).

We have, however, also identified exceptions to these clusters and traits and tendencies which are (potentially) bridging the classical cleavages. The shared features which are found in the way in which the CEOs view their own work situation may similarly be explained by "huge" structures. Thus, the way in which they interpret the overall function and legitimacy of both the public sector and the challenges to their own position points in such directions. One of these huge structures has to do with the fact that they are all top executive officers in the public sector, meaning that the public context (the legal and the political environment etc.) is all-important. Thus, we cannot confirm the generic assumptions about leadership being the same in every context (public, private and voluntary). Other, and new huge structures which encourage the bridging of classical cleavages are the above-mentioned new megatrends, the new dynamics of change in western local government. It can of course be disputed (as we mentioned in the introductory chapter) to which extent these new megatrends are in fact being looked upon and implemented in much the same way or if these are also nationally, regionally and locally plural. Nevertheless, they are found and are talked about in much the same way. The old, huge structures produce and explain some of our findings, namely the old clusters while the new, huge structures provide the bridges.

The New Mandarins – Contours of a New Professional Identity
We have identified both similarity and diversity among our CEOs. To use the old Chinese label (as did Dogan ed. 1975) they are the mandarins of local government. While the overall picture allows for an identification of shared trends

which bridge old cleavages and pave the way for the "new Mandarins" (who increasingly serve and are expected to serve as discreet local political advisors and entrepreneurs), it may be difficult for some local government CEOs to adopt and identify with the new fads and ideas about management and to conform to the new and at times diverging expectations from various groups in their environment.

As the qualitative part of the Portuguese research shows, the CEOs present themselves as partisans of modernization, while at the same time having to live with the legacies of past oligarchic, paternalistic and clientelistic traditions. To operate under such diverging cognitive and empirical circumstances is possible only by decoupling them over time, depending on the issue and between saying and doing. Thus the recognition of new management ideals among the CEOs has an important symbolic function.

It should also be noted that the new managerial fads should of course be understood in their proper context. Despite marked trends in the direction of New Public Management, the public sector is not simply becoming "private" in its way of functioning. This is clearly stressed by Magnier in the Italian case. While there is a general trend caused among other things by new functions to be attached to the Italian "Segretario Communale", a trend which changes the role from being a "quiet supervisor" towards a more active organizational leader, it is important to observe the specific context. Rather than being simply an example of a generic application of a New Public Management approach inspired by a narrow "private" interpretation of management, Magnier emphasizes that it is a specific aspiration towards public administrative leadership.

Nevertheless, the overall picture is quite clear. We can identify clusters of countries which share common features in regard to the relative power of the CEOs, their preferred roles and the way in which they see the roles of the politicians. Yet at the same time, there are features bridging these (classical) cleavages. Local government CEOs of the Western world are becoming professional managers. Both the Danish and the Belgian cases describe the transformation as one from being the town clerk to becoming the manager. And as Baldersheim and Øgård conclude in their national analyses, NPM measures are being taken and the Norwegian CEO is still an apolitical bureaucrat struggling to become more of a modern manager. They become professional managers, however, within a public context as undercover leaders in a political system where they are not the boss. To anyone else but their employees, they are the anonymous leaders.

New professional norms are slowly penetrating the world of the CEOs. Being a local chief executive is gradually being a part of a genuine profession, a far cry from being first among equals. We see the contours of a new and widely shared professional identity of appointed CEOs in Western local government.

Bibliography

Aberbach, Joel D., Robert D. Putnam and Bert A. Rockman (1981): *Bureaucrats and Politicians*, Cambridge: Harvard University Press.

Dogan, Mattei (ed.) (1975): *The Mandarins of Western Europe: The Political Roles of Top Civil Servants*, Beverly Hills: Sage.

Huntington, Samuel P. (1996): *The Clash of Civilizations and the Remaking of World Order*, New York: Simon & Schuster.

Tilly, Charles (ed.) (1976): *The Formation of National States in Western Europe*, Princeton: Princeton University Press.

Technical appendix

by Lene Anderson and Poul Erik Mouritzen

Content

1. The survey
2. The intensive interviews
3. Analysis of jobpostings
4. The calculation of indices
5. Questionnaire for Chief Executives in Local Government

The survey

From November 1995 until May 1997, 14 countries conducted the survey. A joint questionnaire was proposed during 1995. In January of that year the first joint meeting among the researchers was held in Odense, Denmark. At this meeting the terms for the project and the survey were decided. During the following months, the Odense team prepared a draft of the questionnaire, which was presented and discussed at a meeting in Bordeaux (France) at the end of April. The comments and ideas from the Bordeaux meeting were embodied in the questionnaire during the Summer, and the first surveys were carried out by the end of 1995.

The common questionnaire consists of 54 core questions with 254 variables. Each country were allowed to add country specific questions. These questions are not part of the joint datafile.

The third joint project meeting was held in Odense in January 1996. During this meeting a coding workshop was conducted with student assistants from nine countries. During the week spent in Odense, the coders participated in the development of general coding principles as well as in the development of categories for open-ended questions. The coders were very competent and returned to their countries to finish the job in an efficient way guided by the common principles. Those countries, which did not participate in the coding workshop were each given individual advice as to how to code the questionnaires and how to work with the datafile.

The table below gives information about the survey in each of the 14 countries. It is important to note that the response rates vary considerably across countries. In order to increase the representativeness of the samples, weights have been created along two dimensions. The first dimension takes care of the problem with representativeness within each county with regard to size of municipality. The second dimension takes care of the differences between the countries with regard to sample size. Due to the time schedule for the present book, it was not possible to use the weights in the calculations made. However, at a late stage a test was conducted for countries which exhibited a small response rate or had a skewed sample due to stratification. In no case did this test indicate problems of any significance. The weighting procedures will be described in detail in the books to come (cf. the introduction).

Table 1 Response rates

Country	Survey conducted	Sent out	Returned	Response rate	Comments on population
Australia	Oct 96	670	246	37	All local governments with the exception of Aboriginal community governments in the Northern Territory
Belgium	Nov-Dec 95	589	351	60	All municipalities are included in the survey. Questionnaire mailed in both a Dutch and a French version
Denmark	Nov 95	275	200	73	All Danish municipalities
England	Dec 95-Feb 96	511	284	56	Full population less city of London
Finland	March-April 96	439	308	70	All municipalities except those of the Åland Islands
France	Dec 95-Jan 96	772	266	35	A stratified disproportionate sampling drawn among municipalities with more than 5000 inhabitants.
The Nederlands	March-May 96	584	404	69	All municipalities, except 59 which do not have an appointed CEO
Ireland	May-June 96	34	21	62	All municipalities are included
Italy	Dec 95-March 96	2000	541	27	Italy has 8100 municipalities, but only 6100 CEOs. Several CEOs work in two or three small municipalities. The sample is 50 pct. of all municipalities with more than 10,000 inhabitants, and 50 pct. of a random sample of municipalities with less than 10,000 inhabitants
Norway	Jan 97	434	325	75	All municipalities are included
Portugal	Dec 95	275	104	38	All municipalities except the Island of Madeira and the Azores
Spain	Nov 95	5000	366	7	The actual population is 8120. Questionnaire distributed with newsletter to CEOs
Sweden	Nov-Dec 95	279	224	80	The actual population is 288, but 9 municipalities did not have an appointed CEO at the time
USA	Jan-May 97	1178	697	59	CEO/CAO in all cities with more than 50,000 inhabitants and a sample of one quarter of the cities with a population between 2,500-50,000.

Intensive interviews

To get a more detailed knowledge of the work of a CEO a series of intensive interviews were conducted in some of the participating countries (cf. table 2). Most of the interviews were taped and transcribed. In some cases English summaries were made and distributed among participants.

Table 2 Number of intensive interviews conducted

Country	Number of interviews
Australia	Interviews conducted Fall 1998
Denmark	3 (+15 in a previous study)
England	7
France	17
Holland	6
Ireland	6
Norway	Interviews conducted Fall 1998
Portugal	2
USA	5 (incl. two former mayors)

All interviews have been conducted after the same interview guide according to which the following items/questions were covered:

1. INTRODUCTION
    1.1. Presentation of the U.DI.T.E project
    1.2. Issues of anonymity, how data are dealt with
    1.3 Plans of publication (broadly)
    4 Questions raised by interviewee

2. BACKGROUND (some of these items can be filled in by the researcher, just make sure all are registered)
    2.1. Country, age, gender
    2.2. Career background
    2.3. Characterization of municipality as area
    2.4. Characterization of municipality as administrative structure
    2.5. What are the most important recent problems in the municipality (external and internal)?

3. JOB AS CEO
    3.1. How would you broadly characterize your job as a city manager?
        (Tasks, dilemmas, problems, opportunities, cross pressures, predictability, active/reactive, external relations, rules/administration versus entrepreneurship, leader versus manager, fire-fighting?)

4. RELATION TO POLITICS/POLITICIANS IN GENERAL
    4.1. How would you describe the general political climate in the municipality?
        (conflict? stability? fixed majority? who runs things?)
    4.2. What are the effects of this climate on your role as CEO?
    4.3. How would you describe the ideal politician seen from your position?
        (related to: ideal definition of politics versus administration)
    4.4. How and to what extent do the politicians differ from this ideal?
    4.5. Effects thereof on role as CEO?
    4.6. Any attempts by CEO to influence style/behaviour of politicians?

5. RELATION TO MAJORITY/ MINORITY
    5.1. Please describe broadly your relations to both political majority and minority
    5.2. Effects of majority/minority issues on role as CEO?

6. RELATION TO MAYOR
    6.1. How would you broadly characterize the mayor?
        (relation to voters, to party, to whole political body..)
    6.2. Please describe the division of tasks between the mayor and the CEO
    6.3. Please describe the type of advice you may give the mayor
    6.4. What are the effects of your relation to the mayor on your role as a CEO

Analysis of jobpostings

The last source of data to be described is jobpostings. The term "jobposting" refers to advertisements that provide information about a municipal vacancy. Briefly explained jobpostings provide information about job content, professional and personal qualifications required etc. This information is – in contradiction to survey data – independent of the perspective of the person who actually performs the CEO job. Jobpostings may also be seen as a way of communication used by municipalities to create or sustain a certain public impression of the particular municipality and its administration.

Before using jobpostings some methodological considerations have been done. Jobpostings should not be read directly as valid indicators of what the CEO job requires technically. On the other hand jobpostings are not purely symbolic either. The hypothesis behind analysing jobpostings is, that changes in institutional settings and norms in time define varying socially appropriate standards for municipal leadership.

The job adds were collected during three periods: all of 1975, all of 1985 and the period between October 1st 1994 until September 30st 1995.

The criteria for participating are that the jobpostings are available in one or a few journals, and that the jobpostings display enough variation in content/form within each country to be seen as interesting objects of analysis.

Table 3: Number of jobpostings per country and period

	1970's	**1980's**	**1990's**	**Cases in total**
Denmark	23	39	35	97
Finland	35	36	25	96
France	15	39	59	113
England	25		19	44
Norway	1	9	40	50
Sweden	16	16	32	64
The Nederlands	38	53	24	115
Cases in total	153	192	234	579

The 579 job postings have been coded with respect to the following eight main categories (involving 77 variables per job posting):

1. Identification (country, year ect.)
2. The specific add in total (size, number of words, illustrations, logos)
3. Job content and functions
4. Abilities, experience, formal qualifications
5. Personal qualifications
6. Job benefits, salary, terms
7. Municipality as area
8. Municipality as administrative organisation

Lene Anderson and Poul Erik Mouritzen

The calculation of indices

Many of the questions posed to the CEOs in the survey involved five response categories, cf. the questionnaire below. In order to simplify the presentation of the results, indices taking values from 0 to 100 were constructed. An example will illustrate this procedure:

> The CEOs were asked to indicate how much emphasis they assigned to different tasks in their daily work (questions 23, cf. below). They were further asked to respond on a scale going from "of utmost importance", "very important", "moderate importance", "little importance" to "very little or no importance". In order to present the exact results from a country, it was necessary to show how large a percentage of the respondents had chosen each of the five categories. In order to simplify the comparison among countries, the index method was used. If a respondent had answered "of utmost importance", he was assigned a value of 100, the answer "very important" was given a value of 75, "moderate importance" a value of 50, "of little importance" a value of 25, and if the respondent had answered "of very little or no importance", he was assigned the value 0.

For this book two different sets of composite indices have been constructed. The first refers to the weights assigned by the CEOs to different tasks which involve two indices for the classical and "the political" bureaucrat, respectively (based on question 23, cf. below). The second set focuses on how the CEO thinks the politicians should act. In this connection we used the four indices for administration, representation, governance or stability (based on question 36, cf. below).[1]

---

[1] In the chapter about the Swedish CEOs the use of the role concept is different (cf. chapter 9). Australia, Ireland and Spain did not include the role concepts of the ideal politician in their chapters.

Questionnaire for Chief Executives in Local Government

C1 1. **Please indicate the number of inhabitants in your municipality:**

- ☐ 1   Below 1.000 inhabitants
- ☐ 2   1.000–   2.000 inhabitants
- ☐ 3   2.000–   5.000 inhabitants
- ☐ 4   5.000–   10.000 inhabitants
- ☐ 5   10.000–   15.000 inhabitants
- ☐ 6   15.000–   20.000 inhabitants
- ☐ 7   20.000–   30.000 inhabitants
- ☐ 8   30.000–   50.000 inhabitants
- ☐ 9   50.000–   100.000 inhabitants
- ☐ 10 100.000– 200.000 inhabitants
- ☐ 11 200.000– 500.000 inhabitants
- ☐ 12   Above 500.000 inhabitants

C2 2. **How many people are employed by the municipality (please convert to full-time equivalents)?**

Total number of employees in the municipality: _____

How many are employed in administrative functions: _____

C3 3. **What is your official title:** _____

C4 4. **When were you born?** 19 _____

C5 5. **Are you**

- ☐ 1 Male
- ☐ 2 Female

C6 6. **How many years of full-time education have you had (including primary school)?**

_____ years

C7 7. **Please state your education (more than one entry if necessary)**

- ☐ 1 Municipal apprenticeship
- ☐ 2 Private administrative education
- ☐ 3 Middle range education (teacher, social worker etc.)

Please state: _____

University degree:
- ☐ 41 Law
- ☐ 42 Economics/finance
- ☐ 43 Political science/administration
- ☐ 44 Technical degree (engineer, architect)
- ☐ 45 Natural science
- ☐ 46 Humanities, history etc.
- ☐ 47 Other university degrees

    Please state: _____

Other education

    Please state: _____

C8 **8. What was your first job after you left full-time education?**

C9 **9. What was your last job before your present post? Please give details: title, place of employment and number of years employed:**

C10 **10. For how many years have you held your present position?**

    _____ years

C11 **11. Do you consider your present position as the last one in your career, or do you intend to seek another job?**

- ☐ 1 I do not intend to seek another post
- ☐ 2 I may seek another post if the right opportunities arise
- ☐ 3 I am definitely planning to seek another job sometime in the future

C12 **12. We kindly ask you to indicate the reason(s) why your immediate predecessor left his/her position (you may mark more than one item if necessary).**

- ☐ Career (advancement to higher or better paid office)
- ☐ Problems of cooperation with politicians
- ☐ Problems of cooperation with bureaucrats
- ☐ Workload and other pressures stemming from the job
- ☐ Age
- ☐ Illness/death
- ☐ Don't know
- ☐ Other reasons (please state): _____

C13 **13. Please estimate of how many local associations or local pressure groups you are a member.**

Number of associations: _____

C14 **14. Are you a member of any professional bodies? Please give details.**

_____
_____

C15 **15. Are you now or have you been a member of a political party?**

☐ 1 I am presently a member of a political party
☐ 2 I have previously been a member of a political party
☐ 3 I have never been a member of a political party

C16 **16. Please estimate the number of hours you work in a typical week:**

_____ hours

C17 **17. Did you spend part of your childhood (0-18 years) in the county/region where you presently work?**

☐ 1 Yes
☐ 2 No

C18 **18. Do you live within the boundaries of your employing authority?**

☐ 1 Yes
☐ 2 No

C19 **19. What was the household head's occupation when you were around 15 years old:**

Self-employed
  ☐ 1 Farmer/fisherman
  ☐ 2 Professional (lawyer, medical practitioner, accountant etc.)
  ☐ 3 Shop/company owner, craftsman, self employed person
  ☐ 4 Business proprietor, owner (full or partner) of a company

Employed
  ☐ 5 Employed professional (employed lawyer, practitioner, accountant)
  ☐ 6 General management, director or top management
  ☐ 7 Middle management
  ☐ 8 Employed position, working mainly at a desk
  ☐ 9 Employed position, not at a desk, but travelling
  ☐ 10 Employed position, not at a desk, but service job (hospital, restaurant, police, fireman)
  ☐ 11 Supervisor
  ☐ 12 Skilled manual worker

☐ 13 Other (unskilled) manual worker, servant
☐ 14 Other occupation/unemployed/retired

C20 **20. Please think of an ideal job – disregarding your present job. In choosing an ideal job, how important would it be to you to:**

	Of utmost importance 1	Very important 2	Of moderate importance 3	Of little importance 4	Of very little or no importance 5
1. Have sufficient time for your personal or family life	☐	☐	☐	☐	☐
2. Have good physical working conditions	☐	☐	☐	☐	☐
3. Have a good working relationship with your direct superiors	☐	☐	☐	☐	☐
4. Have security of employment	☐	☐	☐	☐	☐
5. Work with people who cooperate well with one another	☐	☐	☐	☐	☐
6. Be consulted by your direct superiors in her/his decisions	☐	☐	☐	☐	☐
7. Have an opportunity for advancement to higher level jobs	☐	☐	☐	☐	☐
8. Have an element of variety and adventure in the job	☐	☐	☐	☐	☐
9. Work closely with politicians	☐	☐	☐	☐	☐
10. Have the possibility of influencing the development of the municipality	☐	☐	☐	☐	☐

C21 **21. How often do you feel nervous or tense at work?**

☐ 1 Never
☐ 2 Seldom
☐ 3 Sometimes
☐ 4 Usually
☐ 5 Always

C22 **22. How frequently, in your experience, are subordinates afraid to express disagreement with their superiors?**

☐ 1 Very seldom
☐ 2 Seldom
☐ 3 Sometimes
☐ 4 Frequently
☐ 5 Very frequently

C23 **23. Chief executives must necessarily decide the priority of various tasks. Please indicate how much emphasis you in your daily work put on each of the tasks listed below. Make your entries on a scale from 1 (attach very little or no importance to) to 5 (attach utmost importance to).**

	Of very little or no importance 1	Of little importance 2	Of moderate importance 3	Very important 4	Of utmost importance 5
1. Solve problems and conflicts of human relationships	☐	☐	☐	☐	☐
2. Stimulate cooperation between departments	☐	☐	☐	☐	☐
3. Formulate ideas and visions	☐	☐	☐	☐	☐
4. Guide subordinate staff in day-to-day handling of cases	☐	☐	☐	☐	☐
5. Promote and encourage new projects in the community	☐	☐	☐	☐	☐
6. Be informed about the viewpoints of the employees	☐	☐	☐	☐	☐
7. Develop and implement new routines and work methods	☐	☐	☐	☐	☐
8. Manage economic affairs, accounts and budgetary control	☐	☐	☐	☐	☐
9. Ensure that rules and regulations are followed	☐	☐	☐	☐	☐
10. Give the Mayor legal, economical and other kinds of technical advice	☐	☐	☐	☐	☐
11. Give the Mayor political advice	☐	☐	☐	☐	☐
12. Be informed about citizens' viewpoints	☐	☐	☐	☐	☐
13. Develop and implement norms concerning the proper roles of politicians vis-à-vis the bureaucrats	☐	☐	☐	☐	☐
14. Influence decision-making processes in order to secure sensible and efficient solutions	☐	☐	☐	☐	☐
15. Attract resources from external sources like the national/regional government, funds, private investors and business	☐	☐	☐	☐	☐
16. Make sure that resources are used efficiently	☐	☐	☐	☐	☐

With regard to the following two questions, we would like you to indicate the importance of different aspects of your work. Please indicate the priority you give to these aspects by giving the most important aspect a 1, the second most important a 2, and the third a 3.

C24 **24. If there is a clash between different considerations in your daily work, what priority do you give to the following? (Please write 1, 2, 3)**

_____ Observing the established rules and procedures (e.g. laws, regulations and internal procedures)

_____ Accomplishing tasks efficiently and quickly

_____ Ensuring everybody involved are satisfied with decision-making processes and their outcomes

C25 **25. Among other things, leadership and management is about the distribution of work and ensuring cooperation between people and different parts of the organization. However, leadership skills may be necessary in ones daily work as well as in crisis situations. What priority do you give to the following aspects of leadership? (Please write 1, 2, 3)**

_____ Formal power and authority

_____ Motivation through commendation and reward of the individual

_____ Personal relations (friendship, respect, trust)

C26 **26. Chief executives may find inspiration in their daily activities from many sources. To what extent have you found the following sources useful concerning your ability to develop your skills as a leader?**

	Extremely useful 1	Very useful 2	Somewhat useful 3	Of little use 4	Of no use 5
1. Inspiration from executives in other municipalities	☐	☐	☐	☐	☐
2. Own schooling/educational background	☐	☐	☐	☐	☐
3. Inspiration from consultants	☐	☐	☐	☐	☐
4. Inspiration from training courses, seminars etc.	☐	☐	☐	☐	☐
5. Professional journals, magazines and the like	☐	☐	☐	☐	☐
6. The general management literature	☐	☐	☐	☐	☐
7. Inspiration from managers in private business	☐	☐	☐	☐	☐
8. The activities and meetings of the association of chief executives	☐	☐	☐	☐	☐
9. The activities of other professional associations	☐	☐	☐	☐	☐
10. The Local Government Associations	☐	☐	☐	☐	☐

C27 **27. One aspect of the work of the chief executive is the management of organizational change. How would you weight the circumstances mentioned below as part of such a process of organizational change? Please indicate on a scale from 1 (attach very little or no importance to) to 5 (attach utmost importance to).**

	Of very little or no importance 1	Of little importance 2	Of moderate importance 3	Very important 4	Of utmost importance 5
1. Wide-ranging involvement of the employees	☐	☐	☐	☐	☐
2. Careful preparation with a small number of executives	☐	☐	☐	☐	☐
3. A quick reorganization	☐	☐	☐	☐	☐
4. Secure trade union support	☐	☐	☐	☐	☐
5. Achieve incremental reorganization rather than an extensive reform	☐	☐	☐	☐	☐
6. Create a broad consensus among elected politicians	☐	☐	☐	☐	☐

C28 **28. To what extent do you agree or disagree with each of the following statements?**

	Strongly agree 1	Partly agree 2	Undecided 3	Disagree 4	Strongly disagree 5
1. Most people can be trusted	☐	☐	☐	☐	☐
2. One can be a good manager without having precise answers to most questions that subordinates may raise about their work	☐	☐	☐	☐	☐
3. An organization structure in which certain subordinates have two bosses should be avoided at all cost	☐	☐	☐	☐	☐
4. Competition between employees usually does more harm than good	☐	☐	☐	☐	☐
5. The rules of an organization should not be broken – not even when the employee thinks it is in the bestinterest of the organization	☐	☐	☐	☐	☐
6. When people have failed in life it is often their own fault	☐	☐	☐	☐	☐

C29 **29. Do you think that the job as a local government CEO is more attractive today than it was ten years ago?**

- ☐ 1 Yes, much more attractive
- ☐ 2 Yes, somewhat more attractive
- ☐ 3 More or less the same as ten years ago
- ☐ 4 No, the job has become somewhat less attractive
- ☐ 5 No, the job has become much less attractive

Please give the reasons for your assessment:
_____
_____
_____

C30 **30. Does any one party presently have an overall majority of seats on the local council?**

- ☐ 1 No party has an overall majority
- ☐ 2 One party has an overall majority

Please indicate which party: _____

C31 **31. All in all, do you think there are many conflicts between the major political parties in your municipality, some conflicts or few conflicts?**

- ☐ 1 Many conflicts
- ☐ 2 Some conflicts
- ☐ 3 Few conflicts
- ☐ 4 No conflicts at all

C32 **32. For how many years has the present Mayor held the position as Mayor?**

_____ years

C33 **33. How would you evaluate the chances of the Mayor in the next local election if he/she decides to run again?**

- ☐ 1 The Mayor is almost sure to continue in the position
- ☐ 2 The Mayor stand the best chances of all candidates but he/she cannot be sure to continue
- ☐ 3 The Mayor is likely to lose his/her position in the next election
- ☐ 4 Don't know

C34 **34. How would you evaluate the Mayor's position within her/his own party and party group?**

- ☐ 1 The Mayor is the unchallenged leader of the party
- ☐ 2 The Mayor's position as the leaders of the party is under attack but he still runs affairs
- ☐ 3 The Mayor has a rather weak position within the party
- ☐ 4 Don't know

C35 **35. Please indicate the extent to which the following describes the Mayor's behavior.**

	To a very high extent 1	To a high extent 2	To some extent 3	To a little extent 4	Not at all 5
1. The Mayor is very much engaged in the details of the daily work of the administration	☐	☐	☐	☐	☐
2. The Mayor is a visionary person who constantly initiates new projects and policies in the locality	☐	☐	☐	☐	☐
3. The Mayor has excellent relations with the public and knows what concerns the citizens	☐	☐	☐	☐	☐
4. The Mayor is primarily a politician engaged in policy making rather than administrative details	☐	☐	☐	☐	☐
5. The Mayor merely reacts to the circumstances when new policies are formulated	☐	☐	☐	☐	☐
6. The Mayor emphasizes the promotion of the party program and the interests of his fellow party members	☐	☐	☐	☐	☐

C36 36. Politicians must give priority to different tasks in their daily work. As a local government official, to which tasks do you think the leading politicians ought to attach particular importance? Please make your entry on a scale from 1 (very little or no importance) to 5 (of utmost importance).

	Of very little or no importance 1	Of little importance 2	Of moderate importance 3	Very important 4	Of utmost importance 5
1. Be informed about citizens' views	☐	☐	☐	☐	☐
2. Represent the municipality to the outside world	☐	☐	☐	☐	☐
3. Create stability for the administration	☐	☐	☐	☐	☐
4. Formulate exact and unambiguous goals for the administration	☐	☐	☐	☐	☐
5. Defend the authorities' decisions and policies externally	☐	☐	☐	☐	☐
6. Implement the program on which he/she has been elected	☐	☐	☐	☐	☐
7. Be a spokesperson for local groups or individuals who have issues pending decision by the authority	☐	☐	☐	☐	☐
8. Decide on major policy principles	☐	☐	☐	☐	☐
9. Be a spokesperson for their political party	☐	☐	☐	☐	☐
10. Have a vision of the way in which the municipality will develop in the long run	☐	☐	☐	☐	☐
11. Lay down rules and routines for the administration	☐	☐	☐	☐	☐
12. Making decisions concerning specific cases	☐	☐	☐	☐	☐
13. Be a spokesperson vis-à-vis the press	☐	☐	☐	☐	☐
14. Procure resources from upper-level governments	☐	☐	☐	☐	☐

C37 **37. Chief executives may have different opinions about the way in which their relations with politicians ought to be organized. Below are some statements which touch upon this subject in different ways. Please indicate whether you agree or disagree with them:**

	Strongly agree 1	Partly agree 2	Undecided 3	Disagree 4	Strongly disagree 5
1. It is the politicians' duty to decide only on major principal issues and not on routine matters	☐	☐	☐	☐	☐
2. Certain groups in society are so weak that it is the duty of the administration to be a spokesman for them	☐	☐	☐	☐	☐
3. Administrative officials should make themselves aquainted with the intentions of the politicians and put forward proposals in line with these intentions only	☐	☐	☐	☐	☐
4. The administration must be a prime mover in adapting the local authority to changes in society	☐	☐	☐	☐	☐
5. It is an advantage if the chief executive is of the same political opinion as the majority of the local council	☐	☐	☐	☐	☐
6. The administration should not undertake major policy reviews without political direction	☐	☐	☐	☐	☐
7. The administration should be non-partisan and only base its recommendations on expert opinion	☐	☐	☐	☐	☐
8. The chief executive officer should be primarily responsible to the political leadership and only secondarily to the local population	☐	☐	☐	☐	☐

C38 **38. To what extent has your ability to perform your job as chief executive been affected *negatively* by the following factors during recent years?**

	To a very high extent 1	To a high extent 2	To some extent 3	To a little extent 4	Not at all 5
1. Financial problems in the municipality	☐	☐	☐	☐	☐
2. Lack of clear political goals	☐	☐	☐	☐	☐
3. New regulations from upper-level governments	☐	☐	☐	☐	☐
4. The demands of the population for better service	☐	☐	☐	☐	☐
5. Demographic changes	☐	☐	☐	☐	☐
6. Conflicts between the political parties	☐	☐	☐	☐	☐
7. Unemployment and social problems	☐	☐	☐	☐	☐
8. Central and/or regional government control of local government finances	☐	☐	☐	☐	☐
9. Conflicts between the various departments and/or department heads	☐	☐	☐	☐	☐
10. Pressures from local organized interests, business and the like	☐	☐	☐	☐	☐
11. Unclear division of labour between politicians and the administration	☐	☐	☐	☐	☐
12. Cuts in grants from upper-level governments	☐	☐	☐	☐	☐

C39 **39. Has the municipality during the last decade privatized or contracted out functions?**

☐ 1 No
☐ 2 Yes

If yes, how important do you think this privatization/contracting out has been in terms of reducing the number of municipal employees?

☐ 1 Of utmost importance
☐ 2 Very important
☐ 3 Of moderate importance
☐ 4 Of little importance
☐ 5 Of very little or no importance

C40 **40.** An organization may be characterized as more or less centralized, regarding the degree of discretion delegated to the lower levels of the hierarchy. Please indicate whether your municipality has become more or less centralized over the past decade.

Much more centralized	More centralized	No change	More decentralized	Much more decentralized
☐	☐	☐	☐	☐

C41 **41.** The relationship between politicians and administrators may be characterized by more or less delegation from the former to the latter. Please indicate whether there has been more or less of such delegation in your municipality over the past decade.

Much more delegation	More delegation	No change	Less delegation	Much lesser delegation
☐	☐	☐	☐	☐

C42 **42.** The relationship between the municipality and upper levels of government may be characterized as more or less decentralized. Please indicate whether there has been more or less decentralization to local government over the past decade.

Much more centralization	More centralization	No change	More decentralization	Much more decentralization
☐	☐	☐	☐	☐

C43 **43.** When setting priorities, municipal authorities must consider numerous performance goals. Please indicate whether there have been changes in the importance attached to each of the following goals in setting priorities in municipal decisions?

	Much more importance 1	More importance 2	No change 3	Less importance 4	Much less importance 5
1. User participation	☐	☐	☐	☐	☐
2. Citizen participation	☐	☐	☐	☐	☐
3. Efficiency of service production	☐	☐	☐	☐	☐
4. Protection of minority interests	☐	☐	☐	☐	☐
5. Speed of decision-making	☐	☐	☐	☐	☐
6. Equal access to services	☐	☐	☐	☐	☐
7. Due process	☐	☐	☐	☐	☐

C44 **44. Please indicate the extent to which you agree or disagree with the following statements:**

	Strongly agree 1	Partly agree 2	Undecided 3	Disagree 4	Strongly disagree 5
1. The need for changes and reorganization of the local government sector has been greatly exaggerated	☐	☐	☐	☐	☐
2. The public sector has grown too large compared to the private sector	☐	☐	☐	☐	☐
3. In general, the private sector is more efficient than the public sector	☐	☐	☐	☐	☐
4. There are very few benefits from contracting out or privatizing services in the municipality	☐	☐	☐	☐	☐
5. The smaller municipalities are too inefficient and ought to be amalgamated into larger units	☐	☐	☐	☐	☐

C45 **45. Many actors may influence local policy-making. Please indicate how influential the following actors are regarding the BUDGET. Make your entries on a scale from 1 (high influence) to 5 (no influence).**

	High influence 1	2	3	4	No influence 5
1. The Mayor	☐	☐	☐	☐	☐
2. Private business interests	☐	☐	☐	☐	☐
3. The committee chairs	☐	☐	☐	☐	☐
4. The local political parties	☐	☐	☐	☐	☐
5. The department heads	☐	☐	☐	☐	☐
6. The media	☐	☐	☐	☐	☐
7. The majority group on the council	☐	☐	☐	☐	☐
8. The chief executive officer	☐	☐	☐	☐	☐
9. Trade union leaders	☐	☐	☐	☐	☐
10. Upper level governments	☐	☐	☐	☐	☐
11. Users/clients	☐	☐	☐	☐	☐
12. Voluntary associations	☐	☐	☐	☐	☐

C46 46. Please also estimate how influential the following actors are regarding the ECO-NOMIC DEVELOPMENT OF THE COMMUNITY (please make your entries on a scale from 1 (high influence) to 5 (no influence).

	High influence 1	2	3	4	No influence 5
1. The Mayor	☐	☐	☐	☐	☐
2. Private business interests	☐	☐	☐	☐	☐
3. The committee chairs	☐	☐	☐	☐	☐
4. The local political parties	☐	☐	☐	☐	☐
5. The department heads	☐	☐	☐	☐	☐
6. The media	☐	☐	☐	☐	☐
7. The majority group on the council	☐	☐	☐	☐	☐
8. The chief executive officer	☐	☐	☐	☐	☐
9. Trade union leaders	☐	☐	☐	☐	☐
10. Upper level governments	☐	☐	☐	☐	☐
11. Users/clients	☐	☐	☐	☐	☐
12. Voluntary associations	☐	☐	☐	☐	☐

C47 47. How often do you normally communicate (oral communication including meetings, telephone calls, etc.) with the following persons/groups of persons? (One cross per row, please.)

	Daily 1	2-4 times per week 2	Once a week 3	1-3 times a month 4	Seldom/ never 5
1. The Mayor	☐	☐	☐	☐	☐
2. Leaders of the political opposition	☐	☐	☐	☐	☐
3. Other politicians in the municipality	☐	☐	☐	☐	☐
4. Heads of departments in the municipal organization	☐	☐	☐	☐	☐
5. Other employees in the municipal organization	☐	☐	☐	☐	☐
6. Citizens in the municipality	☐	☐	☐	☐	☐
7. Journalists	☐	☐	☐	☐	☐
8. Chief executives in other municipalities	☐	☐	☐	☐	☐
9. Regional government officials	☐	☐	☐	☐	☐
10. Central government officials	☐	☐	☐	☐	☐
11. Officials of other public sector bodies	☐	☐	☐	☐	☐
12. Officials from the national association of local authorities	☐	☐	☐	☐	☐
13. Union representatives regarding salaries and other employee-related issues	☐	☐	☐	☐	☐
14. Union representatives regarding other isssues	☐	☐	☐	☐	☐
15. Private business interests	☐	☐	☐	☐	☐
16. Other leading actors e.g. from voluntary and other nonprofit organizations	☐	☐	☐	☐	☐

C48 **48. To what extent are these relations important for your ability to perform your functions as a chief executive officer? (One cross per row, please.)**

	To a very high extent 1	To a high extent 2	To some extent 3	To a little extent 4	Not at all 5
1. The Mayor	☐	☐	☐	☐	☐
2. Leaders of the political opposition	☐	☐	☐	☐	☐
3. Other politicians in the municipality	☐	☐	☐	☐	☐
4. Heads of departments in the municipal organization	☐	☐	☐	☐	☐
5. Other employees in the municipal organization	☐	☐	☐	☐	☐
6. Citizens in the municipality	☐	☐	☐	☐	☐
7. Journalists	☐	☐	☐	☐	☐
8. Chief executives in other municipalities	☐	☐	☐	☐	☐
9. Regional government officials	☐	☐	☐	☐	☐
10. Central government officials	☐	☐	☐	☐	☐
11. Officials of other public sector bodies	☐	☐	☐	☐	☐
12. Officials from the national association of local authorities	☐	☐	☐	☐	☐
13. Union representatives regarding salaries and other employee-related issues	☐	☐	☐	☐	☐
14. Union representatives regarding other isssues	☐	☐	☐	☐	☐
15. Private business interests	☐	☐	☐	☐	☐
16. Other leading actors e.g. from voluntary and other nonprofit organizations	☐	☐	☐	☐	☐

C49 49. Relationships to these actors may be marked by more or less conflict or cooperation. How would you describe your relationship with the following persons or groups of persons?

	Very conflictual 1	Conflictual 2	Neutral 3	Cooperative 4	Very cooperative 5
1. The Mayor	☐	☐	☐	☐	☐
2. Leaders of the political opposition	☐	☐	☐	☐	☐
3. Other politicians in the municipality	☐	☐	☐	☐	☐
4. Heads of departments in the municipal organization	☐	☐	☐	☐	☐
5. Other employees in the municipal organization	☐	☐	☐	☐	☐
6. Citizens in the municipality	☐	☐	☐	☐	☐
7. Journalists	☐	☐	☐	☐	☐
8. Chief executives in other municipalities	☐	☐	☐	☐	☐
9. Regional government officials	☐	☐	☐	☐	☐
10. Central government officials	☐	☐	☐	☐	☐
11. Officials of other public sector bodies	☐	☐	☐	☐	☐
12. Officials from the national association of local authorities	☐	☐	☐	☐	☐
13. Union representatives regarding salaries and other employee-related issues	☐	☐	☐	☐	☐
14. Union representatives regarding other isssues	☐	☐	☐	☐	☐
15. Private business interests	☐	☐	☐	☐	☐
16. Other leading actors e.g. from voluntary and other nonprofit organizations	☐	☐	☐	☐	☐

The National Association of Local Government Chief Executives

C50 **50. Have you been a member of committees, commissions, professional groups, or working groups appointed by the National Association of Local Government Chief Executives within the last five years?**

☐ 1 No
☐ 2 Yes

If yes, please indicate for what purpose the work is/was. Make more entries if necessary.

☐ Influencing national/regional legislation
☐ Implementing national/regional legislation
☐ Internal affairs of the CEO Association

C51 **51. Below are listed a number of tasks which may be of importance for the National Association of Chief Executive Officers. Please indicate how the Association, in your opinion, should decide on priorities in the future compared with the present.**

	Lower priority 1	Same priority 2	Higher priority 3
1. Communication to members on current trends and important national initiatives	☐	☐	☐
2. Influence the "local government agenda" in the country	☐	☐	☐
3. Professional training of members	☐	☐	☐
4. Exert influence on the implementation/-administrative adaption of national laws	☐	☐	☐
5. Exert influence on legislation through membership of committees etc.	☐	☐	☐
6. Comment on law proposals directly to Parliament, ministries, government departments and agencies	☐	☐	☐
7. Ensure that members' interests are heard in the media	☐	☐	☐
8. Strengthen the professional networks between members	☐	☐	☐
9. Promote social relations between members	☐	☐	☐
10. Engage in union functions such as negotiations about members' salaries and working conditions	☐	☐	☐

C52 **52. How satisfied are you with the way the CEO Association carries out the following tasks?**

	Very satisfied	Fairly satisfied	Not satisfied	Don't know/ irrelevant
	1	2	3	4
1. Communication to members on current trends and important national initiatives	☐	☐	☐	☐
2. Influence the "local government agenda" in the country	☐	☐	☐	☐
3. Professional training of members	☐	☐	☐	☐
4. Exert influence on the implementation/-administrative adaptation of national laws	☐	☐	☐	☐
5. Exert influence on legislation through membership of committees etc.	☐	☐	☐	☐
6. Comment on law proposals directly to Parliament, ministries, government departments and agencies	☐	☐	☐	☐
7. Ensure that members' interests are heard in the media	☐	☐	☐	☐
8. Strengthen the professional networks between members	☐	☐	☐	☐
9. Promote social relation between members	☐	☐	☐	☐
10. Engage in union functions such as negotiations about members' salaries and working conditions	☐	☐	☐	☐

C53 **53. In the future, what priority should the CEO Association, in your opinion, attach to these tasks compared to the present?**

	Lower priority 1	Same priority 2	Higher priority 3
1. Communication to members on current trends and important national initiatives	☐	☐	☐
2. Influence the "local government agenda" in the country	☐	☐	☐
3. Professional training of members	☐	☐	☐
4. Exert influence on the implementation/administrative adaptation of national laws	☐	☐	☐
5. Exert influence on legislation through membership of committees etc.	☐	☐	☐
6. Comment on law proposals directly to Parliament, ministries, government departments and agencies	☐	☐	☐
7. Ensure that members' interests are heard in the media	☐	☐	☐
8. Strengthen the professional networks between members	☐	☐	☐
9. Promote social relation between members	☐	☐	☐
10. Engage in union functions such as negotiations about members' salaries and working conditions	☐	☐	☐

C54 **54. Finally, in your private life, how important is each of the following to you?**

	Of utmost importance 1	Very important 2	Of moderate importance 3	Of little importance 4	Of very little or no importance 5
1. Personal steadiness and stability	☐	☐	☐	☐	☐
2. Thrift	☐	☐	☐	☐	☐
3. Persistance (perseverance)	☐	☐	☐	☐	☐
4. Respect for tradition	☐	☐	☐	☐	☐

Participants in the U.DI.T.E. Leadership Study

Australia:	Rolf Gerritsen, Michelle Whyard – Australian Centre of Regional and Local Government Studies – University of Canberra
Belgium:	Thierry Laurent, Rudolf Maes, Yves Plees – Department Politieke Wetenschappen – Katholieke Universiteit Leuven
Denmark:	Lene Anderson, Peter Dahler-Larsen, Niels Ejersbo, Morten Balle Hansen, Kurt Klaudi Klausen, Poul Erik Mouritzen – Department of Political Science and Public Management. Mikael Søndergaard – Department of Management – Odense University
England:	Michael Goldsmith and Jon Tonge – Department of Politics and Contemporary History – Salford University
Finland:	Sari Pikkala, Siv Sandberg, Krister Ståhlberg – Department of Public Administration – Åbo Akademi
France:	Katherine Burlen, Jean-Claude Thoenig – GAPP (Groupe d'Analyse des Politiques Publiques) – Cachan
The Nederlands:	Marcel van Dam, Geert Neelen, Anchrit Wille – Department of Public Administration, University of Leiden. Jaco Berveling – Dutch Transport Research Centre
Ireland:	Andy Asquith – Department of Politics and Public Policy – University of Luton. Eunan O'Halpin – Dublin City University Business School
Israel:	Nahum Ben-Elia – Policy Analysis, Strategic Urban Planning – Rehovet
Italy:	Maurizio Gamberucci, Annick Magnier – Dipartimento di Scienza delle Politico e Sociologia Politica – Universita degli studi di Firenze
Norway:	Harald Baldersheim, Morten Øgård – Department of Political Science – Oslo University
Portugal:	Manuel da Silva e Costa, Joel Felizes, José P. Neves – Instituto de Ciências Sociais – Universidade do Minho
Spain:	Irene Delgado, Lourdes López Nieto, Eliseo López – Departamento de Ciencia Politica – Universidad Nacional de Educacion a Distancia
Sweden:	Folke Johansson, Roger Haglund – Department of Political Science – University of Gothenburg
USA:	James Svara – Department of Political Science and Public Administration – North Carolina State University

Down to

Previous books by Neil Paynter include:

Lent & Easter Readings from Iona
This Is the Day
Gathered and Scattered
Blessed Be Our Table
Holy Ground, with Helen Boothroyd
Growing Hope
Iona Dawn
Iona: Images and Reflections, with David Coleman
Going Home Another Way (Wild Goose Publications)

Iain Campbell has illustrated a number of books, including:

Will You Follow Me?
The Widening Road
Breaking Down Walls
Gaun Yersel Moses
Parable Patter (St Andrew Press)

Down to Earth

Stories and sketches

Neil Paynter

Illustrations by Iain Campbell

WILD GOOSE PUBLICATIONS
www.ionabooks.com

Text © 2009 Neil Paynter
Illustrations © 2009 Iain Campbell

First published 2009 by
Wild Goose Publications, Fourth Floor, Savoy House,
140 Sauchiehall Street, Glasgow G2 3DH,
the publishing division of the Iona Community. Scottish Charity No. SCO03794.
Limited Company Reg. No. SCO96243.

ISBN 978-1-905010-47-9

The publishers gratefully acknowledge the support of the Drummond Trust,
3 Pitt Terrace, Stirling FK8 2EY in producing this book.

All rights reserved. No part of this publication may be reproduced in any form or by any means, including photocopying or any information storage or retrieval system, without written permission from the publisher.

Neil Paynter has asserted his right in accordance with the Copyright, Designs and Patents Act, 1988, to be identified as the author of this compilation.

A catalogue record for this book is available from the British Library.

Overseas distribution
Australia: Willow Connection Pty Ltd, Unit 4A, 3-9 Kenneth Road,
Manly Vale, NSW 2093
New Zealand: Pleroma Christian Supplies, Higginson St., Otane 4170,
Central Hawkes Bay
Canada: Novalis/Bayard Publishing & Distribution, 10 Lower Spadina Ave.,
Suite 400, Toronto, Ontario M5V 2Z2.

Printed by Bell & Bain, Thornliebank, Glasgow

CONTENTS

Foreword   13
Introduction   15

NURSE'S NOTES   19
Introduction   20
Grace   21
Amazing grace   21
Kate   22
Elma   23
Paul   23
Emily   24
He still remembers that day   25
Margaret   25
Suddenly a joke about chickens   26
Oh boy   27
Home   27
Mr Hicks   28
Watching TV with Mr Wilson   29
Tillie   30
A 93-year-old woman talking about apples   31

VETERANS: THE ROUNDS   33
Introduction   34
A room   35
George   37
Eddie   40
Paddy's visit   44
Andrew and Jessie   46

THE RAINBOW MAN   51
Introduction   52
The Rainbow Man   53
Donald Duck   54
Gary   59
The Rainbow Man 2   63
The busker   66
Hush puppies   70
Homelessness is …   71

SITTING   75
Introduction   76
Sitting with Mr Fenton   77
Esme and Peter   79

LEONARD AND MARK: DANCING INFINITY   83
Introduction   84
Leonard: a Christmas story   85
Mark: an Easter story   94

BINGO IN THE BASEMENT   99
Introduction   100
Muriel   101
Kenny   103
Maggie   107
Sarah's deep handbag   108
Peter's journal   108
Elizabeth   112
Lester   114
The professor   115
Doreen   117
The prayer wheel   118
Snack time   119
Meeting Sybil one day outside of Starbucks   121

Mable and Ha   125
Maggie and Walter   125
From Resurrection to Apocalypse   127
Outside (Into the night)   128

FUNNY THESE THINGS COME TO YOU   131
Introduction   132
Eating a kiwi fruit noisily   133
Wendell's first farm   133
A 'Spring Tooth Arrow'   135
Persimmons   136
Katherine's plants   139
James the Second   140
Birds and trees and a long, long road   141
Three breeds are smart   143
I've got news for you   145
Looking at the moon with Wendell   146
A good joke   147
Vera's second husband   147
Treasure chest   148
Wendell's last dog   150
The good, not the bad   151
All these years   152
A skein   153
A flower in the kitchen   154
Wendell's other neighbour   155
A tea party   156
The birdman   162
Train to Winnipeg   163
She knows   164
Womb of darkness   164

WORKING THE DOOR   165
Introduction   166
Working the door 1   168
The man with his heart on the wrong side   177
Working the door 2   181
Abbot and Costello Meet The Mummy   191
Working the door 3   199
Sweeping up   208

IT SMELLS LIKE LONELINESS   211
Introduction   212
Mikehead   213
Gerry   215
Helping Gordon with his Christmas decorations   219
I know a cat whose name is …   223
The lonely caribou   230
Tree says   231
Everybody knows that cats like to rumba   231
A psalm   234

An invitation   235

Everything around me was half asleep, every sound was muffled. Things moved reluctantly, just out of sheer necessity and not from any passionate love of movement and life. And I dearly wanted to give that earth a hard kick – and myself as well – so that everything, myself included, would start spinning round in one joyful whirlwind, in a festive dance where people were in love with each other, in love with a life … which was beautiful, bold and honest. And I thought: I must do something, or I'll be finished …

Maxim Gorky, My Apprenticeship

Why on earth are we here?
Surely not to live in pain and fear.

John Lennon, Instant Karma

And the Word became flesh and lived among us …

John 1:14

In the true life of prayer we are forever on the knife-edge. We move in the light and shadow of Him who is born Son of God and Son of Man. Manifestly there is a new prayer life demanded: not stationary times with God, but living, flowing times when, by His Spirit, we are exercised in unravelling the mystery of that apex of majesty which is His humanity.

George MacLeod, Only One Way Left

To beautiful Helen (Lambie)

Thank you so much to (in no particular order):

Bill and Lisa, Simon and Shonna
Rick, Bethany
Jeff, Jonathan
Mike K, Yoshiki
Nicole
Yvonne
Karen Massey
Peter and Dorothy Millar, Brian and Sheila Woodcock, Anna, Scott Blythe, Jane Bentley, Helen Boothroyd, Ruth Burgess, Ian Fraser, Kathy Galloway, Kath O'Neil, Jan Sutch Pickard … and many other people I met on Iona
Iain Campbell
Sandra Kramer

And, of course, thanks to my family: my mom, dad, grandmother and brother, Matthew

Thanks to all the amazing people I met in nursing homes, rest homes, night shelters and on street corners …

Thanks to friends at Wild Goose Publications: Alex O'Neill, Jane Riley, Lorna Rae Sutton

FOREWORD

After I read some of Neil's stories in this profound but wonderfully readable book, I had some hesitations about writing a foreword. What could I say in the face of such wisdom, truth and vitality being revealed through the lives of women and men who have experienced great human suffering? Folk who live on the margins of our societies and who are often forgotten, even by those of us who are concerned about other people.

But, as I thought about it, I suddenly knew what I wanted to say! This book is here to remind us, powerfully but with tenderness, poetry and laughter, that people matter more than status and possessions – and that they matter not just to us but to God. The God whose image is in us all. In a world of easy compromises and much false posturing in which the rich, the often corrupt, and the people with power keep telling us how to live and what to strive for, Neil writes about a world where hearts matter and in which vulnerable folk can teach us much.

These pages carry a basic truth – that, ultimately and when it really matters, the unbelievable richness of our lives is to be measured by our stories. And the stories here are about people who live on the knife-edge. These are strong stories at a time when so many of us seek only to be comfortable. And that's why they are both important and prophetic. And extraordinarily beautiful. Through the telling of these stories, Neil invites us to see our world differently: to realign our perceptions. He does this brilliantly as we enter into the lives of many he has met on his own journey working alongside those who are homeless and those who have experienced the dark night of the soul.

As I thought about this book, I understood that there are at least two ways of reading it. We can read it as 'observers' of the human condition, or we can read it recognising in its pages something of our own vulnerabilities and uncertainties, and our own need for healing. The women and men who people these pages are not 'out there' – for much of their struggle is in every human heart. We all long for love, acceptance and affirmation – even those who have achieved all the glittering prizes.

If we think about what is happening in our world at this present time, this book's publication is timely. It allows us to look again at our true humanity, and to reflect on those qualities of the spirit which enable human beings to survive against all the odds. And not only to survive, but to live with the ability to dance in the storm.

Neil's friends whose stories have made this book possible have often been through many dyings. They have known overwhelming darkness as well as powerful light. We can so often pass them by on the other side, but when we stop and listen to their heartbeats, as Neil has done over many years, our souls are refreshed and our ability to care deeply is enlarged.

I hope these great contemporary stories, told with love, will bring new strength, understanding and wisdom for your own journey. They certainly have done that for me.

Thank you, Neil.

Peter Millar

INTRODUCTION

When I left university I had no idea what to do with my life. I'd only gone to university because there was nothing else to do, or so it seemed. It was the early 1980s and the beginning of post-industrialism. There weren't a lot of jobs around and I had no 'bankable' skills.

I left university with an English degree – and still no bankable skills. I loved words and music. I was also very interested in people, and in myself.

I started doing nurse's aide work. For about fifteen years I worked as nurse's aide, as a companion aide, as a 'counsellor' in post-psychiatric 'rest' homes, and as a worker in shelters for homeless men.

I think I chose to be around people who were 'broken' because I felt broken myself; I still feel broken, though I'm gentler with myself now, and have a little more understanding. I somehow felt a sense of solidarity with these people; I felt a part of their tribe. I felt on the outside and on the edge, and wanted to be with people who were outside and on the edge. During one period, I was working in a nursing home for veterans, in a post-psychiatric rest home for women and in a night shelter for homeless men; sometimes on different days, sometimes at different times on the same day. I also did volunteer visiting. I did all this because I wanted to help people and to work for social justice; but I also did it because I wanted to test the boundaries of myself and of reality: I was exploring. One thing I quickly discovered was that many of the people who are labelled as 'disabled' have great gifts and wisdom. I learned so much from the people I worked with. Jean Vanier, founder of L'Arche Community (where I have also worked), wrote: 'The weak ones of our society have taught me so much. They have shown me what it is to live simply, to love tenderly, to speak in truth, to pardon, to receive openly, to be humble in weakness, to be confident in difficulties and to accept handicaps and hardships with love.'

I did this work because I wanted, in my small way, to help build a world where people mattered – the Kingdom. I saw the world – and still see the world – as a place where you don't matter unless you have money and property. Capitalism is a system that throws not only things but people away. In capitalism, if you don't 'work', if you are 'faulty', you are thrown on the garbage heap. In one post-psychiatric rest home I volunteered in, three people shared each tiny room. Recreation was bingo in a square, low-ceilinged basement: it felt like they were stuffing us all into a box (or a train car). Conditions were filthy all over: mice lived in bathtubs and disappeared down hairy drains; disturbed people were straitjacketed with heavy drugs. It amazed me that in a 'developed', 'first-world' country people were treated like that. My eyes were opened. Capitalism is such a short-sighted system. I don't want to romanticise people, but so many of the folk I met in my work, so many of the discarded people, were to me the most prophetic and Christ-like. It was a privilege to know them.

I wanted to live in a world where heart matters, not money. Where richness is measured in stories. Where people are valued for their life experience. That was naive, I guess. Still, we move further and further away from that human world, don't we? I never thought things could get more money-driven and Conservative than life in the 1980s under Reagan, Thatcher and Canadian Prime Minister Brian Mulroney. I was wrong – that was only the beginning. Who knows where it will end? Maybe we'll all be thrown into a basement somewhere. All of us poetic, useless ones. Well, I won't go without a fight. Money is not all that matters. I'm on the side of Spirit. I saw the work I was doing as counter-cultural, I guess.

Sometimes I took breaks – travelled and worked: on a farm, as a fruit-picker, as a cleaner, as a bookseller, as a musician … Sometimes I felt empty and burnt out. Sometimes I felt crazy and over the edge. These days I work as an editor and writer – and I'm grateful. It was time for a change.

I didn't think of myself as a Christian when I started this work. That is the reason why some of these stories are more 'religious' than others. Some of the stories (like those in the Working the Door sequence) don't (on the surface anyway) seem 'Christian' at all. But I don't believe Jesus lives in a church, or is very dogmatic about the language he wants us to use – I think of him as very down to earth, open and understanding. I think he cares that we use language well though – he was a poet. I think he wants us to tell good stories.

I hope you like these stories. Human beings are infinite. We rarely get close to the core of even people we think we know well – partners, family, friends. We understand each other in glimpses; ourselves in glimpses. People are so complex and mysterious and so frustratingly wonderful. Jesus, Buddha, Mohammed ... understands. The best we can do is help one another. Have patience. Not expect too much, or anything. Not get disillusioned. That's hard to do – with work, our busy lives, our many moods, our personal suffering. Easier said than done. (I seldom do it.) It is hard to stay open to the mystery of people, mystery of life. We can go for years feeling dead – then resurrect again. I guess this book is a sort of testimony to the times I've stayed awake and alive over the years.

These stories come out of experiences working in Canada and in the United Kingdom. The language reflects this.

The artwork is by Iain Campbell, whom I met working at the Iona Community office in Glasgow. Iain was a youth worker with the community, visiting Polmont Young Offenders Institution and schools throughout Scotland; today he works as a secondary-school art teacher. One of the things I love about Iain's sketches is the strong line. That's the way I've tried to sketch the characters in this book. With little that is superfluous.

These stories can be used in personal meditation and in group reflection. If you like, you could use some in church worship, though you might have to adapt bits, depending on your church. (A lot of churches don't like too much reality though, so be careful, and gentle.) Many of these pieces were used in Iona Abbey: The Rainbow Man, George, Leonard, Mark, Elizabeth, Maggie ...

Neil Paynter,
Biggar, Scotland,
Easter 2008

NURSE'S NOTES

Introduction

A series of pieces about working as an aide in nursing homes. These were taken from my diary and from letters and emails to friends.

> *The glory of young men is their strength, but the beauty of the old is their grey hair.*
>
> Proverbs 20:29

Grace

The nurses were dolling everyone up for the Christmas party. Putting on make-up. Giving manicures. So I grabbed an emery board, and sat and filed and shaped Grace's jagged, cracked, thick yellow fingernails that had been soaking soaking … Not bad. We had a good chat.

'And, so what about a little Christmas glitter on those nails, Grace?'

'Oh, no thanks, dear – I've never been the flashy type.'

Everyone was having a good time. I gave a facial. Smoothed and massaged Pond's cold cream into a ninety-one-year-old woman's tired, dry wrinkles. She closed her eyes – it must have felt good. I wondered how long it had been since somebody had touched her (not counting turning her to change her, not counting wiping her rear). How long had it been? How long since someone had touched her? It felt good. I wondered if she remembered a lover; a son; the summer breeze – fragrant as Pond's cold cream. Or nothing: just a relaxed, full, soothing feeling sinking in …

Amazing Grace

Jane is far away in her interior landscape. She sits in her room all day. Locked in a wheelchair. Hums and sings to herself. Loudly sometimes, as if saying: 'I'm still here. I'm still fucking here.'

I glanced at her case file. A hell of a life – deaths, deaths, alcohol …

There's a piano in the Alzheimer's unit. I played 'Amazing Grace' – and Jane sang along.

Amazing how someone who can't remember their daughters' and sons' and spouse's names – their own name some days – can remember all the words to some old song. Music is holy. Music is the voice of God.

I played Jane 'Summertime'. And she sang along – her voice rough and broken and sore and beautiful. Tears in her throat.

Kate

Helping Kate get dressed. Talking about stiff things – the weather, current events …

'Did you hear about the two hunters up in Red Bay?' she suddenly asks me.

'No. No, I haven't.'

'Yeah, two hunters up in Red Bay. And the one was going hunting – for bear or deer, I guess – and was saying to his friend that what if he got bit by a rattlesnake up there? Cause he was feeling a little perturbed about it, you know. What to do.'

'There are a lot of rattlesnakes up there I've heard.'

'Right, a lot of rattlesnakes. So his friend told him, no problem, that it's no problem – you just slit it open with your hunting knife and suck the poison out. Suck out the poison.'

'I've heard that –'

'Right, no problem. So his friend goes out hunting – for bear or moose, I guess – and comes back and his friend asks him, when he sees him, so how'd it go? How his hunting trip went. "Did you have any problem with rattlesnakes?" he asks him. "Oh good – no, no problem," his friend tells him. "Oh, I got bit when I was out." "Oh yeah? Where?" his friend asks him. "In the backside," he says, "but, no problem, I did what you told me. And gosh, you sure know who your friends are."'

And Kate laughs and I smile and she beams up at me – a roguish, lopsided smile. And I think: she's paralysed all down one side but still full of flowing spirit. And I stop trying so hard and relax. Take it natural. And from then on the conversation flows easy. Easy as a good joke.

Elma

Sitting in the dining room, trying to help Elma eat:

> 'I can't eat, I'm dead, oh, please, no.'
> '… You can't eat because you're dead?'
> 'Yes … I can't even pick up that glass there.'
> 'You can't pick it up because it's too heavy? … You can't pick things up because you're dead?'
> 'Yes. I'm hollow inside. I'm living in a dead body.'
> 'Your body is giving out on you.'
> 'I'm dead. See, I can't pick it up – I wish someone would believe me.'
> 'Because you're dead everything is so heavy?'
> 'Yes.'

Paul

'Everyone's dead,' Paul says.

I'm feeding him in the dining room.

'Everyone's dead up here, you know,' and I look around at everyone staring with fish eyes and understand what he means.

'But you're not,' I say. 'You're not, Paul – you're full of spirit yet.'

'You bet cha. You *bet* cha!' And he eats everything on his plate. Has me scoop up the crumbs.

Paul was in the war. Afterwards, played guitar and harmonica and rambled round. Then settled down and farmed.

I push him back to his room after lunch. He can't sleep any more, he tells me. Just ten or fifteen minutes at a time. Like he's afraid of going to sleep and waking up dead.

During the afternoons he likes to just sit and think, he says. To just sit, and look at his pictures up on his wall, and think.

Paul lost his arms somehow. Housekeeping keep putting his

clothes and blankets and soaker pads on his nightstand – keep blocking his view of his pictures. He curses and shakes his head. I pick up the stack and move it out of the way for him. Set it on his bed.

He smiles – cries out because he can suddenly see the vista of his life now …

There are framed photos of his dashing older brother who was in the Air Force and got shot down 'too young, too young' …

'I guess any age is too young,' I say.

'You bet cha. You *bet* cha.'

His wife riding a pinto horse: beautiful, smiling cowgirl with a lasso.

'Well, she sure lassoed me,' Paul says.

He and his army buddies who got killed, or else lost on the way …

I leave Paul with his memories and thoughts.

'Thank you!' he calls. 'Thanks.'

Later I have to come back in and give him an enema.

Emily

Helping Emily to wash her hands and face after lunch:

'This always reminds me of being a child,' she says.

'Why?' I ask, thinking it's because I'm *treating* her like a child – washing her hands with a face cloth.

'Peanut butter and jelly sandwiches,' she smiles. 'When you eat them they're *sooo* good. And you get it all over your hands like that. Remember?'

'Yes, yes – I remember picnics.'

'Oh yes, picnics!' exclaims Emily, and we giggle. And I glance up, and the whole dining room is looking over at us – like we're crazy.

He still remembers that day

Sitting in the common room talking about things like where the flour mill used to be, the dance hall …

About the day May's mother replaced the icing sugar with baking soda, to teach her a lesson.

About the day she lost her good hat over a bridge – and stood and watched the wind carry it away … And how there used to be logging; and how as kids they'd ride the logs down the river; fall off sometimes and scrape themselves up on the knots. 'That was fun!'

'Remember all the pulp and wood shavings.'

'And coal. The coal from all the big boats that used to come in. Remember the big boats?'

'Oh, yes!'

About the day Oscar went to the pier and all his friends laughed at him because of his knees. 'Washerwoman's knees, washerwoman's knees!' they chanted. From helping his mother scrub kitchen floors – his father was away at the war. He still remembers that day.

Sitting in the common room talking about some of the things old people remember.

Margaret

Getting Margaret up for the day:
'Wow. You seem happy today, Margaret. All smiley.'
'I was dreaming about dancing with my husband.'

Suddenly a joke about chickens

People can seem so disoriented – calling out for the dead. Then suddenly start reciting a poem they learned in grammar school, word for word; or, out of nowhere, suddenly start telling you a joke about chickens:

'Farmer buys two chickens and puts them in his basement, and weeks pass and he has a whole bunch of chickens. Flock … Yeah, but then it rains and the basement floods and they all drown one night. So, he calls up his alderman and says: "I bought chickens and now they all drowned." And the alderman says: "I can't do anything, call the mayor." So the farmer calls the mayor and says, "I bought chickens and now they're all drowned – what am I supposed to do?" And the mayor says, "Geez, I'm sorry, try the president, try the President of the United States." So the farmer calls the President and the President says: "I can't do anything, my hands are tied. Next time buy ducks."'

Oh boy

One of the nurses brought her little boy in. He was helping to feed one of the residents at lunchtime. An old old woman who never speaks much, makes sounds. She had a smile in her eyes – a sudden smile; there was a glimmer of awareness, and humour.

'Oh boy,' she said, as he shakily offered up a spoonful of puréed meat and mashed potatoes.

The moment was beautiful, sad, fragile, human ... – so many things at the same time. It made me want to give up; it made me want to live.

A little boy feeding an old old woman – what a picture!

'Well, Jessie certainly came alive anyways,' someone said.

Home

I visit Vera in her bedroom. She sits in her chair, with her 'posture pal'. Vera only ever comes out of her room for meals.

'Hello, Vera!' I call. 'So how are you today?' ...

She sits gazing. Out the window. In at the past. Chants rhythmically at intervals: 'Are-e, Are-e, Are-e, Are-e ...' – to stimulate and comfort herself I guess. 'Are-e, Are-e, Are-e ...' To help relieve the boredom, the isolation.

I touch her arm ... Make eye contact.

'Oh, hello,' she says, and smiles. She tells me that she's sitting waiting for Philip to come and take her home. 'Are-e, Are-e, Are-e, Are-e, that's all.'

I ask her who Philip is and she tells me her brother.

'Your little brother?'

'Are-e, Are-e, Are-e ... I think so. I want to go home in the worst way. I want to go home in the worst way now.'

'It's hard ...'

'Are-e, Are-e, Are-e, Are-e ...'

'Is Philip at home?'

'Are-e, Are-e, Are-e, I guess he'd be home now. At the house.'

'… What kind of house? What kind of house is it?'

'Not a big house, but it's a nice house. Are-e, Are-e, Are-e, Are-e, that's all.'

'A nice house.'

'Nice house … Warm … I wanna go to my bed.'

'Warm like your bed?'

'Yes … Are-e, are-e, are-e. Not a lot of rooms but a nice house. Flowers.'

'Flower gardens?'

'Yes … Are-e, Are-e, Are-e, Are-e. It's way out in Hanover. I'm Hanover. It's outside of Hanover. I want to go home in the worst way. I want to go home in the worst way now.'

'To the nice warm house with Philip.'

'Yes … I wish Philip would come and take me home. So, I sit and wait for him to take me. I sit and wait for him. Are-e, Are-e, Are-e, that's all.'

Everyone here longs to go home. Home to their home – their real home. Home to the past. Home to their mother and father. Home to their brothers and sisters. Home to their husbands and wives and children. Home from here, from this place called a home. Home to God. Home to Mother earth.

Alzheimer victims wander up and down the long, narrow hallways, searching for a way out, a way home. All the doors are locked.

'Are-e, Are-e, Are-e, Are-e, that's all.'

Mr Hicks

In his life Mr Hicks worked as an engineer; sailed yachts down the Nile … But there are few to talk with about it here. The nurses are too busy.

'You know, I'm just another horse in a stable to them anyway!' he wails.

He's surrounded by the senile and the drugged, he says.

'Zombies, zombies, all around me – it's like the fuckin' *Night of the Living Dead!*'

Like in that film, he fears being 'captured' and becoming one of them.

(I pass by them and smile. Nothing. I touch them. I caress them. Nothing. I don't know how to reach them. I don't know how to wake the dead.)

But it is not those lost and groping in their interior landscapes for whom I feel the most compassion. It's the living.

Mr Hicks may sleep all day. Sometimes he reads. Books ordered from the library: *A History of the English People*, *The Wisdom of the Great Teachers*, *Keeping Your Mind Alive* …

Sometimes he goes out, and comes back drunk. Once the police found him three days later, travelling in his wheelchair down the parkway 'on the road to China'.

Watching TV with Mr Wilson

'Robberies, earthquakes, floods … You want to know why I watch this? Do you *really* want to know why I watch this every night? It's terrible but … I watch the TV news every night because it keeps reminding me – it keeps reminding me that there are actually people in the world who are worse off than me … That's terrible, isn't it? … No? Well, I think it is. Ah, change the station – please! … Anything but a game show. Anything but that *Wheel of Fortune* – that programme is so inane it makes me want to tear my hair out.' …

Tillie

Playing bingo with a reserved air is Tillie.

One evening after bingo, Tillie told us all about the heavenly trip she'd taken to Hawaii a couple years ago with her son and daughter-in-law: Evenings on the balcony of the posh hotel overlooking the ocean; the gentle, fragrant breezes; the feeling of the world slowing down; and the waves, thrusting.

'God, just lovely,' she sighed … 'And the prostitutes,' she giggled.

'What?'

'Pardon, Tillie?'

She'd surprised us. She had always given us the impression of being very prim and proper. Someone you'd be careful not to swear around: a homey quilt on her neat bed, walls covered in little birds singing sweetly on branches, embroidery in progress … Yet it seemed Tillie got a kick out of watching the girls down on the boulevard, down on the strip fighting over territory, cars and Johns. 'Tugging and pulling at each other's hair some of them. Kicking each other in the shins!'

Tillie leaned across the fold-up table and confided that, one evening, when her son and his wife had gone out for a night on the town, she switched off the television and went down in the elevator to the hotel bar. There Tillie laughed and drank creamy drinks with an elderly gentleman and after last orders seduced him up to her room.

'I lost my virginity that night,' she cackled. 'Well, not exactly, but it had been so long it seemed so!' Tillie leaned over the table farther, her voice a whisper, a mischievous glimmer in her old eyes. 'You know, it takes a long time to get those old ones up, this one anyway, but once they're up! … And I loved the thought of the kids walking in. It made it more exciting. I would have loved to see their faces.'

Bless her, I thought. She could still enjoy life. She had not lost that art in this place.

A 93-year-old woman talking about apples

'In ancient times we used to get all types of apples. We used to get Thamey Sweets, St Lawrence, crabs, russets, candy-striped, sheep's nose. Like a sheep's nose, yes. Sort of tapered. My mother would bake Thamey Sweets – and the skin would shine. So sweet you didn't need sugar. You just left the stem on and added cloves. A squatty kind of apple. God – the smell when they're baking,' sighed the old woman, and closed her eyes. Like it suddenly all came back to her. On a wave.

Prayer

Thank you, God,
for the wisdom of 93-year-old women:
food for thought.

Thank you for apples. For Thamey Sweet apples,
St Lawrence apples, crab apples,
russet apples, candy-striped apples,
sheep's nose apples …

For the precious and amazing
diversity of your world.

May we never take that wealth for granted.
May we work to guard and secure it.
May we be full of wonder.

This we pray,
in the name of the One God:
the One God of many apples.
Amen

VETERANS: THE ROUNDS

Introduction

When I was working in nursing homes and homeless shelters, I met many veterans of the Second World War, also some veterans of the First World War, the Korean War and Vietnam. I was a pretty average nurse's aide and shelter worker, but I was good at listening to people's stories. Or at least that's what I enjoyed the most. There are a million stories in nursing homes and shelters – and people are dying to tell them.

Listening to people's stories was a huge privilege. The whole point of being alive, it seems to me, is to listen to each other's story. There never seems to be enough time though. We are all too busy – listening to ourselves, making money; surviving.

If I'd really listened to people in my work, this book would be a lot longer, and better.

A room

From a nursing home

Matthew 26:36–46

This is a big room really. It's because there are six beds. It's because there are six beds that it looks small. I start at the back and with my cart – diapers, creams, lotions, baby powder – work my way up, from bed to bed. Rouse the old men gently and get them ready for the long day – wash, dress, transfer to wheelchair.

There is Gordon. He had to flee his home town out East after returning from the war. 'It was just too much,' he told me one morning as I was giving him a quick bed bath, the curtain drawn around us. Without Gordon's knowledge, someone in a local recruiting office had used his eager face on a local poster. And when he landed, victorious and whole, all the mothers who had lost sons, and all the girls and wives who had lost lovers descended on him like a pack. Blamed him. Took their anger out on young Gordon. On the streets the townspeople called him a Judas. Asked him straight out: 'So, where's your thirty pieces of silver, Gord?' Threw dirty pennies at his feet.

There is Mr Eliot. He was a graduate student in philosophy at the University of Toronto. Then wrote several novels; later in life, children's books. But he can't see well enough now – almost not at all. His cataracts are ripe but the doctors don't think it's worth operating.

He's messed his bed again. He says he's sorry. I tell him it's all right, not to worry about it. As I change the bed I change the subject, telling him that I'm a writer, too. We sit and talk about authors. We chat about Somerset Maugham and agree that *Of Human Bondage* was his most mature. He touches my face with his cold fingertips. Then smiles. 'You have a beard, too. Can't you sit and talk with me a while longer?' I explain that I have to move on.

'Could you come back later, after you've finished?'

I explain that I've been up all night. And that I really must go home. But maybe some other time. For sure some other time.

There is Mr Finny. There's a car on the roof, he says. Horses thundering in the yard. In the war he defused mines – 60 cents a day. He motions me aside and reports, whispering hoarsely, that guns are pointing at us from out of the wall sockets. Then he squints suspiciously at my cart. He's convinced there's a bomb buried beneath the heap of bleached blankets. Won't get up until I prove all is safe. Until I've defused it. He'll explain to me how. 'Now go slow, boy. Go slow.'

There is Mr Hamilton. Years ago he lost his legs due to diabetes and drinking. Due to neglect. Now his stomach is swollen. He's pregnant with bile. He tells me they're admitting him for tests tomorrow and thanks me for being so patient with him last night. For mopping his burning brow with a cool cloth. For mopping up when he was sick. The head nurse takes me aside and whispers they suspect stomach cancer. Mr Hamilton has drunk himself to death and won't be here when I come back next week. I say goodbye. Wish him luck. 'Hang in there, you salty old mariner,' I call. He laughs. It hurts him to laugh now. 'Ouch, ya thanks, see ya, skipper.'

This bed is empty. Ron Shepherd died last week. He kept calling for me in the night. When I finally came, he'd forgotten what he wanted. I offered him a sip of cool water. He gulped it greedily through the plastic straw. The moment I stepped out of the room he'd bellow again, madly sounding the call buzzer safety-pinned to his pillow. Finally, I told him off. Finally, I ignored him. I had no idea how bad he was. No idea death was stalking him when I was sitting down the hall reading the newspaper.

Jack is sleeping. He's always sleeping now. It's less painful. We used to talk a little. About his son out in Vancouver. Now he only wakes for his pills. Stricken with a rare form of muscular dystrophy, his sets of ribs stick up like sharp fins threatening to pierce through his thin skin. It's as if he'd swallowed sharks. I turn him to change his pad. He doesn't wake. I see black blood beginning to leak. I see thick blood beginning to flow. I call a nurse. She calls a doctor.

I leave the room with six beds thinking: this is only one room in a world full of rooms.

The world itself like one big, cramped room.

George

From a night shelter

Luke 24:13–16

I met George when I was going to college and working part-time at a shelter for homeless men. When I wasn't busy, and he was free, we'd sit and talk together, about art and classical music. As a young man, George had studied oil painting. He'd wanted to learn to draw like the old masters, he told me. He loved the art of portraiture especially, and had dreamed of, just once, capturing a face so that it 'mirrored the soul'.

At first it seemed a little surprising to be talking about art and music in the cacophony of a night shelter, surrounded by bare, nicotine-yellow walls and ugly, orange linoleum scarred with cigarette burns.

I'd heard that George had been a soldier, too, that he'd fought at Normandy and in the Desert campaign, later again in Korea, but when I asked him about that period of his life, he said he didn't like to talk about it.

Once when Tommy was having a seizure, and lay writhing on the cold floor like he'd been shot, I glanced up and saw George. He gazed down at Tommy and kept shaking his head; it was like he was away some place else. His face expressed infinite pity.

Blood drooled from the corner of Tommy's mouth; his body kept flailing and churning. 'Gonna be alright, Tom,' said George. Tommy roiled and writhed, his boyish, trenched face contorted, tortured-looking. George handed me his suit jacket, balled-up for underneath

Tommy's head. I tried to keep Tommy over on his side between attacks; with a tender, sore, caressing voice, George told Tommy that he was going to be all right, that he was just going to see the nurses. 'Just goin' to see the nurses,' the crowd of tough, scared men started up in a chorus. 'Tommy's just going to see the nurses.' 'Luck-y.' 'Some nice ones there, I'll bet ya.' 'Oh yeah, for sure.' 'Be alright now, Tommy.' 'Tommy, be alright.' And, finally, the ambulance screamed up with a stretcher the paramedics rolled Tommy on to like a bag of loose sticks.

My colleague Phil, who'd been working on the front line for years, and knew George better than anyone probably, said that George felt profound guilt for having survived the wars – that George couldn't understand why he'd lived when all his good friends, and so many other good people, had been blown away or left crippled for life, had been taken prisoner and tortured, had gone missing and never been found … He carried the question like a cross, Phil said.

'You see him alone sometimes, talking to himself, talking to God. Shouting at the heavens; praying for peace.'

A tabloid newspaper portrayed George as a dirty old drunk, on its front page one day. Some photojournalist shot him as he sat alone out on the front stoop of the shelter with a 'dead soldier' beside him. He looked like a poor, pathetic soul: dressed in a crumpled tweed jacket, bowed down by drink. The angle and light didn't do him justice, made his face look ugly and guttered. 'A Skid Row Alcoholic', the title underneath the picture read. There was a story concerning the growing number of homeless and the face of downtown. There was no report of him talking gently, humanly to Tommy as he lay writhing in hell, of the wars of liberation and absurdity he'd fought in through deserts and jungles and back streets; no mention that he had a wife and grown children somewhere, or of his dreams to become a fine artist who mirrored the soul.

No quote of him speaking knowledgeably, sensitively, passionately about the rich, beautiful, soaring music of Gustav Mahler.

The guys were mad. Somebody wanted to go down and teach the reporter a lesson. 'Give the poser a slashin'.'

Phil said it didn't surprise him. 'People have been painting him like that for ages now. Still hurt him though, I bet.'

George had one of the most beautiful faces I've ever seen. Sitting across from him one night, I told him that; I'd felt overwhelmed. He said thank you, that I was a gentleman.

It was hard to express with words. George's face was like grainy, grey rock, its features sculpted and etched by wind and rain, pocked and scarred by ice and snow; like an ancient landscape that had experienced fecund, young times of flowers; sudden rifts; slow, glacial change. George's face shone with the experience and wisdom of ages –

'Maybe that's what they mean,' said Phil. 'About suddenly seeing the face of Christ.'

Eddie

From a nursing home

Isaiah 2:4

Returning from my rounds, I discover Eddie's up. Oh, he's up all right – naked, streaking up and down the cold narrow hallway, chanting, 'Jumpsuit, jumpsuit!'

I quickly catch up and direct him into a washroom.

Eddie's mind works in ruts it's difficult to jolt it out of – onto a different track of thought, onto a different subject.

'Jumpsuit, I want my jumpsuit or somethin'.' Eddie speaks with a lilt, a poet's rhythm – Bob Dylan at seventy-five.

I corral him into a stall and, as gently as possible, both dry rough hands on his broad, bare shoulders, push him firmly down onto a cold toilet seat.

'Yes, Eddie, I know you want to get dressed' – again he tries to rise. I hold him down with just enough pressure to let him know who's boss; that's how I've been instructed to handle Eddie.

'We'll put your jumpsuit on in just a minute. And it's the green one, the one you like best, the one we didn't shrink. But, first … see if you can go, OK?' As I'm talking, I surreptitiously pull a thick leather restraint across Eddie's lap, chaining him to the toilet. Now that he is sitting it should be a great deal easier to communicate with Eddie. In just a few minutes after sitting down, Eddie's mind usually settles, clears, and then one is able to have quite a good chat with him about, say, politics, baseball, Chinese cooking, philosophy, gardening …

He continues straining against his tether, while stroking his fuzzy, sagging breasts with the calloused tips of his burnt fingers. (Eddie smokes a pipe, and has a collection of over twenty, one from every country he visited.) Occasionally he tweaks his cold, erect nipples.

'Come on, jumpsuit. Goddamn jumpsuit.'

'So, Eddie …' – I see the concentration and strain on his old but still somehow boyish face as he works the muscles in his swollen abdomen – 'how's your garden coming along, any results?' Eddie helps the groundsman, Hal – 'Hal's my pal, Hal's my pal' – and has his own little plot out back.

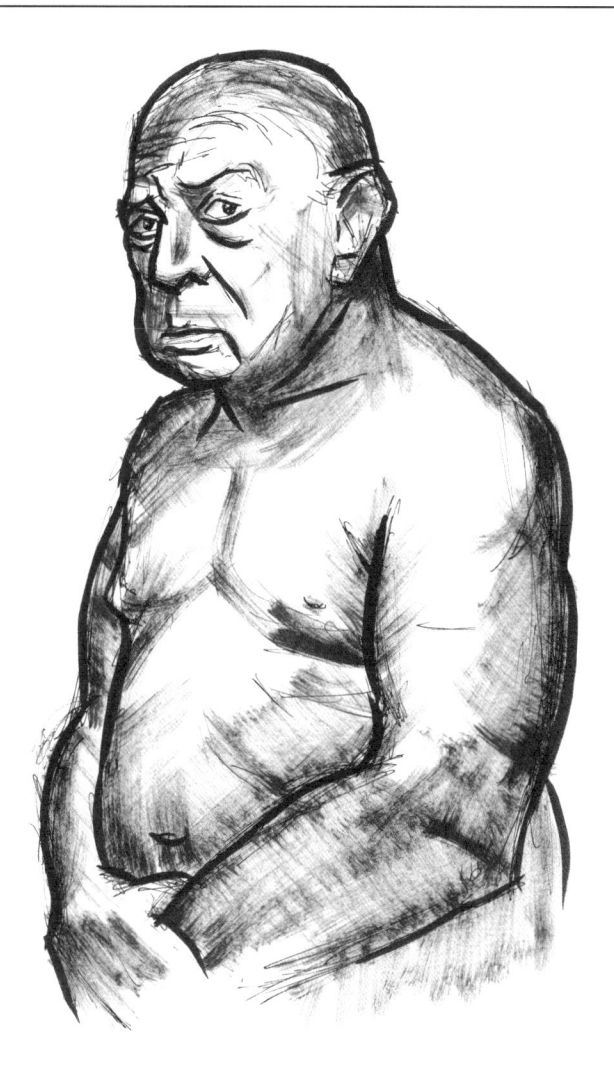

'Like to kill that goddamn groundhog. The cute little bugger's been eatin' up all my lovely lettuce. Can't crap or somethin'.'

Most of the hospital garden's grown over now. Rumours are they're going to close this place. After the World War One vets have all passed on, someone was saying at caffeine break the other day.

'Ya, saw a rainbow in the garden yesterday, in the spray, after it rained. Just stared. It was so goddamn beautiful. You don't see that too often. Too much goddamn pollution … Ya, like to shoot that gopher – the cute little bugger's been eatin' up all my lovely lettuce. Can't crap.'

I ask Eddie what books he's been reading lately. He reads war literature mostly – fiction, non-fiction – and devours several thick books a week. Last Sunday he'd just finished an epic Russian novel about the First World War. 'Solzhenitsyn's a goddamn good writer,' he advised. I ask Eddie again what he's been reading but he doesn't answer me. He seems far away.

Eddie was a tail gunner in the Second World War. Stationed in England, he did runs over Germany and won eight medals. One for landing a crippled plane after his pilot was shot – at 18! (At 18, I couldn't even drive a car.) After the war he lived in big cities, at Sally Ann missions mostly, and, in the summertime, alone at a dead friend's cottage up north (so I read in his file). Finally, because he moved around so much, the Veterans' Affairs stopped issuing him cheques.

They found him in the fall of 1963, at the crumbling cottage. He'd stopped eating and 'looked like an inmate from a concentration camp'. The place was stinking, the report said, littered with his faeces.

The toilet flushes. I turn from the sink where I'm assembling towels and a facecloth for Eddie. Eddie fiddles with himself underneath; he begins flushing the toilet repeatedly – frantically rattling the handle. 'Can't crap. Can't crap or somethin'!' And I realise he isn't wiping himself but fingering himself. The toilet overflows. I unchain Eddie and pull him off the toilet and out of the stall. He stands there naked, and again reaches up inside himself for his waste matter, for the poison that won't come.

I hurriedly put an Attends on Eddie.

'Don't need a goddamn diaper!'

'I'm sorry, Eddie.'

No matter how many times I do it, it feels wrong putting a baby-blue diaper on a man. On a man who was a hero.

'I'm sorry.'

'Don't need a goddamn diaper.'

I wash Eddie's hands and face; tell him to step into his jumpsuit; comb his thin head of hair; tie his new white runners; then send him away to play outside in the garden.

'Be back by lunchtime, Eddie,' I remind him, as he trots off with excitement.

Out in the day room, a company of men sit underneath the television waiting for their maple-flavoured oatmeal; droop like cut flowers in stagnant water. I gaze red-eyed out the window and suddenly see Eddie – running across the dewy bright lawn in his green jumpsuit. The summer sky is a deep, clear blue, and it looks like he wants to take off into it.

Paddy's visit: a monologue

From a night shelter

Mark 14:37

Don't worry about it, don't worry about it, I'm just comin' in for a visit. Just 'til eight o'clock, then I'm goin' back to watch the telethon. Wouldn't let me in down at detox to see the boys. Got my own place now. Jesus, been in bigger boxing rings. And you don't have to search me for Christ's sake, I got nothin'. Nothin'. No booze or dirty books up my sleeve, don't worry. Be friskin' and feelin' me up before they let me climb in my casket. I'm just comin' in for a visit, just 'til eight o'clock then I'm goin' back to watch the telethon. It's for the kids! It's for the kids! The telethon for all the sick children. I'm gonna call in and pledge ten bucks. Ten bucks, ten bucks, I'll just drink it anyway. There's gonna be singing, what's-his-name's gonna be emcee. What's-his-name, you know… No, no, not fuckin' Jerry Lewis. Don't you think I know Jerry Lewis?! The guy. The guy on the news, you know. The guy on the news who does the weather with the bird. I'm gonna call in and pledge ten bucks. Ten bucks, ten bucks, I'll just buy a bottle anyway.

What's-her-name, Pauline in the office? … Leo 'round? … David upstairs? Jesus Christ, where the hell is everyone?! … Gone home? Well, I guess so, I guess so. Well, might as well come sit with me then, but bring the cards, bring the cards. Just 'til eight o'clock. Well, don't just stand there like a dead dick, get the cards, get the cards …… So whadda you know kid, crib? … Been a while? Whadda ya mean, since ya got any? Euchre? No, no, I'm not gonna teach nobody, forget it, forget it, doesn't matter, doesn't matter. I don't know, fish?! Fish?! … Rummy? OK, then rummy. Rummy, rummy, I'm just an old rummy, Jesus …

Put your hand here. Put your hand on my neck for Christ's sake, I don't got the plague. No, no, higher, lower, there, feel that there, lump? … Blood clot, tumour, cancer … I don't have to ask no doctor.

Don't you think I know what it is for Christ's sake?! ... I'll tell ya honest, kid, I'm scared. I'm scared a dyin'. You only go one a two places – up, or down. I don't wanna go down. There's too much suffering on earth. I want peace ... I could go to my sister's. Patricia. I miss her. She makes me soup. She makes my bed. I could jump on a Voyageur bus and be in Montreal in a couple hours. It's good but I can't go there. Just when I'm sober. And at Christmas. It's an agreement. My brother-in-law – he's a little nervous, eh – he never drank. He's a nice guy but – Jesus, he goes to bed at nine o'clock at night and you can't play the television. And he's younger than me, younger than me. That's what happens ... I could get a bus, be there in a couple hours. Time you got now? Just 'til eight o'clock. Ten bucks, ten bucks, just blow it anyway. It's for the kids! For the kids ...

Jesus, will ya look at these people. Look at these people. Jesus, what are ya, gone blind or somethin'?! Bald guy baptising himself with milk. Guy over there with his mouth all wired shut – how's the poor bastard supposed to eat – that's what I wanna know? Guy talkin' to hisself in the windows. Mr Solitaire over there. You know it's the war that got his leg, eh? I know what that's like. Didn't lose my goddamn leg but I know what that's like. I fought in the war too, you know. From the beginning. Right from when we got into it over there. Then in Montreal after. Was a middleweight. Too short though, didn't quite have the reach. Ya, but I did alright, I did alright. Finally I was gettin' beat up so bad I hadda quit. Patricia was happy anyway. 'What do you think you'll do now, Patrick?' she asked me. She was the only one. So I started writin' these songs. Pawned this trophy – too much to lug around anyway, boxing gloves, some other stuff I didn't think I'd need no more – and bought a guitar. Saw it sittin' in this window. Six strings with a strap, you know. Saw it sitting there. Geez, it looked good. Started kickin' around with that a while. Writing songs. About people and things I saw mostly. Troubadour I thought. Sent a bunch of 'em to this big shot in Toronto. Never heard nuthin' ... I dunno, why's there so much suffering in the world? Why?! ... Dunno neither? Well, I guess so, I guess so. If you'll excuse my language this world's a fuckin' mess. Why's there so much suffering? Bangladesh. They're all starving over there. Sick children. That tornado down in, in, what's it, what's it? ... Texas, Texas. You know I ask some people sometimes. David. What's-her-name. These people upstairs. Religious people – excuse me if you're one a them. I used to stay in Toronto a lot, eh. At this place, I forget the name. Doesn't matter. It was on the waterfront. Don't know if it's still there. Doesn't matter. I stayed there two years on and off. Two years. They were good to me. Gave me extra blankets. Let me stay in. I was laid up a while. Bout a TB. There was this preacher there. A young guy. And we'd sit and talk sometimes. He was a nice guy but ... 'Patrick,' he'd say, 'you see we can't understand God's order. We don't have the capacity to fathom his divine plan.' You're tellin' me! 'Everything has a reason.' Things like that. Jesus. Finally I got fed up. 'Yeah, well if we don't understand God's plan then why don't you stop talkin' about it!' He was always talkin' about it. Easy for him, sittin' upstairs. Ah, it was never the same after. I got fed up. Never went back. They were good to me ... This world's a fuckin' mess. Bangladesh – they're all starving over there. Sick children. That tornado down in Texas. Terrible, terrible ... You can only go one a two places. Up, or down. I don't wanna go down. I want peace. I could go to my sister's. I miss her. I could grab a bus, be there in a couple hours. Time you got now? Just 'til eight o'clock then I'm goin' back to watch the telethon. Ten bucks, ten bucks. There's gonna be singin'. What's-his-name's gonna be emcee ...

Andrew and Jessie

Before I started working in the social service field, I was a volunteer visitor in a nursing home. I used to go to the home on Sunday afternoons, just to sit around and chat with the residents, or to help the nurses in whatever tiny ways I could. In the home I met Andrew, who was a veteran of the First and Second World Wars. Andrew was the first person in my life who overwhelmed me with his presence, with his story. My first living icon. Andrew inspired me to start working with people and to write. He died before I could tell him how much he had inspired me. I went into the home one day and he was gone. His wife, Jessie, was still there, strapped into her wheelchair, but I couldn't tell her.

People don't realise how amazing they are. We think we're failures – carry guilt and shame around for years. But we touch people in ways we don't even realise. It would be good if we could talk to each other. It would be good if we could tell one another how much we mean to each other before we die. It's a tragedy that we often don't. But that's life, isn't it?

Psalm 30:10–12

'I'll make my pass on your starboard side,' Andrew calls out to me down the long narrow hallway. 'You know your starboard, don't ya? … Oh, you landlubbers,' he says with mock disgust, 'I tell ya … I've just been doin' my exercises, you know.'

Andrew travels up and down the hallways of the home to stave off the stiffness of the rheumatoid arthritis creeping, like gangrene, up his sinewy, tattooed arms. He is battling against the paralysis of his independence.

For there are many in the home, strapped into stilled silver wheelchairs. Each alone in his or her little boat. There is little current here. These are the horse latitudes of life: many in the home at the mercy of busy nurses in uniforms white as sails.

'I got to be gettin' back to my Jess,' he says. 'The doctor was in again this week, you know. She's not doin' well.'

Andrew spends his days helping the nurses care for his wife – helping to change and clean and feed her. In his spare time, he talks into the tape recorder by his bed; or to Jessie, who doesn't answer any more; or to God and Jesus in the little stained-glass chapel.

Sometimes when I visit, we sit out on the patio, or in his room, and he tells me his story: About fighting in the First World War as a 'Jack Tar', leaving from Scapa Flow when he was fifteen and a half. About fighting in Gallipoli. About another time, out in the foggy, cold Atlantic, arriving too late to save friends blown to bits by a U-boat; fishing for arms and legs, feeling sick with grief and the horror of war.

About his merchant marine days and going on shore leave in Singapore. Strolling into a brothel there he didn't realise was a brothel (he was only looking for a beer) and suddenly getting caught up in a brawl and getting tossed out a window; falling three stories into a cushioning heap of sewage and rubbish and then having to go back to report to his commanding officer.

About driving a school bus for years, after immigrating to Canada. About getting gangrene somehow and losing his legs. About coming home from the hospital.

Once he told me about a time he was feeding Jessie. They were sitting in the dining area as usual ... And as Andrew was offering his Jess her puréed vegetables and she drooled on her bib, her mind, suddenly, like a shutter in a camera, opened:

'Bonnie Andrew,' she dribbled in an expressionless voice. Her vacant, pale blue eyes staring straight ahead. 'Bonnie Andrew.'

And then, just as suddenly and inexplicably, her mind snapped shut again, and the light it shed upon Andrew was smothered. Jessie was silent. And Andrew was left alone in the darkness again.

Like an overloaded automaton recalling a program from another time, Jessie's only communication now being: 'The doggy's in the basement. The doggy's in the basement.' Her little dog is long dead. Their little house was sold. Sold so that they could be together here.

Andrew and I talk a while; then sit in silence, watching the sunset. Occasionally, he puts some music on his phonograph, and dances. Balances, graceful as any dancer, on his bed, his shorts rolled up, free leg stubs swinging gaily to and fro to a recording of Scottish folk music.

I watched him dancing one day and he was like light to me. Amazing – how someone can go through so much in their life and still dance. Lose their wife, lose friends, lose their legs, and still dance.

'Any regrets?' I asked him, up over the spirited music.

'I saw the world,' he said. 'And had a warm, wee house ... I'm thankful,' he sang.

THE RAINBOW MAN

Introduction

All the stories in this section were inspired by people I met in homeless shelters. I worked in night shelters in Canada, in Scotland and in London, England.

Someone who was homeless once told me this: 'Homelessness, it can happen to anyone, people don't realise – lose your family, your job, your mind ... People have no idea – how close to the edge they're walkin'.'

As Ed Loring of the Open Door Community in Atlanta, Georgia wrote: 'Homelessness is you, homelessness is me.'

We are all so infinitely fragile and our situations are transient. We believe we are solid and deathless and that our life situations are secure. But it could all change in a second. We are just flesh and blood, grass in the wind (Psalm 103) ... That's scary; but the realisation might also help us to live more in the here and now, and to appreciate the people around us – to see the beauty of individuals and experience the miracle of every day – the holy gift and grace of it all. It might also help us to empathise and connect more with sisters and brothers who are suffering.

Well, that's how I think sometimes anyway.

The Rainbow Man

John 9:13–17

I met the rainbow man in a night shelter for homeless men. The rainbow man dressed in bright colours – tie-dyed T-shirts, purple hair, pink nail polish. Spoke in colours. It was a depressing, colourless place – dingy, dirty yellow walls; clouds of grey smoke hanging. He was labelled mentally ill, schizophrenic. At one time he had studied fine arts at college, somebody said, had worked masterfully in oils and acrylics. Now, he worked in Crayola crayon. Drew like a child: dogs and cats and upside down pink-orange flowers planted in clouds. He got beat up by the men a lot.

One day he brought a leaf in from a walk he took (he was always taking long walks) and held it up to me and said *to look, see the light in the leaf pulsing, dancing still.*

I was busy and tired and had forgotten how to see, and said: 'Yeah, it's a maple leaf, so what' – there was someone buzzing at the door again, paperwork, so many important things to do. 'The light in the leaf,' he said again and danced away in a whirl of wind.

And when I sat down and stopped, I realised that what he meant was: to look and see that energy, that essence, alive in the leaf. He could see it. He was supposed to be disabled but he was able to see the light of God in a leaf and to wonder at it. After weeks of running blind through my life, the rainbow man taught me to open my eyes and heart again.

Donald Duck

Isaiah 43:1–4

It was my job to ask anybody new their name. There was a tough-looking young man shovelling sugar onto his bowl of cold cereal. I went over and introduced myself. He didn't answer, or look up. When I asked him his name he told me to fuck off.

The next night, I approached him again.

He growled, and said his name was Donald. When I asked him his surname, his hands clenched into fists.

'Duck,' he said.

Though he made me want to keep a safe distance, I'd try to make some contact when he came to the shelter. I'd offer him something to eat. I'd ask about the weather.

It was some time before we had our first true conversation:

'Fuckin' brilliant dumplings,' he said one night, 'these home-made?' He tried another spoonful and his dead eyes lit up. 'So who made these?' he asked, and glanced around.

I sat down beside him.

He told me he'd lived with his granny when he was a boy, and that she would make him beef stew with dumplings.

'Brilliant,' he sang, digging in.

It took a long time before he really opened up:

It took the homey smell of Norman's cooking.

It took people remembering his name, and giving him a warm welcome when he trudged in from the cold.

It took Ray's knock-knock jokes.

It took straight talk.

It took Sue finding him clean clothes and a decent, warm coat.

It took a long time.

Then, one summer evening, he told me his story:

We were sitting out on the church steps. He told me that he was a professional chef, and that he'd worked in a restaurant in the city centre. He'd worked his way up from porter, he said, but then lost his job when the place went bust. After that, he lost his flat and started sleeping on the streets.

He nursed a tall can of Strong Brew – he was rattling, he said, and took a hit.

I asked him what sort of food he'd cooked and he said he could cook anything and everything, but that cakes were his speciality.

'That's my real talent. Layer cakes, cheesecakes, sponges. Birthday cakes, wedding cakes – you name it.'

I thought of this tough, hard man baking cakes: the hands that had looked like they wanted to strangle the life out of me, squeezing out thick icing; piping delicate rosettes.

He wanted to start his own business, he told me. His own business selling cakes – cakes by mail order, cakes on the internet; that was his dream, he said, and shrugged.

I thought of a cake falling. 'No – why don't you?' I said.

He took another hit of Strong Brew – the inside of his arm was bruised and marked, pasty and weak – then told me about the time a famous TV chef had visited the restaurant. At the end of the meal the chef asked to shake the hand of the person who had made the raspberry soufflé – and he got called out.

'You must have felt proud,' I said.

'I felt brilliant,' he answered, sitting, working the empty, crushed can.

He started to give us a hand around the shelter, running boxes and crates into the kitchen whenever there was a delivery or donation.

Another evening out on the steps, he told me that he had a five-year-old son.

I asked him his son's name and he said: 'Rory.'

His son was in care. His girlfriend was in detox. (I imagined him for a moment, back in the world of birthdays and weddings.) He'd been on the streets a year in September, he announced, and fell silent.

'Rory … That's a beautiful name,' I said.

It took a long time to build trust:

It took Ray who'd lived on the streets and was a counsellor now.

It took Ray and Jane and Tony and people who had been there.

It took people who had never been there exactly but who could empathise.

It took Anne mothering him when he was sick, and people treating him like a human being again.

It took accepting him at the door, drunk and difficult and out of his head.

It took us barring him for a week for throwing an empty plate and calling Rahim 'Paki bastard'.

It took tough love.

It took Father William's understanding, gentle way.

It took giving him a home address so he could finally get a pay-book sent.

It took a long time.

Then, one Tuesday night, he told us that his name wasn't Donald, by the way. It was Brendan.

'Brendan Matheson,' he pronounced, and watched me write his name down in the book. 'Here,' he said, and took the pen.

I wondered if it was a sign. A sign he was growing more accepting of himself; a sign he was ready to begin dealing with his past, and future?

'Brendan,' I said. 'It suits you.'

He smiled.

He became protective of us. One night when someone was giving Anne a hard time on the door, he came out and told the guy to show the woman some respect – that, or he'd be out on his arse: it was *his* choice, he told him.

As the months passed he seemed to be feeding his addictions less; there was a mischievous glimmer in his eyes – he traded jokes with Ray, recipes with Norman. It felt like you weren't always reaching out to him down a long deep depression; inside of a black hole.

Then one day he told us that we probably wouldn't be seeing him for a little while. There was a warrant with his name on it, he explained. 'Can't keep your head down for ever,' he said, and walked up the road to the cop shop.

Ray and Jane visited him.

When he got out, he landed a job cooking in the shelter kitchen. He wanted to give something back, he said.

'Fuckin' brilliant,' all the guys raved. He was teaching Norman some things. On Christmas day, he and Stormin' served up an awesome and legendary feast: turkey with all the trimmings; roast potatoes; brussels sprouts; chipolata sausages and rolled bacon – and for dessert, out of this fuckin' world Christmas pudding topped with cream and brandy butter.

Brendan said his plan was to save his wages and get some gear together – piping bags, tubes, syringes, a decent set of knives and spoons.

Three years later, he stopped me in the street. He called my name and I turned around. I didn't recognise him at first. 'Brendan!' I cried.

He looked like a different person. He looked brand new.

It was a bright warm spring day and we shared our news:

He was a pastry chef at Costco supermarket, he told me; he was in charge of cake decoration and of interviewing and training bakery staff. He was living with his wife, Jamila, and his step in a little house outside the city.

He'd been through some ups and downs – rehab twice. It ha~~ been easy. He told me about trying to go cold turkey; about the hunger pain of withdrawal. He was feeling brilliant now. Life was sweet. Jesus Christ had called him, he revealed – and proudly, soberly showed me his tattoo of a Celtic cross. His arms were hard with muscles – cook's arms – sinewy from the push and pull of hard work, clean except for a couple recent burn marks from the oven.

It was the last time I saw Brendan.

I think of him sometimes: icing names onto birthday cakes in the brilliant light of Costco; living in a house with his wife, Jamila, and stepdaughter, Kate.

Gary

Acts 9:17

'People ask me how I can always be so happy,' says Gary, and tells me his story. About how some junkies broke into his flat and stole his TV and music system. Stabbed him in the head and ribs sixteen times.

'I thought I was falling asleep, but I was really dying.'

'During it I had this feeling,' he says. 'Like someone suddenly reached out and touched me. My guardian angel, my mom said. And I knew I was safe and held in love.' Sunlight falls on Gary's face and he closes his eyes; he says the stabbing helped to clear away the fog.

'People ask how I can always be so happy – I'm back from death.'

He looks like he's on permanent vacation – standing in flowery knee-length shorts, leather sandals, and a T-shirt proclaiming LIFE'S A BEACH; a great smile across his broad tanned face.

We're standing in the middle of the city sidewalk. People rush across to important meetings; wait with clouded looks. Gary's bopping and dancing away …

I remind him about the last time I saw him. Down at the drop-in centre: pale and shivering in a corner, hugging himself.

'I wasn't pretty picture, eh?'

Gary tells me he's moved across town and hardly goes there now, except to visit friends. He likes to go on long walks instead – round Gilmour Park, the market, the botanical gardens … He's got energy to burn – energy he never knew he had.

'Here, look,' he says, and shows me the camera his father sent him, turns it over in his knuckly hands like treasure. He laughs: 'I used to hate people taking *my* picture. I used to think I was ugly. Ugly inside and out, you know? Now I wear my shorts, take my shirt off. Why not?' he says, and shows me his zoom lens, 'there's nothing to be ashamed of.'

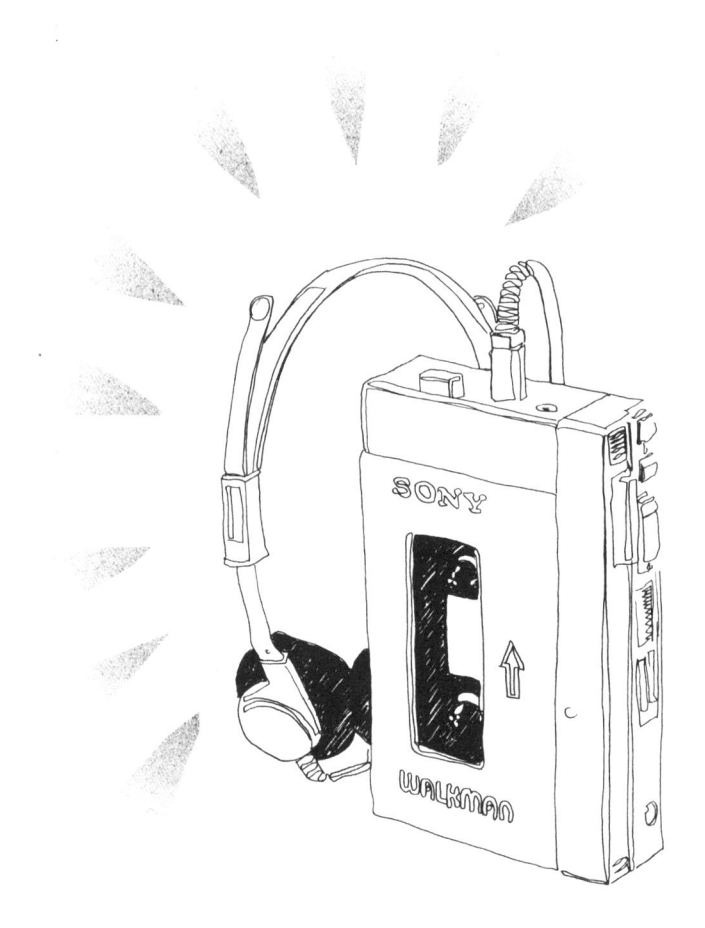

Gary doesn't care if people see his scars, or think he's crazy or stupid.

'God thinks I'm beautiful. Jesus calls me his beloved son,' he says, standing openly – like he has stood in front of God's gaze and grown bright with it. Like something brilliant has happened, and he'll never feel ashamed again.

I ask him what he likes to take photos of, and he says people he loves, things he loves. 'Sunsets and sunrises. Squares and fountains. Faces and flowers ... I used to sit and watch TV. Now I wanna take pictures.'

Gary tells me he loves the way the light changes and is everywhere. 'There's so much I never even noticed before. You know?

'So, that's why I listen to jazz,' he says, and excitedly shows me his Walkman now. 'I used to listen to basement music – Black Sabbath, Iron Maiden. Now I listen to jazz. Walk around everywhere and take pictures and listen to jazz. I used to hate it. I didn't understand. The joy. The joy – but sadness too. Jazz people went through a lot, suffered. But it's the joy that comes through stronger in the end – Louis Armstrong, Ella Fitzgerald. I listen to the words. I never did before. They sink in. I used to hate it. I used to hate everything ... Life was a bitch. I was sour, sittin' in a basement. I didn't understand.'

Gary shrugs. 'Sometimes you gotta die to be born,' he says, and starts showing me the stack of photographs he keeps in his rucksack with a bottle of water; drops one the Spirit catches and carries off. 'Oh well, someone'll find it,' he says as it wings away.

Gary says he was dead. Dead when they climbed in his casket and stole his buried treasure. Now his treasure is the light that glitters. Each new day. 'I just thank God ... See, listen,' he says, and reaches up and lays his hands on me, gives me his headphones.

'Can you hear? ...... See – light and dark. Sorrow and joy ... Can you hear?' he trumpets. People passing glance around, wondering if he's talking to them. I listen. And can hear: the bluesy key, the brassy joy.

While I'm standing listening to the music of life, Gary stands out on the street corner handing out photographs: waxy, shiny leaves of grass breaking up through the cement; blazing heads of flowers in the ruined shell of a building; the radiant dome of sky arching over office towers and apartment blocks ... Gives one to a woman who stops, suddenly surprised ... then smiles as something slowly sinks in. Hands one to a man who lights up and laughs. He seems to know who to give them to: people stopped or slowed with care or worry; people in a hurry who only have time for a bite. He seems to know: who needs energy, who needs some hope. I close my eyes – and can see pictures in the music ...

I hand him back his halo.

Gary says when he walks through the mean street valley now he feels protected. 'Not wrapped in fog, tangled in sweat.' He smiles – the lines and wrinkles around his eyes all crinkly, radiating out. He looks lit up from within, his face beaming, his Hawaiian shorts like stained glass glowing.

The sun's come out and the world is full of light. It seems to me that Gary is making it that way – and he is. We shake hands like brothers and he strolls off, listening to the sea of life.

I watch him disappear down the street, taking pictures of everything in the world he nearly lost.

Heading uptown everything is lit up from within. The crucified, leafy trees; the lined faces of souls ... Like a saint has passed this way trailing and spreading light. Like the fog has cleared.

There's a smell of tar; dazzle and glitter of sand dunes on a building site. There's a soft breeze, a warm, embracing feeling – I can feel the sun, sinking into my bones and heart. I want to run home and put my shorts on.

So why are you so happy? people passing seem to ask.

I'm back from death.

The Rainbow Man 2

The rainbow man comes out into the shelter lobby sometimes when I'm working the door. I give him scrap paper. He shows me his jumbo box of Crayola crayons, the bright shavings clinging to the built-in sharpener. Flips open the pack and, with his long crayon-stained fingernails, picks out some of his favourite colours. Holds them up so that I can read their names.

Mulberry

With gentle taps, puts it back before drawing out another.

Vivid Tangerine

'Nice colours, eh,' he says, then goes back to humming to himself. 'They're beautiful,' I tell him. 'Beautiful.'

Dandelion

Titanium

Orange Sunset

The rainbow man holds his open box of crayons out to me, inviting me to close my tired red eyes a moment – and to smell: my nose accustomed to the assault of rotten breath, raw alcohol, fuming vomit; Mr Fitzgerald's gangrenous toe workers take turns carefully swathing in gauze bandages.

I lean forward and breathe in, inhaling deeply: childhood. Rainy Saturday afternoons in the yellow kitchen – running outside after it stopped in my red Spiderman rubber boots.

'Wow!' … I smile.

He starts laughing, can't stop. 'Yeah. Remember that time, remember that time when you and your Aunt Mimi went picking bouquets of flowers in the meadow and John Lennon came along, and Paul Klee and Miro and late Picasso on a glossy red bicycle with a bell? I don't eat using a knife and fork any more also a palette knife, when's the bird supposed to swoop down like Jesus Christ, do you know?' he asks me, his sky-blue eyes beginning to cloud over. 'The pink and orange and turquoise and scarlet bird of paradise. The sweet bird of sorrow, the Birdman of Alcatraz, Big Bird, Big Bird …'

The rainbow man's sky-blue eyes start raining tears.

He drifts off, yellow thongs slap slapping drab linoleum …

'Ain't no beaches round here, you crazy fucker.'

Sometimes I bring a cup of powdered orange juice over to where he's sitting, with his head down, and ask him what's wrong, what's the matter? He rarely answers. In five or ten minutes the spell usually passes and he goes back to drawing; the tip of his tongue set between his brown-yellow teeth; his waxy black hair scribbled all over his face.

The rainbow man tacks his pictures up on the bulletin board. Around postings and notices: Where you can go for a free pair of shoes. Or anonymous AIDS testing and syringes. Who you can call if you have a drug or alcohol problem, or are feeling depressed and alone and suicidal. With my roll of tape, sticks them up over dirty-yellow walls. Critics trash them or hork greenies. Post-psych patients stand in the road and stare … Most people just pass his works by. On their way to the coffee urn hearth, or up to the dark dormitories where they pull night over their heads.

When the rainbow man isn't colouring, he sits silently, gazing at designs of light and shadow sketched onto the tables or floor, or at his peanut butter and jelly sandwich, or at his wriggling toes … Sometimes he goes upstairs and rearranges the rations of shampoo we set out on the table outside the showers. Out of phalanxes of Dixie cups, creates a gentle spiral, or a pentagram, or a crescent moon … Picks up the tubes of Crest he seems to like the squishy squashy feel of, or the little bars of rose-scented soap donated by a downtown hotel. Picks them up; sets them down. Picks them up; sets them down, at a certain angle. Walks away; then comes right back to perch a bar of soap on top of the can of shaving cream …

'Don't those soaps smell nice?' I coax sometimes, up on shower duty. 'Hey, why don't you have a nice hot shower then? There's no one in there hardly.'

'Ya, neat, eh? … The jewels, jewels falling in those little plastic baggies –'

One time he hissed at me the way he does at some of the men. It had been an especially stressful evening at the shelter – a grand mal seizure, two fights, the fire alarm … I told him to listen – that I didn't care about 'eider ducks shedding in the deep blue meadow of rain', what I cared was that he showered for once.

'You haven't had a shower in – I don't know how many days,' I lectured, uncreatively consulting the clipboard. 'So, what I suggest is that – if you don't want to be barred – you stop playin' around and pick up that shampoo there – right there!'

I'd poured him a brimming capful of Kwellada – the men were complaining he had head lice. I pushed a towel and pair of pyjamas across the desk at him, and felt a fine spray of spit wash across my face. I dried myself off with his towel …

The rainbow man was on anti-psychotic medication for a time.

'Nice colours, huh?' we'd say, trying to get him to take the pills. He didn't laugh or draw as much, but was easier to communicate with: his speech was toned down, his crying spells less frequent. We could talk about the weather. Mostly he'd just sit and stare. At the coloured TV bolted high up on the wall. When he stopped coming to the office at the prescribed times, we had to start calling him in. Finally, we told the nurse and social worker we couldn't force him.

The busker: a monologue

I used to meet the busker on a street corner when I was coming back and forth from working at a nearby shelter. Later, in the wintertime, the busker lived at the shelter.

Psalm 57:7–10

But what I really wanna do – and I'll be the first to admit it sounds kinda strange, kinda weird when you think about it but ... See, like I was telling you, I play all this other stuff, eh. You know, rock, folk, blues, jazz, classical. Everything 'cept country and western. That's a whole different thing. I don't play country. I respect it and everything but – what I really wanna do, is to merge, is to fuse the musical stylings of Jimi Hendrix and, you know Bach? ... Gotta light, by the way? ... Hey, thanks, man.

See, cause, like, what people walking around don't realise is that those guys had a lot in common. Both those guys, they were both, well, it's hard to explain ... virtuosos, well ya sure, they were both virtuosos on their instruments. Hendrix on the electric guitar, or the acoustic guitar. Bach on his well-tempered clavier, or harpsichord or Weimar pipe organ. Incredible virtuosos. But it's more than that really. It's hard to explain ... See, I heard it all in a dream once. That's how I know it can be done. Merging, uniting the musical stylings of Johann Sebastian Bach and James Marshall Hendrix. See? And shit, I'm the first to admit, it may take me all my life to do this thing. I, I may never do it!

I was out in Vancouver last month. Ever been to Vancouver? ... Fuck, those mountains, eh? Incredible. And, OK, so you're probably asking yourself, so, like, what's this guy, what's this guy doin' freezin' his tattered, blue-jeaned butt off here, when he could be back in good old Van where it's probably at least a balmy fifty or sixty degrees right now? I been askin' myself the same question. But, see, it's I don't necessarily follow the seasons as they occur per se. The seasons

I follow are the ones I feel change inside myself, if you can understand. So, like, while it's getting winter here, I'm still spring. I'm still spring ... Fuck, that smoke hits the spot bull's eye, thanks again, man. Nothing like a good smoke. The simple, everyday pleasures. Like that first cup of coffee in the morning, you know? Ever go down to Duke's Coffee Shop on Dalhousie? Now Duke makes a good cuppa coffee!

But, like, when I was out in Vancouver, I think I mighta got some ideas on how I could do this thing. See, out here busking I keep pretty much to my set list. Little tattered, but it serves my purposes. You know, rock, folk, blues, jazz, classical. Everything 'cept country and western. But in my head, it's something else: I can always hear this Bach/Hendrix thing playin' on up inside my head somewhere. So, now it's just a matter of gettin' it all to flow down through my arm and out my fingertips.

See, to me, to me Hendrix was incredible. And Bach, Bach was like, like fuckin' water, man. Like cool, delicious water. Like some pure, pure stream, you know? Like some purling beautiful stream you just sit and watch flow by and shake your head at and smile cause it's just so incredible. Then maybe further along there are some rocks it rolls over or maybe leaps up against and does a little dance and maybe some leaves get caught or something ... No way, fuck Mr George Frederick Handel. Don't mean to profane him but – Bach is water. Rollin' on to the sea. Never gets there but it must I guess. But the fun of it, the fun's just watchin' it roll by. That's the beauty he understood.

And Jimi – I wasn't really alive when he was playing or anything. I was what, three, four years old? I wasn't really alive but, you know – they still don't even know how it was he was able to make those sounds that he did. He built his own guitar, eh. And when that man passed on, they all went lookin' for it. Fanned out, hither and thither. Cause they all wanted to find out how it was he made all those incredible sounds. Sounded like the fuckin', fucked-up world burning. Like everything on fire finally. They were gonna pick it up and pull it apart and dissect it and give it a lobotomy. But know what? ... Nothing, nowhere to be found. Gone. Poof! Magic ...

They got all this crap now, eh. I was down at this music store the other day. Leo's. Lee's, is it? Alright, so I was down at Bruce Lee's Music Shop and they got all this crap. You know, pedals for this, pedals for that, little gadgets – buncha junk. All this shit, and they *still* can't make it sound like Hendrix did. All I got's this acoustic here. Little battered up but it serves my purposes.

And, OK, so, you may be thinking, well, Hendrix and Bach. James Marshall Hendrix and Johann Sebastian Bach. Hendrix is 1960s and Bach, Bach's like 1720s. That's pretty old, how's that all gonna sound? But, see, what people walkin' around don't realise is that Bach is *now* man. He's now. Just like Hendrix'll be now two hundred years from now. Bach too. Know what I'm sayin'? I mean, they can never stop those guys. The only plausible way they could ever stop those guys is to turn out the lights. And they will, you know. They'll put out the lights. Like one big, greedy, clawed paw slappin' ...

And so that's why I'm doin' all this I think really. Just hope I can while we can all still see. I spend almost all my time on this thing, this merging, coalescing of Bach and Jimi Hendrix. All my time: waking, sleeping, psychic, stellar, sidereal, you name it. And you may be saying: Well, that sounds a little selfish. But everyone's got their thing to do. All these lunch-break business men. 'Point on, Mr Business Man, you can't dress like me.' Sluggishly flowing on down the street here. They got theirs, I got mine. They got their mergings and dealings and fusings in the sun (I got no right to say really), I got mine. See, me, I just wanna live in a world where it's just as valid to be a business man as it is to spend your time trying to fuse Bach and Jimi Hendrix. I mean, in the end, when we go up to heaven and the Big Man asks: 'OK, so what have you been doing? What have you been doing with your precious time on Earth?' what would be the best answer? 'God, your Holiness, I spent my time trying to sell insurance'? Or, 'God, I spent my time trying to merge Bach and Jimi

Hendrix'? What would God find more interesting for one thing? … Not sure? Maybe she'll say: 'Trying to sell insurance? Are you mad?!' Or maybe he'll say: 'Bach and Jimi Hendrix? – that's like tryin' to mix fire and water. Are you mad?!' Or maybe it would be better to say to God: 'I tried to help people. I lived for others.' Maybe *that* would be the best answer. Probably. Probably it would. But, hey, I try to do what I can. I try to be gentle and humane, you know. Try to give people music to soothe and feed their souls … Anyway, I got no judgements. I leave that to God. I leave that to the Maker. Everyone's got their mission. And I'm an artist – I can't sell insurance – no one would believe me. It's like playing country and western – no one would believe me.

I was reading this Buddhist book in the library the other day. Opened it just anywhere. Heavy, smelled about a thousand years old. 'Everyone must work out their own salvation,' it said. And that's all I'm standing here sayin' really. What I've been thinking my whole life long ever since I can remember. And it may take me my whole life long. I may never do it. It may take generations or when the dust clears. You know? That can happen too. Or I can, say, give the idea to you and maybe you'll do it or pass it on as you see fit. You never know. Who knows, maybe we're talkin' generations for this thing. But I don't think so. I got it all in my head. It's just a matter of gettin' it all out onto the fret board … And anyways, I better stop standin' here talking like the crazy son of a bitch that I am and get back to it … Hey, it's been real good talkin' to you, man. Probably see you around again sometime. You never know. But, hey, before you go, you wouldn't happen to have another cigarette on you, would you? … Ah, God bless you, man. Shantih.

Hush puppies

1 Corinthians 13:4–7

One night at the shelter, Lee, who's 17, told me about the problem he was having with his new girlfriend:

'It's cause of the abortion, eh. It wasn't my baby. It was the guy before me. He took off out West. Jerk. Or scared, I dunno. So now whenever I try to get close to her she just starts wailin' me in the shins. She's got these big, kick-ass, steel-toed boots – man, it hurts. It's just when she's drinking. I don't know what I'm gonna do. She won't let me near her. And I can understand – I always say to her: "Look, I wanna understand, let me in, let me in on about how you're feelin" … But she doesn't believe me. Can't blame her really. I don't know what I'm gonna do. I need my hugs, man.

'Then I was walking through the mall the other day, you know, and stopped in front of this store window. And looked in and all of a sudden it came to me – hush puppies, yeah, hush puppies. Shoe store. Hush puppies, get her some hush puppies – soon as my next welfare cheque comes. I need my hugs … It's only when she's drunk but, man, it hurts – take a look at my shins. See – all bruises … I'm gonna buy her some hush puppies – soon as my next cheque comes.'

The poem that closes this section was written while I was working in a night shelter in Leith, just outside of Edinburgh. The shelter ran over the winter months and was held in a different church each night. All denominations were involved in the project, and the staff team ranged from 'Marxist-Christians' like myself to those on the far right of the Church. We worked well together – even after some heated discussions about theology in the middle of the night. We worked well together because at heart we all shared the same core belief – that Jesus came to serve: to feed the hungry, to welcome the stranger, to clothe the freezing … I learned a lot about ecumenism while working in that shelter, and a lot about people of course:

Homelessness is you, homelessness is me

Homelessness is you, homelessness is me
Homelessness is Dan who was a miner
Homelessness is Eric who was a computer programmer
Homelessness is Emily who was a student
Homelessness is Brian who worked packing meat for a while,
and worked picking fruit for a season,
and works in construction when they can use him
Homelessness is you, homelessness is me

Homelessness is Jack who fought in the Falklands War
Homelessness is Harry who fought in Normandy and in Korea
and in the east end of Glasgow
Homelessness is Jane who fought and survived
    the mental health system
Homelessness is Maggie who says:
If there's one thing she's learned – it's that she's a survivor
Homelessness is you, homelessness is me

Homelessness is David who sees guardian angels in the trees;
seraphim perched on fences
Homelessness is Sarah who sees no way out
Homelessness is Eric who jumped from a bridge in London
Homelessness is Chan whom they found frozen in a dumpster
Homelessness is you, homelessness is me

Homelessness is Ewan who has travelled to South America and
    China and Alaska,
and has so many stories he could fill a book
Two books!
Homelessness is Victor
who has a tattoo of a butterfly he reveals –
like he's baring his soul
Homelessness is Jenny who is dying of AIDS,
and whose last wish is to travel to Skye …
to sit on a beach near Portree
and watch the sun setting
Homelessness is you, homelessness is me

Homelessness is Mohammed who sleeps in his car,
and has to keep moving on when the cops come
Homelessness is Ray who sleeps in the graveyard
Homelessness is Vernon who lives in a tidy squat where he likes to
    read the *Evening Times* and cook sausages
Homelessness is you, homelessness is me

Homelessness is Sittina who escaped the war in Sudan
and is scared of being deported by the Home Office
Homelessness is Susan who escaped her husband in Manchester
and is scared of being found and killed
Homelessness is Jessica who escaped her stepfather
Homelessness is Curtis who works at a charity shop
    and can fix anything –

radios, TVs, bicycles, washing machines …
Homelessness is Curtis who has lived for forty years with the labels
    stupid, defective, disabled, broken …

Homelessness is Neil who loves to sit and talk about '60s' music –
and knows his stuff
Homelessness is Nicola who loves the ballet
Homelessness is Sylvester who plays joyful, jangly ragtime piano in
    the shelter chapel
Homelessness is Paul who writes the most sensitive,
    beautiful poetry
Homelessness is you, homelessness is me

Homelessness is Craig who never speaks or smiles
and has an abused collie dog he takes excellent care of
Homelessness is Ian who wanders the streets looking for a hit –
and has a distant light in his eyes when he remembers:
playing football with his mates, walking in the hills,
    fishing for salmon …
Homelessness is you, homelessness is me

Homelessness is Chaz and Barry and Lynne,
who spent their childhoods in and out of foster care,
their teenage years in and out of institutions,
and all of their adult lives inside either jails or shelters
Homelessness is Albert who spent 10 years inside Belmarsh,
where he learned to hate
and how to play
the whole dirty, rotten game

Homelessness is Dave who wants to work with children
Homelessness is Lewis who can't pay his council tax
Homelessness is Norma who can't pay her electric
Homelessness is Elizabeth who is eight months pregnant

Homelessness is Miles who misses tucking his kids in
Homelessness is Robbie who says:
when he wins the lottery he's gonna buy his own tropical island,
and give what's left to the nuns –
who accepted him for who he is,
who treated him like a human being again
Homelessness is you, homelessness is me

Homelessness is Dick who says:
'I was staying with friends but they get sick of you.'
Homelessness is Chris and Nina who take good care of each other
and make love where –
and when –
they can
Homelessness is Matt who says you feel like 'the invisible man'
Homelessness is Vincent who says:
'It could happen to anyone, people don't realise –
lose your family, your job, your mind …
People have no idea –
how close to the edge they're walkin'.'
Homelessness is me
Homelessness is you.

The phrase 'homelessness is you, homelessness is me' is from a story by Ed Loring of the Open Door Community in Atlanta, Georgia
www.opendoorcommunity.org

SITTING

Introduction

For a period, I worked with some nursing agencies, sometimes in nursing homes, sometimes in people's own homes. Here are two pieces about working as a 'sitter'/companion aide with the elderly.

Sitting with Mr Fenton
2 Corinthians 5:1–5

Mr Fenton's existence was limited to his bed, where he spent most of his time – bed rails up and locked like the sides of a crib during the hours no one was sitting with him – his washroom, and his desk where he sometimes, in slow motion, ate his meals.

Just getting Mr Fenton up for lunch was a miracle. We had to go in stages. I'd have to support him, and be very careful setting him down as his bones were brittle as dried-out wood. When he did manage to make it to that other land that held his desk and red velvet chair, I'd arrange his tray for him and cut up any of his food that hadn't already been put through the blender. Though he'd often protest, I'd also straighten out the clutter on his table top, one of the places Mr Fenton was hoarding packets of fine cane sugar, salt and pepper, and little plastic tubs of real butter, blueberry jam, marmalade and cream. I didn't see any point in throwing his mounting treasure out though, it would just upset him.

Bolted to the back of his desk was a mirror. One morning I remember Mr Fenton peering into it and a look of shock washing over his face. He probably hadn't been up for days and had forgotten what he looked like.

'I'm old ... I'm ugly ... I'm miserable ... I'm tired,' he croaked. Then, without swallowing a bite of sustenance, he motioned me to help him back to his bed, which I hadn't had a chance to change yet.

I was the sitter who changed the calendar the Royal Bank had sent him. It was eight months behind. I tried to do it as sensitively as possible. I didn't want to shock him. He became angry with me, and accused me of trying to trick an old man. Finally, he told me I could just go to hell. I scribbled in the Nurses' notes what had happened, and that I thought Mr Fenton should be oriented to time and place every day now.

In these notes were instructions for the sitter to get Mr Fenton up, to the shower, and dressed for the day. In the beginning, I attempted this routine.

'Stop trying to be Florence Nightingale,' Mr Fenton gargled, for the fourth time before I understood him. When he spoke it sounded like water going down a drain. In his pipes were clumps of phlegm. To understand him, I learned to offer him a sip of cool water through a striped straw between phrases; then, later, between words.

I explained, somewhat frustrated, that I just wanted to give him a full life. He laughed at me. At first I thought he was choking. The way he was heaving, for a moment I was afraid his joints might split.

'I haven't had one up till now,' he said in a gravelly voice, 'and it's not about to begin with you … Come here, boy,' he said, motioning to me with a strictured hand.

'Look at me … really look at me.'

I did finally.

'I'm waiting to die … All right?'

I nodded.

I felt ashamed. He shouldn't have had to get my permission. From then on we got along. I stopped believing I knew better. I wasn't dying. When I sat with him, I'd get him what he asked for. 'Water.' And his drops. In the mornings, I'd first, with a warm facecloth, gently wipe the sand from the corners of his eyes. Standing over him with the eyedropper, his starved eyes straining wide, I felt like I was feeding a dying bird.

On Mr Fenton's desk was a gilt-framed photograph of the many-roomed house he had had to sell. I saw it made him happy, proud, to talk about it, so I'd say: 'That's a fine-looking house there, Mr Fenton. Just beautiful …'

Mr Fenton died in a plush, sound-proofed room, leaving rumours of a great treasure buried in a bank vault somewhere; and, as if for banquets in the after world, a hoard of condiments to be excavated from secret compartments. From pockets in suit coats and from dresser drawers.

Esme and Peter

Hebrews 12:1–2

I've been visiting an elderly couple from 9:00am until 9:00pm every day for the last few weeks.

Peter has dementia and Esme's got cancer. Her whole, small shrivelling body racked with the fucking disease. Peter is not very lucid, though once in a while we'll have a short conversation. Or he'll surprise me, suddenly ejaculating: 'Well, let's not sit here all night like dead dicks, boy, let's go for a stroll!'

So, we stride over to the magnificent glittering shopping mall. Peter is a towering, robust old man. We scratch puppies behind the ears in the Little Pals Pet Centre, have a styrofoam coffee in the Food Court, then slowly, silently amble home. I make him his dinner, heaping his plate full because I feel death all around me. Yellow niblets of canned corn, a heap of frozen peas and carrots – even though he only eats his meat and rice pudding. His plate full of colour, grey death all around. After dinner, Peter may bring out a photo album full of old friends and places mostly new to him now. He sits in his chair with the television going, turning the thick pages, yellow photographs falling out onto the green shag. 'It's all right, Peter,' says Esme when he gets confused and upset, speaking his name softly. 'It's all right, dear,' struggling, pulling herself up with atrophied muscles and the trapeze bar. 'It's really all right,' until his face relaxes that awful look of panic and fear and Esme can collapse and close her eyes and breathe. And Peter comes over to the death bed we set up in the living room and bends way down to give her a little hug she can feel in the marrow of bones that ache.

Every evening at twilight, Peter stands gazing out the back window, waiting for the grey squirrel to come to the little tree. Chuckles when it does. When it looks around, eating the walnuts he cracked and left for it. 'Better find somewheres for winter, boy,' he tells him. The backyard squarely fenced, the maple tree dead centre, a puddle of yellow leaves spreading from its trunk, flowing out over the tired grass, rippling in a gust.

At eight o'clock, the last stretch before Denny, their son, gets home, I remind Esme to take her morphine. It pours thickly from the jars the nurse leaves in a row like days. Is sickeningly sweet, Esme says, so she mixes it with the Welch's grape juice I go get her. Esme wakes every ten minutes. Seldom gets a good rest now, yet still manages to smile. Sometimes, I slowly crank the bed up and we talk a little after Peter's gone off to sleep – in his clothes, in his hard shoes. About when she was a young bride and he was off to war for five years. Yes, it was lonely she says, but worse for him. 'I had Denny then … No man should have had to see the things that Peter did.' He wrote her letters, telegrammed when he could.

She nods off in the middle of the story, in the middle of a sentence. I make her coffee and a toasted tomato sandwich. She falls asleep with the sandwich half-eaten in her skeleton hand. I slip it out from between her long fingers trying not to wake her. The strawberry-flavoured energy drink I pour and leave on her bedside table is thick with vitamins, is the colour of her cotton jumpsuit she sometimes finds hot, and sometimes feels cold in. Wisps of winter-white hair stick up around Esme's flowery kerchief. Her skin has turned yellow, is translucent and veiny. Her smile grows more and more distant. Awake or asleep, seems to speak softly of acceptance. There are a couple pictures on the knick-knack-cluttered mantle of her when she was healthy. Wearing make-up and a pinched look. Peter stands impassive in uniforms – Army, Legion, the Greyhound Bus Company.

On Friday I came to the house to find Esme's hospital bed folded up like a dead leaf. On the stormy night before she'd been taken to the General.

I returned Monday to learn she'd passed away. I used to bring her garden flowers. Souvenirs of the walks Peter and I took in the park, where broken brown glass glints in cold sun and the occasional condom lies in a shallow puddle, muddy water reflecting cloudy sky. She used to try to get up and water her plants. I was scared she'd fall and break her hip. 'I'll do it for you, Esme,' I'd tell her. 'It's OK, I'll do it.' Sometimes she'd make it. Sometimes she'd pull herself around with her walker and water her plants; talk to them in a soft, hoarse voice. Rub grey dust off broad, mottled leaves. I'd run and get her shawl. By the end, in the hospital, she slept all day and felt little pain, they said. Body and mind floating in a sea of morphine.

A few days before Esme was taken away to the hospital, I remember Peter looking gently down on his shrunken wife sprawled on the wrinkled bed, and turning and whispering hoarsely: 'Whenever my wife gets sick that woman lying there comes to take her place.' He then went and made us, three people, four cups of instant coffee, one for 'that woman there'.

Now, pacing the creaking, warped floors sensing something is terribly wrong, Peter says, 'Geez, I wish she'd call and let me know.' I ask him if he wants to go for a stroll, see what's happening over at the mall. 'I don't understand it,' he answers, 'she just went out for a few things. That's not like her.' And he goes and lies down again. I put one of Denny's happy movies on. *South Pacific*. It seems so fucking surreal. Denny'll be home soon, I tell Peter. 'Soon, not too long.'

Peter's heavy steps echo, echo because Denny has started selling the furniture.

Peter will be placed in a nursing home in a few weeks. Over a can of Old Milwaukee at the kitchen table, Denny explains that he'll get better care there. 'I mean you've done a great job, don't get me wrong.'

The fridge whirrs, windows rattle. We sit with our thoughts. In a couple weeks I won't have a job, I think; but that is life too.

LEONARD AND MARK: DANCING INFINITY

Introduction

Rubem Alves wrote: 'Hope is hearing the melody of the future. Faith is to dance to it.' Leonard and Mark were labelled 'disabled'. But they knew more about how to open up to the light and to the music of life than I ever will.

Leonard: a Christmas story

A story about working as an assistant in a L'Arche home for individuals with developmental challenges
Matthew 5:14–16; John 1:1–18

It didn't feel like Christmas Eve. I didn't even want to go to mass. I was so tired. So tired of all the hassles and arguments all day. Arguments between assistants and core members, assistants and assistants, core members and core members … The household was divided. It was three against two, two against three. Alfred had thrown himself on the floor, Rita had thrown and broken her cup, Pierrette had cried that Christmas was ruined – and closed her eyes and prayed to God that we'd all just go away, her face scrunched up tight like a fist. Like a discarded invitation, left lying in a ball in the corner.

It had been one long day of frustrated expectation. Like an endless trip to get some place special we never ever arrived at, and that kept receding in flatness. Everybody became twitchy and irritable. We'd been talking about Christmas coming for weeks. It was like we were all sitting waiting for the magic and love to open up and when it didn't we started blaming each other. We tried opening one gift each, to see if that would help – help open the magic and love a crack – but nothing happened. In everything we tried something was missing.

I just wanted to go to bed.

We piled into the van. Didn't speak on the way. Pierrette started to sing along to some radio jingle and Rita told her to shut up I got a headache. With her cleft palette it sounded like 'heartache'. 'I got a heartache.' We couldn't find a place to park, and so had to walk; piled out into the cold. Pierrette forgot her mittens. 'Why do you always forget your mittens, Pierrette?' 'She does it on purpose,' someone accused. Pierrette cried that she did *not* do it on purpose! Alfred muttered and swore under his breath, like he was full up with everything everyone was thinking and feeling all day and it had to come out – in a litany; the winter night clouded with curses.

We met Leonard inside the cathedral. Leonard lived in our house too and shared a room with Matt; he'd been away at a Christmas party for his workshop. He clapped and danced when he saw us (I couldn't understand why); stood wearing a paper hat and a dumb look that made Rita suddenly start laughing. 'Ha, look at Leonard,' she pointed, 'what a fool. You're a fool, Leonard,' she sang, carrying herself along in a huff, then resting. Leonard's workshop made little wooden boats and trains that the community shop sold. He went around shaking all our hands, like he had some good news to share; his grip, rooted and bracing, his breath, warm and sweet, smelling of Christmas cookies and shortbread – fruit cake seasoned with rum. We got all tangled together and touched. The big bell pealed and Leonard led us in through the heavy doors with a dance-walk. He looked brilliant in his party clothes.

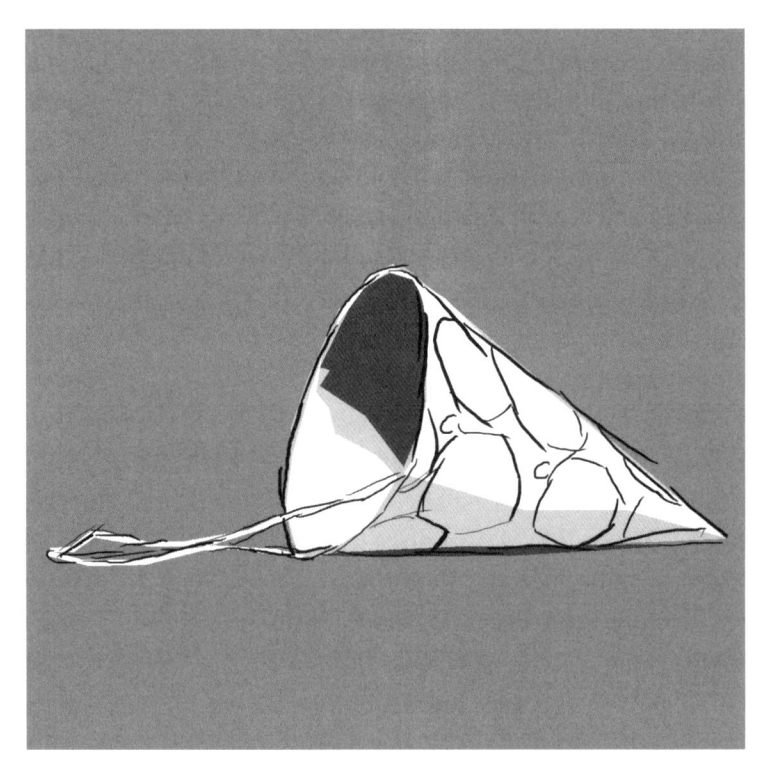

We were late, and slow, and they started without us. We had to find some space in back; God seemed far away. The cathedral domed and towered, and we gazed up at the rich, golden light every place. 'Wow,' said Rita. There were families and couples everywhere, fancy women, children dressed in their nicest clothes, best behaviour. There was a choir of boys somewhere; distant, faint draughts of spicy, sweet incense.

Pierrette closed her eyes when you were supposed to, opened them when you were supposed to, but nothing happened. Her face remained worried. Alfred had to go to the washroom, and Gus, my colleague, took him. Matt kept biting the skin around his fingernails. When it came time for communion at last, Leonard was the only one who stood at the invitation. Rita said: 'No, yeah, you go for us, Leonard,' and slid down in the pew. I said I'd take him, and Leonard led me up the long road of red carpet ...

When we reached the crossing, he stopped by a deserted side chapel and turned and signed to me – signed to me to come, come follow, and ducked inside. The chapel was warm and embracing; stone walls flickered and glowed. I sat down in a window recess to wait. We'd be home soon, I thought, and glanced at my watch.

Leonard stood in front of a crucifix and crossed himself. It was never easy to understand Leonard when he spoke with words; you had to really listen, know him (Christ understood perfectly). Leonard prayed aloud and in the rise and fall of language I recognised the name of his friend Charlie who had died two Christmases ago. Charlie had Down's, and had lived in the same institution as Leonard before coming to live in community. Charlie and Leonard were like brothers, and the loss made Leonard sad and heavy at times – so that he wouldn't come dance in the living room when you put the Bay City Rollers record on; wouldn't change his dirty clothes when you told him to, and turned up your tone.

Leonard prayed for the soul of his friend – his name whispered in the chapel and settled in the arms of Christ, gently, lovingly ... I closed my eyes; and in the peace prayed to Jesus to take away the sadness and weight I still wore like dirty clothes. I could feel myself begin to settle down into a more rooted place. I became aware of my breathing. My busy, frightened mind. After a moment, Leonard tapped me on the shoulder – took my hand.

When we made it to the front finally, Leonard solemnly stepped forward – then suddenly stole the chalice out of the priest's hands and – with his strong thirst, profound spirit – drank the wine down in a few quick gulps! Like he wanted to drink deep the draughts of God alive. Like he'd been sitting in the middle of a desert and it was an emergency, and he had to drink enough for the whole of us.

'Aaaaaah,' he said, and licked his lips. Wore a purple ring.

I started to open in a smile. The priest didn't smile, and carefully, seriously took the cup back (never exactly let go). He signed something in Latin (Christ understood perfectly). I seized the bread and wine of the moment, and Leonard and I walked around the cathedral with our tapers, lit up now. 'Wow, wow,' he kept saying – the eternal 'wow' – gazing around at all the points of light, at all the people: like stars coming out; his boyish face lit up with a zing, like when you helped him shave in the morning and he slapped on Skin Bracer. He stopped and gazed up at his Mother Mary with such a deep, human love that light spilled from his eyes. She held her arms out to the whole world, and Leonard wanted to reach out and hug everybody in the congregation. And some responded warmly, and shook his hand, and others remained seated inside themselves; stared past him like he wasn't there; or smiled politely, faces shining with a clean, hard light: like polished brass, a gold pendant; kept their hearts cordoned. Some treated him like a child and preciously. Others gave him looks that said it was not how they believed people should behave inside this institution. Some glanced away, embarrassed by all his dancing openness, naked feeling showing. And others looked as if they wished they could embrace him, break free. As we passed through the crowd I recognised my frightened selves reflected back. I caught up to Leonard; took his hand.

Leonard loved the children and the little babies, all bundled up. I assured one young mother that it was all right, that he was very gentle, and she let him put his face up and say hallo; he beamed like the sun. The tired woman looked into Leonard's warm, beaming face and handed him her child to hold and rock a minute. Leonard kissed the baby's forehead, left a mark of glistening. The baby stopped crying, and the woman smiled a moment; looked less pursued in that light – more a hopeful follower of the future than a sad-eyed refugee from a past.

 I handed Leonard back his candle; and he turned and carried it to where the others were left sitting; walked with slow ceremony down the long aisle, shielding and cradling the fragile warm flame that trembled and bounced. The priest was declaiming that God was the Light that the darkness could never extinguish, and that Christ was the Light of the world; that we were all light and loved and held in

God's hand, and as he was speaking, Leonard passed the light from the tip of his taper down the dark line of us ... Pierrette gazed down with wonder at the light she was holding and swallowed – then suddenly smiled. Rita looked at her light and laughed – a nervous flicker at first, then out loud, held high. Matt looked at his light, his dark eyes glowing with shy halos inside. Alfred looked at his, and was silent. One by one our faces lit up; with each new light all our separate lights seemed to grow stronger, more confident; there was a warm feeling passed down through us; down the line like forgiveness. I turned to Gus and we looked one another in the eye; shook hands: acknowledging the light in each other. Leonard and Matt embraced. Everyone in the cathedral stood to sing the final hymn, Hark the Herald Angels Sing; held hands, candles aloft. Rita knew all of the words. Didn't need to look at the book like other people did. Gus teased her that she looked like the Statue of Liberty and Rita told him to shut up she was singing; gave him a good slap. He called her it again. Pierrette said she never wanted the moment to end, and closed her eyes down upon it tightly. The bell rang out for Christmas Day and you could feel it shiver all through you.

The priest gave the final blessing, and free of heavy shadow we were vaulted up into the heavenly music. Families and neighbours were all kissing and hugging. 'Wow. Wow,' Leonard kept saying, like he kept seeing shooting stars every place. Suddenly all the lights in the cathedral were switched on from somewhere: like an explosion from a long lit fuse. Down inside I felt the warm, still centre Leonard had led me back to. Like a perpetual light set there.

Leonard went around saluting the priest and altar boys, clapping his hands, drunk on Holy Spirit. Matt copied him. Then found his own style, dance. 'Hey, look at Matt,' cried Rita, 'what a clown. You're a clown, Matt.'

We walked out together, holding hands like one big family. Rita walked with an angel in her step, like her legs weren't bothering her at all any more.

I'd gone into church depressed and exhausted and had emerged with a starry feeling and the energy of love.

'Look it, snow!' cried Pierrette. And suddenly everyone held out their hands; started catching it on their tongues. Strangers. Neighbours we didn't know – big, soft, floaty flakes that hung on to our coats and mittens and eyelashes. It was like the hand of heaven had opened up. There was a life-sized nativity scene out on the front lawn, all lit up. The night was like a million lit tapers and I stopped to breathe in the wonder a moment: the light, rich, heady scent of snow, like bread rising, before we hopped in the van and sang Gloria all the way home. Rita said her headache was gone. 'I'm a good singer,' she told us. 'You're a good singer, Pierrette,' she told Pierrette.

We stayed up late and drank the wine we didn't all have in church. Leonard didn't drink and had Pepsi Cola. The living room was warm and homey and we switched off the lights a moment to see the tree all lit up. 'Wow!' we all cried at once, and sat wrapped in silence, it was so beautiful. Pierrette said it was beautiful the way everyone all helped to decorate the tree. 'I can see where Rita helped, and I can see where Alfred helped, and I can see where Matthew helped …' Red wine glanced and shimmered in my mug; I could smell the cinnamon and cloves, and evergreen. We switched the lights back on and tried to guess our Chris Kinders. Matt and Leonard played Santa. Leonard got jumbo bubble bath. Gus said, 'Great, now we'll never get him outta the tub!' Matt got more Legos. Pierrette got slippers and a cookbook to try. Alfred got new clothes his family sent him. Rita got a new mug that played Jingle Bells. Gus got a funny T-shirt; I got a serious book. Pierrette said we all had gifts, and closed her eyes and prayed for peace and joy for all of God's people this holy night – her beautiful face relaxed and peaceful and open, like it could hold the whole world.

Prayer

Jesus, I think of you as someone
who'd clap and dance and
be happy to see his friends.

Who'd move with a dance in his walk
and open heavy doors.

Who'd wear a party hat and play the fool.

Who'd be unafraid to show love,
who'd reach across and hug everyone.

Who'd grab away the cup and offend the priests.
Who'd be looked upon as simple.

Who'd bring light to the deserted and
help open up the night.
Who'd help open gifts.

Who'd see shooting stars every place
and chant 'Wow!'

Jesus, help me to recognise you
in unexpected people and places.
Amen

Mark: an Easter story

A story about working as a companion aide

John 5:1–12; Mark 16:1–7

It took a long time for Mark to find a church he could dance in. During hymns, through songs of praise. During sermons, sometimes – rocking and turning and spinning in his wheelchair. It took him a long time but finally he found one. 'It disturbs the congregation,' they'd told him. 'Makes people uncomfortable in church.'

'People are afraid I guess,' he told me. 'Afraid of joy.' When Mark first started learning he danced in tight circles. God told him how it meant that God's disabled people are afraid, timid. Not loose. Not free. But then slowly, gradually he wheeled and danced and the circles grew bigger. It's not for himself that he dances, Mark says. It's for God – to dance in front of God – to express his gratitude and thankfulness, and how he's chosen joy finally, and wants others to choose joy too. To dance.

'People just sit in the pews, and benches along the back. And when they stand up to sing finally hardly sway or close their eyes. Like they're crippled and broken.' Dance and help free the disabled, God told Mark.

We're sitting together making decorations for his wheelchair – tissue paper streamers, yellow and gold – for the dance tonight. Mark tells me about how he spent six months in hospital with double pneumonia, and pressure sores from lying that cut to the bone. Just to move was painful. Getting turned like lying on knives. He cried whole days. Asked God, Why? Felt like Job. Like Job did. When can I get up again, he cried, like in some psalm, and God said: When you learn finally, really learn. He wanted to die, just wanted to die. It was too much pain all the time – at one point with his circulation they were afraid gangrene could set in in his foot and they'd have to amputate. But God said: No, you can't die, I'm not finished with you.

You have inner healing to do. Then you can get up. You have work to do but you still won't listen.

'Lying there,' said Mark, 'there's not much to do but think. Think and talk to God. There's no way to get away. You try to, watch the TV and that, but you can't really anyway.'

Mark told me how, lying propped and positioned between locked bed rails, he was forced to really work through his feelings from his past: His separation from a woman born with a disability also, his hurt. His drinking. Above and below all, his broken relationship with God. His anger at God for the way God had made him. For what he put him through to suffer.

Then – after six months lying broken in sorrow, with ulcers and sores eating him – Mark resurrected healed and whole and God said dance. OK, so dance. Stop abusing yourself, stop punishing yourself and others. Stop sitting with words. Dance resurrection. Dance joy. The good news. Dance for all God's disabled people and for their liberation. Mark doesn't care what people think, he has to dance. It's his purpose, his mission. There's a service tonight, a celebration, and we're blowing up and tying on coloured balloons.

Lately he's been dancing figure eights, Mark says. In the crossing – big, free figures. Flowing, spinning, gliding. 'For a while I was trying to figure out why exactly. And didn't know, so then stopped thinking about it and just danced, feeling the flowing freedom of it. But then it came to me: If you put a figure eight on its side, you know what it's the sign of? … Infinity. It's infinity. It's dancing infinity.'

I smile and we sit in silence. Finishing up, Mark says to me: 'I wish my mother was alive.' 'Gets lonely?' I say. 'Yeah, sometimes. And the doctors all told my mother, told mom when I was a child that I'd never walk. That I'd always need a wheelchair …' Mark smiles. 'But they never said I'd never dance. Never said that … Maybe she can see me. Dancing. Dancing now. I like to think of her like that … There, finished, nice huh? Well, I guess that's it. Thanks for the help. So, you dancin' tonight too?'

Communion prayer

We find it so difficult to dance in this life:

Carrying the burden of responsibilities
the pressures of every day
the memory of past partners
the weight of the world, it seems like, sometimes.

Afraid of what people might think
afraid of people judging us
(of God judging us)
afraid of looking foolish out there on the floor.

Afraid we won't get the rhythm right
afraid dancing is for the chosen few
Feeling so weighed down with guilt and sin
we can't move with grace …

O Christ, Lord of the Dance,
in you we live and move and
have our being.

Through your body and blood
our sins are forgiven
and all we carry which is heavy
you take upon yourself.

So that we may dance again
and give thanks
and celebrate life.

Let us celebrate
Let us share the bread and wine –
the bread that dances with the atoms of the revolving Earth
the wine that shimmers with the light of Christ's Love.
Amen

Leonard and Mark: Dancing Infinity   97

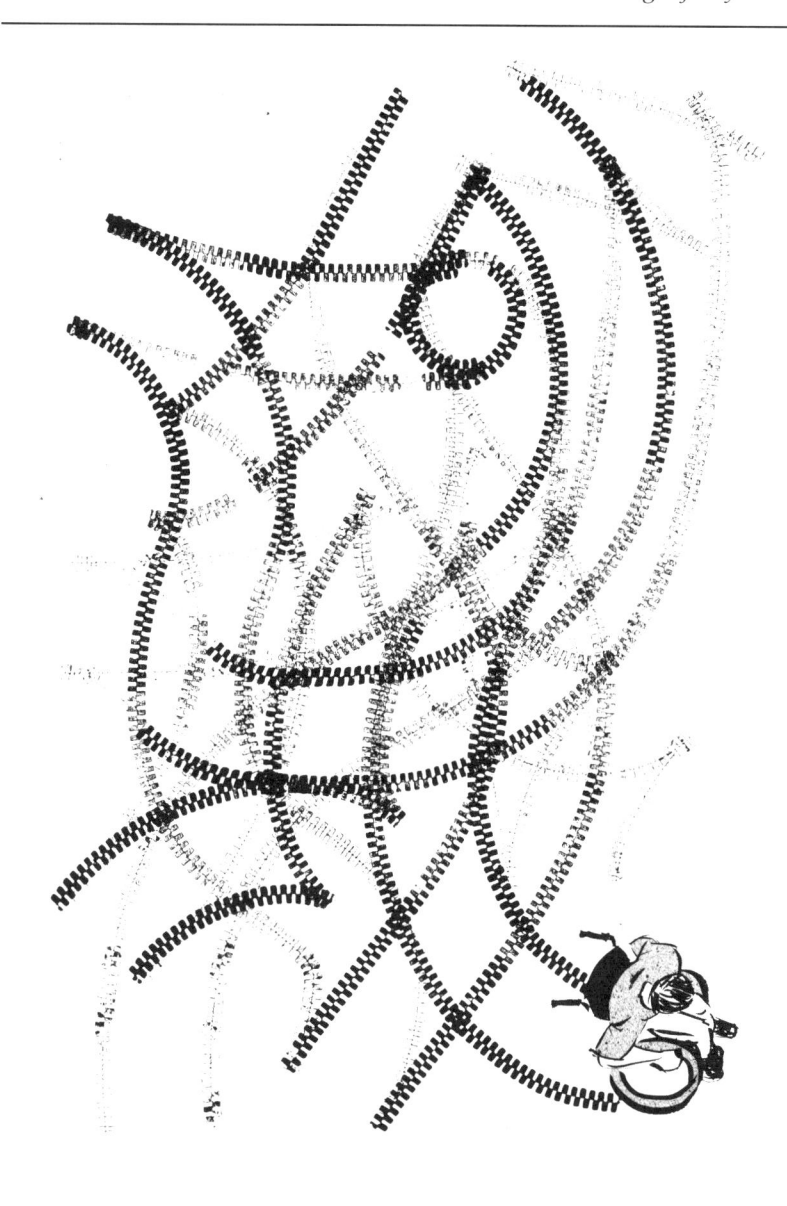

BINGO IN THE BASEMENT

Introduction

This sequence is about working as a volunteer in a 'post-psychiatric rest home'. Most of the folk in the home had been in and out of mental hospitals and institutions all of their lives. Others had less serious mental health problems, or none, and just seemed dumped there. (Everyone in the home just seemed dumped there.) The residents were of all ages, the youngest 18, the eldest 93. I was in my early 20s at this time.

The home was privately owned, a business. Should homes for the mentally ill – or the elderly – be primarily businesses? Great Britain spends 59.2 million pounds a year on war; America spends 528.7 billion dollars every year (Source: SIPRI Yearbook, 2007*). What should our priorities as a society and community be? Caring for our grandparents, parents and neighbour; or threatening enemies/the stranger with oblivion?*

> 'And if anyone's name was not written in the book of life, he was thrown into the lake of fire.'
>
> Revelation 20:15

Muriel

I enter from the outside. (It's getting colder outside.) Then descend through poor, dirty light, down grey cement stairs to the basement where we play bingo. It's only twenty-five minutes to, and already Muriel has limped down from her small, shared room to secure her seat. Just a black plastic chair. One of a bunch jammed around a quivering fold-up card table.

'Muriel's chair' is always the closest one to the door. I guess she feels safer, less trapped, knowing there's a quick exit available. Not that the others – the other residents of the Valley Lodge Rest Home – persecute or tease her so much. They do somewhat. Muriel wants, needs to be among people, but at the same time they terrify her. I've felt like Muriel. It's a vicious circle. Bingo can be a vicious circle.

God – it must be exhausting to be always glancing out of the wrinkled corners of your tired eyes for a predator to pounce. And spooking at the most innocent remarks, harmless gestures. Muriel sitting at bingo like a small thirsty animal at a watering hole, trying to remain inconspicuous, attempting to hide its wounds and tender spots.

'Can I have a cigarette?' Muriel asks me, in her sore, gravelly voice, the second I enter the basement.

'Hullo, Muriel, how are you?'

'Can I have a cigarette?' demanding as a child.

I smile apologetically. 'I'm sorry, Muriel, I don't smoke.'

I see the veins in her hands straining against thin flesh – as if her soul beneath it all were beaten and swelling. Jagged, cracked fingernails. Gaunt fingers stained yellow, and burned in spots.

It can't all be clumsiness, accidental. And I wonder what on earth has generated such intense self-hatred. What in her past had she done, or left undone? What had someone else done, undone?

Though maybe somewhere, far below, Muriel whispers: *Well, at least I am feeling something.* Singeing her fingers an ironic form of self-preservation. A desperate method by which to keep herself oriented to a torturous but somehow still sacred reality. A desperate, stubborn unwillingness to surrender life. Like jabbing oneself with a pin to keep from closing heavy eyelids.

And feeling something – anything – is a great accomplishment here at the Valley Lodge. God, so many – numbed, catatonic, given the symbolic lobotomy. Day after day, dumped underneath the television bolted up on the dirty wall, blazing on the horizon like a one o'clock sun. As if at a seaside resort, they bask in its rays, burning their brains, scorching their vision.

So many poor paling bastards – their dead lives like lifeless stars revolving around a sun radiating a light, blue as ice.

Muriel should remember by now I don't smoke. Still, she begs me for a cigarette every week when I descend to the basement. I shake my fat finger at her, scolding, trying to look comical, desperately, trying … 'Um, and I don't appreciate you always encouraging me to start, young lady!'

I am attempting to make the atmosphere lighter. A little joke, harmless teasing I had thought. But my routine falls flat. Muriel is clearly not amused – she'd surely pelt me with rotten fruit if she had it handy. She has her face though. Muriel throws me a sour look. I see her sharp hip bones jutting beneath her stretchy brown, Salvation Army-bin slacks. Muriel's body like shrivelled fruit.

I ask Muriel how her week was. But she won't talk to me now – glares down at the floor. I should have known better really, to rub it in. To flaunt and dance my youth.

I should have known better. One must be very careful handling the people of the basement. They've little skin left to protect themselves, and the last layers are always the most sensitive and raw. The slightest scratch will make them bleed. The lightest touch will make them cry. The people of the basement – with blood and tears running so close to the surface.

Kenny

On the other side of the basement, alone at another fold-up table, is, of course, Ken – Kenny. His mouth gaping so wide it must hurt him.

Kenny leads the simple life. Mornings – 6:30am – they gently rouse him from the refuge of sleep; there is (they hope) just a short stopover in the toilet; and then, an aide on each flabby arm, he is escorted down to the basement and dropped into that chair: his throne where he is eating.

I have never seen him anywhere different. I'd bet my life that he'll be sitting in that chair, at that table, every day now for the rest of his slowly waning life.

Kenny had an accident long ago which left him with limited control of his limbs. It may take him hours to finish eating. I don't know why no one here helps him. I guess they feel they are preserving his independence, that it's therapeutic in some way. I think they just want to keep him occupied. Keep him out of their hair. Give him food to play with. Maybe they feel they do enough changing him. And though Kenny is lucid, he cannot speak. Kenny can only protest with his paling, blue eyes; and with grunts that sound like they take some effort.

Kenny wears a tattered baseball cap (a team he pitched for ages ago), a red-checkered shirt, and blue jean overalls with red-white-and-blue suspenders. He looks like he belongs in a little wooden rowboat in the middle of a small clear northern lake, enjoying retirement, spending his days fishing. The lures festooning his cap tell me he probably had such dreams once. He does fish his days away now, but not for trout or salmon (unless it comes from a can). Kenny fishes all day for the food on his paper plate. And when he does manage to catch a school of peas, or to spear a small, wriggling strip of cold meat, his hand trembles so much that the prize, many times, falls off the hook. Gets away.

Food – all colours – sprinkled on the black fold-up table and dirty floor: green peas; yellow kernels of canned corn; orange carrot – like a rainbow had shattered and fallen, steadily, in broken bits around Kenny.

He motions to me when I enter the slowly cracking basement. Like a friendly gorilla with mashed potatoes smeared on its face. He has the same build – short and stocky; sagging breasts; potbellied; moist, monkey lips. He is so convincing that it's almost as if he believed himself to be some lower primate. It would be easy here where all you do is eat, sleep and defecate.

Once, when I played the piano that wastes away in a corner of the fusty basement like a resident in the corner of a room, its voice becoming distorted, slurred as if it too were on medication, Kenny was happy.

Christ, I thought as I chorded – wonderful! I felt useful. Other residents were enjoying the music too. The radio in the basement had been broken for months.

I could hear Kenny behind me, jerking up and down in his squeaking seat in rhythm to the jaunty counterpoint. And throughout quiet, contemplative movements – swaying, cooing, moaning, groaning …

'Music charms the savage beast,' one of the aides joked, loudly thumbing a worn pack of playing cards. She smiled, proud of her wit. Strange how a smile can be so full of malice, I thought.

'It's after eight o'clock, time to pack it up,' she commanded in the middle of the finale, the most emotional part of the piece, as if she were afraid of emotion, then walked away to the back room, cracking sunflower seeds between her dull, yellow teeth.

Muriel has forgotten about me by now. That I'm here, that I exist at all probably. Muriel trapped in herself again: staring down at the cigarette-scarred linoleum.

Peter sits in a far corner, crossing and uncrossing his legs. Tangling, and untangling, himself. Peter usually stays in his room. Once in a while he descends to our bingo games to watch from his distant corner, peeking over the edge of the book he's nestled in (usually something like *The Stranger* or Sartre's *No Exit*); sometimes he writes in his journal. Tonight he does neither, and his white, long-fingered hands flutter and flit, like rare birds that can't settle. I wave, and he waves back.

I enter the 'Nurses' room', a back room off the basement. (None of the workers here are actually nurses.) The room is claustrophobic, not conducive to mental health. And I think that maybe someone is trying to drive the help here over the edge too. After all, there are always spaces to fill.

A couch with a faded floral pattern fills the back wall. It looks harmless enough. But when you try to find comfort in it, you are unexpectedly prodded by springs and sharp coils which hide like snakes underneath the worn-thin fabric.

One of the aides lounges languidly upon it, immune to its stings, cracking and eating sunflower seeds. With careless ceremony she spits out the shells, frequently overshooting an overflowing garbage pail planted just in front of her. Wet husks glisten in glaring fluorescent light on a grimy, once-white carpet. And as I watch her carelessness, I remember the night I played my music for Kenny and how she cracked and ate seeds then.

Tonight she looks more surly than usual, as if the salt stinging her thin chapped lips was also burning into the chancre of her heart.

On a little table crushed into a corner, someone from another shift has left behind a half-eaten apple. It's well-oxidised; dead brown.

And I wonder, is it the pay, tiredness, the weight of personal problems, ignorance, complacency, boredom …?

The little table's all knocked and beaten, so that countless coats of paint can be distinguished; like raw layers of personality chiselled and chipped away.

I hang my coat and scarf up in a locker. There's a notice up that informs me that I MUST SECURE ALL ARTICLES IMMEDIATELY UPON ENTERING THE INSTITUTION. THE VALLEY LODGE REST HOME CANNOT BE HELD RESPONSIBLE FOR LOST OR STOLEN PERSONAL ITEMS … No one here would steal my heavy coat anyway. Hardly any of the residents ever go out. Into the sunlight. Into the moonlight. Into the world. Out of themselves.

I escape the back room and, back out in the basement, meet up with Sarah and Heather.

Sarah is the inspired soul who came in off the street and initiated bingo in the basement at the Valley Lodge, every Wednesday evening from 6:00pm to 8:00pm. She suggested to her friend Heather that it might be good for her to come along too; I came on my own, having seen Sarah's posting up at the Volunteer Bureau.

Though my apartment's across town, Sarah usually gives me a lift home after bingo, and Heather, too. On the way we talk about the friends we've left behind in the basement; or they ask me how university's going; or, lounging in the backseat of the Toyota, I listen to the two of them talk about their teenage daughters and sons. About which boyfriend or girlfriend they don't trust and wish their son or daughter would stop seeing; about whether or not they're using birth control …

Occasionally the three of us go out to a folk club downtown for a couple draft beers. It was there that Sarah told me about her ex-husband, Larry, who became an alcoholic; and how his touch grew repulsive to her, and how, at one time, she would sleep all day.

It was at the folk club, while a guitarist strummed quietly, simply, sadly, that Heather confided that she was trying to leave her husband, too. And I realised then, watching the two old friends with their arms around each other, giving support to one another and to the singer's chorus, how important Sarah was to Heather; and something more about what their work in the basement was about.

Maggie

'Maggie, you've got your teeth!'

Maggie stands in the basement and smiles, modelling them for us. 'Madonna, eat your heart out,' she says, and laughs in her husky, earthy way.

It's quite a contrast: the false perfection of the new, white-white teeth against the brown, wrinkled background of her crooked, beaten face.

It only took a year. 'Wait for your cheque.' 'Wait for your teeth.' Maggie has learned patience. (Like everybody here, she's had to.) She knows it takes a long, long time for anything to trickle down to a basement in a valley. Maggie accepts she is decaying, knows parts waste away – genitals, minds. Having no teeth is a trial, but after so many trials and losses – abusive men, dead-end jobs, poor housing and rich landlords, psychiatrists and social workers, breast cancer; a best friend who lost all hope; a good friend who was murdered – you learn to endure, and to live with little things like having no teeth.

'You really look great, Mags,' I say.

'Well, thank you, dear, but they're just a plug in a leak, you know. The body dies, the soul is eternal, as they say. But at least I can chew now – no more soup and mush,' she says, and smiles brightly again.

'Alleluia,' I answer, and stop and gaze at her ... But it's not her new white-white teeth I'm struck by – although I'm very happy she finally has them – it's her old laughing eyes – and the light that has never left her. The beautiful, strong light that no one has been able to blacken, or rob, or put out, or take away – that no force can kill. The miraculous, amazing light she has, somehow, never lost faith in.

Maggie invites Sarah, Heather and me out for fish and chips after bingo – to celebrate Walter's birthday and her new teeth.

Sarah's deep handbag

'Can I have a cigarette? …'

Sarah reaches deep in her flowery cloth handbag, and rummages around … Then – like a magician pulling something miraculous out of a hat – suddenly reveals a pack of Camels; cellophane catches the fluorescent lights and glitters – Muriel's old eyes wide as a child's. Sarah unwinds the wrapping and holds out … a long, clean white cigarette … Not a thin roll-up. Not a crushed butt picked up off the street.

'Here, dear.' Muriel snatches it.

We talk amongst ourselves, and out of the corner of my eye, I watch Muriel, the cigarette quavering in her cracked lips. And I remember suddenly that Sarah doesn't smoke (she quit after leaving Larry).

It would have been so easy to grant happiness. The small joy of a cigarette, monumental.

Muriel leans back in her chair. She smokes, not furiously and anxiously, but slowly, puffing with pleasure, stick legs crossed. She looks at peace, maybe for the night, maybe less. Peace fleeting as a cigarette …

Peter's journal

'H-H-H-Hell-Hell-Hell-o, S-S-S-Sarah … I-I-I r-r-r-ran out too, c-c-c-could I-I-I bum-bum-bum a smoke too, p-lease?'

Peter stands looking down at the floor – his stuttering like the sound of an airplane that can't get up off the ground. He wasn't born with a stutter. One night he told me that his father used to beat him with a bicycle chain.

'Of course, Peter, here you go … And are you playing bingo tonight? We'd love to have you come sit in.'

'I-I-I d-d-d-on't know m-m-maybe. Thanks, Sarah' – walking

directly back to his distant corner. 'Think I'll just watch a-gain.'

Peter is not much older than myself, his face written over with lines. Sometimes the two of us sit and talk together in his corner, about books and music mostly. Occasionally he shows me his journal.

One evening, during bingo, he copied down a passage that I'd told him I especially liked, and gave it to me to keep. He told me that if I ever wrote my own book, I had his permission to include it. So, with Peter's permission, I share it here:

… A big deal – not knowing what the hell to do with your free hands. You fidget fingers and twiddle thumbs. It's like you've actually been forced to hold time there in your hands and you're fumbling with it. And you don't have a goddamn clue how to handle it and feel so inadequate. At least with a smoke you rid yourself of the responsibility for a while.

A cigarette kills time. (Kills me too!) But without something to kill the time the ticking can drive you crazy – crazier. Ha! Each tiny tick, each tiny tock like a drop of water falling on your tired head. Like the Chinese water torture. It can drive you crazy – you'll crack.

Without something to kill the time it all becomes just too obvious. You're reminded that when you were young you prayed for more time and planned how you'd use it, how you'd become more complete. How you'd 'become'. Time was the sacrament. Time, the holy water. Now you're less complete. And you realise you shouldn't have waited for it to come at all, because when it comes – if it comes at all – it always comes too late – to mock – like when you're rotting away in a rest home. And you realise you should have demanded it when you were young – right then and there – demanded payment right then and there – went and got it – tore it out of their fat fists without so much as a thank you. Now, you're old – you're old. And thinking back to when you weren't – to when you were young – to the intensity you felt – when you were young – and to how you'd become more complete – to all the plans you made – when you were young – it all seems, from this distance – lies – obvious lies – something you failed to act on – had no intention of acting on – just a way to get you through to now – to now: the first time you've looked yourself full in the face – well, not really, there were other times – will be other times – but you'll never change – you haven't the strength – the faith – the strength and faith to break entrenched dirty habits – you'll always find ways to deny your youth is soiled – you'll always find ways to deny your age has no wisdom – no wisdom – except in these painful, clear moments – when you admit you're a liar – when you feel like a coward – when you feel you've failed – when you feel the worst you can – when you feel dirty and you think and you think and you think and you think – you couldn't possibly be scrubbed clean – not in a million years – not in a million births.

So, what the fuck do you do in the painful, clear moments when your life seems a parody – is a parody – when you look yourself full in the face? You have to go out – get away from yourself (if possible) – or go out to the library – or to the corner – buy something – a magazine – and thumbing through it – it's like you're suddenly knocked over – pounced upon by a gigantic wave – 'Oh God!' you scream – under your breath. And drowning, you look around the store – at everyone – on the shore – calmly buying – and you think you're alone – but you don't realise: everyone's screaming and drowning – maybe once a day – that beautiful, confident blonde there paying for the milk – last night – alone – screaming drowning – and that man there – paying for the cigarettes – like you – and you come up for air – and buy too – and go back to the rest home. Rest home? – tell me – what have you ever done? – what need do you have of 'rest'? There – it's not the earned rest – the rest that feels good – that refreshes. There it's the rest of the dead. The Valley Lodge Rest Home – where they 'rest in peace' – Ha! – that basement – below ground – like a fucking tomb. But you go back anyway – and read all about the happy plastic people over last night's dinner heated up – maybe later you'll masturbate – what the hell can you do – in the painful clear moments? – you'll find more and more ways to deny – and forget – while Life is being aware of each moment – you'll find more and more ways to forget – to deny – you're constantly fleeing (like a criminal) from life.

Quit fleeing – it's your only hope.
Quit denying – it's your only hope.
Quit denying you're sinning – it's your only hope.
Quit denying you're lying – it's your only hope.
Quit denying you're denying – it's your only hope.
Quit lying – you're denying.
Quit denying – you're lying.
Quit lying – you're dying –
quit fleeing – start being –
quit fleeing – start seeing –
start seeing – start being –
God! – start being –
God! – start seeing –
God!

God, forgive me – grant me grace
I've been stuttering my life away …

Elizabeth

Few residents in the Valley Lodge keep track of the days. Either they are unable to – lost in a fog of heavy drugs – or, since the days are all the same, they don't bother.

Elizabeth has an amazing and inexhaustible wardrobe and makes a point of dressing up extravagantly. She sometimes changes as often as four times a day! And standing, smiling, in a long, flowing, golden gown; a floppy hat – both too big for the short old woman who looks like a little girl trying on her mother's outfits – long, white gloves;

bright-red lipstick; costume pearls; dangling earrings in the shapes of moons and fishes, she explains proudly: 'I dress this way, darling, because the days are all the same. And if the dirty old days won't change then, by Jesus, I will!'

Through the long afternoons she dances. In the dirty, fold-up dining room. To a music only she can hear. All around her gather the ghosts of this place – the suicides, the walking dead …

I've danced with her on occasion during bingo, over the rhythm of numbers being called, and she's taught me new steps. Taught me how to open up and hear the music. Taught me how to dance no matter what …

Each week, we must mount the grey cement stairs to scour the four floors of the Valley Lodge for many of our bingo in the basement regulars.

The corridor walls on all floors are a dirty yellow. Like the colour of Muriel's fingers or of rotten teeth.

Halfway up the dirty yellow walls hang paintings. Crooked clichés: a ship tossed in a storm, then a bowl of fruit. A ship tossed in a storm; then a bowl of apples, oranges and bananas. A ship, a bowl of fruit … ad infinitum. Like a bad dream. The heap probably bought at some cheap department store's clearance sale. It drives me crazy as I search for our regulars – it can't help them.

The hallways smell of toilets. On each floor are two washrooms where everyone's smell mingles.

One evening Heather peeked into a dark washroom, switched on the naked light and shrieked, seeing a dirty grey mouse darting back down its hole – the hairy drain of the rusty chipped bathtub.

Lester

I wonder what in hell is happening behind all the closed doors of the home. I want to knock, my trembing hand on a cold doorknob, but my arm falls impotently to my side. There is enough out in the open to terrify those of us from the outside. And when doors are shut here people can't really be pulled out anyway. It's as if they had fallen into a void in the earth and it had closed upon them. Locked them inside.

A few doors along the hallway are open. 'Hello, Lester. Coming down for bingo?'

I peek through the fissure into his chamber.

Lester is usually a very jovial fellow, with bright eyes and laugh; streaming, magical white hair, and a snowy, bristling beard he twists or drags his little hands comb-like through, peering down at his bingo card, contemplating strategies. He looks like he just stepped out of a folktale: short and merry as a leprechaun; jolly dance-walking, barely touching the earth, as if he were about to jump up and click his heels – or fly away.

But tonight we see that Lester has crashed. The wreckage sprawled on his unmade bed.

'… Lester, coming down for bingo?' we try again.

He doesn't answer – tucks himself into a ball. We say nothing more, realising we're poking and prodding. Lester won't be playing tonight. We must abandon him. And it's hard leaving Lester behind on his unmade bed, darkness, like rock gathering speed downhill, falling upon him. It's hard leaving Lester to the avalanche of night.

I look in a last time through the cleft. A breeze and bird songs seep in through his rotten, cracked window. I can smell the sudden spring; and I wonder if the change has caused the sudden change in him. Curtains flap sadly, fitfully, like the wings of an exhausted bird.

'Is there anything we can do?' I whisper to Sarah.

'Shut the door.' Lester's words muffled in the soiled sheets, smothered as if someone were shovelling dirt on him. I shut the door. The earth closes upon him. On the joyless leprechaun wondering where in hell he has lost his pot of gold.

The professor

Another room we pass on our rounds – can't miss – is the old professor's.

The professor was once a doctor of psychology, his diplomas hanging crooked and upside down on his cracked wall. He lectured at the university in town; ten years ago or so, someone said. I don't know what happened to the professor. Some people carry so much weight around with them that it is inevitable they collapse under it all.

His room looks like a bomb was dropped on it. It's hard to give a full picture: broken chairs and tables; a cracked full-length mirror reflecting a thousand different perspectives; food welded on paper plates; heaps of clothes like dirty mountain ranges; a hundred books of different sizes and subjects scattered north, south, east, west, in different regions of the landscape, in various stages of being read and not read; thin patches of topsoil upon the wooden floor; and faded orange-brown pine needles sprinkled, like ashes, over the entire expanse of the room, from the three small, dead evergreen trees the professor, nevertheless, stubbornly, faithfully replants from flower pot to flower pot: like a scientist pouring from test tube to test tube; like an alchemist searching for the mythical mystical reaction.

It's as if, after the Bomb was dropped, the professor believed himself to be the only survivor left on earth, and to be charged with the enormous, profound responsibility of salvaging through the dross and reordering the world.

And the earth was without form and void.

He sits cross-legged like a monk – he's shaved his head – in the midst of the rubble of his darkened room, amongst the remains of the silent world – and moves his trembling hand over the landscape.

And the Spirit of God moved upon the face of the waters.

Then, he suddenly acts. He picks up this (an umbrella, a chicken bone) and places it there, there, at a precise angle, within degrees, as if it must be positioned just so in order to receive certain cosmic vibrations and signals which run up through it and into the receptive professor. He lifts up that (a pine cone, a running shoe) and sets it down way over there ... no, way over here. On the way the professor trips over a teapot, upsetting the order of the world ... The professor scratches his chin. The professor scratches his head. He squats down beside an empty bookcase, which stands like a central monolith, and sits and contemplates its tall, smooth back, as he waits to become pregnant with inspiration again ...

There was a period of about three weeks when we never saw the professor at the home. Then, one evening, he appeared in the basement for bingo! He'd never come down before; had never spoken to us, or recognised us, I thought. I was surprised.

It was good to see him. 'Hello ...' I said.

'I won't win,' he answered, 'but I came down to be around people.'

Later, we discovered he'd been in the hospital for the three weeks we hadn't seen him. One night at the home he ate a tube of Super glue. Maybe the despair of not being able to reorder the world had finally got to him; or it was a last, desperate act. But glue is not strong enough to hold the world, or even yourself, together, from falling into ragged pieces. One never knows, it might have just been an accident: maybe the professor thought it was a tube of toothpaste, or God knows what. The professor was rushed to hospital and pumped out; then shocked into sense with a dose of ECT.

Now, John plays bingo with us every week. Getting five in a row, or even four corners, is a much simpler order.

The staff said, 'Let there be light', and there was light. They pulled open his heavy drapes and let the face of the real world in; blitzed and gutted his bedroom. (Since then, John has developed a neatness fetish. He's become obsessive. His room is immaculate. Maybe he fears having to fight Chaos again.)

Everyone tells him that he's doing so much better. I say it too.

But it's sad, in a way, seeing the professor's room like everyone else's. Sad, in a way, seeing the humbled professor meekly following the established order, waiting in line at medication times, hair grown back, combed neat. The professor: just another cowed old man playing bingo and winning soda pop. The professor, John, ageing now.

Doreen

Doreen is on the landing, just come in from an evening walk. One of a handful here who, once in a blue moon, do go outside.

Last week I saw Doreen on a sedate side street nearby, hugging a broken old tree. Another evening I watched her petting an invisible animal, an imaginary friend.

Doreen, just inside the heavy door, looking down ashamedly. The cool breeze has made her cheeks ruddy. Has made her look healthier than she really is.

'Hello,' I say, about to pass her on the landing and descend the stairs back down to the basement. 'How was your walk?'

'I don't do anything right I don't do anything right I don't do anything I try and I try and I try and I try nobody likes what I do nobody likes it nobody likes what I do I try and try but nobody loves me I try nobody loves me no one loves I don't do anything right ...'

Doreen's coat is frayed. Doreen's hair is frayed. Nerves too. Doreen frayed from the inside out. She has stopped flagellating herself and is waiting for me. She wants to cry. But won't cry unless I give her permission. Unless I give her a hug.

I feel awkward. And I hate myself for feeling this way. For the thought that I can slip by her and escape, effortlessly, down the stairs without making a scene.

I touch her, cautiously, one hand on her padded shoulder. And she feels it: my timid touch through her heavy coat, woollen sweater, faded shirt. And sobs. She wants to cry. Needs to cry. She is waiting for me still. I haven't given enough. My soul, which should be flowing out to others, is dammed up; diverted – severed from the sea. It's flow choking, coughing. I can't act. Have I been lying to myself all this time? Am I full of ideals or full of shit?

Or, is it that I'm afraid? Afraid of rejection? Or afraid of emotion? I've been weaned by a society that is uncomfortable with emotion, that worships reason.

That may be but, in the end, I am responsible.

She is still waiting, cheeks paling.

Resolutely I put my arms round her, and she cries.

My eyes water, as I feel the coldness in me melting. The emotion I was protecting myself from sweeping away the shit from my dammed, severed soul.

I tell her: 'It will be all right.' It sounds trite. It *is* trite. She should slap my face for telling her something like that. And: 'I understand.' I don't understand. Not really. Only a little. She should slap the other cheek. But Doreen spares me. She is very forgiving of people from the outside.

Through her thin, quaking body, wrapped in a thick, ragged bandage of clothes, run only occasional tremors now. 'I'm going down to the basement, Doreen. Why don't you come and play bingo?'

It is a pathetic suggestion, but all I can propose. Yet she assures me she will; after collecting herself.

The prayer wheel

There is a feverish anticipation in the air. It is six o'clock and, like a prayer wheel, the bingo wheel is turning.

Without extending my arm fully, I can reach up and touch the smoke-stained, water-marked basement ceiling. It seems to creep a little lower each week.

Everyone puffs incessantly, and soon Sarah is calling numbers through a haze which hangs thickening into a fog, unable to escape. The two small windows at ground level are stuck somehow. Patients ever inhaling, exhaling stale air. Air polluted with not only the poisonous gases of cancer-sticks, but the past. Air clouded with sighs, with old sorrows ... Air stagnant as a swamp, teeming with anxieties that multiply and infect. Patients trapped in the trapped past. I want to break a window with my fist.

Because the windows can't be prised open, in the summertime we sweat, suffocating. While in the winter, because of a heating system we can't control, we shiver. Fragile old women wear their sweaters – sometimes coats and gloves. Life never seems to settle into an equilibrium here; there are always extremes.

I mark Kenny's card for him, as he is not coordinated enough to keep up to our furious pace, and is still eating anyway, struggling away. I circulate, helping any others who are having difficulties, for whatever reasons, but who want to be – must be – away from their merciless, cornering selves for an evening. Some even go so far as to feign they're having trouble to get my attention. So that I'll sit beside them for a moment.

Doreen has just come down. She wants me to choose her bingo card. 'It'll be lucky,' she says confidently. I do. She loses. That's all right though. Doreen is used to losing. In a child's sing-song voice, she teases me: 'You made me loo-oose, you picked my car-ard.' I admit it. 'But thanks anyway,' she says.

She wants me to pick another. I close my eyes and choose her another 'lucky card', praying to all the patron saints of bingo that she'll win.

Everyone wants cream soda. The establishment grants us four or five cans of soda pop; these are our bingo prizes. Everyone wants cream soda. After all, it has a palm tree on a beach on the front. So, because the two or three cans usually don't hold out for more than the first few games, it is important to come out fighting. Otherwise, one must be content with Orange Crush or No Name Ginger Ale, or, at 7:00pm – the midway point of bingo in the basement when there is a pause in the action and the aides trundle in a cart of refreshments – with powdered juice in little throwaway cups.

Snack time

Minutes prior to the aides parading in the feast, residents who don't play bingo descend from their little rooms, knowing the customary time for 'treats'. The braver among them come in and sit with us for a moment; maybe even play a game or two. Others peek in from doorways, or pace the narrow hallway outside.

We stop the game and they enter, quickly but cautiously, glancing from side to side, advancing directly to the refreshment cart where they stand in line for cherry Kool-Aid and chocolate chip cookies.

Self-consciously they drink.

Heather, careful not to make any movements that might startle, points out to Sarah and me two or three we rarely see in the basement. And suddenly it feels ridiculous – like we're naturalists viewing frightened deer at a watering hole. And then I feel anger. A hot flood of anger. Watching a man. A man timidly snatch a hard cookie out of a nurse's gloved hand, and then scurry out of the basement …

At the back of the line stands young David. Young David is far away. Awareness has eked from his once-bright blue eyes, leaving them dull-pale. As if some force has slowly wrung them out.

We ask him questions which must travel a great distance before reaching him. And if David does finally send a reply, it is an incomplete, jumbled communication. As if the words, having to trudge and crawl to us from such a great distance, get separated, lose each other, or die on the way.

At the head of the line stands 'The Hawk'.

'Did you know I can see auras?' The Hawk once asked Heather.

'Pardon? … No, no I didn't … So, what are auras exactly?'

'I can see colours.'

'Colours?'

'Yes – I can see colours. Colours around people. A force enveloping them … You're red,' he told her, moving in close, thrusting himself into her personal space.

'So … does that mean anything?' asked Heather with a gulp.

'Well, it might, and it might not,' The Hawk replied. 'It depends – and you've got holes.'

'Holes?!'

'Yes, holes in your aura. Your energy's leaking. I can see through your aura.'

'Hey – now that sounds obscene,' interposed Sarah, trying to lighten the atmosphere. 'Careful he doesn't try to look up your aura, Heather!' …

When he left, Heather admitted: 'He frightens me.'

'Don't worry about him, Heather. He just wants a little attention. To feel special in some way.'

'Or maybe it's difficult to believe this is all there is to life,' I said, with a sweeping glance around the dirty, grey basement. 'There's got to be more to *this* life than meets the eye.'

'Yes … And then again, maybe he actually sees something,' suggested Sarah.

'I don't have holes,' said Heather.

We've all got holes, I thought.

Meeting Sybil one day outside of Starbucks

'Hey, where's Sybil?' I asked everyone in the middle of a game, after juice and cookie break one Wednesday. 'I haven't seen her around in a while, she in hospital or something?'

'Sybil? … Sybil moved out,' called Maggie between numbers. 'Bingo!'

The story was that some mysterious old woman – someone who had had some connection with Sybil's dead father and had known Sybil as a child – had suddenly got in contact with Sybil, and asked her if she'd like to come move in with her. She had a big old house out in Hampton Park. A mansion. The lady's husband had died of cancer and she was living all alone.

I ran into Sybil one day outside of Starbucks. I told her I'd treat her to a coffee – I owed her for keeping me supplied evenings when I was calling bingo, I said. Sybil laughed.

The Starbucks used to be 'Duke's' – Duke's 24 Hour Coffee Shop;

but Duke's closed (and then re-opened as a chain store) when the neighbourhood was being gentrified. Sybil and her friends were cleared out: property developers and young professionals moved in.

I held open the heavy door for Sybil and she tripped in.

Sybil – a glaring outcast: six-foot-four-inches-tall; long, thin legs quavering in steel braces. Sybil – like a crumbling, condemned building. The manager studied us. Previous times, he'd taken me for a university student, doing some reading, taking notes.

Sybil clumped and shuffled inside, armoured in size twelve and a half shoes. Heavy, black, men's shoes – tragic as Frankenstein's. She fumbled her cane. I picked it up before she began the epic task of bending her stiff, creaking body. She dropped it again. I felt everyone looking at us from over their newspapers and froth.

I asked Sybil what she fancied. She looked up at the board.

'I just want a coffee,' she said.

'Same here,' I told the manager, and picked up some sugars. I remembered Sybil liked four sugars.

Sybil smelled of urine. One side effect of being on so many prescription drugs was a problem controlling her bladder; another was being thirsty all the time. (Another was the shakes. Another was double vision …)

'Is this for inside, or out?' the manager asked, in a whiffy manner.

At the table, Sybil sat shifting her cramped legs, excitedly telling me about her new home and the lonely old woman who had taken her in, and who was going through such a difficult transition in her late life.

'I can manage the dishes for her and help her with the cooking, and we talk … It's good to feel useful again … She says to call her 'mother' – and *I* was a good mother too, ya know!' Sybil protested suddenly. 'No matter what they said in court!' …

We sipped our coffees slowly.

Sybil also told me that Ken (not Kenny 'the fisherman') had moved out of the basement, too. Ken, though 38, looks about 60. In the good weather he sleeps on the streets, and in the winter resorts to a shelter or the rest home. Ken crashed our bingo games from time to time, hurling himself through the basement, flinging little old ladies out of their chairs and asking them to dance, telling dirty jokes. At our Christmas party, he slipped his harmonica (his 'harp') from the front pocket of his grimy denim jacket and performed excerpts from the 1st movement of Beethoven's 5th symphony! Then, some downright dirty twelve-bar blues. And then (as an encore) 'All I Want For Christmas Is My Two Front Teeth', as he'd had those kicked out in a fight down on the fruit market.

With his short hair standing straight up on end, Ken hammered out sixties' rock 'n' roll on the decaying piano, rasping songs of his heyday.

While I supported him with some harmony vocals, Ken howled:

How does it feel? …
How does it feel?!
To be on your own …
With no direction home …
Like a complete unknown …
Like a rolling stone!!

'Ken's goin' out West,' Sybil told me.
'Way out there? … To Vancouver?'
'Ya, he joined up with some church or something.' She grinned. 'The Church of the, of the … what was it? He's changed his name to Ezekiel – The Church of the Universe – that's it! And they're all going out West to pick magic mushrooms … Did you know I picked tobacco for thirty years? That was before all this happened to me, before I walked into the plough. And those bastards – they wouldn't give me my pension. Not 'til the social worker I had and I took 'em to court. Never got all of it though … But at least now that I'm outta that home, I can keep the little I *do* get for myself … and,' Sybil smiled, 'for mother.'

Sybil explained that the rest home had had her monthly cheque endorsed to them and had kept her on an allowance of twenty-five bucks a week. 'And you know you can't go anywheres on that!'

'Listen,' Sybil advised me very seriously, 'if you're goin' into a new home – make sure you get someone you trust to check it out first, eh, before you move in.' (I'd mentioned to Sybil earlier in our conversation that I was going into another home, but she had misunderstood.)

'You're still young, and still together – but no matter how sane you are goin' into some of them places, you're bound to come out nutty in the end. Be careful, and get someone you trust,' she counselled me tenderly.

Sybil had seen me at the rest home on Wednesday evenings playing bingo. I was familiar to her but she had forgotten, maybe never realised, that I was a volunteer, not a fellow resident. When I'd mentioned I was going into another home, I'd meant that Sarah, Heather and I had been asked by Community Mental Health to go out into the community and to convert other post-psychiatric rest homes – to spread the good news and salvation of bingo.

Milling around, the manager had overheard our entire conversation, and for a moment I writhed in embarrassment. And I hated myself for my reaction to him. For almost interrupting Sybil and saying, loud enough for him to hear: 'Oh, no, no, Sybil, you've got it all wrong. No, no, I'm a volunteer, remember? I have my own apartment. I'm a respectable student, a promising young man, a part of society, blah, blah, blah ...' But I kicked myself in the ass.

Sybil and I finished our coffees in silence. Then she pulled herself up and shuffled slowly, painfully to the door; her leg braces clanked like fetters.

Out on the street she gave me a hug goodbye. Then she launched out into the flow of humanity and time and disappeared.

I wandered down to the public library, where I hoped to find some sanctuary in a book. I sat in a study carol, but couldn't help noticing all the ripped and tattered people from the streets hiding in corners, drooping and snoring in soft chairs behind yesterday's news.

Mable and Ha

… Ha laughing. And beatific old Mable Green smiling … I pour the ginger ale I've won for her. 'You like ginger ale, don't you, Mable? …… Mable just smiling, smiling …

'Ah, pour it on her head,' a fellow resident sneers, and laughs.

I caress Mable's bony shoulder and she smiles up at me. If I kicked her she'd smile.

Ha came from Hong Kong to attend university. But he never completed his degree, or returned home. I don't know what happened to Ha. They say he started laughing and couldn't stop, got stuck. Like Mable, his smile is perpetual. One number called on his bingo card enough to generate in him a feeling of bliss. Mable and Ha sit together, beaming like holy idiots, the happiest souls in the basement.

Walter and Maggie

Doreen won twice tonight!: 'I won once for you; once for me,' she says. We both smile.

Walter hadn't won once. And that was enough to make him believe he was a total loser in life. But Maggie, reading this in his fallen face, hands him the last prize of the night.

Walter and Maggie are an item here. The sweethearts of the basement. Teased, though good-naturedly.

They sit beside each other; and the simple beauty of the battered, old couple holding hands like young lovers moves me. One evening I watched them comb each other's thin hair.

Outside of the home, Walter and Maggie have joined a social club called 'Good Company'. There they play cards, do crafts, bake, or go on day trips to places like Niagara Falls. Once they saw a play. It was Shakespeare. The club pulls them out of the basement three times a week.

And on Thursdays, when the weather's good, they take their

sandwiches and go over to the park to feed the pigeons around the fountain.

Walter is the gentleman of the basement. Courteous, chivalrous. At the Christmas party, in contrast to Ken's ragged version of 'Like A Rolling Stone', Walter crooned old standards, full 'from the diaphragm'. I accompanied him, chording compositions like 'Moon River' and 'My Funny Valentine' on the decomposing piano.

'Wow! Nice voice, Walter!'

'As a young man I sang lead tenor in the church choir,' he said proudly.

Maggie looked smitten.

From Resurrection to Apocalypse

The nurse who crushes seeds hurriedly rolls in the cart, cleared of hard cookies and Kool-Aid, and covered now in phalanxes of inch-high plastic cups, full and half-full of assorted candy-coloured pills.

She visits certain residents to make sure they've swallowed … the rebellious, the comatose; checks under thrush-coated tongues. She wants some peace tonight. 'Nurse', I think, wondering what she's nursing.

Curious how with some people, their pain and misery sours into spite. While others are somehow able to transmute their darkness into light, into compassion and empathy. These are the wise souls who realise that under all our many sorrows lies one suffering. And I am silent and still for a moment, and pray that my troubled soul one day comes to understand the one suffering under all our many sorrows.

Sarah, Heather and I pack up. It's after eight o'clock and time to go. We fold chairs, collect abandoned bingo cards, and say our goodbyes. Goodbyes to some through a thickening fog of medication. And they wave back vaguely to the friends they are quickly losing sight of onshore.

'See you all next week!'

A week – anything could happen here in a week. Anything from Resurrection to Apocalypse.

Outside (Into the night)

I tell Sarah I want to walk home tonight. From the slowly cracking basement, I climb the murky, grey cement stairs. Opening the heavy door, I am back outside in the night. Out of the underworld and in the dark world again. There's a smell of snow in the air. Clean and sharp as a knife.

Plastic bags and scraps of newspaper tumble across roads. And stepping cautiously into the deserted suburban street, I suddenly feel like an outlaw intruding upon a law-abiding town in the old West, and fear the gunning down.

Like boulders in the moonlight – the heaps of garbage stacked and waiting on the fringes of each manicured lawn. I walk quickly, contemplating this throwaway society – there a TV, a bed, a box of books; a family of chairs put out on the sidewalk; a ripped-open bag of half-eaten food spilling out on to the street … The most arrogantly wasteful in history. And it is not only things we discard when they become 'useless'; it is people. People we bury below ground in basements.

I walk away thinking about my English degree. (Perhaps Sybil saw something in Starbucks. Was not mistaken when she, like an elder, counselled me as one of her tribe.)

As I'm crossing the road a car speeds up, charging at me with its horn down, forcing me to dart across. I am almost struck down! Suddenly, it doesn't look like an automobile to me at all – but like a nightmare monster: a creature of flesh and metal intermingling. Like man and machine have finally bred. Multiple heads poking out of its lurching shell. 'Get a job!' one drunk, flailing head roars at me.

And as it screeches away into the night, kicking up dust like a big dumb beast, I stop and catch my breath, thinking about the access to movement here, outside. Cars and trains and planes and space capsules. And my friends back in the basement where the windows are at ground level and do not open. Where the sagging, smoke-stained, water-marked ceiling seems to be falling, creeping a little lower each week. Where the front door is heavy. My friends in the basement – below ground like a fucking tomb. As if society is quietly sequestering all the useless people, plotting a mass grave. A pogrom. A holocaust. Conspiring to silently slide a stone slab across the exit one Wednesday evening when I am in there calling out bingo numbers.

Gazing up, the moon. Full and crazy. And I feel as if I've stepped from the basement into just another ward of a labyrinthine madhouse. Here, fat residents – swollen full of another kind of sickness – a respectable sickness.

I drag myself into a park, and flop down under a big old tree. Tuck myself up into a ball ……

In my nose there's a spicy, damp smell of wet leaves, rotting into earth; I could just lie here and let the snow cover me.

After a while, I sit up, and lean back against the tree.

Yet there have been moments, I admit. When I've felt so profoundly connected. The beauty. The joy. In the forest up on the moonlit mountain – running between the great pillars of trees. Energy surging. Spirit resonating in my soul. And suddenly all seemed right with the world.

And sometimes, playing piano. Improvising. Music giving an order to the chaos. Again, in touch with the Spirit. Letting it flow through me. I live for those moments.

I think of Doreen, and turn and hug the tree; and, for a moment, it hugs me back. With its great, deep heart …

I run my hands through the cold wet grass. Somewhere far away a bird is calling, and another answering …

I touch the bark of the great tree … take a deep breath … then lift myself up and begin to walk slowly, tentatively into the night again …

FUNNY THESE THINGS COME TO YOU

Introduction

For a time, I worked in a beautiful old three-storied house in a little country town in North America. The house had been converted into a rest home for the elderly, and I worked there as a sort of nurse's aide/ cook/cleaner/landscaper/snow-shoveller ... As a sort of jack-of-all-trades (master of none). The residents were more independent than folk in institutional settings. Runa, Wendell, Vera, Katherine, Molly and Elmer all had their own bedroom in the home.

'Funny These Things Come to You' is a sequence of pieces about memory. 'What's left of us after memory is gone?' someone once asked. I guess only God can answer that.

> *Surely goodness and mercy shall follow me all the days of my life; and I shall dwell in the house of the Lord for ever.*
>
> Psalm 23:6

Eating a kiwi fruit noisily

Runa asks for a kiwi fruit. (She's allergic to bananas.) When she was a little girl her parents would give her bananas to eat and she would go into seizures. 'They didn't know about allergies in those days. They thought that bananas were good for me, that it was just nerves.'

I pass her the fruit basket; ask her how old she is now, ninety-three?

'Yes, I think so,' she says.

There's something beautiful and moving about a ninety-three-year-old woman eating a kiwi fruit, noisily. Everyone else is sitting around the table eating dry silence.

'I guess you must have seen a lot of changes,' I say.

'Oh yes …When I was nursing my second husband he looked up at me and asked: "Will it be long?" I didn't know what to tell him. I couldn't say.'

'Did he … live very long?'

'I really don't know. Things are getting vague, you know … My first husband died and left me with four children.'

'That must have been hard.'

'Oh, if they told you what you'd have to go through in life,' says Runa. But laughs, kiwi juice trailing down her old veined hand, shining on her chin.

Wendell's first farm

Wendell comes down at eleven o'clock every day to watch *The Price Is Right* and *Wheel of Fortune*, and for his hot water and milk. Sometimes hot water and blackstrap molasses, he stirs slow, talking slow. About how he used to give molasses to his cows. He'd mix it in water and sprinkle it onto their hay. It came in a big wooden barrel then. (A little clear plastic tub now.) They liked it better then, their hay. Ate more of it – and it was good for them too.

'Sweeter?'

'Oh,' he laughs, 'they liked it all right. Oh, they liked it,' stirring, smiling to himself.

We sit at the kitchen table and talk about the weather; about farming ... Wendell worked on his father's farm until he was almost thirty years old: His father wouldn't help him to start his own farm – told him he'd never make it on his own – that he'd lose all the money he had. He wanted Wendell to work on *his* farm only.

Finally Wendell found someone who had some faith in him, a man he was working for on the side, who covered his first mortgage.

So, he bought his first farm. Then another.

His first farm was best. 'Oh, that was a good farm.'

'Big?'

'Oh, a good farm. Good heavens! – a hundred and thirty acres. Fields stretching ...... half a mile. And that was stony fields out there,' says Wendell. 'So that was rare. One hundred and thirty acres of good land.' Wendell tells me that he's got a picture of it somewhere. And of a stone fence he made.

'With the Indian?'

Wendell smiles. 'So, you know a stone boat?' he asks.

'For clearing stones?'

'Yep.'

About the size of the kitchen table, Wendell says. With runners on the bottom. Two pieces of wood put together. A good farmer would clear his field some each year, add to the stone fence. He built one with an Indian one year. 'He wasn't fast, but he knew how to build a stone fence!'

Wendell explains that you build it so that the cattle can't see over to the other side, and so then won't jump over. 'So ... that's how you build a stone fence,' he says.

'Well, thank you.'

He's got a picture of it (somewhere in his room scattered with boxes, clothes, envelopes, jumbled memories ...).

He paid all his mortgages back, he tells me.

Wendell laughs: 'In those days the cows would stand and graze by the side of the roadway. They couldn't do that now.'

'They'd get hit by tourists,' I reply.

'Yes, that's right, that's right!'

The Price Is Right is on in the living room. Bob Barker in Hollywood. He looks like he's had some plastic surgery. Wendell's face like a furrowed field.

A Spring Tooth Arrow

Wendell and I get talking again before lunch. I'm heating up the leftover soup, setting out soda crackers, bread, Libby's Fruit Cocktail … Wendell tells me that he worked on a farm around here for a time – and once harvested 60 acres of grain in two weeks!

You didn't have a plough then, but a cultivator. And couldn't sit down.

'Could you stand on the back going along at least?'

He laughs: 'Nowhere to stand.'

'So you had to walk all the way?'

'Yup.'

He had one with three horses.

Then they invented one with four horses. He can't recall the name. He gazes off, wandering in the field of memory.

'A Spring Tooth Arrow,' he digs up suddenly, and smiles.

He thought that if four horses could walk twenty miles pulling, he could walk twenty behind it! Wendell hobbles across the kitchen floor to get the bagged milk from the refrigerator. At some point in his life, Wendell lost the toes of his right foot. I'm not sure how: the war, frostbite, diabetes, the Spring Tooth Arrow …? Over his foot, he wears a knitted, red-white-and-green bootie.

'So, did you like tractors and that when they came along?' I'm getting the bowls and plates out.

'Well, yes! Of course. Why sure.' He laughs. 'Why sure … But they were good horses. Good horses. Well, they had to be.'

'Yes – walking all that way.'

'Animals are smart,' says Wendell. 'Smarter than people. They know, they know' …

Persimmons

I'm in cleaning Vera's bedroom. Dusting, vacuuming …

'So, is that a tomato?' I ask her. There's an orange, and two pieces of fruit that look like tomatoes sitting on her bedside table.

'You know what that is?'

'Um … pomegranate?'

'Persimmons.'

'Oh, persimmons.'

Her daughter left them for her, Vera tells me. 'Ever taste one?' she asks.

'I don't think so. No.'

'You have to wait until they're ripe, so it's sweet, you know … The last one I had – it was good – but at the end it tasted like powder in my mouth.'

Vera tells me that she ate persimmons all the time when she was a little girl living in California. 'Gosh, all sorts of fruit. Coming out of your ears!'

'I bet.'

There was a fruit stand across the boulevard from school. 'They called them boulevards. They were highways really, you know, but they called them boo-levards.'

'Boo-levards.'

'There was an old man with a cart across the boo-levard, and he'd come with his cart, you know, and the school kids would buy fruit for their lunch. 5 cents a piece.'

'Wow.'

'Oh, and sooo good.'

'I bet.' (There's a bruised banana left behind on Vera's lunch tray, eyeing me.) …

Vera tells me she got a call from her sister-in-law this morning: she puts her hand up and makes a yap-yapping sign. 'Gossip, eh. She goes to the shoe store. And she goes to the hairdresser. For gossip, eh – like shopping. She had a friend once who'd always come and see her. And she'd leave, and right away she'd talk about her. I wonder what she says about *me*. "Why don't you ever call me?" she says. Then I call and she never calls back. So I said to myself: OK, I'll wait for *her* to call. She said: "Oh, I'll call you when I get moved." So, good. She can call me when she gets moved.' Vera rolls her eyes. 'Keeps you on the phone for hours, eh. I was hoping you'd come in with the vacuum so I could say I had to get off.'

'I was going to – but then I heard you on the phone!'

'Oh God, you should have! You should have …… Yeah, that's a persimmon.'

Vera reaches for it. 'My mother used to work in a fruit plant too.'

The persimmon is a warm colour; Vera's hand is cold blue.

'Really?'

'Fruit down the conveyor, you know. Then you wrap it in paper and put it in a box.'

Vera worked at the plant, too, for a summer.

'You must start seeing oranges and lemons everywhere.'

'Yeah, you do. It was all right though – I liked it.'

Vera even had fruit trees growing in her backyard, she tells me. 'Orange and lemon trees.'

'In your backyard. Wow.'

'Yeah. Just walk out in the sun and pick one – just like that.'

Vera had a friend in the same grade all the way through; and after school they'd go and pick lemons. 'You cut it in half, eh, then sprinkle salt on and eat it. Mmmm, so good.'

Then there was a bully in the neighbourhood who one day stole their salt cellar.

'"You're not gettin' any salt!" she said. She made us eat it without salt.' Vera makes a sour face. 'It was the only time she did it. She left us alone after that. I don't know why.'

Vera says she thinks about her friend sometimes. Wonders what happened to her; if she's still alive. 'She'd be about the same age.'

'Maybe she thinks of you, too, sometimes,' I say.

'Oh well,' Vera sighs. 'Maybe.' …

I continue vacuuming her room …

'That quilt … That quilt there is a hundred years old. Would you believe it? Well, not all of it. But some pieces.' Vera explains that her mother didn't have time left to sew it, after collecting all the pieces, so gave them to her, and then she gave them to *her* daughter and *she* finished it. 'She's clever.'

'She the one who brought the persimmons?'

'Yeah. Does embroidery, ceramics. You know, anything like that. She made that poodle there. Knits. Like this … chain stitch. And that's not easy. I could do plain stitching but that's it. I don't have the patience.'

I empty the wastepaper basket; gather up her lunch tray.

Vera tells me she had a visit from her grandson the other day.

'Oh yeah?!'

'He's cute … I don't see him much.' Vera explains that her daughter works long hours: 'In a carpet factory. A lot of heavy work. She doesn't like it, but what can you do? It's work.'

'Yeah. Yeah.'

Her husband has a truck and works part-time. 'Doing odd jobs and that, I guess.' Vera has four daughters.

'Four?'

'Oh, I don't mind being a loner,' she says. 'I'm used to it. I like it … And you can't worry about them,' Vera tells me. 'I've learned *that* the hard way. Oh, sometimes you still do. You have to keep it aside though.'

She's got herself to worry about, she says, and reaches for her oxygen mask.

Vera leans back in her lazy-z-boy and breathes in deeply; closes her baggy eyes. The oxygen machine hums like a hive of bees.

Before I leave her room, Vera hands me a warm red persimmon to take and try. 'Wait till it's ripe though, else it's too sour. It's OK, I've got two.'

Katherine's plants

I peek in on Katherine; ask her how she's doing today.

She sits in darkness; doesn't seem to know.

'How are your plants doing?'

There's an amaryllis, and a poinsettia in a basket with a big red bow.

She answers with a shrug and limp wave of her hand. 'Oh, they're just, you know … surviving. They're not … flourishing or anything.'

On her dresser stands a gilt-framed photograph of her and her late husband, young and smiling with children and books gathered round them. In the picture, Katherine's hair is done up elegantly.

Katherine's plants haven't been watered in ages, the soil all hard and cracked. I grab the empty water glass on her night table.

'Don't worry, Katherine,' I say, all sunny and breezy (and hopeful and young), 'we'll have those thirsty leaves smilin' again soon.' She smiles, weakly.

Back with the water, I suggest that we tie back her curtains and 'let the face of the world in'. 'Come on, it's a nice bright day outside, Katherine. See?' I hate the way my voice lilts, thinly.

Katherine tells me she doesn't care any more – wishes she could just die.

I water her dusty plants, while she blinks and winces against the light. Finally, I leave her alone.

I stand outside in the hall for a moment and listen to her breathe.

'Close the door,' she sighs.

James the Second

I'm in cleaning Molly's room. She's in bed, snuggled up with the cats. There are two cats at the home: a calico and a patched black-and-white with a longish face.

Setting up the vacuum I ask Molly if she had any animals when she was a little girl.

'No … I guess my father always thought they'd get run over or something.'

But she always had them when *she* had kids, she tells me. 'At the house there's a whole graveyard in back!'

Molly tells me about the time her son ran in with his dog who had got run over. '"Mom, mom, he dead, he dead, isn't he?" "Yes, lad," I said. "But you have lots of good memories of him." He could have got run over himself – the way he ran out there on the road.'

The cats look up at me with sleepy half-shut eyes; they keep kneading and nudging Molly.

They had a funeral for her son's dog in the backyard.

'I'm just glad they didn't ask me to sing! I woulda woke him up. Brought him back from the dead. Now watch your claws, don't get excited.'

Molly tells me that the cats come in every morning at 6:30 and wake her up.

I laugh.

'You laugh – well, did you see what they did to my curtains?' Molly scolds them; waves a stiff finger.

The cats purr.

I think of the cats' nice purr and the awful roar of my vacuum cleaner.

'I shouldn't waste your time with stories of my dogs and cats.'

'It's a lot more interesting than cleaning, Molly.'

'We had another dog named Lassie. Like the TV programme, you know; and I swear you couldn't tell the difference.'

Molly remembers how Lassie 2 kept taking the cat's dish and

dropping it behind the water heater. 'No, no, now that was James, James the Second. Jealousy, eh.

'So, one day I got the kids off to school and hid and saw him do it. I talked to him: "Now, don't be jealous," I said. "There's no need, we love you too." And after that he didn't!'

The morning sun's streaming in and the calico is soaking it up; the black-and-white reaching for it with his paws.

'They're still babies in lots of ways,' says Molly.

I vacuum up; and find a pill Molly dropped.

'Were you playing with that?' she asks the black-and-white. 'I was looking for that.'

I move Molly's wheelchair. Her walker.

'If you're vacuuming …… I was just saying: if you're vacuuming one day and you ever see a great big grey blob lying on the floor. That'd be me. I just *have* to use my walker more, or these legs will never work.'

Birds and trees and a long, long road

'That sure is a beautiful painting,' says Runa.

We're all sitting around the dining room table again – Runa, Molly, Katherine, Wendell and Elmer – eating lunch: soup and sandwiches. Munching silence: dry soda crackers.

'There's so much depth. It's *amazing* what people can do,' says Runa with appreciation and perspective.

'Um hmm,' I answer.

She used to paint at one time, she remembers.

I ask her what kind of things she liked to paint and she says she can't recall. 'Still lifes? … When you get old, things go blank. And when you don't have a family around to remind you.'

'It's frustrating forgetting,' I say, stupidly.

'More or less,' answers Runa, and reaches for a ripe kiwi fruit. She's allergic to bananas. When she was a little girl her parents would give her bananas because they thought they were good for her, and she would go into seizures. They didn't know about allergies in those days.

'Some things you never forget. When I was nursing my second husband he looked up at me and asked: "Will it be long?" I couldn't say. When he died I straightened his limbs and waited for the undertaker.'

I say: 'That's something you never *could* forget. It's always with you. I guess it must take a long time to get over.'

'I choose not to think about it,' interposes Katherine from across the table. 'So are you on duty *all* day?' she asks me.

'I guess you never really do get over it ... It's amazing what people can do. When we were young we had a maid, you know. And one day we were walking along the road, and I was trying to show her the beauty in nature: the trees, the flowers, the grass, the sky ... And all she kept saying was, "Um hmm. Um hmm". I coulda kicked her behind. But, I guess it takes all kinds to make the world go round.'

'Or none,' croaks Elmer from the head of the table, gnawing on a bread crust.

Runa makes a slurping sound. Wipes kiwi juice off her chin.

Molly says: 'There's beauty in everything, if you want to see it.' And, as if on cue, the calico takes a sudden tear up the living room drapes. Molly laughs. 'They're just like little gymnasts.'

'Should get *that* one fixed,' Elmer mutters; while Runa sits savouring the painting: birds and trees and a long, long road.

Upstairs, Katherine has everything from her dresser drawers dumped out onto her unmade bed.

'I'm throwing it all away,' she tells me.

I sit down on the edge of the bed and try to help her sort through it all, try to show her there are some nice things there.

'Nice things. See, look here, Katherine.'

Letters, cards from people. Scented soaps from Christmas time.

'Remember? Here, smell ...'

Combs, ribbons, hairpins. 'You need those, Katherine. For your nice hair.' Photographs. 'Nice photographs.'

'I'm just getting to the point where I can't – it's too … Oh, I don't know!' she stamps suddenly, two different pairs of slippers on.

'Where does it all come from?!' she demands, strands of her beautiful long, thick white hair lashing out. 'Where?!'

'From people … people who care about you.'

'Care about me?' Like she doesn't believe it, remember.

Katherine forgets more and more. About what happened yesterday. About how her husband and eldest daughter died in a car crash three years ago.

A snow-white veil hangs across her wintery face.

'Come on, Katherine,' I coax, 'let me help you with your hair. Let's do it up nice. OK?'

She looks terrified.

'Come sit, Katherine,' I tell her, as she stands, holding an empty drawer.

Three breeds are smart

Wendell comes downstairs for *The Price Is Right*.

He says hullo to the cats, sitting keeping me company. 'They're good cats … good cats,' he says, scratching them under their chins so that they purr.

He used to keep barn cats, he tells me. Fed them good. Good on all the cow's milk they wanted. 'Well, not *all* they wanted,' he says. 'Twice a day … Animals are smart.'

He had a friend once who had had a hip operation: 'And his dog would follow him to the washroom at night – to make sure he was all right. He *knew* something,' says Wendell.

Stirring his hot water and milk, Wendell tells me that he had a dog once, a dog that was three breeds. 'Terrier, hound …' He can't remember the third breed. Shrugs. 'Three breeds are smart.'

He slept with her out in the barn when he first got her. In the hayloft. He got her from her mother at six weeks old, which is the right time. 'But gosh, they get some lonesome. So lonesome ... She was good dog. A good dog.'

He built a kennel for her. Then he looked out the window one day and she was playing with another dog – she'd got loose somehow; then looked out again and she was gone.

'Oh no. So did you get her back?'

He went looking for her all up and down the hill. Finally, she was on the other side of the street as he was coming home.

'I didn't say one word. Not *one* word.'

She went and lay down and Wendell didn't talk to her until the next day. 'She knew. I didn't say a word. Not *one* word.'

Then he was going to play shuffleboard one day. Behind the cenotaph. 'I said to her: "Now, don't you follow me," and kept looking back. Then I got to the shuffleboard and she was there already, waiting for me. Laughing, wagging her tail.'

Wendell smiles. They had a little room in back, so he put her in there until he finished his game. 'There was a short, ill-tempered fellow. I said: "She was looking for a bank and made a deposit – in the room." "She better not!" he said. "She better not!" And she would *never* do that. Never. Never in the house. She just wouldn't. No sir ... She was a good dog. A good dog.'

Someone on *The Price Is Right* has just won a brand new Deluxe-Dishwasher-Toaster-Oven-Microwave-Trip-To-Paradise-In-A-Box.

Wendell stays in the kitchen and tells me about his relatives, who one winter once drove a horse and cutter right across Lake Simcoe.

'Right across?'

'Right across.'

Wendell once did it from across the bay here. 'The horse, he didn't want to go. No sir. He kept turning and turning to go back. We got halfway across before he liked the idea. He could see the other side then ... But, that horse *knew*. He knew he was on ice and wasn't supposed to be ... Terrier, hound ...'

When he first got her from her mother he slept with her out in the hayloft. 'They get so lonesome. So lonesome.'

'Like people.'

'Even more – more so.'

His neighbour had a dog, and he made her sleep on a cement floor in the barn. 'In wintertime.' Wendell shakes his head. As a Christmas gift, Wendell gave her a rug to sleep on.

'You feed the cats chicken bones? Wendell asks me.

'No way!'

'Well, he did. Fed his dog chicken bones and that's what happened. She choked on one and died … I was with her. You couldn't do a thing. Couldn't do a thing … Just be with her … Animals, animals are smarter than people.'

I've got news for you

I'm tidying and straightening the living room.

'Hello, Runa, and how are you this afternoon?'

'Oh, pretty good. Not bad for an old lady … It's all right if you have your health,' she tells me, digging deep into the dish of peppermints … 'Once I was so sick – once I was so sick I had tubercular peritonitis. And people came to visit. "You think I'm going somewhere, that this is it, huh? I've got news for you – I've got four children to raise" … I have two left. And two gone now.'

Runa tells me how they used to go to church together and sit in the back pew, two on each side of her.

'I remember two of them had to sing a song one time and the young one got the giggles. Oh boy, was the other one mad. But it was just nerves, you know … Oh, I've been through the mill I guess. When I was nursing my second husband he looked up at me and asked, "Will it be long?" I didn't know what to say. When he died I straightened his limbs, put a diaper on him and waited for the undertaker. Oh, if they told you what you'd have to go through in life,' says Runa, and gazes out the living room window … 'Good Lord,' she laughs, after a silence, 'if all this snow melts at once we're gonna have floods!'

Looking at the moon with Wendell

'Elmer, Elmer! Come see the moon!'

Wendell and Elmer have known each other since they were youngsters. They listen to the obituaries together on Wendell's little radio, mornings after *The Price Is Right*.

Elmer says: 'I'm not seein' no moon. Haven't seen no moon for thirty years, and I'm not seein' no moon now.'

I come to look.

Wendell tells me it's a dry moon.

'A dry moon?'

Wendell explains that when the moon's like this:

🌙

it holds water. And the other way:

🌙

it's a wet moon.

'See? Cause water would spill out … I believe it.'

He planted by it, he says, the moon. Although he'd plant more by when he had the time, he admits, and laughs.

We gaze out the kitchen window: country dark – the icy world glinting like magic.

'Gosh, it's sooo orange.'

'Yep.'

A good joke

I'm in the dining room clearing away the wieners and beans, bread, soda crackers, silence …

'Did you hear about that fellow? That fellow who retired?' Wendell asks Elmer with a smirk.

Elmer has trouble hearing.

'Did you hear about that fellow?! Who retired?!' I repeat back to him.

'Fellow who retired?'

'He worked in his wife's honey dew shop.'

Elmer looks at me, the sides of his mouth going; he looks pained.

'Worked at his wife's honey dew shop.'

'Honey dew?'

'Honey dew *shop*! … And yeah, it was "Honey, do this" and "Honey, do that".' Wendell laughs.

'Yeah, women are always like that,' Elmer (who hasn't seen the moon in over thirty years) says.

Wendell says he heard the joke on the radio. He likes to listen in the mornings. Likes to start his day off with a good joke. 'With a laugh.'

The funnies, *The Price Is Right*, the obituaries, *Wheel of Fortune* …

Vera's second husband

I'm in cleaning Vera's room again: feather-dusting, vacuuming; scrubbing out her sink with lemon-scented cleanser … We get chatting:

About how she used to live down on Murray Street. That was her first house. 'Way back when.'

No water, no electricity. 'That was how it was then, eh.'

She had to go out and chop and carry wood – up until the time she was about to have her first child: her husband was away working on the ships.

'He never sent any money … He sent *one* cheque.'

She stayed in the house alone until her father came and told her that she had to go on welfare. 'I was down to one loaf of bread – I always wanted to be independent, to take care of *myself* … My father came and said: "We're taking you back with us – *and don't you argue.*"'

Then Vera's husband came back.

'"So, why aren't you home to welcome your husband?" My father told him to get out: "And she won't be back until you get it together and get a job!" And … he never did.'

Vera left her daughter with her parents and went away to find work.

'To Montreal?'

'Yes, that's right.'

She worked as a maid for a Jewish family. 'And when I met my second husband I told him: "I have a daughter and she'll always be with us wherever we go." And she was … Then I had one child after another: Then I had Ellen, and Jane, and Sandy. Then Bob.'

'Not bad for an old lady.'

'No, not bad at all.'

Treasure chest

I ask Runa if she's ever seen so much snow! She's gazing out the dining room window at the street, and at the big flakes, swirling wildly again.

She laughs and says that if all the snow melts at once we're going to have floods!

'When you get old you see things change a lot,' she tells me.

'I bet … I guess when you were a little girl you travelled by horse and buggy. Horse and cutter?'

'Oh yes, a car was a rare thing … When we were children we had a horse that a drunkard once owned. And it would get cold from sitting, you know, when the man was in the tavern or whatever – so that when you got in the buggy to start him up he'd go off lickety-split. Just rare up – like this. My brother would get the giggles and I'd have to grab on to the reins … Oh, the things you remember. That stick with you. My father raced horses and I remember the tears just coming down his face, hoping his horse would win. And I had a sister, younger than me, and she would go into the stalls, you know, and those horses they wouldn't move a muscle. They wouldn't move a muscle.'

'They knew,' says Wendell, between slurps of soup.

'Oh yes, they sensed she was gentle.'

Molly says that probably her best, most fun day was when she was a young girl and her aunt sent her family a box from India, and they kept taking different things out of it. 'All afternoon long, it seemed like. Gosh – such beautiful things … It wasn't really a box exactly,' says Molly. 'It was more a … Oh, what would you call it?'

'A crate like?'

'Sort of. But more. Oh God, isn't that stupid? I can't even think of the word. Oh, shut up, Molly.'

Runa's father was in charge of the livery stable, and one day a man was looking for him for something.

'I told him that my father had just gone down the road: "He's a short man with a crooked nose," I said – I never lived *that* one down.'

'And did he find him?'

'I don't remember.'

'The box was just *full* of things. Chest! Chest. Like treasure chest. Oh gosh, wonderful things – like the most beautiful, colourful cloth, and plates, and strange brass statues, and the smell of spice – I was just fascinated. For a young girl, that was the most fun day of my life.'

Molly pours Runa and herself another cup of tea from the china pot. Her father lived in India too, Molly tells us, and used to have stories about him riding elephants. '"Didn't they get mad, dad?" we used to ask him. "Didn't they get mad at you, riding on their backs through the hot jungle all day?" He said no, that they were used to it.'

'Oh, a lot of changes.'

'I'll say.'

'I guess we've been through the mill.'

'Some days it feels like it.'

'When I was nursing my second husband he looked up and asked, "Will it be long?" I couldn't answer.'

'It's hard.'

'When he died I straightened his limbs, put a diaper on him and waited for the undertaker.'

Wendell's last dog

Wendell's had a bad night. The staff member I'm relieving thinks he's had a stroke maybe. The ambulance is on its way.

Wendell's upstairs, sitting on his commode – still telling jokes:

'Do you know why Santa has such a nice garden … You don't? Cause he loves to hoe, hoe, hoe.'

I smile. 'Do you need a hand to stand up now, Wendell?'

'Well … I could … I always say: "Need a hand?" Well, I could use a foot.'

The paramedics come, and ask Wendell to squeeze their fingers. 'Can you squeeze my fingers, Wendell?'

'Well … I don't want to hurt you.'

The young one gets down on one knee and asks Wendell how he's feeling. Wendell answers that he's feeling a little strange. Weak. Down his side.

'Which side? This side here?'

'I don't really know … Tingly.' He laughs.

The paramedics leave us alone so that Wendell can finish. '… Did I ever tell you about my last dog?' he asks … 'Part terrier, part hound, part … collie.'

'Oh, collie! Collie.'

'Three breeds. Three breeds are smart.'

'You slept with her in the barn. Up in the loft.'

'They get so lonesome. *So* lonesome.' …

Wendell says that he kept her until she couldn't jump up into the truck any more. 'She just couldn't,' he cries.

Then he took her to the vets. 'She knew. She knew …'

Burying his last dog was the hardest thing he ever did in his life. 'The hardest thing …'

The paramedics knock on the door: 'Finished, Wendell?'

As they bear Wendell out on a stretcher, I think of the things he has loved in his life: his first farm, his last dog …

The good, not the bad

Vera never went to high school. She was supposed to.

'I was scared.'

She was tall, well-built.

'I didn't know anything! I was still playing with dolls up until then – if you can believe it.'

Vera remembers giving her dolls away before she moved, to a girl she knew. It rained, and she looked out the window and saw her favourite doll: 'Lying there in the rain. God, I cried.'

When she arrived here from California her mother told her: 'Go out with your cousins.'

She didn't want to go. They drove out into the country. '*What is this*? I thought.'

They stopped and parked. 'In the rubble seat, you know?'

A boy tried to kiss her and she moved away. '"Take me home!" I said … They thought I was fast, eh. From California.'

Then her brother's friend got into the house one day and got into the home-made beer under the bed. 'Boy, was I scared.'

The guy made a move on her and she cried. Her brother told them all to leave.

Vera tells me that she was kind of 'sucky' when she was a kid; and cried, too, every time her brother got blamed for things at school.

She remembers him drawing pictures of airplanes in the back of the class.

'Mrs Byng was the only one who could reach him. Funny what you remember. They say it's not good to remember, but I like to – the good, not the bad. And there were plenty – believe you me …

'Speaking of which … I got a call from my second husband the other day out of the blue. He's in a home. He's a nice guy, I just couldn't live with him in the end.

'My third husband. Now, that wasn't so good … He was always taking pills. Pills for this, pills for that. Then getting in his car and driving. "Look, you can't drive. You *can't* drive." Well …'

Vera reaches for her oxygen mask. She's got herself to worry about, she says.

All these years

'If you've got time, and you're not too busy,' says Molly.

'Gosh – from the chest your aunt sent from India?!'

'Beautiful, isn't it? I kept it all these years.'

'Wow …'

Molly sits in her wheelchair, in front of her dressing table, cradling a long, shimmery silk scarf – like a rainbow in her stiff grey hands.

(I've just been cleaning, and clutch a wad of wet rags.)

'Look, see all the work … all the tiny stitches all over.' She caresses it … 'Gosh, someone a long time ago, far away, did this. Probably they're dead now. My God …' She shakes her head.

Molly has carried it with her all these years. Brought it with her from the house she had to sell … to take out sometimes and touch. Hold.

She looks at it a moment longer. Then folds it up in tissue paper and sets it away in her drawer.

A skein

Wendell is back from the hospital: He had a 'mini-stroke', they said.

He sits in the kitchen, stirring his hot water and milk. Yesterday was his birthday. Someone sent him a nice bouquet of balloons.

'So, how old exactly?' I ask.

'I won't tell. But I'll tell you what year … I was born in 1907.'

'So, you're …… eighty-nine?'

'Yup.'

His brother was born in 1906.

'The one in Orillia?'

'He's locked in. He got out once. He got out once and it took a while. A while to catch him.' Wendell smiles, remembering. Remembering them chasing his brother all over town.

Wendell goes and sees him sometimes. On holidays.

'Does he … remember you all right?'

'Oh, he remembers *me*.'

Wendell sits and stirs.

He had a friend who was locked in once, too. The woman from the farm near him. He went to visit her one time and she wasn't doing very well.

'A fellow there, working there – a nurse I guess – said, "Why don't you do something together?" She had some wool there with her, for knitting … It was all tangled. So I helped her make a skein. A skein, you know it? It took a long time, all afternoon, and was hard work, hard work at first, but we finally got it all back into a ball. And, geez, she was happy. She could smile. I really did something. I really helped her that day!'

Wendell saw her in town just last week. 'She was going to a meeting at the Women's Institute when I met her.'

'That must be good to see.'

'Great to see … She had the farm next to me. And then her husband died, eh.'

'That the couple you helped with the mortgage that time?'

'They started out with one bag of seed grain, some farm implements. No cows even – you need a cow. For milk – you can always sell that.'

Wendell got them a couple cows, pigs.

'Farmers like to have some hens too. You can make some money. Not much, but some, a little.'

'Hard life. Hard work.'

'You clear the fields first. Make a stone boat. Size of this table. Square, with runners.'

A good farmer would clear his field some each year; add to the stone fence. Wendell built one with an Indian one summer.

'He wasn't fast – but he knew how to build a stone fence.'

A flower in the kitchen

'That's a beautiful flower –'

I'm in the kitchen, doing supper clean-up – wrapping leftovers in clingfilm, loading the dishwasher, scouring soup pots – running around, busy busy. One loud-red, tropical bloom trumpeting in the middle of a long, white winter. Right underneath my nose on the window ledge and I never once noticed it.

Runa says to look, see, other buds coming, too. I watch her old hands, moving gently, confidently amongst the flower's heart-shaped leaves, and feel blind and deaf as an old man. She bends down to breathe in its perfume, mixed with the dark rich scent of earth.

'When I was a girl, we had a maid and we'd walk along the road and I'd try to show her the beauty in nature – the flowers, the trees, the grass, the sky … And all she'd ever say was, "Um hmm. Um hmm". I coulda kicked her behind. And you wonder who her parents were, how they taught her to look at the world.'

'It's all there if you just open your eyes,' I say, 'nature, beauty, wonder …'

'Yes, it's really what makes life,' says Runa.

'If you can just pull away the veil,' I motion, but still feel it there.

'But I guess it takes all kinds to make the world,' Runa says.

'Um hmm. Yes,' I reply; and stand and gaze at the red bloom a moment longer. Then go back to scouring soup pots. I can hear Runa above the struggle, digging in the dish of peppermints: cool peppermint; ripe kiwi fruit; a graceful, defiant red blossom against the deep, dark, dead wintertime …

'That'd make a good painting,' I call. 'That flower.'

'Yes, it would,' says Runa. 'It sure would.'

Hairpins

'What 'cha doin', Katherine?' She sits in the living room with a box of hairpins in her lap. She keeps sticking hairpins in her hair.

'I'm putting hairpins in my hair,' she answers, irritated, like I'm stupid. 'If I keep on doing this … it will be all right,' she says.

'Oh,' I answer … and stand and watch her trying to keep herself together. Trying to keep time from unravelling and her life from falling apart.

Wendell's other neighbour

Wendell remembers his other neighbour – who never used a litter tray for manure. Wendell shakes his head, stirring. 'You know a litter tray? … Like a box, but with a round bottom.'

Instead, he made his wife and sister use a wheelbarrow: 'Up the plank with a wheelbarrow, pushing and carrying the manure.' Wendell shakes his head. 'A litter tray's easy. Just attach it on the chain and dump it – and it gets pretty slippery on the plank in wintertime.'

Wendell laughs. He remembers there was a guy out in Copper Kettle who used a wheelbarrow, and one time his feet slipped backwards, and his face fell forwards.

'Not too fun.'

'Nope.'

His neighbour was an auctioneer, too.

'He was always crowing … Crowing, bragging about how smart he was. He wasn't smart. Making his wife and sister use a wheelbarrow in winter … He cut Christmas trees. You know, for winter, make some extra money. He'd go off in the bush and start here and go there, and so end up at the hotel drinkin' with the boys. And then they put his picture in the paper. He used to keep sheep. A picture of him with a wolf he shot.' Wendell shakes his head: 'I always said they shoulda had a picture of his wife and sister using a wheelbarrow while he was drinking at the hotel.'

A tea party

Molly's up from her catnap, the cats on her bed, yawning and stretching awake with her. She missed lunch; so I go and make her a cheese-and-jam sandwich: one piece of bread folded over. The secret is not too much strawberry jam, but just enough to make it nice and moist. I tease Molly about her taste in sandwiches. I wonder if it's comfort food. Something her children liked and she made for them. Summer afternoons, long ago.

'I don't remember how I got on to them. Well, anyway, I'm coming out to see the world,' she says, and wheels out into the dining room in her housecoat. Molly keeps to her bedroom mostly. Calls it 'Siberia' out here. Today it feels more spring-like. The old house less draughty. A different, stronger, clearer light streaming in through the windows.

Outside, the snow's still all heaped up, a dirty brown colour.

Molly says it looks like a man out there, in a brown coat digging. 'That'd be me,' I tell her.

We chit-chat. She didn't get a lot of sleep last night. 'Do you sleep well at night?' she asks me.

I say usually, unless there's something on my mind.

'Are you a worrier? I am. I worry. I'm a worry wart.'

The kettle's singing, so I go make her a cuppa. Molly always likes her tea.

'God, it's so quiet. Like a morgue.'

'I know.' …

I sit with her while she eats her lunch.

Starving for some conversation, Molly asks me what my age is again.

I tell her that I'm thirty-four. She says that thirty-four is a good age.

I ask her what decade she thinks is best: 'Your 20s? 30s? 40s? … I hear your 40s.'

She says it all depends. 'I liked my thirties. Then again, I had my accident in my thirties.'

It happened during the war years, she tells me. It wasn't her fault. An old man was driving down the road from a garage and slammed into her car. He wasn't looking. Molly broke her spine and had to have an operation. Then another operation. She was in hospital for six months in total.

She was sitting sideways, she remembers, and could see him coming towards her. 'You couldn't do a thing. "Quick, give me, James", I told my brother John up front, and so he did. He didn't argue – just reacted. So I could just wrap him up in a blanket before it happened.'

When Molly came to, she was up at the steering wheel and her son was still all wrapped up in the blanket. 'Kicking and crying "Lemme out!" He only got a cut across his face – thank God – but he could have been killed!'

Molly's grown-up son, James, visits her every week. Brings her comforters, warm clothes, whatever she needs. Hostess chips and dip. (Comfort food, I vacuum up.)

She could have sued the man, says Molly. 'For everything he had, I guess, but I'm not that type.'

Sunlight falls on Molly's face and she closes her tired eyes a moment. Outside, icicles drip; thawed patches of snowy streets glisten.

'And we could have used the money then. But then I thought of the man, old and worrying about his farm.'

I nod. Molly winces.

A couple of mornings ago she fell out of bed. (She's been falling more lately.)

She tells me she's been getting shooting pains down her legs.

'Last night?'

'Like a knife keeps jabbing in … Oh well, just my arthritis,' she says.

She kisses and licks strawberry jam off her fingers. The tablecloth's stained with food, dappled with sun.

Molly asks me what my family background is again: 'Did I tell you that someone on my father's side made a history of our family that went all the way back to the 1500s?'

'The 1500s. Wow.'

'Columbus's time just about, I guess.'

'That's interesting.'

'Yes. It is.'

'So any important or notorious relatives?' I ask. 'Any outlaws?'

Molly laughs. She says no – but that she thinks that one of her relatives was a mayor of Edinburgh.

'Mayor of Edinburgh! That's something.'

She forgets just who now exactly.

'So, we're both Scots,' I say.

'Yes. I guess we are.'

'Do you like haggis?'

'Eeeee! No! … Well, actually, I've never really tried it. Have you?'

Katherine wanders down in her housecoat; she asks where she's supposed to be. 'There must be a way of knowing why, how …?' Her hair hangs in confusion.

'Come sit with us here, Katherine,' Molly invites warmly. 'Come have a cuppa.'

'Yes, come sit, Katherine.'

I try to keep the conversation flowing. I ask Katherine *her* family background.

Irish … she thinks.

'And have you seen your family lately, Katherine?' Molly asks.

'Yes, oh, I think so … I tell them not to bother too much. I'm all right. You know.'

'It's hard in the wintertime,' I answer, 'with the roads and that.'

Runa shuffles by on her way to the bathroom.

'So how are you today, Runa?!'

'Oh, not bad for an old lady.'

She joins us on her way back, and I go make a pot of tea in the good teapot. Bring back some ginger snaps and Dare chocolate chip cookies on a nice flowery plate.

'So, what's *your* family background, Runa?'

I explain that my family background is Scottish/Irish. And Katherine, her background was Irish –

'Pennsylvania Dutch. And I still remember it.'

'Really? That's interesting. Do you speak it?' asks Molly. 'Like swear words?'

Runa laughs. 'Oh, I don't know.'

'And do you know about your ancestors, Runa? Can you tell us about them?'

'I used to. Maybe I did at one time. Maybe I didn't. Things get vague, you know … Oh, thank you.'

'Danke,' I say.

'Yes – that's right.'

Wendell and Elmer come down from listening to the obituaries on Wendell's radio.

Wendell pulls up a chair.

Elmer stands, chewing the corner of his mouth. 'Doin' 'er in style today, eh,' he says. 'Umm hmm. Um hmm.' …

There's a silence. Then Molly asks me if I ever played hookey when I was young.

'Hockey?' says Elmer, planting himself.

'Hookey.'

'Oh, hookey … Hookey?'

'You tell me first.'

'Once …' And Molly tells us about the time her mother was out, and she and her friend stayed away from school for the afternoon and made candy at her house. She laughs: 'And it was so stiff you couldn't even get the spoon around.'

Then, all of a sudden, there was a knock on the door – and so they ran upstairs and hid in the bathroom.

'We thought it was the School Police, I guess.'

Molly sat on the toilet seat and stirred and stirred the candy. 'Well, the seat was down … We just stayed there. My friend tried to open the door a little, to see who it was.'

I look around at Katherine and Runa and Wendell and Elmer and they're all leaning in, listening. It's nice to be sitting around drinking tea together, telling stories. A tea party.

'Oh the things!' laughs Runa.

'We just stayed up there and ate candy all afternoon.'

'So, did you ever find out who it was at the door?'

'No. Never. We just sat up there eating candy. And gosh – were we sick after.'

Smiles all around.

'So, did you ever play hookey, Elmer?' I try.

'No.'

Wendell says: 'You couldn't wait to get away *from* home, eh, Elmer?'

Elmer doesn't answer; clears his throat of phlegm.

Molly asks Elmer how his family are doing these days. The two of them talk about where their relations are living now … Some folk they both know … Someone in Elmer's family who was killed in a house fire …

I refill everyone's cup. The conversation is suddenly stopped. Like a teabag across the spout.

'That tea looks like it could use a transfusion – I like to tease him.'
'Well, I won't say anything about your taste in sandwiches, Molly.'
'Well … Do you like garlic then?'
'I *love* garlic.'
'*Fresh* garlic.'
'Oh, garlic,' says Runa. 'Yes! I remember garlic.'
'Do you like garlic at all, Katherine?'
'Oh, yes, I think so. Yes.' …

Molly glances round the room.

She was listening to her radio the other night, she tells us:

'They were airing a programme about the Canadians who liberated the Netherlands during the Second World War. Now that must have been wonderful to see! I remember when it happened. I wish I had been there. It must have been such a feeling – such a feeling you'd never forget in your life.

'There was an American on the programme who made it sound like *they* were responsible. And it's not true. I was going to write in. But I can't write any more. "Great, Molly," I said to myself. "Write in and you can't even write any more. Oh, shut up, Molly."'

I ask if anyone remembers that song by Vera Lynn from the war years. And I start singing: 'Don't know where/Don't know when … But I know we'll meet again some sunny day …'

Molly joins in, then Runa and Wendell. We're all singing together for a moment. Even Elmer, moving his mouth.

At the end, Katherine starts to cry.

Molly takes her hand.

'Well, I don't know,' Katherine sobs …

'It's hard,' says Runa. 'Life's hard.'

'Maybe we shouldn't sing,' whispers Elmer.

'No, it's good,' says Wendell, 'it's good to sing.' …

Trying to change the subject, I ask Elmer if he thinks that spring's around the corner. 'The light's suddenly so much different today. All the ice melting. See?'

'Be six more weeks of winter anyway. At least. It's only February.'

'If all this snow melts at once we're gonna have floods!'

'Um hmm.'

We talk about the weather a little more, before the tea party breaks up, and everyone goes off to their separate rooms, selves.

The paperboy comes – everyone looks forward to the newspaper coming. Wendell picks it up from between the doors, and flips through for the funnies.

I stand and look out the living room window; at the icicles dripping. At the roof of the house across the street, steaming in the sun.

The Birdman

Wendell's off the telephone from speaking to his sister in the city (he folds his fragile phone list away and slips it back in his wallet).

His sister's boy was a schoolteacher. He tried it for a year but couldn't take it, Wendell tells me. So then he went to Mr Grocer – and now he's their top man in the Dairy department.

Wendell asks me if I know the Birdman.

'The who?'

'The Birdman: He was a schoolteacher too and couldn't take it.'

'Oh.'

And Wendell tells me the story of the Birdman; and how, one night, Wendell heard him talk to a bird.

'There was this bird, high up in the branches of a spruce tree. The Birdman was standing on a balcony. Did I say what kind of bird? … Owl, owl I guess. And he talked to it. It was over on the south side and he talked to it to come over to the north side tree. He called me over then, but I couldn't talk to it so … it flew away.'

The Birdman worked for the Ministry of Natural Resources and knew every trail in the woods. Like the back of his hand.

'So, did he actually … talk to it?'

'Why sure! You have to speak the language. You have to speak owl, I guess.'

Train to Winnipeg

I get talking to Wendell about what the town used to look like when *he* was young. He explains to me where the livery stable used to be. How the window place used to be a sugar beet factory.

I ask him what the grocery store was, and he says that that would be getting down near the stockyards. The fire hall was the train station. No trains run now, the tracks all torn up.

Wendell remembers how you could take a train to Winnipeg for fifteen dollars. One summer he and his cousin found a job working on a dairy farm out there. His cousin found a farm where he made ten dollars and Wendell found one making fifteen … No, *he* was making ten, his cousin was making fifteen. Wendell laughs: 5am wake-up – and he hadn't milked in months.

'God, your wrists! The muscles. Here … Two hours straight. God, sore.'

'Do you get calluses too?' I ask, naively.

'No, cow's teats are soft.'

After a year and a half they came back to nothing.

'Well, we left with nothing,' he shrugs.

He laughs – his cousin's car was a wreck. 'He didn't take care of it. After two years you have to change the oil! … Funny these things come to you. I don't remember two weeks ago but I can remember *these* things like yesterday.'

Wendell tells me about selling his '29 Chev; his father breeding horses; getting kicked by a horse …

'Where'd it kick you?' I ask.

'Out in a field,' Wendell answers.

She knows

I come in early Sunday morning to find Wendell lying on the living room rug. He doesn't want to get up. Can't. I don't want to move him. I call an ambulance; stay with him ……

The calico pads by and tilts her head, looking concerned; she sniffs something in the air and miaows. She knows.

Wendell's dentures are loose. I pray he doesn't start choking on them. The pendulum of the dining room clock keeps ticking – so loudly, slowly. I keep talking to Wendell, as his eyes flicker shut. The ambulance screams up finally.

Later, I hear that Wendell's had another stroke. He stays in hospital for a month; then moves into a nursing home in the city.

Womb of darkness

Up on my evening rounds, I check in on Runa.

It's going down to twenty below, the radio says, so I cover her with an extra blanket.

She smiles up at me, and I reach over and switch off her bedside lamp.

'Night, night, Runa,' I call, into the womb of darkness. 'God bless.'

WORKING THE DOOR

Introduction

For a number of years I worked in a shelter for homeless men in a Canadian city. When I wasn't working down in the kitchen or up on the showers, when I wasn't sitting out in the common room talking to the men and playing cribbage, I was 'working the door'. My job working the door was to greet and welcome the men coming in for the night and to assign beds, and also to be a sort of gatekeeper: anyone too drunk or high I'd have to stop at the inside door – or at the outside *door preferably – and send down to detox, which was just down the street; anyone too disturbed or violent, or who was 'barred', I'd have to gently turn away. Many times they wouldn't want to go and I'd have to call the police for back-up. I never got knifed or shot at working the door but did get hit a couple times. You never knew what was going to happen next working the door, who was going to ring the buzzer; it was intense and exciting for a time, but after a few years the work made me feel shell-shocked.*

I learned a lot about seeing 'Christ in the stranger's guise' while working the door. Other times it was hard to turn the other cheek.

Another part of working the door was giving out sandwiches (baloney, egg salad, cheese or peanut butter and jam). People would come to the shelter 24 hours a day – people whose money and groceries had run out, people starving for conversation and human contact. I had some good conversations at four in the morning, and some surreal ones too.

Working at the shelter, I learned that the reasons why people are homeless can often be very complicated and layered. But what was/is much harder to understand is our heartlessness as a society. Why are there still people starving in such a rich, bloated society? Why are there still people freezing to death in the dead of night? Why are there still people dying of loneliness?

Why are there still sisters and brothers lacking the basics of life? Food, shelter, love.

Then the king will say to those at his right hand, 'Come, you that are blessed by my Father, inherit the kingdom prepared for you from the foundation of the world; for I was hungry and you gave me food, I was thirsty and you gave me something to drink, I was a stranger and you welcomed me, I was naked and you gave me clothing, I was sick and you took care of me, I was in prison and you visited me.' Then the righteous will answer him, 'Lord, when was it that we saw you hungry and gave you food, or thirsty and gave you something to drink? And when was it that we saw you a stranger and welcomed you, or naked and gave you clothing? And when was it that we saw you sick or in prison and visited you?' And the king will answer them, 'Truly I tell you, just as you did it to one of the least of these who are members of my family, you did it to me.' Then he will say to those at his left hand, 'You that are accursed, depart from me into the eternal fire prepared for the devil and his angels; for I was hungry and you gave me no food, I was thirsty and you gave me nothing to drink, I was a stranger and you did not welcome me, naked and you did not give me clothing, sick and in prison and you did not visit me.' Then they also will answer, 'Lord, when was it that we saw you hungry or thirsty or a stranger or naked or sick or in prison, and did not take care of you?' Then he will answer them, 'Truly I tell you, just as you did not do it to one of the least of these, you did not do it to me ...'

Matthew 25:34–46

Working the door 1

Jimmy comes in with a radio. 'I was born broken. Oh well, I think it's still good,' he says, and twiddles the silver knobs on it. The aerial's half-snapped; medical tape holding the back on.

Jimmy searches in the garbage and dumpsters for stuff and brings it round to fix and give to people. Or donates it for broken people. He can repair anything – Jay's ten-speed, my Walkman. One winter Mel was on sanity leave and no one could get the boiler in the basement going, and everybody was starting to freeze their asses off till Jimmy came in.

'Guy may be retarded – what's the word?' said Jay, 'but he ain't dumb.'

Jimmy sticks his arms up and I frisk him. His eyes are all red but his fingers are clean, and steady. He smells of chlorine.

'Sorry, Jimmy.'

'It's O-K,' he sings … 'I gotta go to court tomorrow. That's just a yo-yo.'

'That's tomorrow already?'

'Yeah. That's just my Phillips. Phillips Multipurpose Screwdriver. See this pin I found?'

'Hey, yeah.'

'He's a runner.'

'Hey, yeah. That's all right. That's nice.'

'I found it so pinned it on my ski jacket here that Fred got me. Hope some kid didn't lose it and is sitting crying now. Oh well.'

I hand Jimmy back his stuff: his screwdriver, yo-yo. Lucky rock, acorn, rusty length of chain …

'I gotta look for a television for Fred still – Fred gets me warm clean clothes. Fred takes care of me. Fred Flintstone I call him. Yabadabadoo. Hope he doesn't mind. Oh well.'

Jimmy starts off, then comes back with a peanut butter and jelly sandwich.

'They're gonna decide what to do with me. I gotta get all dressed up and stuff. Fiona's bringing my new clothes – my new clothes *with* her, she says.'

Jimmy looks down and shuffles. 'Sometimes I think she gets a little mad at me. Oh well, she's nice, she's nice too. "So, what am I going to do with you, Jimmy, hmm?" I dunno,' answers Jimmy.

Fiona is Jimmy's social worker; Fred works down at detox mostly.

Jimmy licks jam off his fingers: 'Fiona's just kidding and gonna have a little baby. I have to stand in front of the judge and say what I want. She doesn't know what name yet.'

I ask Jimmy how he's feeling about standing up in front of the judge and he laughs; chews his sandwich.

While we're talking I sort out the bed list. Jimmy's got bed #15. A top bunk near the window – his initials bored in the wooden frame, his body worked deep in the mat.

'She's going away on leave for a year at least. You have to give him a name, I said. Or for a girl if it's a girl.'

Jimmy's face violently twitches and winces at times, like he's got a faulty connection somewhere; as he talks he rocks himself gently back and forth.

'Fiona says to just stand up and say that I want to move into the group home. I fixed her car. On the John Allen Memorial Parkway. The John Allen Way. Allen's Apple Juice, I call it. Oh well.'

Her car broke down coming back from taking him swimming, Jimmy explains.

'It's a Plymouth Dodge Duster. They're gonna teach me how to budget my money. I gotta go to a day programme. *Every day*, Fiona says. It was just the gas line loose. "No, be careful, careful. Here, use a rag – take a rag." Jimmy waves his hands.

'You're good at fixing things,' I say.

'Yeah, I dunno ... It's not really hard or anything. I like doing it for people if I can. Life's a lot easier if you've got a television ...... Or a radio at least,' says Jimmy, playing with the silver knobs, making sounds to himself: the lonely static between stations. His runner pin is one of those little figures stamped out of pewter, like a badge.

'Sometimes *I* feel like running,' Jimmy says, stroking it with his wrinkled fingertip. 'Sometimes I feel like running far away.' He laughs. 'Oh well, swimming's OK.'

'Where do you feel like running?' I ask.

'I dunno. Just keep on running I guess. I dunno.' He looks down and shuffles. 'Swimming's OK, I guess … They use a lot of chlorine though, geez, it burns my eyes. The pool man says they use it to kill germs. And for people that pee in the pool and that. Oh well. Fiona doesn't come in or anything. It's all just swimming for retards and that, eh. Fiona says they don't call it that any more, they call it something else. Something, I dunno, I forget, oh well …

'Fiona says I got a dolphin named Flipper stitched on my swimsuit, and that if I want to I could train for the Olympics again. The Special Olympics.'

'Hey, yeah, that'd be good – the medal you won that time.'

'Yeah.'

'That'd be good.'

'Yeah, I dunno, it's been a long time though. I dunno. Oh well, maybe. It's OK. Everyone wears water wings. Well, almost everyone. I gotta stand up in front of everyone and tell the judge what I want. And promise not to do things any more … I'll miss Fred and all them. Fred says, Fred says it's cool to still come visit here anytime I want to.'

'Sure.'

'Cept the home's way out in Park Meadows, and I'd have to take about ten buses to get here at least. It's a nice place though, you should see. Fiona took me. It's a big house with trees and everything. There's only gonna be three of us, so I'd get my own room and that, so that'd be cool I guess. Three of us, plus counsellors of course. It's not like the John MacLean Memorial Centre, that was big. Huger than here. Like a hospital almost. I remember we used to race down the hallways, that was fun. Wheelchairs got a head start but some were fast anyways, geez, you shoulda seen. I liked that OK. 'Cept I was born there practically when my mother left me and that and can't remember her. Well, sometimes I think I can. And had friends and that there – lots till it closed. Oh well. I hope they're happy. Sometimes I think of them. Sometimes I don't any more. Sometimes in dreams. Oh well.'

Jimmy peers inside the broken radio. Picking at the medical tape, he says he guesses he could help fix things at the group home too maybe when they break down in the middle.

'Yeah, you probably could. Sure – I bet they'd love to have someone handy like *you* around!'

'Cept it's so brand new it'll probably be a long time before anything does or anything. Oh well … Fiona says to meet her tomorrow. Nine o'clock. *Nine o'clock.* She's bringing my new clothes with her. I tried them on in Jack Fraser's. Jack Fraser's Men's Wear Store. Jack and the Beanstock, I call it. We laughed and laughed. Me standing in the big long mirror there. That was funny. Like at the amusement park one time. I got a haircut, see? The Golden Comb. "Honeycombs, honeycombs from Post," I call it. She says she thinks I'm ready. I dunno. I guess so.'

Jimmy shrugs. 'Oh well,' he says – and dashes off.

Glyn at the door: draped in a crumpled black T-shirt. I ask him how it's going – he looks crushed.

Glyn writes science fiction novels and short stories. Lives in one room in Lower Town. In a study carrel down at the public library: Lives trapped in poverty and his self – dreaming of infinite space and possibility, and of other worlds. He comes to the shelter for the sandwiches we hand out; the tins of pork and beans he eats cold from the can.

He's been working all day on a story, he tells me – on one part. On one sentence.

'You've been stuck before.'

'Not like this,' he says, and unwraps a stale cheese sandwich.

He hasn't eaten since yesterday. He just sat and stared at the blank page: 'Like an abyss. Like a black hole … I just can't figure it out.

Where I'm going – it's all wrong … I got another rejection letter today.'

'I'm sorry.'

'I'm getting tired,' Glyn says, and chews.

He looks exhausted. Like he hasn't slept in days, shaved; washed his confused hair. He looks thinner.

'Sitting in the study carrels in the library,' says Glyn, 'you feel like a frog in a jar. There's, like, this faint chemical smell. From the furniture and carpets, I guess. Like formaldehyde. Like in high school science class, you know? … It gives you a headache. Makes you feel … dead …… Sometimes I wish my soul could start over,' Glyn says … 'Oh well, I'm starting to write poetry again at least.'

'Sometimes that helps. Gets you unblocked.'

Glyn shakes his head.

Glyn writes some powerful stuff. About living with depression mostly:

Morning …
feel it
enter my being

Like cold rain
seeping
into a poorly constructed building.

'This is my *last* one,' he says, with disturbing emphasis, and hands me a crushed-up piece of lined paper.

'Last one?'

'I haven't really finished it yet. To tell you the truth, I'm kinda scared to. Oh well, you can read it on your break if you want.'

As I'm unclenching Glyn's crushed soul, Anton trips in.

'Hi ya, dudes.'

Anton's T-shirt's all streaked and blotted with blood: he looks like he slaughtered somebody out there, but the pain's all his.

Glyn eyes the slash marks up and down Anton's bare arms: like a sore, tangled journey. Ones from before glow green with angry infection.

(Someone on staff said that Anton was abused as a child; and someone else said, no, they do it for attention, 'slashers'.)

'So how's life?' asks Anton thickly, his bottom lip stabbed through with a diaper pin: Anton froze his lip with a Popsicle and then pierced himself with a sewing needle. 'Sweet pain that hurt like a mother fucker.' His fist is tattooed over with I ♥ SCUM.

'Hey look – ripped this fuckin' doll's head off a doll in Wal-Mart. Like it? ... Yeah, me three. Hope some kid don't, like, freak now – ha. Gonna paint it black and wear it around my neck. Think it'll look quite good, whadda ya think?'

Anton drinks till he pukes then finds his way here; most times we have to refer him to detox. Tonight he's OK though, so I look for a bed for him here.

'Like a shrunken head or somethin'. Can I borrow your magic marker there, dude? Promise I won't sniff it.'

Anton wears a striped silk tie noose with his photo card clipped on from when they tried to put him away and he flew out a fifth-storey window; slashed jeans with anarchy signs. He and Glyn get talking about music and books.

Anton's reading *Interview with the Vampire*. 'Yeah coool, my whole life's, like, neo-gothic or whatever. Gothic and surreal and totally, supremely fucked, I'm sure. I'm Frankenstein. Can't ya tell? Aaaaah! My old man sent me away – floating off on an island of ice and fire. So you got a bed there, dude, or what? Sally sucks. I don't care, I'll sleep outside ... Twenty-one? Coool. I'm twenty-one. Cool.'

Big Dean leans into the conversation and says wanna hear something *really* weird?

'Yeah, yeah,' says Anton, and lets him in from the outside, from standing all alone.

Dean says that when he went and had his brain surgery at the hospital, he could feel them playing around in his head the whole time.

'Coool.'

'Cause they gotta ask you questions and stuff,' Dean says importantly.

'That'd be a buzz.'

'Yeah. Perfectly awake all through it … Like that guy over there, poking around in his radio almost.'

'So that means you had a broken radio head,' says Anton and laughs – like a fiend in pain – but Dean doesn't get it.

Dean bends down to show us where they drilled and dug. 'You can smell it burning.' Shows us the dents and crush marks where his hair won't grow any more.

Glyn gently asks him why they did it in the first place, and Dean tells him grand mal epilepsy – an experiment; they were trying to cure him – his brain's in a book!

'Coool.'

He was one of the first. He's still got it though, but not as bad. 'That's why I gotta take pills still. *Every day.*'

'Yeah, like my fuckin' social worker, man. He wants to send me to a shrink and drug all the connections so the light can't get in no more, and I won't remember nothin' – and I'll be walking round the fifth floor like a zomboid. Aaaaaah! … No offence.'

Glyn, Anton and Dean are all around the same age – early twenties – and stand together in the lobby, munching and ripping into cheese and baloney sandwiches.

Dean says: 'My old man doesn't want anything to do with me now, eh – cause of the past.'

'Tell me about it. Burn the past. Burn the fuckin' past.'

Glyn says that he's tried, but it's fireproof.

'Last time I went there,' says Dean. 'Last time I went to my old man's house, he shut the door in my face – right in my face. Like that – you know? And I wasn't even drinking. That's why I went a little nuts here the other night – when I came to the door and they wouldn't let me in. And like *he* doesn't drink ever.'

'Tell me fuckin' about it.'

'Yeah, tell me fucking about it – I try and still he doesn't. I don't care, I give up. I tried. I tried, you know?'

'Yeah.'

'Now is now – all else is burned. All else shall be burned,' pronounces Anton, and grabs the doll's head by its long blonde hair and starts swinging it.

'I told him about how I'm gonna take those classes. About going back to school and all that. The night school. The school at night?'

'"Father?" "Yes, son?" "I want to kill you."'*

'Those classes, I told you about? Hotel Management.'

I nod that I remember.

'"Mother? … I want to … Aaaaaaaah!"'*

'Like I'm tryin', I'm tryin',' cries Big Dean, ducking and dodging Anton's mother's head. 'What else can I do? And he goes – hey, watch it, man, watch my head – goes and shuts the door in my face – watch it, I'm serious – when I'm trying so hard like that! What's he want anyway? asks Dean. 'What's he want?!' his eyes welling with hurt, anger, fear …

'I don't care. I give up. I tried. I tried.' The doll's head whizzing round, its wide blue, blue eyes screaming and snapping shut in their sockets.

Glyn stands watching Anton singing and dancing around … 'The Doors. The End,' he says, as if by naming the song he has made a decision. He says goodnight. Goodbye.

Fumbling through the sandwich bin, I offer him another processed cheese sandwich. 'Donuts?' It sounds absurd. 'Donuts …?!'

Dean gives me a sudden hug – squeezes so hard it hurts. Like he's got so much love nobody wants.

'You'd never shut the door in my face, would you? Would you?!'

I tell him no, I wouldn't.

'I'm sorry, I'm sorry,' he sobs.

He says to not leave him alone. 'The more alone you are, the more

---

* Words from The Doors' song 'The End'.

you get *left* alone. The more no one talks to you ever.'

Over Big Dean's shoulder, I watch Glyn disappear out the door. Into the black hole of the night. I hold Dean together until he stops crying; and then he and I talk about him getting his Grade 12, and about a correspondence course he saw on a book of matches he picked up …

Finally I sit down and read Glyn's last poem:

How shall I say
goodbye to the sky?
Will its blue look
make me cry?

How shall I say
goodbye to the trees –
the stones, the sun
the moon, the breeze …

How shall I say
goodbye to you?
If there was a you to
say goodbye to.

How shall I say
goodbye to me?
And will death finally set
my earthbound spirit
free?

Next day, Fiona comes to the door. Do I know where Jimmy's run off to? He must have climbed out the bathroom window at the courthouse, she says. She managed to get another court date – but she's got to find him.

Two days later, Jimmy comes to the door, waving a sandwich bag of glue, eyes glazed with a wild, long-distanced look; glue caked and cracked round his mouth; stuck on his Jack Fraser's.

We call down to detox but he keeps running out into the middle of the road, laughing and dancing and waving his bag of glue. Finally, he stops, collapsing across a curb onto a patch of waste ground.

Fred goes out to pick him up; and on the steps finds the TV Jimmy left him, wrapped in a suit coat.

Glyn comes in as Fred jogs out: 'Hello! I *think* I figured out a way. Wanna hear? … If my main character, Sebastian, builds a space-time continuum …' And Glyn and I get talking together about the future, while Fred takes care of Jimmy; rolls him over on his side so he won't choke.

But things aren't too bad, things are OK, until Big Dean comes to the door, screaming and crying, and so drunk I have to finally gently, firmly shut the door in his face.

Through the plexiglas window I watch him recede into the infinite night … floating away on an island of ice and fire …

The man with his heart on the wrong side

The man with his heart on the wrong side always asks for donuts. First thing in the door: 'Got any donuts tonight? Got any Timbits?' If we do, I go bag him some. Day-olds we get from the mall. Chocolate-glazed are his favourites. I can seldom convince him to take a sandwich. 'No, I live on donuts,' he tells me – his body doughy; his face round and splotchy.

When things aren't too busy we talk a little; sit together on the sandwich-bag-littered steps between the doors.

One evening – in his slow, low monotone – he told me that his mother died when he was nine years old, and that he never knew his father. I said that that must have been hard. He answered that it *was* hard, very hard; and that he was thinking of going out to Saskatchewan to live.

Another evening, he told me about the experiments they perform on him at the hospital:

'I go there every month. I can't tell you which hospital. There's a doctor there who uses me. Who uses me to trick his students.' And that's when he revealed to me that he had a very rare, rare condition – that he had his heart on the wrong side.

'That's what they call it. They've got a long name in Latin for it but that's what it means: "Heart on the wrong side." See, one out of one-million-five-hundred-thousand-and-fifty-five people are made by God like that. With it beating on the right side and not the left, like in normal people. Like God got bored.

'But, even though it's rare, I bet there's probably someone else like that in here. Because that's the kind of people who come here. If there was someone else, they'd probably be hiding in here. Or else in another place like this one.

'I have to take my shirt and pants off in front of them. Then they lie me down on this steel table. It's cold. Then – I shouldn't be telling you this – the doctor takes his stethoscope out of his ears. They're hairy, his ears. I always think: he has such hairy ears, such hairy ears. And that he mustn't be able to hear or to listen to people right. Your ears are all right. But you're not old yet. And they're all around me, eh? So, it's terrible, it's just this wall of flesh draped by white coats. So I can't go anywhere. And a tray of scalpels and those clamps. And everyone masked with dead, blank expressions in their eyes. I usually count the ceiling tiles. One, two, three, four, five, six, seven, eight, nine, ten, all the way up to twenty-two. One, two, three, four, five, six, seven, eight, nine, ten, up and down, from one end of the room to the other. Then the doctor says that, OK, he wants someone to listen to my heart. "Who will volunteer to step up here and listen to this young man's heart?" And someone raises their hand and he nods and they step up onto the platform, and all you can hear are their shoes squeaking. I keep counting the ceiling tiles and try not to think too much, but my breath gets all snagged and ripped. And the lights are hot. And the stethoscope is as cold as the table, sliding around on my chest like that. And the doctor says, gruff at his intern: "Well, what's wrong, what seems to be the problem now?" Very angry because of his life. "Doctor I, I, can't seem to hear anything. I –" "Well, there's nothing wrong with the stethoscope, lad – what's wrong is wrong with you." And then he asks them did they just start medical school or something? "Step down, please … Step down! Can't even find a man's heart. They send me puppies." He calls them puppies. And he shakes his head and calls for another volunteer. And the same thing happens to them and I feel sorry for them. I feel sorry sometimes for the doctor too. Having to use me to impress other people like that. Some days I feel sorry for everyone in the world. Some days I feel sorry for trees … Then the doctor starts chuckling, then laughing. He enjoys being the only person in a crowded room laughing. Then he finally explains about the one out of one-million-five-hundred-thousand-and-fifty-five people, and that the first thing in the art of medicine to always remember is never to assume any-thing. "Or else you make an ass out of 'u' and me" – and then everyone laughs, even I do because I feel so relieved and can go soon now and get paid. Then everyone claps, even the people whom he tricked clap, and he bows. Some of them ask me questions. Medical questions. About what it's like.

'But, you know … I always look around at them and think that it's not me, it's not me. It's them. These people who keep performing these tests and experiments on me, who keep using me to trick other people, who have their hearts on the wrong side. It's not me at all.' …

I go get the man with his heart on the wrong side some chocolate-glazed donuts. Back with a bagful, I ask him if he's still thinking of moving out to Saskatchewan.

'Yes.'

'Do you know anyone out there at all?'

'No, no … I just think it would be somewhere where you could think. You can't think here. There's too much in the way – too many tall buildings, too many tall people. It's perfectly flat out there. I just want to get out of this city of experiments, and sit on the prairies –

with the tiny, perfect wildflowers and the last, great wise buffalo – and think right.'

I nod.

He smiles, his teeth smeared with chocolate; stuck with rot. 'Well, see you tomorrow, Mr Sandwich Man! Thanks for the donuts. Thanks for listening.'

'No problem. Take care.'

A university student comes in as he goes out: His student loan's all eaten up. Can he have some sandwiches please? Something with meat if possible.

Next, a father who in polite, broken English asks for some sandwiches for his children: he holds up three fingers. He was a doctor in *his* country, I understand.

Next, a guy who's just rolled into town and is crashing out in his Datsun, and could use an extra blanket. Do I know any place where he can park and not get ticketed – he doesn't have much gas left. He glances round. I wouldn't happen to know anyone who wants to buy some wheels, would I? Cause this is the kind of place he's gonna end up living in, if he doesn't get some bread together soon.

Next …

Working the door 2

Ziggy hands me a loose screw he found. 'I don't know,' he says laughing – he never *stops* laughing – 'musta falled off somethin' – better find out,' he says, and floats off ... I set the screw on the window ledge. Go back to my paperwork paperwork ...

Wayne comes in.

'So how was work?'

'Stressful.' He's been having problems with the new cook.

Wayne works at Baudelaire's Café down on the market: university students with black lipstick and black nail polish, at black tables, in black light; washes their dessert plates and coffee cups; makes $4.80 an hour, saving up for his apartment.

Wayne asks me how I am, how *my* job's going. 'It must be stressful sometimes too, huh, with people coming in drinking, and other things.' Wayne's voice is soft, considerate.

I tell him yes, sometimes.

Wayne stands hugging his Bible. He likes to sit in the chapel after work, but can't right now because The General's in there playing the piano.

'Faggot – quit standin' like a girl,' someone passing him says, and Wayne straightens up suddenly.

One night after work, Wayne told me about his life before he came to the shelter. He was married and had gone to university. The marriage was annulled now.

He'd married the daughter of his parents' best friends: his parents had forced him.

At university he'd studied music: his parents were both teachers, and played with the city symphony.

'I got so I *hated* music,' Wayne told me. 'Always picking it apart all the time – voice leading, harmony, orchestration, counterpoint ... Theory theory all the time. Then practising every day for eight hours. By yourself in those little rooms.' He took his glasses off and rubbed his tired eyes. 'It's not healthy for a person, you know? Even the doctor I went to said that. Trying to get Bach or whomever just perfect perfect. It gives you headaches all the time. Then I got a rash all over my hands. At first I thought it was the measles or something … A lot of other people I talked to at the school felt the same way … Music still makes me feel sick sometimes. I've got a peptic ulcer – you know those pills I take? I don't mind church music, hymns. I like the quiet, quietness best.' …

Wayne stares down at the scarred linoleum, studying patterns. The General's in his stride now – he sounds like a circus.

'Well, maybe things at work will look up,' I say. 'Maybe when the new cook gets used to things.'

'Yeah – well, the owner likes me. He always talks to me when he comes in and asks me how I am. Says to grab myself a salad – or whatever I want. He's the one who hired me – he *knows* that I work. I've been working there for eight, almost nine months now … But I know if it's between the cook and me – it's a lot harder to find a cook than what I'm doing … It's never any problem when I'm working by myself, you know? But he's always standing over me. He tells me, no, that I have to do *this* first, then do *that*. I *know* what to do. But I never say anything. He's always pushing me. Pushing me around with his voice, you know? He's always on me to work faster faster. I keep on breaking things. I think he wants me to. I think he wants to hire his stepson … He keeps telling me stories about the women he's met and plays his radio all the time –'

And as if on cue Chas and Murray burst in the door singing, and Wayne gets pushed aside, by guitars and cases and laughter.

They made forty-eight bucks up on the market. In three hours!

'Hey, all right!'

'That's, like, twenty bucks an hour,' says Chas.

'Well, more like fifteen,' says Murray, and they laugh.

'Not too bad though, eh?' Chas says, patting Murray's pocket. (Murray holds the money.)

Murray plays rhythm; Chas fingerpicks and solos – plays some nice slide with his Bic lighter. They both sing.

Chas is in a groove tonight, his body bopping and dancing, like there are waves of music rippling all through him; Chas usually takes the lead in conversation too.

'See, cause life is *for* creativity,' Chas is saying, running his elegant, long-fingered hands through his waist-length, blonde rock 'n' roll hair, tossing it back, 'that's why we're all here, why we're all here on earth for anyways, man. To live creatively. But people don't let you, that's the thing, society don't let you. Plastic money, plastic food, plastic society, plastic soul. And everybody eatin' it up. Fuck, like that song we wrote, eh, Mur?: "Plastic souls /deep black holes /no/controls on me, babe" it goes, I'll play it for you sometime, just need a bridge, a bridge now, eh, Mur? They don't let you – and goddamn, that's what life is for! It's crazy … hazy/ then they say you're lazy/ Goin' down/Goin' dowwwn …'

And Leonard, down from his shower, standing listening says that that's exactly right. 'I've been trying my whole life to live creatively!'

'I believe it, man – I believe it.'

Peering out from behind strands of his thin, tangled wet hair, Leonard tells us how he's been trying to get amnesty as a political refugee. He even went down to the Amnesty International offices here the other day – but they never do anything.

Leonard's face is framed with lines; pocked like he's suffered a lot of hard knocks. (Probably took too much of the brown acid at Woodstock, someone said.)

Leonard explains to Chas and Murray that the CIA is after him – and that if he goes back home to the United States he's a dead man: because he knows too much.

'States suck,' says Chas. 'The government.'

Murray listens politely, then gives me a nod and goes inside the chapel to jam with The General.

Leonard tells Chas that his plan is to go out to New Zealand, the roly-poly General playing Christmas carols now, six months out of season but nice; sprightly – the upright sounding all silvery. The General can play anything from Chopin waltzes to '40s' show tunes.

Sentimental lost love ballads and funeral marches to boogie woogie and ragtime. A moody repertoire expressing how he's feeling that day, what he's been marching around the city recalling. Murray backs him up, grabs chords as he goes along. 'Fall in, Private.' Gets into the spirit. Music flows out into the lobby over the TV crash and burn; shines through the dull pall of cigarette smoke hanging.

'New Zealand, far out,' Chas is saying. 'Far out!'

'Everything's green and honest and *real* out there.'

'Yeah, not like here.'

'That's exactly right. Not like here.'

'Yeah plastic, eh, everything's plastic. People inside now.'

'That's right – and be doing everything they tell them to soon.'

In the chapel Murray's singing. 'Good King Wenceslas looked out'. I go back to my paperwork paperwork. Sounding real good, real good on his own. Deep and crisp and even. His voice has a rooted quality; Chas sings more from the throat. Murray told him that you get nodes that way.

'Good diaphragm technique, put you in the camp jamboree singsong this year, Private. Get a form, get a form, get in formation now, Private – sweetly, sweetly, dolce.'

Leonard is saying to Chas that when he heals, and can travel again, he'll call his sister in Montana from a payphone: They jumped him in an alley behind the fish market, he explains, and broke six of his ribs. He lifts his T-shirt to show Chas the bruises.

'Shit, man. Fuck …'

Like the map of a continent.

Mel the cleaner pops in – 'Howdy do' – jingles his ring of keys. 'So, who's supposed to be on duty with ya? Dave somewhere?'

I shrug.

Chas is explaining to Leonard that he and Mur aren't just bumming around busking – they've got a manager back in Vancouver. Their manager in Van said: travel, expand, write songs. Come back and cut an album.

Leonard doesn't like music. Doesn't like music like that song

Every Breath You Take Every Move You Make I'll Be Watching You.
 'The Police.'
 'What?!'
 'The Police – the band.'
 'Or that, what's it? *A Free Man in Paris*?'
 'Joni Mitchell.'
 'Ya, Mitchell. It's all, it's all cracked half-truths,' says Leonard. 'Cracked half-truths. You know, I was washing dishes in Paris. Sleeping worse than this with rats, you know – with rats. Ya, right – free man washing dishes in Paris watching you.' And Leonard peers through his bent, wire-framed glasses that the CIA agents stepped on.

With one ear I listen to Chas and Leonard, and with the other to The General and Murray, on to Broadway musicals now:
 'There's a bright golden haze on the meadow.'
 'That's it – smell the mornin' notes, Private.'
 'There's a bright golden haze on the mea-dow.' Sunny warm seventh chords, and The General cooing now …
 'So when I get on the plane to New Zealand finally, I'm not looking back.'
 'Oh, what a beautiful mornin'/Oh, what a beautiful day.'
 'Yeah – when we get the album recorded, I said to Mur …'
 'Everything's goin' my way …'
 'Wheat smells sweet, Private, wheat smells sweet! Aaaaah … Feel that earth-fragrant wind on your face? … High as an elephant's eye, Private. Corn high as a white elephant's eye! Oh, I seen it.'
 'No, I believe it – you spend your whole life trying to be creative – and then the government and the Powers-that-be don't let you …'

And as The General and Murray segue into something fast and jittery I don't recognise, there's someone's drum drumming. On the inside door – it booms out with a kick: Lloyd Tolman, I jump – his fist-smushed, ogre's face pressed up against the plexiglas, fogging it with his anger. He wants a meat sandwich. Now!
 'Come on, fuckin' meat sandwich!' Lloyd grrrrs.
 Out of the blue, Big Dean swoops down.

'Hi! Hi!! Hi!!!' He just got back from his flying lesson.

'And it had better be *meat* this time!'

Dean hands me a binder with HOW TO FLY A JET AIRPLANE printed across it in black magic marker; instructs me to lock it in the office with his pills. With his pills he's not taking any more.

'Last time you gave me one with only mus-*turd* and margarine. Can't get very far on that, eh? Can't get very far on *nothin'*!' while Dean follows me into the kitchen, instructing me to put his binder in the office with his pills – with his pills he's not taking any more; Lloyd drumming; and I promise that I will – just as soon as I go deliver Lloyd his meat sandwiches.

I hand them to Lloyd through the half-open door – he tears into the bag and spits it out, rips into a sandwich, meat flopping around in his mouth like it's alive ... He probably hasn't eaten in days.

Dean orders me to go get him the Yellow Pages now because he wants to look up some farms to work on. 'Some farms for now, just for now,' he says.

Farm work sounds like a down-to-earth idea, but Lloyd wants donuts. 'Fuckin' donuts,' through the movie holes; drums his fist CHOC-LATE, CHOC-LATE and the screw rolls off the ledge onto the floor.

'Goofis goofball goof ...' – fuck sakes, and now who let Tommy in the back way?! – 'Goofis goofball goof' – pacing round, calling everyone names, then crying out: 'Mom, where's mom?! Mom, where's mom?! ...' Where the fuck is Dave?

As I snatch some chocolate donuts for Lloyd, and the Yellow Pages for Dean, Ross muscles up to me:

'I'm just warnin' ya, man – if that freak with the stuffed animals looks over at me one more time, I'm gonna fuckin' nail him! Jus' warnin' ya, man,' and stalks off – and immediately comes back: 'That freak sticks his tongue out at me *one more time* – I'm gonna wrap it round his throat!'

Someone's turned the TV up over The General and Murray. A chorus of screeching tires, wailing sirens, gun shots ... Lloyd glaring in over top.

Dean says to show him where the truck driving schools are now: 'Working on a farm was a *stupid* idea. I don't know what I was thinking,' he says, and laughs at himself.

He wants to be a truck driver now: because he looks like a truck driver. 'Don't you think?' juggling through the phone book that keeps shutting on him.

'Goofis goofball goof,' Tommy waving his limbs like a drunken tree.

'Jus' warnin' ya, man.'

'See I told ya! A truck driver, cause I look like a truck driver, right? ... And strong, eh? Strong. Driving an eighteen-wheeler rig with a horn down Highway 401, carrying a load of diamonds. A load of diamonds or something, eh? I'll have to get my F licence.'

Big Dean was in the army for a while; then worked as a janitor. He comes from a rich, well-respected family; his father calls him 'a big, fat zero' – he wants to kill his father. He stands over me grinning – his teeth like rotten columns, his breath a fetid breeze.

Lloyd leaves finally; but others keep coming to the door for sandwiches sandwiches: Ezekiel ... the Bottle Man ... Conrad: a fallen old gentleman with a lifetime of stories I've got no time to sit and listen to now. 'It's OK,' he says with understanding, 'I'm not dying this year – I've made up my mind.'

Oliver minces up to me. He hugs his dinosaur the way Wayne hugs his Bible. 'I'm just warning you,' he lisps ... 'If that Ross person doesn't stop pestering and pestering me – I'm gonna poke his eyeball out with a pencil crayon. I'm just warning you': a pudgy little boy of twenty-two.

I tell Oliver to just ignore Ross. 'Don't start.' All his animals have names; some have several. He places them around his bed at night; we keep him downstairs on a mat so the men won't kill him.

'Don't start?! *I* won't start ... I'll get Pablo to sic him,' and he roars, and coughs and sticks Pablo the Purple Plesiosaurus up in my face. Pablo smells like cigarette smoke. Like night sweats and tears.

'Si, Señor,' says Pablo. 'Si, Señor.' If we don't give Oliver enough attention he falls down the stairs. Says his legs won't work any more and that he's dying.

'Goofis goofball goof ...'

'Tommy, go down to detox, OK? ... No, I told you, Anne's not in – Mom's not working tonight.'

Oliver starts playing in my box of pens and pencils, and I have to sing to him to remember that he's not supposed to hang around the lobby. 'Just ignore him, Oliver. OK?' He walks away – tripping over his shoe laces, tripping over his self ...

Just Conrad between the doors now, sitting on sandwich-bag-littered steps. 'I'm not dying this year!' he proclaims – and holds up his cane – like a victory sign over unemployment, poverty, depression ...

The television makes it sound like the whole shelter's on fire, but the door buzzer's ringing less; and things seem almost under control – until Dean comes flying out of the common room with his arms out, screaming: 'Run, everybody, run! – that guy's got hand bombs! HE'S SADDAM HUSSEIN! HE'S SADDAM HUSSEIN!'

And suddenly the men are scattering every which way – the sound of shoes, the sound of tables. 'SADDAM HUSSEIN – RUN!' The sound of ceramic coffee cups exploding off walls and someone crying they're going to kill now. 'GOING TO KILL!'

The sound of Duane bounding by with his pockets loaded full of arcade change. 'Take cover, Dude' – a rain of quarters bulleting off the floor; ricocheting off walls.

'GOING TO KILL!!': Rejean Mohammed hugging a plastic milk crate loaded with ceramic cups he keeps on launching wildly, screaming: 'KILL!'

I spoke to him over coffee once: about how his brother was taken prisoner and tortured; about walking through the mountains with no shoes.

'Guy's a fuckin' madman – run!'

The General steps out of the chapel with a cigar in his mouth to reconnoitre the situation.

'Hit the deck, boys!' he commands – and pushes Murray down as a cup whistles over his head and explodes, shrapnel flying everywhere, men crawling over the floors. I'm in charge it suddenly comes to me, and I glance around; meanwhile Rejean's grabbed another cache of cups and has me in his sights – his eyes awful: wide and terrified, with nothing in them you can reach any more – cocking his arm back as Mel comes charging down the hall, and dives and tackles Rejean from behind and pins him, and suddenly I'm on top too and we're wrestling and holding him down while he's beating his brains against the floor screaming: 'Going to KILL! KILL!!' – us, if he tears free, himself if he keeps on beating his head like that. Someone throws us their jacket. Someone else drawls: 'So, want me to finish him off for ya?' and steps up.

We slip the jacket underneath Rejean's head, as Dave pops in to see what's going on, and runs away to call the cops; and we keep holding Rejean down. Mel's got a good hold, but mine keeps slipping. Hope the cops get here soon – 'KILLLL!' – and aren't on donut break; and I can feel it – 'KILLLLLLL!': like deadly current coursing through Rejean's wiry body every time he lashes out – his cut-up fingers clawing for cup shards Mel sweeps out of reach.

Rejean lashes and kicks and can't get free, so stops and beats his head against the floor, crying kill. The men gather round:

'Just take it easy, man, it'll be alright – don't, man. Fuck. It'll be alright, don't, don't …'

'Fuckin' cracked – that's what happens.'

Others stand silently, as if praying that it doesn't happen to them too someday; blood drooling out Rejean's mouth now, matted in his dull black hair.

'Better be careful touchin' him at all, dude, he's probably got AIDS.'

Sobbing, beating his head: 'Killll, killl …'

And, finally, the cops come and everybody scatters. They put Rejean in handcuffs and take him away, crying in his mother tongue, blood and sweat tearing down his face – a last last try.

'Fuckin' far out wild!' sings Chas. 'Gotta get this in a song somehow – fuckin' chaos. Hey, that's the bridge, Mur. Mur, that's the bridge …!'

Leonard shakes his head: 'See how those cops grabbed him up like that?'

Mel and I look at each other.

'Just lucky I watched Kojak,' he says.

'Anyone hit?' The General barks out, taking charge. 'Anyone hit? Report if you can do so – send up a flare, radio your position.'

Wayne reports to me, blood trickling through his fingers. He took a coffee cup in the head. He takes his hand away and The General assesses the wound with his fat red face scrunched up.

'Sorry, you can't go home, son,' he says, and claps him on the back.

Deep enough for some stitches though, and Dave's on the phone calling for an ambulance, giving me the sign that everything's OK, everything's cool, while Mel mops up the blood and tears. There's rubble strewn all over; the drywall pocked in places. Like a stone wall in some magazine. Big Dean flips up the picnic table bunkers, while Duane retrieves his quarters. Henry scurries round between them snatching up the playing cards with *SUN* girls on them. 'Wouldn't touch those quarters,' Duane tells him.

I walk Wayne into the chapel and we sit down together. He leans back, a stack of paper towels pressed to his forehead. I tell him to just keep applying pressure.

'Life is very stressful, isn't it?' he says, and closes his eyes.

I move down away from him. Something in his voice: so defeated. I feel fragile. In pieces …

There are dizzying sirens, and then the white-coated attendants lead Wayne out while everyone stands and watches; Ziggy holds the door laughing. Oliver tugs at my sleeve sleeve that he needs his cough syrup – and that I had better come quickly, because Tommy is having one of those seizure thingies again …

Abbot and Costello Meet The Mummy

Roy comes in in a mellow mood, he's gonna see how it goes. 'That's good,' I say. 'Yeah, yeah, all you can do. Why get all worked up about it?' he says. Doesn't do nothin'.'

I nod. He smiles; shakes his head like life's fuckin' crazy but he's still hanging in there. 'One day at a time,' he says.

I ask him how his day went. He was over at the Work Program.

'Well, not all day. Just from ten 'til two. That's all they can keep it open for.' He wishes they could keep it open all day. 'They're lookin' for funding.'

Roy makes trophies out of wood.

'Not easy sometimes with this but' – and lifts up his clawed right hand, paralysed from a knife fight. I can't imagine anyone having the guts to pull a knife on Roy: two hundred pounds solid – easily.

'Severed the tendons and shit … Yeah, but you shoulda seen the other guy. Let's just say he ain't walkin' too well.'

When Roy's low-income housing comes through he can get out of here; go to the Work Program days and make trophies. He'll get faster at it, he says.

'I have no doubt,' I say.

'Oh, neither do I,' says Roy, 'neither do I.'

His girlfriend's living with her mother for now. She's not drinking as much.

'That's great!'

'Yeah.'

Before the baby she drank like no tomorrow. Two forty ouncers a day. Roy says he's anxious to move in with her again and start a new life, but he knows it's going to take time. 'So, the social worker in tonight? Oh no, that's next week, right? Oh well, it can wait, it can wait. No point gettin' all worked up.'

They're thinking of taking Sticks in too; getting a place with an extra room or a pull-out or something. Sticks hitched with him all through the States.

'Crazy … Yeah, but it's only if he can get off coke first. That's the condition. Cause it's just gonna bring us all back down I know.' Roy glances up at me. 'He still feels like a brother, no matter what. Know what I mean?' he asks.

I nod.

'Well, it'll work itself out. One day at a time,' he says. 'So, those movies?' he asks.

Things in the common room are mellow. No fights or arguments.

Someone says should have got *Silence of the Lambs*. 'Guy fuckin' eats people.'

'No, or a porno,' someone else says.

Ollie picked up some classic old comedies. Down at Video Busters. 'Something silly. Give the boys a laugh for a change.' The Keystone Cops, Laurel and Hardy. And for the main feature: *Abbot and Costello Meet The Mummy*.

The buzzer rings (it's Duane I can tell). At the inside door he hands over his switch blade – and some supplies he picked up at the 'five-finger discount store': liquorice, Maltesers, and a jar of Orville Redenbacher Gourmet Popping Corn … all of which he produces, like a magician, from bottomless coat pockets.

'Hey, need some help there, dude?' he calls over to Dave who's having trouble with all the wires, fuckin' wires, in back of the TV.

'Hey, don't let him go anywheres with that VCR, eh,' someone says.

'Yeah, watch the back door.'

'Relax,' says Duane. 'Take a downer. Take a break.'

'We got movies? Movies tonight?' someone asks. And as I go answer the door again I can smell popcorn popping.

'Hey, tell him tons of butter. Tons!'

On the way, I pass by Henry, sitting with his arm round Lola: a life-size – and life-like – blow-up doll he bought at a sex shop in Centretown.

I pass Joseph, and ask him how he's doing.

Joseph used to be a student but dropped out – 'One day one-finger math will be faster than a computer' – graduated here. The professor, they call him. He still carries his briefcase with him everywhere; wears thick, black-framed eyeglasses held together with electrical tape, and a U of T sweatshirt he refuses to change.

'I'm still trying to figure out the epsilon; still working on Pascal's triangle and the repeating enigma of pi. It's all a chess game, it's all a chess game, it's all a game …'

He doesn't have time for a shower.

'Time's a hole you could measure with formulas,' he answers, pacing, his hair out at angles.

He sits down periodically, to play chess with The General. I played him myself one night and he beat me in six moves! I sat dazed, wondering.

'One day one-finger math will be faster than a computer. I'm still working on the epsilon, the enigma, pi, it's all a chess game – an abacus, an abyss, an arboretum …'

It's Tommy at the door. And so I buzz him in.

'Oh boy, oh boy, no more hot water left now, I'll tell ya!'

Tommy loves coming in after being out all day, and jumping in a nice hot shower. Sometimes you can't get him out, with him singing and splashing around.

He strides and paces, his big ears sticking out. 'Oh boy, no more hot water left now, I'll tell ya!' rubbing his cold hands together now like he's about to run and dive in; but before he does he plunges into the common room to see his friends. Pals he's known since grade school – Sylvester, Jake, Danny. The gang of them hang out in the park and pass the bottle round. Shoot up. But no one's in yet.

'Hey, where is everyone? … Where's mom? Ollie the trolley?'

The buzzer rings again – and it's a fancy, fur-lined woman with leftovers from an office party. Her arms are full and Tommy runs to help her.

'There's more in the car,' she sings, and Duane jogs out, while Tommy fumbles and juggles the cases and plastic trays to the kitchen like slapstick.

There are little quarter-cut sandwiches, chips and dip, a couple of cases of Schweppes ginger ale, cheese platters …

'Oh boy, there's a mouse in the house. A mouse in the house now, I'll tell ya!'

Ollie comes out of the kitchen wearing a Simpsons apron.

'Ollie the trolley! Ollie the trolley!'

Ann steps out of her office.

'Mom!'

She stands on her tiptoes and gives Tommy a big hug. He's six-foot-four, and they dance.

'Mom.'

Many nights she's the first person Tommy asks for in the door. Nights when he staggers in clutching his heart; nights when he trembles and shivers and cries.

She cradles Tommy's cold hands and asks him where his mittens are.

Ollie says: 'See, God answers prayers.' And rearranges the crackers and marbled colby cheese, the celery and carrot sticks, picking out the wilted lettuce, filling in the holes, making everything nice.

'Hey, movies tonight, Tommy. We got movies. Videos.'

Tommy blinks.

'Hey, maybe we shoulda got a western too. A western for Tommy.'

'Next time. Maybe have a video night regular.'

'That's what I was hoping.'

'Got a membership card.'

Tommy starts slinking and slanking around the OK corral of the lobby, underneath the fluorescent high-noon lights, hands in his pockets, jangling the silver he made out on the square begging.

Tommy can remember every character in *Gun Smoke*, *Bonanza*, *Have Gun Will Travel* … Remembers when he was a little boy: lying on the rug in his mother's basement before she died, watching television – says ask him a question, ask him a question; peers at us – steely-eyed. Starts singing theme tunes, galloping through them. Then turns and points and fires. Fires – and I so I stagger around the lobby like I've been shot, caught in an ambush.

'Got 'cha. Oh boy, got 'cha, got 'cha.'

But then I turn, and point, and fire – and Tommy acts like he's taken a silver bullet in the chest. Lurches and clutches his heart, staggers and turns in circles. And as I watch him die slow I remember he *is* dying, of AIDS. Tommy has AIDS and is slowly dying.

Mr Johnson signals me over after the dust has cleared and Tommy has gone upstairs.

'I just wanted to tell you that I think you are a nice person ... Well, that's all I wanted to say,' he says. 'You remind me of my brother. He lets me get away with murder too. Lets me in when I've been drinking. But I've made up my mind,' Mr Johnson says with resolve, 'this has got to stop. I'm gonna get a job. Well, that's all I wanted to tell you.'

Mr Johnson spends his afternoons down at the drop-in centre, leafing through the classifieds, sipping tall cans of strong brew. Once he worked one-hundred-and-fifty-foot cranes. Massey Ferguson bulldozers. Built skyscrapers, moved the earth. Now he walks by the offices and towers he built ... and stops and watches people going inside and out.

In the springtime he'll go down and see what's doing, he says. 'There's no point before. When the weather gets better. In the spring. There's no use gettin' all worked up about it ... I used to operate bulldozers. Cranes. Did I tell you? In the springtime they'll be loads of work. That's when things get movin'. There's no point before. Christ sake – there's still six feet of snow out there' ... He glances up at me. 'But I know,' he says soberly, 'that *this* has *got* to stop ... You remind me of my brother. I never really thanked him. He has a wife, kids – I'm here.' Mr Johnson surveys the crowded, smoky room of men; throws up his hands.

'Well, I just wanted to say that I think you are a nice person.'

I thank Mr Johnson, and tell him that I think he is a nice person, too.

There's a silence, and I ask him if he wants to come and watch some movies. 'Ollie's got movies.'

'Movies? ... Movies?' he laughs. 'Sure, why not?'

'Why not.'

'When summer comes I'll go down. See what's doing.' He glances at his wristwatch; stands, and sways, then sits back down. Waits until the lights go out before he lifts himself up again.

'Hey, man, hit them lights!'

'Yeah, make it like a real movie. Like a real movie would.'

Men start drifting over – drawn by the unbelievable smell of hot buttered popcorn. Men who were sitting playing solitaire; men who were comatose.

'God, I thought I was dreaming. Dreaming that smell.'

'Hot buttered popcorn,' smiles Roy, standing with a fistful. And pretty soon we've got a full house. Everybody pushed together in the common room and no one complaining.

The front door again. And by the time I'm back from handing out peanut butter and jelly sandwiches to a hungry family of five, the first feature is rolling.

There's an incredible feeling of tired bodies relaxing and the long day unwinding; of men slowly letting down their guards while, through the grilled windows, the sun melts, like butter, over the snowy city.

Marco's here, in a corner, images flickering over his face. It's great to see him. Usually he paces and paces and can't sit down; stands and cries and won't, can't tell us why.

(One night shift we were talking, and Ollie was saying that he was reading about Marco's home country in the newspaper, and about the death squads there in the 1980s. Maybe Marco had been through something terrible like that, he said; had seen some things he was finding it hard to live with.

I was thinking probably. And that maybe now there were death squads inside his head, because when I'd ask Marco if I could help him somehow, he'd stand and shake his head violently back and forth, back and forth, like he was trying to scatter them, throw them off – my voice just another in an onslaught.)

It's great to see him, sitting, enjoying some escape, peeking through the tangled vines of his hair, his leg pumping like a jackhammer.

'Hey, who's throwin' popcorn? Roy suddenly threatens. 'Warnin' ya, pal, payback's a bitch.' But he's not really serious.

In *Abbot and Costello Meet The Mummy*, the mummy gets all unravelled and one of the men kids: 'Hey, that guy looks a lot like Duane in the morning.'

'Yeah, right, eh,' Duane says, 'dream on. Looks like your mama.'

'Hey, down in front, down in front. Shhh, fuckin shhh, ha, this part.'

It's good to sit with the guys. A lot of nights I stand ready to jump in between them before tempers erupt and fists fly; some nights it's like the Wild West, my body charged with the tension.

Someone pings me in the head – and I'm caught suddenly in the crossfire of a popcorn fight: Duane and Roy vs Kahil and The General, but a truce is quickly called …

'Hey, pass that bowl down here, will ya? Stop hoggin' it.'

'Cheques in this week, eh?'

'Shut up – movie.'

'Cheques in?'

'Yeah. Shhhh.'

Roy smiles up at the screen; shakes his head like life's fucking crazy but he's hanging in there, even starting to enjoy it.

'Too much salt, my lips,' Duane pants, gulping down cold ginger ale.

'So, good movie, Joseph?'

Joseph has stopped trying to solve the enigma of pyramidal forms and the epsilon for a time and is sitting laughing at someone who got a pie in the eye. He laughs out loud. Like a great bird. Everyone turns and looks at each other. Like a great bird.

'Lemon pie in the eye, oh boy!'

Ollie stands in his Simpsons apron, holding the trays the angel woman brought. 'Half time!' he announces, and there's an orderly and polite push.

In the back row Henry's got his arm around Lola, pulling her close, making his move.

Someone has given old Willie a cigarette. A clean, white cigarette: not a rollie, not a dirty, stamped-on butt. He smokes with his tired eyes closed, the calm, quiet dark washing over him. He exhales, and the smoke swirls and hangs.

Tommy stands underneath the ceiling, nibbling crumbly old cheddar cheese, broken Wheat Thins. 'Oh boy, there's a mouse in the house, a mouse in house now, I'll tell ya! ...'

Roy chews on a cocktail stick, puts his feet up.

Back in the kitchen, Ollie's popping up the Orville Redenbacher and whistling 'It's a Long Way to Tipperary'. There's an explosion of laughter, and we turn and look at each other.

Working the door 3

Shane buzzes. And dances in.

'Shane, my man!'

Shane works construction, but his dream is to become a female impersonator. He's a big, well-built black man, so no one intimidates him or yells: 'Hey, shut up you fuckin' faggot – you AIDS,' when he's practising his Diana Ross or Tina Turner. And if somebody new gives him a hard time, he looks them straight in the eye and asks them what their problem is … their problem with the music of Miss Ross or Tina Turner – 'The Queen of Rock 'n' Roll', disarming them with his quick sense of humour, so that they're soon part of the crowd calling out requests. Or so that he's soon sitting down with them over a cup of java, listening to their troubles.

Shane speaks in a tenor, but sings in a breathy, reedy soprano:

'Set me free, why don't you, babe?
Get outta my life, why don't you, babe?
You really don't want me –
you just keep me hangin' onnnn …'

'I know this guy who owns a club up in T.O.,' he told me one night, standing in his work boots and hardhat.

'Don't go up there unless you got something *really* solid,' Francis advised. 'It's a crazy place – *I* should know.'

Shane told him to not get in a tizzy – that this club had class and treated their people right: it wasn't one of those sleazy places up there.

'I could probably work in one of those places right now, but why should I? Anyway, this guy I met, he *really* likes my voice – he heard me at an amateur night when I went up there. On the bus that time? And he says that I just gotta get the moves down better. That it's just the stage show and mannerisms now. I already got the cleavage. That's no problem,' said Shane, thrusting out his chest, his diaphanous white T-shirt still wet with sweat, so that his big, hard nipples stood out. 'Besides, Diana's as flat as my mama's ironing board – Michael Jackson's probably got more up front than *she* does. Tina, now that's a different story. I'd be needin' falsies for her for certain.'

Suddenly serious, Shane said that what he was thinking of doing was getting his own apartment for a while – in the wintertime when things quieted down on site – and getting hold of a VCR, and spending the whole winter studying old music videos.

'Or get a VCR in here,' said Francis. 'Do a show here. Do a show here every night!'

Shane said that he was looking into it practically, and went down to Granada TV on Filmore Street. 'You know, just to see how much a VCR would be if I rented it by the month. There's a nice guy down there. Hmm, yes, very helpful ... Anyway, I think I can swing it – the apartment, the VCR and everything – if I keep on saving. And maybe I'll even qualify for a little unemployment insurance this time. I'm gonna talk to my social worker.'

'Sounds like a solid idea,' I said.

'Yeah, I think so. I wanna lose a little weight too. So that's it – I've gone on a comprehensive diet programme: no more junk food, no more vending machine crap. No more donuts or pogo sticks or grape Popsicles, or poutine with all that melted cheese and gravy. For lunch now I say 'No thanks, Sally' to that catering truck that comes around, and run over and grab myself a salad at this health food place in the mall. They all think it's pretty funny down on site: me sittin' there with a fork eatin' a salad. "So, how's your salad there, Shane" – sittin' there with a foot-long hot dog or something, grinning, lickin' mustard and ketchup off their fingers. "Oh, good, good," I tell them. "And so how'd you like a knuckle sandwich for dessert?" ... Oh, it ain't easy, I'll tell ya, this diet thing, and by three o'clock, I gotta admit, some days I feel like I'm gonna faint, but I think I lost some weight already. Whadda ya think? A few pounds anyway. I think I did.'

I told Shane he looked good.

'Yeah, I think so ... I gotta get me some clothes from somewhere though. Like, I don't mean to sound like Miss Snooty or Miss Queen Bitch or anything – it's nice of folk to give for sure – but … some of the stuff that people donate here – Tacky City. I mean, there was a dress over there in that clothing shed I saw with – I'm serious – pink poodles all over it. I'm serious – I wouldn't lie about something like that. For a minute I thought I might be able to pull them off or something. So, I don't know what I'm gonna do in that department. I mean there's some good stuff over there for mothers I guess, but I need something with some elegance and chic to it. That's what the guy in Toronto said. And I mean – let's face it – that clothing shed ain't where Diana shops. And then there's make-up and false eyelashes and nails and stilettos and all that to find … Anyway – I'm not gonna let it mess my head up: thinkin' about all the details now. That always fucks me up when I do that. That's always my downfall and nemesis. I'm just gonna worry about one thing at a time. *One thing at a time*. And I was thinkin' that anyway maybe they got a whole wardrobe to choose from at the club, or could spot me an advance or something – he likes my voice. Anyway, it's the VCR and videos first thing. Working on the mannerisms and stage show.'

Shane asks me if there's any news on Callum's job yet:

Callum had some work lined up today, helping some guy somewhere dig a basement.

Shane and I took him over to the clothing shed to get him all fitted out. Found him some gloves – and a half-decent pair of steel-toed boots. I marked him down for a 5am wake-up because he'd have to catch the first bus, then have to walk a mile to meet some guy named Nat at a restaurant some place.

'No news yet. But Roy called: he's back with his girlfriend.'

'Good man.'

'Sticks is down on the market – I saw him.'

'Probably shopping for coke. Gotta stay clean – that boy's gonna crash. I told him.'

'Yeah, but what can you do?'

'He's gotta learn for himself. It's a hard thing to say but … Well, I just hope Callum's job panned out. Man needs a break big time ... Well, guess I better hit the showers then. Practise some scales – get at these nails. Scandalous.

'Do you know where you're going to?
Do you like the things that life is showing you?
Where are you going to?
Do you know ... ?'

Shane's voice resonates gorgeously in the stairwell; fades out at the top – like a hit single.

Callum trudges in. He looks tired.

'Callum ... So how'd the job go?'

'It didn't,' beer on his breath.

And signing in, Callum explains that the guy who was supposed to have quit ended up showing up again at the very last minute, and the boss couldn't very well tell him to leave, because the guy already knew the job way better than Callum did. 'So it's not my fault, I guess.'

'No, it's not.'

Over at the head of the sandwich line Ray is stammering and stuttering – trying to explain that he doesn't want a baloney-egg-jam-cheese sandwich like rotten reality stabbing him in the guts all the time – he wants to use the telephone:

'See, they stuck wires in my legs and body back in 1978 and now I can't get a hold of these people. They didn't have to do it. They rewired me back in 1978 – and now what am I supposed to do?! How am I ever supposed to get out of here and get my own home to practise my guitar in when I'm all short-circuited inside? My fingers won't even flow right now, see? It's all on fire inside – and they didn't have to do it, spittin' up blue blood all the time – and that's not right ...'

Ray has a Gibson Les Paul Sunburst he bought with his disability cheque. He has no amp but still plugs a short, coiled cord into the guitar's body. Lays his trembling yellow-brown finger across the 7th or 9th or 13th fret and pings out magical-sounding overtones; closes his tired eyes to listen to them ring out in the stairwell; talks about things like how overtones decaying reflect the crystalline presence of God resonating from the beginning of all time. Sits and stares at his deeply lined face mirrored in the pickups.

One time I found him sitting out on the fire escape. It was a hot, sticky night and it felt like the shelter was about to explode; we sat together in the cool breeze a minute ... Then – perched in midair over the abyss, legs dangling – we had a short conversation about the Andalusian classical guitarist Andrés Torres Segovia. Ray knew a lot! It was good to connect with him for a moment.

'Come on, freak, keep it movin'.'

An automaton drones that the telephone is 'strictly for emergencies only', and Ray cries that this *is* an emergency – they rewired him back in 1978 – and now what's he supposed to do?!

'For *real* emergencies.'

'Yeah, real emergencies, fuck face. Like someone dyin'. Keep it moving – so hungry I could kill.'

Ray hobbles off stiffly.

Callum shakes his head. 'Sometimes I'm afraid I'm gonna end up like that guy.'

Wraiths of smoke wind up round Callum as he stands there. There's a TV show on with an insane laugh track.

'The boss guy gave me fifteen bucks though, for showin' up at least. So that's something – easiest fifteen bucks I ever made.'

'Hey, that's all right. That's something.'

'Broke up the day anyways. It was different. He said to call him again in a month, that maybe he'd have some work then.'

'That's good.'

'Yeah ...'

There's a silence. Callum asks me if I want a cup of tea – he's getting himself one. Callum and I sometimes sit and talk together when he comes in. One evening, he told me about his life in Toronto, before he ended up here:

'First of all, it took me, like, ten days to hitchhike there from Charlottetown. I had to sleep along the highway, in the bush – I didn't sleep too well, I'll tell ya.'

'I bet.'

'There were all these big trucks flyin' past all the time ... Lyin' there in the ditch, I just kept telling myself that – well, number one, at least it's not raining. Number two, I'd brought enough food along. And number three, it wasn't that cold yet cause it was still summer – but there were still enough mosquitoes around anyways, geez.'

In Toronto Callum found a job making hamburger paddies.

'For six days a week, twelve hours a day I did that. Then got laid off after eight months cause I didn't have any real seniority, and because they were putting in more machines. I tried to find other work, but with just your grade twelve it's 'Sorry, Charlie' ... So that's why I decided to come up here. Fat Cat City, I heard.

'I'd never worked in a factory before, eh. You gotta work fast. You get all these blobs of, like, ground-up meat coming down the conveyor belt at you – so you gotta work fast. I had this shaper – a kinda tool that shapes them, you know? You get fifteen minutes break. You can see your breath it's so cold. But it still smells. Pretty soon it's like you can smell it in your sleep.' Callum wriggled up his nose, remembering the raw stink.

'I got to *feel* like a hamburger sometimes, it was kinda weird. I'd never really experienced anything like that before. But, you get used to it.' Callum glanced round. 'Just like you get used to here, I guess ... Especially the money, it was OK money. But geez, it's expensive to live in Toronto, you should see. I was only sharing a place with these two other guys, eh, and it still cost me over five hundred and fifty bucks a month. And that's just for rent, no utilities or hydro or nothin'. But Francis, you know? – he had to work in a slaughterhouse. Had to wade around in these big rubber boots. Up to his knees in guts and blood, he said.'

Callum told me that the worst thing of all about living in the shelter was the boredom – day after day rolling by exactly the same: going from drop-in to drop-in and drinking tons of coffee (then not being able to sleep at night). Staring up at the dormitory ceiling, listening to men talk and cry in their sleep. 'You feel totally exhausted, even though you haven't actually done anything.' …

Back with the teas, he asks me if I want to play a game of golf: Callum spent his basic needs allowance on a 'bored' game about golf. Two to four can play, or you can play it alone, it says on the box. It's not busy on the door so I say sure. I like Callum, and I'm worried about him.

We take our mugs of tea and set up in the common room.

Throwing the dice, Callum says that he'll maybe try to find some work in a greenhouse or something: his father owns a greenhouse.

'I could probably go back home and work there right now – if it weren't that there'd be too many problems. Too many arguments all the time.'

It was just Callum and his father left. His mother had died of cancer when he was fifteen.

'Actually,' remarks Callum, moving his man round the board, 'I should be seeing my father again in October. Yeah, he's got, like, a horticulture show or something he wants to go to near Toronto. So, I'm gonna hitchhike down there and meet him, I guess. He'd be ashamed to find out I was living here. He'd wanna take me back. Probably try to.' Callum shrugs. 'To tell you the truth, he still thinks I'm living in Toronto. The guy I lived with down there sends any mail I get up to me … He doesn't write much.

'So, I told my father I'd be getting my holidays from my job around that time. And that I'd probably catch a ride back to the island with him. Not to stay though. No way. You *do* kinda forget how it was sometimes when you're livin' here, but I know that as soon as I got back – soon as I'm with him for, oh, about a day and a half, I'd say, I know we'll be at each other's throats … See, my mom, she was *so* different from him. She was beautiful. She was always looking on the bright side of things, you know, always joking around. Even when she was lying there sick ... I used to love to hear her laugh. I try to remember to be like her, but it's pretty hard sometimes. Sometimes I think I'm becoming more like *him* ... It was her idea to start the greenhouse in the first place. She used to grow all sorts of different flowers – roses, tulips, daffodils – everything. She *was* a flower ... For my father it was just a business, eh. He thought it was stupid. Ya – stupid until *she* started making money. He was always hassling her. Always on her back. Always putting her down. Even when she was lying there dying. Now he just grows vegetables. For some big supermarket or something ... When mom was alive, she used to plant flowers between the vegetable rows, you know?: "Just to keep the vegetables growin' happy," she used to say.' Callum smiles.

'No way – two weeks is long enough. You know: it'll be good to see some old friends. Go out. Lay some flowers on mom's grave.'

Shane sashays downstairs from the showers, smelling 'fresh and clean as a daisy'. He claps Callum on the back. 'So how'd the job go, my friend?'

'It didn't.'

And Callum explains again about the guy who came back at the very last second.

'Shit, that's not fair. Man! ... I'm still trying to get you in down at the site, you know.'

'I know. The man gave me fifteen bucks though.'

'In August maybe, maybe in August. Fifteen bucks? For what? – so you been drinkin'?!'

Callum shrugs. 'Just one beer.'

But his face falls; spirit slumps ...

Shane sees it, and looks at me ...

'Hey, I almost forgot,' he says, spinning round suddenly. 'I got another question for ya.' (Shane and I regularly play 'music trivia' and try to stump each other with increasingly specialist questions.) 'Someone gave me this one at work.' He snaps his fingers. 'OK, you ready? ... You sure? OK: Who was the producer on the Ike and Tina

Turner classic 'River Deep, Mountain High'?'

'Phil Spector,' I answer without hesitation (just before the door buzzer sounds).

'Not bad ... Pretty good,' Shane concedes. 'Tina's the hardest to get down. She can really strut' – and with a flourish Shane suddenly disrobes – his red silk kimono sailing through the thick, grey air – and launches into a whole Tina Turner medley! Starts bopping and strutting up and down the common room, singing 'What's Love Got To Do With It?' ... 'Private Dancer' ... 'Nutbush City Limits' – men scurrying and dancing out of his path, cigarette smoke billowing like a dry-ice, stage-show effect; Jesus Christ standing, watching from an icon, blessing Shane as he pouts and wags his butt, puts his hands on his head to shake 'em, oooo shake 'em (almost losing his pyjama bottoms in the act).

Shane shimmies, humps, bumps, grinds, digs – a bounce and wag of flesh that shakes the floor – the whole Earth it seems – until, out of breath, he falls back against the far wall panting ...

The room erupts with applause. Shane curtsies and bows. A couple men run in to see what's happening, and clap, even though they missed the show. Then things go back to normal ... Men settle into clumps and the air solidifies.

Callum stands smiling, shoulders shaking – he let's go a loud laugh – like a sudden bloom – can't stop now. 'The man's got talent ... You gotta admit.'

Callum's got the best laugh in the shelter. You always know when he's enjoying a good joke or a video night. It's the kind of laugh that makes you smile to hear it – I was afraid he might be losing it.

Shane and I look at each other.

'So, did you let a *horse* in here or somethin'?' he asks me. 'This is a night shelter, you know, not a barn – such a farm boy.'

'For like the fourteenth time, I told you: my father owns a green horse – house. Oh geez!'

'You put your foot, hoof in it now.'

'Ah ha, farm boy, probably watched *Little House on the Prairie* every day. So honest.'

'Wasn't that *Anne of Green Gables*?'

'Yeah, *Anne of Green Gables* – *Anne of Green Gables*.'

'Oh, come on, stop it,' Callum blushes, and buries his head in his hands.

Catching his breath still, Shane says that that's it – he's *got* to go into training. 'Rent those videos. Lose some more weight.'

Callum says he's got to gain some.

'I'd give you some if I could.'

'I know. I know you would.'

'You gotta eat more, my friend.' Shane gives him playful poke.

'Don't know why – I never do anything. All I ever do is sit around and eat sandwiches and donuts … Maybe it's too much reality, stabbing me in the guts.'

'Huh?'

'Nothing.'

Callum asks Shane if he wants to sit down and play a game of golf.

Shane says sure – anything with balls, he's in.

'… Man, can't believe I'm sittin' here playing golf. Never had no golf where I came from. Never saw no grass!' And between turns he sings.

Sweeping up

There are men who sit. At the same table every day. Same seat. Who sit and smoke ragged cigarettes and look at their hands, maybe wondering if they're really theirs. Who sit and look out the grilled windows at the dying afternoon. At the night … Who get up to get a sandwich, and take what we give them, and shuffle away back to their seats and chew white bread.

Men who have slept in the same bunk for years. Men who are a bed number. Men whom we mark in before we've even seen them standing waiting in the long line at the door. Old men mostly. Nice, quiet old men who never give us any problems. Who just sit and breathe, looking down at the floor … at their hands … at their split shoes.

Sweeping up, I ask Mr Thompson how his day was. 'Wasn't it hot out today?'

We talk about the weather. In the middle he stops, and looks up, and asks me what day it is. 'Is this Sunday?' he asks.

'It's, um, Wednesday, Wednesday today,' I tell him, acting not too sure myself.

'Oh, that's right, that's right, Wednesday. It's Wednesday today.'

'Yeah … Sure was a hot one today …' I laugh: 'You know, I was walking to work and my T-shirt was stickin' to me – it was *that* hot.'

Mr Thompson laughs. 'Oh, it sure is. I think so. Yes, yes, thank you.' …

And we nod and gaze out the window; and at our hands; and down at the floor …

After a couple of minutes, Mr Thompson says that he guesses he'll go up and get his shower now, and thanks me again: carrying on a conversation about the weather, difficult after months of talking to yourself, only yourself, as you walk around downtown picking up dog ends, peeking in bins, glancing in shop windows at your reflection, standing there. As you keep moving so the cops don't pick you up, and shovel you into a cell.

Mr Thompson shuffles off and I go back to sweeping up: sandwich scraps, cigarette butts, orange peels, ashes …

IT SMELLS LIKE LONELINESS

Introduction

These pieces are based on people outside of the social service field, and on myself.

> *Then he said to them, 'My soul is very sorrowful, even to death; remain here, and watch with me.'*
>
> Matthew 26:38

Mikehead

Mikehead owned a beauty salon. MICHEL'S _ _ _ SEX BEAUTY SALON, up on Thompson Street, one of the city's main drags. After meeting Mikehead, I soon suspected him of being the joker who had shinnied up the sign pole and stolen the 'U', the 'N' and the 'I'.

When I turned sixteen my older brother said: 'No, the wet head's dead. It's time I took you for a *real* haircut!'

So I hopped up into his red, rock 'n' roll van. Up until then I'd been going to my dad's Italian barber, who'd parted my hair cleanly down the side. I wanted it layered and feathered and parted down the middle – I was going into grade ten after all.

Instead of *Vogue* and *Vanity Fair* and *Chatelaine* and *Mademoiselle* scattered on the tables to flip through while you waited, like at the salon where my mother went to get her hair done and sometimes took me for an unnecessary trim, Mikehead offered his patrons *Playboy*, *Penthouse* and *Playgirl*. There was a hint of that traditional beauty parlour scent at Michel's, but mostly it smelt of spilled beer and cigarettes. And no more did I have to sit and patiently endure accordion music, or musak, or inane radio talk show chit-chat – because Mikehead tuned in to WRIF. 'The Home of rock 'n' roll – baby! You got Arthur P on your ray-did-i-o – and here's another hour of commercial free tunes!'

And when Arthur P didn't spin what Mikehead wanted to hear – namely the Rolling Stones – Mikehead would slap a crackly album on an old stereo you could write your name on in the dust. *Exile on Main Street*, *Goat's Head Soup*. *Some Girls* had just come out.

Mikehead's imitation of Mick was in great demand down at the Dominion, the neighbourhood bar. He'd seen The Stones sixteen times and knew all of Jagger's dances and moves. Sometimes at work he'd brush up; and miming 'Sympathy for the Devil', would suddenly start strutting and bopping and mincing around the barber's chair.

Physically, Mikehead looked nothing like Mick, or one's idea of a beautician. He had long, thin, very straight dirty blonde hair that looked like it could use a good shampooing; wore little, thick round glasses with amber lenses; and spouted a greasy goatee he'd compulsively clutch and twist, like when he contemplated your bangs.

'He looks more like he belongs on the back of a motorcycle,' my mother said.

Mikehead spoke with a lisp, and had a seemingly endless supply of dirty jokes he relished with a cackle, which had begun as an affectation, I suspected, but soon became his distinctive laugh.

Tucked into his streaky mirrors were different-coloured joke shop cards he'd enjoy with a cackle too.

'Complaint Department? … Talk To My Butt'

'Hairdressers – Do It With Style'

Sometimes down at the bar, or up at the salon, he'd walk around wearing a swastika armband he'd picked up at an army surplus store.

From the time I was sixteen, my barber was this short, paunchy, beer-swilling fascist whose parents had been killed in an automobile accident and had left him with the responsibility of caring for his younger sister. He kept real good care of his sister, people said. When the car-fuelled economy ran out of gas, Mikehead lost his salon and found work as a janitor.

He was still my barber though. I'd go over to his house and he'd charge me beer money. When I was eighteen, he gave me a Jimmy Page perm. It took four and a half hours. I can still smell the caustic chemicals.

'Remember, tell your big brother to *call* me,' he said as I left. 'And, remember, don't wash it for two days – else it'll all fall out. Then you'll look more like the drummer for the fuckin' Lawrence Welk Band.'

I lost touch with Mikehead when I went to university.

I heard he'd worked as a cleaner for years; and that he'd waited until his sister was safely off on her own, before climbing up onto the barber chair in the basement of his parents' old house, and hanging himself.

Gerry

People called you

lazy
weak
a loser
fucked in the head

I used to think

if you were missing an arm or leg
if you had been hit by a car
or had come back from a war

if you had a disease like cancer

they would have felt sorry for you
they would have looked on you as a hero

They would have been more forgiving of you
sittin' there on a bar stool all day long
drinkin' their hard-earned taxes
They would have bought you a beer

(Sometimes they *did* buy you a drink

when they were feeling superior and generous
during lulls in real life when they came slumming
when they needed to stand beside you in order to get
a taller measure of themselves

When they were down and needed some understanding

Besides
you were a good drunk
You were harmless)

Gerry

you lived down the street
with your mom and dad

    'Forty-three years old and still
    living with his parents'

You never said much
but when I was growing up you lent me record albums
Paul Simon's *Still Crazy After All These Years*
Imagine by John Lennon

They said a lot

One day
you took me into your father's dark shed
which smelled of gasoline and grass clippings
(you cut lawns sometimes, did odd jobs)
and you showed me your wood carvings:

    a timber wolf
        a Canada goose
    an old man with a cane
        the face of a Native American woman

carved from pieces of driftwood you collected and
branches broken in storms
Sunlight came streaming in through the single window
and I saw you in a different light

You looked transformed
ascetic

Your work was beautiful and skilful

I said you should sell some
You said you didn't want to sell them. They weren't that good
They *were* good, I said
They were

You smiled
and looked satisfied for a moment
happy

When I was older I used to see you
down at the Dominion Tavern on Saturday nights
You stayed over on 'the dead side',
with veterans sitting alone at sticky tables
and other old people
life had passed by and
left tangled in cobwebs

Sometimes I'd come over and talk to you

Once on your birthday
you gave me some advice:

Don't grow up like me, you said –
and looked me in the eye

Ah, come on, I said
Come on

I wanted to get back to the music and lights

back to my friends
(back to 'the land of the living')
Everybody was there
The Bar Flies were playing
Layla Tajanii was dancing
in the close, summer heat

I stayed a little longer
and left an empty bottle beside you on the bar
I'd come back later to make sure you got home all right
I told myself
When I remembered
you were gone

Gerry
I heard you killed yourself

Slit your wrists in a park one night

(Someone walking their dog found you)

Ray the bartender told me when I came back to town one year
I ran into him walking down by the river
The Dominion was a steakhouse now
'Christ, I felt sorry for the kid,' he said.

'Did anyone keep his wood carvings?' I asked.
'His *what*?' he said.

Gerry, I wish I could have said something to make you believe
you weren't a failure in life

Gerry, you touched me –
I wish I could have told you that

Would it have been enough?

I doubt it
I'm sure it wouldn't have. It never is

Gerry, I think you were heroic
to try to transform your great pain

Strong
to have lasted as long as you did

Gerry
this world is crazy
can't see
the potential beauty
in brokenness

Helping Gordon with his Christmas decorations

Gordon lived in the same seniors' building as my grandmother. One afternoon when I was over helping my gran with her Christmas decorations – out in the hallway hammering her wreath up on the door – Gordon came out and asked me if I could please help him put up his decorations one day. He didn't want to get himself all upset, he said ...

    The TV and radio are conversing loudly when I come in ... Gordon's apartment is crowded with knick knacks: figurines, mugs with faces; things from the house he didn't have the heart to part with, framed photographs of his mother ... Gordon gets me a Labatt's Blue from the fridge, which is bare except for bottles of beer. He's got some leftover Chinese food from the Kgum Go heating up on the stove, on low.

    He's relieved that I'm here to do the lights and decorations because he doesn't want to get himself all upset. Last year he did it all by himself and he got so upset. 'I'm too old,' he says. 'I've made my mind up – I'm not getting myself upset any more.'

He's got a white plastic tree, a garland he bought today over at the Home Hardware, a set of those little blinky white lights tangled frustratedly in a cardboard box ... I get working on it.

'Take a beer break,' he says.

The tree goes up pretty easily, after I figure it out. In a rush of Yuletide inspiration, I duct tape the garland up around his fake fireplace.

'Oh gosh – I'm just thrilled with that!' he exclaims. 'I just love how you've draped it around like that. That's wonderful. See – if I was doing it, I'd be so upset by now. Here, have a beer.' (I'm still working on the first one.)

I sit down for a second, and glance around the apartment. He must have about twenty mobiles hung up: flocks of birds, constellations of stars ... butterflies, doves, mobiles made from seashells ... All twisted and tangled.

He started collecting them after his second wife died, he tells me.

'That's another thing I wanted to ask you to do – I'd do it myself but I'd just get upset.'

So I untwist and untangle Gordon's mobiles for him; walk around the little two-roomed apartment and free them, one by one.

He reaches over and switches on the ceiling fan, and they all start speaking softly. Chimey ones; soft, gongy ones ...

'Oh, I just love this,' he says. 'Sometimes I just sit here and listen. It's so peaceful and calming.'

It's good to see the birds and butterflies and stars swaying and dancing again.

Another Blue – then back to work.

'Have a beer break.'

His duct tape is so old it either doesn't stick at all, or else sticks for a bit then slowly peels away, pulling off paint.

'Oh, don't worry about it,' Gordon says. 'What's a little paint? It doesn't matter. Nothing like that matters in life – believe me!'

After a couple Blues I'm losing my work ethic, and a certain sharpness I feel ... As I untangle the lights, and hang them up around the fireplace with the garland, Gordon tells me about the last Christmas he spent with his mother. 'I was just sitting here remembering,' he says.

He visited her Christmas Eve: she was up at the nursing home by then.

'It was the best place for her ... I asked the nurse if it would be all right if I brought her some liquor in. "Sure, why not?" she said. It was a lovely green colour. I forget what it was now, but this lovely green colour. I had glasses, beautiful glasses along. We sat in the big room that they have there, by the big window, and just watched the snow fall together, and drank a couple glasses. Lovely ... Then the nurse came by and said, "You have to go back to your room now." So, we went back and had one more glass there. Then I put mother to bed. Lovely. I always remember it. Especially now at Christmas time.'

I say that it sounds like he and his mother had a really good relationship.

'Lovely,' he says.

He was adopted, he reveals. 'I think of my adopted mother as my real mother,' he tells me.

The TV's turned down now with just the picture: The Community Listings: ... A country square dance somewhere ... The Distress Line. Easy listening on the radio. 'The relaxing, mellow sounds of WEAZ.'

Gordon asks me what I'm doing for Christmas.

I tell him that I'll be with family.

He'll be here, he says. Enjoying the decorations.

And on Christmas Eve he'll go and visit the woman who used to work as his mother's maid. She's deaf and dumb, but can read lips. She lives just outside of town. He takes a cab over and checks in on her from time to time. Last year she came over and he made a turkey with all the fixings. Cranberry sauce. This year they're going to keep it simple. She gave him the embroidery there on the wall. The papier mâché cat beside the television.

'We're friends. She loved mother, and we've known each other such a long time.'

I finish the decorating. As I'm packing away the boxes, Gordon asks me if I'd like to order a pizza, his trembling, arthritic hand on the receiver. I thank him very much but tell him that I really have to get home (and I do).

'Well, I've got my Chinese food heating.' It smells like loneliness.

'Another beer, then?'

'One for the road.'

I plug in the lights and we sit together a moment; he switches off the high light.

'Oh, that's just beautiful! I just love the way you draped it around like that ... Now I can just sit here and look at it and enjoy it without getting upset.' And underneath, the mobiles make soft, gentle, sad sounds ......

I get up to go. Gordon pulls himself up to say goodbye, and reaches in his pocket and holds out $150 dollars. 'No, here, take it, it's worth it. It's worth it not to get upset.'

I explain I can't – I've only been there a couple hours. Not even. I accept fifteen.

'We're friends,' I say.

He smiles.

I leave, feeling not so much drunk but overloaded with life.

My gran dies in the new year, but I help Gordon with his decorations for a couple more Christmases, until he moves into a nursing home. I visit him there at Christmas once; sneak some whisky in. We sit and watch *It's a Wonderful Life* on the common room TV.

The next Christmas I come again, but he doesn't know me any more. I leave the home, and walking down the dark country road gaze up at the night sky, tangled with stars.

I know a cat whose name is ...

'One in four people will suffer from mental illness in their lifetime.'
Penumbra

John 1:4–5

There's a stigma to mental illness – still. People empathise but then back off. Like they suddenly smell something on you, like they're afraid of contagion.

People wonder why you don't just snap out of it. It's maddening, you can't snap out of it! You can't snap out of hell. On the outside you look in and don't believe, or want to believe, it could happen to you. Well, it can.

In 1996 I went through an 'episode' of clinical depression. I lost all confidence in myself, couldn't work for much of the time; I broke up with my partner – actually, she broke up with me; who can blame her? I'd become irritable, manipulative, needy as a child. At one point the depression got so bad that I started to self-harm, to cut the insides of my arms with kitchen knives. I'd tell people that the cat did it. I was just playing with the cat. I was playing with death.

How did I fall down so far? How did I go from someone who had worked as a nurse's aide and a counsellor, from someone who'd travelled through Yugoslavia solo, to someone who couldn't even take a city bus alone? ... One thing was certain: I was sure that, down below, it was my fault. It wasn't of course, but I couldn't help feeling that I was a very weak person. Weak, defective, lazy, a loser. A failure: the shame of depression on top of the depression.

I did a lot of things to survive during that time: I talked to good friends, I fell back on family, I went through counselling, I took antidepressants. One day, I woke up and started writing children's poems. I had always written, but I'd never once thought of writing children's poems. I was desperate. I was clawing for the light.

The depression lasted for about a year. I've been well since that time. These days I feel blessed: I have work I feel passionate about, a wonderful partner; sometimes I even do gigs as a stand-up comedian. If you had told me, back in the days when it was hard to get out of bed in the morning, that one day I'd be doing stand-up comedy, I never would have believed you.

Sometimes when I'm doing stand-up, I use the following poem in my act – one of the 'children's poems' I wrote when I was clinically depressed. I recite the poem and skip rope. Punters seem to enjoy it. That a poem I wrote when I was clinically depressed now makes people laugh is a miracle to me.

On the surface, this little poem may seem to have nothing at all to do with being a survivor of depression; for me, though, it is an embodiment of 'the light that shines in the darkness' …

Going through depression has rooted my faith, has brought me closer to Jesus Christ – I have no problem in the world now in believing in resurrection.

I used to feel very guarded and ashamed of talking about mental illness. Now I need to hold myself back. I want to shake people awake and tell them how close to the edge we can all come, how normal it is – how human.

Skipping song

This poem is a performance piece. When I recite it in a club, I do things like throw peanuts, drink milk, hand cans of tuna fish and salmon to the audience …

I know a cat whose name is Mimi
she doesn't like tuna fish
I know a cat whose name is Mimi
what's her favourite dish?

(skip)

Pears
Potatoes
Pizza pie
Falafels
Capers
Ham on rye

Olives
Pickles
Fried bananas
Rumballs
Gumballs
Dried sultanas

I know a cat whose name is Mingy
who likes his mozzarella stringy
I know a cat whose name is Leroy
who left the duck and ate
the decoy

I know a cat named Siamese Sam
who's lost his yen for corned beef and Spam
I know a cat named Siamese Sam
what sticks to his chops?

(skip)

Blue cheese
Toasted fleas
Chocolate-covered honeybees
Garter snakes
Frosted flakes
Pistachio-almond honeycakes

I know a cat named Need-a-tail
who's trying to eat a lot of kale

I know a cat whose name is Oopik
who forgets how to hunt walrus and seal
I know a cool cat named Oopik Toopik
what's his favourite meal?

Cheese nachos
All dressed tacos
Enchiladas
Fried iguanas
Beef burritos
Fried Tostitos
Corn tortillas
Margueritas
Hot peppers! *(skip like mad)*

I know a cat whose name is Kate
who plays with the sunlight on her plate

I know a cat whose name's Mad Manx
who struts from his bowl and never says thanx

I know a cat titled Rex the Third
who says that eating canned food's absurd
I know a cat titled Rex the Third
what does he rather fancy?

(skip)

Pheasant
Quail
Chinchilla under glass

Bouillabaisse
Mayonnaise
Refined sugar

I know a Tom who's a tough Maine Coon
who picks at the garbage and cries at the moon

I know a cat named Davy Crockett
who keeps liquorice jerky in his pocket

I know a cat who's an opera singer
and always wears black coat and tail
I know a cat, half-alto, part-tenor
what does he like for dinner?

Rigatoni
Rice-A-Roni
Fried baloney
Cold spumoni
Manicotti
Pavarotti
Late Puccini
Hot linguine
Cannelloni
Macaroni
Vermicelli
Cold spaghetti
Hot peppers!! *(skip like mad)*

I know a cat who likes a good pot luck
I know a cat who likes a good pot lick

I know a cat who smelt the smelts
(in the salty, fishy, kitcheny air)

I know a cat who's fond of airline peanuts

I know a cat whose name is Stevie
who crunches on Spice Mice watching late-night TV

I know a cat called Hate-to-Cook
who'd rather shed on her deep, soft bed
I know a cat named Hate-to-Cook
what does she like instead?

(skip)

Take out
Drive through
Ready to eat
Dine in
Phone-up
Delivery free

I know a cat who likes to lie
and dream of eating pie in the sky

I know a cat called Judy Star
who lives for caviar by soft guitar
I know a feline called Judy Star

I know a cat who's kinda finicky

I know a cat who's kinda picnicy

I know a cat who sucks out the marrow

I know a cat who picks like a sparrow

I know a jaded Abyssinian
who doesn't want to eat the same thing again

I know a cat who hisses at hot dogs

I know a cat who relishes relishes

I know the cat who owns Captain Cat Burgers
(but his name is Ed)

I know a cat who chatters for chocolate

I know a cat who's a milkaholic

I know a cat named Alabamy Sammy
whose vit'ls consist of grits and groats

I know a cat named Hamish McCaindish
who always eats stiff Quaker Oats

I know a cat who skips double Dutch
and never even stops for lunch

I know a cat who skips much double Dutch
and never even stops for lunch
and never even stops for lunch …

Some more children's poems:

The lonely caribou

A lonely caribou
didn't know what to do
so he walked all the way to Kalamazoo
and tried to patch a call to you

But the operator said
her line's gone dead
or else she's wed or
gone to shed so

the lonely caribou
who didn't know what to do

without the you of you
stood beneath the stars in the snow
stood beneath the stars in the snow

Tree says

be rooted
little flower says bloom
bird says fly before it's cold

Wind says float free
sun says Love
rain says it's OK
to cry

Everybody knows that cats like to rumba

Eels like to shimmy
and cows do a hoedown
Rhinos hornpipe and
hippos can hula
but everybody knows that cats like to rumba

Pollywogs can cakewalk
flamingos can cancan
dingos tango
peacocks fandango
mongooseys watoosie
and wapitis dance boppity
but everybody knows that cats like to rumba,
everybody knows that cats like to rumba

Mambas mambo
molluscs mazurka
llamas samba and
pandas La Bamba
wonga-wongas like to conga conga
but everybody knows that cats like to rumba

Foxes like a trot
German shepherds polka
bunnies bunny hop
bugs like to jitter
ducks disco
swordfish sword dance
tapirs caper and civets
and vervets curvet
but everybody knows that cats like to rumba

Chimps do the monkey
worms do the worm
wombats do the Wilde Wildebeest
shaggy horses clog dance
polar bears like a snowball
hairy black spiders tarantella
but everybody knows that cats like to rumba

Emus and gnus boogaloo
rattlesnakes shake their bootys
bees do the honey dance
bears are chained to waltzes
svelte silky impalas saraband
colourful coral fish calypso
but everybody knows that cats like to rumba

Giraffes gavotte and
Guinea pigs dance the Irish jig
lambs do the fling in spring
whales ballet
newborn things do the hokey-cokey
but everybody knows that cats like to rumba,
everybody knows that cats like to rumba

Camels do the bump bump bump
skunks are full of funk funk funk
amoebas pair off
boas hold their last dance close
stinkbugs cut a mean rug
porcupines dance alone mostly
whelks and elks got nothing in common much
but everybody knows that cats like to rumba

Lemmings mosh and
drakes do a slam dance
beetles twist and shout and shake it up baby now
but everybody knows that cats like to rumba

Gypsy moths dance by caravan light
Shetland ponies like a ceilidh
baboons ballroom and
ants like a march tune
centipedes have to be careful and
millipedes have to be carefuller
but everybody knows cats that like to rumba
everybody knows that cats like to rumba
everybody knows that cats like to rimba, rumba, roo!

A psalm

God, I feel I could wear the day
I feel I could wear the day today

like a scarf
(But not because it's cold
'cause it's not)

I feel I could wear the day and
the wind would wrap it around and around me

I feel I could wear the day
I feel I could wear the day today
Like a scarf
and dance it

Yellow with a fringe or two of blue …

An invitation

When Jean Vanier visited institutions in France and saw the lifeless, hopeless conditions that people with developmental challenges were living in, he began L'Arche, an international community where people with learning difficulties and assistants share a life together. We need something similar for the elderly, and for folk with mental health challenges. This would bring about a revolution in care, and help to heal our fractured, individualistic, commodified society.

Why do we spend £53 billion year on armaments and death (UK statistic) and segregate elderly people in boring, sterile, impersonal surroundings? Why not instead use the money to help create and support communities where the elderly and children and young people and others can all live together and share a life and journey?

Author

Neil Paynter has been a farm labourer, a fruit-picker, a teacher, a security guard (reluctantly), a bookseller, a hospital cleaner, a stand-up comedian, a musician and an editor. He lives in Biggar with his partner Helen, his mother and Stevie, his cat.

The Illustrator

After a decade of youth-work (including three years with the Iona Community) and illustrating a little bundle of books, Iain Campbell decided to roll his two careers into one and become an art teacher. However, it's hard to leave the illustration alone and he finds his paintbrush and Indian ink get a bit lonely without him. Iain lives in Glasgow with his wife and their three little girls, who all like drawing too.

Wild Goose Publications is part of
THE IONA COMMUNITY:

- An ecumenical movement of men and women from different walks of life and different traditions in the Christian church
- Committed to the gospel of Jesus Christ, and to following where that leads, even into the unknown
- Engaged together, and with people of goodwill across the world, in acting, reflecting and praying for justice, peace and the integrity of creation
- Convinced that the inclusive community we seek must be embodied in the community we practise

Together with our staff, we are responsible for:

- Our islands residential centres of Iona Abbey, the MacLeod Centre on Iona, and Camas Adventure Centre on the Ross of Mull

and in Glasgow:
- The administration of the Community
- Our work with young people
- Our publishing house, Wild Goose Publications
- Our association in the revitalising of worship with the Wild Goose Resource Group

The Iona Community was founded in Glasgow in 1938 by George MacLeod, minister, visionary and prophetic witness for peace, in the context of the poverty and despair of the Depression. Its original task of rebuilding the monastic ruins of Iona Abbey became a sign of hopeful rebuilding of community in Scotland and beyond. Today, we are about 250 members, mostly in Britain, and 1500 associate members, with 1400 friends worldwide. Together and apart, 'we follow the light we have, and pray for more light'.

For information on the Iona Community contact:
The Iona Community, Fourth Floor, Savoy House, 140 Sauchiehall Street,
Glasgow G2 3DH, UK. Phone: 0141 332 6343
e-mail: admin@iona.org.uk; web: www.iona.org.uk

For enquiries about visiting Iona, please contact:
Iona Abbey, Isle of Iona, Argyll PA76 6SN, UK. Phone: 01681 700404
e-mail: ionacomm@iona.org.uk

Wild Goose Publications, the publishing house of the Iona Community established in the Celtic Christian tradition of Saint Columba, produces books, CDs and digital downloads on:

- holistic spirituality
- social justice
- political and peace issues
- healing
- innovative approaches to worship
- song in worship, including the work of the Wild Goose Resource Group
- material for meditation and reflection

For more information:

Wild Goose Publications
Fourth Floor, Savoy House
140 Sauchiehall Street,
Glasgow G2 3DH, UK

Tel. +44 (0)141 332 6292
Fax +44 (0)141 332 1090
e-mail: admin@ionabooks.com

or visit our website at
www.ionabooks.com
for details of all our products and online sales